Fifteen into one?

MANCHESTER
UNIVERSITY PRESS

European Policy Research Unit Series

Series Editors: *Simon Bulmer, Peter Humphreys* and *Mick Moran*

The European Policy Research Unit Series aims to provide advanced textbooks and thematic studies of key public policy issues in Europe. They concentrate, in particular, on comparing patterns of national policy content, but pay due attention to the European Union dimension. The thematic studies are guided by the character of the policy issue under examination.

The European Policy Research Unit (EPRU) was set up in 1989 within the University of Manchester's Department of Government to promote research on European politics and public policy. The series is part of EPRU's effort to facilitate intellectual exchange and substantive debate on the key policy issues confronting the European states and the European Union.

Titles in the series also include:

The governance of the Single European Market Kenneth Armstrong and Simon Bulmer

The politics of health in Europe Richard Freeman

Immigration and European integration Andrew Geddes

Mass media and media policy in Western Europe Peter Humphreys

The regions and the new Europe Martin Rhodes (ed.)

The rules of integration Gerald Schneider and Mark Aspinwall

Political economy of financial integration in Europe Jonathan Story and Ingo Walter

Extending European cooperation Alasdair R. Young

Regulatory politics in the enlarging European Union Alasdair Young and Helen Wallace

Fifteen into one?

The European Union and its member states

Edited by
Wolfgang Wessels,
Andreas Maurer
and Jürgen Mittag

Manchester University Press
Manchester and New York
distributed exclusively in the USA by Palgrave

Published by Manchester University Press
Oxford Road, Manchester M13 9NR, UK
and Room 400, 175 Fifth Avenue, New York, NY 10010, USA
www.manchesteruniversitypress.co.uk

Distributed exclusively in the USA by
Palgrave, 175 Fifth Avenue, New York,
NY 10010, USA

Distributed exclusively in Canada by
UBC Press, University of British Columbia, 2029 West Mall,
Vancouver, BC, Canada V6T 1Z2

British Library Cataloguing-in-Publication Data
A catalogue record for this book is available from the British Library

Library of Congress Cataloging-in-Publication Data applied for

ISBN 0 7190 5849 X *paperback*

First published 2003

10 09 08 07 06 05 04 03 10 9 8 7 6 5 4 3 2 1

Typeset in Sabon
by Action Publishing Technology Ltd, Gloucester
Printed in Great Britain
by Bookcraft (Bath) Ltd, Midsomer Norton

Contents

List of figures

List of tables

Notes on contributors

Kenneth A. Armstrong is Lecturer at the Faculty of Laws at Queen Mary and Westfield College, University of London

Felipe Basabe Lloréns is Assistant Professor at the Universidad Pontificia Comillas, Madrid

Danielle Bossaert is Senior lecturer at the European Institute for Public Administration, Maastricht

Simon Bulmer is Professor of Government at the University of Manchester and Visiting Professor at the College of Europe in Bruges

Christian Franck is Professor of Political Science at the Institut d'Etudes Européennes at the Catholic University of Louvain-la Neuve

Nikos Frangakis is Director of the Hellenic Centre of European Studies and Research, Athens

Flaminia Gallo is Civil Servant at the European Commission in Brussels

Birgit Hanny is Consultant in Public Administration Affairs, Hamburg

Ben J.S. Hoetjes is Professor at the University of Maastricht and Senior Research Fellow at the Netherlands Institute of International Relations, University of Leiden

Otmar Höll is Director of the Austrian Institute for International Affairs, Laxenburg

Karl Magnus Johansson is Research Fellow at the Swedish Institute of International Affairs, Stockholm

Brigid Laffan is Jean Monnet Professor at the Department of Politics at the University College Dublin and Visiting Professor at the College of Europe in Bruges

Hervé Leclercq is Research Fellow at the Institut d'Etudes Européennes at the Catholic University of Louvain-la Neuve

Finn Laursen is Professor at the Department of Political Science at the University of Southern Denmark, Odense

Andreas Maurer is Senior Research Fellow at the Stiftung Wissenschaft und Politik, Berlin, and Jean Monnet-Lecturer at the University of Osnabrück

Jürgen Mittag is Research Fellow at the University of Cologne

Antonios D. Papayannides is Legal Counsel and Member of the Board of the Greek Centre of European Studies and Research, Athens

Johannes Pollack is Research Fellow at the Austrian Academy of Science, Vienna

Sonja Puntscher-Riekmann is Professor at the Universities of Innsbruck and Vienna

Maria João Seabra is Research Fellow at the Institute of International and Strategic Studies, Lisbon

Andrea Szukula is Research Fellow at the University of Cologne

Teija Tiilikainen is Research Fellow at the Department of Political Science, Co-Ordinator of the Programme on European Policy-Making at the University of Helsinki and Finnish Representative of the EU Convention

Claire Vandevievere is Research Fellow at the Institut d'Etudes Européennes at the Catholic University of Louvain-la Neuve

Wolfgang Wessels is Jean Monnet Professor of Political Science at the University of Cologne and Visiting Professor at the College of Europe in Bruges and Natolin

Preface and major findings: the anatomy, the analysis and the assessment of the 'beast'

Fifteen into one? is the result of a collective reflection by a group of political scientists who are all fascinated and puzzled by the evolution of the EU system and its major features. The study is part of a two-level research project for which the Deutsche Forschungsgemeinschaft (DFG) has given a grant (WE 954/6–1) within the larger research programme 'Regieren in Europa' (Governance in Europe) co-ordinated by Beate Kohler-Koch, University of Mannheim. Our particular project aimed to examine if, and to what extent, the European Union's political system has changed since the Maastricht Treaty came into force. The analysis has been pursued at the 'Brussels–Strasbourg' level as well as at the national levels, where we dealt with the constitutional, institutional, procedural and administrative adaptation and reaction processes.

Taking up earlier work by one of the editors, we follow some conventional and some less tried approaches, identify some strange puzzles and come up with some traditional and some perhaps surprising results. As a starting point, this project took the demands of a multi-level system seriously. The analysis has therefore been pursued both in the 'Brussels–Strasbourg' space as well as at the level of all fifteen Member States. To link the evolution in both arenas we decided to follow a neo-institutionalist approach and – in this line – to take the para-constitutional and institutional evolution of the EC/EU Treaty as the independent variable. The central question was: in what way did the treaty amendments and revisions affect Member States or – to formulate it more concretely – how have groups of actors in the member states adapted their constitutional, institutional, procedural and administrative structures to the common and self-made challenges of the EU polity?

In a country-by-country account the research group has described and analysed who participates in which forms and at which stages of the EU policy-cycle and thus how national actors interact and fit into the Union system. We also addressed the demand for a dynamic approach and the need to analyse the integration process over a longer period. Starting from the impact of the Treaty on the European Union, we discovered that we also had to look back to the set-up and situation prevailing before the European Union was created in Maastricht.

Another characteristic of our approach was the use of quantitative trends including especially a systematic comparison of legal provisions and data about the production patterns and the output of legal acts, provided in raw data from EC institutions. At the end we were able to describe the long-term trends of the integration process some over nearly half a century from the early days of the European Coal and Steel Community (ECSC) until the end of the 1990s. The major findings of this multi-level and multi-actor analysis point to particular features of the EU polity with the Member States as constitutive units:

(1) From analysing the institutional and procedural evolution of the European polity over the last fifty years we realised that the evolution, amendment and revision of the set-up at the European level have been considerable. Of specific relevance were five trends in the growth and differentiation of the EU system. National actors, as masters of treaty-building, have considerably increased the demands on their own set-ups – especially through para-constitutional communitarisation, sectoral and procedural differentiation, institutional and actor differentiation as well as through the burgeoning scope and density of binding obligations in form of the acquis communautaire. The data for the 1990s indicate that *these integration processes have not reached a stage of saturation nor even a 'local optimum'*.

(2) Confronted with these challenges – i.e. the considerable changes in our key variables – we wondered about the patterns of national reaction. The findings of the country reports indicate clear traces of a broad and intensive 'Europeanisation' of national actors in the institutions of members states and a 'domestication' at the European level. As we – in contrast to other approaches – define the ambiguous term 'Europeanisation' as a shift of attention, we observe that national governments, administrations, parliaments, regions, interest groups and courts have mobilised additional resources for their multi-level game. They have adapted their national machinery and invested time in the EU policy cycle at both the national and the EU level. Within this persistent trend the period since the Single European Act (SEA) (1987) has been a time when more and more national actors discovered the importance of the EC/EU polity for their own interests. With increasing salience in more and more sectors national demands for 'voice' opportunities have grown exponentially. Using key concepts such as 'transparency', 'democratic deficit' and 'legitimacy' as pretexts for a higher degree of participation, more and more groups of actors have been included. These processes increase the degree of complexity of the emerging politico-administrative system.

What thus becomes clear at the turn of the millennium is that the European Union has been opened by national institutions and actors. Looking from the other perspective, 'Europeanisation' is closely linked with a 'domestication' of EU institutions, rules and behavioural settings. 'EU-Brussels' is no longer just an arena for diplomats but for all national ministries (since 1999 also for defence secretaries) and an increasing range of policy networks. This process of mutual interaction is significant; it is not a one-way street. *The allocation of competences and the patterns of mutual participation point to a fusion of both levels.*

(3) Given this rise in salience of the EU level many might find the vertical asymmetry between 'Brussels' and the national capitals surprising. Fundamental patterns of national policy-making have not changed: national actors have strengthened existing set-ups to mobilise their resources for 'access' and 'influence' over an increasing range of 'vital' policy areas and over all phases of the policy cycle. We observe some limited constitutional revisions, some minor institutional rearrangements and a lot of procedural and administrative adaptations, but no structural revolution in the Member States. Actors playing on both levels have been ingenious in developing incremental devices without creating new major set-ups at the national level. We could not find indicators of any change in this 'conservative' attitude of major actors. Thus the rate and the degree of para-constitutional, institutional and procedural amendments and revisions of the EC/EU treaty, our independent variable, has not led to respective changes in Member States, and *this vertical asymmetry between the two levels is part of the evolution of the EU system.*

(4) The latter finding might help to explain another counterintuitive observation – that of non-convergence among Member States. The rather uniform patterns of national reactions with regard to the shift of awareness, attention and mobilisation should thus not hide another surprising pattern: the constitutional, institutional and administrative systems, and their relative use, have not clided into one – ideal – model of adapting to the Brussels policy cycle. Given the same kind of institutional and procedural challenges that react on and shape the EU system, the degree similarity among the 'Fifteen' is rather small. Traditional national patterns are resistant and apparently flexible enough to induce complacency about one's own performance. Imports of apparently more competitive set-ups or procedures are rare. *Each member state pursues its own way in the Brussels 'space'*, and a *screening of 'best practices' is not pursued on any systematic level.*

(5) In spite of a general trend towards an increased engagement in the EU policy cycle we find a clear horizontal asymmetry among groups of actors in the adaptation process. Gains and losses in getting access and influence on both levels are not equally distributed among national actors; some are more flexible as well as more forceful, and thus more competitive

than others. Using a fourfold typology of identifying adaptation patterns on both the national and the European level, our reading of the national reports confirms the traditional view that some actors – especially parliaments and some regional administrations – are only weak adaptors whereas others – such as the head of governments, governmental administrations and interest groups – have increased their role as strong and active multi-level players. Though parliaments normally count among the 'losers' in the multi-level game some have at least established a position of strong national adaptors. Though not all effects are directly visible, one consequence is *a shift in the internal national balance of powers towards governments and administrations and thence towards the heads of governments and finance ministers*.

(6) Unlike at the beginning of our project we are now extremely cautious about positing an optimal model or blueprint which would offer 'best practices' in national adaptation and thus serve as an ideal example for 'efficient governance'. Long-established national features make it extremely difficult to offer any valid statements on which structures and procedures are more or less 'fit' for the multi-level game. Any blueprint for an optimal model would be both academically invalid and politically risky. The picture we get from studying the particularities of Member States makes it clear that imitation by straightforward import would be subject to the law of unintended and therefore worrying consequences unless the institutional–procedural environment had been carefully analysed. The limited use of the experience of other Member States is therefore a prudent decision. EU applicant countries should thus be careful in drafting their specific institutional set-up and procedural rules. Present members offer a broad set of variations, which indicates the importance of national actors, but they do not necessarily serve as a good example. Based on these reflections this study refrains from offering a model case for the ideal member of a 'XXL Union' of 25 or more members. One general conclusion, however, is evident for institutional strategies: all existing plans which propose changes in the Treaty text *without discussing national reaction patterns* will remain superficial and may lead to damaging and even counterproductive results.

(7) As a consequence of the dynamic and comparative approach *Fifteen into one?* also tries to contribute to a dynamic theory on the evolution of the (West) European states. Exploiting conventional integration-related theories – in our case, studies of (neo-)realist, (neo-)federal/neo-functional, governance and fusion issues – we found stimulating offers and insights in each of them. Our findings stress, however, that nation states are neither strengthened or 'rescued' in their traditional set-ups. The evolution of the national and the European level does not follow any clear path towards a discernible 'finalité politique'. We are thus observing the creation of a new kind of polity, a mixture of 'Europeanisation' and

'domestication' as described by the fusion thesis. These trends *indicate a new stage in the evolution of West European states, with the EU level as a major component.*

The analysis of the 'Fifteen' and the 'One' could not have been carried out without the help of the contributors. Each of them has dealt for many years with the effects of the process of European integration in his or her particular member state. As is necessary in a volume of this kind, special efforts were made to standardise individual chapters. We therefore discussed the analytical approach and preliminary results during a workshop at the Europa Centre, Bonn, in February 1999 and tried to scrutinise the contributions against a common checklist.

Special thanks should go to Simon Bulmer who linked the editors to the publisher and who gave further helpful advice. We received constructive comments and criticism on earlier drafts of our paper on 'Governance in the EU after Maastricht' from Arthur Benz, Armin von Bogdandy, Geoffrey Edwards, Hans-Ulrich Derlien, Markus Jachtenfuchs, Francis Jacobs, Thomas Jäger, Christian Joerges, Beate Kohler-Koch, Dietmar Nickel, Charles Reich, Roger Scully, Michael Shackleton, Peter Schiffauer, Helen Wallace and Michael Zürn. We are very grateful to our student researchers Jana Fleschenberg, Astrid Krekelberg, Martina Kroll and Sonja Siegert, who helped us in establishing the necessary data bases and in editing the volume. Christine Agius and Richard Whitaker helped us to polish the English. Finally, we would like to thank Pippa Kenyon and Nicola Viinikka from Manchester University Press for their patience and comments.

The relations between Member States and the European Union are an never-ending story. The contributions were written in 2000 and may not therefore encompass subsequent changes in national arrangements. The editors are already planning their next edition on a Union with some twenty countries and working within the constitutional and institutional set-up after further steps in treaty-building. Our joint search into the future indicates another function of this volume. We hope that it offers useful reflections for the applicant countries on how to make their systems 'fit' for a successful and competitive life inside the 'Brussels + X' labyrinth, though no 'easy' lessons can be drawn.

Andreas Maurer
Jürgen Mittag
Wolfgang Wessels

List of abbreviations and acronyms

ACP	African, Caribbean and Pacific countries signatory to the Lomé Conventions
ADM	Area Development Management
ASEAN	Association of South-East Asian Nations
BNC	Beoordelingscommissie Nieuwe Commissievoorstellen (NL)
CAP	Common Agricultural Policy
CC	Coalición Canaria (E)
CDA	Christen Democratisch Appel (NL)
CDS	Centro Democrático Social (P)
CDU	Christlich-Demokratische Union (D)
CEEC	Central and Eastern European Countries
CEN	European Committee for Standardisation
CENELEC	European Committee for Electrotechnical Standardisation
CEUA	Committee on European Union Affairs (D)
CFSP	Common Foreign and Security Policy
CGT	Confédération Générale du Travail (F)
CGTP	Confederação Geral dos Trabalhadores (P)
CIPE	Comitatio Interministeriale per la Programmazione Economica (I)
CiU	Convergencia i Unió
CJD	Creutzfeldt-Jakob Disease
CMO	Common Market Organisation
CoCo	Co-Ordination Committee (NL)
CoCoHAN	Co-Ordination Committee at High Civil-Service Level (NL)
COCOM	International Co-Operation Commission (B)
COES	Cabinet Office European Secretariat (UK)
COPA	Committee of Professional Agricultural Organisations in the European Community

CoR	Committee of the Regions and Local Municipalities
COREPER	Comité des Représentants Permanents/Committee of Permanent Representatives
COSAC	Conference of Committees specialised in EU affairs
CSF	Community Support Framework (IR)
CSU	Christlich Soziale Union (D)
CSV	Chrëschtlech-Sozial Vollëkspartei (LUX)
DATAR	Délégation à l'Aménagement du Territoire et de l'Action Régionale (F)
DEFRA	Department for Environment, Food and Rural Affairs
DFA	Department of Foreign Affairs (IR)
DFG	Deutsche Forschungsgemeinschaft
DG	Directorates General
DIKKI	Dimokratiko Kininiko Kinima (GR)
DL	Démocratie Libérale (F)
DL	The Democratic Left (IRL)
DOP	Defence and Overseas Policy
DREE	Direction des Relations économiques extérieures (F)
DTI	Department of Trade and Industry (UK)
EAEC	European Atomic Energy Community
EAGGF	European Agricultural Guarantee and Guidance Fund
EBRD	European Bank for Reconstruction and Development
EC	European Communities (since 1993) European Community
ECA	European Court of Auditors
ECB	European Central Bank
ECE	Economic Commission for Europe (UN)
ECHR	European Convention on Human Rights
ECJ	European Court of Justice
ECOFIN	Economic and Financial Comittee
ECOSOC	Economic and Social Committee
ECOWAS	Economic Community of West African States
ECSA	European Community Studies Association
ECSC	European Coal and Steel Community
ECT	Treaty establishing the European Community
ECU	European Currency Unit
EEA	European Economic Area
EEB	European Environmental Bureau
EEC	European Economic Community
EFGP	European Federation of Green Parties (EP)
EFTA	European Free Trade Association
EIB	European Investment Bank
EIF	European Investment Fund
ELDR	European Liberal, Democrat and Reform Party (EP)

EMI	European Monetary Institute
EMS	European Monetary System
EMU	Economic and Monetary Union
ENVIREG	Environment and Regional Development Programme
EP	European Parliament
EPC	European Political Co-operation
EPP	European People's Party (EP)
EQO	European Question Official Committee (UK)
ERDF	European Regional Development Fund
ESCB	European System of Central Banks
ESF	European Social Fund
ETG	Expert Technical Group
ETSI	European Telecommunications Standardisation Institute
ETUC	European Trade Union Confederation
EUAC	Ausschuß für Fragen der Europäischen Union (D)
Euratom	European Atomic Energy Community
EUROSTAT	Statistical Services of the European Union
FAO	Food and Agriculture Organisation (UN)
FCO	Foreign and Commonwealth Office (UK)
FF	Fianna Fail (IR)
FG	Fine Gael (IR)
FORPPA	Fondo de Ordenación y Regulación de Productos y Precios Agrarios (E)
FPÖ	Freiheitliche Partei Österreichs (AU)
FRG	Federal Republic of Germany
FROM	Fondo de Regulación y Organización del Mercado de Productos de la Pesca y Cultivos Marinos (E)
FYROM	Former Yugoslavian Republic of Macedonia
G	Green Party (IR)
G 7	Group of seven major industrialised nations
G 8	Group of eight major industrialised nations (G 7 plus Russia)
GAP	Groupe des affairs parlementaires (of the European Commission)
GATS	General Agreement on Trade in Services
GATT	General Agreement on Tariffs and Trade
GDP	Gross Domestic Product
GEM	Groupe d'études et de mobilisation (F)
GNP	Gross National Product
Grüne	Bündnis 90/Die Grünen (D)
GSO	Group of Senior Officials
GURI	Gazetta Ufficiale della Republica Italiana (I)
HSE	Health and Safety Executive (UK)
IBEC	Irish Business and Employers Confederation (IR)

IBRD	International Bank for Reconstruction and Development (World Bank)
IEC	Inter-Ministerial Economic Committee (B)
IFOP	Instrumento Financiero de Orientación de la Pesca (E)
IGC	Intergovernmental Conference
IMF	International Monetary Fund
INEM	Instituto Nacional de Empleo (E)
INJUVE	Instituto de la Juventud (E)
INSERSO	Instituto de Servicios Sociales (E)
IPO	Inter Provincial Consultative Agency (NL)
IR	Ireland
IRYDA	Instituto Nacional de Reforma y Desarrollo Agrario (E)
IU	Izquierda Unida (E)
JHA	Justice and Home Affairs
JRC	Joint Research Centre
Lab	Labour Party (IR)
LCGB	Lëtzëbuerger Chrëschtleche Gewerkschaftsbond
LEADER	European LEADER Initiative for rural development
LEONARDO	Community Vocational Training Action Programme
LIF	Liberal Party/Liberal Forum (AU)
LIFE	LIFE is a financial instrument for three major areas of action: Environment, Nature and Third Countries
LINGUA	EU Programme which supports the following actions: Encourage and support linguistic diversity throughout the Union; Contribute to an improvement in the quality of language teaching and learning; Promote access to lifelong language learning opportunities appropriate to each individual's needs
LSAP	Lëtzëbuerger Sozialistesch Arbëchter Partei (LUX)
MAE	Ministerio de Asuntos Exterior (E)
MAFF	Ministry of Agriculture Fisheries and Food (UK)
MDC	Mouvement des Citoyens (F)
MEH	Ministeria de Economía y Hacienda (E)
MEP	Member of European Parliament
Mercosur	Southern Cone Common Market (Mercado Común del Sur)
MP	Member of Parliament
MPF	Mouvement pour la France (F)
MSG	Ministers and Secretaries Group (IR)
NATO	North Atlantic Treaty Organisation
ND	Nea Dimokratia (Neue Demokratie) (GR)
NGO	Non-Governmental Organisation
OECD	Organisation for Economic Cooperation and Development

OGBL	Onofhëngege Gewerkschaftsbond Lëtzëbuerg (LUX)
OJ	Official Journal of the European Communities
OP	Operational Committees (IR)
ÖVP	Österreichische Volkspartei (AU)
PASOK	Panellinio Socialistiko Kinima (GR)
PD	Progressive Democrats (IR)
PDS	Partei des Demokratischen Sozialismus (D)
PES	Party of European Socialists (EP)
PFP	Partnership for Peace (NATO)
PHARE	Poland and Hungary: Aid for the Restructuring of Economies
PNV	Partido Nacionalista Vasco (E)
PP	Partido Popular (P, E)
PR	Permanent Representation (GR)
PRISMA	Providing Innovative Service Models & Assessments
PS	Parti Socialiste (F)
PS	Partido Socialista (P)
PSD	Partido Social-Democrata (P)
PSOE	Partido Socialista Obrero Español (E)
PvdA	Partij van de Arbeid (NL)
QMV	Qualified Majority Voting
RAN	Réglement de l´Assemblée Nationale (F)
R&D	(Community) Research and Development
RECHAR	EU Programme of support for coal-mining areas
REIA-E	Council on International and European Affairs – Sub-Division on Europe (NL)
RPR	Rassemblement pour la République (F)
RS	Réglement du Sénat (F)
SCA	Special Committee on Agriculture (UK)
SEA	Single European Act
SECE	Secretaría de Estado para las Comunidades Europeas (E)
SEM	Single European Market
SEPEUE	Secretaría de Estado de Política Exterior y nova la Unión Europea (E)
SERCE	Secretaría de Estado para las Relaciones con las Comunidades Europeas (E)
SEUE	Secretaría de Estado para la Unión Europea (E)
SGCI	Secrétariat Général du Comité interministériel pour les Questions de Coopération Economique Européenne (F)
SGG	Secrétariat Général du Gouvernement (F)
SME	Small and medium-sized enterprise
SOCRATES	EU Education and Training Programme

SPD	Sozialdemokratische Partei Deutschlands (D)
SPÖ	Sozialdemokratische Partei Österreichs (AU)
SSEA	Secretariat of State for European Affairs (P)
STRIDE	Science and Technology for Regional Innovation and Development in Europe
TACIS	Technical Assistance to the Commonwealth of Independent States
TEMPUS	A cooperation programme in Higher Education managed by the European Commission, Directorate General for Education and Culture
TEU	Treaty on European Union (Maastricht Treaty)
TREVI	TREVI group, part of a 1975 Council initiative to convene home affairs ministers for regular public order and internal security discussions
UDF	Union pour la Démocratie Française (F)
UGT	União Geral de Trabalhadores (P)
UKREP	UK Permanent Representation
UN	United Nations
UNICE	Union of Industrialists of the European Community
VAT	Value-added Tax
VNG	Dutch Association of Municipalities
VVD	Volkspartij voor Vrijheid en Democratie (NL)
WEU	Western European Union
WTO	World Trade Organisation

I

Introduction

1 *Wolfgang Wessels, Andreas Maurer and Jürgen Mittag*

The European Union and Member States: analysing two arenas over time

Our puzzles: traditional approaches and beyond

Fifteen into one? takes up traditional approaches to political science. Since Aristotle it has been considered useful to compare constitutional and institutional dimensions of polities and not least to discuss 'optimal' models of policy-making. In view of the European Union's multi-level and multi-actor polity, we add to a vast literature[1] by highlighting the complex procedural and institutional set-up of nation states preparing and implementing decisions made by the institutions of the European Community (EC).

Unlike volumes on the general structure and culture of European political systems, this volume focuses on *reactions and adaptations to a challenge* which is common to all – i.e. the policy-cycle of the Union. We thus intend to explore structural commonalities and differences with a common point of reference. Fifteen traditional systems and their variations may be better explained when the comparison is based on the fact that they are reacting to the same challenge. In looking at the emerging and evolving realities of the European polity we are interested in how European institutions and Member States (re-)act and interact in a new institutional and procedural set-up. Thus, our major puzzle is: how do governmental and non-governmental actors in different national settings – involving different national traditions – adapt to common challenges, constraints and opportunities for which they are mainly themselves responsible?

Given the features and the dynamics of the evolution of the EU system, we expect to find generally observable trends in the ways that national systems meet the demands of the Union. How do actors perform when they become objects and subjects of the same interaction structure?

Fifteen into one? aims to offer a mixture of conventional and specific analyses and insights for different groups of readers. For scholars of international relations, European integration and comparative politics, these evolutions are of specific interest:[2] they involve looking at both the national level, as in comparative studies,[3] and at the European level, as in integration-related approaches.[4]

We thus try to identify from our comparative research some general trends that can be drawn from our analysis of the Member States. These expectations are based on the assumption that, in response to para-constitutional changes – the SEA, the Maastricht, Amsterdam and Nice treaties – national institutions and actors will have altered their roles, rules and interaction patterns during the period of research. Are we witnessing – owing to the similar pressure for adaptation in each Member State – a trend towards a common and unique model, or rather towards the reinforcement of existing divergences? Will national institutions converge towards one multi-level EU system or will national variations remain? Are the institutions resistant to change or are they subject to a trend of 'Europeanisation'? Does a consideration of national institutions enable us to draw some final conclusions on the future of the Member States – that is, will the European choir sing with one voice or will there still be fifteen distinct sounds in future?

The 'One': evolution into what?

Fifteen into one? goes beyond a strictly comparative approach of academic curiosity. It deals with the issue of how traditional institutions of the West European nation states are shaped by becoming part of one new and different polity. This issue is of growing relevance as frequent institutional and procedural revisions and amendments of the Treaty on European Union (TEU) have provided the Union's members with additional rights and obligations. With respect to their history, West European states have – in the last half of the twentieth century – created a new and particular kind of political system, which offers opportunities and incentives for making public policies beyond the borders of individual countries.

We follow the conventional wisdom that in studying the EU polity it is also necessary to look at the national – constitutive – parts of the EU system. Since the early days of studying the integration process it became obvious that the political system of the Member States could not be treated as a 'black box', which would be irrelevant for the Brussels arena.[5] As a logical consequence academics and practitioners have chosen to analyse how national governments, parliaments and interest groups react on the national level.[6]

Major areas of decision-making have shifted partly or mainly from the state arenas to the EU 'space' in recent years. Many key issues – of utmost political sensitivity – have become part of the subject matter of the European Union. Even if one discounts how the features of 'governance' in the emerging EU political system have been analytically appraised by academic scholars,[7] one fact has become obvious: the European integration process has had a significant impact on the characteristics of national political systems. This is not merely because the individual Member States have to implement Community legislation, but also – and even more importantly – because national institutions are increasingly involved in preparing and making binding decisions. Within the individual Member States there is an ongoing reaction to the challenges of the evolving EU system. National institutions have made substantial efforts to cope with the self-made and challenging devices of the European Union. Some indicators highlight the validity of the impact of the European Union for the national political systems.

Within the Union, institutions take decisions which are binding on the fifteen Member States and their citizens. The dynamics of recent decades are considerable: in amending the original treaty via the SEA (1987), the Maastricht (1993) and Nice (2001) versions of the EU Treaty, Member States – acting as 'masters of the treaties'[8] – have enlarged the scope of policy fields for common activities. They have added new articles which define specific competencies and procedures (from 86 in the EEC treaty of 1957 to 254 in the EU Nice Treaty of 2001) and have revised again and again the institutional and procedural set-up. The overall output of their activity – taking various forms from regulations and directives towards legislative programme decisions and non-binding recommendations – has evolved from 1952 to 1998 towards a total of 52,799 legal acts in December 1998. Many of these decisions apply to relatively short time periods or are regularly replaced by new legislation.[9] If we focus on the total amount of 'legislation in force' – the 'acquis communautaire' with which the Member States must comply and which applicant countries have to adopt – we observe a smaller number of legal acts, but even the acquis communautaire more than doubled from 4,566 legal acts in 1983 to 9,767 in 1998 (Figure 1.1).

In other words, the treaties and their policy provisions have been extensively exploited by the Member States acting jointly within the Council of Ministers and with the European Commission and – to a growing extent – together with the European Parliament (EP).[10]

The 'Fifteen': 'Europeanisation' as a key feature of mutual reinforcement
The Union is considered to have made a marked difference to its constituent units. In this way, the 'masters of the treaties' challenge their other role as 'masters of their own constitution'. Although Member States have been the architects of the emerging EU system, the challenges for their own traditional polity were and are considerable. Not only has the scope and intensity of EU decision-making increased, but also its complexity. It is thus not surprising that national actors of several kinds and levels have pursued different strategies to retain or even increase their say – at both the European and the national or regional level. This volume

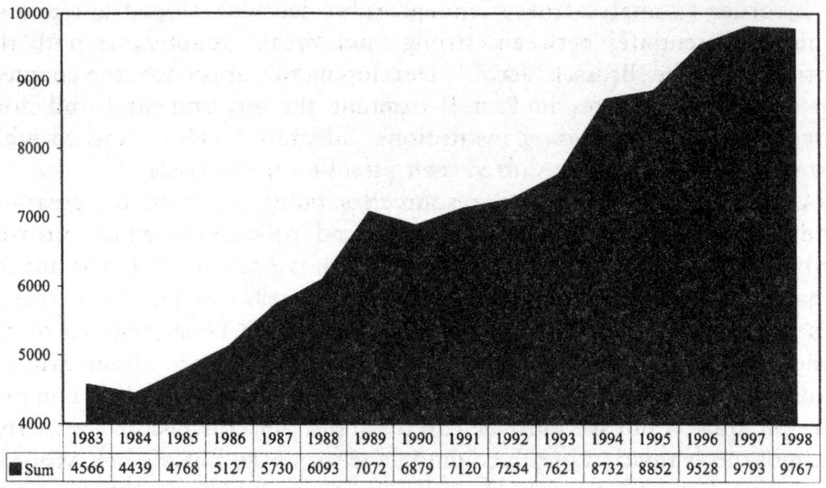

Figure 1.1 Evolution of the European Union's legislation in force, 1983–98
Source: Directories of Community Legislation in Force (Luxembourg, 1984–99, December issues).

points to a considerable variety in these approaches. Through various loops of push–pull dynamics between the European and the national levels, the struggle for a voice[11] has even increased the institutional and procedural differentiation in the national as in the European arenas. Consequently, we anticipate that we shall witness a further stage in the evolution of the West European state.[12]

Comparative studies of the fifteen political systems of EU Member States can thus no longer remain separate from the emerging 'One' – i.e. the evolution of the Union. The exclusion of the European dimension from research into the major trends of national systems will increasingly lead to distorted results.

Fifteen into one? thus discusses the 'into' – i.e. the actual process of integration and what we call 'Europeanisation'. Europeanisation of national actors and procedures is measured first by a shift of attention and participation.[13] With regard to its processual character, 'Europeanisation' means 'the incremental process of reorienting the shape of politics to the degree that EC/EU political and economic dynamics become integral parts of the organisational logic of national politics and policy-making'.[14] At one extreme, 'Europeanisation' could lead to a full synchronisation of national politics with EC/EU imperatives. National institutions would turn into strong multi-level players using their access and influence in one arena for improving their role in others. Actors would profit from a *mutually reinforcing virtuous circle*, upgrading or at least retaining the opportunities to have a say in 'their' European business.

In order to analyse these tendencies we have developed a typology which differentiates between 'strong' and 'weak' adapters at both the national and the 'Brussels' level.[15] Developing this approach, the chapters on the Member States in Part II examine the governmental and non-governmental structures of institutional adaptation. How, and to what extent, have these actors shifted their attention to 'Brussels'?

Given that time is a scarce resource for political actors, the creation, and especially the use, of institutions and procedures which provide linkage to the EU machinery should be seen as relevant. But relevant for what? What we cannot offer, with the modest means we have available, is a socio-psychological analysis of the attitudes and belief systems of the individuals involved.[16] We assume that they learn more about Brussels and their partners in Europe – an important part of some kind of community-building,[17] but we must be careful about our conclusions – in terms both of the evaluation of the common endeavour and of the behaviour of the actors involved. Nevertheless, the chapters on the Member States in Part II indicate that those elites involved in the EU policy-cycle seem to develop some kind of positive 'orientation'[18] towards European governance; they certainly invest a considerable amount of their time in dealing with the Brussels–Strasbourg arena.

Linking two arenas

In analysing this process we focus on two research areas – the European and the national – and compare evolutions on the European level with those in the national setting. In this regard, several developments point to a kind of 'parallel' and simultaneous evolution owing to the creation and use of opportunity structures at the EU level. The evolution of the Council and of the Committee of Permanent Representatives (COREPER) and its related working groups went hand in hand with the creation of 'European' departments in more and more ministries of the Member States. Similarly, new demands for joint problem-solving induced institutional differentiation in the Commission (new Directorates General), the Council (new Council formations) and in the Member States (new services within existing ministries). To a certain extent direct elections to the EP and the successive allocation of powers to Members of the European Parliament (MEPs) have generated the institutionalisation of European Affairs Committees in the parliaments of the Member States. Early attempts at regional and structural policies induced institutionalisation processes at both the European and the national as well as the regional levels. Institutional adaptations to a changed or changing environment are reactions to demand 'pulls' from the Brussels arena, which are by them selves the results of the 'push' of actors from Member States. In other words, multi-level governance creates a 'loop' of adaptation.

'Fifteen' and the 'One': a new kind of relationship?
Fifteen into one? aims to provoke a debate on what the evolution of the state in Western Europe will look like. Will the EU bodies dilute and replace national institutions which are the product of centuries-old evolutions and revolutions? Or will the latter dominate the Union without being seriously affected by the Brussels arena in their day-to-day activities? Thus as shapers which are not shaped by themselves, the 'Fifteen' would remain unaffected by a rather less important or even marginalised 'One'. Or have the 'masters of the treaties' created additional and essential incentives to alter their own politico-administrative set-up in order to strengthen their problem-solving capacity? Several actors would then have to mobilise energy and attention in order to play a game in an arena which offers more effective instruments for solving problems. For this purpose they have to gain additional material knowledge, procedural skills and political sensitivity. National actors have to enlarge their channels for action and their style of interaction. Existing machineries will at the same time increase their functional differentiation and their co-operation mechanisms. The 'One' would become a major force for the evolution of the 'Fifteen'. Thus, the very process of European integration raises the even more demanding issue of linking trends on both arenas in a multi-level analysis.[19] *Fifteen into one?* is thus more than a comparative study: it raises the issue of how a linkage between several levels of government can be established within a novel mode of governance beyond the nation state.

Such an issue is not only of academic interest. If the constituent cornerstones of the EU system – the 'Fifteen' and the 'One' – become more heterogeneous, the structures, processes and networks which link the different branches and layers of governance will become even more complex for the policy-makers as well as for the citizenry.

Which direction? Expectations from theories

To orient our analysis we look at a set of theory-led expectations about the evolution, the patterns and their impact on Member States and their structural frameworks for the EC/EU policy-cycle.[20] The 'acquis academique' on European integration delivers an ever-increasing variety in the concepts and terms used for identifying major characteristics of the EC/EU. It seems that Donald Puchala's elephant[21] is apparently a beast with more and more parts which are quite often looked upon separately. But there seems to be a broad consensus that although the elephant is slow-moving, he is still far from moribund.

One can distinguish between approaches which concern the conceptualisation of the EU's organisational nature, the actual process of integration, and specific policies, institutions and decision-making networks. Among the most prominent concepts include those referring to the Union as a 'quasi-state',[22] a 'regulatory state',[23] or a 'supranational federation'.[24] Perhaps highest on the current political science list are the conceptual models of multi-level,[25] supranational,[26] network (without government),[27] 'polycratic'[28] or multi-tiered governance.[29] Other terms identify core features, such as 'layered intergovernmentalism',[30] 'deliberative supranationalism'[31] and 'multi-level constitutionalism'[32] or concentrate on the Union's political and socio-economic processes following the Treaty of Maastricht.

This range of characterisations demonstrates the difficulties in applying the traditional categories of territorial 'state' and 'international organisation'.[33] However, in spite of the manifold approaches which refer to governance in the Union as 'sui generis', there is one common feature which almost all scholars of European integration studies share: unlike other international organisations, the EC/EU system takes binding decisions which affect the way of life of its citizenry. Legal acts – regulations, directives, decisions, etc. – and the evolution of the actors involved in the production of commonly defined measures, are thus major characteristics of the EC/EU construction. They can therefore be used as significant indicators for the evolution of the political system[34] which is permitted to authoritatively allocate values.[35] Given that we identify this feature almost everywhere within the ruling paradigms, we can link these characteristics with traditional elements of political science and in particular the political system approach.[36]

Whatever the language used, political scientists and lawyers classify the EC/EU as a system for *joint decision-making* in which actors from two or more levels of governance interact in order to solve common (and commonly identified) problems. Whereas the areas of co-operation and integration were originally restricted to the coal and steel industry and its related labour markets, the European Union of the third millennium pertains to a much wider scope of potential action: nearly every field of traditional state activity can become subject to policy-making beyond the nation state. The intensive research on operating networks, single institutions and policy fields as well as on multi-level governance has contributed considerably to our understanding of the post-Maastricht system. But what kind of systemic dynamics can we observe in an overall view over the last fifty years?

(Neo-)functional and (neo-)federal expectations: downgrading and superseding national actors

From the well-known neo-functional or neo-federal lines of argument one could expect a linear or even exponential growth in the making of a sui generis European polity, i.e. a rather smooth process upwards towards some kind of a federal union. In this case, the very nature of integration follows the stimulating definition, which describes 'the process whereby political actors in several distinct national settings are persuaded to shift their loyalties, expectations and political activities towards a new centre, whose institutions possess or demand jurisdiction over the pre-existing national states. The end result of a process of political integration is expected to lead to a new political community, superimposed over the pre-existing ones.'[37] The main feature of integration here is the concept of functional, institutional and procedural spillover: a process which refers 'to a situation in which a given action, related to a specific goal, creates a situation which the original goal can be assured only by taking further actions, which in turn create a further condition and need for more action, and so forth'.[38] Consequently, spillover gradually involves 'more and more people, call[s] for more and more inter-bureaucratic contact and consultation, thereby creating their own logic in favour of later decisions, meeting, in a pro-community direction, the new problems which grow out of the earlier compromises'.[39]

Neo-functionalism would thus predict that actors tend to expand the scope of mutual commitment and intensify their commitment to the original sector(s).[40] In the view of this approach, the revisions of the European treaties are the legally sanctioned products of spillover processes which provide the EU institutions with more exclusive powers for shaping outputs which bind the Member States. The latter accept their roles as part of a process the final outcome of which is not fixed. The 'finalité' is not officially declared. Neo-functional spillover or Hallstein's 'Sachlogik'[41] within policy fields and from one policy area into another would lead to a widening of the functional scope of EC/EU law – i.e. to an increasing number of treaty provisions for a growing number of policy fields. The EC/EU-related structures and procedures of Member States would be oriented to an emerging supranational bureaucracy.[42] The latter would be expected to act as a 'political promoter' which formulates far-reaching policy agendas, articulates ideals and brokers strategies for the deepening of the integration process. The influence of national actors would wither away.

According to federalist thinking, national actors' struggle for access, voice and veto powers, e.g. for an effective control of the Brussels arena, has not been, is not and will not become, successful.[43] Instead, Member States' institutions and actors will become increasingly marginalised and substituted by EC/EU bodies. Such Member State institutions will be transformed from arenas for national actors into autonomous bodies replacing national influence. Each step of treaty (constitution)-building would increase the role of supranational institutions and decrease the veto powers of Member States. The behavioural pattern of the Council of Ministers would be dominated by the use of articles which allow for qualified majority voting (QMV). Where the treaty permits strong parliamentary involvement, co-decision would replace other weaker procedures for parliamentary participation. Those EU-related bodies which bring the national actors together (Council, COREPER and its related working groups) would be seen as primarily serving parochial national interests and as a limited part of a proper federal system which alone could guarantee efficient, effective and legitimate European policies. Concomitantly, the attempts of national administrations to lock into the EC/EU system of a supranational governance evolving towards a real government are rejected as a strategy against the real will of the European people (demos) and the desirable path to a federal union.[44] In this view the EP is a key institution of the constitutional set-up of the (future) EU government. Federalism assumes a legitimate supranational order in which the EP formulates far-reaching policy agendas, articulates ideals and brokers strategies for the deepening of the integration process. As weak adapters, the national actors – governments, administrations and their EC/EU-related agencies – would be downgraded to secondary actors.

(Neo-)realist assumptions: strengthening or rescuing the nation state

In contrast to this approach (neo-)realist thinking conceives the sovereign nation state as the authoritative actor in cross-border interaction.[45] Although various intrastate actors participate in the making of political decisions, the nation state is identified as a unified defender of clearly defined interests and preferences.[46] Following neo-realist assumptions, the Union and its institutional set-up are products of a general strategy of national governments and their administrations to gain and to keep influence *vis-à-vis* other countries.[47] 'The fundamental goal of states in any relationship is to prevent others from achieving advances in their relative capabilities.'[48] Within the framework of the Union, the principal task of Member States is to retain their supremacy as 'masters of the Treaties'.[49] National actors defend and shape an institutional balance favouring the Council and – to a growing extent – the European Council. The Council's infrastructure is then considered as an addition to national institutions sharing the control of the Commission's activities and thus preventing an evolution towards an unrestrained supranational bureaucracy: 'The influence of supranational actors is generally marginal, limited to situations where they have strong domestic allies.'[50] The style of European law-making is characterised by conflict between Member States in which zero-sum games predominate. Accordingly, the behavioural pattern of actors in the Council of Ministers would be characterised by unanimous decision-making and distributive – 'quid-pro-quo' – bargaining.

Strictly Realist expectations for post-'Maastricht' developments stress that the 1989 'geopolitical revolution' and the subsequent radical transformation of the international system makes West European integration look like a child of the Cold War period.[51] From this perspective the Maastricht Treaty was already outdated at the time of its signature.

Neo-realists, however, could interpret 'Maastricht' as the product of a new 'integrative balancing'[52] between Member States. The provisions of the Treaty on European Union (TEU) would reconstitute the ultimate power of Member States: more veto rights for Member States, a benign neglect of the EP and reduced influence for the European Commission. The use of 'Maastricht' and its new or revised provisions – however supranational they might look – will follow an intergovernmental regime of domination by national governments. With regard to the EP, Member States would rather try to exclude MEPs than allow the involvement of a new set of actors who are difficult to control. Instead, neo-realism would expect national parliaments to provide the necessary means for democratic scrutiny of EU business. National administrations would be regarded as essential in maintaining the 'institutional balance' and overall legitimacy in the Union. The interaction style between the two levels of a co-operative governance would follow a model of diplomatic administration. Civil servants – usually seconded from foreign ministries and prime ministerial departments – would prevent any attempts among supranational actors to gain influence. Thus national administrations remain the key protagonists, strengthening or at least 'rescuing the nation state'.[53] The European Commission and the EP would remain 'weak' European actors.

Unlike classic realism, the liberal intergovernmentalist variant of neo-realism analyses the construction of national preference-building. 'National interests are . . . neither invariant nor unimportant, but emerge through domestic political conflict as societal groups compete for political influence, national and transnational coalitions form . . . new political influence, national and transnational coalitions form, and new policy alternatives are recognised by governments.'[54] The analysis of the configuration of national interests therefore includes a consideration of how groups of actors beyond the core of governments and administrations steer the definition or – as regards public opinion – the background of interests and preferences: 'Groups articulate preferences; governments aggregate them.'[55] Liberal intergovernmentalism therefore shares the (neo-)realist assumption of the centrality of Member States' actors within the EC/EU and it explicitly 'denies the historical and path dependent quality of integration',[56] which neo-functionalism stresses as the rationale behind the very process of 'supranational governance'[57] in the Union. In following these assumptions, few national institutions would become 'strong' multi-level players, most would simply have to play the role of strong national actors.

Views of governance approaches: polycentric, non-hierarchical multi-level co-ordination

In view of the major approaches within the modern (i.e. post-1989) school of governance, the institutional and procedural changes in the EU treaties should be analysed as one particular element of rather minor relevance within the complex multi-level game of the Union. The EU polity is seen as a 'post-sovereign, polycentric, incongruent' arrangement of authority which supersedes the limits of the nation state.[58] Assuming a non-hierarchical decision-making process, the EU does matter but only as one realm of collective decision-making and implementation. In other words, 'policy-making in the Community is at its heart a multilateral inter-bureaucratic negotiation marathon'.[59] Given that formal and informal networks[60] among different groups of actors are the decisive arenas for decision-making, formal rules are generally seen as a less important factor.

The 'governance-inspired' pendulum thesis then assumes some kind of cyclical up and down between 'fusion and diffusion'.[61] This 'pattern of the pendulum varies over time and across issues, responding to little endogenous and exogenous factors, and including shifts between dynamics and static periods or arenas of co-operation'.[62] With 'Maastricht' as a more permanent fixture, this to-ing and fro-ing[63] leads to an 'unstable equilibrium'[64] where trends of 'Europeanisation' and 're-nationalisation' come into close competition. In clear contrast to neo-realism and intergovernmentalism, some contributions of multi-level governance would conceive the EP as an active player in the game. 'Irrespective of whether the EP provides legitimacy of European executive decisions, it certainly interferes with the negotiating process.'[65] It can, and sometimes does, overturn the results of negotiation in and around the Commission and the Council. 'Maastricht' would not however constitute a major structural change for the daily governance of the Union. Even if the EP is seen as 'perhaps the largest net beneficiary of the institutional changes in the TEU',[66] multi-level governance would not view the EP as a key player in the EU arena.

From the perspective of this school of thought, Member States are not seen as unified actors. Rather, they are viewed as arenas of collective decision/preparation and implementation, thus indicating a new stage for both administrations and for the state. European governance therefore contributes to a 'decrease in the unilateral steering by government, and hence an increase in the self-governance of networks'.[67] National actors follow a plurality of different adaptation strategies and so we would expect to see weak and strong multi-level players. In any case the monopoly of the state in steering this process would wane. Accordingly, we would expect an 'erosion' of the traditional politico-administrative systems of nation states and a shift of the EU towards a new 'middle ages'[68] of overlapping complex authority structures and divided loyalty configurations. We would then discover a 'post-modern state'[69] in a 'post-national constellation'.[70] Eventually, national administrations might need to rearrange their relationship with both the Union and the national core channels for policy-making.

The fusion view: Europeanisation and communitarisation
The fusion theory[71] goes beyond the analysis of integration at a given (set of) time(s) and tries to offer tools for understanding the dynamics of the EU system over time. It regards EU institutions and procedures as core channels and instruments by which national governments and administrations, as well as other public and private actors, increasingly pool and share public resources from several levels to attain commonly identified goals. Institutional and procedural growth and differentiation – starting from the ECSC – signals and reflects a growing participation of several actors from different levels, which is sometimes overshadowed by cyclical ups and downs in the political and public mood. However, each 'up' leads to a ratchet effect by which the level of activities in the valley of day-to-day politics will have moved to a higher plateau of a supranational communitarisation. The major feature of this process is a transfer and a 'fusion' of public instruments from several state levels linked with the respective 'Europeanisation' of national actors and institutions. The steps of treaty-building are typical products of the attempt by the 'masters of the treaties' to improve their capacity for effective problem-solving and, at the same time, for retaining and even improving their national 'voice'. The result is a new degree of institutional and procedural complexity which is documented in the treaties. From this view the legal output would be expected to increase; the EP would become a real 'co-legislator',[72] and the speed of decision-making would depend on procedural frameworks, national and cross-national interest formation as well as on external pressure.

On the national level the fusion thesis suggests a significant trend towards 'Europeanisation'.[73] EU policy-making thus triggers institutional adaptation in the Member States and alters domestic rules and the inter-institutional distribution of the means for effective participation in European governance. National and regional actors are socialised into the EU legislative process, and continue to adapt to the procedures. Thus, in this view, institutions from both arenas would become strong multi-level players, able and willing to pursue an ongoing positive-sum game.

Grasping the 'One' and the 'Fifteen': on method and approach

In a historic retro-perspective, as well as in terms of shaping the future of Europe, the subject of our research is both rather unique and yet also 'in the making'. We therefore face a dual methodological challenge: that of analysing a rather unfamiliar polity which at the same time has not remained static but is undergoing considerable change. Unless we focus on the process, we risk missing some basic features of the dynamics of European integration. Static analyses and evaluations might be outdated by the time of their publication.

The quantitative exploration of the 'One'

Our approach is to analyse expectations of how national actors have behaved in EU governance after 'Maastricht'. The method applied is deduced from our reading of historical neo-institutionalist theory.[74] We thus use a 'macro-political' perspective within a systematic institutional framework that transcends policy fields and permits an analysis of the Union's politico-administrative system and its procedural features over time. In this first step[75] we focus on the evolution of the para-constitutional and institutional set up and of the de facto use of legal and procedural instruments at the disposal of Member States and EU institutions. We look at the essential features for understanding the actual process of EC/EU integration and co-operation as well as at the different devices used to shape the 'legal' constitution of the Union. Accordingly, we proceed to analyse the effective use of structures for joint problem-solving by the key actors concerned. We try to give answers to the question whether para-constitutional revisions, such as Treaty amendments, matter and how they matter for the set-up and evolution of policy-making structures. Finally, we use the results to readdress the question of whether integration-related approaches provide evidence to support some of the theoretical assumptions elaborated by the academic community.

For the purpose of this volume these trends are taken as independent variables. In Part II, we look at how national institutions and intermediary actors (re-)act to the constraints and challenges from the EC/EU level.

Taking issues seriously: considering the fifteen 'national appendages' of the moving 'beast'

Our analysis focuses on the overall relevance of the EU evolution for each national system. The central question which arises is: does, and in particular *how* does, the Union matter for the national systems in general? After a brief overview of the historical path of the respective country into the European integration process, each chapter in Part II refers to the basic attitudes towards, and concepts of, European integration in the Member State, and also considers parties, interest groups and public opinion, which potentially play important parts in the formation of a European polity. In this context, special attention is given to the development of public opinion. Apart from (neo-)functionalist approaches – which tend to stress only the role of elites – we must also take into account the role of the citizenry in European affairs because 'public opinion applies not just to formal processes of regional integration or specifically to the development of the European Community but applies right along the continuum of internationalised governance'.[76] What is the attitude of the general public in the national systems towards the European Union? How is this orientation expressed? Has the mindset changed over the years?

The analysis leads to the question of whether there are substantial differences between individual Member States and how these background variables might affect the politico-administrative set-up. Thus, we considered it essential to link fundamental patterns of Member States' positions on the European Union with the efforts of governments, parliaments, administrations, regions and courts to adapt to European integration. This issue is highly salient: how do Eurosceptic states fare in the multilevel game?

Closely linked to the issue of public opinion is the analysis of political parties and party systems. In connecting the state with society and interest groups, parties act either as intermediary structures, which express society's interests and needs,[77] or as a 'linkage between institutions and constituencies within the Polity'.[78] Parties represent, aggregate, articulate and adapt conflicts, acting on the basis of social cleavages. With regard to West European societies, these cleavages are subject to ongoing change. Thus, another requirement is to show how far the European integration process has affected parties and party systems. Has European integration led to ideological changes at the national party level[79] or is the traditional set of cleavages complemented by a European cleavage – leading to a system of anti- and pro-integrationist parties?

Interest groups provide another link between state and society. How do such groups react to the European integration process? How do they formulate concepts and strategies with regard to secondary EU legislation? Are they still orientated towards the national level or do they devote more attention to European issues?

If parties and other intermediary actors shape the 'background' of interests and preferences we also need to look at specific national priorities with regard to European integration. Given the socio-economic heterogeneity of and the geographical distance between Member States, one could expect different governmental interests with regard to European integration policy projects. Thus, we also look at the questions: since 'Maastricht', and in comparison to the pre-Maastricht era, what are the main policy areas of the Member States? Which European topics are discussed in national debates? Is there any evidence to suggest that major political events or national conflicts – such as national elections, changes in government, etc. – produce important changes in the tone or style of EU policy-making at the national level?

National adaptation: structures and procedures for European policy-making

A second – and, for us, highly salient – set of questions concerning the Member State level relates to the national structures and decision-making processes in relation the European Union and its institutional framework. The fifteen chapters on the Member States in Part II explore the roles and behaviour of institutions in the national policy-cycle, i.e. from the perspective of the national – and, where relevant, from the regional – capitals. The focus will be on the extent and intensity of participation by national institutions in the process of preparing, making, implementing and controlling EC/EU-generated decisions. Our central question is: to what extent are national institutions involved in the policy-cycle of the European Union? We look both at the Member States and how they interact with Community bodies. Special attention is given to the impact of the (Maastricht) Treaty on the European Union. Did 'Maastricht' matter for the single Member States, at least those twelve signatory states of the EU treaty? What constitutional, institutional and procedural changes have taken place since 'Maastricht'? How relevant are the EC/EU oriented procedures as well as the institutional and administrative set-ups for the Member States and for their constituencies? What highlights – in quantitative as well as in qualitative terms – can we observe with regard to what is new or what seems to be strange in individual Member States? Has the Maastricht Treaty had any major impacts, such as leading to the establishment of new administrative units and co-ordinating bodies?

In this second step, opening up the 'black box' of the EU-related policy-cycle involves analysing the patterns of interaction between governments, parliaments, administrations, regional entities, constitutional courts and other actors, while bearing in mind how allies and competitors perform in the political space. The chapters in Part II describe who is involved at each stage of the policy-cycle.

We thus look into the manner in which the 'established' members shaped their institutions and procedures in the light of the major constitutional amendments and revisions of the (Maastricht) Treaty. As for the Member States that joined as part of the 1995 enlargement (Austria, Finland and Sweden), the authors analyse both the institutional–procedural structures and the adaptation and transformation processes.

The investigations in Part II also refer to the co-operation and interaction of national bodies with the European institutions in the Brussels sphere. We analyse how national institutions, especially governments or administrations, deal with European affairs. In this regard, the involvement of national parliaments in European affairs and the subsequent changes affecting the procedures of national parliaments is also examined.[80] How do national parliaments deal with European affairs, particularly since 'Maastricht'? Which methods of parliamentary participation have been used? With regard to regional actors the authors studied which channels of information and policy co-ordination have been set up by regional institutions. Finally, we take a look at the constitutional complaints and judgements of national (constitutional) courts and their interpretations.

We want to know if and how some well-known specifics of some member countries survived the 1990s. Did the Danish parliament secure its gatekeeper role? What is the updated record of the renewed SGCI, which gained the reputation of representing an efficient, centralised system in France? How much success have the German Länder really achieved in the march towards Brussels and Bonn/Berlin? Which formula of national participation in the EC/EU policy process have the Swedish or the Austrian systems adhered to?

The search for best practices: what lessons can be learned?

One intriguing issue frequently present in political and academic debates is the question of the 'best practice' of adaptation to the EC/EU structures. Comparing the structures and processes in the fifteen Member States, we examine the national institutions in terms of a comparative performance test. Based on our findings, the foremost question of Part II is how well the individual Member States have adapted. Can we identify Member States which look more efficient than others? Why do some states succeed and others fail to reach their goals? Have the national institutions undertaken serious innovations? Thus, do the common challenges of handling the Brussels set-up lead national systems to adopt similar methods of organising the essential constitutional and institutional dimensions of their polity? Or do the reactions to these challenges lead to a strengthening of national approaches so that the traditional specifics of Member States turn out to be more relevant than the similarities?

For both the next round of newcomers to the Union and for the founding members we take up Aristotle's vocation of going beyond description and analysis towards discussing improvements. If we focus on the multiple ways in which Member States have developed their systems, can we identify an optimal model which would serve as a reference point, or do we need to be more modest?

This enquiry refers to the debate about whether certain actors and – more importantly – whether certain Member States are more able than others to attain their goals or to cope with the challenges coming from the EU level. Is there a model of the most competitive Member State or institutional actor which might therefore serve as a point of reference for other members and for the institutional and procedural designs of the newcomers? Have institutional features such as the role of the Danish parliament, the UK cabinet system or the strategies of the German Länder served as models for other Member States? Remarks about the 'unfair' advantages of some partners are not unknown in Community circles. The Council's internal debates about necessary reforms to streamline the co-ordination among its various formats and subordinated bodies lead directly to the question about which national model(s) of EC/EU-related policy co-ordination would fit(s) into an arena of twenty or more participants.[81]

Patterns of adaptation might also be identified in terms of certain basic models: *Fifteen into one?* develops a typology of different ways in which national actors (re)act within and adapt to European integration. Will such an adaptation be asymmetrical? Will the point of convergence be dominated by specific structures of one Member State or a group of Member States?

The 'goodness of fit' category considers positions expressed by academics and political actors with regard to each Member State, thus permitting each author a – necessarily subjective – analysis concerning the 'performance' of his or her Member State.

Methodological risks

The methods used in this volume might be seen as conventional. Authors from the fifteen Member States analysed 'their' respective country on the basis of a semi-structured outline, which was collectively discussed and elaborated. The approach has its merits and limitations. It helps us to compare the structural and organisational reactions of a certain set of important actors but has the limitations of more subjective assessments, the latter being especially visible when authors analyse the extent to which a system has adapted to European integration. Given the limits of time and resources, an in-depth study of Member States' relative competitiveness in different policy fields could not be pursued. However we hope that our findings may serve as a starting point for a broader set of case studies.[82]

There are further caveats. The evolutions and changes in states' politico-administrative spheres are usually continuing, gradual and time-consuming. Tracing back an ongoing process of interaction and mutual adaptation between various actors always risks a timebound, backward-looking view. Accordingly we might need a longer-term perspective to identify the key patterns of evolution. However, using the 1960s–90s as a basis for our observations, we take the risk of privileging certain educated expectations about institutional trends within the emerging multi-level and para-constitutional system.

We realise that the EU system cannot be described and analysed simply by looking at the institutions of the EU and their policies in a narrow sense and from a sectoral perspective. Case studies on governance within different policy fields and related networks provide an essential intellectual input to our understanding about the evolution of multi-level and multi-actor governance.[83] We admit that the links between the 'constitutive' elements of the Union cannot always be easily assessed. In this respect, scrutinising the institutional adaptation of national and sub-national actors to a 'moving target' beyond the boundaries of traditional policy making – the Union in recent decades – is subject to an obvious risk. Hence, we may observe different speeds of adaptation. We may also need to take into account the slower reactions of some Member States at the national level. Member state A may remain immune to a new external input whereas Member State B is characterised by a dynamic set of changes in the politico-administrative system owing to European demands. Member States C and D, at the same time, might not alter their formal rules of EC/EU participation. However, the public discourse on policy-making and administrative participation is characterised by an ever growing 'de facto internalisation' of European issues into traditional 'national' spheres. Analyses of common trends of Europeanisation need to account particularly for the roots of change.

Institutional adjustments may not automatically lead to a direct and swift alteration of policy processes in all areas simultaneously. There may be fundamental hidden patterns which we are not able to not grasp through our empirical data.

Notes

1 See e.g. Helen Wallace, *National Governments and the European Communities* (London: Chatham House, 1973); Christoph Sasse, Edouard Poullet, David Coombes and Gérard Deprez, *Decision Making in the European Community* (New York, London: Praeger, 1977); Spyros Pappas (ed.), *National Administrative Procedures for the Preparation and Implementation of Community Decisions* (Maastricht: EIPA, 1995); Kenneth Hanf and Ben Soetendorp, 'Small States and the Europeanization of Public Policy', in: Kenneth Hanf and Ben Soetendorp (eds), *Adapting to European Integration, Small States and the European Union* (London: Longman, 1998); Yves Mény, Pierre Muller and Jean-Louis Quermonne (eds), *Adjusting to Europe. The Impact of the EU on National Institutions and Policies* (London: Routledge, 1996); Johan P. Olsen, 'Europeanization and Nation-State Dynamics', in: Sverker Gustavsson and Leif Lewin (eds), *The Future of the Nation-State* (London: Routledge, 1996); Robert Ladrech, 'Europeanization of Domestic Politics and Institutions. The Case of France', in: *Journal of Common Market Studies*, No. 1/1994, pp. 69–88; Klaus Götz, 'National Governance and European Integration. Intergovernmental Relations in Germany', in: *Journal of Common Market Studies*, No. 1/1995, pp. 91–116; Wolfgang Wessels, 'Institutions of the EU System: Models of Explanation', in: Dietrich Rometsch and Wolfgang Wessels (eds), *The European Union and Member States, Towards Institutional Fusion?* (Manchester: Manchester University Press, 1996), pp. 20–36; Caitríona Carter and Andrew Scott, 'Legitimacy and Governance beyond the European Nation State: Conceptualizing Governance in the European Union', in: *European Law Review*, No. 4/1998, pp. 429–445.

2 For the debate about the usefulness of International Relations (IR) and Comparative Politics approaches see Simon Hix, 'The Study of the European Community: The Challenge to Comparative Politics', in: *West European Politics*, No. 1/1994, pp. 1–30; Markus Jachtenfuchs, 'Theoretical Perspectives on European Governance', in: *European Law Journal*, No.

2/1995, pp. 115–133; Thomas Risse-Kappen, 'Exploring the Nature of the Beast: International Relations Theory and Comparative Policy Analysis Meet the European Union', in: *Journal of Common Market Studies*, No. 1/1996, pp. 53–80; Andrew Hurrell and Anand Menon, 'Politics Like Any Other?: Comparative Politics, International Relations and the Study of the EU', in: *West European Politics*, No. 2/1996, pp. 386–402; Simon Hix, 'CP, IR and the EU! A Rejoinder to Hurell and Menon', in: *West European Politics*, No. 4/1996, pp. 802–804; Gary Marks, 'Comparative Politics and International Relations: Suggestions for a Unitary Approach', in: *ECSA Review*, No. 2/1997, pp. 1–2; Simon Hix, 'The Study of the European Union II: The 'New Governance' Agenda and Its Rival', in: *Journal of European Public Policy*, No. 1/1998, pp. 38–65.

3 See Ulrich Battis, Dimitris Tsatsos and Dimitris Stefanou (eds), *Europäische Integration und nationales Verfassungsrecht* (Baden-Baden: Nomos, 1995); Thibaut de Berranger, *Constitutions nationales et construction communautaire* (Paris: Librairie Générale de Droit et de Jurisprudence, 1995); Francesco G. Duina and John A. Hall, *Harmonizing Europe: Nation-States within the Common Market* (New York: State University of New York Press, 1999); Hanf and Soetendorp (eds), 1998, *op. cit.*; David Hine and Hussein Kassim (eds), *Beyond the Market. The EU and National Social Policy* (London: Routledge, 1998); Wolfgang Ismayr (ed.), *Die Politischen Systeme Westeuropas,* Second Edition (Opladen: Leske & Budrich, 1999).

4 See Kenneth A. Armstrong and Simon J. Bulmer, *The Governance of the Single European Market* (Manchester: Manchester University Press, 1998), Simon Hix, *The Political System of the European Union* (New York: St Martin's Press, 1999); Hussein Kassim, Guy Peters and Vincent Wright (eds), *The National Co-Ordination of EU Policy* (Oxford: Oxford University Press, 2001); Beate Kohler-Koch and Rainer Eising (eds), *The Transformation of Governance in the European Union* (London: Routledge, 1999); Beate Kohler-Koch, 'Framing: The Bottleneck of Constructing Legitimate Institutions', in: *Journal of European Public Policy*, No. 4/2000, pp. 513–531; Neil Nugent, *The Government and Politics of the European Union,* Fourth Edition (Durham, Md.: Duke University Press, 1999); John Peterson and Elizabeth Bomberg, *Decision-Making in the European Union* (Houndsmills, London: Macmillan, 1999); Jeremy Richardson (ed.), *European Union. Power and Policy-Making* (London: Routledge, 1996); Helen Wallace and William Wallace (eds), *Policy-Making in the European Union*, Fourth Edition (Oxford: Oxford University Press, 2000).

5 See Wallace, 1973, *op. cit.*; Sasse *et al.*, 1977, *op. cit.*

6 See Rometsch and Wessels, 1996, *op. cit.*

7 See for a general overview Markus Jachtenfuchs and Beate Kohler-Koch, 'Regieren im dynamischen Mehrebenensystem', in: Markus Jachtenfuchs and Beate Kohler-Koch (eds), *Europäische Integration* (Opladen: Leske & Budrich, 1996), pp. 15–44; Gary Marks, Liesbet Hooghe and Kermit Blank, 'European Integration from the 1980s, State-Centric vs. Multi-Level Governance', in: *Journal of Common Market Studies*, No. 3/1996, pp. 341–378; Gary Marks, Fritz W. Scharpf, Philippe C. Schmitter and Wolfgang Streeck, *Governance in the European Union* (London: Sage, 1999); Fritz W.

Scharpf, *Governing in Europe: Effective and Democratic? (*Oxford: Oxford University Press, 1999). Note also the European Commission's recent attempts on the White Paper on European Governance, Brussels, 11 October 2000, Document SEC(2000) 1547/7Final.

8 German Constitutional Court, 'Judgement of October 12, 1993 on the Maastricht Treaty', in: Andrew Oppenheimer (ed.), *The Relationship between European Community Law and National Law: The Cases* (Cambridge: Cambridge University Press, 1995).

9 See Edward C. Page and Dionyssis Dimitrakopoulos, 'The Dynamics of EU Growth. A Cross-Time Analysis', in: *Journal of Theoretical Politics*, No. 3/1997, pp. 365–387; note that one-half of all EC legislation lasts for less than two years.

10 See for Figure 1.1 in detail Andreas Maurer and Wolfgang Wessels, 'The European Union matters: Structuring Self-Made Offers and Demands', Chapter 2 in this volume, pp. 43–45.

11 See Albert O. Hirschmann, *Exit, Voice and Loyalty: Responses to Decline in Firms, Organisations and States* (Cambridge, Mass.: Harvard University Press, 1970).

12 See for such an approach, see: Charles Tilly (ed.), *The Formation of National States in Western Europe* (Princeton: Princeton University Press, 1975) and Stein Rokkan, 'Dimensions of State Formation and Nation-Building: A Possible Paradigm for Research on Variations within Europe', in: Tilly (ed.), 1975, *op. cit.*, pp. 562–600.

13 See Wolfgang Wessels, 'The Growth and Differentiation of Multi-Level-Networks: A Corporatist Mega-Bureaucracy or an Open City?', in: Helen Wallace and Alasdair A. Young (eds), *Participation and Policy-Making in the European Union* (Oxford: Clarendon Press, 1997), p. 36.

14 Robert Ladrech, 'Problems and Prospects for Party Politics at the European Level. The Case of Socialist Transnational Party Development', Paper presented to the 4th Biennial ECSA Conference, 11–14 May 1995, p. 68.

15 See for more detailed conclusions: Jürgen Mittag and Wolfgang Wessels, 'The "One" and the "Fifteen"? The Member States between Procedural Adaptation and Structural Revolution', Chapter 18 in this volume, pp. 413–414.

16 See in this respect Jarle Trondal, 'Integration through Participation – Introductionary Notes to the Study of Administrative Integration', in: *European Integration online Papers*, No. 4/1999 www.eiop.or.at/eiop/texte/1999–004a.htm.

17 See Karl W. Deutsch, Sidney A. Burrell and Robert A. Kann, *Political Community and the North Atlantic Area* (Princeton: Princeton University Press, 1957).

18 Oskar Niedermayer and Bettina Westle, 'A Typology of Orientations', in: Oskar Niedermayer and Richard Sinnott (eds), *Public Opinion and Internationalized Governance* (Oxford: Oxford University Press, 1995), pp. 33–50.

19 See Beate Kohler-Koch, 'Catching up with Change: The Transformation of Governance in the European Union', in: *Journal of European Public Policy*, No. 3/1996, pp. 359–380; Wolfgang Wessels, 'An Ever Closer Fusion? A

Dynamic Macropolitical View on the Integration Process', in: *Journal of Common Market Studies*, No. 1/1997, pp. 267–299.

20 See for a first overview Helen Wallace, 'Institutions, Process and Analytical Approaches', in: Helen Wallace and William Wallace (eds) *Policy-Making in the European Union*, Fourth Edition (Oxford: Oxford University Press, 2000), pp. 3–81; Laura Cram, 'Integration Theory and the Study of the European Policy Process', in: Jeremy Richardson (ed.), *European Union. Power and Policy-Making* (London: Routledge, 1996), pp. 40–58; Andrew Moravcsik, *The Choice for Europe. Social Purpose and State Power from Messina to Maastricht* (London: UCL Press, 1999); Wolfgang Wessels, 'Die Europapolitik in der wissenschaftlichen Debatte', in: Werner Weidenfeld and Wolfgang Wessels (eds), *Jahrbuch der Europäischen Integration, 1980* ff. (Bonn: Europa-Union Verlag 1981 ff.).

21 See David J. Puchala, 'Of Blind Men, Elephants and International Integration', in: *Journal of Common Market Studies*, No. 3/1972, p. 267: 'The story of the blind men and the elephant is well known. Several blind men approached an elephant and each touched the animal in an effort to discover what the beast looked like. Each blind man, however, touched a different part of the animal, and each concluded that the elephant had the appearance of the part he touched ... The total result was that no man arrived at a very accurate description of the elephant.' A similar story can be found in 'Nathan the Wise' by the German drama author Gotthold Ephraim Lessing (1729–81), which focuses – in the so-called 'Ringparabel' – on the way different persons look at the same thing. See Peter Demetz (ed.), Nathan the Wise, Minna Von Barnhelm, *and other Plays and Writings by Gotthold Ephraim Lessing*, German Library, Vol. 12 (London: Continuum Publishers, 1991).

22 William Wallace, 'Government without Statehood', in: Helen Wallace and William Wallace (eds), *Policy-Making in the European Union*, Third Edition (Oxford: Oxford University Press, 1996), pp. 439–460.

23 Giandomenico Majone, 'The Rise of the Regulatory State in Europe', in: *West European Politics*, No. 17/1994, pp. 77–101.

24 Armin von Bogdandy, 'Die Europäische Union als supranationale Föderation', in: *Integration*, No. 2/1999, pp. 95–112; Armin von Bogdandy, *Supranationaler Föderalismus als Wirklichkeit und Idee einer neuen Herrschaftsform. Zur Gestalt der Europäischen Union nach Amsterdam* (Baden-Baden: Nomos, 1999).

25 See Gary Marks, 'Structural Policy and Multilevel Governance in the EC', in: Alan W. Cafruny and Glenda G. Rosenthal (eds), *The State of the European Community 2: The Maastricht Debates and Beyond* (Boulder, Co.: Lynne Rienner, 1993), pp. 391–410; Marks, Hooghe and Blank, 1996, *op. cit.*; Fritz W. Scharpf, *Community and Autonomy, Multilevel Policy-Making in the European Union*, European University Institute, Florence, EUI Working Paper, No. 1994/1.

26 See Wayne Sandholtz and Alec Stone Sweet (eds), *European Integration and Supranational Governance* (Oxford: Oxford University Press, 1998).

27 See Beate Kohler-Koch, 'The Evolution and Transformation of European Governance', in: Beate Kohler-Koch and Rainer Eising (eds), *The*

Transformation of Governance in the European Union (London: Routledge, 1999), p. 15.

28 Christine Landfried, 'The European Regulation of Biotechnology by Polycratic Governance', in: Christian Joerges and Ellen Vos (eds), *EU Committees: Social Regulation, Law and Politics* (Oxford: Hart Publishing, 1999), p. 173.

29 See Simon Bulmer, 'The Governance of the European Union, A New Institutionalist Approach', in: *Journal of European Public Policy*, No. 4/1994, pp. 351–380.

30 Deirdre Curtin and Ige Decker, 'The EU as a 'Layered' International Organization: Institutional Unity in Disguise', in: Paul Craig and Cráinne de Búrca (eds), *The Evolution of EU Law* (Oxford: Oxford University Press, 1999), pp. 83–136.

31 Christian Joerges, 'Good Governace through Comitology?', in Christian Joerges and Ellen Vos (eds), *EU Committees: Social Regulation, Law and Politics* (Oxford: Hart Publishing, 1999), p. 312.

32 Ingolf Pernice, 'Multilevel Constitutionalism and the Treaty of Amsterdam: European Constitution-Making Revisited?', in: *Common Market Law Review*, No. 36/1999, pp. 703–750; see also: Beate Kohler-Koch, *A Constitution for Europe?*, Mannheimer Zentrum für Europäische Sozialforschung, Working Papers, No. 8/1999 (Mannheim: MZES, 1999).

33 See Brigid Laffan, 'The European Union: A Distinctive Model of Internationalisation?', in *European Integration online Papers*, No. 18/1997: http://www.eiop.or.at/eiop/texte/1997–018a.htm.

34 See Hix, 1999, *op. cit.*

35 See David Easton, *The Political System* (New York: Knopf, 1953), pp. 129–134.

36 See Easton, 1953, *op. cit.*; Hix, 1999, *op. cit.*; David Coombes, *Seven Theorems on the European Parliament* (London: Kogan Page, 1998), pp. 1–15.

37 Ernst B. Haas, *The Uniting of Europe*, Second Edition (Stanford: Stanford University Press, 1968), p. 16; see also Kalypso Nicolaidis and Robert Howse (eds), *The Federal Vision – Legitimacy and Levels of Governance in the United States and the European Union* (Oxford: Oxford University Press 2001).

38 Leon N. Lindberg, The Political Dynamics of European Economic Integration (Stanford: Stanford University Press, 1963), p. 10. See also Robert O. Keohane and Stanley Hoffmann, 'Institutional Change in Europe in the 1980s', in: Robert O. Keohane and Stanley Hoffmann (eds), *The New European community, Decisionmaking and Institutional Change* (Boulder, Co.: Westview Press, 1991), pp. 1–39.

39 Haas, 1968, *op. cit.* p. 372.

40 See Philippe C. Schmitter, 'Three Neofunctional Hypotheses about International Integration', in: *International Organisation*, No. 23/1969, p. 162.

41 Wolfgang Wessels, 'Walter Hallstein's Contribution to Integration Theory: Outdated or Underestimated?', in: Wilfried Loth, William Wallace and Wolfgang Wessels (eds), *Walter Hallstein: The Forgotten European?* (London: Macmillan, 1998), pp. 229–254.

42 See Andreas Maurer, Jürgen Mittag and Wolfgang Wessels, 'Theoretical Perspectives on Administrative Interaction in the European Union', in: Thomas Christiansen and Emil Kirchner (eds), *Committee Governance in the European Union* (Manchester: Manchester University Press, 2000), pp. 23–44.

43 See Richard Mayne and John Pinder, *Federal Union: The Pioneers, A History of Federal Union* (London, New York: Macmillan, 1990), pp. 214–215; John Pinder, *European Community: The Building of a Union* (Oxford, New York: Oxford University Press, 1995); John Pinder (ed.), *Foundations of Democracy in the European Union. From the Genesis of Parliamentary Democracy to the European Parliament* (London: Macmillan, 1999).

44 See Altiero Spinelli *et al.*, The Manifesto of Ventotene www.let.leidenuniv.nl/history/rtg/res1/histdoc.htm; Altiero Spinelli, *Manifest der europäischen Föderalisten* (Frankfurt a.M.: Europäische Verlags-Anstalt, 1958); Heinrich Schneider: 'Föderale Verfassungspolitik für eine Europäische Union', in: Heinrich Schneider and Wolfgang Wessels (eds), *Föderale Union – Europas Zukunft? Analysen, Kontroversen, Perspektiven* (München: Beck, 1996), pp. 21–50.

45 See Kenneth N. Waltz, *Theory of International Politics* (Reading, Mass.: Addison-Wesley, 1979); Peter B. Evans, Dietrich Rüschemeyer and Theda Skocpol, *Bringing the State Back In* (Cambridge: Cambridge University Press, 1986); Thomas Volgy, Lawrence E. Imwalle and John E. Schwarz, 'Where is the New World Order? Hegemony, State Strength, and Architectural Construction in International Relations', in: *Journal of International Relations and Development*, No. 3/1999, pp. 246–262.

46 See Joseph M. Grieco, 'Anarchy and the Limits of Co-Operation: A Realist Critique to the Newest Liberal Institutionalism', in: *International Organisation*, No. 3/1988, p. 494.

47 See Grieco, 1988, *op. cit.*, pp. 485–587; Werner Link, *Die Neuordnung der Weltpolitik. Grundprobleme globaler Politik an der Schwelle zum 21. Jahrhundert* (München: Beck, 1998).

48 Grieco, 1988, *op. cit.*, p. 498.

49 German Constitutional Court, Judgement of October 12, 1993, *op. cit.*

50 Andrew Moravcsik, 'Liberal Intergovernmentalism and Integration: A Rejoinder', in: *Journal of Common Market Studies*, No. 4/1995, pp. 611–628 (here p. 612); Andrew Moravcsik, 1999, *op. cit.*

51 See John Mearsheimer, 'Back to the Future. Instability in Europe After the Cold War', in: *International Security*, No. 1/1990, pp. 5–56.

52 Link, 1998, *op. cit.*, pp. 148–150.

53 Alan S. Milward, *The European Rescue of the Nation State* (Berkeley: University of California Press, 1992); see also Stanley Hoffmann, 'Obstinate or Obsolete? The Fate of the Nation State and the Case of Western Europe', in: *Daedulus*, No. 3/1966, pp. 862–915.

54 Andrew Moravcsik, 'Preferences and Power in the European Community: A Liberal Intergovernmentalist Approach', in: *Journal of Common Market Studies*, No. 31/1993, p. 481.

55 Moravcsik, 1993, *op. cit.*, p. 483: 'The most fundamental influences on foreign policy are, therefore, the identity of important societal groups, the

nature of their interests, and their relative influence on domestic policy.'

56 Moravcsik, 1995, *op. cit.*, pp. 612–613.

57 Alec Stone Sweet and Wayne Sandholtz, 'Integration, Supranational Governance, and the Institutionalization of the European Polity', in: Wayne Sandholtz and Alec Stone Sweet (eds), *European Integration and Supranational Governance* (Oxford: Oxford University Press, 1998), p. 5, who view 'intergovernmental bargaining and decision-making as embedded in processes that are provoked and sustained by the expansion of transnational society, the pro-integrative activities of supranational organizations, and the growing density of supranational rules'. Consequently, they argue, 'these processes gradually, but inevitably, reduce the capacity of the Member States to control outcomes'.

58 Philippe C. Schmitter, 'If the Nation-State Were to Wither Away in Europe, What Might Replace it?', in: Sverker Gustavsson and Leif Lewin (eds), *The Future of the Nation-State* (London: Routledge, 1996), p. 136.

59 Kohler-Koch, 1996, *op. cit.*, p. 367.

60 See Adrienne Héritier, 'The Accommodation of Diversity in European Policy-Making and Its Outcomes: Regulatory Policy as a Patchwork', in: *Journal of European Public Policy*, No. 2/1996, pp. 149–167.

61 Helen Wallace, 'Politics and Policy in the EU: The Challenge of Governance', in: Helen Wallace and William Wallace (eds), *Policy-Making in the European Union*, Third Edition (Oxford: Oxford University Press, 1996), p. 13.

62 *Ibid.*, p. 14.

63 See Jachtenfuchs and Kohler-Koch, 1996, *op. cit.*

64 William Wallace, 'Government without Statehood: The Unstable Equilibrium', in: Helen Wallace and William Wallace (eds), *Policy-Making in the European Union*, Third Edition (Oxford: Oxford University Press, 1996), pp. 439–460 (here p. 439).

65 Wallace, 1996, *op. cit.*, p. 33.

66 *Ibid.*, p. 63; Andreas Maurer, *What Next for the European Parliament?* (London: Kogan Page, 1999).

67 Kohler-Koch, 1996, *op. cit.*, p. 371.

68 David Held, *Democracy and Global Order. From the Modern State to Cosmopolitan Governance* (Cambridge: Polity Press, 1995), p. 137, referring to Headley Bull, *The Anarchical Society* (London: Macmillan, 1977), pp. 254–255; see also David Held, 'Changing Contours of Political Community: Rethinking Democracy in the Context of Globalisation', in: Michael Greven (ed.), *Demokratie – eine Kultur des Westens? 20. Wissenschaftlicher Kongreß der Deutschen Vereinigung für Politikwissenschaft* (Opladen: Leske & Budrich, 1996), pp. 137–138.

69 James Caporaso, 'The European Union and Forms of the State: Westphalian, Regulatory or Post-Modern', in: *Journal of Common Market Studies*, No. 1/1996, pp. 29–52.

70 Jürgen Habermas, *Die postnationale Konstellation* (Frankfurt a.M.: Suhrkamp, 1998), pp. 94–96.

71 See Wessels, 1996, *op. cit.*; Wolfgang Wessels, *Die Öffnung des Staates, Modelle und Wirklichkeit grenzüberschreitender Verwaltungspraxis 1960–1995* (Opladen: Leske & Budrich, 2000), pp. 122–137; Ben

Rosamond, *Theories on European Integration* (Houndsmills, London: Macmillan, 1999), p. 140.

72 Maurer, 1999, *op. cit.*

73 See Götz, 1995, *op. cit.*; Carter and Scott, 1998, *op. cit.*; Christoph Knill and Dirk Lehmkuhl, 'How Europe matters. Different Mechanisms of Europeanization', in: *European Integration online Papers*, No. 7/1999 www.eiop.or.at/eiop/texte/1999–007a.htm.

74 See Guy Peters, *Institutional Theory in Political Science. The 'New Institutionalism'* (London, New York: Pinter, 1999); Peter A. Hall and Rosemary C.R. Taylor, 'Political Science and the Three New Institutionalisms', in: *Political Studies*, No. 5/1996, pp. 936–957; James March and Johan P. Olsen, *Rediscovering Institutions: The Organizational Basis of Politics* (New York: Free Press, 1989).

75 Andreas Maurer and Wolfgang Wessels, *The European Union Matters: Structuring Self-Made Offers and Demands,* Chapter 2 in this volume, pp. 32–33.

76 Richard Sinnott, 'Bringing Public Opinion Back in', in: Oskar Niedermayer and Richard Sinnott (eds), *Public Opinion and International Governance* (Oxford: Oxford University Press, 1995), *op. cit.* pp. 11–32 (here p. 31).

77 See especially with regard to this function Leon D. Epstein: *Political Parties in Western Democracies*, Second Edition (New Brunswick, New York: Transaction Books, 1980); Gunter Jasmut, *Die politischen Parteien und die europäische Integration* (Frankfurt a.M.: Peter Lang, 1995), p. 23.

78 John Gaffney, 'Introduction: Political Parties and the European Union', in: John Gaffney (ed.), *Political Parties and the European Union* (London, New York: Routledge, 1996), pp. 1–2.

79 See Simon Hix, 'Parties at the European Level and the Legitimacy of EU Socio-Economic Policy', in: *Journal of Common Market Studies*, No. 4/1995, pp. 525–554. See also Simon Hix and Christopher Lord, *Political Parties in the European Union* (London: Macmillan, 1997), pp. 7–10.

80 For a recent analysis on the roles of national parliaments in EC and EU affairs, see: Andreas Maurer and Wolfgang Wessels (eds), *National Parliaments on their Ways to Europe: Losers or Latecomers?* (Baden-Baden: Nomos, 2001).

81 See European Council of Helsinki, 10/11 December 1999, 'Conclusions of the Presidency, Annex III: An Effective Council for an Enlarged Union, Guidelines for Reform and Operational Recommendations'. See also the report submitted by the Secretary-General in March 1999, Document No. SN 2139/99.

82 See in this respect Hine and Kassim (eds), 1998, *op. cit.*; Hussein Kassim and Anand Menon (eds), *The European Union and National Industrial Policy* (London: Routledge, 1996); Beate Kohler-Koch and Rainer Eising (eds), *The Transformation of Governance in the European Union* (London: Routledge, 1999); Andrew McLaughlin and William A. Maloney, *The European Automobile Industry. Multi Level Governance, Policy and Politics* (London: Routledge, 1999); Sandholtz and Stone Sweet (eds), 1998, *op. cit.*

83 See Tanja A. Börzel, 'What's So Special about Policy Networks? An Exploration of the Concept and its Usefulness in Studying European

Governance', in: *European Integration online Papers*, No. 1/1997 http://www.eiop.or.at/eiop/texte/1997–016a.htm; Tanja A. Börzel, 'Rediscovering Policy Networks as a Form of Modern Governance' (book review), in: *Journal of European Public Policy*, No. 2/1998, pp. 354–359; Adrienne Héritier, 'Policy-making by Subterfuge. Interest Accommodation, Innovation and Substitute Democratic Legitimation in Europe – Perspectives from Distinctive Policy Areas', in: *Journal of European Public Policy*, No. 2/1997, pp. 171–189.

2 *Andreas Maurer and Wolfgang Wessels*

The European Union matters: structuring self-made offers and demands

Self-made demands from the EU: analysing the impact of Maastricht

The evolution of European integration since 1950 has been considerable. The European Union has gained in stature, taking on and aspiring to new functions across the policy spectrum and challenging the conceptualisation of the evolving structure for joint problem-solving, deliberation and decision-making.

The evolution of the Union: stages of constitution-building

To test different theory-led expectations and their impact on the Member States,[1] in view of the Maastricht Treaty, we proceed in two steps. First, we explore the evolution of EC/EU primary law, e.g. treaty provisions. With regard to the institutional and procedural design 'before' and 'after' the TEU we scrutinise forms of decision-making rules within the EC/EU from its foundation. More precisely, we look at the evolution of decision-making rules in the Council of Ministers and the decision-making procedures involving the Council and the EP. We thus sketch the evolution of our independent variables. As a second step, we take the legal output of the Council of Ministers, the EP and the European Commission as dependent variables in order to identify fundamental trends in the 'demands' made by political actors to use or to refrain from using the EU's para-constitutional resources and opportunities.

When exploring the relationship between the European and national levels of governance,[2] we assume that one important variable is to be found in the creation and subsequent development of EU institutions as well as in the increasing differentiation of procedures within the policy-cycle of the Brussels arena. In addressing the specific interaction mechanisms between treaty reform and Member State adaptation to new European 'opportunity structures',[3] this chapter investigates the latter's fundamental nature.

We therefore try to offer answers to four sets of questions:

- What kind of essential features can we identify for grasping the EC/EU on the move? How do the 'masters of the treaties'[4] shape the 'legal' constitution of the EU? Which indicators permit an analysis of fundamental trends and structural evolutions?
- How do institutional actors use self-made structures for joint problem-solving? Do para-constitutional revisions such as treaty amendments matter – and how do they matter – for the set-up and evolution of the policy-making structures of the EU's 'living constitution'?[5]
- What are the EU-related challenges to national systems?
- How can the results be explained in terms of general, integration-related approaches? Do they support or dismiss some of the theoretical assumptions elaborated in the academic community?[6]

The shape of the Maastricht Treaty on European Union

The Maastricht Treaty of 1992 was designed to give a renewed contractual input into the West European multi-level and multi-actor machinery of common problem-solving and joint decision-making between Member States' governments, their politico-administrative substructures and the EU's institutions. Five years after the entry into force of the SEA[7] and the accession of Portugal and Spain to the then European Communities, the 'masters of the treaties' agreed to a revision of the founding treaties as well as to the creation of two distinct pillars for intergovernmental co-operation in the fields of Foreign and Security Policy (CFSP)[8] and Justice and Home Affairs (JHA).[9] The result was a kind of 'Russian doll': a new TEU integrating the three existing Paris (1951) and Rome (1957) treaties. Encompassing EC-generated supranationalism and EU-related intergovernmentalism, the Maastricht Treaty committed the Member States as well as the European institutions to a 'single institutional framework' embodying a broadly defined set of aims and tasks as well as common procedures.[10]

The road to Maastricht[11] was marked by important, somewhat unintended and unpredictable circumstances. The treaty reform was originally aimed at a policy-based Intergovernmental Conference (IGC) on the three-phased movement towards Economic and Monetary Union (EMU).[12] But the end of the Cold War and German unification pushed the heads of state and governments towards other, though not completely new, themes of political union: policy and institutional reform – including CFSP, social policy and JHA – as well as a revision of rules governing the EC/EU policy-cycle from decision preparation to decision implementation and control.

Treaty revisions: creations and creators

Like its predecessor and successors – the SEA of 1986, the Amsterdam Treaty of 1997 and the Nice Treaty of 2000 – the Maastricht Treaty has to be interpreted as but one 'grand bargain' decision[13] among Member States along an uncharted path of European integration and co-operation. In this perspective, Maastricht needs to be read as a peak within a fluid landscape, moving with regard to time, the functional, institutional and geographical dimensions of supranational integration and interstate co-operation and co-ordination. Member States – governments, administrations, parliaments, parties and other 'collective actors'[14] – were and still are important but not exclusive players of the game: their preferences provide an input or a 'voice'[15] on the basis of experience gained while crossing the landscape between the 'peaks' of IGCs.

We then conceive of treaty revisions and amendments as initial 'offers' to actors working within the EU institutions. Placed within this multi-level and multi-actor framework for governance they create incentives and disincentives to use or to refrain from using treaty articles – legal empowerments provide the skeleton of a 'living constitution'.[16] Institutions and procedures provide arenas and rules for making binding decisions. One could therefore argue that treaty-building has a significant effect on the day-to-day output of the Union and thus on the evolution of the system in general; we therefore consider the evolution of para-constitutional patterns within the integration process over the Union's whole history. Starting from this assumption, we expect to be able to identify five periods which are defined by historical decisions either to create, amend or re-design the treaties: the ECSC Treaty, the Rome Treaties establishing the European Economic Community (EEC) and the European Atomic Community (Euratom), the SEA, the Maastricht Treaty and the Amsterdam Treaty. As a concluding point we will refer also to the reforms of the Nice Treaty (2001).

It is our view that relations between treaty reform and treaty implementation are not uni-directional. Treaty reforms do not emerge from nowhere as a 'deus ex machina', rather they represent reactions to prior developments and trends, reflecting both the complex day-to-day machinery at all relevant levels of policy-making as well as the reaction of socio-political actors which do not or only rarely intervene during the 'implementation' of a given set of treaties. Quite often these contractual treaty foundations simply formalise institutional evolutions which have been developed either within existing treaty provisions, through inter-institutional agreements, institutional rules of procedure and codes of conduct, or outside of the treaties, through bilateral or multilateral agreements between EU members.[17] Treaty amendments also attempt to address institutional and procedural weaknesses identified during the implementation of previous adjustments to the 'rules of the game'. Treaty revisions are thus endemic parts of the process; they are not only independent variables affecting the nature and the evolution of the system but also become dependent variables themselves. Institutions and procedures

– 'formal rules, compliance procedures, and standard operating practices that structure the relationship between individuals in various units of the Polity and economy'[18] – are creations and creators at the same time. In this regard, one specific feature of the Union should be addressed: in negotiating and ratifying treaty amendments, Member States *challenge their own politico-administrative systems*. The effect of these challenges varies according to the nature of the political systems in the Member States.

The EU: a multi-level and multi-actor system ... in process: an institutional approach

We assume that institutions do matter. Historical neo-institutionalist theories[19] and the path-dependency approach[20] to policy preferences, institutions and procedures, policy outcomes and policy instruments offers a possible starting point. The institutional and procedural design of the EC/EU is subject to new circumstances, political and institutional changes over time – a 'stickiness in movement along the continuum'.[21] Accordingly, Member States seek not only functional, i.e. policy-based, but also institutional solutions to shared problems on the basis of what already exists. Critical junctures – revisions of the treaties or exogenous developments affecting the EC/EU or a major part of it – offer Member States and institutions the chance to adapt and re-design the existing arrangements.[22] The logic of path dependency suggests that in such an institutionalised arrangement as the EC/EU, 'past lines of policy [will] condition subsequent policy by encouraging societal forces to organise along some lines rather than others, to adapt particular identities or to develop interests in policies that are costly to shift'.[23] Institutions, rules and procedural routines at both the national and the European levels of governance therefore become able to 'structure political situations and leave their own imprint on political outcomes'.[24] In other words, institutional arrangements affect the range of future developments insofar as they narrow down the areas for possible change and oblige Member States incrementally to revise existing arrangements.

Within these processes, national interests and preferences – as they are the articulated products of shared beliefs – 'act as "focal points" around which the behaviour of actors converges'.[25] This process presupposes interest aggregation by national governments.[26] They are widely perceived as 'unified actors'[27] and remain key interlocutors for the EC/EU institutions and arenas. They are important targets of Non-Governmental Organisations (NGOs) and other functional 'demoi'.[28] They provide essential resources for the system not only with respect to the financial basis of the Union, but also with regard to the effective functioning of the institutional setting. Hence, Member States second civil servants to the Council of Ministers and the Commission, and provide important intellectual and managerial resources for Council Presidencies and coercive resources for pushing the Council to reach agreements.[29] However, as with institutional and policy developments, national interest formation is 'locked in': the preference aggregators and articulators of the EC/EU system, especially national governments, use the channels which they have created themselves. Concomitantly, societal preference-builders – parliaments, political parties, NGOs, public opinion and the mass media – also become involved in the process. Some of them, such as parties and NGOs, may be fully aware of these interaction mechanisms because they are mirrored directly by similar or corresponding entities within the Brussels and Strasbourg arenas. Others, especially public opinion, may only react to European policy and institutional outcomes. In any case, the complex mechanism between institutions, interests and ideas needs to be taken into account.

As we are interested in the long-term trends of the EC/EU system and the respective impacts on EC/EU policy-making in the Member States, we look at the effective use of treaty provisions. For this purpose, we explore the real 'demand' for different procedural 'offers' or opportunity structures at hand.

We take the changes, which the architects of the treaties have included within primary law, as independent variables. Of course, we do not expect that the intentions of the treaty architects will be fully met. Fifteen national, aggregated interpretations of the treaties[30] produces a productive ambiguity[31] which itself serves as a driving force behind subsequent reforms of the EU's para-constitutional setting. The 'masters of the treaties' might revise the formal rules through informal arrangement (at European Council level) or – together with the constitutive elements of the Union's 'single institutional framework' – by the adoption of inter-institutional agreements (between the Council of Ministers, the EP and the European Commission).[32] Even if Member State governments are in full agreement about the respective interpretations of treaty implementation, they cannot guarantee a full and comprehensive use of new articles. The treaty provisions do not prescribe actors' subsequent behaviour; new governments and new political coalitions may prefer other areas and methods of co-operation to those used by their predecessors – thus one might expect to see the law of unintended consequences at work.

The evolution of the EU system

Incentives and disincentives for bringing the treaty rules into play do not exclusively depend on procedural and institutional opportunities but depend also on the political context of the day and the time. Preferences of Member States and other actors matter, although they cannot be taken as fixed. Time lags in making use of amended treaties are imposed by the treaty provisions themselves.[33] However, we argue that the usefulness of new opportunities is proved either early or never. It is the period between the conclusion of an IGC and a rather short period afterwards where actors set precedents which set out the 'path'[34] or at least the range of possible behaviour for implementing the treaty. We assume therefore that during five years (November 1993–December 1998) of the application of Maastricht, possible effects should have become apparent.

The extension of scope and actors involved: trends and patterns of constitution-building

As a first step, we concentrate on the development of the EC/EU's rules between 1951 (ECSC Treaty) and 2001 (Nice Treaty). We observe that the total number of treaty articles dealing with specific competencies and decision-making rules – the *enumerative empowerments* – in an increasing amount of specific policy fields, has grown considerably from 86 (EEC Treaty 1957) to 254 (Nice Treaty 2001). Further illustrations of this broad scope can be seen in the expansion of the number of Commission Directorates-General (DGs) (from nine in 1958 to twenty-four in 1999) and of autonomous executive agencies (from two in 1975 to eleven in 1998);[35] the agendas of the EP at its plenary sessions and especially the presidency conclusions published after each session of the European Council.[36] The increasing number of sectoral forms of the Council of Ministers (from four in 1958 to twenty-three in 1998)[37] as well as the extension of the administrative sub-structure, indicates that governmental actors have become more and more involved in using their Brussels networks extensively and intensively.[38]

As for the provisions governing the decision-making system within the Council of Ministers, Figure 2.1 shows the absolute proportion of the Council's internal decision-making modes between 1952 until 1999. It can clearly be seen that the total number of rules providing for unanimity and QMV has considerably increased over time. If we focus on the relative rates of the treaty-based provisions in the Council (Figure 2.2), we also notice an over-proportional growth in QMV voting up to Amsterdam.

The EP was not originally designed along the lines of national legislatures in the EU Member States. Given its original lack of legislative powers, Parliament's influence on important decisions in traditional policy areas remained limited, although MEPs engaged in trials of strength with the Council in the context of the budgetary procedures. Since 1979 Parliament has expanded its role as a watchdog by making intensive use of its right to ask questions, by keeping a close eye on EU expenditure (through the Committee on Budgetary Control) and by setting up temporary committees of inquiry. Since 1986–87, EC Treaty amendments have introduced important changes concerning the role and position of the EP. On the basis of the positive experiences gained with the co-operation procedure after the entry into force of the SEA (1987), the Maastricht Treaty widened the procedure's scope and in also created the so-called 'co-decision procedure'. The EP obtained the right to block a proposed legislative act without the Council having the right to outvote

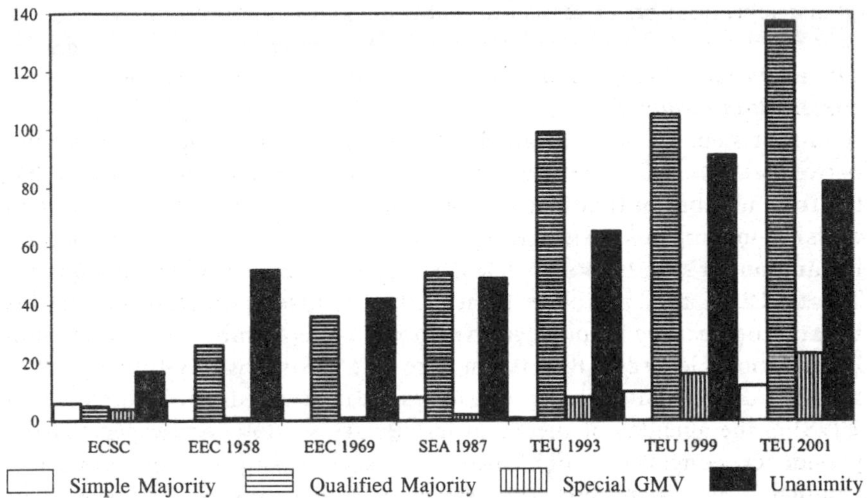

Figure 2.1 Decision-making modes in the Council of Ministers, 1952–2001, absolute numbers
Source: Original ECSC, EEC, EC and EU Treaties (by time of their entry into force).

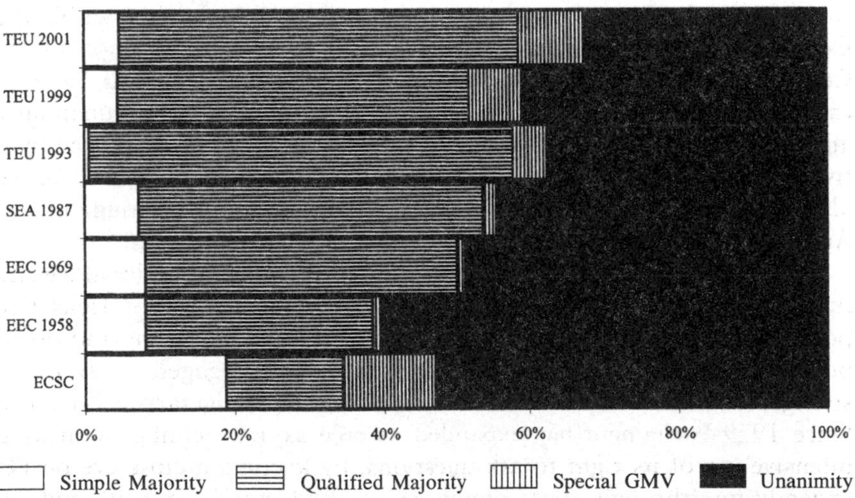

Figure 2.2 Decision-making modes in the Council of Ministers, 1952–2001, per cent
Source: Original ECSC, EEC, EC and EU Treaties (by time of their entry into force).

it at the end of the procedure. The Conciliation Committee was to be the nucleus of the co-decision procedure. Apart from co-decision, Maastricht extended the assent procedure to a wide range of international agreements and other sectors of a legislative nature. As regards the implementation phase of the EC/EU policy-cycle, Parliament was given the formal right to set up temporary Committees of Inquiry in order to investigate maladministration in the implementation of EC law. Finally, and with a view to the early stages of European decision-making, Parliament gained the right to request the European Commission to submit legislative proposals.

Commentators on the Maastricht Treaty have argued that the EP 'was perhaps the largest net beneficiary of the institutional changes in the TEU'[39] and that the treaty 'marks the point in the Community's development at which the Parliament became the first chamber of a real legislature; and the Council is obliged to act from time to time like a second legislative chamber rather than a ministerial directorate'.[40] Understanding the slow but steady move to include the EP into the EU system therefore necessitates a perspective which departs from orthodox realism. On the other hand, the co-decision procedure could well be depicted as symptomatic of the 'general trade-off' between the 'problem-solving capacity'[41] of EU decision-making on the one hand and parliamentary involvement on the other: 'Expanding the legislative ... powers of the European Parliament could render European decision processes, already too complicated and time-consuming, even more cumbersome'.[42] As for the roles provided by the treaties for the EP, the relative dimension of its 'exclusion' from the EC/EU policy-making process has considerably diminished (Figure 2.3). However, in view of the absolute increase in treaty-based decision-making procedures (Figure 2.4), the growth in consultation, co-operation and co-decision procedures is balanced by a small augmentation of 'non-participation' in the Council's rule-making process. The main reasons for this development are the dynamics of subsequent treaty reforms widening the functional scope of European integration and co-operation into new areas. Of specific interest in this regard is the combination of both the respective powers of the Parliament and Council, which shows a remarkable increase in procedural complexity over time. There is no typical procedure which clearly dominates the political system, e.g. QMV and co-decision as the general rule.

An ideal three-step model towards communitarisation

To explain these trends we can construct an ideal type of a three-step evolutionary pattern by which governments create competencies and respective procedures in policy fields (Figure 2.5).

- *Intergovernmentalisation:* to achieve objectives of joint interest and to reduce transaction costs, Member States agree to pool resources in a loose form which might be outside the E[E]C Treaty (e.g. European Political Co-Operation, the Exchange Rate Mechanism (ERM) of the European Monetary System (EMS),[43] the TREVI[44] network providing a collective intellectual capacity to combat international crime); or by referring to Article 308 (ex Article 235) ECT (the treaty establishing the European Community), which requires unanimous decision-making in the Council of Ministers.

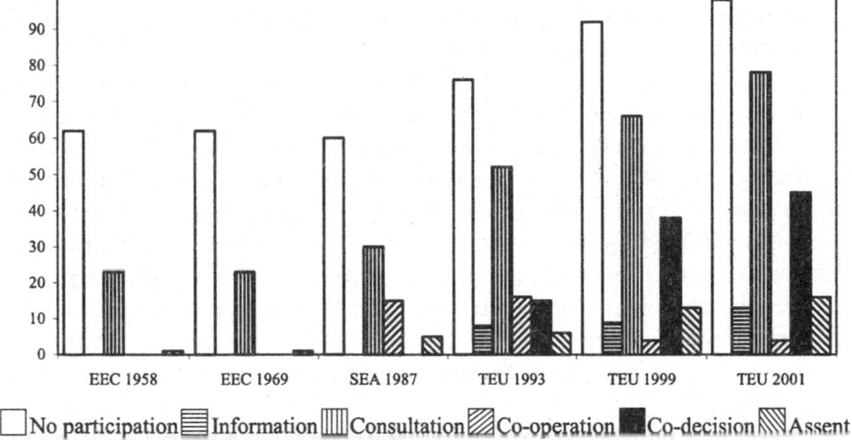

Figure 2.3 Decision-making procedures in the European Parliament/Council, 1958–2001, absolute numbers
Source: Maurer (1999), new data added, based on original EEC, EC and EU treaties.

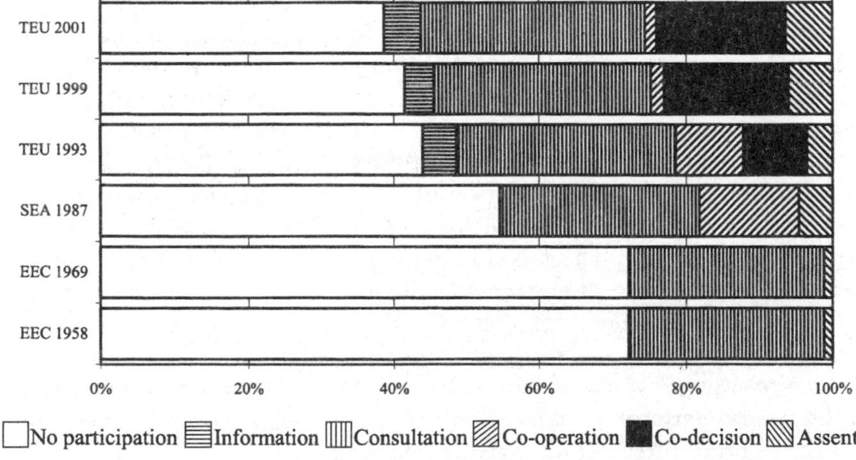

Figure 2.4 Decision-making procedures in the European Parliament/Council, 1958–2001, per cent
Source: Maurer (1999), new data added, based on original EEC, EC and EU treaties.

- *'Treatyisation'* by 'hard' intergovernmental structures and procedures: In a second phase governments include the new policy area(s) *expressis verbis* into the treaty, perhaps with formulas limiting the roles of EC/EU bodies or securing Member States' veto powers (such as unanimity in the Council), since they remain hesitant to cede too much power to non-national actors or to risk being outvoted by majority decisions and restrictive rule interpretations.
- *Communitarisation:* in a third phase of treaty amendment, governments then commit themselves to QMV instead of unanimity, for the sake of efficiency and effectiveness. As for the EP and the European Court of Justice (ECJ), Member States are, in the first phase of policy-building, rather reluctant to allocate powers to other actors. Only in the subsequent phases of treaty amendments has the EP been granted some powers – ideally consultation in the second phase and co-operation, co-decision or assent in the third phase of constitutional revision. As to the ECJ, similar empowerments evolve over time. In a first phase, judicial control is excluded, then narrowed down to some specific policy fields and/or behavioural settings. If trust in the system and the Court precedes compliance with its decisions, governments agree in subsequent phases to widen and/or to strengthen its powers.

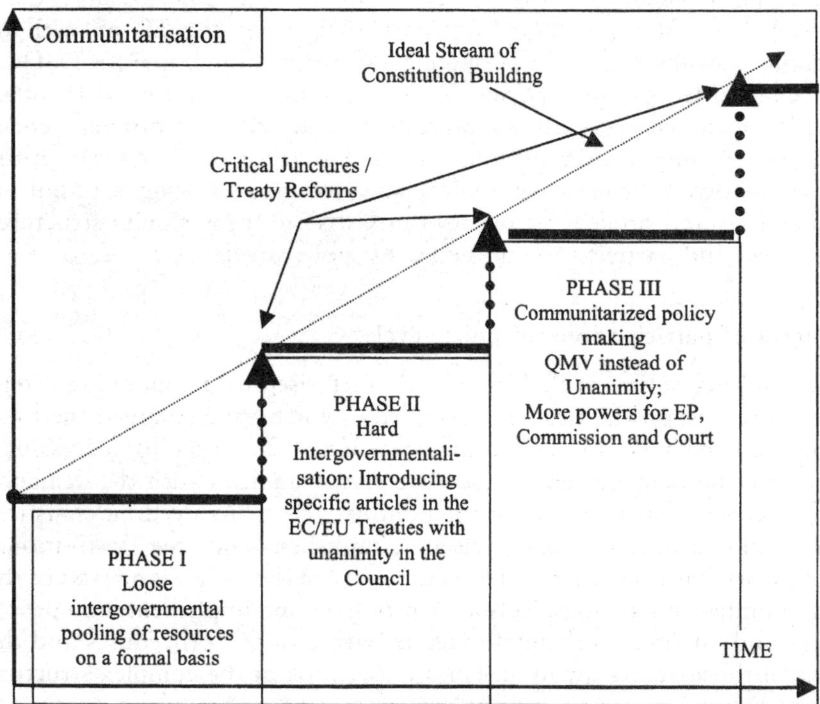

Figure 2.5 Three steps towards communitarisation

Over recent decades, we thus witness a strong centripetal trend towards 'communitarisation': a push and pull of provisions towards the EC treaties or, within the treaties, towards supranational procedures,[45] or towards EC-like rules within the intergovernmental pillars of the Union[46] – even if it is with many derogations, such as the case of the area of 'freedom, security and justice' (Title IV ECT)[47] and even if, in terms of community orthodoxy, 'dirty' communitarisations[48] and institutional anomalies[49] take place.

Towards procedural ambiguities

The character of treaty provisions is reinforced by a specific legal feature: if we take a closer look at the treaties, we can identify a trend towards *procedural ambiguity* over time. Whereas the original treaties foresaw a restricted (clear) set of rules for each policy field, subsequent treaty amendments have led to a procedural differentiation with a variety of rule opportunities. As a result, the treaty provisions do not dictate a clear nomenclature of rules to be applied to specific sectors. Instead, since the SEA, Member States and supranational institutions can, in an increasing number of policy fields, select whether a given piece of secondary legislation – a regulation, a directive or another type of legal act – should be decided by unanimity, simple or qualified majority voting in the Council; according to the consultation, co-operation or (after Maastricht) the co-decision procedure; without any participation of the EP or with or without consultation of the Economic and Social Committee (ECOSOC), the Committee of the Regions (CoR) or similar institutions. In other words, different procedural blueprints and interinstitutional codes compete for application and raise the potential for conflict between the actors involved. From a national perspective, this growing variation of institutions and procedures means a mixed set of opportunity structures for access and participation in the EC/EU policy-cycle.

Patterns of participation: the policy-cycle

The resulting nature of the Union is characterised by a continuing extension of its responsibilities and authorities, which have enlarged the total range in which EC/EU institutions are active. In order to successfully reconcile the management of growing responsibilities with the demands for functional participation of the political actors involved, new institutions and procedures have been established and the institutional framework has been altered. The complexity of the Union is a result of the huge number of its duties, legislative processes and implementation procedures and, at times, the unfathomable nature of the procedures and the roles of those actors involved. For a closer look at the complex structure of the Union we use the policy-cycle as a scheme for observing fundamental patterns of the Union's living constitution (Figure 2.6).

Phase / Level	I. Decision preparation		II. Decision-making			III. Decision implementation		IV. Control	
	(a) Initiation	(b) Preparliamentary deliberations	(c) Parliamentary deliberations	(d) Preparation	(e) Decision-making	(f) Transposition	(g) Implementation	(h) Execution	(i) Verification and Sanction
EC/EU Level	COMMISSION 20 members Cabinets (20) DGs (24) Other Services (12) Expert groups (around 700)	Committee of the Regions (222 members) ECOSOC (222 members)	EUROPEAN PARLIAMENT (626 members) Party Groups (7) Committees (17) European Political Parties	COUNCIL Secretariat General COREPER and Working Groups (around 250) Advisory Committees (Economic and Finance Committee, Employment Committee)	COUNCIL Presidency A + B Points EUROPEAN PARLIAMENT MEP, Committees Administration Commission DG's	COMMISSION Supervision of transposition calenders (for directives, recommendations and decisions)	COMMISSION Implementation 'Comitology' Committees (around 420)	COMMISSION Supervision of execution, continuous monitoring of application of EC law	COMMISSION Rule application divisions EUROPEAN COURT OF JUSTICE Jurisdiction EUROPEAN PARLIAMENT Temporary Committees of Inquiry
National level	Civil servants and interest groups Regions, European Associations / Federations		COSAC and Joint committee meetings National parliaments Political parties	National Ministries, Administrations and Parliaments		National Governments, Parliaments and Administrations	Civil servants for 'Comitology' committees	Execution through national (incl. regional) administrations	National Courts

Figure 2.6 The EC/EU policy-cycle, November 2001

Rules for decision preparation, decision-making, implementation and control differ both across the policy fields in which they are applied, and in terms of the institutions and bodies involved. Furthermore, Maastricht introduced new bodies such as the CoR and the European Central Bank (ECB). These developments – repeated in the Amsterdam Treaty by the creation of new institutions such as the Employment Committee, CFSP, the Policy Planning and Early Warning Unit within the second pillar, and procedures such as the closer co-operation clauses[50] – are an expression of the growth and differentiation of European integration. New institutions are established not for the purpose of furthering the institutional complexity of the Union, but because they are required to deal with the Union's new policy duties and tasks, to give it a single voice or interface for dealing with third countries and organisations, or to become its formalised feedback system towards the specific geographical or functional levels of governance. New institutions do not operate in a political vacuum but in a closely connected system and balance of power in which the architects of the treaty have positioned them. Whenever new institutions gain autonomy, they do not use it in isolation but in a framework of established rules and centres of political power. This process of institutional growth thus attains a higher degree of complexity, potentially mirrored by new structures and processes in the Member States.

Considering institutions as 'systems of rules', institutionalisation is the process by 'which rules are created, applied, and interpreted by those who live under them'.[51] One characteristic of this institutionalisation is – as Figure 2.6 suggests – the comprehensive and intensive participation of national governments, parliaments and administrations in nearly all phases of the policy-cycle, the intensity of participation varying according to constraints which are to be found in EC/EU treaty law as well as in the rules governing the political systems in the Member States. The use of these bodies, as well as the tendency towards procedural differentiation, has increased significantly. The extension of the scope of trans-border co-operation has resulted in a growing number of separate and specialised arenas for interaction and law-making. New Council formats and related working groups have been created, new Commission services installed, new parliamentary committees set up and new consultative bodies placed within the existing 'institutional terrain' of the Union.[52] If the various Council voting procedures are combined with the different forms of involvement and methods of the EP in the policy-cycle, it is possible to identify more than thirty distinct procedures for the process of decision-making[53] (this number excludes the roles foreseen for the ECB, the ECOSOC, the CoR and the new Employment Committee, as well as the non-treaty-based 'soft law' extensions and mutations such as the increasing number of interinstitutional agreements and codes of conduct).

Administrative involvement and interaction modes

However, the considerable and increasing role played by EC institutions has not automatically led to the substitution of national actors. Even 'exclusive EC competencies' in the fields of agriculture, fisheries and trade require meetings of the Council of Ministers or its working groups in which national civil servants shape the exact scope of the Commission's authority. Thus, the growing role of de-nationalised and supranational actors is leading to a more intensive and differentiated incorporation of national actors in the whole EC process.[54] In pursuing their strategies for access and influence, Member States have become intensively involved in those phases of the policy-cycle where the Commission enjoys rather exclusive prerogatives, such as the right of initiative. As part of the Commission's internal procedure for using this monopoly (see phase I of the policy-cycle), this 'epistemic community'[55] draws on some 700 expert groups. The involvement of national civil servants is important for the Commission in its tasks of identifying problems, collecting first-hand information and examining options for possible legislative proposals. Expert groups advise the Commission on the basis of the Member States' interest or perspectives. They act as 'early warning units' for the Commission. This growing network provides the Commission with extended and timely information. Expert groups indicate a Member State's willingness to incorporate a given issue into their national rolling agenda: will Member State X and its administration be able to transpose the directive within a given time period? Will the envisaged legal act have an effect on the administrative law of Member State Y?[56]

The overall proportion of civil servants with immediate access to the EU cycle is considerable and probably even larger within smaller member countries and those with a federal system of shared competencies between different levels of governance (Belgium, Germany, Austria). To these agents directly participating in the Brussels arena we must add their colleagues who are indirectly involved in national preparation and implementation procedures. These domestic spillovers are difficult to calculate, not least because each country has different internal methods of co-ordinating EC/EU business.

National officials work closely together on preparing Council of Ministers' decisions in approximately 250 working groups under the Council and COREPER[57] (see phase II of the policy-cycle). These interaction patterns involve many sectors and levels of national administrative hierarchies.[58] The Council's working groups have a significant impact on the decision-making arena; around 90 per cent of EC legislation is prepared at this stage.[59] As for the implementation of EC regulations or directives (see phase III of the policy-cycle), the Council has created around 420 comitology committees involving national civil servants. There are more than ten different formulas for these committees characterised by different rights of national civil servants to delay or to block operational decisions by the Commission.[60] These committees fulfil rule-interpreting, fund-approving or rule-setting functions. They therefore act both as 'regime-takers' and 'regime-makers'.[61] Furthermore, the Brussels-based infrastructure is surrounded by consultative and advisory committees made up of non-governmental and sectoral specialists who provide expertise at both the decision-preparation and implementation phases. Reflecting the EC/EU's external policy activities, one can also find joint committees, bringing together administrators from the EU institutions, the Member States and third parties. The potential influence of committees differs largely according to the phase of the policy-cycle and the policy sector.

The involvement of national civil servants in the policy-cycle is not simply a 'watch-dog exercise' because for the Commission and the national institutions, the 'engrenage'-like[62] interlocking of actors is an important part of the joint management of the policy-cycle. If any major element could be held responsible for the bureaucratisation[63] of Brussels, it is this network of multi-level administrative interpenetration. However, this bureaucracy is not an accidental product of personal mismanagement or just another example of Parkinson's Law which assumes that expansion takes place simply for the personal advantage of the civil servants involved. This trend is an ultimately unavoidable result of the intensive propensity of national politicians and civil servants to comprehensively participate in the preparation, making and implementing of those EC/EU decisions which directly affect them.

Empirical trends of the Union: divergent patterns

Policy-making in the Council: using opportunities and output production

After sketching the evolution of procedural opportunities and the basic structures of the involvement of national actors in the EC/EU policy-cycle, we now consider the patterns of their usage in an aggregated form. How have the actors within the institutions exploited the opportunities provided by the original treaties and their subsequent amendments? Can we identify any relationship between the stages of EC/EU constitution-building and the evolution of the Union's policy output?

Altogether, we can list a total sum of 52,799 legal acts adopted between 1952 and December 1998 (Figure 2.7).

Of course, the 52,799 legal acts are not of equal rank in terms of their legal relevance. Besides regulations, directives, decisions and recommendations authorised by the Council alone, the EP and the Council or the Commission, the Union's data bases also include a set of political events which are less binding (Council conclusions of a political nature,

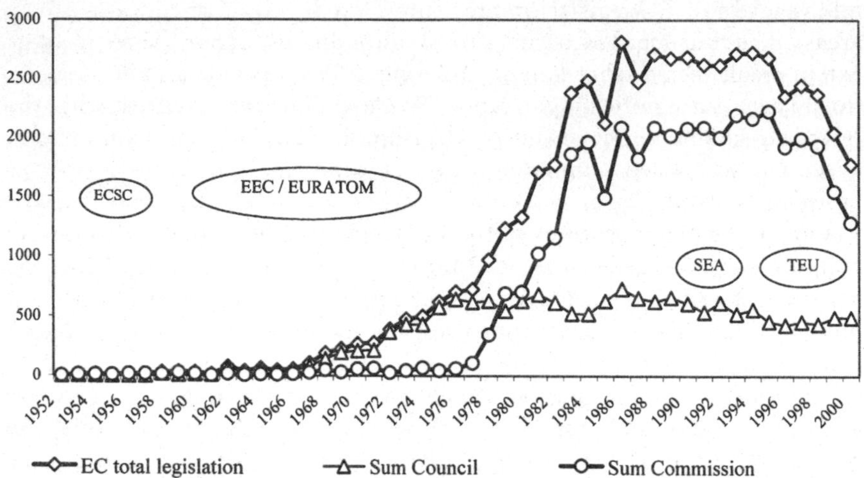

Figure 2.7 Legal output of Council and Commission, per year, 1952–2000
Source: Maurer 2001 based on CELEX.
Note: Sums represent every legal event as noted by CELEX. Apart from 'real' secondary legislation, CELEX also refers to executive acts by either the Commission or the Council. Note that from November 1993 onwards, Council legislation also comprises legislative acts by the EP and the Council (co-decision procedure).

etc.). Figure 2.7 indicates a quasi-linear growth with regard to original secondary legislation and other legal events from 1961 until 1987 with some significant drops between 1964 and 1965 and between 1983 and 1984, but a constant stepwise decrease from 1987 onwards; the Council of Ministers' output shows a steady decline from 1986–87. Furthermore the Maastricht provisions did not lead to an increase in output. Hence, the legal acts which arose from the new Maastricht pillars – CFSP and JHA – did not change the overall trend. Within the two intergovernmental pillars, the Council issued only 287 legal acts between 1993 and December 1998 (compared, for the same period, with 7,518 legal acts under Agricultural and Fisheries policy). The European Commission's output began to grow from 1976 onwards, although the relative growth remained stable between 1980 and 1993. With the coming into force of the Maastricht Treaty, output decreased dramatically, thus reflecting the net decline in Council legislation after 1986–87.

Our interpretation of the fall in the Council's output after 1987 is based on a consideration of three major policy areas of the EC – that of the Common Agricultural Policy (CAP) and Fisheries policy, external trade policy and customs policy, which together constitute 41,886 legal acts or 79.3 per cent of all measures produced up to December 1998. Given their age, one can assume a saturation of these policies; in fact, the falling levels of EC legislation are almost exclusively due to these policy areas. The European Commission's autonomous activities to a large extent result from earlier Council (or since 1993, Council and EP) legislation. There is a significant gap from 1952 to 1979, which suggests that the relatively small amount of Council legislation required fewer Commission executive acts when compared with legislation passed from the 1980s onwards (Table 2.1).

One of the major features of the EC's legal output is the variation with regard to the binding nature of legal acts. From this perspective, the nature of the Council's legal acts is characterised by a decrease in the most binding measure – i.e. regulations outside the policy sectors of CAP and trade policy after 1987. On the other hand, the SEA apparently affected matters insofar as the number of directives per year increased between 1987 and 1993, i.e. during the final phase of the Single European Market (SEM) programme. Since 1993, the use of directives decreased slightly until 1996; subsequently, the number remained fairly stable. Interestingly, one can also witness an increase in decisions from 1961 to 1982 and then again from 1986 to 1998. The first phase concerns the Council's regulatory decisions in the strict sense of Article 249 (ex Article 189) ECT on the definition of the different legal instruments available within the EU system. The second phase includes another type of decision, so called 'legislative decisions' in the framework of policy programmes (SOCRATES, Ariane, Research Framework Programmes, etc.).[64]

Another issue concerning the production of binding EC/EU law needs to be addressed. So far, we have focused at the dynamics of the Council in the EU system. We referred to the total output of legal acts irrespective of whether the different items were still in force or not. A large proportion of these decisions are in force for relatively short time periods or are regularly replaced by new legislation. However, during the 1990s the acquis communautaire – the legislation in force at a given moment – more than doubled from 4,566 legal acts in 1983 to 9,767 in 1998.[65] Thus there has been a substantial increase in overall legal activity within the Union in recent years (Figure 2.8).[66]

Voting procedures in the Council

When representing their interests, positions and preferences, national actors are faced with specific rules, of which QMV is considered the most significant. Statistical data on the use of QMV within the Council of Ministers have been published only since the coming into force of the Maastricht Treaty on 1 November 1993, but some raw data are available for earlier periods (Table 2.2).

Table 2.1 Legal output per year of Commission, Council and Parliament, 1952–98, according to policy areas

	1952–86			*1987–93*			*1994–98*			*Totals*	
Policy domains as identified by CELEX	*Total*	*Acts per year*	*% of Legal output*	*Total*	*Acts per year*	*% of Legal output*	*Total*	*Acts per year*	*% of Legal output*	*Legal acts: total*	*% of Legal output*
General financial and institutional affairs	610	17.42	2.8	476	68	2.57	693	138.6	5.51	1779	3.36
Customs policy	4347	124.2	19.97	2496	356.57	13.50	1021	204.2	8.12	7864	14.89
Agriculture	9274	264.97	42.62	8435	1205	45.63	5310	1062	42.28	23019	43.59
Fisheries	798	22.8	3.67	1325	189.28	7.16	800	160	6.36	2923	5.53
External relations	3549	101.4	16.31	2963	423.28	16.03	1568	313.6	12.48	8080	15.30
Competition	384	10.97	1.76	474	67.71	2.56	854	170.8	6.79	1712	3.24
Industry and internal market	1004	28.68	4.61	528	75.42	2.85	582	116.4	4.63	2114	4.00
Taxation	80	2.28	0.36	84	12	0.45	63	12.6	0.51	227	0.042
EPC/CFSP	0	0	0	6 (1 Nov. 1993)	0.85	0.03	161	32.2	1.28	167	0.031
Justice and Home affairs	0	0	0	1 (1 Nov. 1993)	0.14	0.005	119	23.8	0.94	120	0.022
Freedom of movement and Social Policy	397	11.34	1.82	237	33.85	1.28	143	28.6	1.13	777	1.47
Right of establishment	119	3.4	0.54	89	12.71	0.40	67	13.4	0.53	275	0.52
Transport policy	258	7.37	1.18	186	26.57	1.01	139	27.8	1.10	583	1.10
Economic and monetary affairs	130	3.71	0.59	32	4.57	0.17	56	11.2	0.44	218	0.41
Regional and structural policy	126	3.6	0.57	439	62.71	2.37	256	51.2	2.03	821	1.55
Environment, consumer, health	248	7.08	1.13	379	54.14	2.05	358	71.6	2.85	985	1.86
Energy policy	284	8.11	1.30	116	16.57	0.62	118	23.6	0.93	518	0.98
Education, science, information	119	3.4	0.54	177	25.28	0.95	206	41.2	1.64	502	0.95
Law relating to undertakings	25	0.71	0.11	35	5	0.18	39	7.8	0.31	99	0.18
People's Europe	5	0.14	0.02	5	0.71	0.027	6	1.2	0.047	16	0.030
Sum	21757	621.62	100	18483	2640.42	100	12559	2511.8	100	52799	100

Source: CELEX data base as at 1 December 1999.

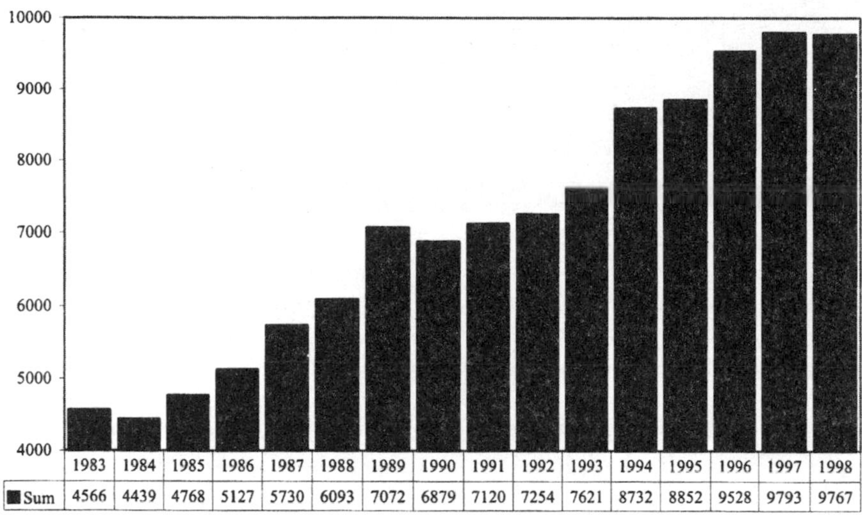

Figure 2.8 European legislation in force, 1983–98
Source: Directories of Community Legislation in Force (Luxembourg, 1984–99, December issues).

Table 2.2 'Real' use of QMV, 1985–99

Item	*1985*	*1986*	*1994*	*1995*	*1996*	*1999*
Total sum of Council legal acts	615	731	561	458	429	327
Number of cases where 'real voting' occurred	approx. 70[a]	approx. 100[b]	64[c]	54[d]	45[d]	31[e]
Percentage: number of cases of voting/council legal acts	approx. 11.38	approx. 13.67	11.4	11.84	10.48	9.78

Notes: [a] Answer to Written Question No. 1121/86 by James Elles to the Council of the EC; *OJEC*, No. C 306/42, 1 December 1986. [b] Answer to Written Question No. 2126/86 by Nicole Fontaine to the Council of the EC; *OJEC*, No. C 82/43, 30 March 1987. [c] Answer to Written Question No. E-1263/96 by James Moorhouse to the Council of the EU; *OJEC*, No. C 305/71–75, 15 October 1996, and: Answer to Written Question No. E-858/95 by Ulla Sandbaek to the Council; *OJEC*, No. C 213/22, 17 August 1995. [d] Commission Européenne (Secrétariat Général): Analyse des décisions adoptées à la majorité qualifiée en 1996, Bruxelles, 14 July 1997. [e] Monthly Summaries of Council Acts, January–December 1999, http://ue.eu.int/en/acts. Data for 1997 and 1998 were not available.

Among the 561 legal acts of the Council in 1994, a total of 64 (11.4 per cent) was subject to real voting. Of the 458 legal acts adopted in 1995, the relative share of 'real votes' increased slightly to 54 (11.84 per cent). In 1996, the Council referred 45 times to having voted by QMV in a total of 429 cases (10.48 per cent). Altogether, the rather small share of 'real voting' indicates the underlying 'culture of consensus'[67] within the Council and its component members. However, the average rate of QMV also suggests a belief among national actors that, ultimately, the use of voting is an acceptable way out of a deadlock. In addition, the data on the real use of QMV are based on the total volume of the Council's legislative activity. Accordingly, the basis also includes legal acts where the treaties oblige the Council to act by unanimity.

Voting risks problems in the later stages of the policy-cycle. Given that since 1993 voting results have been published by the Council, the views of out-voted Member States are therefore visible to interest groups from all sides – governmental as well as non-governmental. Thus, Member States which find themselves in a minority position may come under pressure from domestic actors to oppose the legislation and then to block the timely enforcement of the legal act in question. However, one should not underestimate the impact of 'real voting', despite the small extent to which it is used. Hence, the idea behind QMV is not exclusively its routine practice but its potential power as a 'sword of Damocles'[68] that pushes Member State actors to concede in order to reach agreement. What QMV certainly implies therefore is the need for governments to clarify, at an early stage of the policy-cycle, the domestic 'common position' between the actors involved. QMV may thus increase the pressure on national administrations and their EC/EU-related policy co-ordination systems. If this argument holds, one would expect to see changes in such systems after the SEA and/or after the Maastricht Treaty, since both revisions induced a considerable transfer of unanimity rules into QMV opportunities. We will see in the chapters on the Member States in Part II, if and how governments, administrations and their related agencies have reacted to these potential challenges.

The efficiency of the Council: frequency of sessions and productivity

One way of observing behavioural patterns in the EC/EU policy-cycle is to analyse both the frequency with which national ministers and their representatives use the Council of Ministers and their capacity to reach agreement within the time they spend in the relevant institutional structure. The number of Council meetings per year has grown constantly from twenty meetings in 1967 to ninety-one in 2000. The relatively high number of Council meetings per year is related in particular to new Council formats rather than to higher frequencies of meetings among existing ones (Figure 2.9).

As we know from the well-documented agricultural sector, the frequency of meetings in the Council of Ministers, on the one hand, and its working groups, on the other, has grown considerably. Many civil servants meet twice monthly on average.[69] If one also includes unrecorded informal meetings, it becomes quite clear that the intensity with which

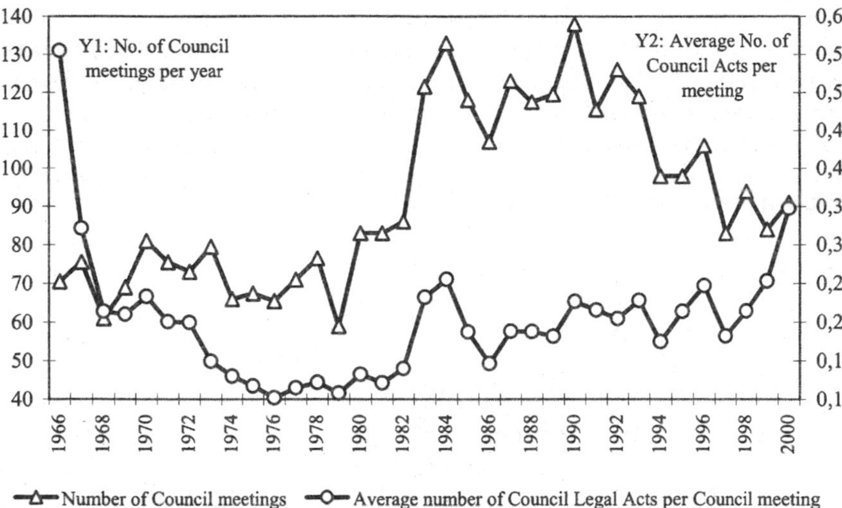

Figure 2.9 Productivity of the Council of Ministers, 1966–2000: legal acts per year against meetings per year

some civil servants deal with European affairs in their daily agenda is remarkable. This level of activity is not only a characteristic of the mid-1990s but has grown constantly over recent years. Has the frequency of meetings led to greater efficiency? Certainly not. Between 1976 and 1998, the Council's productivity – defined as the ratio between its legal output and its meetings per year – declined from ten legal acts per session in 1976 to three acts per session in 2000. In other words, the greater number of Council meetings has not led to a growth in the Council's output. The Internal Market programme (legislative proposals of the Commission prior to the SEA) led to a higher productivity from 1984 to 1986. However, after the entry into force of the SEA, not only the Council's overall output, but also its productivity per session, fell again.

Are we therefore witnessing the evolution of a growing 'participation bureaucracy',[70] whose major interest is to get involved at any expense without considering the potentially damaging effects of its size and complexity? Or is our observation of the Council's productivity mainly due to the constitution of new policy areas which, given their nature and technical specificity, cannot be dealt with by existing staff at the governments' disposal? Instead, new policy areas require new expertise and adequate personnel input, which thus leads to an ever-growing network of ministries and governmental agencies. Chapters on the Member States in Part II will thus address the question of under which circumstances national actors – located either in the permanent representations or at their home bases – have and will become involved in the EC/EU policy-cycle.

The evolution of the EP's involvement
Given that national governments and administrations have to co-operate with the EP as an established actor, we have also looked at the evolution of the different procedures which govern this special kind of a bicameral relationship (Figures 2.3 and 2.4). We note that between 1987 and December 1993, more than 30 per cent of Commission proposals which addressed the EP fell under the co-operation procedure (Figure 2.10).

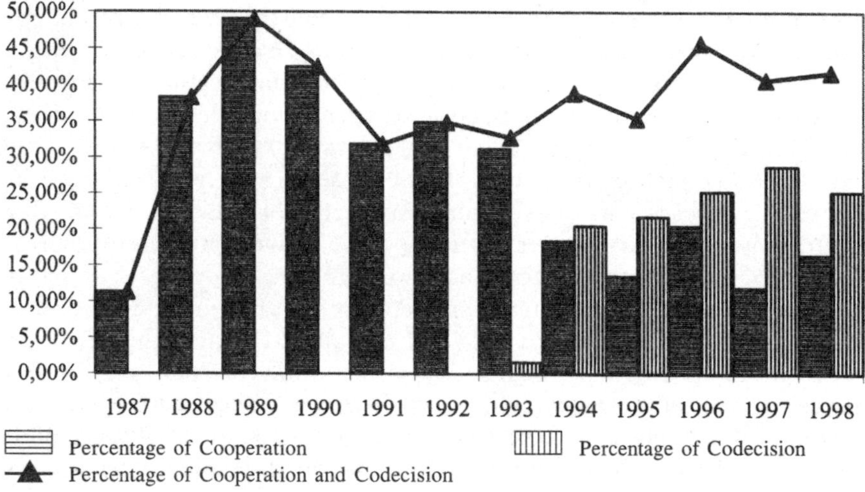

Figure 2.10 Parliamentary involvement in EC legislation, 1987–98: real use of procedural empowerments
Source: Maurer (1999), based on the OIEL data base.

Following the Maastricht Treaty, the share of legislation falling under co-operation declined to 13.6 per cent (1995) whereas the share under co-decision rose to 21.8 per cent. The main reason for the substitution of co-operation by co-decision lies in the procedural change applied to Article 95 (ex Article 100a) ECT which was and still is the general legal basis for harmonisation measures in the framework of the Internal Market.[71] Hence, around 66 per cent of all co-decision procedures concluded between November 1993 and December 1998 fell under Article 95. In spite of the fact that co-decision was to apply to only 9.25 per cent of all EC treaty provisions containing procedural specifications (see Figures 2.3 and 2.4), nearly 25 per cent of the European Commission's initiatives submitted to both the Council and the Parliament up to December 1998 fell under this procedure.[72] This is not only the result of an EP-friendly attitude but is also due to the fact that these provisions are mainly ruled by QMV (except for cultural policy and research policy programmes). The demand for this kind of legislation was thus much higher than the original – treaty-based – supply would have suggested. The Maastricht Treaty clearly led to a strengthened legislative role for the EP regarding the internal market and the areas of environment, research and education policy. This trend will continue under the Amsterdam Treaty as most co-operation procedures (except for four related to EMU) have been replaced by a simplified and shortened co-decision rule.[73]

Has the slow but steady inclusion of the EP affected the national systems? The participation of Parliament in co-decision may induce new institutional settings within those national ministries which are directly concerned: ministries of economics and/or industry, environment, consumer protection and health policy, telecommunications, transport, education and youth. Alternatively – or even in parallel to the national EP-related bodies – the permanent representations of the Member States may reinforce their contacts with the EP by setting up special units or by providing civil servants to as 'points of contact' for MEPs. It may be that there are no formal changes owing to the 'parliamentarisation' of the EC/EU but a smooth de facto inclusion of EP-related concerns within existing ministerial or parliamentary departments. However, we may also identify similar evolutions at the level of national parliaments. Do they view the EP as a new or familiar but stronger ally or alien? Or do they perceive their European colleagues as illegitimate intruders? Have they introduced new means of digesting the growing role of the EP in EC/EU politics, such as involving themselves in a meaningful dialogue, at the very least with their respective national party's MEPs?

The speed of policy-making: the learning curve of the Council and the EP

One major indicator of the demands made of national and supranational actors in the EC/EU policy-cycle is their performance in terms of time needed to adopt binding legislation, i.e. the *procedural efficiency* of the system. In operational terms, we concentrate on the application of the co-decision procedure and analyse the speed of decision-making over time. With regard to the EP's increased powers following Maastricht, and therefore its contribution to the 'output legitimacy'[74] of the EU's multi-level governance framework, co-decision was expected to be a complex, lengthy, cumbersome and protracted procedure.[75] Indeed, the procedure could well be depicted as symptomatic of the 'general trade-off' between efficiency and the 'problem-solving capacity'[76] of EU decision-making on the one hand and parliamentary involvement on the other. This argument is also stressed by the fusion theory.[77]

However, in contrast to these predictions, co-decision does not appear to have led to serious delays in the final adoption of EC legislation. The average total duration of the 152 procedures concluded prior to April 1999 was 737 days. In contrast, the average length of time taken for acts adopted under the co-operation procedure was 734 days. In other words, co-decision has exceeded the time length of co-operation by only three days on average (Figure 2.11).[78]

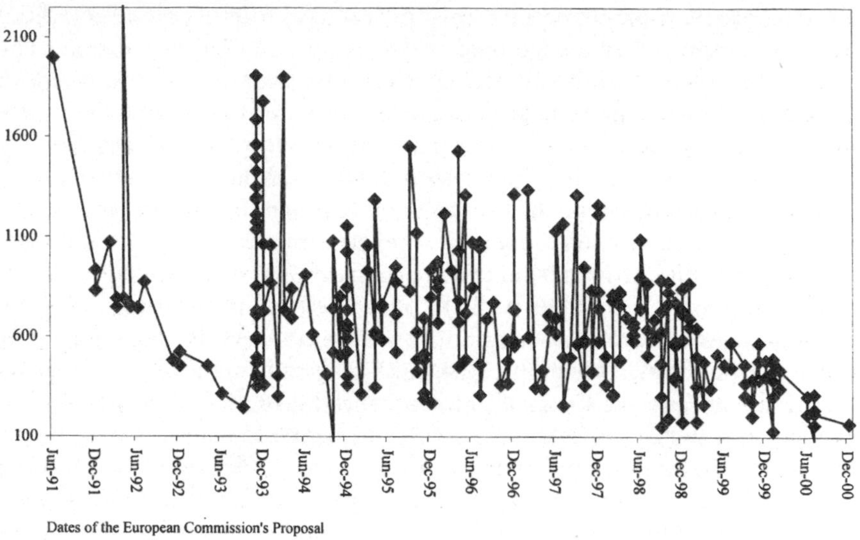

Figure 2.11 Co-decision procedure, 1991–2000: time periods between Commission proposal and final adoption of the legal act, December 2000
Source: Maurer (1999, 2001).

How can we explain the shortening of these time spans and the fact that the time needed for co-decision does not differ as much from co-operation, as was expected in the aftermath of Maastricht? One explanation could be that the two chambers directly involved in co-decision act not as adversaries but as problem-solvers who are interested in de-dramatising political conflict. Another – less idealistic – suggestion would be that there is an aim simply to produce some output, to attain public attention and to gain legitimacy. That is to say that either the EP or the Council prefer the adoption of second-best solutions rather than exhausting their negotiations and battling for long periods in order to reach a joint agreement. If this argument holds we would expect a decrease in the number of meetings of the conciliation committee in relation to the adoption of joint legislation over time. However, the empirical reality shows an increasing number of conciliation meetings in relation to legal acts completed between 1994 and 2001.[79] Thus, the time efficiency of co-decision is not rooted some kind of low-level confrontation between the institutions involved. Both the Council and the Parliament have learned to negotiate and develop a specific type of communitarian '*Streitkultur*'.[80]

We offer a different explanation for the trend towards efficiency. The most important delays in co-decision occur owing to lengthy procedures before the adoption of Parliament's first reading and the Council's common position where the treaty provisions do not set any deadlines. Even before the Commission's formal proposal, the actors involved aim to achieve substantial influence over the Commission's proposed text. The various groups of Member States' civil servants and private industry meet within a highly elaborate network of working groups where the substance of the Commission's drafts is fine-tuned by a wide range of civil servants and lobbyists. MEPs meet with Council of Ministers and COREPER representatives, Commissioners, Commission cabinet members and other officials to indicate their potential amendments and ideas on the draft. Moreover, MEPs are contacted to a growing extent by members of national parliaments who aim to draw their colleagues' attention to the potential consequences of European legislation and to possible EP amendments.[81] Once the Commission has officially published and submitted its proposal to Parliament and the Council, informal meetings take place in which EP rapporteurs and civil servants, COREPER members, Member State representatives and interest groups deliberate on the draft.[82] Hence the EP's first reading and the subsequent adoption of the Council's common position are subject to informal deals between the institutions on matters such as the legal basis, the financial resources necessary or available for implementing the act, or some its major aspects. In line with governance approaches we identify the effects of a growing and rather effective set of networks in an 'iron quadrangle'[83] between the Commission's services, national administrations, lobbyists and EP committees.

Theoretical and operative conclusions

Revisiting expectations: controversies surrounding an emergent system

Through negotiating and ratifying para-constitutional treaty amendments, Member States affect their own politico-administrative systems. For that purpose we have looked back over the last fifty years in order to identifying the relevant features of an emergent system. Some are counterintuitive especially in view of historical accounts of the EC/EU's developments. However, the empirical results do not point in one clear direction. We observe divergent trends, between both indicators and policy fields. The institutional and procedural opportunities on the European level are employed to differing degrees. The impact of these challenges varies according to the nature of Member States' political and administrative systems. According to this assumption our question is: do para-constitutional revisions matter – and how do they matter – for the set-up and functioning of national, sub-national and non-governmental policy-making structures?

Following theory-led expectations we can observe different degrees of validity. Thus we identify some spillover processes when looking at the para-constitutional dynamics of the Maastricht Treaty. However, they have not operated convincingly according to the expansive logic in neo-functional assumptions: the real use of the new treaty-based competencies has not lived up to the prediction of a quasi-exponential ('spillover'-related) exploitation. For neo-federalist approaches, the EP has used its powers rather effectively but undramatically and in a business-like way. However, there are insufficient cross-institutional and cross-policy field indications of a clear, linear shift towards the strengthening of a supranational state-like and purely parliamentary system. Finally, the observations concerning efficiency point to methods of collective bargaining *and* learning processes which could be interpreted as steps towards a new kind of bicameral system at the EU level.

(Neo-)realist views of a decline of the Union following the demise of superpower bilateralism have been falsified by the revisions to the ECT, including those at Amsterdam and particularly the measures increasing the EP's powers. When considering only the Council's output, this school of thought might claim that the overall 'use' of EC/EU institutions by governments has declined. However, a closer look reveals that this decrease is mainly caused by a 'saturation' in traditional EC fields such as agriculture and trade policy and where new legislation is short-lived (e.g. price-fixing regulations).[84] Governments have even used the articles for taking politically and – at least with regard to the third pillar – legally binding decisions in the new pillars although the procedures are clearly intergovernmental. The net decline in productivity could be interpreted as reflecting an increasing difficulty in balancing interests between Member States, but this school of thought might have difficulties in explaining the increasing role of the EP.

The observed macro-political patterns resemble most clearly the expectations deduced from governance approaches. In the overall figures the 'pendulum' metaphor might be useful in capturing general impressions. For many of the indicators we do not find a significant impact which could be attributed to the procedural revisions and amendments of the Maastricht Treaty. The treaty revisions of 1987 and 1993 – at least those concerning the EC Treaty – provided for more efficient procedures, but the exploitation of these provisions was mainly concentrated in some policy fields. In this view, the extension of the number of policy areas in which the Council may act by QMV has not resulted in more 'real' voting in the 1990s. Although the treaty revisions provided for more parliamentary procedures, the day-to-day inclusion of the EP remains an issue of controversial debate. Therefore, governance analyses might need to take greater account of the role of this institution. The increase in the EP's power, however, is linked to a rise in procedural complexity, leading to an erosion of the traditional cornerstones of democratic legitimacy, the national parliaments of the Member States. European parliamentarians are therefore becoming an active part of the highly specialised interaction that takes places within informal non-hierarchical networks.

As to the fusion view, the empirical record is also mixed. Overall figures point to national governments' decreasing interest in using EC/EU instruments. However, we need to qualify this assessment in view of the limits of quantitative analysis. We would draw attention to a non-linear relationship between para-constitutional developments and the exploitation of treaties. On the other hand, we identify a dynamic process of treaty modification and change brought to the institutional and procedural set-up of the Union – a regular pattern of remodelling institutions, procedures and competencies.[85] A closer look also indicates that the new provisions of the Maastricht Treaty have been used across the board; as an explanation we could point to the saturation in traditional fields like agriculture policy. The increasing role of the EP fits the expectation of a dual legitimacy of European decision-making and the execution of sectoral authority in the name of the citizenry. The creation of the Conference of European Affairs Committees of the national parliaments (COSAC) in 1989 and its formal recognition by the Amsterdam Treaty, the instalment of national parliament liaison officers within the EP buildings and the increasing importance of meetings between corresponding committees of both the national parliaments and the EP indicate a trend towards an embryonic kind of multi-level parliamentarism.

Increasing demands: trends of growth and differentiation

What are the operative challenges to the Member States and their politico-administrative systems? We might point to a set of trends from the Brussels arenas which need to be analysed in terms of their potential effects on national systems. Of particular relevance are:

- The dynamic evolution of new and refined treaty provisions leading – in a typical pattern – to an ever-increasing set of communitarised frameworks for policy-making: para-constitutional communitarisation with a growing role for all Community institutions.
- The subsequent widening of the functional scope of integration: sectoral differentiation concerning an increasing variety of policy fields and thus involving more and more actors.
- The creation of institutions by subsequent treaty amendments: institutional differentiation, which increases the range of interaction styles among relevant actors in the policy cycle.
- The creation and cross-institutional combination of different kinds of procedures, which provide actors with opportunities to take binding decisions: procedural differentiation, which increases complexity and

the need for national actors to improve their procedural skills; with majority rule as an acceptable method of decision-making and given the speed of the co-decision procedure, national actors cannot adopt an attitude of 'wait and see'.

- The activation of networks and procedural mechanisms which allow a growing set of interest and preference articulators outside the official array of institutions, to participate in EC/EU policy-making: actor differentiation, which leads to the need to take into account political sensitivities in broader coalition games.
- The increasing scope and density of legal obligations: the doubling in size of the acquis communautaire from the early 1980s to 1998 (see Figure 2.6) also indicates both the rise of the para-constitutional set-up as well as the invasion of the 'legal space' of Member States.

In view of these trends, does the Union require governments, parliaments and administrations to adapt at the national level? Given the evolution of the functional scope of EU policy-making over time, do new policy areas, altered instruments and reformed institutions mobilise national actors and lead to adaptation at the national level? Is the evolution of the EP viewed as a challenge which must be dealt with, or are Member States' systems immune to such a group of new players?

In the following chapters we will scrutinise the roles and behaviour of institutions at the national level, i.e. from the perspective of the national capitals. The focus will be on the extent and intensity of participation by national institutions in the process of preparing, making, taking, implementing and controlling EC/EU-generated decisions. Given the features and the dynamics of the EC/EU evolution, we expect to find generally discernible trends in the ways national institutions react and adapt to the challenges of the EC/EU. In line with the fusion approach, we look for trends of 'Europeanisation' defined as shifts in the attention of national institutions caused by the growth and differentiation of the para-constitutional and institutional set up of the EC/EU. We are curious as to how we can witness emergent or convergent patterns.

Notes

1 See Wolfgang Wessels, Andreas Maurer and Jürgen Mittag, 'The European Union and Member States: Analysing Two Arenas over Time', Chapter 1 in this volume, pp. 8–14.

2 See e.g. Tanja Börzel and Thomas Risse, 'When Europe Hits Home: Europeanisation and Domestic Change', in: *European Integration online Papers*, No. 15/2000 http://eiop.or.at/eiop/texte/2000–015.htm; Simon Bulmer, 'Domestic Politics and EC Policy-Making', in: *Journal of Common Market Studies*, No. 4/1994, pp. 349–363; Werner Feld, 'Two-Tier Policy-Making in the EC: The Common Agricultural Policy', in: Leon

Hurwitz (ed.), *Contemporary Perspectives on European Integration* (Westport, Conn.: Greenwood, 1980), pp. 123–149; Klaus Goetz and Simon Hix (eds), 'Europeanised Politics? European Integration and National Political Systems', *West European Politics*, Special Issue, Vol. 23, No. 4/2000; Johan P. Olsen, 'Europeanization and Nation-State Dynamics', in: Sverker Gustavsson and Leif Lewin (eds), *The Future of the Nation-State* (London: Routledge, 1996), pp. 245–285; Johan P. Olsen, 'Organising European Institutions of Governance. A Prelude to an Institutional Account of Political Integration', ARENA Working Paper, No. WP 00/2 (Oslo: Arena, 2000); Robert D. Putnam, 'Diplomacy and Domestic Politics: The Logic of Two Level Games', in: *International Organisation*, No. 3/1988, pp. 427–460; Jarle Trondal, 'Integration through Participation – Introductory Notes to the Study of Administrative Integration', in: *European Integration online Papers*, No. 4/1999 http://eiop.or.at/eiop/texte/1999–004a.htm; William Wallace, 'Collective Governance', in: Helen Wallace and William Wallace (eds), *Policy-Making in the European Union*, Fourth Edition (Oxford: Oxford University Publishers, 2000), pp. 523–542.

3 Christoph Knill and Dirk Lehmkuhl, 'How Europe Matters. Different Mechanisms of Europeanization', in: *European Integration online Papers*, No. 7/1999 http://eiop.or.at/eiop/texte/1999–007a.htm., p. 1.

4 German Constitutional Court, Judgement of October 12, 1993, in: Andrew Oppenheimer (ed.), *The Relationship between European Community Law and National Law: The Cases* (Cambridge: Cambridge University Press, 1995).

5 See Olsen, 2000, *op. cit.*, p. 6; and Johan P. Olson, 'Europeanisation and Nation-State Dynamics', ARENA Working Paper, No. 3/1996 (Oslo: Arena, 1996).

6 See for the identification and analysis of these approaches: Wessels, Maurer Mittag, *op. cit.*

7 See for a comprehensive analysis of the SEA: Jean de Ruyt, *L'Acte Unique Européen* (Bruxelles : Bruylant, 1987).

8 See on the evolution of CFSP: Martin Holland (ed.), *Common Foreign and Security Policy, The Record and Reforms* (London: Pinter, 1997); Simon Nuttall, *European Foreign Policy* (Oxford: Oxford University Press, 2000); Elfriede Regelsberger, Philippe de Schoutheete de Tervarent and Wolfgang Wessels (eds), *Foreign Policy of the European Union, From EPC to CFSP and Beyond* (Boulder, Co.: Lynne Rienner, 1997); Ramses A. Wessel, *The European Union's Foreign and Security Policy, A Legal Institutional Perspective* (The Hague: Kluwer Law International, 1999).

9 See on the evolution of JHA: Malcolm Anderson, Monica de Boer, Peter Cullen and William C. Gilmore, *Policing the European Union* (Oxford: Clarendon Press, 1996); Serge A. Bonnefoi, *Europe et Sécurité intérieure. TREVI – Union Européenne – Schengen* (Paris: Delmas, 1995); Elspeth Guilde (ed.), *The Developing Immigration and Asylum Policies of the European Union* (The Hague: Kluwer Law International, 1996); Jörg Monar and Roger Morgan (eds), *The Third Pillar of the European Union* (Brussels: European Interuniversity Press, 1994).

10 See Article 3 (ex Article C) TEU.

11 See Finn Laursen and Sophie Vanhoonacker (eds), *The Intergovernmental Conference on Political Union* (Maastricht: EIPA, 1992); Richard Corbett, *The Treaty of Maastricht* (London: Cartermill Publishers, 1993).

12 See Kenneth Dyson and Kevin Featherstone, *The Road to Maastricht, Negotiating Economic and Monetary Union* (Oxford: Oxford University Press, 1999); Daniel Gros and Niels Thygesen, *European Monetary Integration, From the European Monetary System to European Monetary Union* (London: Longman, 1992).

13 See Andrew Moravcsik, 'Taking Preferences Seriously: A Liberal Theory of International Politics', in: *International Organisation*, No. 4/1997, pp. 513–553.

14 See Helga Haftendorn, 'Zur Theorie außenpolitischer Entscheidungsprozesse', in: Volker Rittberger (ed.), *Theorien der Internationalen Beziehungen: Bestandsaufnahme und Forschungsperspektiven* (Opladen: Westdeutscher Verlag, 1990), pp. 401–423.

15 See Albert O. Hirschmann, *Exit, Voice and Loyalty: Responses to Decline in Firms, Organisations and States* (Cambridge, Mass.: Harvard University Press, 1970), p. 19; Joseph H.H. Weiler, 'The Transformation of Europe', in: *The Yale Law Journal*, No. 8/1991, pp. 2403–2483.

16 See Olsen, 2000, *op. cit.*, p. 6; and Olson, 1996, *op. cit.*

17 See Thomas Christiansen, 'Bringing Process Back In: The Longue Durée of European Integration', in: *Journal of European Integration*, No. 1/1998, pp. 99–121; Thomas Christiansen and Knud E. Jorgensen, 'The Amsterdam Process: A Structurationist Perspective on EU Reform', in: *European Integration online Papers*, No. 1/1999 http://eiop.or.at/eiop/texte/1999–001a.htm.

18 Peter Hall, *Governing the Economy: The Politics of State Intervention in Britain and France* (Cambridge: Polity Press, 1986), p. 19. David R. North offers a similar definition. Institutions are 'the rules of the game in a society or, more formally ... the humanly devised constraints that shape human interaction'. See David R. North: *Institutions, Institutional Change and Economic Performance* (Cambridge: Cambridge University Press, 1990), p. 3. See also: James G. March and Johan P. Olsen, *Rediscovering Institutions: The Organisational Basis of Politics* (New York: Free Press, 1989), p. 167.

19 See Guy Peters, *Institutional Theory in Political Science. The 'New Institutionalism'* (London, New York: Pinter) 1999; Peter A. Hall and Rosemary C.R. Taylor, 'Political Science and the Three New Institutionalisms', in: *Political Studies*, No. 5/1996, pp. 936–957; March and Olsen, 1989, *op. cit.*; Paul J. DiMaggio and Walter W. Powell, 'Introduction', in Walter W. Powell and Paul J. DiMaggio (eds), *The New Institutionalism in Organizational Analysis* (Chicago: University of Chicago Press, 1991), pp. 1–38; Bulmer, 1994, *op. cit.*; Wayne Sandholtz, 'Membership Matters: Limits of the Functional Approach to European Institutions', in: *Journal of Common Market Studies*, No. 3/1996, pp. 403–429; Mark Pollack, 'The New Institutionalism and EC Governance: The Promise and Limits of Institutional Analysis', in: *Governance*, No. 4/1996, pp. 429–458; Simon Hix, 'The Study of the European Union II: The "New

Governance" Agenda and Its Rival', in: *Journal of European Public Policy*, No. 1/1998, pp. 38–65.

20 See Paul Pierson, 'The Path to European Integration: A Historical Institutionalist Analysis', in: Wayne Sandholtz and Alec Stone Sweet (eds), *European Integration and Supranational Governance* (Oxford: Oxford University Press, 1998), pp. 27–58; see also Pierson's recent article, 'Increasing Returns, Path Dependence, and the Study of Politics', in: *American Political Science Review*, No. 2/2000, pp. 251–267.

21 Alec Stone Sweet and Wayne Sandholtz, 'Integration, Supranational Governance, and the Institutionalization of the European Polity', in: Wayne Sandholtz and Alec Stone Sweet (eds), *European Integration and Supranational Governance* (Oxford: Oxford University Press, 1998), p. 19; and Alec Stone Sweet, Wayne Sandholtz and Neil Fligstein (eds), *The Institutionalization of Europe* (Oxford: Oxford University Press, 2001).

22 See Pierson, 1998, *op. cit.*, p. 131.

23 Hall and Taylor, 1996, *op. cit.*, p. 941.

24 Bulmer, 1994, *op. cit.*, p. 356.

25 Geoffrey Garrett and Barry R. Weingast, 'Ideas, Interests and Institutions: Constructing the European Community's Internal Market', in: Judith Goldstein and Robert O. Keohane (eds), *Ideas and Foreign Policy. Beliefs, Institutions and Political Change* (Ithaca: Cornell University Press, 1993), p. 176.

26 See Robert D. Putnam, 'Diplomacy and Domestic Politics: The Logic of Two Level Games', in: *International Organisation*, No. 3/1988, pp. 427–460; Andrew Moravcsik, 'Preferences and Power in the European Community: A Liberal Intergovernmentalist Approach', in: *Journal of Common Market Studies*, No. 4/1993, pp. 473–524; David Skidmore and Valerie Hudson (eds), *The Limits of State Autonomy: Societal Groups and Foreign Policy Formulation* (Boulder, Co.: Westview Press, 1993).

27 See Joseph M. Grieco, 'Anarchy and the Limits of Co-Operation: A Realist Critique to the Newest Liberal Institutionalism', in: *International Organisation*, No. 3/1988, p. 494.

28 See Heidrun Abromeit and Thomas Schmidt, 'Grenzprobleme der Demokratie: konzeptionelle Überlegungen', in: Beate Kohler-Koch (ed.), *Regieren in entgrenzten Räumen* (Opladen: Westdeutscher Verlag, 1998), pp. 293–320 (on the concept: pp. 301–303); Heidrun Abromeit, *Democracy in Europe – Legitimizing Politics in a Non-State Polity* (Oxford, New York: Bergahn, 1998)

29 See, with further references on the theory of leadership in international negotiations, David Metcalfe, 'Leadership in European Union Negotiations: The Presidency of the Council', in: *International Negotiation*, No. 3/1998, pp. 413–434.

30 See Moravcsik, 1993, *op. cit.*, p. 483.

31 See Heinrich Schneider, 'Europäische Integration – die Leitbilder und die Politik', in: Michael Kreile (ed.), Die Integration Europas', *Politische Viertelsjahresschrift*, Sonderheft No. 23 (Opladen: Westdeutscher Verlag, 1992), p. 11.

32 See Jörg Monar, 'Interinstitutional Agreements: The Phenomenon and its

New Dynamics after Maastricht', in: *Common Market Law Review*, No. 4/1994.

33 Note that in this respect, the treaty provisions of the co-decision procedure (Article 251, ex Article 189b) permitted a scenario involving three Council and three parliamentary readings, plus two conciliation procedures. If all possible additional months and weeks were agreed throughout, the procedure could take up to fifteen months from the date of the transmission of the Council's common position (= approx. 475.5 days); see Andreas Maurer, *What Next for the European Parliament?* (London: Kogan Page, 1999).

34 See Pierson, 1998, *op. cit.*; Hall and Taylor, 1996, *op. cit.*, pp. 941–942.

35 See Alexander Kreher (ed.), *The EC Agencies between Community Institutions and Constituents: Autonomy, Control and Accountability, Conference Report* (Florence: European University Institute, 1998).

36 See, for example, the Presidency conclusions of the Cologne (June 1999) and Helsinki (December 1999) summits http://ue.eu.int.

37 See Martin Westlake, *The Council of the European Union* (London: Cartermill, 1995), pp. 164–167.

38 See also: Wolfgang Wessels, *Die Öffnung des Staates. Modelle und Wirklichkeit grenzüberschreitender Verwaltungspraxis 1960–1995* (Opladen: Leske & Budrich, 2000), pp. 195–260.

39 Helen Wallace, 'Politics and policy in the EU: The Challenge of Governance', in Helen Wallace and William Wallace (eds), *Policy-Making in the European Union*, Third Edition (Oxford: Oxford University Press, 1996), p. 63.

40 Andrew Duff, 'Building a Parliamentary Europe', in: Mario Télo (ed.), *Démocratie et Construction Européenne* (Bruxelles: Bruylant, 1995), pp. 253–254.

41 Frank Schimmelpfennig, 'Legitimate Rule in the European Union. The Academic Debate', *Tübinger Arbeitspapiere zur Internationalen Politik und Friedensforschung*, No. 27 (Tübingen, 1996), p. 19.

42 Fritz W. Scharpf, 'Community and Autonomy: Multi-Level Policy-Making in the European Union', in: *Journal of European Public Policy*, No. 1–2/1994, p. 220.

43 See Kenneth Dyson, *Elusive Union. The Process of Economic and Monetary Union in Europe* (London, New York, Longman: 1994).

44 On a joint Dutch and UK initiative, the Heads of States and Governments meeting at the Rome European Council in 1975 decided to hold regular meetings between the ministers for the interior in order to discuss common concerns with regard to police co-operation against international terrorism. The ministerial meetings of this 'TREVI' network were prepared and co-ordinated by a set of six different working groups at a high adminstrative level (state secretaries and senior officials). See Serge A. Bonnefoi, *Europe et Sécurité intérieure. TREVI – Union Européenne – Schengen* (Paris: Delmas, 1995); Tony Bunyan (ed.), *Key Texts on Justice and Home Affairs in the European Union, Vol. I (1976–1993): From TREVI to Maastricht* (London: Statewatch, 1997).

45 QMV instead of unanimity; co-decision instead of co-operation for the EP.

46 See, for example, Article 34 TEU on JHA instruments and procedures as amended by the Treaty of Amsterdam.

47 See Jörg Monar, 'Justice and Home Affairs in the Treaty of Amsterdam: Reform at the Price of Fragmentation', in: *European Law Review*, No. 4/1998, pp. 320–335; Monica den Boer and William Wallace, 'Justice and Home Affairs. Integration through Incrementalism?', in: Helen Wallace and William Wallace (eds), *Policy-Making in the European Union*, Fourth Edition (Oxford: Oxford University Press, 2000), pp. 493–519.

48 See Wolfgang Wessels, 'Der Amsterdamer Vertrag – Durch Stückwerksreformen zu einer immer effizienteren, erweiterten und föderalen Union?', in: *Integration*, No. 3/1997, pp. 117–135.

49 'Institutional anomaly' was the term used by the Portuguese Council Presidency within the framework of the 2000 IGC. See Conference of the Representatives of the Governments of the Member States, Presidency Note on 'IGC 2000: Possible Extension of Qualified Majority Voting – Articles which could Move to Qualified Majority Voting as they Stand', CONFER 4706/1/00, Brussels, 11 February 2000.

50 See Helen Wallace and William Wallace, 'Flying Together in a Larger and More Diverse European Union', Working Documents (The Hague: Netherlands Scientific Council for Government, Working Documents, No. W 87, 1995); Eric Philippart and Monica Sie Dhian Ho, 'From Uniformity to Flexibility – The Management of Diversity and its Impact on the EU System of Governance', in: Gráinne de Búrca and John Scott (eds), *Constitutional Change in the EU: From Uniformity to Flexibility* (Oxford: Hart Publishing, 2000); Wolfgang Wessels, 'Flexibility, Differentiation and Closer Cooperation. The Amsterdam Provisions in the Light of the Tindemans Report', in: Martin Westlake (ed.), *The European Union beyond Amsterdam. New Concepts of European Integration* (London: Routledge, 1998), pp. 76–98; Christian Deubner, *Enhanced Cooperation of EU Member States after Amsterdam. A New Tool to be Applied or to be Avoided?* (Ebenhausen: Stiftung Wissenschaft und Politik, 1999); Eric Philippart, and Monica Sie Dhian Ho, *The Pros and Cons of 'Closer Cooperation' within the EU* (The Hague: Netherlands Scientific Council for Government, Working Documents, No. W 104, March 2000).

51 Stone Sweet and Sandholtz, 1998, *op. cit.*, p. 16.

52 See Neil Fligstein and James A. McNichol, 'The Institutional Terrain of the European Union', in: Wayne Sandholtz and Alec Stone Sweet (eds), *European Integration and Supranational Governance* (Oxford: Oxford University Press, 1998), pp. 59–91.

53 See Wolfgang Wessels, 'The Growth and Differentiation of Multi-Level Networks: A Corporatist Mega-Bureaucracy or an Open City?', in: Helen Wallace and Alasdair R. Young (eds), *Participation and Policy-Making in the European Union* (Oxford: Oxford University Press, 1997), pp. 17–41.

54 Wessels, 2000, *op. cit.*, pp. 251–252.

55 Peter Haas, 'Introduction: Epistemic Communities and International Policy Co-Ordination', in: *International Organization* No. 1/1992, pp. 1–35 (here p. 3).

56 See Christoph Sasse, Edouard Poullet, David Coombes and Gérard Deprez, *Decision Making in the European Community* (New York, London: Praeger, 1977).

57 The German Presidency of the Council (January–June 1999) listed 351 operating working groups. See Andreas Maurer, 'Germany: Fragmented Structures in a Complex System', Chapter 5 in this volume; Andreas Maurer, 'The German Presidency of the Council: Continuity or Change in Germany's European Policy', in: *Journal of Common Market Studies*, The European Union. Annual Review of the EU 1999/2000, pp. 43–47. In its November 2001 summary, the Antici group of the Council lists 257 working groups. See Council of the European Union: Council Preparatory bodies, Document No. 14132/01, Brussels, 16 November 2001.

58 See the individual chapters on the Member States in Part II of this volume.

59 See Sasse *et al.*, 1977, *op. cit.*; Peter van der Knaap, 'Government by Committee: Legal Typology, Quantitative Assessment and Institutional Repercussions of Committees in the European Union', in: Robert Pedler and Günther Schäfer (eds), *Shaping European Law and Policy: The Role of Committees and Comitology in the Political Process* (Maastricht: EIPA, 1996), pp. 83–116 (here p. 114). The Council itself notes that some two-thirds of its rolling agenda is closed by COREPER, out of which 70 per cent are agreed at the working groups level. See Rat der EG, Der Rat der EG (Luxembourg: Amt für amtliche Veröffentlichungen, 1990), p. 22; See also Wessels, 2000, *op. cit.*, pp. 228–229.

60 See Robert Pedler and Günther Schäfer (eds), *Shaping European Law and Policy: The Role of Committees and Comitology in the Political Process* (Maastricht: EIPA, 1996); Christian Joerges and Ellen Vos (eds), *EU Committees: Social Regulation, Law and Politics* (Oxford: Hart Publishing, 1999); Thomas Christiansen and Emil Kirchner (eds), *Committee Governance in the European Union* (Manchester: Manchester University Press, 2000). The structure of the Comitology network was amended and simplified by Council Decision 1999/468/EC of 28 June 1999. Following the Decision, the Commission published, on 8 August 2000, the list of existing Comitology committees according to the policy fields in question, and their dates of creation. See *Official Journal of the EC*, No. C 225, 8 August 2000, pp. 2–18.

61 See Stephan Haggard, 'Integrating the Two Halves of Europe: Theories of Interests, Bargaining, and Institutions', in: Robert O. Keohane, Joseph S. Nye and Stanley Hoffmann (eds), *After the Cold War: International Institutions and State Strategies in Europe, 1989–1991* (Cambridge, Mass.: Harvard University Press, 1993), p. 191.

62 See Sasse *et al.*, 1977, *op. cit.*

63 See Guy Peters, 'Bureaucratic Politics and the Institutions of the European Community', in: Alberta Sbragia (ed.), *Euro-Politics: Institutions and Policymaking in the 'New' European Community* (Washington, DC: Brookings, 1992), pp. 75–122; Wolfgang Wessels, 1997, *op. cit.*, pp. 17–41.

64 We base these observations on ongoing research by Armin von Bogdandy, Felix Arndt and Philipp Dann, University of Frankfurt and their interim report 'Strukturen des Unionsrechts', mimeo (Frankfurt, 1999).

65 According to the annual reports of the Commission the number of legal acts adopted by the EC institutions per year is much higher. The reason for this discrepancy is that the annual reports also list all internal administrative acts

including appointments, decisions regarding salaries, etc. On the other hand, if we refer to the Community legislation in force, the overall number is much smaller. Calculating on the basis of different times of publication of the Directory of European Community Legislation in Force (DECLIF), we find 5,127 legal acts for the period between 1952 and December 1986, 7,621 for the period until 1993 and 9,767 for the period until December 1998. These numbers are well below the total sum of EC/EU legislation across the period 1952–99. The difference between these rather low numbers and the overall legal output is rooted in different statistical methods. Whereas studies based on the DECLIF are mainly interested in the structure of the EU legal corpus, counting the legislative activity over time provides us with the necessary data for exploring the dynamics of the system. Therefore, we organise our data basis on the overall amount of legislation produced over time. The methodological problem is that 'legislation in force' does not take into account the very process of decision-making and legal output over time. Since the DECLIF is updated twice a year, it has to be understood as a snapshot of EC/EU output at a given time. What cannot be derived from these data is the dynamic of the system which produces legislation across time. See also Edward C. Page and Dionyssis Dimitrakopoulos, 'The Dynamics of EU growth. A Cross-Time Analysis', in: *Journal of Theoretical Politics*, No. 3/1997, pp. 365–387; Mark Pollack, 'The End of Creeping Competence? EU Policy-Making since Maastricht', in: *Journal of Common Market Studies*, No. 3/2000, pp. 519–538.

66 Special thanks go to Astrid Krekelberg for the compilation and initial analysis of the raw data.

67 See Hix, 1998, *op. cit.*, p. 73.

68 See for this kind of Council policy-making 'in the shadow of the majority vote', Fritz W. Scharpf, *Games Real Actors Play, Actor-Centered Institutionalism in Policy Research* (Boulder, Co.: Westview Press, 1997), pp. 191–193.

69 See Josef Falke, 'Comitology and other Committees: A Preliminary Empirical Assessment', in: Robert Pedler and Günther Schäfer (eds), *Shaping European Law and Policy: The Role of Committees and Comitology in the Political Process* (Maastricht: EIPA, 1996), pp. 117–165; Ellen Vos, 'The Rise of Committees', in: *European Law Journal* No. 3/1997, pp. 210–229; Wessels, 2000, *op. cit.*, pp. 200–221, 225–229 and 232–240.

70 Thanks for this specification to the members of the Friedrich-Ebert-Foundation Study Group on European integration and Klaus Suchanek. The term is a free translation of the German term 'Mitwirkungsbürokratie'.

71 See Maurer, 1999, *op. cit.*; Andreas Maurer *(Co-)Governing after Maastricht: The European Parliament's Institutional Performance 1994–1999*, European Parliament, Working Paper, No. POLI 104/rev. EN, Brussels 1999, pp. 24–31.

72 See Maurer *(Co-)Governing*, 1999, *op. cit.*, p. 26.

73 See e.g. Simon Hix, 'How MEPs Vote', ESRC One Europe or Several? Programme, Briefing Note 1/00 (London, April 2000); Amie Kreppel, 'What Affects the European Parliament's Influence?', in: *Journal of Common Market Studies*, No. 3/1999, pp. 521–535; Michael Shackleton, 'The Politics

of Codecision', in: *Journal of Common Market Studies*, No. 2/2000, pp. 325–342; Amie Kreppel, *The European Parliament and Supranational Party System: A Study in Institutional Development* (Cambridge: Cambridge University Press, 2002).

74 Fritz W. Scharpf, 'Introduction: The Problem-Solving Capacity of Multi-Level Governance', in: *Journal of European Public Policy*, No. 4/1997, pp. 520–538; Fritz W. Scharpf, *Governing in Europe: Effective and Democratic?* (Oxford: Oxford University Press, 1999).

75 See David Earnshaw and David Judge, 'From Co-Operation to Co-Decision: The European Parliament's Path to Legislative Power', in: Jeremy Richardson (ed.), *Policy Making in the European Union* (London: Routledge, 1996), pp. 96–126; Martin Westlake, *A Modern Guide to the European Parliament* (London: Pinter, 1994); Neill Nugent, 'Decisionmaking Procedures', in: Desmond Dinan (ed.), *Encyclopaedia of the European Union* (Boulder, Co.: Lynne Rienner 1998).

76 Scharpf, 1997, *op. cit.*

77 See Wessels, 1996 and 1997, *op. cit.*

78 The total average duration of co-decision varies considerably, depending on the legal bases applied for. See: Maurer, 1999, *op. cit.*

79 See Andreas Maurer, '(Mit)-Regieren nach Maastricht: Die Bilanz des Europäischen Parlaments nach fünf Jahren Mitentscheidung', in *Integration*, No. 4/1998, pp. 212–224.

80 See Wolfgang Wessels and Udo Diedrichs, 'The European Parliament and EU Legitimacy', in: Thomas Banchoff and Mitchell P. Smith (eds), *Legitimacy and the European Union. The Contested Polity* (London: Routledge, 1999), pp. 134–135.

81 See Andreas Maurer, 'National Parliaments in the European Architecture: From Latecomers' Adaptation towards Permanent Institutional Change?', in: Andreas Maurer and Wolfgang Wessels (eds), *National Parliaments on their Ways to Europe: Losers or Latecomers?* (Baden-Baden: Nomos, 2001), pp. 27–76; Andreas Maurer, *Perspectives for Co-Operation between the European Parliament and the National Parliaments, European Parliament*, Working Document: Political Series W-19 (Brussels/Luxembourg, 1996).

82 See Beate Kohler-Koch and Christine Quittkat, *Intermediation of Interests in the European Union*, Working Papers, Mannheimer Zentrum für Europäische Sozialforschung, No. 9/1999 (Mannheim: MZES, 1999).

83 See in this respect on the concept of the 'iron triangle': Guy Peters, 'The European Bureaucrat: The Applicability of Bureaucracy and Representative Government to Non-American Settings', in: Andre Blais and Stéphane Dion (eds), *The Budget-Maximizing Bureaucrat. Appraisals and Evidence* (Pittsburgh: University of Pittsburgh Press, 1991), p. 313; Wolfgang Wessels, 'Comitology: Fusion in Action. Politico-administrative Trends in the EU System', in: *Journal of European Public Policy*, No. 2/1998, pp. 209–234 (here p. 223).

84 On the issue of the longevity of EU legislation see especially Page and Dimitrakopoulos, 1997, *op. cit.*

85 In the words of the Report of Richard von Weizäcker, Jean-Luc Dehaene and David Simon to the European Commission on 'the institutional implications

of enlargement': 'The present [1999] situation is typical: the treaty of Amsterdam entered into force on May 1st, and, on June 4th, the Cologne European Council called for a new intergovernmental conference.' See this report of 18 October 1999, p. 12.

Select bibliography

Hix, Simon (1999) *The Political System of the European Union* (London: Macmillan). Jachtenfuchs, Markus and Kohler-Koch, Beate (eds) (1996) *Europäische Integration* (Opladen: Leske & Budrich).

Maurer, Andreas (1999) *What Next for the European Parliament?* (London: Kogan Page).

Maurer, Andreas (2001) 'National Parliaments in the European Architecture: From Latecomers' Adaptation towards Permanent Institutional Change?', in: Andreas Maurer and Wolfgang Wessels (eds), *National Parliaments on their Ways to Europe: Losers or Latercomers?* (Baden-Baden: Nomos).

Olsen, Johan P. (1996) 'Europeanization and Nation-State Dynamics', in: Sverker Gustavsson and Leif Lewin (eds) (1996) *The Future of the Nation-State* (London: Routledge).

Wessels, Wolfgang (2000) *Die Öffnung des Staates, Modelle und Wirklichkeit grenzüberschreitender Verwaltungspraxis 1960–1995* (Opladen: Leske & Budrich).

II

Member States and the European Union

3 *Christian Franck, Hervé Leclercq and Claire Vandevievere*

Belgium: Europeanisation and Belgian federalism

Introduction: European integration as a historical lesson of neutrality

For about fifty years, the Belgian policy toward European integration is the most significant demonstration Belgium has made of its commitment to multilateralism and international co-operation in security as well as in economic affairs. Even if Belgium had already illustrated such an orientation through its participation in multilateral trade and monetary co-operation before the Second World War, its security policy, by contrast, had been shaped by the compulsory neutrality imposed on Belgium from 1830 to 1914. To escape from being involved in a new war caused by the rivalry of its great neighbours, Belgium, had returned to neutrality by the so-called 'politique d'indépendance' in 1936 – with the well-known consequences when the turmoil of 1940 began.

European orthodoxy and political pragmatism

It was the Belgian government in exile in London (1940–44) which initiated the new course of Belgian foreign policy for the second part of the century. Security was to be ensured through collective security and collective defence, hence the active commitment to the United Nations (UN) and the North Atlantic Treaty Organisation (NATO). Belgium has searched for a 'voice' in politico-strategic and economic diplomacy through multilateralism and through participation in a decision-making process which rested not on directoires by the great powers but on the institutional rules of international organisations. Even if both the UN and NATO have offered forums of great importance for its foreign policy, it is European integration that has been the central focus for Belgium since the creation of the Council of Europe and the strengthening of the Europe of the Six in the early 1950s. Despite divisions in the Belgian political elite between defenders of national sovereignty and supranationalists led by Paul-Henri Spaak, it was the latter that had a greater role in shaping Belgian European policy. The long-term aim of this policy is the achievement of a federal union, so Belgium has pushed for a widening of the scope of EC competencies and a strengthening of supranationalism in EC decision-making. Belgium has thus favoured the Commission's monopoly in policy initiation (that is, its role as 'the motor' of integration), the extension of QMV in the Council, a growing role for the EP and full powers for the ECJ in ensuring that European law is observed. Nevertheless, the story of Belgian diplomacy is also one of pragmatism in its attempts to bypass obstacles on the road to the integration.

In 1972 the Belgian government supported French President Pompidou's attempts to give a new impetus to the European unification. However, it was not certain that the French proposals made at the 1972 Paris Summit were an attempt to pave the way towards a federal Europe. Having been against the proposal in the early 1960s, by December 1974, Belgium had agreed to the direct involvement of heads of state or prime ministers in EC affairs through the European Council. The Tindemans Report (December 1975) was another illustration of Belgium's pragmatism in looking for incremental progress at a time when substantial moves towards a federal Europe were not forthcoming. However this pragmatism was also visible in Belgium's efforts to preserve and to reinforce the supranational elements of the EC's institutional system whenever such opportunities arose. For instance, the Belgian presidency pressed for voting on agriculture issues in the first half of 1982. Furthermore, following 'the night of the long knives' during the 1997 Amsterdam European Council, Belgian Prime Minister Jean Luc Dehaene insisted there was no point in re-weighting the votes within the Council of Ministers' QMV system without extending it to cover new competencies.

The priority of EMU

In the 1990s, movements towards EMU formed the strategic priority for pushing forward European integration, but the objectives of political unification were also constantly relevant. Belgium has remained among those who support a common defence policy and a common defence which would fully consolidate a political role for the European Union in international affairs. And the final aim of federalism has not been abandoned even if Dehaene insisted more on federative elements of the institutional system than on a definite federal system. This federalist attitude, associated with Belgium and the Netherlands, explains their unhappiness with the pillar structure of the TEU and their support during the 1996–97 IGC for a progressive inclusion of the two intergovernmental pillars into the supranational pillar one. Since the Maastricht Treaty has entered into force, membership of the Euro-Zone has been the main priority for the Belgian government. The latter took important measures to decrease public debt which fell from 7.2 per cent in 1993 to under 3 per cent in 1997 (in fact, 2.1 per cent). Although the overall trend was downward, the debt ratio of 135 per cent in 1993 was still at 123 per cent in 1998. The European Monetary Institute (EMI) has asked that Belgium retain a positive balance (net of debt) that could lead the country, as foreseen in the Treaty of Maastricht, to a debt ratio of 60 per cent by 2031. At the time of joining the Euro-Zone, Belgium aimed to maintain a positive balance of 6 per cent for several years.[1]

Furthermore, an administrative service (Commissariat général à l'euro) has been created as an instrument to prepare and adapt the banking, financial and economic sectors to the use of the Euro. Its activities are organised around the following themes: preparation for and adaptation to the Euro by public administrators (non-)financial enterprises and consumers, and communication policy. The aim of the Commissariat was not to substitute private initiatives but to co-ordinate and provide information and recommendations about how to follow the guidelines. It began, for instance, with an inventory of all the measures necessary to ensure a harmonious and efficient introduction of the Euro within Belgium between 1999 and 2002. Each measure is explained in the form of an up-to-date file which deals with the relevant sectors, the state of the work, the timing and, in some cases, recommendations. Leaflets and colloquia are also supplied. The possibility of enlargement in the year 2000 placed Belgium at a crossroads. A fear of losing its influence within EU institutions led Belgium to defend its position and to adopt a reluctant attitude towards following the 'larger' Member States who press for institutional reforms. Might Belgium take on a rigid if not conservative approach to institutional issues? At Amsterdam, it aimed to maintain the minimum ratio of one commissioner per Member State and was reluctant to see a re-weighting of votes in the Council of Ministers – arguing, as mentioned above, that this reform would prove necessary only if QMV was significantly extended. The Belgian government, however, reacted promptly to overcome the Amsterdam failure on institutions by proposing a declaration which links the re-weighting of the voting in the Council of Ministers, the composition of the Commission and an extension of QMV. This initiative was also supported by France and Italy.

Political parties and public opinion: from permissive consensus to issue-related 'voice'

Belgian political parties, in general, are still in favour of a federal Europe but are critical of recent developments and suggest that the Union should be more democratic, more social and more efficient. Hence the Green Party voted against the Treaty of Amsterdam and the federal parliament adopted a resolution supporting the Belgian government in its proposal for institutional reforms. In the Senate on 4 June 1998, 49 members voted in favour of the Treaty of Amsterdam and 13 voted against. In the Chamber of Representatives on 9 July 1998, 105 members voted in favour and 23 voted against. In party terms, the Social-Christians, Socialists and Liberals voted in favour while the Green Party voted against. Also voting negatively were 'Volksunie', a party that favours Flemish autonomy, and the 'Vlaams Blok', the separatist and extreme-right group, both of which favour a 'Europe of the Peoples'.

Public opinion has naturally moved in the same way. From a general permissive consensus, the attitude of the population has become more critical depending on policy issues. Two major events put Europe on the agenda: the bankruptcy of Clabecq Forges and the closing of Renault-Vilvordre. Europe was seen at the same time as both a scapegoat and a forum in which a social dimension should be developed. However, beyond such circumstances as these, public opinion is not usually significantly mobilised. The Maastricht criteria were synonymous with restrictions but have nevertheless been accepted. However, from 1980 to 1996, those who believed that belonging to the Union was a good thing became a minority according to Eurobarometer data (57 per cent in 1980 and 42 per cent in 1996). The majority of interest groups are in favour of European integration though there are differences among various types of groups and subjects.

Belgian federalism

The major institutional feature that influences Belgian European policy is its *federal structure* completed after the Treaty of Maastricht. The specific character of Belgian federalism lies in the co-existence of two different kinds of federated entities: regions and communities. There are three regions: the Wallonian Region, the Flemish Region and the Brussels-Capital Region. They are territorial entities created essentially as a response to aspirations of socio-economic autonomy. They have major power in the fields of town and country planning, economic policy, public industrial initiatives, infrastructure, employment, environment, energy policy and transport. The Kingdom of Belgium also has three communities, which express cultural autonomies: the French Community, the Flemish Community and the German Community. They have authority in education, cultural matters, broadcast media, use of languages and policies with a personal impact (personal assistance, health, policy concerning persons with disabilities, protection of young children, etc.). These federated entities have become increasingly involved in the EC decision-making process, both at the preparatory stage and, since the Maastricht Treaty, with regard to final decision-making. This is due to the change of Article 203 (ex Article 146) ECT, advocated mainly by Belgium and Germany. The Council of Ministers is no longer formed strictly by members of the national government but is composed of representatives of each Member State at 'ministerial level', entitled to take decisions for the government of that Member State. A member of a federated government can legally represent Belgium but this must be on the basis of a consensus which can sometimes be difficult to attain. A co-operation agreement was signed on 8 March 1994 between the federal state and the regions and communities to establish the rules for the representation of Belgium. The Flemish Parliament passed a resolution in 1996 requesting separate votes for the Belgian federated entities in the Council of Ministers on matters which concern them.[2] However, the federal state did not defend this proposition during the 1996 IGC which would have divided the Belgian vote in the Council of Ministers. The Belgian state therefore remains the only interlocutor although some entities would like more power. This could be possible only within the fundamentally changed Belgian framework brought about by Belgian federalisation. Co-operation and co-ordination have become essential at the administrative and political levels. Federated entities are very sensitive on specific issues such as culture, the right of European citizens to vote in local elections, and the concept of subsidiarity.

In its memorandum for the 1996 IGC (October 1995), the Belgian government pointed out that subsidiarity is not only a 'downward' principle – from Union to States – but also an 'upward' principle if action at the Union level is appropriate. Being a federal state, the government sees in subsidiarity a crucial principle in the relations between the Union, the federal state and the communities and regions. The CoR and the use of Article 203 ECT are expressions of this subsidiarity. However, according to Belgium, subsidiarity should be applied in all Member States. A renegotiation of subsidiarity at the 1996 IGC was conceivable only if it did not damage further developments in European integration or interfere in the sharing of competencies within Member States. The federal government's support for the specification of subsidiarity in the Treaty of Amsterdam was mainly an attempt to please the federated entities.

The national policy-cycle: the complexity of horizontal and vertical co-ordination

Actors and co-ordinating bodies

Some ministerial departments at the federal level, which are particularly involved in European integration, have their own European co-ordination structures. All, however, have assigned one of their staff members to act as a 'European co-ordinator'. Currently, the regional or community ministries are striving to organise European co-ordination in the same way by designating either a person or a unit to this role. In addition, there are many interdepartmental co-ordination bodies. At present, no ministerial department has been created in Belgium to deal specifically with European issues. Rather, the existing bodies have been adapted to participate in drawing up and implementing Community decisions. At the

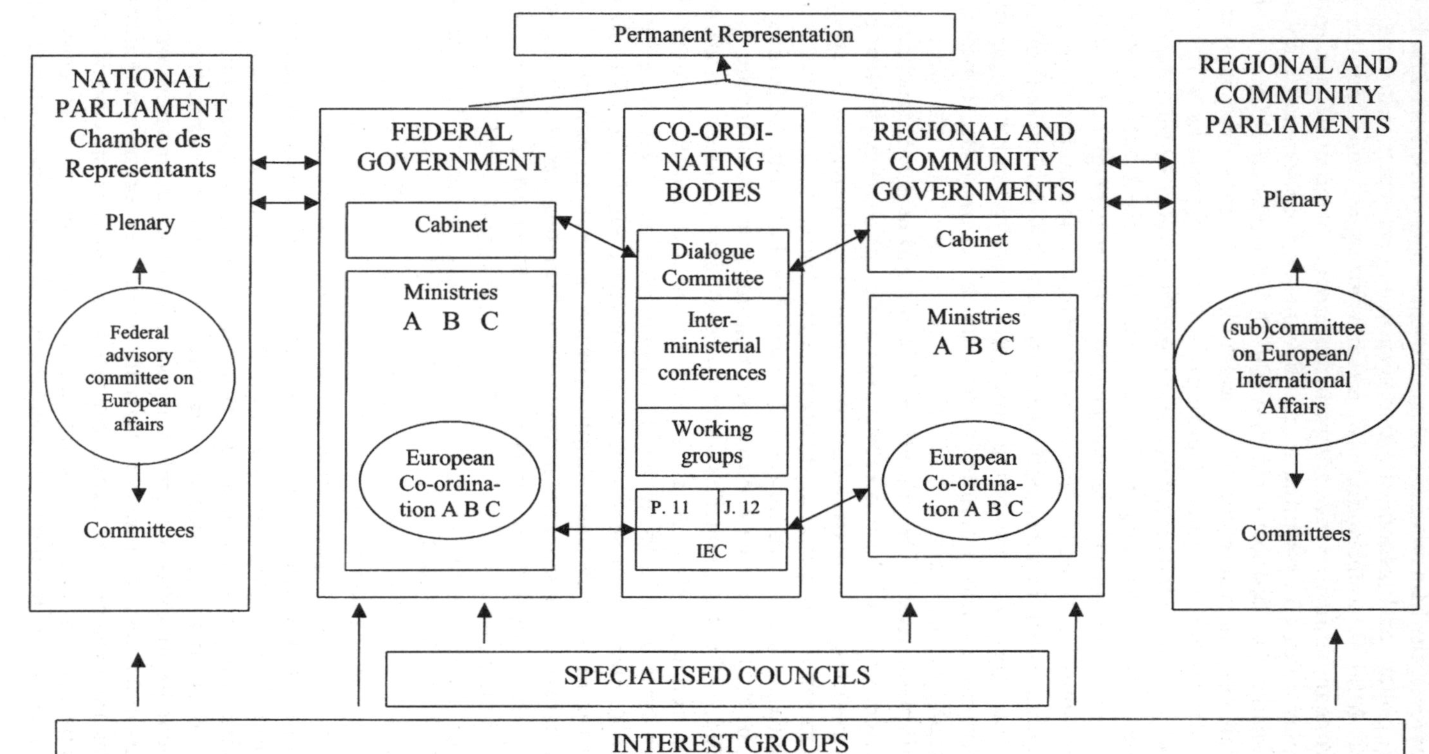

Figure 3.1 The national level of European decision-making – Belgium

political level, the Minister for Foreign Affairs is responsible for Belgium's foreign policy and general European policy. He participates in the 'General Affairs' Councils and sits together with the Prime Minister on the European Council. At the administrative level, two ministerial departments play a key co-ordinating role: the Ministry for Foreign Affairs and the Ministry for Economic Affairs. The former has two services for European co-ordination: the P.11 and J.12 services. In the Economic Affairs Ministry consultation takes place in an interdepartmental committee known as the Inter-Ministerial Economic Committee (IEC), which is composed of representatives from several ministries. Above all these administrative bodies act as federal co-ordinators; representatives of both the communities and regions are also invited to IEC meetings whenever an issue of concern to them has been put on the agenda. As for P.11, it holds ad hoc 'European Co-Ordination' meetings, to which it invites representatives from the various ministerial cabinets and departments concerned; occasionally a delegation from the Commission of the European Communities attends. The composition of the group varies according to the subjects studied. The process of co-ordination involves preparing the Belgian position to be defended in the Community institutions – upward co-ordination – and giving momentum to the transposition of EU law – downward co-ordination. Upward co-ordination falls within the jurisdiction of the P.11 service while downward co-ordination is dealt with by the P.12 service. The IEC, which co-ordinates the various ministerial departments in economic matters, is chaired by the Secretary-General of the Ministry for Economic Affairs and is composed of high-level civil servants from departments with economic responsibilities (in the broad sense of the word) and never includes members of the ministerial cabinets.

In principle, the 'European Co-Ordination' meetings in the Ministry for Foreign Affairs deal, as a priority, with the political and institutional aspects of the matters involved while the IEC provides a forum for co-ordination of a more technical nature. Besides those general co-ordination groups, there are sectoral co-ordination bodies which act to overcome the combination of ad hoc meetings, for example at the Department of Agriculture or at the Department of Public Health and the Environment. Like other Member States, Belgium uses its Permanent Representation to the Communities in Brussels for all communications between the European institutions and the Belgian administrations. The Permanent Representation participates in the co-ordination of the preparation of national positions in relation to Community law. Civil servants from the Permanent Representations and in some cases other designated officials from the ministries are present in the working parties that prepare Council decisions and even possibly in expert groups convened by the Commission. It takes part in negotiations in which it expresses Belgium's standpoint. In addition to career diplomats, the Belgian Permanent Representation also comprises officials seconded from the Ministries for Economic Affairs, Communications and Infrastructure, Finance, Agriculture, Employment and Labour, and also from the National Bank. The communities (except the German-speaking community) and the regions have also designated 'attachés'. They receive instructions only from the minister to whom they are answerable but are under the authority of the Ambassador.

Procedures

The lengthy preparation of the legislative process starts, as a general rule, with a Commission proposal. This proposal is actually the outcome of work during which the Commission calls upon, in particular, consultants or experts from the national administrations. For the preparation, the Belgian experts included in a COREPER working party are specialised officials appointed by the department which has been contacted by the Permanent Representation. In most cases it is easy to find the competent service. The co-ordinator will intervene only when the decision proposal does not clearly fit into a section of existing Belgian law: he has then to designate an official to participate in the work or, if several ministries can claim jurisdiction in the matter, he will attend a European co-ordination meeting in the P.11 service which will determine the department to be the so-called 'pilot department'.

A form of post hoc control of the position adopted by the expert is the regular report s/he has to submit to her/his minister. In addition, coherence of the Belgian position is guaranteed by the presence, within the working party, of officials from the Permanent Representation who act as spokespersons for Belgium. At this stage, the Representation is actually responsible for the co-ordination but if necessary, it is assisted by the pilot department. After COREPER, when the matter goes back to the Council of Ministers, the experts gathered in the P.11 service then prepare the Council meeting by charting the main lines of the position to be defended by the minister, accompanied by a member of his cabinet, the Permanent Representative and the Deputy Permanent Representative.

For implementation, the department or departments concerned make plans that are communicated to the European co-ordinator or co-ordinators. The J.12 service ensures that the deadlines for the transposition of directives are observed. Given that European rules generally encompass the responsibilities of several ministerial departments of the federal state, the regions and the communities, co-ordination at this level is required. The pilot departments are entrusted with an initiating role and are charged with contacting the other ministerial departments concerned and following the action through. These departments are chosen because of their responsibility and those most often charged with implementing directives are Economic Affairs, Agriculture, Social Affairs, Public Health and Environment, and Finance.

Regular meetings are held at the Ministry for Foreign Affairs to ensure that the follow-up is supervised. At these meetings the co-ordinators of the departments concerned evaluate the progress of the transposition or implementation procedure. Actually, in many fields basic legislation makes all later rules subject to consultation by some specialised council. These councils are either bodies composed of scientific specialists (e.g. the High Council for Hygiene in Mines), consumers and social partners (e.g. the Public Contracts Commission) and sometimes only of social partners (e.g. the National Labour Council), or bodies with a socio-economic composition (e.g. the Consumers' Council or the Central Council for the Economy). They are not bound by any deadlines within which they must give their opinion. As is customarily the case in Belgium, they also enjoy a considerable amount of autonomy in organising their work. It seems therefore that the process is ruled more by officials than by the government. The minister representing Belgium is fully informed at the end of the elaboration process before attending the Council of Ministers. There is also some reluctance among those with political authority to act on instructions from the administrative level. As a consequence officials do not receive any instructions and a minister may change Belgium's position at the very end of the negotiations. When a matter causes conflict or has a political significance, it is dealt with at the governmental level.

Political parties are rather excluded from this game which is dominated by officials, at least in terms of legislation of lesser importance. When it appears that a matter has political relevance, political headquarters come in to defend a particular position. Their involvement is however, modest because of the technical, and the evolutionary character of European negotiations, the lack of transparency and the priority given to national issues. As far as transposition is concerned, one could equally make the distinction between those measures which are of political importance and those which are not. The former are dealt with at the political level in the government or among political parties; the latter at the administrative level but both cases require the government's intervention. The preliminary draft of the law of transposition is discussed in the Belgian Council of Ministers. The government may change its draft according to the suggestions contained in the opinion of the Conseil d'Etat without being bound. The draft order is submitted to the King to be signed (or the competent minister of a federated government). As for the draft law, this is presented to the competent legislative assemblies. Ratification, promulgation and publication are still required for the law to be applicable in Belgium. Once the transposition has been completed, the Belgian Permanent Representation is informed so that it can then notify the Commission.

The specifics of regional and community involvement

Co-operation on European policy-making between the federal state, regions and communities is facilitated by co-ordination procedures which are formalised through legal rules and which are designed to promote dialogue between the three levels. The 'comité de concertation' comprises six national ministers – including the Prime Minister who chairs the committee – and six ministers representing the Flemish government, the government of the French Community, the Wallonian regional government and the Brussels regional government. Originally set up to settle 'conflicts of interest', this committee is now an important meeting place where general co-ordination problems arising from the drafting and implementation of Belgium's European policy can be raised and may be solved. The 'comité de concertation' may set up specialised committees, called 'inter-ministerial conferences', to promote consultation and co-operation between the state, communities and regions. Consultation takes place between the relevant members of the federal government and the community and regional governments, not between the members of their staff. The 'conferences' can however set up working groups on a permanent or ad hoc basis. The Inter-Ministerial Conference on Foreign Policy takes a prominent part in European affairs. The permanent representative and the deputy representative are the only persons entitled to take the floor within COREPER. When preparing meetings, they have the option of assistance from the Belgian 'spokesperson' from one of the working parties set up by the committee. It is usually the permanent representative who designates an official from the Representation to play this role in each working party. If appropriate, such an official can be chosen from among the regional or community 'attachés'.

The federal authority, the regions and the communities concluded on 8 March 1994 an agreement 'relating to the representation of the Kingdom of Belgium within the Council of Ministers of the European Union'. The aim of this agreement was to organise a general co-ordination mechanism ensuring unity in the views expressed by Belgium. 'Co-ordination' must take place before each session of the Council of Ministers, whatever the field may be. Such co-ordination is the responsibility of P.11 in the federal Ministry for Foreign Affairs, 'both from a general point of view and in respect of each point of the agenda of the European Communities Councils meetings'. Positions are adopted by consensus but if this cannot be reached, the case in hand is referred to the Inter-Ministerial Conference for Foreign Policy, which also acts by consensus. If agreement still cannot be achieved then the matter is submitted to the 'comité de concertation'. This co-ordination process must result in the adoption of a single position so that Belgium can take part effectively in Community decision-making. Without a consensus the Belgian representative has to abstain from voting or from taking a position within the Council of Ministers.

By virtue of Article 146 of the Treaty of Rome, as reformulated by the Treaty of Maastricht, representation of Belgium within the Council is possible through 'a representative ... at ministerial level' from all the competent regions and communities, 'authorised to commit the government' of Belgium. Article 81 of the Special Act on Institutional Reforms of 8 August 1980 authorises the regional or community governments 'to commit the State within the Council in which one of their members represents Belgium', in accordance with an agreement to be concluded between the federal authority, the regions and communities. The agreement signed on 8 March 1994 reiterates the point that only one minister may hold the Belgian seat and is authorised to commit the State by his or her vote.[3] As for Belgium's representation, the agreement distinguishes between four categories of Councils:

- Councils concerning exclusively federal competencies (general affairs, economy and finance, justice, telecommunications, consumers, development, civil defence and fishery) in which Belgium is led by the federal authority.
- Councils concerning chiefly federal competencies (agriculture, internal market, public health, energy, environment, transportation and social affairs) in which Belgium is represented by the federal authority in the presence of an assessor representing the constituent units.
- Councils concerning chiefly regional or community competencies (industry and research) in which Belgium is represented by one of the constituent units, helped by a federal assessor.
- Councils concerning exclusively regional or community competencies (culture, education, tourism, youth, housing and land planning) in which Belgium is represented by one of the constituent units.

The 'assessor-minister' assists the minister representing Belgium. When matters deliberated in the Council of Ministers do not correspond exactly to the attribution of competencies in the Belgian system, the 'sitting-minister' representing the predominantly competent collectivity will be assisted by a minister from one of the other collectivities which shares this competence in an ancillary fashion. With regard to their representation, Belgian regions and communities have organised a half-yearly rotation system for the assessor or sitting-ministers entitled to act on behalf of Belgium. An annex to the agreement details a rotation system for informal Councils as well. This process of co-ordination prior to meetings of the Council of Ministers allows for the establishment of instructions from which the Belgian representative cannot depart except if the evolution of the discussion in the Council demands adaptation. If this is the case then decisions have to be taken urgently without consultation and with the representative defending the general interest. As far as implementation is concerned, the transposition of directives in Regional and Community fields – within the terms of Belgian law – depends solely on the communities or regions themselves. The federal authority is not able to force the latter to fulfil their European obligations. However, at an international level, the Belgian state could be held liable, as in the case of environmental protection, a field in which regions often fail to act or are late or negligent.

Under Article 169 of the constitution, the federal authority can take the place of the region or community which has not fulfilled an 'international or supranational obligation', provided that beforehand the state has been 'sentenced by an international or supranational court for not fulfilling' this obligation. The state then has the power to implement 'the enacting terms of the decision' of the court but the effect of such measures ends as soon as the community or region concerned has complied with the enacting terms of the judgement.

Parliamentary participation

The parliamentary assemblies, in particular the Federal Parliament and to a lesser extent the regional and community councils, have striven to increase their control over European integration. For example, since April 1985, within the Chamber of Representatives, there has been an Advisory Committee on European Issues. In March 1990 the Senate also set up such a committee. The two bodies have worked together in the form of the Federal Advisory Committee on European Issues. This is composed of ten deputies, ten senators and ten Belgian members of the EP. The main tasks of this committee are to inform the Parliament on Community affairs and to control the government's action at the European level as regards preparation and implementation of Community law. The committee produces reports and recommendations.

Some federated Councils have set up similar committees but their members do not often meet and therefore they play only a minimal role in parliamentary scrutiny and in the transposition of directives. Nevertheless these initiatives accurately reflect the reactions of most national parliaments in the face of what is called the "European democratic deficit". However, they have had only a limited influence on the Belgian administration. Legal provisions have been adopted since the last Belgian Constitutional reform in 1993, the year in which the Maastricht Treaty entered into force. Article 168, §6 of the constitution states that 'The Chambers shall be informed of any revisions to the treaties instituting the European Communities, or to the treaties and acts amending or supplementing them, as of the moment that the negotiations concerned are opened. They shall be fully aware of the draft treaty before its signature.' Article 16(2), of the Special Act on Institutional Reforms gives the regional and community councils the same prerogative. Regular meetings on the IGCs have been held in practice in the federal parliament, mainly with the Minister for Foreign Affairs. This practice, however, is not frequent in the Regional and Community Councils, where European affairs are not high on the agenda. For secondary law, the Special Act on Institutional Reforms also includes a section dealing with the 'Information of the Chambers and the Councils on the proposals for acts with a normative character of the Commission of the European Communities'. Article 92 provides that: 'as soon as they are sent to the Council of the European Communities, the proposals for regulations or directives and, if necessary, other acts with a normative character of the Commission of the European Communities are communicated to the federal legislative chambers and to the regional or community councils, depending on the subject matter.'

Attempts to exercise some control over these proposals have been very sporadic in the councils but there is actually a procedure in the federal parliament. Indeed the Federal Advisory Committee on European Issues regularly receives a list of the European Commission's proposals.

Each political group chooses one proposal that should be dealt with as a priority. The subject has to refer to a federal competence and to be relevant for the Committee. After the redaction of a technical sheet on each selected proposal, the Committee has different possibilities related to the relevance of the matter: the procedure can be brought to an end or a report on the subject can be elaborated by collecting information and organising hearings – this can lead to a resolution by the Advisory Committee. Another possibility is that a permanent committee of the Chamber or of the Senate would want to study the matter, which hardly ever takes place because this kind of committee is usually overloaded. In any case the technical sheets collected in a parliamentary document are a source of information for all the deputies who can use them for classical scrutiny.

Any deputy indeed can formulate (written or) oral questions in the commissions or in the plenary session on European matters. Although only the Chamber of Representatives has the political control (the Senate no longer has this), such questions rarely endanger the government's position. The latter informs and listens to the parliament and takes good note of comments made but is not compelled to take account of them in forming a negotiating stance. The efforts of deputies to exert control during the early stages of decision-making result from a realisation that such deputies have lost any control over the implementation of EU law. The latter is usually carried out through governmental orders and legal acts which leave very little room for important changes. Only a few matters such as the right to vote at municipal elections are subjected to important debates that cause some difficulties to the government. But again, the precise terms of the directive in question have to be respected.[4]

Participation of other actors

As regions and communities are direct institutional actors involved in European policy through co-operation, co-ordination and representation, they have been included in the general organisational set-up. With regard to political parties, there is an evolution towards a reduced consensus on European affairs (see the Introduction). Governments are coalitional and one could argue that tensions arise more as a result of conflicts of interest between portfolios than between political tendencies. For instance, within the framework of Agenda 2000, differences have arisen between the Social-Christian Prime Minister – who favours maintaining the EU budget at 1.27 per cent of EU GNP), the Socialist Minister for Foreign Affairs – who supports CAP reforms – and the Social-Christian Minister for Agriculture – who, by contrast, wishes to defend the agricultural sector. Turning to the role of lobbyists, who relay public opinion and interests, one could make the distinction between socio-economic interests – such as workers and employers, agricultural organisations, services and professional groups and political–cultural interests – such as human rights, ecology and consumers' rights. The level of lobbying for these particular interests depends on the resources that lobbyists have available at the European level, and on the potential benefits that such lobbying can bring.

National survey data show that interest groups' communications networks are limited.[5] Such organisations mainly look for contacts with actors that have only a limited influence on the European decision-making process such as the EP, the media, national political parties and federal or regional deputies. Even then, contacts are not that frequent (although a comparative study would be useful). On the contrary, actors such as the European Commission, the Permanent Representation or the Ministry for Foreign Affairs, are neglected. The media, however, can be a good means of pressurising or 'waking-up' the government. However, socio-economic groups with a direct European interest seem to find their way more easily to the Commission and many such organisations are members of interest groups that act at the European level. This is an advantage when interests coincide, but this is not always the case.

The majority of these organisations are in favour of an increase in the EU's competencies. Practical reasons such as efficiency explain this attitude. However, this is not the case with the CAP, where many interest groups see the amount of money spent on this particular interest as exaggerated. By contrast, EMU is accepted, particularly among socio-economic interests who recognise its economic advantages. While social policy is seen as a necessary complement to EMU (except among employers and business interests) this is viewed as a defence reflex to preserve social benefits rather than in terms of a European ideal of solidarity. EMU and social policy are in that respect two major topics among the Belgian population. This is not to say that there is a major social mobilisation in Belgium around the Union. Indeed the debates on the Amsterdam Treaty, for instance, might be seen as particularly shallow.

The control of EC law: the Belgian legal order and the supremacy of EC law

The milestone decision of the Belgian Cour de Cassation on this point is that taken in the case of *Le Ski* on 27 May 1971. In this case, the Cour de Cassation gave up the former adage of 'Lex posterior derogat legi priori' in favour of the Supremacy of EC law over Belgian legal acts. The reasoning of the Cour was the following:

> In the event of a conflict between a norm of domestic law and a norm of international law which produces direct effects in the domestic legal system, the rule established by a treaty shall prevail. The Primacy of the treaty results from the very nature of international law. The reason is that the treaties which have created Community law have instituted a new legal system in whose favour the member-states have restricted the exercise of their sovereign powers in the areas determined by those treaties.[6]

Thus, by recognising the ceding of sovereignty, the Cour de Cassation proclaimed a fortiori the supremacy of both the primary EC treaties and secondary EC legislation. The terms of the judgement are obviously borrowed from the leading ECJ case of *Costa* v. *ENEL* (1964), except in the reference to the limitation of the exercise of sovereign powers, where *Costa* v. *ENEL* invoked a definitive limitation of sovereign rights. But the Cour de Cassation did not address the question of whether EC law should prevail over Belgian Constitutional provisions. As regards the Conseil d'Etat, whose role is to assess the constitutionality of administrative acts, in the *Orfinger*[7] case it clearly held that the supremacy of EC law was based on Article 34 of the Constitution and implied that provisions of the European treaties should prevail over Belgian constitutional law. This statement is rather unsatisfactory, for the simple reason that Article 34 of the Constitution can be modified under certain procedures to the extent that the supremacy of EC law can be challenged in the future.

Concerning the Cour d'Arbitrage, whose role is to monitor the constitutionality of legislative acts, it has up to now argued that the Constitution should prevail over conventional provisions of international law. But the current case law concerns only classical international treaties, and not those which deal with a supranational structure such as the European Community. In a report (10–13 May 1993), the Cour d'Arbitrage addressed the question of conflict between Belgian constitutional provisions and Community law, and held that this problem could not be solved without referring to Article 25 of the Constitution (new Article 34) which provides that the exercise of the powers of national institutions can be delegated by a treaty to institutions bound by public international law. This assertion opens the door to the possible recognition by the Cour d'Arbitrage of the supremacy of EC law over the Belgian Constitution.

The Belgian legal order: direct applicability and direct effect

In its report on Belgium, Hervé Bribosia made a very good summary:

> The point of view of the Belgian legal order is in accordance with that of the EC: national courts admit the supreme jurisdiction of the ECJ – by virtue of Article 177 – to rule on the direct effect of EC law in the domestic legal order ... The decision of the Conseil d'Etat in the case of *Corveleyn* in 1968 deserves to be mentioned as it precedes by a few years the ECJ's decision in the *Van Duyn Case* (1974) asserting the principle of the direct applicability of directives ... Indeed, the Conseil d'Etat annulled a ministerial order of deportation that violated the 1964 directive, which, at the time, had not been transposed ... Since then, the Belgian courts have with a few exceptions, supported the direct application of directives, at least in their vertical dimension, in accordance with the ECJ's decision in *Marshall.*[8]

Appeals to the ECJ

There is one pending case based on Article 227(ex Article 170) ECT that should be judged in 1999; there are no cases under Article 232(ex Article 175) ECT but, since 1993, ninety-nine cases have been introduced or are pending before the ECJ under Article 234(ex Article 177) ECT. Article 227(ex Article 170) is very rarely used by the Member States for political reasons, which is understandable; they prefer to call upon the Commission to pursue a Member State for non-compliance with community obligations under Article 226(ex Article 169) ECT. In spite of this, Belgium introduced an Article 227(ex Article 170) ECT action before the ECJ against Spain concerning the importation of Rioja wine. The facts of this case can be summarised as follows: Belgian importers would like to import Rioja in bulk. But a Spanish decree, in order to guarantee the appellation of origin, obliges bottling within the region concerned, and thus forbids the importation of Rioja in bulk. Moreover, importers have contested this legislation on the grounds that it infringes the principle of the free movement of goods. The ECJ has already decided in favour of *Delhaize* in a former case under Article 234(ex Article 177) ECT but, in practice, the Spanish authorities have not back-pedalled. It is now up to the ECJ to confirm its interpretation of Community law, despite the fact that Spain, with the clemency of the Austrian presidency, has attempted to bypass the ECJ by trying to convince the Council of Ministers to adopt a resolution stating that the production of wine must include bottling within the region of production. As regards Article 234(ex Article 177) ECT, the ninety-nine cases that are or have been brought before the ECJ since 1993, can be classified as in Table 3.1.

Table 3.1 Cases that are being or have been brought before the ECJ, 1993–98

Area (in alphabetical order)	*No.*	*Area (ordered by importance)*	*No.*
Agriculture	5	Social welfare	22
Brussels convention	1	Free movement of goods	14
Competition law	4	Fiscal affairs	9
Consumers	1	Supremacy of EC law	1
Co-operation agreement	1	Freedom of establishment	8
Environment	2	Free movement of workers	7
Fiscal affairs	9	Free movement of services	6
Free movement of goods	14	Agriculture	5
Free movement of persons	1	Sex discrimination	5
Free movement of services	6	Competition law	4
Free movement of workers	7	Social policy	4
Freedom of establishment	8	Environment	2
Free trade agreements	1	Intellectual property	2
Intellectual property	2	Transport	2
Protocol on privilege and immunity	1	Brussels convention	1
Public health	1	Consumers	1
Sex discrimination	5	Co-operation agreement	1
Social welfare	22	Free movement of persons	1
Social policy	4	Free trade agreements	1
State aid	1	Protocol on privilege and immunity	1
Supremacy of EC law	1	Public health	1
Transport	2	State aid	1

It is interesting to note that the more sensitive areas are mainly social policy, fiscal affairs and working environment issues (which involve mutual recognition of professional qualifications, degrees and working conditions). The importance of social policy is not a coincidence. It highlights the social consequences of economic globalisation with its plethora of mergers, restructuring and 'delocalisation' of undertakings. In *Office National de l'Emploi* v. *Heidemarie Naruschawicus*,[9] for instance, the ECJ was questioned on the interpretation of Article 3 of Directive 77/187 regarding the maintenance of workers' rights following the transfer of undertakings.[10] In this case, the ECJ held that the rights of workers deriving from their contractual relationships were transferred to the transferee. Both the globalisation of the international economy and the requirements of the Euro have led the Member States to attempt to cut down their social expenditure one way or another, and in the meantime to increase their incomes in order to ensure a balanced budget. This attitude is illustrated in many cases dealing with pensions (twelve cases), indemnities for disability (six cases), doles (three cases). Those cases often take the shape of a conflict of law applicable to the facts at stake or a conflict of interpretation of a regulation or directive. The importance of fiscal affairs is mainly owing to the directives on VAT harmonisation; the problems raised often refer to the interpretation of a specific provision that has an important implication for the undertakings concerned. Because of the importance of the economic consequences for these actors, it is not surprising that they have a very good knowledge of Community law themselves or, through their advisers, of well-known law firms specialising in these matters. With regard to the working environment, a distinction has to be drawn between the problems linked to freedom of establishment and free movement of services and those linked to the free movement of workers. The former problems can be divided into two categories: first, those concerning the mutual recognition of qualifications and conditions of access to professions – affecting doctors, veterennaries, architects, lorry drivers – and secondly, those relating to the legal standing of migrant workers.

With regard to the latter problems (those concerning the free movement of workers), particular importance must be attached to the '*Bosman Case*' in which it was confirmed that EC law in general and the free movement of workers in particular, applies even to sporting activities and should prevail over sporting regulations whenever those regulations are contrary to EC law. But, once again, there were important financial interests at stake which justified Mr Bosman's determination to continue his legal struggle to the end, and his decision to employ the services of legal experts. Otherwise, it is often surprising to see how few Belgian citizens and even lawyers, are aware of EC law: although citizens have heard about EC law, it remains the domain of specialists and a legal 'elite'.

Conclusions: the Europeanisation of a small declining federal state

Given its political landscape, Belgium is well trained in the process of compromise. Belgium often plays a conciliatory role between the divergent, even antagonistic, positions of Member States. Being a small country, however, Belgium rarely takes the initiative for new Community rules. Rather, it tends to follow others and for much of the time considers the Commission as an ally. However Belgium holds some winning cards such as the stability of its prime ministerial office, its ministers who know their dossiers and their European partners very well, the presence of some strong personalities and the alliance with other small countries, in particular the Benelux nations. One could argue that Benelux co-operation was not at its best during the last round of the Amsterdam negotiations. However, it did not prevent the prime minister from blocking institutional reforms because of his dissatisfaction with regard to the extension of majority voting.

As a federal state with important competencies devolved to its constituent units, Belgium has created elaborate procedures to achieve a delicate balance between the existence of federated authorities and the need to preserve its unity as a single Member State within the Union. The main aspect of achieving this balance is the co-ordination and the co-operation between the federal authorities, the regions and the communities. They participate in the elaboration of Community policies thanks to co-ordination within Belgian's political and administrative system and representation at the European level, not only in the consultative CoR but especially in the Council of Ministers. This is owing to the fact that the last constitutional reforms in Belgium favoured greater visibility of the regions and the communities at the international and European level. By 'visibility' we mean presence and competencies. This respect for the federated entities' autonomy causes some problems of efficiency but growing claims for autonomy have been satisfied.

This political reality sometimes preoccupies the other Members States that recognise one single political entity: the Kingdom of Belgium. When signing the Amsterdam Treaty on 2 October 1997, Belgium had to reassure its partners by stating that it was in all cases the Kingdom as such which was bound in respect of its entire territory by the Treaty and would bear full liability for compliance with the obligations entered into the Treaty. A temporary substitution procedure is a partial solution to allow the state to implement Community law when regions or communities are delaying this process.

Belgium's credibility as a pro-European is also harmed by its reputation of being tardy where implementation of Community law is concerned. Belgium has striven and is still trying to ameliorate the situation, but the results remain unsatisfactory. The comparatively poor position of Belgium can be explained to some extent by a number of factors: the federal system, the poor performance of some administrations owing to shortage of staff, lack of pressure and motivation, the strict separation between officials in charge of preparing Community law and those responsible for its implementation, the absence of a European culture among many officials and the obligatory consultation of many specialised consultative councils.

The levels of 'Europeanisation' within the Belgian administration

The first difficulty in determining the degree of 'Europeanisation' is the danger of generalisation. One could indeed identify at least two types of officials: full-time officials working on European matters and part-time officials. Diplomats and officials from the Permanent Representation are an elite that have fully integrated themselves into European policy-making. (Delegates from communities and regions are still in a learning process.) At the other extreme, there are national officials that are very occasionally in touch with European matters – when, for instance, transposing a directive without having had anything to do with the negotiation process. Personal factors and the frequency of European matters dealt with by officials influences the degree of European culture. In the negotiation process, the presence of a member of the Permanent Representation or a national official in working parties is due to practical necessity, depending in particular on the technicality of the matter. Audio-visual issues, for instance, are so technical that national experts dominate the relevant working party.

Apart from this distinction, three factors particular to Belgium could be identified in determining the degree of 'Europeanisation' – that is the closeness of the Belgian administration to European institutions and culture: geographical proximity, ideology and Belgian federalisation. The proximity of Belgian and European institutions facilitates the involvement of national officials in the European policy-cycle. The Belgian Permanent Representation has thus a comparatively smaller staff than other Permanent Representations but there are proportionally more Belgian officials. Proximity also means that such officials keep in close contact with their ministries.

The ideological factor influences matters in two ways. Survey data show that the full-time Belgian Euro-officials are considered to be the most supranationalist.[11] This explains not only their constructive behaviour and their willingness to reach agreement at the European level, but also their confidence in the European Commission. This confidence leads Belgian officials to have less involvement in the Commission's networks, in contrast to their British counterparts. In addition, as a small state, Belgium cannot afford to have officials in every body but does not prevent them from maintaining specific contacts.

Belgian federalisation also plays an ambivalent role. It has meant that some national officials have become community or regional ones but also that many new officials have been employed. As a whole, it has led to more people being involved in European matters who want to assert their authority. Sometimes, for example, one can see within the Permanent Representation an objective alliance between community and regional officials aiming to assert themselves ahead of experienced federal officials. Federalisation also means that new political entities are keen to preserve the autonomy they have recently acquired. Officials can thus be unwilling to play the European game. With regard to the Amsterdam Treaty, for instance, Flanders was absolutely against majority voting on cultural matters and the French-speaking Community succeeded in having a protocol inserted on the financing of public broadcasting.

Federalisation has also brought with it new officials who are inexperienced in European affairs and structures. The learning process is sometimes difficult and can cause reticence. The lack of staff is also an important obstacle. The German-speaking Community in particular does not yet have any delegate at the Permanent Representation and never attends COREPER meetings. The Brussels-Capital administration does not yet have any official specifically in charge of European affairs, rather each official attempts to deal with the European aspects of her/his own competencies, but this is rarely a matter of priority.

Beyond the 'Europeanisation' of the administration, it is also significant to underline the extent to which European and Belgian policies increasingly interact. From 1992 to 1996, when the budget deficit had finally fallen to reach the target of 3 per cent of GDP, compliance with Maastricht's economic convergence criteria was the dominant determinant of government policy (since 1992) led by Prime Minister Dehaene. Another more recent illustration of this ever closer interaction has been provided by the linkage between the Belgian plan for employment prepared in early 1998 according to the guidelines of the special employment summit of November 1997 held in Luxembourg and the interprofessional agreement of November 1998. By incorporating employers and trade unions in the drafting of the Belgian document delivered in April for presentation in the Cardiff European Council (June 1998), the government has helped bring about a new social dialogue between these two groups. This opened the way to the November 1998 interprofessional agreement for 1999–2000 and created a new impetus for professional training, flexibility and the reduction of labour costs – linked to the creation of jobs. According to Dehaene, no interprofessional agreement in Belgium would have been possible without the European framework and process.[12]

Another example of the influence of European affairs in domestic politics is the acceptance of the Amsterdam Treaty by the Brussels COCOM gathering together the two linguistic wings of the Brussels regional assembly. A majority in each linguistic group is required on cultural issues. The Brussels Regional Executive, supported by a large majority of the 65 French-speaking representatives, was lacking one vote in the Flemish group. However, two representatives of the opposition Flemish Liberal Party chose to side with the executive, thereby ensuring that support for the Amsterdam Treaty was forthcoming from both linguistic groups.

While the 'Europeanisation' of politics and policies is increasing, a final question may be raised concerning the parallels between Belgian federalism and European federalisation. Such parallels have recurrently been drawn by the Belgian authorities, namely by Kings Baudouin and Albert II.[13]

While this 'official' approach might be seen as an attempt to legitimise the Belgian federal experiment as part of the broader European experience, one may also suggest that the two processes are actually moving in opposite directions, the first representing a case of 'centrifugal' federalism while the second illustrates a 'centripetal' or associative federalism.

Notes

1 See Déclaration de politique générale du Premier ministre à l'ouverture de l'année parlementaire 1998–99, 13 October 1998.
2 See Parliamentarian document of Vlaams Parlement, stuk 226 (1995–96) – No. 6, p. 45.
3 See *Moniteur belge*, 17 November 1994.
4 Article 19 (ex Article 8 b) of the Maastricht Treaty creating the right for European citizens to vote and to be elected at local elections provoked strong reactions among Flemish political parties, which feared that the voting of the European citizens would reinforce the French parties in Brussels and its neighbourhood.
5 See Les groupes intermédiaires belges et la politique européenne. Survey carried out the Belgian Ministry for Foreign Affairs with the universities UIA, KU Leuven and with the collaboration of UCL and ULB, 1998.
6 Cass., 27 May 1971, Pas., 1971, I, 886.
7 See Conseil d'Etat (6ème chambre), 5 November 1996, J.T., 1997, 254.
8 See Anne-Marie Slaughter, Alec Stone Sweet and Joseph H.H. Weiler, *The European and National Courts. Doctrine and Jurisprudence* (Oxford: Hart Publishing, 1998), p. 10.
9 ECJ, 14 November 1996, Case C-305/94, ECR, I-5927.
10 There are four other similar cases that have been introduced, before the ECJ.
11 See Guido Dierickx, 'De Euro-Belgische ambtenaren. Een paradoxale prestatie', in: *Res Publica*, No. 2/1998, pp. 219–222.
12 See 'La Libre Belgique', 18 December 1998.
13 See Christian Franck and Claude Roosens, 'Le roi Baudouin et la politique', in: Christian Franck and Claude Roosens, *Le roi Baudouin, Une vie, une époque* (Bruxelles: Racine, 1998), Chapter VII, esp. pp. 147–151.

Select bibliography

The text (English translation) of the constitution of Belgium can be found at the University of Richmond's constitution finder at http://confinder.richmond.edu/. Further sources on government and parliament of Belgium can be found at Government http://belgium.fgov.be or at Parliament http://www.fed-parl.be.

de Wilde d'Estmael, Tanguy and Franck, Christian (1996) 'Belgium', in: Dietrich Rometsch and Wolfgang Wessels (eds), *The European Union and Member States, Towards Institutional Fusion?* (Manchester: Manchester University Press), pp. 37–60.

Dierickx, Guido (1998) 'De Euro-Belgische ambtenaren. En paradoxale prestatie', in: *Res Publica*, No. 2/1998, pp. 219–222.

Franck, Christian (1997) 'La Belgique', in: Rudolf Hrbek (ed.), *Die Reform der Europäischen Union, Positionen und Perspektiven anläßlich der Regierungskonferenz* (Baden-Baden: Nomos), pp. 37–50.

Franck, Christian (1998) 'La politique européenne de la Belgique. Les années 1970–1996: entre orthodoxie et pragmatisme', in: *Res Publica*, No. 2/1998, pp. 197–212.

Franck, Christian and Roosens, Claude (1998) 'Le roi Baudouin et la politique étrangère', in Christian Franck and Claude Roosens, *Le roi Baudouin, une vie, une époque (*Bruxelles: Racine).

Lejeune, Yves (1994) 'The Case of Belgium', in: Spyros A. Pappas (ed.), *National and Administrative Procedures for Preparation and Implementation of Community Decisions* (Maastricht: EIPA), pp. 59–110.

Lejeune, Yves and Vandevievere, Claire (1998) 'Administrative and Procedural Structures for the Implementation of Community Policies: The Case of Belgium', within the framework of the conference 'The Regional Impact of Community Policies', Mid Sweden University, 23–25 April.

Ministry for Foreign Affairs (1998) 'Les groupes intermédiaires belges et la politique européenne'. Survey carried out by the Universities UIA, KU Leuven and with the collaboration of UCL and ULB, 1998.

4 *Finn Laursen*

Denmark: in pursuit of influence and legitimacy

Introduction: a reluctant but serious player

Attitudes to European integration in Denmark are very complex. A majority of the Danish people support economic integration in Europe as long as it does not affect Danish autonomy too much. Denmark joined the EEC in 1973 after a referendum in October 1972 where 63.4 per cent of the Danish people supported membership. The SEA was ratified after 56.2 per cent of the Danish people supported it in a referendum on 27 February 1986. But the Maastricht Treaty was first voted down by a narrow majority of 50.7 per cent on 2 June 1992. By the time it was accepted in a second referendum on 18 May 1993 by 56.7 per cent of the electorate, Denmark had secured four exemptions or reservations at the Edinburgh summit in December 1992.[1] One of these dealt with EMU, where Denmark decided not to take part in the third phase.

The three other reservations dealt with citizenship of the Union, JHA co-operation and defence policy. Denmark would not join the Western European Union (WEU) and would take part only in intergovernmental JHA co-operation. The four areas were those where a deepening of integration was taking the process closer to the traditional symbols of the nation state: citizenship, money and defence. The hesitancy of the Danish public should be contrasted with an economic and political elite that is much more pro-integration. In 1972, 141 members of the Danish parliament voted in favour of membership, against 34 'no' votes. In 1992 and 1993 there were quite large majorities in the Parliament as well. The only exception from the rule was January 1986, when the opposition denied the Conservative-Liberal government a majority in favour of the SEA. However, after a referendum a substantial majority did vote for the Treaty. On 12 May 1992, the Folketing authorised ratification of the Maastricht Treaty with 130 votes in favour, with only 25 voting against (23 members were absent and a Faroese member abstained). This meant support from the Conservative-Liberal minority government at the time, as well as the leading opposition parties, the Social Democrats, the Social-Liberals, the Centre-Democrats and parts of the Christian People's Party. Only the right-wing Progress Party and the left-wing Socialist People's Party did not support the Treaty. Still, a small majority of the people rejected it on 2 June 1992.

After the four Edinburgh exemptions prior to the second referendum, 154 members voted for ratification of the Maastricht Treaty as supplemented by the reservations. The Treaty was now supported by the new government coalition of the Social Democrats, the Social-Liberals, the Centre-Democrats and the Christian People's Party as well as the Liberals and Conservatives, which had in the meantime moved into opposition. An important difference compared with 1992 was the support from the Socialist People's Party, which had been actively involved in finding the so-called 'national compromise', which became the basis for the Edinburgh exemptions (three MPs from the People's Socialists voted against the Treaty in 1993). The Progress Party remained opposed, but the total of 'no' votes was only sixteen (also including one Social-Liberal MP).

The shift in attitude of the Socialist People's Party in 1993 to the Maastricht Treaty had been a traumatic event for the Party. In the elections to the EP in June 1994, its percentage of votes fell to 8.6 from 9.1 per cent in 1989. The People's Movement against the Union claimed 10.3 per cent, and the slightly more pragmatic EU opponents in the new June Movement received 15.2 per cent of the votes, taking the total anti-EU vote to 25.5 per cent, up from the 18.9 percent the People's Movement got in 1989.[2] The Danish electorate had sent a signal to the politicians. At the elections to the Folketing in September 1994 a new radical left-wing party the Red–Green Alliance or the Unity List, entered the Parliament, creating extra pressure within the Socialist People's Party (Table 4.1).

The next election to the Folketing took place on 11 March 1998, just prior to the referendum on the Amsterdam Treaty. In the new Folketing, the following parties opposed the Amsterdam Treaty: the Socialist People's Party, the Danish People's Party, the Unity List (Red–Green Alliance) and the Progress Party. The Socialist People's Party, however, was split on the issue. The Danish People's Party was a splinter group from the Progress Party. The Amsterdam Treaty was accepted by 92 votes after the third reading in the Parliament (Social Democrats, Liberals, Conservatives, Centre-Democrats, Social-Liberals and Christian People's Party) against 22 votes (Socialist People's Party, Danish People's Party, the Unity List, the Progress Party and one Conservative MP, Frank Dahlgaard). Four members of the Socialist People's Party later indicated that they would have voted for the Treaty, had they been present.[3]

The referendum result on 28 May 1998 was a 'yes' vote of 55.1 per cent.[4] The hesitancy of the Danish public has in many ways made Denmark a 'minimalist' state regarding European integration. Danish EU

Table 4.1 Parliamentary representation of Danish parties and groups, 1998

Seats won in the election and % of total votes in Denmark	*Folketing election, 11 March 1998*		*EP election, 9 June 1994*		*Folketing election, 21 September 1994*	
	Seats	*% of vote*	*Seats*	*% of vote*	*Seats*	*% of vote*
Social Democrats	63	36.0	3	15.8	62	34.6
Liberal Party	42	24.0	4	19.0	42	23.3
Conservative Party	16	8.9	3	17.7	27	15.0
Socialist People's Party	13	7.5	1	8.6	13	7.3
Danish People's Party	13	7.4	NP		–	
Centre-Democrats	8	4.3	0	0.9	5	2.8
Social-Liberal Party	7	3.9	1	8.5	8	4.6
Red–Green Alliance	5	2.7	NP		6	3.1
Christian People's Party	4	2.5	0	1.1	0	1.9
Progress Party	4	2.4	0	2.9	11	6.4
June Movement	NP		2	15.2	NP	
People's Movement against the EC Union	NP		2	10.3	NP	
Greenland[a]	2				2	
Faroe Islands[a]	2				2	
Total number of seats	179		16		179	

Notes: NP: did not participate.
[a]Greenland and the Faroe Islands have home rule and are not members of the European Union.
Source: Ministry of Foreign Affairs, 'Political Parties in Denmark' www.um.dk/english/danmark/ om_danmark/partier/, and 'The Referendum in Denmark on 28 May 1998 on the Ratification of the Amsterdam Treaty' www.um.dk/english/udenrigspolitik/europa/vurderinguk/.

policy is domestically driven. Pro-integration parties fear retribution at the polls if they become too pro-European. Whereas Denmark's original reasons for joining the EEC were based on the interests of Danish agriculture and industry, there is now an increasing range of issues where Denmark actively seeks European solutions, for instance, the environment, consumer protection, social policy and employment. Since the beginning of 1993, Denmark has had Social Democratic-led governments which have actively sought to give the EU a more 'progressive' face in the hope of making the two-level game between the domestic constituents and the European partners easier. This has also included support for increased transparency in EU decision-making and support for subsidiarity – or 'nearness', as it is usually translated in Danish.

The basic attitudes of the established political parties have not changed fundamentally in recent years. The Liberal Party and the smaller Centre-Democrats remain the strongest pro-integration parties. The Social Democrats and Social-Liberals are in favour of integration, but have minority factions that are sceptical. These two parties remain committed to the four Edinburgh exemptions, for the moment at least, although leaders of both parties have recently mentioned the possibility of a referendum about the EMU reservation early in the twenty-first century. The integration of the Schengen acquis into the Union by the Amsterdam Treaty is also creating pressures on the JHA exemption, and the new British attitude to a common European defence policy has placed pressure on the Danish policy on European defence.

The Conservative Party is also pro-integration, but less so than the Liberal Party. It is the smaller parties on both the left and the right that have tried to exploit the public's scepticism by advocating anti-integration policies. These smaller parties have sometimes been very successful in setting the agenda of the Danish EU debate. As we have seen, Social Democratic-led governments since 1993 have tried to give the Union a more 'progressive' face. A good indication of this were the proposals made by Denmark during the 1996–97 IGC. There were seven listed, dealing with employment, environment, openness, consumer protection, fraud, subsidiarity and national parliaments.[5] After the negotiation finished in Amsterdam in June 1997, the Danish government went further by stressing the Danish recommendations in the Treaty and emphasising the Treaty's preparations for Eastern European enlargement. It was expected that this could help 'sell' the Treaty to the Danish public.

When the Folketing opened in October 1997, the prime minister said of the Maastricht referenda: 'We have learned, and we have listened. The Danes do not mind being a part of Europe. Europe may also be a part of Denmark, but only a part. For the government, therefore, it was decisive to reach a result in Amsterdam, where the Danish people can recognise the values that society in Denmark is built on. We succeeded, we succeeded.'[6] He went on to give three reasons why the Danes should vote 'yes' for the Treaty: the Amsterdam Treaty was the basis for widening the Union to include the Central and Eastern European Countries (CEECs), a precondition for a peaceful Europe; the Amsterdam Treaty was better than the Maastricht Treaty in respect to the Danish central values (mærkesager); and in terms of democracy, human rights, better co-operation regarding the environment and employment. The four Danish exemptions were intact and secure. He went on to explain that the Union was an association, but not an association where we should co-operate about everything: 'We should co-operate about the necessary.'[7]

The national policy-cycle: complexity at work

It is recognised that EU legislation increasingly penetrates Danish society. The government has responded with elaborate co-ordination mechanisms between the different ministries and agencies, as well as private interests affected by EU legislation and decisions. Further, the Parliament has tried to keep a relatively tight control of the EU policies of successive governments. Both the governmental/administrative and parliamentary mechanisms changed somewhat after Maastricht, partly in response to the request for more transparency and partly in response to the expanded agenda and increased majority voting in the Union. Yet the changes have not been major.

The general outline of the flow of EU decision-making in Denmark is given in Figure 4.1. Proposals from the Commission first go through thirty-one Special Committees with civil servants from the ministries affected by the proposal.[8] At this preparatory stage, interested organisations are usually heard; often they are directly represented on the Special Committees themselves.

The next stage is the high-level EC Committee of Heads of Department from the ministries most affected by EU matters. This Committee is chaired by the Head of Department from the 'Northern' division of the Ministry of Foreign Affairs. Many questions are usually settled before this stage, and if there are still problems they often have to be resolved at the political level. This happens through the government's own Foreign Policy Committee chaired by the Foreign Minister.

Since 1994, the Parliament has had a powerful committee role in dealing with EU matters, in the form of the European Affairs Committee (Europaudvalget). It comes at the end of the process, which is true in the sense that the government seeks a mandate just prior to the final negotiations in the Council. However, the European Affairs Committee is informed about new Commission proposals earlier, and earlier deliberations in the Committee or discussions in political circles can have affected the government's position by the time it seeks a mandate.

The role of government: towards prime ministerial government

It is difficult to separate the role of the government from the role of the administration. The stage at which the responsible minister gets involved varies from case to case. Formally the Danish position is established at cabinet level in the Foreign Policy Committee (Regeringens Udenrigspolitiske Udvalg), which normally meets on Thursdays. It consists of 12 ministers: the Foreign Minister (chairman), the Prime Minister, and the Ministers of Economy, Finance, Justice, Environment and Energy, Labour, Taxation, Transport, Health, Research, and Food, Agriculture and Fisheries. Other ministers can take part as required.[9] This

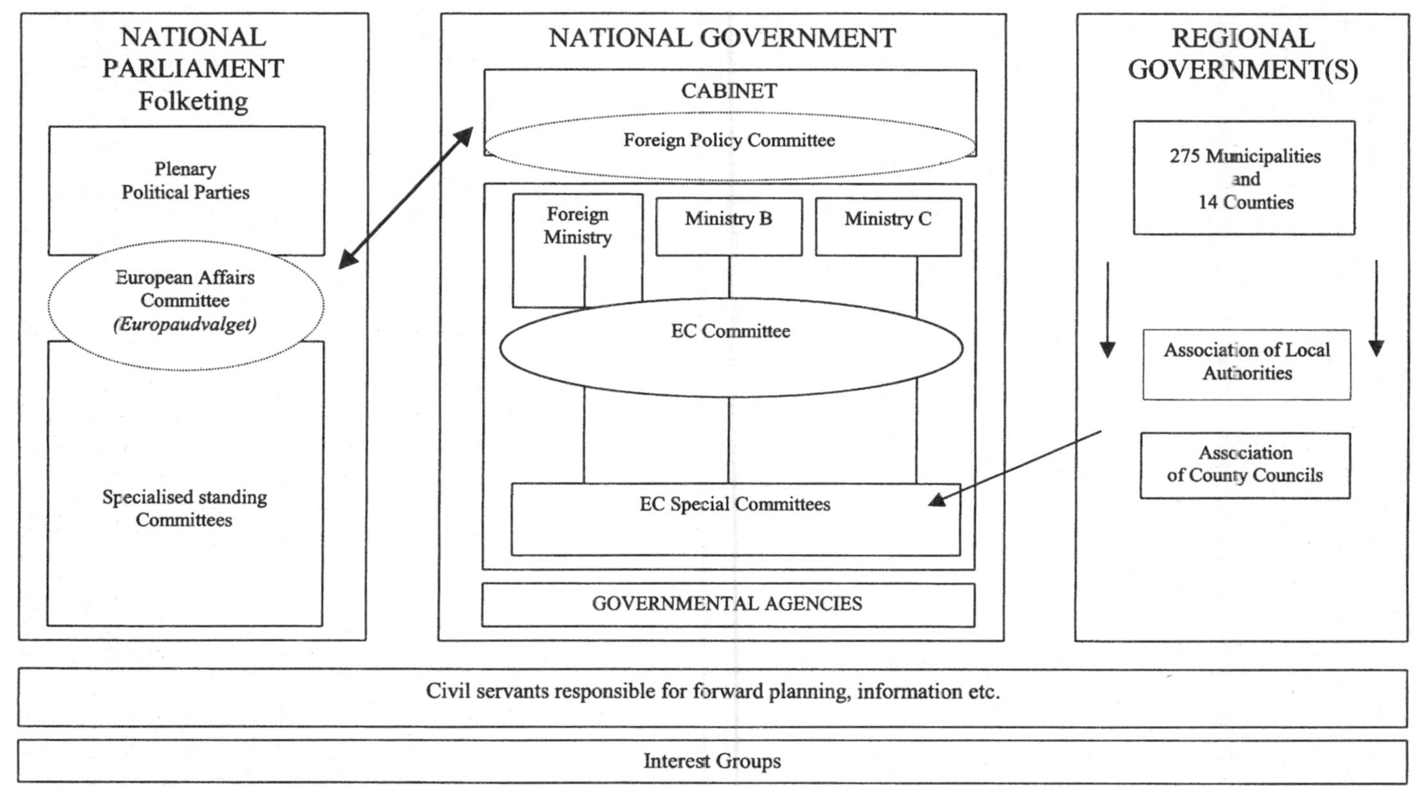

Figure 4.1 The national level of European decision-making – Denmark

committee was formed by merging the government's Common Market Committee and Foreign and Security Political Committee. It deals with the issues of all three pillars of the Union, dividing them into Part I (EC matters) and Part II (Common Foreign and Security Policy (CFSP) and JHA matters).[10] The group of ministers taking part is smaller for Part II than Part I matters: the Foreign Minister (chairman), Prime Minister and Ministers of Economy, Environment and Energy, Development Aid, Interior, Health and Defence. The Minister of Justice takes part in deliberations concerning JHA.

The positions established by the government's Foreign Policy Committee are presented to the Folketing's European Affairs Committee on the Friday the week before the Council meets to discuss the issue in question. If accepted by the European Affairs Committee, the position will constitute the negotiation mandate for the government in the Council of Ministers.

Part II issues related to CFSP also go to the Parliament's Foreign Affairs Committee, and issues related to JHA co-operation go to the Legal Affairs Committee. At the administrative level these issues are co-ordinated through the Foreign and Security Political Committee of officials (Udenrigs- og sikkerhedspolitiske embedsmandsudvalg), not the EC Committee which deals only with pillar one issues. Thus, there are no Special Committees dealing with second and third pillar issues as such. The government emphasises that this is intergovernmental co-operation. For these issues of 'high politics', decision-making is more centralised. The Minister of Defence also participates in Part II co-ordination.

The Government's Foreign Policy Committee mainly concentrates on three types of case. The first concerns concrete cases of great political importance for Denmark, including specific Danish initiatives. Second, it discusses cases for the next Council meeting in Brussels. Discussion is usually limited to cases of a more principled nature or cases where the EC Committee did not reach an agreed position. Finally, bigger issues or cross-cutting topics form part of the Foreign Policy Committee's role. The aim of the discussion can be to formulate either a general Danish attitude or general political guidelines.[11] Generally, change at the level of central government can be detected in the increased role of the prime minister. This is due to a number of factors, such as increased summitry in the Union, and the Prime Minister's wish to control matters that are politically sensitive and can affect the survival of the government. However, the Foreign Ministry remains the most important co-ordinating body.

In the case of the Amsterdam Treaty negotiations a special mechanism was established. All interested ministries were represented in the 'EC Committee in special session' (EF-udvalget i særlig samling) at the level of head of office (kontorchef) and chaired by the Head of the Northern division in the Ministry of Foreign Affairs. Above this was the Summit

Committee (Topmødeudvalget) in which all interested ministries were represented by the Head of Department (departementschef). The interesting thing was that this committee was chaired by the Head of Department from the Prime Minister's Office, which meant a somewhat weakened position for the Ministry of Foreign Affairs. About half the ministers took part in the government's own Summit Committee (Regeringens topmødeudvalg).[12] All in all this meant a broader involvement compared with the 1991 IGC. The purpose was to capture as many of the domestic implications as possible and avoid the problems of Maastricht Treaty ratification. Prime Minister Poul Nyrup Rasmussen's personal interest might also help explain the greater involvement by the Prime Minister and his Office.[13]

The government's interest in this is clear. It wants to control the politically sensitive aspects of the decision-making process. Since even technical details, such as which food additives are allowed or prohibited, can become political issues, getting input from experts and affected interests is important. The administrative system of co-ordination, which will be described in greater detail later, has been set up to include these relevant inputs. At the same time, the system is fairly centralised through the Foreign Ministry to ensure that Denmark gets as much influence in Brussels as possible. So there are both consensus and efficiency considerations behind the organisational set-up.

The role of parliament: towards transparency

Since the very beginning of Danish membership of the EC in 1973 the Folketing has exercised more control over European policy than any other national parliament in the EC/EU.[14] A Market Relations Committee (markedsudvalg) was established in 1972. From the spring of 1973 a system developed which in reality included the issuing of binding mandates to ministers negotiating within the Council of Ministers. The original name of the committee corresponded to the original concept of integration in Denmark. Integration was seen as a relatively limited economic matter. As mentioned earlier, in 1994 the committee changed its name to the European Affairs Committee (Europaudvalget) which, especially after the entry into force of the Maastricht Treaty, seems more appropriate. After the entry into force of the Maastricht Treaty the government has continued to seek a mandate for important matters falling under the EU's first pillar. For CFSP matters the government informs the European Affairs Committee, but the Parliament's Foreign Affairs Committee is also told about these matters. Similarly, JHA matters are dealt with both by the European Affairs Committee and the Legal Affairs Committee of the Parliament. Whenever a mandate for negotiation is needed, however, it has to be given by the European Affairs Committee.[15]

The European Affairs Committee has extensive access to EC documents. Documents that touch on the security of other Member States can be read in the office of the Chairman of the Committee. For this reason members have to accept an obligation of secrecy. The government has the obligation to keep members informed about current proposals for EC legislation; the Committee can request a written orientation from the government about the negotiation situation related to any issue and it can request a meeting with the competent minister at any time.[16] The European Affairs Committee has seventeen members chosen proportionally among the parties represented in the Folketing. Politically the Committee thus mirrors the Chamber. The Committee normally meets on Fridays; ministers will appear before the Committee and present their proposals verbally. 'If there is no majority against the mandate, the Government negotiates on this basis.'[17] Since 1973 the practice has developed that the chairperson counts the votes of the parties represented by the members of the European Affairs Committee. It takes 90 votes or more against to refuse a mandate for negotiation – i.e. more than half of the 179 members of the Folketing.

Usually between two and four ministers attend a meeting, each going through 10–20 points, including proposals on the agenda of the Council meetings in Brussels for the following week. Ministers are accompanied by civil servants. The Prime Minister's Office and the Foreign Ministry have civil servants permanently present.[18] Apart from presenting the negotiation positions the government also informs the European Affairs Committee about proposals under consideration. It is usually only during the last part of the legislative process in the Union that the government presents a negotiation position. By starting the discussion earlier in the European Affairs Committee the government can try to be sure that it knows the feelings and attitudes of the parliamentarians. By the time a negotiation position is put forward it is accepted in more than 90 per cent of the cases, more so under majority governments than minority governments.[19]

However, as outlined in an information brochure produced by the Secretariat of the European Affairs Committee, 'it does not happen infrequently that the Government changes its original mandate for negotiation during the talks with the Committee – or at least adapts it to meet the points of view which are likely to attract a majority in the Committee'.[20] The same text goes on to say that 'the Danish civil servants who take part in the negotiations at an early stage – often before the Commission submits its proposal – take into consideration the fact that the Government shall at a given hour have the result approved by the political forum constituted by the European Affairs Committee'.[21] In other words, anticipated reactions are important in the policy-making process. Civil servants have developed a keen feeling for the interests of their political superiors.

It should be mentioned that the European Affairs Committee receives deputations, as do other standing committees of the Folketing. This gives interest organisations an additional point of access to the policy-making system. The 'no' vote in the Danish referendum on the Maastricht Treaty in June 1992 led to a discussion about transparency in the Union. This discussion also affected the Danish system to some extent. In March 1993 it was decided to have a press briefing after each meeting of the Committee. At this briefing the Chairman of the Committee informs the press about the cases where the government has had its negotiation position accepted, and normally also gives the main lines of that position. Information is also given about the cases where there is a majority against the government position. The briefing also includes information about the position taken by the political parties whose representatives can participate in the press meeting and explain their positions. In cases where there is a decision about secrecy the Chairman will simply state that the government has received a negotiation mandate but that it is confidential until a final decision has been made. When a final decision is made, the stances adopted by the different parties to the negotiation mandate are made public.[22]

Meetings of the European Affairs Committee until 1999 took place behind closed doors. Shorthand minutes have been taken since 1984, but they go only to the Chairman and one representative of each party represented. The lack of openness of the meetings of the Europe Committee has been regularly criticised, especially by the Socialist People's Party. Another type of criticism has come from the other side of the political spectrum, with the Progress Party saying that the Committee is the only parliamentary control on hundreds of changes in Danish law, which cannot even be changed later by the Folketing.

The Danish system has not answered the question whether EU policy is foreign or domestic policy. A particular issue that rises from this tension is the question of which role the specialised standing committees (fagudvalg) of the Folketing should play. These committees will usually have more technical expertise that the more 'generalist' European Affairs Committee. A first response to this problem was sharing of information. A practice was started whereby the agenda of the European Affairs Committee was sent to the chairpersons on the other standing committees. In the case of the Environment and Regional Planning Committee a practice of systematically asking for an opinion on proposals for environmental legislation developed in the 1980s during the years of a 'green' majority of Social Democrats, Social Liberals and People's Socialists under the Conservative-Liberal government of Poul Schlüter.[23]

In March 1993 it was also decided to draw in these specialised committees to a greater extent.[24] A report from the European Affairs Committee of 20 May 1994 continued this trend and sought further association of specialised committees in the process of considering EU legislative matters.[25] A system of parallel information was put in place for new Commission proposals affecting the level of protection in Denmark in the areas of health, environment, labour market and consumer policy. According to the 1994 arrangement, elementary notes were sent concurrently to the European Affairs Committee and to one or several relevant specialised committees as soon as possible after the Commission had put forward a new proposal. Similarly information from the Foreign Ministry later in the process, including the topical notes usually sent at least a week before the meeting of the European Affairs Committee prior to the deciding Council meeting, would be forwarded to relevant specialised committees.

This system was evaluated two years later and some further changes were introduced by a report from the European Affairs Committee of 27 September 1996.[26] The 1996 arrangement decided between the government and the European Affairs Committee extended the parallel information system to all new proposals for directives. Basic notes (grundnotater) are prepared for all new directives as well as Green and White Papers. Basic notes should be ready at least ten weeks after the Commission proposal reaches the Council. A topical note (samlenotat) is still due a week before the meeting of the European Affairs Committee, giving the minister a mandate. Basic notes and topical notes are all factual. They do not reveal the government's stand, which is revealed only orally at the meeting giving the government a mandate.

The general public now has access to 95 per cent of the notes received by the European Affairs Committee. The European Affairs Committee also decided to introduce public hearings in 1996. Hearings and subsequent readings can be conducted in co-operation with the specialised committee in question.[27] Concerning implementation, the 1996 report mentioned the problem that most implementation in Denmark takes place through administrative decrees (bekendtgørelser), i.e. not legislation. This is possible because basic legislation empowers the government to do so. The European Affairs Committee has been kept informed about implementation through short notes. There was now also a need to send these notes to the specialised committees, and the government agreed to do this.

The main purpose of the 1996 reform thus was to get information as early as possible and get it to the specialised committees. It was not a radical reform. Indeed the report had minority views which indicated some problems that still exist. The Socialist People's Party suggested that all Commission proposals should immediately be dealt with by relevant specialised committees. The Unity List and the Danish People's Party went further and suggested that the Folketing should have a full public first reading of EU legislative acts in the Chamber. Specialised committees should be drawn in formally and the meetings of the European Affairs Committee should be open.

The Unity List also criticised the arrangement concerning implementation whereby the specialised committees are informed only after implementation has taken place. For directives where the government had required a negotiation mandate from the European Affairs Committee, it should be possible for a political party to demand that implementation be dealt with by Parliament. Of 127 directives during the period 1994–95, only twenty-seven resulted in laws adopted by the parliament. No less than 141 administrative acts were issued to implement these directives.

Two other changes have taken place more recently. One concerns World Trade Organisation (WTO) matters and other Schengen matters. According to a report of 14 March 1997, the government will provide the European Affairs Committee with half-yearly reports on developments inside the WTO, especially developments that affect the level of protection in Denmark on health, environment, labour market and consumer policy. The government will also provide continuous information about the WTO's work when important decisions of a political character are prepared. The European Affairs Committee will be informed if the Commission needs a negotiation mandate for WTO negotiations. The same procedures as for normal EU cases will be followed.[28] Denmark's decision to accede to the Schengen Convention was confirmed by the Folketing on 10 June 1997. On 27 November 1997 the Minister of Justice suggested a procedure for informing the European Affairs Committee and Legal Affairs Committee prior to meetings in the Schengen Executive Committee. The procedure agreed with the Parliament includes first of all a commitment to send a note concerning the points that are expected to be dealt with, as far as possible a week before the meeting of the European Affairs Committee which takes place the week before the meeting in the Schengen Executive Committee. At the meetings in the Legal Affairs Committee (usually Thursday) and European Affairs Committee (usually Friday) the Minister of Interior and/or Justice will make oral accounts of the essential cases according to the same procedures as for EU matters. After the meeting in the Executive Committee the government will send a written account of the meeting to the two committees.[29] This procedure for Schengen matters is comparable to the procedure already adopted for pillar three JHA co-operation after the entry into force of the Maastricht Treaty. Prior to Denmark's accession to Schengen being fully ratified by the other parties to the Convention, however, the government was not seeking a negotiation mandate, since Denmark was only an observer.

Before getting to the Parliament JHA cases have gone through the Preparatory Committee concerning Legal and Police Co-operation of civil servants (Forberedelsesudvalget vedr. Rets- og politisamarbejde), the Foreign and Security Committee of civil servants (Udenrigs- og

Sikkerhedpolitisk Udvalg) and the government's Foreign Policy Committee (II) (Udenrigspolitisk Udvalg). [30]

The role of the administration
Relevant ministries are represented in the Special Committees where most of the preparation of legislation takes place. The number of Special Committees has increased over time. It started with eighteen in 1972; by 1977 there were twenty-five and by 1982 twenty-seven,[31] and in 1994 there were thirty.[32] As mentioned earlier, there are currently thirty-one. Obviously this increasing number of Special Committees testifies to the increasing functional scope of European integration. This increase in scope has been part of the process since Denmark joined in 1973. New issues, such as environment, energy and research, gradually became part of the agenda, sometimes through the use of Article 235 of the Treaty of Rome. The SEA and the 1992 Internal Market programme boosted the process. This is particularly the case for the latter, with its vast legislative programme and 'the new method' of establishing European standards involving private standards organisations such as CEN, CENELEC and ETSI. This has affected the Danish system and led to an increased involvement of private interests. This has blurred the distinction between the state and society especially at the level of the Special Committees, where private organisations are heard or take part in meetings (Table 4.2).

Table 4.2 Ranking of Ministry involvement in Special Committees

Ministry	*No. of permanent memberships*	*Ministry*	*No. of permanent memberships*
Foreign Affairs	31	Labour	10
Finance	22	Research and Information Technology	9
Business and Industry	12	Health	8
Justice	17	Prime Minister Office	7
Economy	16	Housing and Urban Affairs	6
Food, Agriculture and Fisheries	16	Social Affairs	6
Taxation	13	Education	5
Transport	11	Culture	4
Environment and Energy	10	Interior	4

Source: Computed from 'Specialudvalg under EF-Udvalg (prior. 1 January 1999)', kindly provided by the Foreign Ministry.

The officials of the Special Committees also take part in Commission expert committees while Commission proposals are being prepared. Once the proposals arrive in the Specialised Committees they are usually already known and will be considered by partly the same officials. This has meant a blurring of the distinction between the Danish state and the EU system as such.

The Special Committees play a central role in establishing the Danish positions. Only when there is disagreement in a Special Committee will the higher-level EC EU Committee and the government's Foreign Policy Committee become actively involved.[33] The Special Committees have developed into real negotiating bodies where private and public interests are normatively merged.[34] For instance, the Danish Employer's Association (Dansk Arbejdsgiverforening) and the Danish Confederation of Trade Unions (Landsorganisationen i Danmark) are both currently represented, or at least normally invited to meetings of Special Committees dealing with Labour Market and Social Conditions, Establishment of Services, Transport Questions, Industry and Regional Political Co-operation, Education, Technical Trade Barriers for Industrial Goods and Information Technology and Telecommunication.[35]

The EC Committee, on the other hand, never became a very important committee. Real disagreements can be solved only at the government level. So the EC Committee has become a formal link that expedites cases and distributes information; over time, its influence has probably decreased. One suggestion is that the participants in the co-ordination system have developed a kind of 'EC culture' that includes a good sense of what can be achieved in Brussels.[36] The EC Committee never became the high-ranking committee that it was intended to be.[37]

Højbjerg and Marcher (1995) have suggested that the Danish co-ordination system has gone through three phases: formal institutionalisation (1970–73); a period where more sectors became involved (1974–85); and a period where it became more independent or autonomous (1986–95). This raises the question of whether the post-Maastricht period will become a fourth phase. Based partly on work by Grønnegaard and Christensen,[38] they suggest that the specialised ministries (ressortministerier) and the Special Committees will gain increased importance and that the role of the Foreign Ministry will decrease. The knowledge required to establish the Danish negotiation positions exists at the lower sectoral level in the co-ordination system. However, overall co-ordination through the Foreign Ministry, the government's Foreign Policy Committee and the Parliament's European Affairs Committee will continue to be necessary to ensure coherent positions and to enhance influence in Brussels.

The role of regions

Denmark is divided into fourteen counties (amter) and 275 municipalities (kommuner). These lower levels of government are not major actors in the policy-making process, but they implement and administer much of the ensuing legislation. They are especially responsible for health, social policy and environmental policy. Since some of these areas have been further developed as EU policies since the Maastricht Treaty entered into force, they are, of course, affected. Municipalities and counties have established their own associations and they lobby both the government in Copenhagen and the Commission in Brussels. Indeed, the largest cities have their own lobbyists in Brussels.[39]

In 1994 the Association of Local Authorities (Kommunernes Landsforening) took part in three Special Committees, namely those concerning Labour Market and Social Conditions, Environment, and Health, and it was usually invited to the Special Committee on Education. The Association of County Councils (Amtsrådsforeningen) was an ad hoc member of the Special Committee for Labour Market and Social Conditions, a member of the special committees on Transport and Environment and was usually invited to the Special Committee on Education. There was also a joint communal EC/EU Secretariat (Det Fælleskommunale EF-Sekretariat) which was an ad hoc member of the Special Committee on Industrial and Regional Political Co-Operation.[40] This secretariat, however, was dissolved in 1994.[41] At the beginning of 1999 the Association of Local Authorities took part in meetings of the following Special Committees: Food and Agriculture, Labour Market and Social Conditions, Establishment of Services (as ad hoc member), Transport Questions (normally invited), Industrial and Regional Political Co-Operation, Research, Education (normally invited), IT and Telecommunications. The Association of County Councils also took part in most of these, plus the Special Committee on Health.[42]

The establishment of the EU CoR has also given a more formal avenue of influence for these lower regional Danish levels. Denmark has nine representatives in the CoR. Four are nominated by the Association of Local Authorities, four by the Association of County Councils and one by the Copenhagen and Frederiksberg municipalities.[43] Among the issues traditionally dealt with by municipalities the following are directly affected by EC legislation: environment, public procurement, social and labour market policy, and regional policy. The following areas are said to be under indirect influence: education, trans-European networks (transport, telecommunications and energy), culture, and information technology.[44]

In conclusion, the sub-national level is increasingly involved in EU policy-making in Denmark at the level of Special Committees and through representation in the CoR. Yet they have not become major players. In the spring of 1988 the Association of County Councils produced a proposal for debate.[45] The paper suggested participation by Association experts already in relevant Commission expert groups. The Danish Special Committees were said to be dominated by business interests and hearings usually took place late in the process, thus limiting the possibility of influence. A closer direct co-operation with the government was also suggested; however, the paper is said to have been met by total silence.[46]

Conflicts between EC law and national law

Whereas the Parliament is supreme in Danish politics, the Danish courts have tried to stay away from politics. When the Danish Supreme Court decided to look into a complaint about the Maastricht Treaty it was therefore a surprise for many. The Court delivered its judgement on 6 April 1998, dismissing the case. Neither the additional powers that have been delegated to the Council in pursuance of Article 308 (ex Article 235) ECT, nor the law-making activities of the ECJ can be regarded as incompatible with the demand for specification in Section 20(1) of the Danish Constitution.[47] The Danish Constitution allows the transfer of powers to international organisations 'to such an extent as shall be provided by statute'. The appellants had pleaded that this condition had not been met. The Court went far in deferring to politics – it must be considered to be assumed in the Constitution that no transfer of powers can take place to such an extent that Denmark can no longer be considered an independent state. The determination of the limits to this must rely almost exclusively on considerations of a political nature.[48]

Afterwards the prime minister stated that he was 'satisfied that the matter [had] been closed with a clear and unanimous decision'.[49] In terms of implementing EU directives Denmark is doing quite well. Of 1,378 directives applicable at the end of 1997 Denmark had implemented 1,337, i.e. 97 per cent. Only Sweden had a slightly better record, and the EU average at the time was approximately 94 per cent. Denmark had implemented 100 per cent of the directives dealing with customs, pharmaceutical products, cosmetics, textiles, rights of residence, recognition of qualifications, financial services, company law, intellectual and industrial property, public procurement, direct taxation, indirect taxation, consumer protection and product safety, competition, and environment. Denmark's lowest score was for telecommunications, with nine out of fifteen directives implemented, i.e., 60 per cent, despite the EU average being only 70 per cent. The date for the creation of a liberalised and harmonised European telecommunications market, indeed, was 1 January 1998.[50]

If we look at infringement cases between 1993 to 1997, Denmark also does well. Although there were a number of Article 226 (ex Article 169) letters sent to Denmark, most cases were solved quickly. Only few reasoned opinions followed, and there were no referrals to the ECJ (see Table 4.3). Only Sweden and Finland came through the same period without referrals to the ECJ.

Table 4.3 Danish infringements, 1993–97

	Article 226 letters	*Reasoned opinions*	*Referrals to Court*
1993	66	3	0
1994	57	14	0
1995	42	1	0
1996	22	0	0
1997	63	1	0
Total	250	19	0

Source: 'Fifteenth Annual Report on Monitoring the Application of Community Law – 1997', COM (1998) 317 Final, *OJEC*, C 250, 10 August 1998.

Overall trends: the impact of the Maastricht Treaty

The most direct effect of the Maastricht Treaty was an increased emphasis on policies that could make the whole integration process more legitimate in Denmark. Thus there was more emphasis on environment, consumer protection, social policy, employment, and openness ('nearness'). Institutionally the two new pillars required some adaptations, involving also the Foreign Affairs and Legal Affairs Committees of the Parliament, respectively, in CFSP and JHA matters. Similarly, there has been an effort to involve the functional specialised committees in the parliament earlier and to a greater extent in first pillar legislation. The government and the political parties all talk about making decision-making more open and democratic, but in practice this has turned out not to be so easy so long as there is a concept of 'national interests' to be defended in Brussels. The 'diplomatic' approach to intergovernmental negotiations calls for some secrecy.

However, many day-to-day decisions are made at the level of Special Committees that involve representatives from interest organisations, thus blurring the distinction between the state and the civil society. At the same time the experts in the Special Committees are also involved in the Commission expert committees when proposals are prepared and in working groups under the Council when the final decisions are prepared. This has blurred the division between the Danish and EU institutions. A multi-tiered system that crosses national borders has emerged. Danish officials have become enmeshed in wider transnational networks. One should expect some learning and actor socialisation in these networks. Yet the government's political prerogatives remain strong. Table 4.2 (p. 104) gives a more detailed account of the institutions involved, but it does not include everything: it basically covers pillar one cases, and it also leaves out the EP on the EU side.

Perspectives for the future

We should expect the tension between central co-ordination and input of expertise at the more decentralised level to continue in the future. Perceptions of legislative failure should lead to more involvement of the Special Committees on the administrative side and specialised standing committees in the Parliament. Furthermore, the question of legitimacy in the integration process will remain central for Danish politicians. More openness will be sought in the EP. To the extent that the 'democratic deficit' cannot be resolved at the Danish level, perceptions of the role of the EP may change and become more positive. Indeed, on these points, we recently have seen further efforts and changes.

In November 1998 the European Affairs Committee put forward a draft report concerning greater openness in Danish EU decision-making.[51] The main proposals were to increase further the involvement of the specialised committees (fagudvalg) of the Folketing at an early stage, to open some meetings of the European Affairs Committee to the public, and to invite Danish MEPs to some meetings of the Committee. According to press reports, the prime minister decided after the Supreme Court case about the Maastricht Treaty to make decision-making more democratic. Some EU legislation concerning food additives, where the otherwise environmental and consumer-friendly EP did not ask for high levels of protection, had also inspired the proposals. Getting the Parliament's expertise involved early and creating a stronger link to the EP was seen as a way to improve EU legislation. Further, it was argued that a public debate on important proposals should take place. The government would be asked to present such proposals to open meetings of the European Affairs Committee soon after they were made by the Commission.[52]

The Amsterdam Treaty also influenced thinking in Copenhagen with respect to the role of the Danish MEPs. The increased use of the co-decision procedure implies that the role of the EP will increase. The government therefore began regular meetings with the Danish MEPs in the summer of 1998. The proposal from the European Affairs Committee gave MEPs access to open meetings of the committee in the future with a right to speak; these open meetings, however, would not take decisions. Decisions, including mandates for negotiations to the government, would still be taken in closed meetings.

According to the proposal, the basic notes regarding Commission proposals should be ready two months (rather than ten weeks) after the Commission proposal is received.

On 19 February the European Affairs Committee issued its report on greater openness in the Danish EU decision-making process;[53] the government had agreed to the parts that affected its involvement. The general lines of the draft proposal from November 1998 were confirmed; since 1 March 1999, when the report entered into force, it has become possible to have open meetings in the European Affairs Committee including the presence of Danish MEPs. MEPs can also send proposals to the other standing committees of the Folketing, and efforts to involve these specialised parliamentary committees early in the process have been reinforced. Basic notes from the government must be sent to the EP at the latest two months after the proposal from the Commission has been received by the Council. Therefore, in many ways the Amsterdam Treaty has reinforced trends from the Maastricht Treaty – and, with some cognitive lag, led to increased contacts with MEPs. The integration of the Schengen acquis and the movement of some JHA matters to the first pillar under the Amsterdam Treaty, where Denmark still has an exemption from taking part in supranational co-operation, threatens to place pressure on the Danish system, but no institutional adaptation has yet taken place.

The impact of EMU and accession of new Member States

EMU has been widely discussed in Denmark in connection with the start of the third phase and the introduction of the Euro. It seems that public opinion is becoming more favourable towards Danish participation. The political debate has mainly been about the timing of the referendum. The government seems to regret the marginalised position it is in with respect to the ECB and the making of European monetary policy, but the debate does not seem to have indicated any implications for Danish institutions at present.

Enlargement has also been discussed in Denmark, in particular the accession of the Baltic states, where the government has tried hard to get Latvia and Lithuania into the group of front runners together with Estonia. Three of the existing Special Committees deal with Central and Eastern European Countries – committees on Enlargement, Co-Ordination Concerning Nuclear Safety in Central and Eastern Europe, and the Ad Hoc Special Committee concerning the White Paper on the Participation of Central and Eastern European Countries in the Internal Market.

Conclusion: struggling with the not-so-permissive consensus

Denmark has established a complex policy co-ordination system that usually allows it to speak with one voice in Brussels. It has also established a system with more democratic political control than exists in most other EU countries. Seen in connection with the continued scepticism among the Danish electorate about further integration, this has occasionally made Denmark a difficult partner. The other side of the story, however, is that Denmark has been good at implementing EU legislation. The early involvement of the interest organisations and administrative agencies that will implement legislation has made this part of the process a success story. Where the Danish system still fails, it can be argued, is its lack of success in communicating the rationale of the continued process of integration in Europe to its citizens in a convincing way. Trying to give the EU a more 'progressive' face has become part of the government's strategy to create more legitimacy for the process. Yet the government has not yet dared to make a direct attack on the Danish exemptions from the Maastricht Treaty. These increasingly shackle the government. It can thus be concluded that the Danish political leadership is still struggling with a not-so-permissive consensus among the Danish public when it comes to European integration.[54] Or, put differently, the quest for legitimacy remains somewhat illusory.[55]

Notes

1 See for more background Finn Laursen, 'Denmark and European Political Union', in: Finn Laursen and Sophie Vanhoonacker (eds), *The Intergovernmental Conference on Political Union* (Dordrecht: Martinus Nijhoff, 1992), pp. 63–78 and Finn Laursen, 'Denmark and the Ratification of the Maastricht Treaty', in: Finn Laursen and Sophie Vanhoonacker (eds), *The Ratification of the Maastricht Treaty* (Dordrecht: Martinus Nijhoff, 1994), pp. 61–86.

2 See Thomas Pedersen, 'Denmark', in: Dietrich Rometsch and Wolfgang Wessels (eds), *The European Union and Member States. Towards Institutional Fusion?* (Manchester: Manchester University Press, 1996), pp. 197–215.

3 They had claimed that it was owing to an error that they were not present to vote. See Folketingets Forhandlinger, 1997–98, 7 May 1998.

4 As reported in the Danish press, e.g. *Jyllands-Posten*, 30 May, 1998.

5 The proposals can be found on the Foreign Ministry's internet site www.um.dk.

6 Author's translation from the Danish text which can be found on the internet site of the Folketing www.folketinget.dk.

7 *Ibid.*

8 The number of Special Committees has been increasing over the years. These figures date from 1 January 1999, according to a list provided by the Foreign Ministry.

9 See Foreign Ministry, *UM-tema: Den danske beslutningsprocedure i EU-sager*, August 1997, p. 11.

10 See Peter Nedergaard, *Organiseringen af Den Europæiske Union* (Aarhus: Handelshøjskolens Forlag, 1994), pp. 300–301.

11 See Foreign Ministry, *Den danske beslutningsprocedure*, p. 11.

12 Foreign Ministry, *Den danske beslutningsprocedure*, gives the following group of participants: Prime Minister (chairman), and Ministers of Economy, Finance, Foreign Affairs, Environment and Energy, Business and Industry, Justice, and Food, Agriculture and Fisheries.

13 See Nikolaj Petersen, 'Denmark, the IGC 1996 and the Future of the

European Union', in: Bertel Heurlin and Hans Mouritzen (eds), *Danish Foreign Policy Yearbook 1998* (Copenhagen: Danish Institute of International Affairs, 1998), pp. 43–59.

14 See in general: Finn Laursen, 'Parliamentary Bodies Specializing in European Union Affairs. Denmark and the Europe Committee of the Folketing', in: Finn Laursen and Spyros A. Pappas (eds), *The Changing Role of Parliaments in the European Union* (Maastricht: EIPA, 1995), pp. 43–54.

15 See Nedergaard, 1994, *op. cit.*, p. 302, and the information brochure from the secretariat of the European Affairs Committee, 'The European Affairs Committee', Copenhagen, October 1996, p. 10.

16 See Nedergaard, 1994, *op. cit.*, pp. 305–306.

17 See Report of the Market Relations Committee of 29 March 1973, English translation quoted from 'The European Affairs Committee', Copenhagen, October 1996, p. 3.

18 See also Ove Fich, 'Markedsudvalget – dets styrke og svagheder', in: *Udenrigs*, Vol. 48, No. 4/1993, pp. 63–64.

19 See Nedergaard, 1994, *op. cit.*, pp. 307–308.

20 See 'The European Affairs Committee', *op. cit.*, p. 4.

21 *Ibid.*

22 See 'Beretning om regeringens orientering af Folketinget om EU-sager', 20 May 1994.

23 See Fich, 1993, *op. cit.*, p. 66.

24 See also Hjalte Rasmussen, *EU-Ret i Kontekst*, Third Edition (Copenhagen: GadJura, 1998), pp. 113–114.

25 See Nicole Ameline (rapporteur), 'Les Parlements et l'Europe. Les leçons de l'experience danoise', Rapport d'information, No. 1437 (Paris: Assemblée Nationale, Délégation pour l'Union européenne, 1994), p. 22; English version of the report as appendix in Laursen, 1995, *op. cit.* A collection of the reports in Danish by the European Affairs Committee is available from Folketingets EU-Oplysning.

26 See Europaudvalget, 'Beretning om Folketingets behandling af EU-sager', Beretning No. 6, 27 September 1996, Folketinget 1995–96.

27 See 'The European Affairs Committee', *op. cit.*, p. 6.

28 See: Europaudvalget, 'Beretning om Folketingets behandling af WTO-sager', Beretning No. 7, 14 March 1997, Folketinget 1996–97.

29 See Europaudvalget, 'Beretning om Folketingets behandling af Schengensager', Beretning No. 2, 7 May 1998, Folketinget 1997–98 (2nd session).

30 See Justitsministeriet, Civil – og Politiafdelingen, Det Internationale Kontor, 'Notits', 27 November 1997.

31 See Erik Højbjerg and Frank Marcher, 'Den danske centraladministration og EU. En institutionel-historisk analyse af koordination og forhandling med særlig henblik på Miljøministeriet', *CORE arbejdspapir*, Copenhagen 1995, p. 119.

32 Listed in Højbjerg and Marcher, 1995, *op. cit.*, pp. 226–239.

33 See Nedergaard, 1994, *op. cit.*, p. 297.

34 See Højbjerg and Marcher, 1995, *op. cit.*, p. 136.

35 According to the list 'Specialudvalg under EF-Udvalg (prior 1 January 1999)'.

36 See Nedergaard, 1994, *op. cit.*, p. 300.

37 See Søren von Dosenrode, 'Den optimale minimalløsning i Danmarks administrative tilpasning til EF', in: *Nordisk Administrativt Tidsskrift*, No. 4 (1993), pp. 454–465.

38 See Jørgen Grønnegård Christensen *et al.*, 'Åbenhed, offentlighed og deltagelse i den danske EU-beslutningsproces'. Report for meeting of Rådet for Europæisk Politik, Copenhagen, 18 April 1994.

39 See Pedersen, 1996, *op. cit.*, pp. 197–98. See also Kurt Klaudi Klausen, 'Danish Local Government: Integrating into the EU?' in: Michael J. F. Goldsmith and Kurt Klaudi Klausen (eds), *European Integration and Local Government* (Cheltenham: Edward Elgar, 1997), pp. 16–38.

40 According to the list in Højbjerg and Marcher, 1995, *op. cit.*

41 See also Kurt Klaudi Klausen, 1997, *op. cit.*, pp. 16–38.

42 According to the list 'Specialudvalg under EF-Udvalg (prior 1 January 1999)', provided by Foreign Ministry.

43 Information from web site of the Association of Local Authorities http://www.kl.dk.

44 Information at www.kl.dk/eu/eukommuner.shtm.

45 See Amtsrådsforeningen, 'Den amtskommunale medvirken i EU-beslutningsprocessen – behov for nye samarbejdsformer. Et debatoplæg', April 1988.

46 See Communication from Association of County Council official to the author, 2 February 1999.

47 Text of The Danish Supreme Court's Judgement of 6 April 1998 at www.um.dk/ udenrigspolitik/europa/domeng/. The Danish version, 'Udskrift af Højesterets Dombog. Højesterets Dom af 6. April 1998', is also available from the EU Information of the Folketing.

48 Text of the Danish Supreme Court's Judgement of 6 April 1998, *op. cit.*

49 See: Press release at www.um.dk/udenrigspolitik/europa/domeng/prerel.html.

50 See European Commission, 'Fifteenth Annual Report on Monitoring the Application of Community Law', 1997, COM (1998) 317final, *Official Journal of the European Communities*, C 250, 10 August 1998.

51 See Folketingets Europaudvalg, 'Udkast til beretning fra Europaudvalget om større åbenhed i den danske EU-beslutningsproces m.v.', Alm. del – bilag 225, 26 November 1998.

52 See Jens Bostrup and Nina Vinther Andersen, 'Folketinget vil tage magt fra regeringen', *Politiken* 31 December 1998, p. 6, 1st section.

53 See 'Beretning om større åbenhed i den danske EU-beslutningsproces m.v.', Beretning afgivet af Europaudvalget den 19. February 1999.

54 The author has dealt with this question in: Finn Laursen, 'The Not-So-Permissive Consensus: Thoughts on the Maastricht Treaty and the Future of European Integration', in: Finn Laursen and Sophie Vanhoonacker (eds), *The Ratification of the Maastricht Treaty* (Dordrecht: Martinus Nijhoff, 1994), pp. 295–317.

55 See Niels-Jørgen Nehring, 'The Illusory Quest for Legitimacy. Danish Procedures for Policy Making on the EU and the Impact of a Critical Public', in: Georg Sørensen and Hans-Henrik Holm (eds), *And Now What? International Politics After the Cold War: Essays in Honour of Nikolaj Petersen* (Aarhus: Politica, 1998), pp. 60–81.

Select bibliography

The text (English translation) of the constitution of Denmark can be found at the University of Richmond's constitution finder at http://confinder.richmond.edu/. Further sources on government and parliament of Denmark can be found at Government: www.statsministeriet.dk/ or at Parliament www.folketinget.dk.

Haahr, Niels Henrik (1997) 'Trends in Danish Party Attitudes Towards European Integration', CORE Working Paper, No. 6/1997.

Hedetoft, Ulf (1997) 'The Interplay Between Mass and Elite Attitudes to European Integration in Denmark', CORE Working Paper, No. 2/1997.

Klausen, Kurt Klaudi (1997) 'Danish Local Government. Integrating into the EU?', in: Michael J.F. Goldsmith and Kurt Klaudi Klausen (eds), *European Integration and Local Government* (Cheltenham: Edward Elgar), pp. 16–38.

Laursen, Finn (1992) 'Denmark and European Political Union', in: Finn Laursen and Sophie Vanhoonacker (eds), *The Intergovernmental Conference on Political Union* (Dordrecht: Martinus Nijhoff), pp. 63–78.

Laursen, Finn (1994) 'Denmark and the Ratification of the Maastricht Treaty,' in: Finn Laursen and Sophie Vanhoonacker (eds), *The Ratification of the Maastricht Treaty* (Dordrecht: Martinus Nijhoff), pp. 61–86.

Laursen, Finn (1995) 'Parliamentary Bodies Specializing in European Union Affairs. Denmark and the Europe Committee of the Folketing', in: Finn Laursen and Spyros A. Pappas (eds), *The Changing Role of Parliaments in the European Union* (Maastricht: EIPA).

Nedergaard, Peter (1995) 'The Case of Denmark', in: Spyros A. Pappas (ed.), *National Administrative Procedures for the Preparation and Implementation of Community Decisions* (Maastricht: EIPA, 1995), pp. 111–132.

Nehring, Niels-Jørgen (1998) 'The Illusory Quest for Legitimacy. Danish Procedures for Policy Making on the EU and the Impact of a Critical Public', in: Georg Sørensen and Hans-Henrik Holm (eds), *And Now What? International Politics After the Cold War: Essays in Honour of Nikolaj Petersen* (Aarhus: Politica), pp. 60–81.

Pedersen, Thomas (1996) 'Denmark', in: Dietrich Rometsch and Wolfgang Wessels (eds), *The European Union and Member States. Towards Institutional Fusion?* (Manchester: Manchester University Press, 1996), pp. 197–215.

Petersen, Nikolaj (1998) 'Denmark, the IGC 1996 and the Future of the European Union,' in: Bertel Heurlin and Hans Mouritzen (eds), *Danish Foreign Policy Yearbook 1998* (Copenhagen: Danish Institute of International Affairs), pp. 43–59.

von Dosenrode, Søren Z. (1998) 'Denmark: The Testing of a Hesitant Membership', in: Kenneth Hanf and Ben Soetendorp (eds), *Adapting to European Integration. Small States and the European Union* (London: Longman, 1998), pp. 52–68.

5 *Andreas Maurer*[1]

Germany: fragmented structures in a complex system

Introduction: preferences of a tamed power[2]

Germany's political class is marked by a positive and constructive attitude towards European integration. The main objective of European policy was and still is to achieve effective and democratic European co-operation and integration.[3] All governments and the vast majority of political parties contrive their general European policy agenda around the fundamental aim of far-reaching integration towards some kind of political union. Although the diplomatic class does not follow any kind of altruistic or 'naive' European policy geared to achieve a European federation, the majority of political actors are reluctant to explicitly play a leading role within the evolving European Union. That is not to say that they are immune from searching ways to influence the European agenda. But German initiatives regarding 'great bargain' decisions (IGCs, CAP reforms, decisions on the Union's financial resources)[4] are generally prearranged jointly with other Member State governments. Until 1989, this 'leadership avoidance reflex'[5] was a typical feature of Germany acting under the paradigm of a 'semi-sovereign' state.[6] 'Deutschlands Interessen liegen in Europa' (Germany's interests lie in Europe) – this paradigm reflects the political elites' view of Germany's potential leadership in Europe, the mediation of its power within the EC and its institutional arrangements.[7] With its large industrial sector and dependence on foreign trade, Germany is largely linked to the Common Market. Establishing close economic links within the EC is therefore politically advantageous as it demonstrates the FRG's commitment to economic and political integration.[8]

Time is another country: the impact of the Maastricht Treaty and German re-unification

The end of the Cold War decisively changed the fundamental parameters for the European Union and its Member States. Given the objective changes for Germany – its size and population, its 'geo-political centrality' between West and East Europe and its economic power – one could have suggested that the re-unified Republic would act as a dominant leader in the Union.[9] However, as the Maastricht and the more recent Amsterdam IGC process of 1996–97 revealed,[10] Germany did not aspire to use its potential to engage in unilateral power politics. Despite domestic concerns especially on EMU, neither the federal government nor the parliamentary opposition parties attempted to exploit Germany's potential against its traditional role of an important but 'tamed power'.[11] The political class is associated with the 'traditional' set of priorities in EU politics: achieving and consolidating EMU and political union in institutional as well as in substantive terms, i.e. economic policy co-ordination at the EC level and a coherent and effective CFSP; the continuation of Franco-German co-operation; and a strengthening of the military capacities of the Union through the integration of the WEU into the EU ambit.[12] The basic perception of European integration remains unchanged, particularly with regard to the role of the EC institutions. The German political elite continues to aim at the phased creation of a legally independent, state-like political entity with some kind of a structured multi-levelled – 'two-chamber' system whose members shall – on the basis of equal rights and obligations – co-operate through the adoption of binding law. The Social-Democrat/Green government does not depart from this conception of European integration. On the contrary, compared with the Kohl era, the coalition additionally focuses on social and employment policy, and the formalisation of citizen rights within the corpus of the EU Treaty.[13]

Until 1991–92 public opinion in Germany appeared to conform to the so-called 'permissive consensus'.[14] However, during the 1991–92 IGC, public opinion became somewhat more critical[15] – a development in line with the broader trend towards 'Euroscepticism' which can be observed in all member-states.[16] The negotiations on EMU and the critique of this process articulated by the Bundesbank (during the IGC process), the Social Democratic Party and the Christian Social Union (CSU) (during the ratification process) and a wide range of academics (during ratification and after the Maastricht decision of the Constitutional Court) affected the way in which the 'finalité politique' of European integration was presented. Hence, Chancellor Kohl repeatedly made clear that German European policy had changed since 1990 by admitting that his previous calls for establishing a 'United States of Europe' were a mistake and that he implicitly no longer supported this idea.[17] Although a favourable attitude towards European integration remains, the political parties are gradually adopting more controversial positions with regard to the method of integration and the competencies to be conferred on the European institutions in specific policy areas, especially on those which are also debated at the national level. Hence, one can identify some kind of 'Europeanised' party cleavages which have developed along the path of European treaty reforms in the areas of social and employment policy, equal opportunities policy, environment policy and home and judicial co-operation. [18]

This change in tone reflects a more pragmatic and less 'idealistic' approach towards European integration. German political players try to increase their influence on the implementation and the execution of policy fields and programmes, especially with regard to their financial implications.[19] Given the political environment of the Union after Maastricht (Agenda 2000, reform of the Union's own resources), the economic recession of 1992–93, high and persistent unemployment rates and the extensive transfers to the Eastern Länder, cost-benefit analysis becomes more important and – with view to the interaction between government and the citizenry – also more relevant for German EC/EU policy-making (Figure 5.1).[20]

The national policy-cycle: multi-level complexity and segmentation

Our study of the participation of German institutions in EC/EU decision-making concentrates on the country's political system and institutional design. In that respect the following question has to be addressed: if the relationship between the FRG and the Union can be described as a 'complex interdependence',[21] is this exclusively due to the history of Germany and the institutions involved or did the path of European integration as well as the institutional set-up of the Union also contribute to this interdependence? Moreover, do changes in the basic perceptions of European integration impact on the relationship between Germany and the Union?

The interinstitutional set-up of German EU policy-making features a hierarchy of policy-making powers and functions according to the institutions involved as well as to the different phases of the EC/EU policy-making cycle. Evidently there are 'winners' and 'losers' in terms of participation in EC/EU decision-making.[22] How has this setting evolved over time?

Germany is a federal state. Owing to this constitutionalised structure collective players intervene at different levels in the political process. The Basic Law (Grundgesetz) attributes specific competencies and functions to these levels. The vertical division of powers between the federal level and that of the 'federated states' – the Länder – leads to a complex system of 'political interwovenness' or 'interconnectedness' (Politikverflechtung).[23] Basically, there is no single decision-making centre but different levels interact in the decision-making process and compete for access and participation. In addition to this vertical distribution of 'openings', there is a horizontal division of influence between the different ministries and

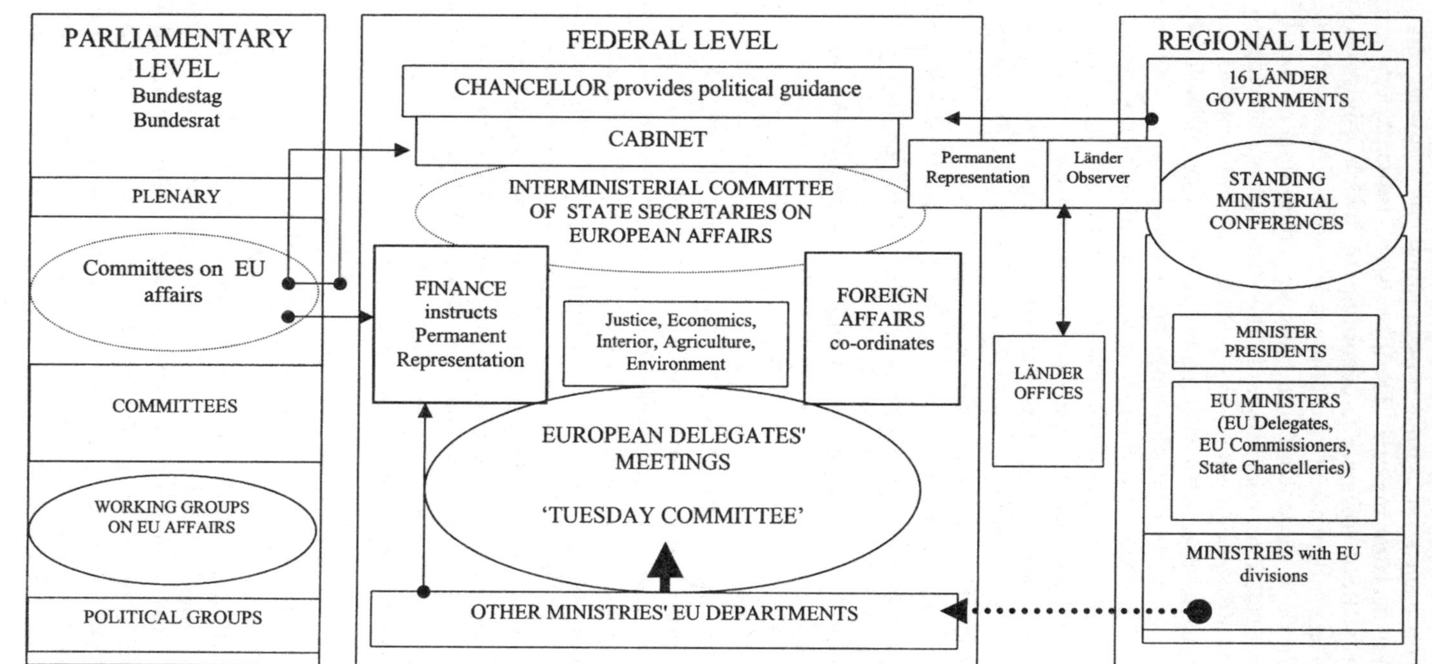

Figure 5.1 The national level of European decision-making – Germany

institutions on each level. Three constitutional rules govern this framework of joint decision-making. The first is the principle of ministerial responsibility ('Ressortprinzip'), according to which ministries at the federal level are independent and competing actors. Unlike the situation in France or the United Kingdom, this principle hinders the different branches of the German government in their attempts to develop coherent approaches to EC policy-making.[24] Secondly, the framework of joint decision-making is influenced by the chancellor principle ('Kanzlerprinzip'), which empowers the Chancellor to guide the government and to define the ministerial portfolios, and which can be mobilised when serious challenges and interministerial bottlenecks occur. However, the Chancellor is not entitled finally to decide on matters where ministers battle for different views or positions. Hence the collective government principle ('Kabinettsprinzip') ensures that open conflicts between ministries are decided by the whole cabinet of the federal government.

Interest groups are involved only in the preparatory and implementation phases of the EU's policy-cycle. Playing a decisive role during the decision-making phase is the exception rather than the rule. Finally the German political parties have very limited institutionalised functions in the policy-cycle.

The federal bureaucracy

Germany's EU administrators have a poor reputation. A growing literature focusing on the efficiency of Germany's European policy-making has detected structural handicaps and 'failures' owing to the institutional design. The conventional wisdom[25] identifies a comparatively low degree of effectiveness and competitiveness. Compared to its French and British counterparts, the performance of the German interadministrative process suffers from horizontal and vertical fragmentation,[26] old-fashioned and cumbersome procedures, 'negative co-ordination',[27] 'institutional pluralism',[28] and 'institutional cannibalism'.[29] Hence, the powers conferred to the different levels of policy-making are not co-ordinated by a central agency responsible for formulating a coherent European policy. These features highlight a lack of clear strategy and of rapid position taking-leading which can leave the German delegation in a minority position in the Council of Ministers. On the other hand, this politico-administrative system features flexible working and co-ordination structures. One of the persistent advantages of the German political system is the decentralised and departmentalised scheme of administrative interaction. Decision-making is filtered from the lowest level towards the highest administrative and political levels.[30] In a manner which resembles the hidden logic behind the decision-making in the EU Council of Ministers, the bureaucracy tries to solve conflicts at the earliest and lowest level possible.

The federal government is composed of the Chancellor, ministers,

ministers of state and the ministerial bureaucracy which are directly involved in the EU's Council of Ministers, its subordinate working mechanisms, but also in the Commission's comitology committees. The Chancellor claims a certain 'domaine résérvé' within the European Council. He disposes of a so-called 'guidance competence' ('Richtlinienkompetenz'),[31] which can be defined as a capability to set the strategic guidelines of the federal government in general, to resolve interministerial disputes (decisions of the Chancellor in this regard are binding for ministers), and to determine the final governmental approach on a given issue.[32] The guidance competence on European affairs was only rarely used until the formalisation of the European Council in 1974. However, since then German Chancellors have made use of this power on several occasions (EMS, Schengen co-operation, IGCs, enlargement). The European Council's tendency towards 'de facto intrusion' into the competencies of the Council of Ministers under the EC Treaty has reinforced the Chancellor's potential to influence the broad but decisive outlines of EU policy-making.

On the other hand, the ministers of the cabinet and the ministerial bureaucracy are highly involved in the preparatory drafting of EC legislation within the working groups of the Council of Ministers and the European Commission as well as within COREPER. The principle of ministerial responsibility would suggest that all ministers are equal in the face of the Union. However, some are more equal than others. This is due to the evolution of EC/EU policy fields, but also results from the historical evolution of the ministries in the FRG. With the exception of the Ministry for Defence, every German ministry contains at least one special division for European Affairs (Table 5.1).

The information provided by Table 5.1 has to be understood as a snapshot taken from the ongoing 'EC/EU reality show' of scope enlargement and institutional as well as procedural differentiation.[33] In comparing the 2001 picture with the institutional design of the German federal government in earlier periods of European integration (our reference period here is 1982–88),[34] we can see that EC/EU membership has had a considerable impact upon the institutional and procedural aspects of German politics and policies. Moreover, by taking the overall number of national administrative units which deal more or less exclusively with European affairs as an indicator for the dynamic 'Europeanisation' of Member States,[35] we can assume that some ministries seem to be more closely involved in EC/EU policy-making than others. Owing to the original ECSC and EEC treaties with their concentration on a few – economic – policy areas, only the Ministry for Economics had established a European affairs division. In the absence of a foreign minister until 1955,[36] the Federal Ministry for Economics took on the lead-role in the day-to-day policy management for the ECSC.[37] These original arrangements established the Ministry of

Table 5.1 The Chancellory, the Ministries and their European Affairs Units, March 2001

Chancellory	*Department 2* *Department 4*	*Group 21* *(Foreign Affairs)* *Group 41* *(Economic Affairs)*	*Division 211* *Divisions 411 and 412*
Ministries	*EU related Departments*	*EU-related directorates*	*EU-related divisions*
Foreign Affairs Provides chairman of the Committee of State Secretaries for European affairs	Department E Political Department (CFSP–COREU)	2 Directorates	4 Divisions each and Task Force (1995–97) on the IGC and (since 1997) on Enlargement. In July 1998, the Political Affairs department's Divisions dealing with EU Member States shifted towards the E Department. Since October 1998 the E Department also provides for the Secretariat of the Committee of State Secretaries on EC Affairs.
Interior	Department V Department P (Police) Department A (Asylum and Foreign Nationals)	–	Working group V I 4 (EC law), Division V I 5 (EP election law), Division V II 4 (German Internal Affairs Unit to the Permanent Representative), Division P6 (Police co-operation), Division A6 (EC-Harmonisation of Treatment of Foreign Nationals)
Justice	Department E	2 Directorates	6 Divisions each
Finance Provides deputy chairman of the committee of state secretaries on European affairs since 10/1998	Department E on European Policy	3 Directorates + Task Force EMU + Task Force on Enlargement	16 Divisions directly linked to Department E since October 1998 representation of the FRG towards the ECJ
Economics Provided deputy chairman of the Committee of State Secretaries on European affairs until October 1998	Department V on Foreign Trade and European Policy (former E department)	1 Directorate on European Policy	5 Divisions directly related to the Directorate on E policy + 2 Divisions substantially related to the Directorate on E policy.
Agriculture	Department 6	2 Directorates	13 Divisions and Project Group 33 (BSE)
Labour and Social Affairs	Department VII	1 Directorate	5 Divisions
Family Affairs, Senior Citizens, Women and Youth	–	–	Divisions for European and International Women and Family Affairs, Politics for Senior Citizens, and Youth Policy
Health	–	1 Directorate	
Transport	–	–	1 Division (EU, OECD, Council of Europe, ECE and OSCE)
Environment	–	–	1 Division (EU, Council of Europe, OSCE, Bilateral Co-Operation with EC Member States)
Education, Science and Technology	–	Directorate 12 Directorate 31 Directorate 42	5 Divisions dealing with EC affairs 1 Division on Higher Education and EC affairs 1 Division on European Science co-operation
Economic Co-operation	Department 4	Directorate 40	2 Divisions
Regional Planning, Building and Urban Development	–	–	Division on Harmonisation of technical norms and Working Group on European Co-Operation

Sources: Organisation plans of the Federal ministries and the Federal Chancellery (December 1997–March 1999) and Auswärtiges Amt/Bundesministerium der Finanzen; Verfahren der Koordination der innerstaatlichen Willensbildung in der Europapolitik (Berlin, 1 December 2000).

Economics in a strong position on matters of functional – economic integration, although there was no formal agreement on the division of labour with the Chancellor's Office. The entry into force of the Rome Treaties pushed the Ministries of Economics and Foreign Affairs into an agreement on European policy responsibilities, reached in 1958.[38] The Ministries for Agriculture, Finance and Foreign Affairs created European departments and directorates during the 1960s. In 1993 – after the entry into force of the Maastricht Treaty – the Ministry of Foreign Affairs established a separate European Affairs division. In addition, the Ministries of Justice and of the Interior provide legal expertise to the so-called 'Four Musketeers'. The involvement of other ministries became relevant only within the context of the SEA and – with regard to the creation of divisions dealing with substantial aspects of co-operation in the JHA field – with the entry into force of the Maastricht Treaty.

Reflecting one of the main characteristics of the EC/EU integration process over time – the incremental enlargement of the substantive scope of policy-making and the institutional as well as procedural growth – German ministerial involvement in European Affairs can be characterised as a process of horizontal differentiation and segmentation. This process becomes perceptible in comparing the division of the workload among the national ministries during EC/EU presidencies. Table 5.2 indicates that the number of working group meetings involving federal ministries outside the club of the 'Four Musketeers' has considerably increased over time. Neither the Ministry for Foreign Affairs nor the Ministry of Economics nor – since October 1998 the Ministry of Finance – has a monopoly in giving Germany a 'voice' in the Brussels arena.

These figures not only mirror the policy preferences of the European Commission and the Council of Ministers at a given time,[39] but also indicate a shift in the competencies of the ministries within the German government. Interestingly, a comparison between the Presidency's draft plans of August 1998 (Kohl government) and of December 1998 (Schröder government) demonstrates the shift in the relative importance of the Ministry of Finance at the expense of the Ministry of Economics to only a very limited extent. The organisational changes of the new government (reallocation of European affairs co-ordination competencies between the Ministries of Economics, Finance and Foreign Affairs) did not spill over into their activity with regard to the Council's working groups. My conclusion would be that ups and downs in the activity of some ministries are mainly rooted in the rolling policy agenda of the Commission and the Council and are not exclusively a result of the policy preferences of the German government. The role occupied by the Ministry for Labour in 1999 confirms this argument, since the Presidency foresaw only one working group dealing with social affairs. Thus, the policy priorities of the Schröder government with regard to employment policy in

Table 5.2 Division of labour among presidents and representatives of the FRG in the working groups of the Council of Ministers during German presidencies, 1988–99

Ministry	*1988*		*1994*		*1999*	
	PRE	*SGD*	*PRE*	*SGD*	*PRE*	*SGD*
Foreign Affairs	2	1	22	22	30	25
Economics	29	48	23	49	38	46
Agriculture	18	23	42	51	63	64
Finance	13	30	2	30	19	48
Justice	24	25	20	22	33	31
Interior	3	3	18	21	33	33
Labour	3	4	4	5	1	1
Transport	4	4	3	8	1	6
Youth, Family, Health	3	13	23	28	35	28
Education, Science, Technology	1	2	4	6	2	0
Environment	2	3	2	6	8	8
Economic Co-Operation	0	5	0	4	1	1
Regional Planning	2	4	1	2	1	2
Permanent Representation	91	26	96	30	84	49
Others	2	3	4	13	2	1
Sum	197	194	264	297	351	343

Sources: For 1988 and 1994: Rometsch and Wessels (1996); for 1999: Draft minutes of the European Delegates' meeting of 15 December 1998, Auswärtiges Amt, Bonn (18 December 1998).
Notes: PRE = Presidency of the Council. SGD = Speaker of the German delegation in the Council.

general (Luxembourg process) and the European Employment Pact (Cologne process) are not reflected in a strengthened role for the relevant ministry. On the contrary, the Pact was, together with the whole policy agenda on employment, one of the areas which Chancellor Schröder reserved for the Chancellery.

Near to the problem – far from the centre: the co-ordination of policy-making

The roles and functions of the different levels within the federal government vary according to the phases of the EC policy-cycle. During the preparation phase, the bulk of activities are carried out by the heads of department, who are involved in long-term policy planning and co-ordination, and by the heads of division, who focus on the technical details of EC/EU legislation. In this phase, ministers of state and parliamentary state secretaries trade political issues whereas in general, the ministers themselves do not intervene. As far as the decision-taking phase is concerned, it is up to the relevant minister to decide on a given issue. However, each ministry's representative from the working groups in Council of Ministers has the task of closing as many dossiers as possible before transferring them to the rather political COREPER and to the Council of Ministers' level.[40]

Horizontal policy co-ordination overarching the different policy fields plays an important role in EC/EU affairs. The principle of ministerial responsibility can account for the fact that the Ministry of Foreign Affairs does not play a preponderant role in EC affairs. However, as far as participation in CFSP is concerned, it is the Foreign Ministry's European Affairs Division which together with the Political Division that shapes Germany's position. Moreover, one of the two Parliamentary State Secretaries of the Foreign Affairs Ministry acts as the Chairman of the Committee of State Secretaries on European Affairs and as the main interlocutor in dealings with the Cabinet of the federal government. For historical reasons – the Ministry for Foreign Affairs was established only in 1955, after the Ministry of Economics[41] – and because of the fact that the main focus of European integration until 1993 was economic rather than political, the Foreign Minister, when acting as a co-ordinator, has always been assisted by the Minister of Economics. Until the end of the Kohl government, it was the latter ministry which was mainly responsible for representing the FRG at the ECJ as well as for the distribution of EC/EU documents to the other actors involved in the German European policy process. Of greater importance to the co-ordination of German European policy-making is the fact that the European Department in the Ministry of Economics chaired the inter-ministerial committees on EC affairs, formulated and transmitted the negotiation instructions to the diplomats in the Permanent Representation of Germany in Brussels, and finally, disposed of the Secretariat of the Committee of State Secretaries on European Affairs.

How did the evolution of the EC/EU influence the powers and responsibilities of these two ministries? The Ministry of Economics developed its role as the central interface between Brussels and Bonn from the time of the founding European Treaties through to the SEA. The Ministry for Agriculture established its 'own' contacts with the relevant players on the national and European levels. In this phase, the Ministry for Foreign Affairs was mainly responsible for macro-political issues such as institutional reform, European Political Co-Operation etc. There was thus a sector-specific partnership between the two ministries. This changed when the Maastricht Treaty entered German politics. The new policy agenda of the Union included many issues which were not exclusively related to the traditional role of the Ministry for Economics. Consequently, the Ministry for Foreign Affairs and other ministries restructured their administrations according to their new tasks in the field of European policy-making. As a result, the trend of 'sectorised policy making'[42] in German European affairs considerably increased.

The ongoing dynamics of segmentation, institutional pluralism and the potential for conflict between the governmental actors dealing with EC/EU affairs suggest that co-ordination mechanisms and institutions across the different phases of the Brussels policy-cycle are highly important. Seen from a French or a British perspective the lack of a central agency which regularly co-ordinates the German European policy may be interpreted as one of the most considerable weaknesses in the political system. Even prior to the first fundamental reform of the EEC, Regelsberger and Wessels described the German co-ordination mechanisms as indicators of 'negative co-ordination': each ministerial actor tries to protect his or her sphere of competence instead of choosing an empathetic approach aimed at adopting coherent German policy preferences across the different EC/EU policy fields.[43] However, one should not jump to conclusions and assume a chaotic regime in European affairs.

The co-ordination of EC/EU policy-making in the Federal Republic is ensured at different levels of government by a set of institutions in the broad meaning of the term,[44] that is, formalised conferences, committees and informal but regular contacts on the administrative level. In the absence of a central interface between Brussels and Bonn/Berlin, channels of information, instruction and communication have been established at each level of the administration. Commission drafts of proposals for new or amended EC legislation are transmitted from the Permanent Representation to the Ministry of Economics and, since October 1998, to the Ministry of Finance.[45] The proposals are then advanced to the lead-department ('federführende Ressort'). The re-transmission of proposals and amendments as well as the instructions for German delegations to the Council of Ministers and its subsequent bodies is therefore the outcome of a complex co-ordination mechanism.

The most political institution is the Cabinet Committee on European Affairs, established in January 1973.[46] Until the Schröder government came into office, the Cabinet Committee had met only twice – at its inaugural session and at the beginning of Helmut Kohl's Chancellorship. Given that since January 1973 the Cabinet of the federal government discussed EU business (under the topics of 'European Questions' and 'International Affairs') on a weekly basis, the Cabinet Committee became a rather artificial instrument. As a consequence, Chancellor Schröder and his government abolished it.[47] In the absence of a formalised and efficient co-ordination structure at the ministerial level, the bulk of the political co-ordination is carried out by the Inter-ministerial Committee of State Secretaries on European Affairs. This committee was set up in 1963 in order to deal with controversies in relation to European affairs.[48] Meeting approximately on a bi-monthly basis, it brings together the State Ministers and State Secretaries of the 'Four Musketeers' in European affairs as well as the State Minister dealing with European Affairs in the

Chancellery and the Permanent Representative of the FRG in Brussels. Other ministries participate in the meetings when the chair (Foreign Affairs) considers it as appropriate. Although the structure of this committee is rather flexible, becoming a permanent member is of political importance.[49] In October 1998 the secretariat shifted from the Ministry of Economics to the Ministry for Foreign Affairs, underlining the latter's strengthened role in co-ordinating German EC/EU policy.[50] The committee's main task is to settle controversial questions and to prepare dossiers of a political and strategic nature with regard to the Council of Ministers' meetings. Decisions of the committee are taken by common accord and are politically binding for the ministries;[51] it does not adopt a pro-active policy approach on the basis of the Council of Ministers' agenda.[52] Besides co-ordinating the internal agenda of European policy-making, determining the German representatives in Brussels is another area of complexity and incoherence. The German Permanent Representation cannot act on its own account. Instead, the Bonn/Berlin-based institutional pluralism and segmentation in European affairs is mirrored in the Permanent Representation in Brussels. Ministries send their civil servants to the Permanent Representation (in 1998 the two core ministries occupied 57 per cent of the posts).[53] The total number of civil servants working in the Permanent Representation indicates an intensive involvement of the German ministerial administration (Table 5.3).

Table 5.3 Evolution of German personnel in the Permanent Representation in comparison to the number of days spent in the Council and its preparatory bodies, 1958–2000

Policy area	*1958*	*1960*	*1969*	*1975*	*1988*	*1995*	*1998*	*2000*
Germany's Permanent Representation staff	5	19	28	39	42	59	87	107
Council meetings	21	44	69	76.5	117.5	98	94	91
Council Meetings/Permanent Representation staff	4.2	2.3	2.5	1.9	2.8	1.7	1.1	1.08
COREPER meetings	39	97	129	118	104	112	116	130
COREPER Meeting/Permanent Representation staff	7.8	5.1	4.6	3.02	2.5	1.9	1.3	1.2
Working group meetings	302	505	1412.5	2079.5	2000.5	2364.5	3140	3537
Meetings/Permanent Representation staff	60.4	26.6	50.4	53.3	47.6	40.1	36.1	33.05

Source: Web site of the Council; *43rd Review of the Council's Work* (Brussels, 1995); *European Commission: General Report of Activities of the EU 1998* (Brussels/ Luxembourg, 2001).

With a view to instructing the Permanent Representation of the German position in Brussels, the Ministry of Finance – until October 1998 the Ministry of Economics – co-ordinates the meetings in relation to COREPER I, whereas the Ministry of Foreign Affairs is responsible for the management of the Bonn/Berlin-based work in relation to COREPER II.[54] In order to give instructions to COREPER I and its subsequent working units, every ministry has a European Delegate ('Europa-Beauftragter'). They meet on virtually a monthly basis; since October 1998 the location and the chairmanship have been transferred from the Ministry of Economics to the Ministry of Foreign Affairs. Below this level, there are regular contacts between the heads of division ('Ressortleiter') in order to settle disputes between the ministries concerned on issues related to the Council's working group meetings. The so-called 'Tuesday Committee', which meets on a weekly basis, focuses on the technical aspects of a given issue. The co-ordination of the European Delegates and the Tuesday Committee, and the informal contacts between civil servants, are aimed at settling disputes of a technical rather than political nature. As regards timing, these bodies focus on the working groups of the Council of Ministers and COREPER I. As far as the meetings of the European Delegates are concerned, the deputy permanent representative for COREPER I is always involved. The relative autonomy of the actors indicates the problem of achieving coherent policy approaches; although the Europe Delegates and the Tuesday Committee give each ministry an opportunity to discuss its position on the COREPER agenda, it remains up to each responsible ministerial administration to formulate the instructions for the working group level.

Although the different co-ordination mechanisms have not been officially established by law, they have a long tradition and have influenced the structure of the federal government's decision-making process to a considerable extent. Ministerial self-interest prevails but given the Chancellor's 'Sword of Damocles', i.e. the 'guidance competence', the competition between the ministries does not lead to anarchy. Autonomy and segmentation are counterbalanced by the possibility that the Chancellery may intervene in order to dispel conflict. Nevertheless, as the working group level is the 'most vital'[55] of all the Council's component parts[56] and given that between 70[57] and 90 per cent[58] of the Council's agenda is dealt with at this level,[59] the fact that there is apparently no effective co-ordination mechanism between the relevant ministerial bodies indicates clearly the problem for European policy-making in the FRG.

The parliamentary dimension

Unlike in the United Kingdom and France, the overall mentality of members in the German two-chamber parliament – Bundestag and Bundesrat – is characterised by co-operation and less by partisan structures and conflict between loyalty and discipline. Co-operation between government and parliament leads to what is classically identified as the German 'working parliament' (Arbeitsparlament), in which the opposition tries to influence the government's decisions by a wide range of technical–concrete rather than political–general instruments.[60] This 'working parliament' function has considerable implications for the organisation of parliamentary activities. For instance, decision-making shifts from the plenary towards the huge range of committees, sub-committees and various working groups within the parliament, all of which are subject oriented. Decision-making has also moved towards parliamentary groups (organised according to subject and cutting across committee spheres), working parties (also cutting across committees) and coalition groups (which themselves are established according to subjects and committee duties). This process of shifting the parliamentary legislative and control functions towards a multitude of sub-structures leads to an 'atomisation'[61] of the Bundestag, with serious implications for the handling of European affairs. Given that the committee structure of the German Bundestag follows the differentiation of the executive branch, one can suggest that the co-ordination mechanisms at the federal government level amplify the process of atomisation at the parliamentary level.

Originally, the Bundestag disposed of very limited scrutiny powers; the federal government had to inform the two parliamentary chambers before any decision that would become binding law in Germany. These general rules were never applied effectively for three reasons: first the 'Article 2 [of the EEC ratification act] procedure' focused on informing parliament about European affairs but did not foresee a right of consultation. Consequently the parliament could not affect the federal government's stance in the Council of Ministers. Secondly both houses were informed about relevant EC documents only at a rather late stage. About 65 per cent of EC documents debated on the Bundestag's floor between 1980 and 1986 were already in force at the time of debate.[62] Consequently, scrutinising the government in EC affairs was limited to some kind of '*ex post*' control and did not provide parliamentarians with an effective involvement in EC policy-making. Thirdly, the Bundestag had shown little interest in scrutinising European affairs. Instead, the overall majority of its members supported the EP's claims for more powers and considered the Bundestag as a temporary substitute for the EP in the treatment of EC documents.[63] Furthermore the first fully-fledged and regular parliamentary institution for dealing exclusively with EC affairs – the so-called EC Committee (EG-Ausschuß, set up in 1991) – faced almost the same structural problems as its predecessors,[64] since it was not empowered to give the Bundestag a central voice *vis-à-vis* the government. Owing to the reluctance of other committees (especially Economics and Foreign Affairs) to share their powers with another body, the EC Committee was only rarely nominated as committee-in-charge ('federführender Ausschuß').[65] A major change in these mechanisms took place with the ratification of the Maastricht Treaty. The amended Article 23 of the Basic Law calls 'the federal Government [to] inform the Bundestag and the Bundesrat comprehensively and as quickly as possible'. Moreover, it obliges the government for the first time since 1957 to 'take account of the opinion of the Bundestag in the negotiations' (of the Council and its subsequent operative structures). In other words, Article 23 opens the door for some kind of a 'parliamentary scrutiny reserve mechanism' similar to that which operates in Denmark and the United Kingdom. But the need to take the Bundestag's view 'into account' is ambiguous and could mean anything between accepting the institution's view, incorporating elements of it or ignoring it altogether with an explanation as to why the government has decided to take a different course of action. Thus, the amendment to the Basic Law had to be combined with several reforms which sought to adapt the relevant institutions to the new situation. First, the government and the Bundestag agreed on a so-called 'co-operation law'. Secondly, both houses of the German Parliament amended Article 45 of the Basic Law to provide a constitutional basis for setting up a Committee on European Union Affairs (CEUA) in the Bundestag. The latter amended its Rules of Procedure in order to define the operational framework for the CEUA as well as the rules for the movement of documents between the different bodies of the house.

Given these shortcomings of the 1992 constitutional reform, it took the Bundestag two years to officially establish the CEUA on 14 December 1994. With fifty full members (thirty-nine members of the Bundestag and eleven German Members of the European Parliament), it is one of the largest committees in the House.[66] The prominent role of the committee is also underlined by the fact that – deviating from the general principle according to which committees shall only prepare decisions of the plenary – the CEUA can be empowered to exercise the Bundestag's rights in relation to the federal government or address its recommendations directly to the government unless another committee opposes. The CEUA acts as a specialist 'clearing house' of parliament. The government has no influence either over the selection of topics for deliberation in the committees or on the way in which the committees organise their work. If the EU Committee is designated as the committee-in-charge, it may submit a draft resolution to the Bundestag.[67] It is responsible for the receipt of all EU documents from the government and for filtering them into the other specialist committees. At first glance this innovation may suggest a major step towards a unified parliamentary position *vis-à-vis* the government. In this regard it was argued that, until 1992, the government 'operated as a unified actor *vis-à-vis* the Bundestag which was divided along departmental lines. Each departmental standing committee could only communicate its views with, and obtain information from, "its" department. Integrating departmental considerations into a broader European policy was difficult.' Now, since the establishment of the CEUA, the argument was that the Bundestag had a body which '– like the federal government, the Chancellor's Office and the Foreign Office – is able to deal with German policy comprehensively'.[68] Of course, comparing the CEUA's powers with its predecessors from a government perspective, one could presume that the committee is identified as 'the' central hub between the Bundestag and the government. However, given our findings on the characteristics and operation of the federal government in European affairs, one might have serious doubts concerning the view of the government as a 'unified actor', since the organisational segmentation and sectorisation of European politics in Germany was reinforced in the post-Maastricht period.

The implications of parliamentary scrutiny differ in every parliament of the Union. Following the Co-Operation Law of 12 March 1993, the German government is obliged to give the Bundestag full information on all EU documents in advance of the preparation for meetings of the Council of Ministers.[69] Unlike in most of the other parliaments of the Union, this rule applies to all three pillars of the Maastricht Treaty. Moreover, once the Bundestag has adopted a position on an EU document, the government has to base its position in the Council of Ministers on the Bundestag's decision. The Bundestag may ask the government to postpone the adoption of a common position in the Council of Ministers. In this case, the government is required to table a 'parliamentary scrutiny reserve' in the Council. In addition to this general rule, the Bundestag's Act of Ratification of the TEU obliged the government to consult the parliament prior to any decision by the Council of Ministers with regard to entry into the third phase of EMU.[70]

The EU Committee has succeeded in broadening the instrumental scope of its scrutiny mechanisms. During the 13th legislative term, it held eighty-four meetings and considered 903 of 2,955 EU documents forwarded to the Bundestag (30.6 per cent). In 174 cases the committee acted as committee-in-charge. This function was not limited to the deliberation of EP documents but extended to some of the most important items of the Union's rolling agenda – the EU Committee took up the lead for the IGC leading to the Amsterdam Treaty and for its ratification, for Agenda 2000, employment policy, the enlargement of the Union as well as for other institutional changes (the European Investment Bank (EIB), establishment of EU agencies, etc.). Even on monetary integration where it acted only as a joint-deliberative committee ('mitberatender Ausschuß'), it contributed significantly to the Bundestag's decision of 23 April 1998 on the approval of Germany's entry into the third stage of EMU. The committee chose the option of directly addressing the German government on three occasions:

on the proposal for a Council regulation on combating fraud, on the creation of an agency for the surveillance of racism and xenophobia and – together with the Committee on the Rules of Procedure – on the resolution of the XVth meeting of COSAC.[71] This last case is particularly illustrative since the vast majority of the Bundestag strongly opposed any upgrading of COSAC in order to control the Council of Ministers collectively. The roots of this critical posture *vis-à-vis* more formalised arrangements for inter-parliamentary scrutiny are to be found in both the positive attitude of German parliamentarians *vis-à-vis* the EP and in the fear that COSAC or similar institutions may aggravate the complex structure of European decision-making at the 'Brussels' and at the 'Bonn/Berlin' level.

The Bundestag arranged a rather timely management of the scrutiny process. Unlike its predecessors, the EU Committee became politically recognised by its 'competing committees' as a useful instrument for holding the government to account. Although the segmented structure of parliamentary activities still dominates the operation of the Bundestag in EU affairs, the EU Committee and its activities have helped to provide a broader range of the Bundestag's members with an understanding of the long-term and horizontal issues in European affairs. The activities of the EU Committee spilled over into other committees insofar as the latter began to invent new mechanisms of scrutiny only after the EU Committee started to work. For example, while the Committee of the Interior did not participate actively in supervising the government's stance in the implementation of the Schengen agreement,[72] it did oblige the government to report on each meeting of the relevant EU Council of Ministers' groups including the K4 Committee.[73] This change of approach occurred after the Bundestag's EU Committee had submitted, for the first time in the Bundestag's history, a 'parliamentary scrutiny reserve' on the signature of the Europol Convention.

The federal state: European policy-making down to earth

As federal states, the sixteen Länder have the quality of 'autonomous statehood' ('Eigenstaatlichkeit'). Two factors define the prominent character of the Länder as entities with an autonomous statehood: first, they possess their own competencies and are thus able to structure politics and policies autonomously within their territory. Secondly, they participate in the legislative and administrative process of the federation and thus play an important role in the decision-making system of the 'whole state' (Gesamtstaat). However, the 'process of European integration has posed a persistent challenge to the legal status of the Länder and their political quality as constituent states, and therefore also to the fundamental federal structure of the Federal Republic'.[74] Thus, whereas federal statehood is still guaranteed as a central and irrevocable structural principle of the Basic Law, the question has repeatedly been posed as to how far the balance between federation and Länder may shift without undermining the essence of federal statehood.

Whereas the Act of Ratification of the Treaty of Rome was combined with an obligation of the federal government to inform the Bundesrat only on legislative proposals issued by the European Commission, the establishment of the European Regional Development Fund (ERDF) resulted in the 'Länder participation procedure'.[75] The federal government declared itself prepared to follow the Länder views strictly if their competencies were affected by a draft legislative act of the EEC. During the negotiations on the Rome Treaties, the Länder and the federal government also agreed on the institution of a 'Länder-Observer' (Länderbeobachter), who is located in Bonn/Berlin as well as in Brussels, to provide information to the Bundesrat and the Länder.[76] The Länder-Observer is entitled to participate at each meeting of the Council of Ministers and to report on the latter's proceedings to the Länder and the Bundesrat.[77] However, owing to its rather modest administrative support – until 1998 there were only two full-time and one part-time civil servants working in its Bonn/Berlin and Brussels offices[78] – the Länder-Observer did not become a key position in the decision-making process between Brussels and the Länder governments.

Considering the complex structure that characterises European policy-making at the 'Brussels' and the 'Bonn/Berlin' levels, it came as no surprise that the primary strategic response of the Länder to the SEA was the establishment of some kind of co-ordination mechanism with regard to the federal state level as well as to the wider arena of policy-making in Brussels. Apart from the different participation procedures in EC/EU affairs, the Länder developed various activities to entrench their rights and to generate an independent capacity in the making of European law and politics.

The Länder established a dense network between Bonn and their respective capitals in order to manage the growing input from the Brussels arena. The most important developments occurred at the ministerial level. During the 1980s the first European policy divisions were created in those ministries which were indirectly affected by EC regulations or directives; this evolution followed the growing scope and differentiation of EC competencies. Both the SEA and the Maastricht Treaty induced a new momentum in this development insofar as every ministry nominated its own desk officers for European affairs ('Europareferent'). In August 1998 the 'Ministry' (Senator) for the Interior of Bremen was the only Länder ministry without a European policy desk officer.[79] The main activities of such officers are centred around the distribution among ministers of the European documentation which enters their ministry from either the Bundesrat's administration or the liaison offices of the Länder in Brussels. As regards the co-operation between the ministries (interministerial co-ordination), the European Affairs desk officers meet on an irregular basis in order to settle disputes and to prepare the draft positions of their Land government at the upper decision-making levels.

To co-ordinate European policy-making between the federal state and the Länder more efficiently, every Land government nominated its own European Affairs Commissioner (Europabeauftragter) or European Affairs Delegate (Europabevollmächtigter), occupying a post either as a minister or as a state-secretary. Such delegates act as a 'bridge' between their Land and the other levels of European policy-making by representing their Land in the 'Europe-Chamber' of the Bundesrat (a special institution for the co-ordination of the Bundesrat's European policy) and *vis-à-vis* the federal government. For this reason, most of these posts have been located at the Representation of the Länder at the federal state level in Bonn/Berlin.

As a response to the growing amount of EC legislation after the entry into force of the SEA, the Länder opened information or liaison offices in Brussels between 1985 and 1987; initially criticised by the federal government as instruments of an 'auxiliary' or 'competitive foreign policy' ('Nebenaußenpolitik'),[80] they quickly became a useful tool for the Länder to secure and pass on information from the European Commission and the German Permanent Representation during the decision-preparation phase. The liaison offices have also proved useful as a tool for advancing the specific interests of each individual Land *vis-à-vis* the European Commission, especially with regard to the management of the ERDF and to the settlement of disputes on state aid and the granting of subsidies with the European Commission's DG for Competition. Compared with the Länder-Observer, the Länder offices have far more administrative staff. In autumn 1997, there were 141 civil servants working in the offices of which 90 belonged to the higher service.[81] Finally, the creation of the CoR also prompted the offices to assist their Länder representatives in the preparation of the committee's meetings.[82]

Based on the Act of Ratification of the SEA, the federal government and the Länder agreed on a co-operation agreement which gradually extended Länder rights of participation in terms of the extent to which their powers and interests were affected by proposed EC legislation. The agreement also officially allowed the participation of Länder representatives in the working groups of the Council of Ministers and the European Commission. Building on these procedures at the Maastricht IGC, the Länder went a step further and successfully sought entrance into the core of the Council of Ministers as equal partners with the other Member States. With the amendment of Article 203 (ex Article 146) ECT and the revision of Article 23 of the German Basic Law, the Länder and the Bundesrat achieved new and important instruments for a more effective and direct interest mediation in the Union. In fact, the new provisions of the Basic Law opened the door of the Council of Ministers to the Länder insofar as it allowed for the appointment of a Länder minister (or another representative of equal rank) to represent the Federal Republic in the Council in cases where the exclusive competencies of the Länder were involved.

In clear contrast to the Bundestag, the Bundesrat adapted its institutional structure and instruments at a rather early stage of the European integration process. The European Union Affairs Committee – EUAC (Ausschuß für Fragen der Europäischen Union) – was established on 1 November 1993, though its general tasks and structure date back to 20 December 1957 when the Bundesrat created the first parliamentary Committee for European Issues in the then EEC. Unlike in the Bundestag, the members of the committee can be replaced by civil servants.[83] The EUAC normally holds a meeting every three weeks to prepare the decisions of the Bundesrat; if a decision must be made on an EU document before the next Bundesrat plenary session is scheduled then the so-called 'European or EU Chamber' (Europa- or EU-Kammer) will be convened. If operating, the chamber replaces and acts on behalf of the Bundesrat's plenary. As a general rule, the EUAC is always nominated as committee-in-charge. It consequently exercises much more power in setting the Bundesrat's EC/EU agenda than its counterpart in the Bundestag. As regards the scope of scrutiny, the federal government adopts a broad interpretation of the concept of 'EU proposals' to be forwarded to the Bundesrat. The latter receives virtually all documents concerning the European Council and the Council of Ministers.[84] Within the framework of the third pillar (JHA) where the Länder have considerable legislative, executive and operative powers, not only the proposals and documents of the Council of Ministers, but also unofficial papers drawn up by other Member States are transmitted to the Bundesrat.[85]

The obligations of the government *vis-à-vis* the Bundesrat are graded depending on the matter and the competencies of the Länder. Where EC or EU legislative proposals fall within the sole jurisdiction of the Federation but where the interests of the Länder are also affected, the federal government is required to take account of the opinion of the Bundesrat when adopting its negotiating position. Where a proposal is concerned essentially with the competencies of the Länder and their administrations, the federal government is obliged to respect the views of the Bundesrat. Concerning EC legislative proposals based on Article 308 (ex Article 235) ECT, the government must come to an agreement (Einvernehmen) with the Bundesrat in instances where the latter's approval is required by domestic law. Consequently the government cannot vote in favour of a proposal before the Bundesrat has given the green light. Where exclusive competencies of the Länder are involved, the

FRG is represented in the Council of Ministers by a minister of the Länder nominated by the Bundesrat. Finally, Article 23 of the Basic Law rules that laws transferring sovereign powers always require the consent of both houses of parliament. More importantly and especially with regard to EU action under the third pillar, Article 23 states that for 'the establishment of the EU as well as amendments to its statutory foundations and comparable regulations which amend or supplement the content of this Basic Law or make such amendments or supplements possible' a two-thirds majority is needed in both houses.

What has been the experience with these innovations so far? As far as the participation of Länder civil servants in the Council of Ministers' and the Commission's working groups is concerned, Weber-Panariello reported that in April 1994 250 Länder civil servants were nominated for the Brussels-based working groups.[86] This number steadily grew from 354 in 1995[87] to 450 in 1996. Since then, Knodt notes that the internal workload of the Länder has lead to a reduction in the number of Länder representatives.[88] Hence, for the 1999 presidency, the Länder appointed officials for 314 working groups, of which 189 are attached to the Commission and its comitology network, and the remaining 125 to the Council of Ministers' working groups. Accordingly, the Länder are present in 38 per cent of the Council's working groups. As regards the implementation of the Co-operation Law of 1993,[89] it seems to have functioned quite efficiently. During the 13th electoral term of the German Bundestag (1994–98), the Bundesrat considered 746 EU documents of which 124 were subject to resolutions covering qualified participation rights of the Bundesrat.[90] The latter asked the federal government to take its view into account in the case of sixty-three EU proposals. In twenty-three of these documents, the Bundesrat also called for the conduct of negotiations to be transferred to a representative of the Länder. Interestingly, the federal government accepted a decision of the Bundesrat in 1995 which called for the transfer of responsibility for negotiations in connection with all discussions surrounding 'audio-visual media', although no specific EU proposal was under consideration by the Bundesrat at the time. The wording of the Basic Law and its list of competencies would suggest a clear-cut distinction between 'federal government-related' and 'Länder-related' policy areas. However, apart from media policy where the federal government always transferred to the Bundesrat the responsibility for negotiations in the Council of Ministers, we cannot identify any other areas where a general rule is applicable. Hence, the transfer of negotiation powers remains a matter of dispute on a case-by-case basis. On the other hand, it should be noted that of the twenty-six decisions where the federal government initially doubted the Bundesrat's view of the applicability of §5–2 and §6–2 of the Co-operation Law, in most of these cases it proved possible to reach agreement either through mutual compromise or by offering the Länder joint membership of the German delegation to the Council of Ministers. With regard to EU legislative acts based on Article 306 (ex Article 235) ECT, the Bundesrat issued twenty-two resolutions. One could have suggested that the Bundesrat would adopt a rather restrictive view on the application of this article, since it always appears to extend the EC's scope of activity without amending the Treaty. In fact, in the vast majority of its '235-resolutions', the Bundesrat agreed on the federal government's line to adopt the legislative act under consideration. Conflict between the Bundesrat and the federal government generally occurred on the application of Article 23(1) of the Basic Law, i.e. on the transfer of sovereign powers. However, in three of the four cases from 1994 to 1998 the dispute mainly focused on the question of whether a simple or a two-thirds' majority was necessary to approve the ratification laws. Since the Bundesrat agreed on all of these laws by unanimity, the matter was always solved without involving a legal dispute.

Complying with European law: the challenge of bananas

The observed trends of institutional differentiation, specialisation and segmentation spill over into the implementation area. Institutional proliferation from the preparation, making and implementation of decisions stems from the fact that the decisive actors involved are the same in the three phases of the EC/EU policy-cycle. A civil servant responsible for the preparation and negotiation of a draft legislative act is also likely to draft the implementation measure ('Referentenentwurf'). These actors tend to be oriented towards the first two stages of European decision-making and are less sensitive to what comes after a given decision[91]: Civil servants would rather act in political than judicial frameworks. However, as the majority of them have studied law, they are aware that a potential dispute between Germany and the Union can be settled in the Courts. Accordingly, their orientation is focused on the early stages of the policy-cycle where they try to avoid conflicts which might later occur owing to their own failure.

More than 90 per cent of all EC measures requiring further transposition into national law fall within the competence of the federal State.[92] In these cases, implementation measures are adopted by a law of the Bundestag and the Bundesrat. In most of these cases, the legislator first creates the legal basis for implementing measures through a special law on the policy field concerned. Only after this law has entered into force can special regulations be passed in order to fulfil the substantive terms of the directive concerned. This process may involve considerable time lags, especially when the Bundestag and the Bundesrat – when there are specific Länder concerns – have to settle their dispute in the conciliation committee between the two chambers. As the EU moved beyond the peak of the 'internal market programme' legislation,[93] one could also assume that the implementation problem became less serious than it had been in previous periods.[94] Obviously, it makes a difference whether the actors concerned have to transpose 123 directives (as in 1992) or seventy-one (in 1995). Moreover, given that the Länder are more deeply involved in decision-making on EC directives and recommendations than any other regional entity in the Union, one could also assume a gradual evolution towards a better implementation record in those areas where the Länder have to transpose EC directives.

Table 5.4 Implementation record for Germany, 1991–2000

Year	*EU average implementation record %*	*Germany: Article 226 ECT Letters of Formal Notice*	*Germany: Reasoned Opinions*	*Germany: Cases referred to the Court*	*Judgements against Germany*	*Article 234 ECT: Germany*	*Article 234 ECT: EU 12*
1991	68.13	60	13	1	5	50	186
1992	82.27	97	18	5	6	62	162
1993	85.00	120	35	4	3	57	204
1994	88.59	90	66	5	7	44	203
1995	89.88	92	25	10	0	51	243
1996	93.45	62	37	8	0	66	243
1997	93.53	116	35	19	0	46	191
1998	96.71	88	46	5	6	49	240
1999	95.70	84	30	9	9	49	190
2000	93.81	92	40	11	12	47	184

Sources: European Commission, *Annual Reports on Monitoring the Application of Community Law* (1992–2001).

The information provided by Table 5.4 seems to confirm this line of argument. Germany's implementation rate steadily grew from 68 per cent in 1991 towards nearly 97 per cent in 1998.[95] However, implementing a directive – notifying the Commission that the legal transposition of a piece of EC legislation has been completed – does not automatically mean adequate execution. Furthermore, it does not prevent the national courts from clarifying whether and how far national case law has to be cleared according to EC law: problems with EC compliance arise in Germany where any law can be reviewed against the Constitution. German case law has gradually accepted the ECJ's theory of direct effect, the supremacy of EC law and therefore the capacity of a norm of Community law to be applied in domestic court proceedings and to overrule inconsistent norms of national law in these events.[96] However, the Constitutional Court regards itself as having the right to review EC law against the fundamental rights laid down in the Basic Law.[97] In this regard, the Constitutional Court's Maastricht judgement had a considerable impact, since it stressed the court's intention to review the respect, by EU institutions, of the limits to their powers, and that this examination may also apply to individual

EC acts. Hence, the ongoing litigation on the compatibility of parts of the EC Banana Regulation[98] with the Basic Law seems to indicate an attempt by German courts to challenge the supremacy of EC law. It remains to be seen if the Constitutional Court will decide against the general principles of the Union which serve as one of most important tools for establishing mutual trust between the Member States.

Conclusion: failing successfully?

In sum, both the constitutional patterns and the evolution of Germany's institutions dealing with European policy indicate an increasingly complex system which is characterised by an ongoing trend towards institutional and political pluralism. This process goes hand in hand with a segmentation of policy-making. Each ministry – both at the federal and the Länder level – shapes European dossiers in its own way and on its own account. The multi-level and multi-actor system clearly testifies a lack of long-term-based policy approaches and strategic policy planning, projection and policy-making. The broader involvement of the federal parliamentary chambers in EC/EU decision-making reflects the fundamental patterns of the governmental level (elements of segmentation and fragmentation) without 'parliamentarising' German EU politics in a way comparable to the Danish Folketing's approach (see Chapter 4 in this volume). In contrasting some of these characteristics, we can also observe a recovery of the 'Kanzlerdemokratie'[99] marked by a high strategic planning input from the Chancellery in European affairs. Especially during the IGCs, the power of the Chancellor to determine policy guidelines prevails over the principle of ministerial responsibility. Hence, the moves towards EMU and Political Union at Maastricht as well as the initiatives on flexibility and the partial communitarisation of the third pillar at Amsterdam were strongly influenced by the Chancellor, acting closely with the French President.

Major institutional and constitutional decisions significantly mobilise the German political system. In this regard, the last two IGCs were also stirred up by the German Länder which successfully asked for a firm recognition of the subsidiarity principle in the EC Treaty, the creation of the CoR and for direct participation of representatives of the Bundesrat in the Council of Ministers when it deals with matters concerning exclusive Länder competencies in Germany.

Apart from these developments which have amplified the complexity of the German EU policy structure, party politics and coalition dynamics have exacerbated the European policy-making style since the introduction of the Maastricht Treaty. In this regard, the trend towards 'institutional pluralism' in particular can also be explained by the fact that coalition governments do not adopt a coherent approach in day-to-day policy-making during their term of office. Instead, they aim to define the broad guidelines for the envisaged legislative term. But during this period, ministers have to balance the objectives of their political party on the one hand and the need to find compromise positions with their coalition partners on the other. Thus in the daily life of EC law-making, a minister may sometimes prefer to adopt a policy approach which corresponds to his or her party position and which may differ from that of the coalition partner and vice-versa. The patterns of decentralisation and segmentation may lead scholars to characterise the German system as unsuitable and as one of the main causes of the relatively weak German stance in the daily life of the Union.[100] Some therefore propose the creation of a Ministry for European Affairs or the assignment of a minister or state minister from within the Chancellery to deal specifically with European matters. The puzzle of German incongruity in the EU system begins, however, when looking at the outcome of German EC/EU policy-making. In spite of all the apparent competitive disadvantages, German politicians and civil servants show a comparatively high success rate in defining the fundamentals of the Union in most treaty amendments and revisions. Not only the principles of a social market economy and monetary stability but also subsidiarity, the 'parliamentarisation' and the 'regio-institutionalisation' of the EU's institutional–procedural system have been 'exported' into the Union.

Any attempt to concentrate European policy planning and policy-making within the federal government and/or between the government and its interlocutors (parliament, Länder, etc.) would interfere with the basic feature of the German politico-institutional system, namely its federal and decentralised structure, in institutional as well as in party political terms. Moreover, given the flourishing of network-building in European affairs across Brussels and Bonn/Berlin, it is far from clear that a central policy-planning and co-ordination agency would automatically lead to more consistent European strategies. Hence, one of the astonishing facts of the development of the Brussels-based and the German problem-solving arenas is the growing movement towards decentralised policy making at both levels of governance.

German EU politics face persistent patterns of interdependence – politically as well as economically. The institutional penetration of the German political system by European integration is considerably high. In exchange, the EU's institutional structure and mechanisms correspond to a considerable extent to the German arrangements. Bulmer defined this process as an emerging congruency between the Union and Germany – congruence with regard to the constitutional macro-structures, the normative rules which shape the decision-making processes (package-dealing, decentralised decision-making, coalition-building), the long-term policy programme (segmented, sectorised and sometimes even fragmented policy processes) and the substantive level (high-ranking policies and policy contexts at the two governance levels),[101] patterns of congruency developed over time. Germany's institutions have adapted to the multi-hierarchical and multi-centred structure in a rather effective way: they have not merely reacted to European integration as one of its 'subjects', rather they were and still are an important component of this structure.

Perspectives for the future: the shortcomings of centrality

What would be the consequences of creating a French-like central co-ordinating structure within the German system? The new body wherever it was located (Chancellery, Foreign Ministry or in a separate ministry) would be torn in two directions. One would be the improvement of mutual information and of horizontal co-operation without any ambitions of shaping a single German position and a coherent strategy. Hence, as in all collective organisations, internal communication could always be improved, but the competition among the actors of the German administration would set clear limits, at least in most policy areas. Moreover, there is no obvious, clear national interest which overarches sector-specific policy ambitions. Furthermore, the very process of European integration indicates that preference-building is not simply a matter of unilateral power politics, but is in itself a substantial part of the cyclical processes concerning politics and policies which move beyond the logic of the nation state.

The alternative role of a central body would be that of achieving a stronger vertical co-ordination backed by the highest political authority – the Chancellery. Such an approach would open a new way of dealing with EU affairs. However, given the deep-rooted features of the German administration, it is likely that such a step would lead to interbureaucratic fights – between and within ministries – which would spill over into the political realm of coalition governments. The battles would presumably reduce the mobilisation of civil servants and their day-to-day effectiveness in dealing with the Union's rolling agenda. Competition in political and administrative terms would become endemic, and with substantial authority, the Minister for European Affairs could become a 'threat' to the key ministries. Consequently, the specific legitimising power of the Chancellor would be needed in everyday life, according to her/his own will, and not only on major bargaining occasions. Besides the issue of internal competition for access to the Union, any conceivable permanent hierarchy could not be more successful given the complexity of the EU system. Whatever the abstract charm of organisational simplicity, such a solution may simply not fit in the complex system that has evolved to steer European integration.

Notes

1 I would like to thank Simon Bulmer, Beate Kohler-Koch, Carl Lankowski, Klaus Suchanek and Albert Statz and the members of the Friedrich-Ebert-Foundation's working group on European integration for their valuable comments on the chapter.
2 See Peter J. Katzenstein (ed.), *Tamed Power. Germany in Europe* (Ithaca: Cornell University Press, 1997).
3 See Simon Bulmer and William E. Paterson, 'Germany in the European Union: Gentle Giant or Emergent Leader?', in: *International Affairs*, No. 1/1996, p. 10.
4 See Andrew Moravcsik, *The Choice for Europe, Social Purpose and State Power from Messina to Maastricht* (London: UCL Press, 1998).
5 William E. Paterson, 'Muß Europa Angst vor Deutschland haben?', in: Rudolf Hrbek (ed.), *Der Vertrag von Maastricht in der wissenschaftlichen Kontroverse* (Baden-Baden: Nomos, 1993), p. 10.
6 See William E. Paterson, 'Beyond Semi-Sovereignty: The New Germany in the New Europe', in: *German Politics*, No. 2/1996, p. 170.
7 See Jeff Anderson and John Goodman, 'Mars or Minerva. A United Germany in a Post-Cold War Europe', in: Robert Keohane, Joseph Nye and Stanley Hoffmann (eds), *After the Cold War. International Institutions and State Strategies in Europe 1989–1991* (Cambridge, Mass.: Harvard University Press, 1993), pp. 23–24.
8 See Paterson, 1996, *op. cit.*, p. 168.
9 On the characterisation of Germany after 1989 see Bulmer and Paterson, 1993, *op. cit.*, pp. 9–31; and – with further references – Wolfgang Wessels, 'Zentralmacht, Zivilmacht oder Ohnmacht? Zur deutschen Außen- und Europapolitik nach 1989', in: Peter Weilemann, Hanns Jürgen Küsters and Günter Buchstab (eds), *Macht und Zeitkritik. Festschrift für Hans-Peter Schwarz zum 65. Geburtstag* (Paderborn, München: F. Schöningh, 1999), pp. 389–406.
10 See Rita Beuter, 'Germany', in: Finn Laursen and Sophie Vanhoonacker (eds), *The Intergovernmental Conference on Political Union* (Maastricht: EIPA, 1992); Andreas Maurer and Thomas Grunert, 'Der Wandel in der Europapolitik der Mitgliedstaaten', in: Mathias Jopp, Andreas Maurer and Heinrich Schneider (eds), *Europapolitische Grundverständnisse im Wandel* (Bonn: Europa Union Verlag, 1998), pp. 213–300; Mathias Jopp, Andreas Maurer and Otto Schmuck (eds), *Die Europäische Union nach Amsterdam* (Bonn: Europa Union Verlag, 1998).
11 Katzenstein (ed.), 1997, *op. cit.*, pp. 49–79.
12 See the coalition agreement of the CDU/CSU–FDP government of November 1994 and its paragraph on the 'Guidelines of European Policy'.
13 See the coalition agreement between the SPD–GREENS government entitled 'Aufbruch und Erneuerung – Deutschlands Weg ins 21. Jahrhundert', 20 October 1998.
14 See Leon N. Lindberg and Stuart A. Scheingold, *Europe's Would-Be Polity. Patterns of Change in the European Community* (Englewood Cliffs, NJ: Prentice-Hall, 1970).

15 See Oskar Niedermayer, 'Trends and Contrasts', in: Oskar Niedermayer and Richard Sinnot (eds), *Public Opinion and Internationalized Governance* (Oxford: Oxford University Press, 1995), pp. 53–72; Oskar Niedermayer, 'Die Entwicklung der öffentlichen Meinung in Europa', in: Jopp, Maurer and Schneider, 1998, *op. cit.*, pp. 419–448.
16 See Niedermayer, 1995, *op. cit.*, pp. 68–69.
17 See Helmut Kohl, 'Die einigende Kraft des kulturellen Erbes im zusammenwachsenden Europa', in: *Bulletin des Presse- und Informationsamtes der Bundesregierung*, No. 29, 17 May 1992, p. 343.
18 See Andreas Maurer, 'Der Wandel europapolitischer Grundorientierungen nationaler Parteien in der Europäischen Union', in: Jopp, Maurer and Schneider, 1998, *op. cit.*, pp. 301–364.
19 See Rita Beuter, 'State Strategies after the End of the Cold War. The Case of Germany', No. 28/97 of the TKI Working Papers on European Integration and Regime Formation, South Jutland University Centre, 1997.
20 See Peter Hort, 'Die deutsche Europa-Politik wird 'britischer', Bonn stellt das Integrationsmodell in Frage und orientiert sich mehr an Kosten und Nutzen', in: *FAZ*, 30 October 1997, S. 16.
21 Simon Bulmer and William E. Paterson, *The Federal Republic of Germany and the European Community* (London: Allen & Unwin, 1987), p. 13.
22 See Dietrich Rometsch, 'The Federal Republic of Germany' in: Dietrich Rometsch and Wolfgang Wessels (eds), *The European Union and Member States. Towards Institutional Fusion?* (Manchester: Manchester University Press, 1996), pp. 61–104.
23 See Jens Joachim Hesse (ed.), *Politikverflechtung im föderativen Staat. Studien zum Planungs- und Finanzierungsverbund zwischen Bund, Ländern und Gemeinden* (Baden-Baden: Nomos, 1978); Fritz Scharpf *et al.*, *Politikverflechtung. Theorie und Empirie des kooperativen Föderalismus in der Bundesrepublik Deutschland* (Kronberg/Ts.: Scriptor, 1976).
24 In addition, the German Central Bank acts as an autonomous institution.
25 See Christoph Sasse, *Regierungen, Parlamente, Ministerrat: Entscheidungsprozesse in der Europäischen Gemeinschaft* (Bonn: Europa Union Verlag, 1975); Elfriede Regelsberger and Wolfgang Wessels, 'Entscheidungsprozesse Bonner Europapolitik – Verwalten statt Gestalten?', in: Rudolf Hrbek and Wolfgang Wessels (eds), *EG-Mitgliedschaft. Ein vitales Interesse der Bundesrepublik Deutschland?* (Bonn: Europa Union Verlag, 1984), pp. 469–499; Elfriede Regelsberger and Wolfgang Wessels (eds), *The Federal Republic of Germany and the European Community. The Presidency and Beyond* (Bonn: Europa Union Verlag, 1988); Josef Janning and Patrick Meyer, 'Deutsche Europapolitik – Vorschläge zur Effektivierung', in: Werner Weidenfeld (ed.), *Deutsche Europapolitik. Optionen wirksamer Interessenvertetung* (Bonn: Europa Union Verlag, 1998), pp. 267–286.
26 See Judith Siwert-Probst, 'Die klassischen außenpolitischen Institutionen', in: Wolf-Dieter Eberwein and Karl Kaiser (eds), *Deutschlands neue Außenpolitik*, Bd. 4: Institutionen und Ressourcen (München: Oldenbourg, 1998), p. 15.
27 Fritz W. Scharpf, *Games Real Actors Play: Actor-Centred Institutionalism in Policy Research* (Boulder, Co.: Westview Press, 1997).

28 Bulmer and Paterson, 1987, *op. cit.*, p. 17.

29 Interview with a civil servant of the Ministry for Foreign affairs, 14 January 1999.

30 See Eckard Gaddum, *Die deutsche Europapolitik in den 80er Jahren. Interessen, Konflikte und Entscheidungen der Regierung Kohl* (Paderborn/München: F. Schöningh, 1994), p. 71.

31 See Article 65 of the German Basic Law.

32 The rules of procedure of the federal government define the Chancellor's Richtlinienkompetenz in §1 and §2.

33 See Wolfgang Wessels, 'An Ever Closer Fusion? A Dynamic Macro-Political View on Integration Processes', in: *Journal of Common Market Studies*, No. 2/1997, pp. 267–299.

34 See Gaddum, 1994, *op. cit.*, pp. 73–77.

35 On the concept of the 'Europeanisation' of domestic politics and institutions see Andreas Maurer and Wolfgang Wessels, 'The European Union Matters: Structuring Self-Made Offers and Demands', Chapter 2 in this volume and Robert Ladrech, 'Europeanization of Domestic Politics and Institutions. The Case of France', in: *Journal of Common Market Studies*, No. 1/1994, p. 68; Klaus Goetz, 'National Governance and European Integration. Intergovernmental Relations in Germany', in: *Journal of Common Market Studies*, No. 1/1995, pp. 91–116; Wolfgang Wessels, 'Institutions of the EU System. Models of Explanation', in: Dietrich Rometsch and Wolfgang Wessels (eds), *The European Union and Member States. Towards Institutional Fusion?* (Manchester: Manchester University Press 1996), pp. 20–36; Caitríona Carter and Andrew Scott, 'Legitimacy and Governance beyond the European Nation State. Conceptualizing Governance in the European Union', in: *European Law Review*, No. 4/1998, pp. 437–445; Jarle Trondal, 'Integration through Participation – Introductionary Notes to the Study of Administrative Integration', in: *European Integration online Papers* olymp.wu-wien.ac.at/eiop/allg/aktuell.htm, No. 14 April 1999; and Christoph Knill and Dirk Lehmkuhl, 'How Europe Matters. Different Mechanisms of Europeanization', in: *European Integration online Papers*, No. 15 June 1999.

36 Chancellor Adenauer was responsible for Foreign and European policy.

37 See Jens Joachim Hesse and Klaus Goetz, 'Early Administrative Adjustment to the European Communities. The Case of the Federal Republic of Germany', in: Erk Volkmar Heyen (ed.), *Jahrbuch der Europäischen Verwaltungsgeschichte*, No. 4 (Baden-Baden: Nomos, 1992), pp. 181–205.

38 See Daniel Koerfer, 'Zankapfel Europapolitik. Der Kompetenzstreit zwischen Auswärtigem Amt und Bundeswirtschaftsministerium 1957/58', in: *Politische Vierteljahresschrift*, No. 4/1988, pp. 553–568.

39 The creation of Council working groups is both a reaction to the Commission's policy in initiating new legislation and a mirror of the Council's activity with regard to the post-initiative stages in European decision making.

40 See Fiona Hayes-Renschaw and Helen Wallace, The Council of Ministers (London: Macmillan, 1997); Wolfgang Wessels, 'The EC Council: The Community's Decisionmaking Centre', in: Robert O. Keohane and Stanley

Hoffmann (eds), *The New European Community, Decision-Making and Institutional Change* (Boulder, Co., San Francisco, Oxford: Westview Press, 1991), pp. 133–154.

41 On the initiative of Chancellor Adenauer, the first FRG Minister for Foreign Affairs and the Minister for Economics concluded an agreement in 1958 on the repartition of competencies in European Affairs: accordingly, the Foreign Ministry only provided the speaker for the General Affairs Council. See Organisationserlaß [Organisational Decree] des Bundeskanzlers, in: *Bulletin des Presse- und Informationsamtes der Bundesregierung*, No. 203, 30 October 1957, p. 1864; Lisette Andreae and Karl Kaiser, 'Die Außenpolitik der Fachministerien', in: Wolf-Dieter Eberwein and Karl Kaiser (eds), *Deutschlands neue Außenpolitik*, Bd.4: Institutionen und Ressourcen (München: Oldenbourg, 1999), pp. 29–46.

42 Bulmer and Paterson, 1987, *op. cit.*, pp. 25–42.

43 See Regelsberger and Wessels, 1984, *op. cit.*, pp. 480–481.

44 See John G. Ikenberry, 'Conclusion. An Institutional Approach to American Foreign Economic Policy', in: John G. Ikenberry *et al.* (eds), *The State and American Foreign Economic Policy* (Ithaca: Cornell University Press 1988), p. 226; James G. March and Johan P. Olsen, *Democratic Governance* (New York: Free Press, 1995), p. 27.

45 See Organisationserlaß des Bundeskanzlers, Bonn, 27 October 1998; and the 'Vereinbarung zwischen dem Auswärtigen Amt und dem Bundesministerium für Finanzen', Bonn, 20 October 1998.

46 See Sasse, 1975, *op. cit.*, p. 28.

47 See Kabinettsbeschluß [Cabinet Decision] vom 16. Dezember 1998 zur Neuordnung der Kabinettsausschüsse, in: *Bulletin des Presse- und Informationsamtes der Bundesregierung*, Nr. 81, 22 December 1998, pp. 987–988.

48 See Sasse, 1975, *op. cit.*, p. 27.

49 See Note that the State Secretary of the Ministry for Environment Affairs was nominated as permanent member of the committee in December 1998.

50 See Organisationserlaß des Bundeskanzlers, Bonn, 27 October 1998.

51 See Sasse *et al.*, 1977, *op. cit.*, p. 12.

52 See Bulmer and Paterson, 1987, *op. cit.*, pp. 19–20.

53 This calculation is based on the data provided by the Union's Interinstitutional directory, Luxembourg, Office for Official Publications of the EC, March 1998.

54 There are exceptions: COREPER II meetings with regard to the Councils on ECOFIN, Budget, Finance and Tax policy are co-ordinated by the Ministry of Finance. The same rule applies to the instructions for the German COREPER II.

55 See Martin Westlake, *The Council of the European Union* (London: Cartermill, 1995), p. 312.

56 The ratio between Council and working group meetings has nearly doubled from 1/12.6 in 1958 towards 1/24.5 in 1995!

57 See Fiona Hayes-Renshaw and Helen Wallace, 'Executive Power in the European Union. The Functions and Limits of the Council of Ministers', in: *Journal of European Public Policy*, No. 2/1995, p. 562.

58 See Wessels, 1991, *op. cit.*, pp. 133–154.

59 See Jan Beyers and Guido Dierickx, 'The Working Groups of the European Union: Supranational or Intergovernmental Negotiations?', in: *Journal of Common Market Studies*, No. 3/1998, pp. 289–317.

60 See Phillipe A. Weber-Panariello, *Nationale Parlamente in der Europäischen Union* (Baden-Baden: Nomos, 1995), p. 198; on the term 'Arbeitsparlament' see Winfried Steffani, *Parlamentarische und präsidentielle Demokratie, Strukturelle Aspekte westlicher Demokratien* (Opladen: Leske & Budrich, 1979), p. 77–79.

61 See Wolfgang Ismayr, *Der Deutsche Bundestag. Funktionen – Willensbildung – Reformansätze* (Opladen: Leske & Budrich, 1992), p. 205; and: Steffani, 1975, *op. cit.*, p. 175.

62 See Ismayr, 1992, *op. cit.*, p. 330.

63 See Phillipe A. Weber-Panariello, *The Integration of Matters of Justice and Home Affairs into Title VI of the TEU. A Step towards More Democracy?*, EUI Working Paper, RSC No. 95/32, Florence 1995, p. 69.

64 See on the 'Integrations-Ältestenrat' (Council of the Elders on Integration): Uwe Leonardy, 'Bundestag und Europäische Gemeinschaft. Notwendigkeit und Umfeld eines EG-Ausschusses', in: *Zeitschrift für Parlamentsfragen*, No. 4/1989, pp. 527–544; on the 'Europa-Kommission': Peter Mehl, *Die Europa-Kommission des Deutschen Bundestags. Eine neue Einrichtung interparlamentarischer Zusammenarbeit* (Kehl, Arlington: Engel, 1987); on the 'Sub-Committee on European Affairs of the Foreign Affairs Committee': Leonardy, 1989, *op. cit.* and Alwin Brück, 'Europäische Integration und die Entmachtung des Deutschen Bundestages', in: *Zeitschrift für Parlamentsfragen*, No. 2/1988, pp. 220–224; on the 'EG-Ausschuß': Meinhard Hilf and Frank Burmeister, 'The German Parliament and European Integration', in: Eivind Smith (ed.), *National Parliaments as Cornerstones of European integration* (London, The Hague: Kluwer Law International, 1996), pp. 67–75.

65 See Sekretariat des Ausschusses für die Angelegenheiten der Europäischen Union: *Der Ausschuß für die Angelegenheiten der EU* (Bonn: Europa Union Verlag, 1998), p. 6.

66 The Members of the EP are entitled only to propose subjects for discussion and to give their opinions on issues of the agenda. Since they have an observer status, they are not allowed to vote.

67 The plenary concerns itself solely with Commission proposals which are submitted to it by the committee responsible together with a report and a recommendation for a decision.

68 See Thomas Saalfeld, 'The German Houses of Parliament and European Integration', in: Philip Norton (ed.): *National Parliaments and the European Union*, Special Issue of the *Journal of Legislative Studies*, Vol. 1, No. 3/1995.

69 See Gesetz über die Zusammenarbeit von Bundesregierung und Deutschem Bundestag in Angelegenheiten der Europäischen Union, 12 March 1993, *Bundesgesetzblatt*, 1993, I, p. 311.

70 By the Minister of Finance's reference made to the resolution, the German Constitutional Court, in its Maastricht ruling, 'constitutionalised' this special parliamentary scrutiny reserve.

71 On COSAC and other forms of interparliamentary co-operation, see Andreas Maurer, 'National Parliaments', in: Desmond Dinan (ed.), *Encyclopaedia of the European Union* (Boulder, Co.: Lynne Rienner, 1998).

72 See Raimund Schütz, 'Europaweite Freizügigkeit ohne demokratische Kontrolle? Überwachung der Schengen II-Konvention durch die nationalen Parlamente', in: *Archiv des Öffentlichen Rechts*, No. 4/1995, pp. 509–548; Andreas Maurer and Jörg Monar, 'Parlamentarische Kontrolle und Innere Sicherheit im Prozeß der Europäisierung', in: Hans-Jürgen Lange (ed.), *Kontinuitäten und Brüche – Staat, Demokratie und Innere Sicherheit in Deutschland* (Opladen: Leske & Budrich, 1999).

73 See Innenausschuß des Deutschen Bundestages: Ausschußdrucksache 13/47, adopted on 6 March 1996.

74 Rudolf Hrbek, 'The Effects of EU Integration on German Federalism', in: Charlie Jeffery (ed.), *Recasting German Federalism. The Legacies of Unification* (London: Pinter, 1999), p. 218.

75 This procedure was based on an exchange of letters between the Chancellor and the President of the Conference of Minister-Presidents in 1979.

76 See Elisabeth Dette-Koch, 'Die Rolle des Länderbeobachters im Rahmen der Mitwirkung der Länder an der Europäischen Integration', in: *Thüringische Verwaltungsblätter*, 1997, pp. 169–175. The Länder-Observer is based in the Permanent Representation but with a separate entry – symbolism matters!

77 See Günter Jaspert, 'Der Bundesrat und die europäische Integration', in: *Aus Politik und Zeitgeschichte*, No. 12/1982, pp. 24–26; Fritz Stöger, *Aufgaben und Tätigkeit des Beobachters der Länder bei den Europäischen Gemeinschaften*, unpublished paper, Speyer 1987, p 6.

78 See Stöger, 1987, *op. cit.*, p. 4.

79 See Christoph Schönberg, 'Europabeauftragte in den deutschen Bundesländern', in: *Die öffentliche Verwaltung*, No. 16/1998, pp. 665–672.

80 Ottokar Hahn, 'EG-Engagement der Länder. Lobbyismus oder Nebenaußenpolitik?, in: Rudolf Hrbek and Uwe Thaysen (eds), *Die Deutschen Länder und die Europäischen Gemeinschaften*, Referate und Diskussionsbeiträge eines Symposiums der Deutschen Verlinigung für Parlaments fragen am 20.–21. Juni 1986 in Stuttgart, Baden-Baden, 1986, pp. 105–110.

81 See Hahn, 1986, *op. cit.*, pp. 105–110.

82 See Lorenza Badiello, 'Regional Offices in Brussels: Lobbying from the Inside', in: Paul-Henry Claeys *et al.* (eds), *Lobbying, Pluralism and European Integration* (Brussels: Editions Interuniversitaires, 1998), p. 333.

83 The chairman of the Committee is elected for one year (in general from 1 November to 31 October) by the Bundesrat's plenary, after consulting the EUAC.

84 See the full list in section I of the Agreement between the Federation and the Länder of 29 October 1993.

85 In practice, the Secretary-General instructs the office of the EUAC to prepare the relevant dossiers. The office therefore selects the proposals which might be of interest to the Länder and prepares them for deliberation in the Bundesrat. Each Land and each specialised Committee can request the exam-

ination of further documents. When the EUAC or another committee recommends an opinion on a given proposal, the issue is put on the plenary's agenda for consideration. In practice, the plenary votes on the recommendations for an opinion prepared by the committee concerned. Debates on a recommendation are rather unusual.

86 See Weber-Panariello, 1995, *op. cit.*, p. 288.

87 See Rometsch, 1996, *op. cit.*, p. 90; for July 1995 see Rometsch and Wessels, 1996, *op. cit.*, p. 85, see also Rudolf Hrbek in Charlie Jeffery, (eds), *Recasting German Federalism: The Legacies of Unification* (London: Pinter, 1999), p. 224.

88 See Michèle Knodt, 'Auswärtiges Handeln der Deutschen Länder', in: Wolf-Dieter Eberwein and Karl Kaiser, *Deutschlands neue Außenpolitk*, Bd.4: Institutionen und Ressourcen (München: Oldenbourg, 1999), p. 158.

89 See Gesetz über die Zusammenarbeit von Bund und Ländern in Angelegenheiten der Europäischen Union, 12 March 1993, *Bundesgesetzblatt 1993 I*, p. 313.

90 See Sekretariat des Bundesrates, Qualifizierte Mitwirkung des Bundesrates in Angelegenheiten der Europäischen Union, Bonn, 31 December 1998.

91 See Klaus Winkel, 'Die Umsetzung von EG-Richtlinien in deutsches Recht unter besonderer Berücksichtigung der Erfahrungen in der Praxis', in: *Zeitschrift für Gesetzgebung*, No. 2/1997, p. 118.

92 *Ibid.*, p. 116.

93 In 1992, the Council passed 123 directives; by contrast, the EC adopted only seventy-nine directives in 1994, and seventy-one in 1995.

94 See Winkel, 1997, *op. cit.*; and Martin Gellermann, 'Beeinflussung des bundesdeutschen Rechts durch Richtlinien der EG', in: *Deutsches Verwaltungsblatt*, No. 9/1995, pp. 482–493.

95 Note that even the 1998 rate of 96.71 per cent means that Germany is for the first time above the EU average of 95.7 per cent and therefore went from 10th in 1998 (together with France) to 5th (behind Denmark, Spain, Finland and Sweden).

96 See Bruno de Witte, 'Direct Effect, Supremacy and the Nature of the Legal Order', in: Paul Craig and Craínne de Burca (eds), *The Evolution of EU Law* (Oxford: Oxford University Press, 1999), pp. 177–213, with further references to earlier works on this issue.

97 See the so-called 'Solange'- ('As long as') – judgements of 1974, BVerfGE 37, 271; BverfGE 73, 339.

98 See European Community Regulation No. 404/93, 13 February 1993 on the common organisation of the market in bananas, *Official Journal of the European Communities*, 1993, No. L 47. There is a vast amount of literature on the pending case. See, for example, Reich, 'Judge-made "Europe à la carte", Some Remarks on Recent Conflicts between European and German Constitutional Law provoked by the Banana Litigation', in: *European Journal of International Law*, No. 2/1996, p. 103; Manfred Zuleeg, 'Bananen und Grundrechte – Anlaß zum Konflikt zwischen europäischer und deutscher Gerichtsbarkeit', in: *Neue Juristische Wochenschrift*, No. 11/1997, pp. 1201–1210.

99 For the term, see Karlheinz Niclauss, *Kanzlerdemokratie. Bonner*

Regierungspraxis von Konrad Adenauer bis Helmut Kohl (Stuttgart: W. Kohlhammer, 1988).

100 See Simon Bulmer, Charlie Jeffery and William E. Paterson, 'Deutschlands Europäische Diplomatie. Die Entwicklung des regionalen Milieus', in: Werner Weidenfeld (ed.), *Deutsche Europapolitik. Optionen wirksamer Interessenvertretung* (Bonn: Europa Union Verlag, 1998), pp. 11–102; Josef Janning and Patrick Meyer, 'Deutsche Europapolitik – Vorschläge zur Effektivierung', in: Werher Weidenfeld (ed.), *Deutsche Europapolitik Optionen Wirksamer Interessenvertretung* (Bonn: Europa Union Verlag, 1998), pp. 267–286.

101 See Simon Bulmer, 'Shaping the Rules? The Constitutive Politics of the European Union and German Power', in: Peter J. Katzenstein (ed.), *Tamed Power. Germany in Europe* (Ithaca: Cornell University Press, 1997), pp. 49–79.

Select bibliography

The text (English translation) of the constitution of Germany can be found at the University of Richmond's constitution finder at http://confinder.richmond.edu/. Further sources on government and parliament of Germany can be found at Government www.bundesregierung.de or at Parliament: http://www.bundestag.de.

Bulmer, Simon (1997) 'Shaping the Rules? The Constitutive Politics of the European Union and German power', in: Peter J. Katzenstein (ed.), *Tamed Power. Germany in Europe* (Ithaca: Cornell University Press).

Bulmer, Simon and Paterson, William E. (1996) 'Germany in the European Union. Gentle Giant or Emergent Leader?', in: *International Affairs*, No. 1/1996.

Eberwein, Wolf-Dieter and Kaiser, Karl (eds) (1998) *Deutschlands neue Außenpolitik, Bd. 4: Institutionen und Ressourcen* (München: Oldenbourg).

Gaddum, Eckard (1994) *Die deutsche Europapolitik in den 80er Jahren. Interessen, Konflikte und Entscheidungen der Regierung Kohl* (Paderborn/München: F. Schöningh).

Goetz, Klaus (1995) 'National Governance and European Integration. Intergovernmental Relations in Germany', in: *Journal of Common Market Studies*, No. 1/1995.

Hilf, Meinhard and Burmeister, Frank (1999) 'The German Parliament and European Integration', in: Charlie Jeffery (ed.), *Recasting German Federalism. The Legacies of Unification* (London: Pinter).

Ismayr, Wolfgang (1992) *Der Deutsche Bundestag. Funktionen – Willensbildung – Reformansätze* (Opladen: Leske & Budrich).

Katzenstein, Peter J. (ed.) (1997) *Tamed Power. Germany in Europe* (Ithaca: Cornell University Press).

Paterson, William E. (1996) 'Beyond Semi-Sovereignty. The New Germany in the New Europe', in: *German Politics*, No. 2/1996.

Rometsch, Dietrich and Wessels, Wolfgang (eds), *The European Union and Member States. Towards Institutional Fusion?* (Manchester: Manchester University Press, 1996).

Saalfeld, Thomas (1995) 'The German Houses of Parliament and European

Integration', in: Philip Norton (ed.), *National Parliaments and the European Union*, Special Issue of the *Journal of Legislative Studies*, Vol. 1, No. 3/1995.

Smith, Eivind (ed.) (1996) *National Parliaments as Cornerstones of European Integration* (London/The Hague: Kluwer, 1996).

6 *Teija Tiilikainen*

Finland: smooth adaptation to European values and institutions

Introduction: EU membership as the beginning of a new political era

Finland joined the European Union together with Austria and Sweden at the beginning of 1995. At first glance, Finnish membership might appear as a rapid change of political orientation, given the inflexible policy of neutrality the country conducted until the early 1990s. In spite of the brevity of national adaptation and consideration, the decision to follow Sweden and submit an application for EU membership was based upon an overwhelming political consensus. All the major political elites, including party and interest organisations, the leadership, key actors in the private sector and the media were in favour of Finnish membership. In the referendum for EU membership in October 1994, the elites were supported by 57 per cent of the people which supported membership. One characteristic of the Finnish EU policy thus seems to be that it relies upon a firm and stable popular support. A division of the country, however, took place in the referendum and it is a division that has given expression to the limits of the governmental policy ever since. Membership in the Union was opposed by farmers and the rural population because it was seriously believed to risk their source of livelihood. The Farmers' Union was the most significant unitary force opposing Finnish membership in the campaign preceding the referendum. Its political importance has, however, been reduced by the reluctance of the agrarian Centre Party to join the opposition. The Centre Party leaders seem to have assumed that such a policy would block the party's road to government and, furthermore, the party will be increasingly dependent upon urban voters in the near future.

During the first years of membership the Finnish government adopted an enthusiastic and unreserved line of policy towards the Union. In the core issues of the Union's political future, Finland showed a high degree of flexibility and a preparedness to join the 'deepeners' of the Union rather than its Nordic neighbours conducting a more reserved policy.[1] Despite the generally positive attitude towards the Union, this position cannot be understood without paying attention to a particular factor affecting Finnish political thinking. After the Cold War era, and the difficult position of Finland between the two superpowers, the Finnish decision to join the Union should be seen very much in the light of security policy. It was seen as a decision to join the Western unity that had been beyond Finland's reach during the five long decades of the Cold War. This attitude did not limit itself to political elites but has been shown by opinion polls. Security remains an important factor behind the positive stand adopted.

The main constitutional amendments

The Finnish EU membership is perceived as a new positive challenge in the Finnish political system and seems to be strongly accepted by a majority of its actors. The membership has been put into effect by keeping the constitutional changes to a minimum. The act of joining the Union was not at a general level – for instance in the form of a transfer of powers, written into the Finnish Constitution. EU membership did result in a number of constitutional amendments, mainly concerning the division of powers between the different political organs. These amendments had largely been put into effect in connection with Finnish European Economic Area (EEA) membership in 1992. The main reason for the constitutional amendments can be found in the extensive powers that the president has in foreign policy. According to Section 33 of the Finnish Constitution Act (Form of Government Act): 'the relations of Finland with foreign powers shall be decided by the President, but treaties with foreign powers must be approved by the Parliament insofar as they contain provisions which pertain to legislation or which according to the Constitution otherwise require the consent of the Parliament'. In connection with the EEA membership, a specific Section (33a) was added to the main Section in order to balance the powers of the President and the Council of State in EEA matters, and to prevent the powers that by definition belonged to the sphere of domestic policy from being transferred to the president.[2] The 'Council of State' is the term used in Finland when the legal–institutional framework of the government is referred to. In certain contexts the term 'Council of State' even involves the president. The importance of the amendment increased when Finland joined the Union. The other amendment made to the constitution related to the EEA membership, and gaining more importance as Finland joined the Union, purported to confirm the parliament's participation in the national preparation of EU issues as well as its right to the necessary information. There have also been some institutional changes. The Grand Committee, whose role was to check the legislative process, has now been given a new task as a committee of EU affairs. The prime minister was given the obligation to inform the parliamentary committees of issues that would be handled in the European Council and the Council of State was given the obligation to forward to the parliament propositions to those legal acts. Approval rests with the parliament.

Separate from these EU amendments, there has been a comprehensive modification of the Finnish Constitution, which will result in a new Constitution which entered into force in the year 2000.[3] The amendments made in this new Constitution to the sections related to the Union do not directly originate in membership itself but are rather a reflection of the political aspirations to curtail presidential powers. In the new Constitution, the Council of State is for the first time placed on par with the president regarding foreign policy matters, making it a key actor in EU policy.[4] The Council of State leads the preparations of all EU issues, even those of the CFSP, and is responsible for keeping the parliament informed. Despite the majority of the eight new chapters of the Constitution being related to EU issues (under the title of 'International Relations'), there is a specific section governing the transfer of sovereignty, which is not included. The general articles of the new Constitution, however, reflect the change that has taken place in Finland's international commitments by mentioning international co-operation and giving peace, human rights and the development of society as its objectives.

The political priorities of membership

The Finnish membership in the Union was negotiated by a government led by the agrarian Centre Party and farming and farmers' unions and interest groups. Consequently, this group came to dominate the official agenda when Finland entered the Union. In May 1995, a new government was built on the results of the parliamentary elections which had been won by the Social Democrats. The new 'Rainbow Government' consisted of representatives of all the major parties with the exception of the Centre Party. The government that sat thorough the entire legislative period became famous for its pro-European policy. Unemployment was the key issue that dominated the domestic EU agenda and this issue was emphasised at the IGC.[5] The Finnish government consequently promoted a firmer EU position in the fight against unemployment. In the IGC, the government emphasised other policy areas with a clear connection to Nordic values such as openness and transparency in EU decision-making, the environment, equality between the sexes, and social policy. Institutional questions have been adopted with a more cautious attitude, however. In addition to these general political goals, the Finnish government has taken pains to launch a political programme called 'The Northern Dimension' in the Union. The essence of the programme was defined as emphasising the positive interdependence of the Union, Russia and the Baltic Sea region. The emphasis of the programme is on sectors such as energy networks, trade and environmental protection.

The parliamentary elections of March 1999 gave a clear vote of confidence to the 'Rainbow Government' which, consequently, continued the old party political composition into a new electoral period. There was a reluctance to make far-reaching amendments to the government. The new government also had major challenges to face in its EU policy. Finland's first presidency of the Union commenced in July 1999 and the agenda was expected to be filled with topics from EU enlargement and the implementation of the Amsterdam Treaty to the preparation of a common defence and institutional reform.

The national policy-cycle: towards a new decentralisation of decision-making

The starting point for the national division of labour in EU matters is the division of powers between the President and the Council of State (Figure 6.1). This is reflective of the entire political system. The clarification of this relationship has taken place in favour of the Council of State, implying a reinforcement of the role of the prime minister as the leading actor of Finnish EU policy. As the leader of the general foreign policy the president, however, leads the Finnish CFSP participation. Under the new Constitution, this role will take place in co-operation with the Council of State. The leadership of Finnish foreign policy in general will take place in co-operation with the Council of State, as far as the Constitution is concerned. In the Finnish case the main responsibility for the control of EU issues and the preparation of the Finnish position belongs to the competent ministries.[6] The relevant ministry examines an issue as far as its political, economic and legal aspects are concerned and formulates the Finnish position. The ministries are assisted by a system of sections that refer to different types of working groups with specific areas and issues to cover. These consist of both government officials and representatives of interest organisations. According to a 1998 Finnish study, the key position of ministries and their officials mirrors the practical exercise of powers and influence in the domestic EU process.[7] Interministerial contacts and negotiations seem to be another important channel as far as influence on EU issues is concerned. In addition to the increasing number of international tasks in the ministries, Finnish EU membership has led to the establishment of new co-ordinating bodies in the government. At the lower level there is the Committee for EU Affairs in which the ministries as well as the president's office, the Bank of Finland and the Chancellor of Justice are represented. The Committee deals with issues in which agreement has not been reached in the sections and with issues that demand more wide-ranging decisions. If there is a difference of opinion regarding the Finnish position in the Committee of EU Affairs the matter can be

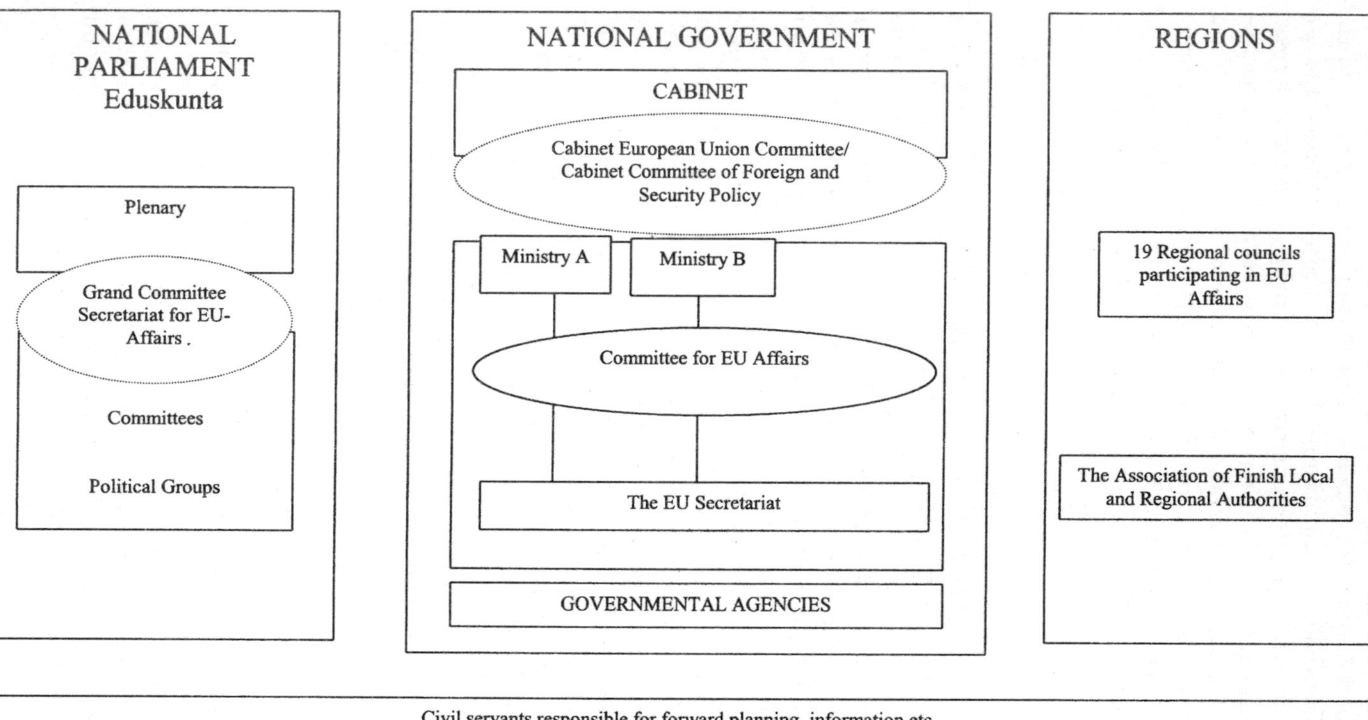

Figure 6.1 The national level of European decision-making – Finland

brought to the leading co-ordinating organ, that is, to the Cabinet European Union Committee dealing with general EU issues of great importance. The Cabinet Committee is led by the prime minister and all the government parties are represented in it. Owing to the division of powers between the Council of State and the president, the issues related to the CFSP are discussed in another Cabinet Committe – in the Cabinet Committee of Foreign and Security Policy that is led by the president.

There was even a new administrative unit established in 1994 to administrate the co-ordinating activities and to function as an administrative secretariat for the two committees. This unit, the EU Secretariat, is located in the Ministry of Foreign Affairs, but as the co-ordinating activities in general are firmly connected with the Prime Minister's Office efforts have been taken to move the EU Secretariat there.[8] A small unit of EU affairs was established in the Prime Minister's Office in 1996. Its main task is to co-ordinate preparations connected with the Finnish EU Presidency. The official Finnish contact to Brussels, the Permanent Representation of Finland in the Union, is the organ that takes the official Finnish position to the EU political machinery. It represents Finland in all EU institutions and supplies information on the activities of the Union to the Finnish administration. It is a large representation with a staff consisting of eighty officials representing different ministries and other governmental bodies. The role of the Permanent Representation has been considered mainly administrative and intermediary and its impact on the substance of the Finnish policy is secondary.[9]

At the level of the Finnish central administration, membership in the Union has implied a remarkable challenge to the traditional position of the Finnish Ministry of Foreign Affairs as the key unit in the administration of international relations. Its role used to be emphasised by the presidential leadership of Finnish foreign policy and by the direct link that used to be established between the Foreign Ministry and the president in the conduct of foreign affairs. At the beginning of Finnish EU membership, the Foreign Ministry had a good grip on its old position owing to the co-ordinating functions it was given in the national EU process. Now, this position is becoming increasingly challenged as it seems to be gradually moving towards the prime minister and his office.

In general, differences in decision-making procedures at the EU level are not taken into account in any systematic way in the national political machinery. The division of EU matters into first and second pillar issues, however, is reflected in the preparation and decision-making in the government as well as in the parliament. In the parliament, the Grand Committee prepares all the other EU issues with the exception of second pillar issues, which are handled in the Foreign Affairs Committee.

The parliament as an active actor in the national EU process
In the Finnish case the parliament can be treated as an active participant in the formulation of Finnish EU policy. Its role is based upon the constitutional amendments connected with Finnish EU membership and is carried out mainly in the form of committee activity. The role of the parliament was one of the major concerns related to the Finnish political system immediately before membership – a fact which still mirrors a certain awareness of the organisation concerning its own position. The system of parliamentary participation that was created in the Finnish EU system is similar to the Danish case with the exception that Finland's system is less centralised to one parliamentary committee. In the Finnish case almost all parliamentary committees are involved in the handling of EU issues.

The constitutional base for the Parliament's participation in EU issues can be found in Section 33 of the Finnish Constitution Act (Form of Government Act), according to which 'the relations of Finland with foreign powers shall be decided by the President, but treaties with foreign powers must be approved by the Parliament insofar as they contain provisions which pertain to legislation or which according to the Constitution otherwise require the consent of the Parliament'. When Finland joined the EEA system, a new sub-section (33a) was added to the main paragraph according to which 'The Parliament shall participate in the approval of those decisions taken by international organs which according to the Constitution require the consent of the Parliament in the manner stipulated by the Parliament Act. The Finnish Parliament shall, consequently, participate in the approval of those decisions taken in the EU which, according to an established interpretation of the constitution, would belong to its sphere of competences.' Provisions concerning the details are included in the Parliamentary Act (Section 54). The government must forward to the Speaker any proposals within the EU organs which the government has notice of and which belong to the parliament's competence. These matters are called 'U matters', referring to the obligatory character of the parliamentary approval. Most 'U matters' consist of Commission proposals for Council regulations or directives. Other categories are proposals for agreements between the European Community and third parties and a group of miscellaneous texts including, for instance, the draft budget prepared by the Commission.[10]

The Speaker shall submit such a matter to the Grand Committee and to any competent specialised committee for analysis and opinion. This takes place in the form of a communication, which also includes a tentative position of the government. The matter is usually handled first in a specialised committee, which gives its opinion to the Grand Committee. On this basis, the Grand Committee then expresses the view of the Finnish parliament.[11]

The position taken by the Grand Committee must be seen to imply a strong political commitment to the government which, in an overwhelming majority of cases, has not deviated from it. It must, however, be taken into account that the government's proposals, when submitted to the parliament, have the support of a parliamentary majority. In this case, the position of the parliament completes rather than modifies them.[12]

According to another paragraph (e) in Section 54 of the Parliament Act, the Grand Committee shall receive information and documentation from the government on any EU matter the Grand Committee requests, or the government itself deems necessary. There is still a particular obligation concerning information dealing with meetings of the European Council and meetings taking the form of an IGC purporting to amend the constitutive treaties of the Union. Concerning these meetings, their agenda, discussions and outcome, it is the prime minister that is obliged to inform the Grand Committee.

The constitutional obligation to inform the Grand Committee implies in practice that the Committee is given information about every Council meeting before and after the meeting. The Committee has a hearing with the competent ministers every Friday, the task being to hear ministers' statements regarding the issues to be decided at the forthcoming week's meetings of the Council. After these meetings, the Grand Committee is provided with a report of them and their results. As was already mentioned, the Grand Committee may even request information on the matters being prepared within the Union or the government may provide information of this kind on its own initiative. These matters are referred to as 'E matters' in which parliamentary approval is not obligatory. The 'E matters' have proved to be a useful instrument in relations between the government and the parliament, reflected among other things in their increasing number. As far as their substance is concerned, the 'E matters' are usually related to the pre-initiative phase of Community legislative procedure or to issues of large political importance in the Union.

The parliamentary activity in EU matters takes the normal forms of questions, interpellations, notices and reports. The number of EU-related notices and interpellations, resulting in a vote concerning the confidence of the government has, however, not been very remarkable. Until June 1999, only two interpellations had been made relating to EU matters and one EU-related notice (dealing with the Finnish participation in the Euro area) given by the government. A report given by the government to the parliament has become a common instrument when the government has been willing to leave its position on a larger EU matter to be discussed by the parliament. A report was given on the Finnish position in the 1996 IGC on EMU and on Finland and the future of Europe. Contacts between the national parliament and the EP seem to be quite modestly institutionalised in the Finnish case. The parliament is represented in COSAC by a delegation nominated by the Grand Committee. The parliament has also employed a special representative in Brussels. He is accredited through the Finnish mission in Brussels although his office is situated in the EP.[13] The secretariats of the Grand Committee, the Foreign Affairs Committee and the special representative together form the Secretariat for EU affairs of the Finnish parliament. The Secretariat is charged with co-ordinating the relationship between the parliament and the EU organs. Relations between national members of the EP and the national parliament could provide an effective link between these two organisations, but in the Finnish case, several problems have been noted in this linkage. The Parliament's relations with the Finnish MEPs are almost entirely carried out through parties and their parliamentary groups, implying that the MEPs do not have any established contacts to parliamentary committees.[14] Even at the party level, contacts to their own representatives in the EP seem to be mostly arbitrary. In small parties co-operation between party organs and MEPs appears to be more systematic than in larger parties that do not seem to be so dependent upon this channel of information and impact.

Other actors: interest groups and regions

In the course of the early years of Finnish EU membership, a majority of social and political actors outside the parliamentary system began to engage, in one way or another, in EU decision-making. Their channels of influence went, however, more often directly to Brussels than to the national system of EU decision-making. Actors from the economic sector adapted themselves most smoothly to the European system owing to their existing contacts and networks. For the time being, many new actors are establishing their positions at the European level. The largest Finnish interest organisations are members of their European umbrella organisations and a great number of actors, from cities and provinces to citizen associations, have established their offices in Brussels. Many actors have even co-ordinated their representation at the European level.

Of the largest Finnish interest organisations, the Confederation of Finnish Industry and Employers, which represents about 5,600 companies in the field of manufacturing, construction, transport and other service sectors related to industry, is a member of the Union of Industrialists of the European Community (UNICE) and is also represented in ECOSOC. The three largest trade unions in Finland, The Central Organisation of Finnish Trade Unions, The Finnish Confederation of Salaried Employees and The Confederation of Unions for Academic Professionals in Finland are all members of the European Trade Union Confederation (ETUC) and have established a common lobby in Brussels in order to promote the interests of Finnish wage-earners. The organisation representing the third main interest sector of the Finnish society, The Central Union of

Agricultural Producers and Forest Owners, is a member of the Committee of Professional Agricultural Organisations in the European Community (COPA). It is even one of the three Finnish organisations represented in the 'Various Interests Group' (III) of ECOSOC.[15] In the political field membership in the Union seems to have brought about a certain division between 'EU elites' and others. A great majority of the active members of the Finnish political parties, for instance, neither engage themselves in EU matters nor have any possibility of following the information flow coming from EU institutions. In spite of the fact that the international connections of the Finnish parties are constantly increasing, most parties have joined their umbrella parties or party federations at the European level.[16] Their international offices, or staff engaged in international activities, are still very modest. The parties' representations in the Finnish parliament have the best access to EU information – a situation which is largely based upon the practice of dividing the parliamentary preparation of EU issues between different specialised committees. Owing to its key position as far as contacts with the government are concerned, the Grand Committee has become somewhat of a parliamentary elite reflecting itself in its member structure.[17] The Finnish regions were not very well prepared to promote their own interests in the Union. One reason for this was that the division of Finland into administrative regions and provinces did not follow the more natural division of the country into cultural or economic regions. Membership in the Union has, therefore, emphasised other regional communities than those brought about by the state. Finland participates in the Union's regional policy in the form of nineteen regional councils that are not identical with state provinces. These regional councils function as promoters of regional interests with respect to the Union and are responsible for the implementation of its regional programmes.

At the lower regional level there is still another interest organisation representing the Finnish cities and municipalities. The Association of Finnish Local and Regional Authorities functions as their interest and service organisation in relations with the Union and provides the secretariat for the Finnish delegation in the CoR. The regional dimension is one of those sectors of Finnish political life that is going through vast changes in part owing to Finnish EU membership. Regional actors are gradually liberating themselves from the strongly centralised state system and are becoming increasingly independent actors with their own interests and identities.

Finally, the role of the Finnish media needs to be briefly discussed as an actor in Finnish EU politics. In general, the Finnish media has adopted a clearly positive attitude towards the project of European integration.[18] The most important daily newspaper, *Helsingin Sanomat*, has been the most explicit with its attitude by declaring openly a positive stand towards the issue. This importance of this attitude is further emphasised when one takes into account the enormous educating and socialising task which the media had during the early years of Finnish membership. The media was responsible for providing ordinary people, usually unversed in the forms and details of integration, with a level of background knowledge in EU affairs. This function reflected itself in a series of textbook-style articles or programmes related to various aspects of the EU system.

Control of EU decisions

Within the Finnish judicial system (which lacks a Constitutional Court), it is the Constitutional Committee of the Parliament of Finland that has the main responsibility for constitutional control over legal acts. In this connection, another legislative peculiarity concerning the Constitution must be noted, namely the possibility for a law to deviate from the Constitution without any explicit amendments being required.[19] Laws that deviate from the Constitution must, however, be predetermined through the same process as explicit amendments to the Constitution. The possibility to make deviations from the constitution without amending its text increases the flexibility of the Finnish constitution *vis-à-vis* international obligations in particular. It has also made the constitutional control connected with participation in European integration much easier. During the early years of Finnish membership the main task of the Constitutional Committee in this respect (that is, the evaluation of the compatibility of the different EU norms and treaties with the Finnish Constitution) was of a mostly technical character. Another important task which it adopted, and which evoked more political controversy, was linked with the division of political powers in Finland and to the implications of participation in European integration.

In the task of controlling the application of EU legislation, the Finnish Courts have not frequently requested a preliminary ruling to be given from the ECJ. By the end of 1998 the number of rulings requested under Article 234 (ex Article 177) was eleven. Of these, two had been requested by the Supreme Administrative Court and nine by other courts and tribunals.[20] The first case, in which a ruling was requested, dealt with the compatibility with Community law of the Finnish energy tax system. According to the claimant, the large Finnish energy company Outokumpu, the tax imposed on imported electricity must be treated as a discriminating tax prohibited by Article 90 (ex Article 95) ECT.[21]

By the end of 1997 Finland had appeared neither as a claimant nor as a defendant in the ECJ. The number of control procedures based upon Article 226 (ex Article 169) EC that the Commission had launched against Finland has increased year by year, as has the number of reasoned opinions given by the Commission.[22] In April 1998 the Commission for the first time decided to bring Finland to the ECJ in a case linked with Natura

2000, according to the Commission Finland having not delivered a complete list of areas to join the Natura 2000 network.

Conclusion: facing challenges owing to Europeanisation

In the Finnish case it is not yet possible to make a long-term assessment of how the process towards the Union has developed and what the role of the Maastricht Treaty was in this development. It is natural that irrespective of the indicators used, the 'Europeanisation' of the political system and the administration should show a more or less linear growth since Finland became a Member State.

During the first years of membership the proper political and administrative machinery was created in Finland for the national handling and co-ordination of EU issues. The key political concerns of this process were to safeguard the role of the parliament in EU decision-making and to guarantee the effective co-ordination of the actors participating in the preparation and decision-making of EU issues at the national level. The 'Europeanisation' of the Finnish political system has reinforced the political pressures towards a change in the division of powers at the highest political level. The prime minister, as the leader of Finnish EU policy, was given a new role in Finnish foreign policy on a par with the president.

The 'Europeanisation' of administration and the huge increase in its international tasks is reflected in an increase of staff and the establishment of new administrative organs. This process has, somewhat surprisingly, been far more modest as far as other social and political actors are concerned. Interest organisations, in general, have not maintained their former positions in the political and legislative process during the EU era; even political parties still have a lot of work to do in the development of their European representations and networks. Even if the referendum held in Finland 1994 on EU membership clearly divided the Finns into two groups, the division did not constitute a permanent new dividing line in Finnish politics. A clear consensus prevails among the parties and other political elites about the advantages of integration. The political campaigns preceding the parliamentary elections of March 1999 indicated that the political preparedness to deal with European themes was still in its infancy. In the second parliamentary elections after Finland joined the Union, national themes were still prevalent.

Perspectives for the future

The Finnish road to the ever-deepening union appears to be open – at least it is not burdened with too many domestic obstacles. The general political opinion in Finland is positive towards the deepening of European integration. It is openly admitted that the national adjustment to integration has demanded a lot of sacrifices, for instance, in terms of reductions made in the welfare state system or in supports given to Finnish farmers. However, it is usually admitted that it remains questionable to what extent these changes are a pure result of EU membership and to what extent they would have had to be effected irrespective of it. Finland's membership in the Union is an expression of the country's new political orientation, distancing itself from its Cold War heritage. This provides the framework in which its future political preparedness must be assessed.

The political debates around EMU and the 1996 IGC reveal the key elements of the Finnish preparedness for integration. From the beginning of its period in office, the Social Democrat-led Finnish government adopted a positive attitude towards the idea of Finland joining the EMU in the first round. From this stage until the summer of 1997, a majority of Finns were against this idea.[23] In spite of this critical opinion among the Finnish people culminating in heavy criticism among the supporters of particular political parties like the Centre Party, the Greens and the Left Wing Alliance, not one of the political parties was prepared to adopt a policy line that would have stood out against the government's position.[24] The EMU case reflected quite clearly the general political atmosphere in Finland *vis-à-vis* European integration. There are political controversies about details but no political will to question the general positive policy adopted towards the Union in general, and the deepening of it in particular. As the political debate around the 1996 IGC revealed, the Finns seem to be less prepared to go ahead with institutional changes in the Union than with other forms of deepening. The government's emphasis was clearly on the citizen issue; Finland supported the Union more strongly in issues such as the fight against unemployment and the promotion of equality between the sexes.[25] The openness and transparency of the Union was another important topic that was given much attention during the IGC. These were, in general, concerns that did not evoke much domestic political controversy. The main party in the opposition, the Centre Party, which takes a more reserved attitude towards integration, criticised the government for its unconditional commitment to the deepening of integration, yet this criticism was mainly directed at other issues than the citizen dimension.

Another issue where the government has taken a very positive stand, and also one of its key concerns in the IGC, relates to the development of the CFSP. In the IGC the Finnish government was in favour of increasing majority decisions in the CFSP and of the conferral of legal subjectivity to the Union. The Finnish–Swedish initiative concerning the reinforcement of the Union's capacity for crisis management was one of the highlights of the domestic debate. The domestic opposition becomes more clear-cut when it comes to second pillar questions. The issue that is most at stake is the future of Finnish military non-alignment. The Centre Party and the Greens have adopted a policy according to which decisions related to national security should be kept on a much more national basis than the government is willing to do.

The most critical question of Finnish EU policy in the IGC, and also afterwards, seems to be connected with the institutional amendments to the Union. In its position in the IGC, the government supported an institutional status quo – being thus unwilling to change either the present division of powers between the institutions nor the structure and decision-making procedures in them. It appears evident that irrespective of the Finnish preparedness to deepen integration, the maintenance of a clear level of intergovernmentalism in the EU's decision-making still forms one of the key Finnish goals. Clear amendments, for instance, in the position of the EP or in the direction of strengthening the second pillar, would be likely to raise heavy opposition throughout the Finnish political field.

Notes

1 The Finnish policy was from the beginning of its EU membership firmly oriented towards taking the country to the third phase of the EMU among the first tranche of countries. This took place while Sweden and Denmark stayed outside. In the issue of EU enlargement, Finland supported the Commission's position according to which negotiations should begin with six applicants while Sweden and Denmark raised a counter-proposition about starting negotiations with all of the applicants.

2 According to the new Sub-section 33§a 'The Parliament shall participate in the approval of those decisions taken by international organs which according to the Constitution require the consent of the Parliament in the manner stipulated by the Parliament Act. The Council of State shall decide on the approval and implementation of the decisions covered by Subsection 1 if the decision does not require the Parliament's approval and does not because of its substance necessitate than an order is issued.'

3 The purpose of this process has been to unite the present four separate constitutional acts into one unitary Constitution, the text of which will be modernised. There was, however, some other political intent connected with the modification process, part of which was to cut down presidential powers.

4 The new Section 93, replacing the old Section 33, states that: 'Finnish foreign policy is led by the President in co-operation with the Council of State.'

5 See e.g. Finland's point of departure and objectives in the Union's 1996 IGC. A Report given to the Parliament by the Council of State, 27 February 1996.

6 See Risto Lampinen, Petri Uusikylä and Olli Rehn (eds), *EU-asioiden valmistelu Suomessa* (Helsinki: Eduskunnan kanslian julkaisu 7/1998), p. 26.

7 *Ibid.* pp. 118–119.

8 The goal of transferring the EU Secretariat to the Prime Minister's Office was even written into the programme of the government that entered into office in April 1999. The change was put into effect immediately after the Finnish EU Presidency in 2000.

9 See Lampinen *et al.*, 1998, *op. cit.*, p. 119.

10 See Niilo Jääskinen and Tiina Kivisaari, 'Parliamentary Scrutiny of European Union Affairs in Finland', in: Matti Wiberg (ed.), *Trying to Make Democracy Work. The Nordic Parliaments and the European Union* (Stockholm: The Bank of Sweden Tercentenary Foundation and Gidlunds Förlag, 1997), pp. 35–36.

11 *Ibid.*, p. 34.

12 See Lampinen *et al.*, 1998, *op. cit.*, p. 125.

13 See Jääskinen and Kivisaari, 1997, *op. cit.*, p. 46.

14 See Mari Linnapuomi, 'Täällä Strasbourg, kuuleeko Helsinki? Suomalaiset europarlamentaarikot eurooppalaisen ja kansallisen tason yhteensovittajina', in: Tuomo Martikainen and Kyösti Pekonen (eds), *Eurovaalit Suomessa 1996* (Helsinki: University of Helsinki, Department of Political Science, *Acta Politica*, No. 10), pp. 247–257.

15 The other two being The Central Chamber of Commerce of Finland and The Federation of Finnish Enterprises.

16 The Finnish Social Democrat Party joined the Party of European Socialists in 1992; The (Conservative) National Coalition Party joined the European People's Party in 1995; The (Agrarian) Centre Party and The Swedish People's Party joined The European Liberal, Democrat and Reform Party in 1995, The Green League joined the European Federation of Green Parties in 1993 and the Left Wing Alliance joined the New European Left Forum in 1991.

17 The Grand Committee includes the chairperson, or the vice-chairperson, of several specialised committees.

18 The positive attitude of Finnish journalists towards European integration has been confirmed in an academic dissertation (Tuomo Mörä, 'EU-journalismin anatomia. Media-sisältöjä muokanneet tekijät ennen kansanäänestystä 1994', Helsingin yliopisto, Viestinnän laitoksen julkaisuja 1A/2/1999).

19 Finland has had four separate constitutions which were unified into the new Finnish Constitution in the constitutional amendment entering into force in March, 2000.

20 See Statistics of the ECJ, http://curia.eu.int/en/stat.

21 Issues related to the ECJ and the control processes launched by the Commission against Finland, Ministry of Foreign Affairs, Legal Department, the ECJ Unit, 1995–30 June 1998.

22 The number of control procedures increased from five in 1996 to eighteen in 1997. The number of reasoned opinions was eight in 1997.

23 In 1996, only 23 per cent of the Finns were in favour of a Finnish participation in EMU whereas 45 per cent were against this policy. A fifty–fifty situation between the two opinions was achieved in the summer 1997 (the opinion polls were conducted by Eurooppalainen Suomi www.eurooppalainensuomi.fi).

24 The Green Party did not take a stand on the EMU question at the party level, leaving the decision to its individual members. The Centre Party and the Left Wing Alliance demanded a referendum on the issue, but took a positive stand at the party level.

25 See Finland's points of departure and objectives at the 1996 IGC; Report to the Parliament by the Council of State, 27 February 1996.

Select bibliography

The text (English translation) of the Constitution of Finland can be found at the University of Richmond's constitution finder at http://confinder.richmond.edu/. Sources on government and parliament of Finland can be found at Government www.vn.fi/vn/english/index.htm or at Parliament www.eduskunta.fi.

Ingebritsen, Christine (1998) *The Nordic States and European Unity* (Ithaca, London: Cornell University Press).

Raunio, Tapio (1999) 'Facing the European Challenge. Finnish Parties Adjust to the Integration Process', in: *West European Politics*, No. 22/1999, pp. 138–159.

Raunio, Tapio and Wiberg, Matti (2000) 'Building Elite Consensus. Parliamentary Accountability in Finland', in: *Journal of Legislative Studies*, No. 1/2000.

Tiilikainen, Teija (1996) 'Finland and the European Union', in: Lee Miles (ed.), *The European Union and the Nordic Countries* (London: Routledge).

Tiilikainen, Teija (1998) *Europe and Finland, Defining the Political Identity of Finland in Western Europe* (London: Ashgate).

Wiberg, Matti (1997) *Trying to Make Democracy Work. The Nordic Parliaments and the European Union* (Stockholm: The Bank of Sweden Tercentenary Foundation and Gidlunds Förlag).

7 *Nikos Frangakis and Antonios D. Papayannides*

Greece: a never-ending story of mutual attraction and estrangement

Introduction: European and Greek identity: an ambivalent relationship and a gateway to modernity

When dealing with Greek attitudes towards the process of European integration, one should still bear in mind that in the 1970s and part of the 1980s, Euroscepticism – or even plain anti-European feelings – reigned in a large segment of both the elites and public opinion at large. Communists and radical Socialists depicted European integration as a subjugation mechanism mainly serving US interests – 'the EEC and NATO are the same barracks', to translate freely a slogan of that times. Given that after the fall of the Colonels' regime in the mid-1970s, there was important anti-American sentiment in Greece, Europe was consequently tainted by the same negative feelings. Moreover, power in the European Communities was perceived as residing in an excluding 'directorate' that was to be impervious to the needs of a small country like Greece.

In the late 1970s and early 1980s, the Conservative/Nea Dimocratia party of Costas Karamanlis, which had the initiative for Greek accession, openly considered integration into the Community as proof that Greece 'belongs to the West'. It was only when the ruling Socialist/PASOK party progressively adopted a pro-European stance – after initiating a much-discussed renegotiation of Greek accession – that the present situation of almost Euroenthusiasm surfaced in Greece. At the end of the 1990s, the Union was seen in Greece[1] as a gateway to modernity, as a source of financial assistance (mainly for infrastructure-building) and as a stabilising force in foreign policy.[2]

Today, only the 'orthodox' Communist Party is openly anti-Union, while a hard-line splinter of the Socialists (DIKKI) also has clearly negative reflexes. Yet these parties are small (in parliamentary terms, the two accumulate seventeen seats out of a total of 300). There is some uneasiness towards European integration from the Orthodox Church, mainly for reasons of cultural/national identity; the Church traditionally has had a subdued political role, but it has begun to adopt a more aggressive stance. Fluctuating Euroscepticism can also be located in dissenting factions of the ruling PASOK party. Under the present leadership of Costas Simitis, the party has a resolutely pro-European official position. Still, the dual shock from the Ocalan affair (the Kurdish leader who had earlier sought asylum in Italy, then was offered sanctuary in Greece, was granted refuge to the Greek embassy in Kenya only to be abducted by Turkish security forces when leaving the embassy) and from the far more important Kosovo crisis (where Greece sided quite reluctantly with NATO, while public opinion was vehemently opposed to NATO/Western intervention against Serbia) has brought to the surface the deeper question whether 'Greece belongs to the West'. The Union was seen in this context as absent and ineffectual in crisis, especially in matters important to Greece.

Among economic elites one finds clear pro-EU reflexes.[3] Intellectual/political elites are less reliable in their European attachment, notwithstanding the fact that it was among academics that much of the early support for European integration was mustered in the early years of Euroscepticism. Foreign policy considerations and the social impact of the protracted stabilisation policies needed to open the way to Euro participation are the main sources of elite scepticism. The press and electronic media provide mainly pro-European coverage. Greek participation in the third stage of EMU in 2001 was generally touted as the paramount policy objective.

Constitutional changes and political adaptations to accommodate the EU legal system

The ratification of the Treaty of Accession of Greece to the (then) European Communities was based on Article 28 §3 of the Greek Constitution passed by a vote of simple majority in Parliament. There was debate over ratification, with arguments that a three-fifths majority or even a constitutional referendum was needed to operate the transfer of sovereignty that accession entailed. This debate was sidetracked when in 1981 PASOK gained government and was keen not to jeopardise Greek accession. Future calls for referendum ratification of the SEA, the Maastricht Treaty and the Amsterdam Treaty were ignored at minimal political cost.[4]

In the first phases of Greek participation, there was some scepticism concerning the eventuality of a federal structure of Europe and support for a more intergovernmental approach to European integration. There was a preference for unanimous voting and/or veto power for a wide range of matters considered of importance to national interests. Nonetheless, since the end of the 1980s, public support for federal-type unification grew. During the negotiation and ratification of the

Maastricht and the Amsterdam Treaties, both the government and the opposition were in favour of increased majority voting, of wider powers to the Commission and a more central role for the EP.[5] Paradoxically this stance has not succeeded in terms of foreign policy issues. EU relations with FYROM/Macedonia or with Turkey have hardened Greek support for the veto mechanism and/or unanimity voting in sensitive issues.

European matters did not play a key (nor even an important) role in the successive parliamentary elections (1981, 1985 or the triple elections of 1989–90). By the time of the 1993 and the 1996 elections an overall consensus towards Europe had been achieved among the largest parties, so any discussion of European matters at election time is now perfunctory. It could be said that even the European elections of 1984, 1989 and 1994 had scant 'European' interest and served mainly as an arena for contesting national issues and rivalries.

Central policy issues and the EU dimension: reflexes and memories carry long shadows

Ever since the Maastricht Treaty, the Greek political system has had to deal with the twin problems of foreign policy and economic stabilisation. Foreign policy issues have been associated with the post-Cold War recasting of Balkan relationships – ominously enough, also of some redrawing of borders – and with the residual enmity with neighbouring Turkey which culminated in the Imia islets incident of early 1996 and remains entangled with the long-simmering Cyprus issue. The belated stabilisation of the economy, as well as efforts to meet convergence criteria that would keep Greek eligible for Euro accession gained importance in public consciousness. The government would like to wish foreign policy issues away, but to the public opinion 'national issues' (as they are characteristically termed) remain a major concern. Steering the Greek economy towards the Union has been a major political gamble for the Simitis government; the fact that foreign policy issues often involve the Union in what is considered a 'Balkan mess' causes further complications, distracting public opinion from Euro objectives.

Having to face acute national phobias and a lack of direction, the government and a large segment of the press explained at great length that the only foreign policy challenge that really mattered for Greece was participation in the third stage of EMU. Once Greece is fully immersed in European integration, the threats and insecurities of the Balkans and the East Mediterranean were expected to dissipate.[6] The far more important disruption brought about by the Kosovo crisis deepened the drift between Greek public opinion and European priorities; while official policy found itself at odds with popular feeling, an identity crisis ensued, influencing the image of Europe in public opinion.

The national policy-cycle: from a closed-circuit business to an open system

Greece is and remains a centralised state, with the government assuming the focal role and parliament used as a means to legitimate choices already made (Figure 7.1). Local or regional government has had little or no worthwhile participation in EC matters. Recent institutional changes in Greece may alter the balance, but until now such tiers of government intervene only in the implementation of (EU-financed) infrastructure-building. This activity is delegated (at EU insistence) by central government to operational mechanisms with local and regional participation along with EU control.

The real 'beneficiaries' of change brought about in Greek decision-making processes by EU participation are administrative bodies involved in EC/EU affairs. The accession negotiations made little use of the competence of Greek administration. Adaptation of the Greek legal order to the 'acquis communautaire' and the transposition of secondary EU legislation usually took place by decree. This occurs under a blanket authorisation voted along with primary law ratification and in the most simplified way (rubber-stamping the translated EU texts, at times with odd results). The assertion that administrations have earned powers and influence may seem odd. However, with the Greek political system's inability to study and deal with technical matters, either of an EU or internal nature, and the parliament's role of a domesticated follower of the government, the administration has seen its effective function devalued Throughout the administration, 'pockets of competence' have been formed and have learned in practice to interact with Brussels. It is through them that the whole system has contact with EU mechanisms.

Ever since the accession of Greece to the then European Community, there has been constant talk of establishing a Ministry for EC/EU affairs, but such projects have never come to fruition. Co-ordinating authority has been shared by the Ministry of Foreign Affairs and the Ministry for National Economy (previously the Co-Ordination Ministry), depending mainly on the personality of ministers. Some co-ordination has at times been exercised at prime minister level. The most enduring form of co-ordination has been the operation of interministerial committees. These meetings have been infrequent at the ministerial level; instead they have worked at the Secretary-General and/or Ministers' assistant level.

The Ministry of Foreign Affairs and the Ministry for National Economy traditionally have Alternate Ministers or Under-Secretaries in charge of European Affairs. Ministries with important European connections, such as the Ministry of Agriculture, and the Ministry of Labour and Social Services, have in their organisational set-up Secretariats-General for European Affairs. Most other Ministries have European Affairs

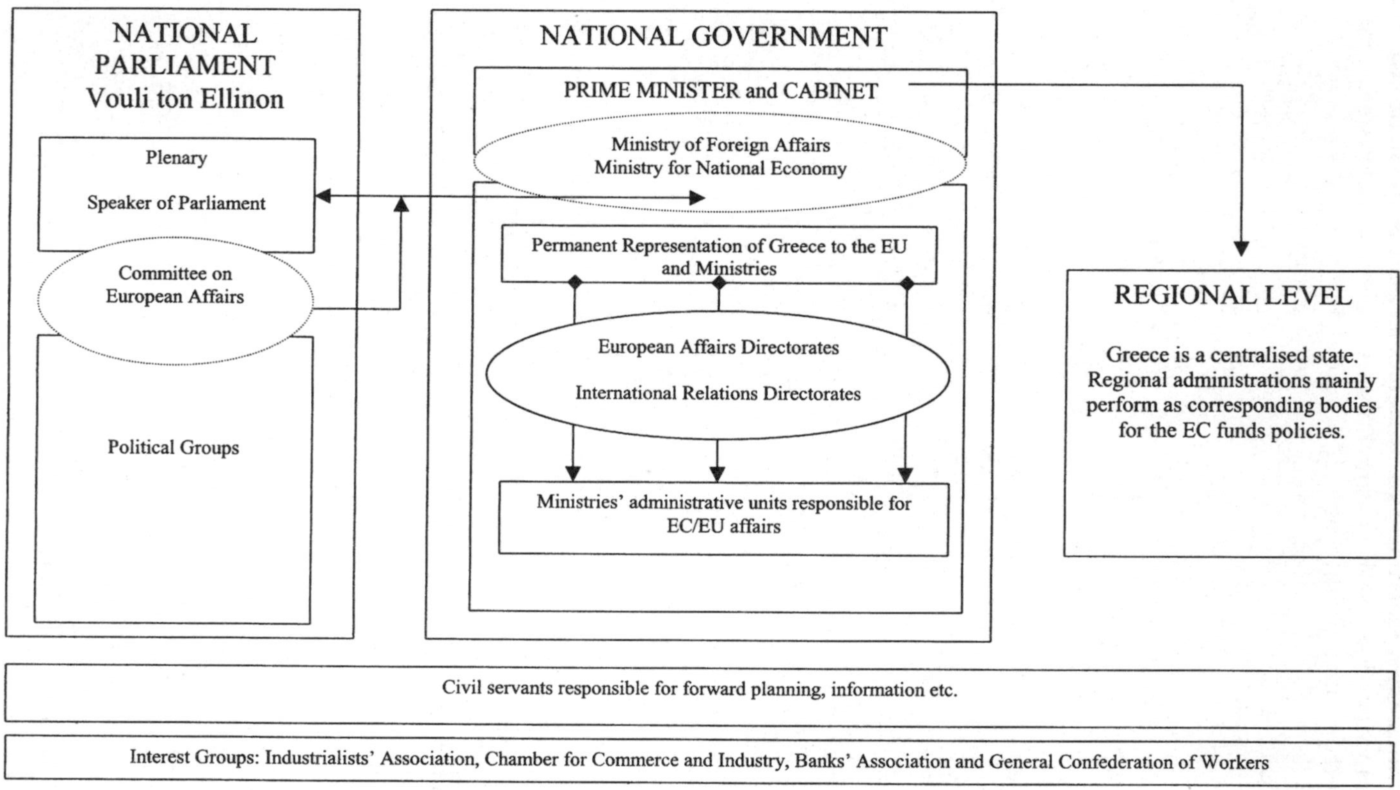

Figure 7.1 The national level of European decision-making – Greece

Directorates, often reporting directly to the Minister or to the Minister's Office. In cases less involved with Brussels, European Affairs are dealt with in the context of International Relations Directorates. Participation in daily Brussels negotiating routines is through expert missions and by the attendance of officials detached at the Permanent Representation. Now numbering some eighty people, the Permanent Representation has a core of some fifteen diplomats and detached officials of Ministries. There have been times where co-ordination has been exercised by the Permanent Representation, to the annoyance of specialised ministries which have occasionally reacted by a form of passive resistance. An example concerns the Ministry of Foreign Affairs, which has had the upper hand in co-ordinating EU policy.

Relations with the EP are conducted sporadically and in no specially organised way, with the exception of foreign policy issues, for which a sort of permanent briefing is usually in place at the Ministry of Foreign Affairs. The Greek Parliament's monitoring of European affairs is conducted mainly through the Parliamentary Committee on European Affairs in a rather rudimentary and unsystematic manner. Greek MEPs are loosely associated with domestic parliamentary activities relating to the EP's competences. The Speaker of Greek Parliament has also created his own mini 'diplomatic' service. In recent years close operational links have been developed at both the Central Bank Governors' and the Monetary Committee level, along with increasing priority given by the government to EMU third-phase participation.[7]

EU decision-making as a 'black box'

The decision-making procedures of the Union are considered by the administration rather in the form of a 'black box'; the emphasis is on forming Greek negotiating positions, securing government approval and adhering to them. Differentiation between the three pillars, as can be found in practice, flows from the 'closed circuit' approach to foreign affairs (and security) matters and internal security/justice issues. CFSP matters are considered 'high politics' and the 'domaine réserve' of a closed circle of diplomats and advisors of the Minister of Foreign Affairs. An important priority is to ensure that no positions are taken that may lead to public or media criticism. Foreign Affairs and the Ministries of Public Order and Justice co-operate – somewhat uneasily – on internal security matters. However, there exists an 'inward-looking' tradition which prefers adherence to positions rather than negotiation. The more central role of the EP in first pillar EU matters is gradually increasing. MEPs are briefed more often, but contacts with them are mainly through the Ministry of Foreign Affairs or the Permanent Representation. Its non-systematic nature, however, means that the potential of influencing decisions has not been fully utilised. National MEPs tend to be consulted and it has only been in vital foreign affairs issues that there has been any systematic links to other European MPs.[8]

The perfunctory function of parliamentary scrutiny

The Greek Parliament has been frustrated by its decreased role in European policy-making and national law-making. Following the ratification of the Maastricht Treaty, a Standing Committee for European Affairs was formed, to which a general report on European issues and government activities has to be submitted annually. Ministers are expected to brief this Committee and be available for specific parliamentary questions and hearings. After some initial enthusiasm, the level of effective scrutiny through the Committee for European Affairs has been rather low and government officials have been reluctant to appear before it. Hearings have grown to be somewhat of a formality. More important, high-visibility issues involving European affairs are dealt with in the normal parliamentary procedure but, again, effective scrutiny is absent. Debates over European affairs are usually exchanges of established party polemics. The government treats the parliament's demands for more information and involvement in European Affairs in a rather detached way.[9] Senior ministers rarely appear to defend or explain position at plenary sessions. EU affairs are usually dealt with long after their newsworthiness has evaporated and debate is usually derailed by general party bickering. Prime Minister's question time rarely touches on EU matters, and when doing so, it does it in a perfunctory way. The opposition also uses this arena to criticise the government and rarely raise questions of essence.

The EU as an awakening mechanism for reluctant Greek actors

Local government has been trying to gain direct access to parts of European decision-making mechanisms. Infrastructure financing and environment are the main fields of such contacts, but research programmes, Social Fund actions or cultural programmes have also proved of growing interest to local authorities. Their efforts to move from rubber-stamping to a more responsible involvement have not so far proved very successful, however. Regions in Greece have yet to obtain an effective political role, so in fact it is first-level local authorities who have been active in EU matters, depending mainly on local politicians' degree of awareness and outward-looking reflexes.

Political parties and the media – who have a tradition of heavily politicised/partisan coverage – have used European affairs as an instrument for political battle; positions used to be more clear-cut and polemical in the 1980s than is now the case. It is interesting to note that 'Europe' or 'Brussels' is often considered by opposition parties or the press as a way to obstruct or influence government decisions. It is even more interesting to see how little the intricacies – or indeed the basics – of EU decision-making are understood. Commission proposals or EP reports are quite often referred to as 'Brussels decisions'.[10] PASOK's shift from Euro-negativism to Euro-enthusiasm has hardly made party debate over 'Europe' more technical in nature. The same goes for the main opposition party, Nea Dimocratia, notwithstanding the fact that it portrays itself as the party that brought about accession to the Union. Likewise, the Eurocommunists have taken a less analytical approach to European affairs.

This reflex of using 'Brussels' as an appeals mechanism was characteristic of interest groups and single economic actors in the first decade of Greek membership. Successive Greek governments and the administration did quite a lot of foot-dragging in adapting to Community rules: the Union was regarded more a 'complaints-receiving apparatus'. More recently, interest groups have been establishing more permanent links with EU institutions. For instance, the Industrialists' Association, the Chamber for Commerce and Industry, the Banks' Association and the General Confederation of Workers established more or less active Brussels offices, and they also integrated Brussels positions and priorities into their way of dealing with policy issues. Both industry and the unions have been increasingly using Europe not only as a lobbying field but also as a source for ideology formation. The whole political discourse about competitiveness, social consensus-building and participation, and the 'modernisation' objective – which has become official ideology – all have been heavily influenced by interaction with Europe and European institutions. When the overall assessment of Greece's participation in the Union is made, this aspect may appear as the most important one for introducing change in Greek political life.

Specific businesses, especially those active in high-technology fields or having undertaken modernisation efforts with the support of EU funding or through R&D in association with EU programmes, have shown an increasing willingness to establish their own links with Brussels and/or to involve themselves in EU-sponsored networks. What began in the 1980s as an interesting but limited phenomenon has grown to quite appreciable proportions, working as a mechanism for modernisation. A similar chain of influence has been working in academia; beginning with science and technology programmes, wider academic circles have been in contact with Brussels. Networks have been sponsored or influenced by the Union; this has provided them not only with financial means, but also with research links and market outlets. At an introspective time for the Greek higher education system, this has proved exceptionally important, reciprocated by increasing involvement of academics in EU-related policy-making.

The gradual introduction of Community law in the Greek legal system: the foundations for acceptance of Community law

Community law had a successful and rather rapid introduction in the Greek legal system. Greek courts, from an early stage in EC membership, deferred to Community law in conflicting cases.[11] Many factors contributed to this. It was the tradition for Greek lawyers to obtain postgraduate training abroad, particularly during the 1970s and early 1980s. Such training is reflected in the reasoning of court decisions but also in the tendency of lawyers to have recourse to Community law as a supplementary means of redress. The legal argument may not have always been very deep, but the use of Community rules is increasingly present. Community law has been mainly used in areas such as equal pay for men and women and the application of Regulation 1408/71, as well as the consequences of Commission agricultural policy decisions (mainly decisions on olive oil, tomato paste and tobacco subsidies). Subsequently, the inventive use of company law directives has been instrumental for testing the legality of a series of de facto nationalisation decisions concerning 'problem undertakings'. The rules on free establishment have helped to focus on contentious issues like the right to private higher education and the acquisition of property in borderline areas or free radio and television services or the opening of public administration to foreign nationals.[12]

The courts get to know Community law: a gradual learning process

Even before accession, the Greek Supreme Administrative Court (Symvoulio tis Epikrateias) largely accepted the mainstream principles of Community law.[13] Soon after accession, the Special Supreme Court adopted the procedure for the election of Greek MEPs to the European Parliament (Ruling 10/1982). Thus, Community competence is readily accepted. When the Greek Supreme Administrative Court had to deal with an equal pay matter, the help of Article 141 (ex Article 119) of the EEC Treaty was invoked by members of the Court to supplement arguments of municipal law.[14] Soon thereafter, with its decision on the *Banana Case*, the Greek Supreme Administrative Court began to make direct use of primary Community law, e.g. the Act of Accession.[15] The case was referred to the Full Court by a ruling of the Fourth Chamber; it was heard twice in Full Court to allow for the argument to be complete. In a case where the self-executing character of a Commission decision was discussed, the Greek Supreme Administrative Court referred to the ECJ[16] for a preliminary ruling under Article 234 (ex Article 177). The ECJ replied with the decision of 28 October 1987,[17] following which the Greek Supreme Administrative Court ruled finally on the matter.[18] From then on, both preliminary rulings under Article 234 and application of Community law have been unimpeded in administrative courts.

The civil courts have been somewhat slower in gaining a sure footing in the application of Community law. There were hesitations about accepting Community law and of adequate argumentation. When cases of equal pay, or of extradition were heard at the Supreme Civil Court,[19] the relevant provisions were examined almost as curiosity items. However, Community law is gradually becoming more familiar.

Both the direct effect and the primacy of Community law has been accepted in the Greek legal order with little resistance from the Courts, although the Greek administration is far less enthusiastic in adopting it. The 'dialogue' between the Greek Supreme Administrative Court and the ECJ in the case of the de facto nationalisation of the Bank for Central Greece shows the limits of a collaboration between judges that has been generally satisfactory.[20]

At the end of the day the comment of Dimitris Evrigenis, one of the most important figures in giving effective content to Greek accession, proved prophetic: 'Good application of EEC rules by the courts means that we do not hear much about them.'

Positions on institutional change: soft landing or hard decisions?

The 1996–97 IGC debate did not generate real interest in Greece, either in public opinion or in the political system. That debate, such as there was, was about concepts like the democratic deficit of European institutions, majority voting, evolution towards federal forms and so forth, which at no time managed to secure any operational content in the minds of those engaged in the debate and were used rather as code-words to prove involvement.

What was more important was the discussion about guarantees that European decision-making would not be detrimental to (perceived) vital national interests. The latter are understood quite widely and have been present to the minds, even of those who have been enthusiastic supporters of QMV and a shift of power to the EP and the Commission. Greece has also been anxious that EU powers might intrude further in the field of foreign policy and, increasingly, defence. It has not been made clear how this extension of EU powers to such sensitive areas could be combined with full respect for veto rights.

Finally, there were also hopes of incorporating into the Treaties some provision for safeguarding the borders of Member States. This point briefly brought the IGC negotiations to the forefront of Greek public opinion, but then it was left to its own devices when it was clear that it would not reach a result deemed satisfactory by a deeply insecure public.[21]

The Greek position on EU enlargement

Let us take as a first example the Greek position on enlargement. Viewed from an EU standpoint, enlargement is an opening of the Union to the countries of Central and Eastern Europe (CEE). The fundamental position of Greece has been favourable to enlargement for the unstated (yet easily perceived, when discussed with policy-makers) reason that enlargement would bring about a dilution of the centralising model of integration. Greece is concerned about the EU moulding itself around a Western or Northern European core. The official Greek position is favourable to a wider integration model for the Union, even with federal overtones, but the expectation is that integration might be more diluted rather than result in a highly structured model.

There is also an intermediate goal for Greece in the enlargement process: how to favour (and be seen to favour) its Balkan neighbours for effective participation and include the Balkan/Southeastern Europe in the Union architecture. Thus, while accepting de facto the 'regatta' approach to enlargement, Greece is a proponent both of an early conclusion of enlargement and the widest possible first wave of new entrants.[22] After the Kosovo crisis, Greece has been advocating the inclusion of Balkan countries, such as Bulgaria and Romania in the enlargement process as part of the stabilisation of the region.

All such motivations towards enlargement retreat once the main concern of Greece comes to the fore: the accession negotiations with Cyprus, and the European future of Turkey, in the background. Greek–Turkish relations can in no way be considered a matter of routine. For Greece, the crisis with its neighbour across the Aegean is the matter of vital national interest. Greece's opportunity to put across its views to its European partners or the international community has usually been in the context of conflagration. However, the policy of improving Greek–Turkish relations as a precondition of closer Union–Turkey ties has been a tactical option, similar to the use of the Cyprus candidacy for accession to obtain some mobility on the Cyprus issue. These tactical moves proved successful at times during the 1990s, but they have been edging towards an impasse. The end result of such efforts has seen Greece view enlargement mainly, if not exclusively, as a chessboard where it can carry on its own game. Greece has increasingly stated that it will block enlargement unless Cyprus' accession is left to proceed unhindered.

France, Italy, the Netherlands, Germany and Sweden have voiced concerns about Cyprus joining the Union. This, along with the suggestion that accession negotiations with Cyprus be suspended pending a resolution of the issue, has only recently been given serious attention in Greek public policy. The expectation is that Greece's attitude towards Turkish and Cypriot accession will be biased.

Agenda 2000: an old game played on a new field

The negotiations over Agenda 2000 offer another example of how Greece views participation in the Union. While Agenda 2000 was a way of simultaneously approaching the impact of enlargement, the own-resources challenge, CAP reform and the future of the Structural Funds, the Greek negotiating efforts have concentrated solely on the level of funds that were to be granted for its furthering structural adjustment. Greek public opinion has altered over the years, from a position of division to enthusiasm. Linked to this is an acute public awareness of the benefits of membership, which includes EU agricultural and Structural Funds. The political system has traditionally used this argument so as to 'easily' win support for European policies. The more articulate notion of interest by participation has gained ground only in the last two or three years, replacing previous notions of a purely financial gain from Europe.

As Agenda 2000 negotiations developed, the Greek position followed the Foreign Affairs Ministry recommendation and refrained from actively participating in the own-resources debate; it focused rather on the spending side, but again opted for a low-profile approach. Following the Spanish leadership on safeguarding Structural Funds financing, Greece put forward the position that any reduction in the 2000–06 package was inconceivable, being the lowest-income region in the Union, despite its wish to be part of the third phase of EMU. At the Berlin Summit, Greece obtained an increase of some 16 per cent (21.75 billion Euros as compared to 18.75 billion Euros). This compares with a 7.46 per cent increase for the whole of the Union. At the same time, the renationalisation of the CAP, which would cost Greece some 200 billion drachma per year, was avoided and Mediterranean-specific products were spared radical reform. Despite Greece's ability to secure a good deal in terms of EU funding, the CAP appears as a separate issue from enlargement or wider budget reforms.

The crux of institutional discussion: is a veto-less future imaginable?

Where decision-making in the Union and the institutional set-up for the twenty-first century is concerned, the Greek position suffers from a case of split personality. Having abandoned its earlier Euro-negativism, Greece has, since the late 1980s, adopted a position favourable to flexible decision-making in the Union, with QMV, increased EP powers and Commission initiative and executive authority. At the same time, Greece has been a proponent of a more active and coherent CFSP, with an active defence element. The centrepiece of Greece's negotiating position in the earlier stages of the Amsterdam Treaty was a CFSP able to allow for the common protection of external borders. Adherence to European institutional 'orthodoxy' and a pro-European integration approach became a fundamental part of both the opposition and PASOK's political profile.[23]

However, Greece's stance in terms of foreign policy has revealed a different attitude. EU relations with Turkey, the S-300 issue in Cyprus, the (forgotten but not totally defused) Macedonian issue, and flare-ups over former Yugoslavia, are recurring examples. Although situations such as the initial Kosovo impasse and the Albanian crisis offered the opportunity for Greece to have a role and use its Balkan experience and advice, Greece's actions have reduced any potential influence it might have had.

Matters of everyday politics have created a deeply rooted mentality whereby the political system and the foreign policy apparatus resort to a blocking and/or veto stance. The ease with which the major pronouncement has been made that Greece will block the whole enlargement process unless Cyprus is allowed to proceed to accession is the most clear-cut example. NATO's military intervention in the Kosovo crisis and Greece's isolationist stance has renewed the push for unanimity in CFSP matters.

Conclusion: creeping 'Europeanisation' – adjusting to difficult policies

The Greek Permanent Representation staff has fluctuated between eighty and 120 persons, of which fewer than twenty are diplomats and the rest are seconded from ministries other than Foreign Affairs. The reason for such a level of Permanent Representation staff is due to the time needed for civil servants to fly in from Greece in order to sit on EU Committees and Working Parties (and to the 'demand' for Brussels postings for money and/or career and/or prestige reasons), more than to any increasing recognition of the role of the Union in Greek administrative mechanisms.

Conversely, civil servants sent to Brussels for Committee and working group business, as well as those seconded to the Brussels' institutions, tend to be fewer than would otherwise be the case. Generally speaking, 'Europeanised' segments of the Greek administration grew rapidly during the first decade of effective membership. This occurred at a time of Euroscepticism on the part of Greek officials; the civil service kept its distance European matters. In the following period and until recently, there has been a de facto segmentation of the civil service, limiting the number of officials to/of European Affairs.

If a process of 'Europeanisation' has occurred within the Greek administration, it is because the EU dimension is increasingly taken into account in legislative and administrative work, almost as a routine matter. Even in areas where the EU dimension was not at first evident, such as environmental matters, infrastructure or local government, the civil service has been integrating EU criteria and priorities into its modus operandi.

There exists an ongoing conflict between the Ministries of Foreign Affairs and National Economy on the one hand (sensitive to EU rules) and Ministries on the other (where national interests persist). This has been noticeably the case in third pillar issues, where the Interior Ministry and Public Order Ministry have been reluctant to follow the latest EU trends. It is also true of the Ministries for Industry, for Public Works, Urbanism and the Environment, and for Education.

The convergence criteria set by the Maastricht Treaty for the third phase of EMU influenced macroeconomic policy-making in Greece, affecting the decision-making mechanisms of economic policy. Foreign policy was also influenced by the Europeanisation process, particularly by the decisions made at Maastricht and Amsterdam. However, the reasons behind Greece's call for a more active CFSP after the Amsterdam Treaty was due more to a 'new European orientation' than to the idea that Greece should project a more European image. Greece advocates a CFSP that protects the external borders of EU Member States, and an integrated, credible defence. In Greece, decision-making mechanisms as such have not been so influenced by EU treaty developments, apart from a willing 'surrender' of rule-making responsibilities to Brussels. It is doubtful whether the Kosovo crisis will still affect the balance achieved in Greece, both at public opinion and elite level, over the Union's foreign policy dimension.

What of the question of the 'fitness' of Greece as a partner in the European common venture in view of the foreseeable evolution of the EU system? Were one to define 'fitness' as the capacity of Member States to adapt to the situation evolving in the wider EU setting by a selective and quite gradual change that caused minimal disruption to their internal equilibria and also, as the capacity to pursue an agenda of its own while not being cut off from the main pack, then Greece appears quite 'fit'.

Notes

1 See Susannah Verney, 'To Be or Not to Be within the EU. The Party Debate and Democratic Consideration in Greece', in: Geoffrey Pridham (ed.), *Security Democracy and Democratic Consolidation in Southern Europe* (London: Routledge, 1989).

2 For the progressive shift in public opinion attitudes and perceptions one can look at a panorama of opinions in: Loukas Tsoukalis (ed.), *Greece and the European Community* (London: Saxon House, 1979), to be compared with the panel discussion between Giorgos Romaios, F. Balshina, G. Vanhaeverbeke and A. D. Papayannides, in: Nikos Frangakis *et al.* (eds), *The Third Greek Presidency* (Athens: HESTIA, 1994), pp. 277 f.; Panos Kazakos and Konstantinos Stefanou, *Greece in the European Community. The First Five Years: Trends, Problems, Perspectives* [in Greek] (Athens: Sakkoulas, 1986), Panos Kazakos, *Greece between Adaptation and Marginalisation* [in Greek] (Athens: Diatton, 1991); Panos Kazakos, *Greece within a Changing Europe* [in Greek] (Athens: Papazissis, 1994); Panayotis K. Ioakimidis, *Europe in Change* [in Greek] (Athens: Themelio, 1990); Panayotis K. Ioakimidis, *European Political Union* [in Greek] (Athens: Themelio, 1993).

3 As a case study, one may compare the positions of the Industrialists' Union and of the Workers' Federation on the priorities of the Third Greek

Presidency with the actual Programme of the Presidency, in: Frangakis *et al.* (eds), 1994, *op. cit.*, pp. 277 f.

4 See Dimitrios Evrigenis, 'Legal and Constitutional Implications of Greek Accession to the European Communities', in: *Common Market Law Review*, No. 17/1, 1980, pp. 161 ff.; Theodora Antoniou, *Europäische Integration und Griechische Verfassung*, (Frankfurt aM, 1985); Ioannis Drossos, *Greek Constitutional Order and the European Communities* [in Greek] (Athens: Ant. Sakkoulas, 1987), pp. 80 ff., Antonis Manitakis, 'The Limits of Community Competence and its Constitutional Reading' [in Greek], *To Syntagma*, 1984, pp. 472 ff., Georgia Papadimitriou, 'The Constitution and the Maastricht Treaty' [in Greek], *Economiocs Tachydromos*, 22 February 1992; A. Plessas and Andreas Loverdos 'The Ratification of the Single European Act: The Missed Debate' [in Greek], in: *Theseis*, No. 23–24, 1991, pp. 69 ff.; Elentherios Venizelos, 'The Maastricht Treaty and the European Constitutional Space. Mutual Influences between the EU and National Constitutions' [in Greek], *To Syntagma*, 1993, 456 ff.

5 See for the official position of Greece to the 1996 IGC, see Mémorandum du gouvernement grec dans la cadre de la CIG sur la PESC, CONF/3861/96, 12.6.1996. The assessment of Amsterdam by central political figures can be found in: Sotiris Dalis (ed.), *From Maastricht to Amsterdam. An Evaluation of the IGC and an Analysis of the New EU Treaty* [in Greek] (Athens: I. Sideris, 1998), Official statement of Prime Minister Costas Simitis, pp. 529–534, articles by Costas Simitis, pp. 31–39, Deputy Foreign Minister George Papandreou, pp. 357–361, and Opposition leader Costas Karamanlis, pp. 69–80.

6 The debate is really about the matter of belonging – to the West, to the Balkans, to the East, to the uneasy in-between bridging continents but also about cultural readings of self – and it is a debate of deep resonance. The articles of Mouzelis, Moulopoulos and Someritis in the high-circulation/high-prestige Sunday '*TO VIMA*' (21 February 1999) mark a watershed in the intensity of this debate.

7 See Panayotis K. Ioakimidis, *European Union and the Greek State, Implications of the Participation in the Integration Process* [in Greek] (Athens: Themelio, 1998), pp. 90–129, 134–141, Panos Kazakos, *Greece within a Changing Europe* [in Greek] (Athens, 1994), pp. 209–212, 213–216, Antonis Makrydimitris, 'Greek Administration and the EU. Convergence or Divergence?', in: Sotiris Dalis (ed.), *From Maastricht to Amsterdam* [in Greek] (Athens: I. Sideris, 1998, pp. 284–294; Themos Stoforopoulos and Antonis Makrydimistris, *The System of Greek Foreign Policy-Making. The Institutional Dimension* [in Greek] (Athens: I. Sideris, 1997).

8 See Antonis Makrydimitris and Argyris Passas, *Greek Administration and the Coordination of European policy* [in Greek] (Athens: A. Sakkoulas, 1994). Interesting case studies on how specific sectors of EC/EU activity have been faced by the administration and the Greek legal system can be found in Nikos Frangakis *et al.* (eds), *National Administration and Community Law* [in Greek] (Athens: A. Sakkoulas, 1993).

9 See Nikolaus Wenturis, 'Greece', in: Roger Morgan and Claire Tame (eds),

Parliaments and Parties: The European Parliament in the Political Life of Europe (London: Macmillan, 1996); Panayotis K. Ioakimidis, *European Union and the Greek State* [in Greek] (Athens: Themelis, 1998), pp. 142–149.

10 See Athanasios Theodorakis, 'The Greek Parliament and the Formation of European Policy: Consequences of Self-Exclusion from the Exercise of Existing Rights' [in Greek], in: *Koinovouleutiki Epitheorissi*, No. 17–18.

11 This point can be traced through the whole two working days of the seminar on the application of Community law in Greece, whose summary is given in Frangakis *et al.* (eds), 1993, *op. cit.*

12 See Introductory comments by Wassilios Skouris, in: Wassilios Skouris (ed.), *Community Law in Greek Jurisprudence* [in Greek] (Athens: A. Sakkoulas, 1994).

13 (Decision) Preliminary assessment 406/1980), *REC* 1980, p. 467 [in Greek].

14 See Decision 520/1983 Fourth Chamber – *R. Hell DE* 1984, p. 191, with comments by Krateros Ioannou [in Greek].

15 See Decision 815/1984 Full Court – *R. Hell DE* 1985, p. 140.

16 Decision 2605/1986 Full Court, after referral from the Fourth Chamber.

17 ECJ 254/86, Rec. 1987, p. 4355.

18 1093/1987 Full Court, *R. Hell DE* 1989, p. 1989.

19 Areios Pagos. Decision 348/1985 Full Court, *R. Hell DE* 1985, p. 148. Decision 891/1985 Fifth Chamber, *R. Hell DE* 1985, p. 150. The Areios Pagos has begun to refer cases to the ECJ under Article 177 (Decision 1124/1986 First Section No. V 36 (1988), p. 1143) and the lower Courts have followed suit.

20 Decision 1544/1992, Full Court-ECJ C-441/93, Rec. 1996, I 1347. See Emmanuel Roukounas, 'Pour le dialogue entre droit communautaire et droit Grec', in: *RHDI*, 1992, pp. 11 ff.; Wassilios Skouris 'Community Law in Greek Legislation and Jurisprudence', [in Greek], in: *R. Hell DE*, 1985, pp. 3 ff., Krateros Ioannou, 'The Greek Judge as Enforcer of Community Law' [in Greek], in: *R. Hell DE*, 1985, pp. 77 ff.; Evangelos Kroustalakis, 'Community Law In Juridical Thinking: The Case of Greece' [in Greek], in: *R. Hell DE*, 1985, pp. 59 ff.; Theodora Antoniou, 'The Legal Foundations of the Direct Effect and the Supremacy of Community Law Rules in the Greek Legal Order' [in Greek], in: *To Syndagma*, 1986, pp. 440 ff., Christos Yeraris, 'The Start of the Dialogue between the Greek and the Community Judge' [in Greek], in: *NoV*, 1988, pp. 1037 ff.; Nikos Frangakis, 'Community law and Us', in: *NoV*, 1988, p. 1025 ff. More hesitant as to the assessment of Greek jurisprudence is: Nicolas Skandamis, *European Law: Institutions and Legal Implications of the EU* [in Greek] (Athens: A. Sakkoulas, 1997), pp. 471–482.

21 For the climate in which the IGC was prepared in Greece see Panayotis K. Ioakimidis, *The revision of the Maastricht Treaty* [in Greek] (Athens: Themelio, 1995). Official Government positions and the position of the main parties are included as Annexes (pp. 87–93). See also Nikos Frangakis (ed.), *Priorities and Strategies for the Revision of Maastricht* [in Greek] (Athens: EKEME, 1996); Nikos Frangakis and Stelios Perrakis (eds), *The Course of the Negotiations for the Revision of the Maastricht Treaty* [in Greek]

(Athens: EKEME/EKEM, 1997). An assessment of Amsterdam by Prime Minister Costas Simitis, opposition leader Costas Karamanlis, Deputy Foreign Minister George Papandreou and Secretary General for Foreign Affairs Stelios Perrakis (who had the most active role in the closing stages of the negotiations) is provided in: Dalis (ed.), 1998, *op. cit.*, pp. 31–39, 69–80, 357–361, 361–368.

22 To get a feeling of the Balkan framework in which Greece is situated, compare *The Southeast European Yearbook 1997–98* (Athens: ELIAMEP, 1998) and previous editions for 1994–95 and for 1991–92. See also Panos Kazakos, *Greece within a Changing Europe* [in Greek] (Athens, 1994), pp. 291–322.

23 For quite optimist assessments, see Panayotis K. Ioakimidis, *European Political Union* [in Greek] (Athens, 1993), pp. 438–452; more tempered in: Panos Kazakos, *Greece within a Changing Europe* [in Greek] (Athens, 1994), pp. 13–17, 179–208, 327–330; also Dalis (ed.), 1998, *op. cit.*, pp. 13–27.

Select bibliography

The text (English translation) of the Consitution of Greece can be found at the University of Richmond's constitution finder at http://confinder.richmond.edu/. Further sources on government and parliament of Greece can be found at Government www.mfa.gr.

Antoniou, Theodora (1985) *Europäische Integration und Griechische Verfassung*, Mineo (Frankfurt a.M. 1985).

Dalis, Sotiris (ed.) (1998) *From Maastricht to Amsterdam. An Evaluation of the IGC and an Analysis of the New EU Treaty* [in Greek] (Athens: I. Sideris).

Drosos, Ioannis (1987) *Greek Constitutional Order and the European Communities* [in Greek] (Athens: Ant. Sakkoulas).

Evrigenis, Dimistrios (1980) 'Legal and Constitutional Implications of Greek Accession to the European Communities', in: *Common Market Law Review*, No. 17/1, 1980.

Frangakis, Nikos, Papayannides, Antonis D. and Apostolides, R. (1994) *The Third Greek Presidency* (Athens: HESTIA).

Frangakis, Nikos and Papayannides Antonis D. (eds) (1993) *National Administration and Community Law* [in Greek] (Athens: A. Sakkoulas).

Ioakimidis, Panayotis K. (1995) *The Revision of the Maastricht Treaty* [in Greek] (Athens: Themelio).

Ioakimidis, Panayotis K. (1998a) *European Union and the Greek State. Implications of the participation in the Integration Process* [in Greek] (Athens: Themelio).

Ioakimidis, Panayotis K. (1998b) *European Union and the Greek State* [in Greek] (Athens: Themelio).

Ioannou, Krateros (1985) 'The Greek Judge as Enforcer of Community Law' [in Greek], in: *R. Hell DE*.

Makrydimitris, Antonis (1998) 'Greek Administration and the EU. Convergence or divergence?', in: Sotiris Dalis (ed.), *From Maastricht to Amsterdam* [in Greek] (Athens: I. Sideris).

Roukounas, Emmanuel (1992) 'Pour le dialogue entre droit communautaire et droit Grec', *RHDI*.

Tsoukalis, Loukas (ed) (1979) *Greece and the European Community* (London: Saxon House).

Verney, Susannah (1989) 'To Be or Not to Be within the EU. The Party Debate and Democratic Consideration in Greece', in: Geoffrey Pridham (ed.), *Security Democracy and Democratic Consolidation in Southern Europe* (London: Routledge).

Wenturis, Nikolaus (1996) 'Greece' in: Roger Mogan and Claire Tame (eds), *Parliaments and Parties. The European Parliament in the political life of Europe* (London: Macmillan).

8 *Felipe Basabe Lloréns*

Spain: the emergence of a new major actor in the European arena

Introduction: the EU as a major step and catalyst in Spain's 'return to Europe'

Spain's accession to the EC in 1986[1] was the result of a long political process and the fulfilment of a historical aspiration for Spanish society. For most internal and external observers, Spain's entry into the Community constituted the final step of the transition process to democracy.[2] Accession to the Community was supported at that time almost unanimously by all political parties and the different societal actors.[3] Such a broad social and political consensus is to be found at the basis of most of the features of the Spanish administrative structure and participation model in the EC/EU decision-making process. Such broad support for the process of European integration has, however, experienced a relative decline in recent years owing to political conflicts on issues such as fisheries, industrial reconversion, reform of olive oil tariffs, and CMO.[4] Also, the rise of interest groups – still on a minor scale – and dissenting opinion within some national political parties[5] has created a climate more critical towards further developments in European integration. However, the perception by the general public and political elites still confirms a very positive attitude and integrationist approach to European issues. EC budgetary reform and the future enlargement to the CEE candidate countries will be a crucial test for such a consensus.[6]

Spain's membership of the Union has had a direct impact on the consolidation of the democratic functioning of its political system, the acceleration of economic development and the modernisation of public administration structures and procedures. The enactment of certain internal policies – particularly environment, regional development, consumer protection and immigration policies – has clearly taken place in a synchronised way and as a consequence of the national implementation of the respective Community policies.

Another direct consequence of Spain's accession to the Union has been the dynamisation of its civil society. This has led to the creation of interest groups, professional associations and co-ordination structures at national, regional and local level in all economic and activity sectors.[7] Spain's role in the international arena has also been considerably enhanced, partly owing to its accession to the Union.[8] Its traditional connections with Latin America and the Islamic world have not decreased, but have altered, mainly because of Spain's economic development and its compliance with EC legislation and the Common Commercial Policy (CCP). Spain's gradual incorporation in the Union has followed parallel trends and patterns to the internal process of territorial redistribution of power and reorganisation of its administrative structure and decision-making procedures. This has facilitated adaptation to the EC/EU decision-making process. In its years of membership, Spain has also contributed to the process of European integration with important initiatives and proposals[9] and has played an active role.

The fact that the Spanish political elites, long before the actual negotiations for accession began,[10] and the general public – despite its lack of in-depth knowledge of the actual functioning and repercussions of EC membership) – shared the same aspirations has clearly facilitated both the adaptation of internal structures and the adoption of unpopular decisions. The EC/EU dimension has been present as an important element of all Spanish major national processes and challenges: economic transformation, social change and regional conflicts.

Political priorities with regard to EU policy-making

Spain's political priorities with regard to EU policy-making have evolved from the first years of membership to the present. The internal process of modernising the administrative and productive structures and enhancing the regionally balanced economic development was the focus of attention prior to the adoption of the TEU. Spain traditionally adopted a very integrationist negotiating stance and tried to cope with the requirements imposed during the long transitional period leading to its full participation in all Community policies.[11] Obviously, all matters related to the definition of a regional development policy at the European level, as well as the subsequent management of the Structural Funds, concentrated Spain's political priorities. Agricultural and fisheries issues were also highly ranked – no doubt owing to the significant and painful restructuring processes undergone by certain Spanish agricultural sectors – within the general preoccupation for Spain's full accession to the SEM.

Spain's political EU agenda has expanded and diversified, for a number of reasons. The TEU was adopted and implemented. In 1991 and 1993, the transitional period for a wide range of economic sectors also came to an end. Finally, the adjustment of the Spanish administration to the usages and practices of the EC/EU decision-making process can also account for the new direction adopted. Agriculture and fisheries[12] have continued to be one of the highest-ranking areas. Regional development policy,[13] particularly the Structural Funds and the Cohesion Fund, and social and economic cohesion, also come into this area. At the same time, the whole process leading to the creation of EMU concentrated Spanish political attention, especially after President Aznar came to power. Spain's entry into the third stage of EMU was the focal point of his electoral programme and the fundamental motivation for his parliamentary alliance with the nationalist parties.[14] Former President González had justified the extension of his government's term in office and his refusal to call for new general elections on the basis of the need for political stability to assume the Presidency of the Council of the EU in 1995.

Another aspect which has immediately attracted Spain's political interest is co-operation in the JHA field, especially those issues related to immigration, external border control and police co-operation against terrorism and drug trafficking.[15] The Ministries of Home Affairs and Justice, traditionally resistant to international co-operation, have developed a new dynamic approach to these issues and even held leading positions and presented initiatives on a European scale in this field. Spain's activity within the CFSP has been less relevant, concentrating its efforts on relationships with the Mediterranean countries and Latin America.

Finally, Spain played an important role in both the 1990–91 and 1996–97[16] IGCs, where it showed its interest in institutional issues – owing to its peculiar position within the EC/EU institutional structure – and those related to the deepening of European citizenship and the fight against unemployment. Spain has always defended the principle of subsidiarity[17] as a means to improve Community action. It played a major role in the 1999 negotiations for EC budgetary reform as a leader of the so called 'cohesion countries' as well as the enlargement negotiations with the CEE candidate countries. Spain has in fact evolved from adapting its internal structures and interests to the EC/EU decision-making process to strengthening its negotiating positions with a view to a wider and stronger defence of its national interests.

Constitutional, institutional and procedural changes

The ratification and implementation of the TEU resulted in a significant number of changes of a constitutional, institutional and procedural nature within the Spanish politico-administrative system.[18] However, most of these changes should be directly ascribed not only to the enactment of the Treaty of Maastricht, but also to the natural evolution and adaptation of the Spanish public administration to the requirements of the EC/EU decision-making process. In fact, smooth adaptation to the new Community institutional procedures has traditionally characterised the Spanish

Government.[19] The ratification process of the TEU[20] was accompanied by the first reform of the Spanish constitutional text of 1978.[21] Article 95 of the Spanish Constitution – not used until now – entitles the Constitutional Court (*Tribunal Constitutional*) to be consulted on the need for reform of the constitutional text prior to the ratification of international treaties, including provisions contrary to the Constitution. This a priori constitutional control was demanded by the government, which limited its request to the study of the provisions related to European citizenship, namely the active and passive electoral rights of EC citizens. The opinion of the Constitutional Court[22] was preceded by the preceptive – and in this case contradictory – opinion of the advisory State Council[23] (Consejo de Estado) and ruled that exclusively Article 13.2 of the Spanish Constitution had to be reformed in order to allow for the inclusion of the passive electoral rights for foreigners in Spain. Such limited constitutional reform was criticised by the legal profession,[24] on the grounds that either it should have been wider, including aspects related to EMU and the transfer of competences in the fields of the second and third pillar, or it could have been avoided with a broader judicial interpretation of Article 13.2.

Both the reform of the Constitution and the ratification of the Treaty of Maastricht were supported by the practical unanimity of all political parties represented in the parliament. Such was also the case for the ratification process of the Treaty of Amsterdam, which was finally approved on 16 December 1998, again with the favourable votes of most congress deputies and senators.[25]

Most of the changes brought by the Treaty of Maastricht refer to the consolidation and widening of the scope of competences of certain interministerial co-ordinating bodies, the extension of the participation in EC/EU affairs to the practical totality of ministries, and the reinforcement of the defining role of the Ministry of Economy and Finance as a co-ordinating actor in determining the Spanish official position. The Spanish Permanent Representation to the Union has also been strengthened by the increase in its high-ranking officials and the improvement of the co-ordination structures with the national ministries via the Secretariat of State for Foreign Policy and the European Union (SEPEUE, Secretaría de Estado de Política Exterior y para la Unión Europea). Such has also been the case of the Joint Committee for the European Union, the most relevant parliamentary body dealing with EC/EU affairs by means of the extension of its powers.

Certain national policies – particularly regional development, police co-operation, immigration, development co-operation and the environment – have received a considerable impetus, partly owing to activities developed at European level. The implementation of the Treaty of Maastricht was accompanied by an increase of regional activism at the European level. Most Autonomous Communities are already represented in Brussels and have created administrative units for the management of EC/EU affairs.[26] Local and municipal authorities still play a minor role in EC/EU affairs, however, and have no global institutional framework to represent their interests at European level.

The political change from the socialist government under Felipe González to the current conservative one under José María Aznar has not been so relevant for the Spanish management of EC/EU affairs, compared to the internal innovations and new political variables brought by the presence of the nationalist/regionalist political parties on the national political arena after 1993 onwards (Figure 8.1).[27]

The national policy-cycle: the slow march towards a decentralised and efficient administrative system

Government and public administration

There is no specific ministry within the Spanish government which vertically co-ordinates and manages all EC/EU matters.[28] The Cabinet of the President of the Government includes a Department of International and European Affairs with a pure advisory and documentary role. Although nearly all the ministries have areas or units – in most cases, Directorates-General dealing exclusively with European affairs – by far the greatest number in the central government have traditionally been located within the Ministry of Foreign Affairs (MAE, Ministerio de Asuntos Exteriores). This ministry formulates Spain's negotiating position in relation to the Union. By holding meetings with other ministries, it also seeks to ensure that no single ministry defends its own interests rather than the interests of the country as a whole. The department within the MAE dealing exclusively with European Affairs is currently the Secretariat of State for Foreign Policy and the European Union.[29] The Secretary of State is assisted by a General Secretary to whom the different directors-general are responsible. Unusually for a government department, there is an extra tier between the Secretariat of State and the Directorates-General, thus reflecting the importance of this area of government. The General Secretary's private office of expert advisers (Gabinete del Secretario General) is in direct line from the General Secretary.[30]

The organisation of SEPEUE was significantly modified at the end of 1998 following the signature of the Treaty of Amsterdam.[31] From 1999 onwards, three Directorates-General (among the seven existing within the SEPEUE) deal with EU affairs. The Directorates-General for Political Affairs and the United Nations (Dirección General de Asuntos Políticos y para las NN.UU.), prepares the meetings of the Political Committee and CFSP issues of the General Affairs Council of the EU. The Directorate-General for Co-Ordination of EU General and Technical Affairs (Dirección General de Coordinación de Asuntos Generales y Técnicos de

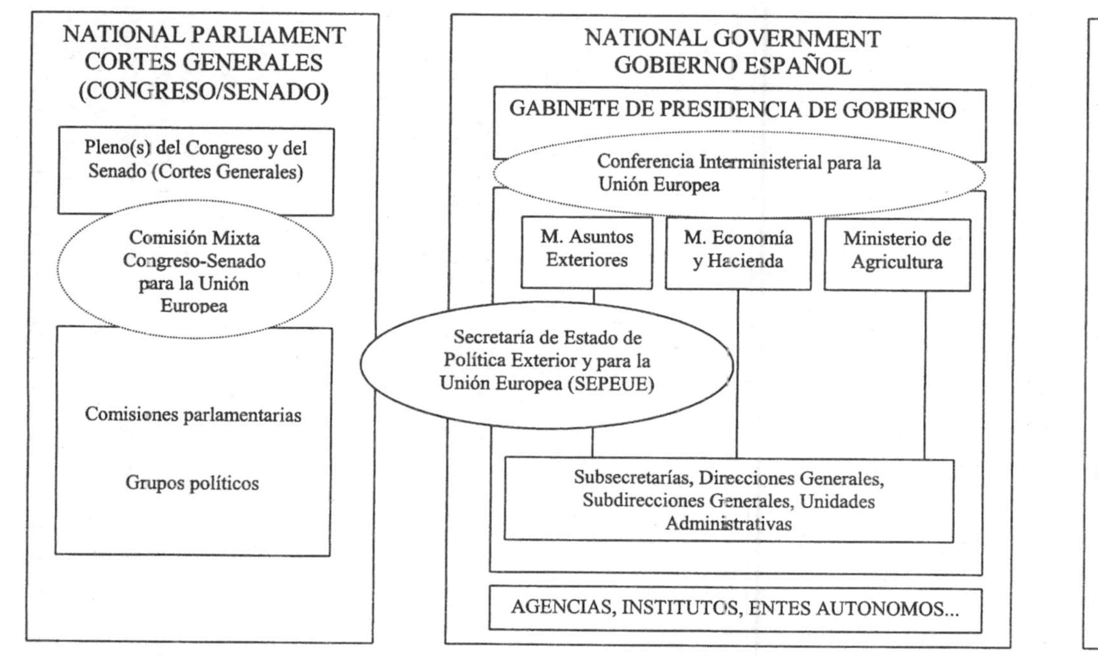

Figure 8.1 The national level of European decision-making – Spain

la Unión Europea), has responsibility for financial, budgetary, economic, commercial and customs issues. Finally, the Directorate-General for Co-Ordination of the Internal Market and other Community Policies (Dirección General de Coordinación del Mercado Interior y otras Políticas Comunitarias), administers agriculture, fisheries, industrial, energetic, transport, telecommunications, environmental, social, education, cultural, health and consumer protection affairs.[32] The new independent Directorate-General for Foreign Policy in Europe (Dirección General de Política Exterior para Europa) is mainly concerned with the relationships with the CEE countries. The new structure tries to rationalise the administrative levels and internal dependencies, creating synergies within the new departments.

After the Ministry of Foreign Affairs, the Ministry of Economy and Finance (MEH, Ministerio de Economía y Hacienda) is the one that has most involvement in EU Affairs. One of its main tasks is to prepare the draft state budget bill which includes the financial flows from Spain to the Union and vice-versa. This ministry is the general co-ordinating agency for all EU Structural Funds and initiatives. It administers receipts from several of these funds.[33]

The major EU-linked activity of the Ministry of Labour and Social Affairs (Ministerio de Trabajo y Asuntos Sociales) is the administration of the European Social Fund, managed by the European Social Fund Administration Unit (Unidad Administrativa del Fondo Social Europeo), located within the Directorate-General for Employment (Dirección general de Empleo).[34] The Ministry of Agriculture, Fisheries and Food (Ministerio de Agricultura, Pesca y Alimentación), through various departments and autonomous administrative bodies, is responsible for the administration of the European Agricultural Guarantee and Guidance Fund (EAGGF).[35] The Ministry of Education, Science and Culture (Ministerio de Educación, Ciencia y Cultura) plays a major role, sometimes in collaboration with other government departments, in the promotion of education, training and exchange links with other EU Member States, as well as a co-ordinating role with reference to the Regional Ministries for Education (Consejerías de Educación).[36] The Ministry of Industry and Energy (Ministerio de Industria y Energía) is responsible for administering EU support for R&D.[37] Finally, the recently created Ministry for Environment (Ministerio de Medio Ambiente) manages the LIFE programme and co-ordinates the selection, evaluation and monitoring of environmental projects to be funded by the Cohesion Fund.[38] The complex management of EC environmental policy has without any doubt been one of the major reasons for the transformation and grouping of several administrative departments, mostly within the former Ministry of Public Works, into the new Ministry for Environment. Institutional participation of the Spanish government in the second and third pillars of the Union varies considerably in each case. While no significant administrative changes were necessary to provide for the Spanish representation in CFSP, a major reorganisation within the then Ministry of Home and Judicial Affairs – currently two separate ministries – was undertaken with relation to Spain's participation in the third pillar.

The autonomous post of the Special Ambassador to CFSP (Embajador en misión especial para la Política Exterior y de Seguridad Común), who attended the meetings of the Political Committee, has now been suppressed and its department ascribed to the Under-Directorate General for CFSP (Subdirección general de Política Exterior y de Seguridad Común) within the Directorate-General for Political Affairs and United Nations.

The Home Ministry created special units to deal separately with Schengen affairs and co-operation in the JHA field. Special units were also created for the National Police (Cuerpo Nacional de Policía) and the autonomous Civil Guards (Guardia Civil), as well as the Ministry of Justice within the Directorate-General for International Legal Co-Operation (Dirección general de Cooperación Jurídica Internacional). They also transformed their internal procedures and specialised their units. For instance, the new Unit for International Co-Ordination and Co-operation (Unidad de Coordinación y Cooperación Internacional) now complies with the different requirements and obligations set within the EU third pillar. Special Counsellors were also appointed at the Permanent Representation of Spain to the Union.[39]

The parliament (Cortes)

The Spanish national parliament (Cortes) has an indirect presence in the EC decision-making process.[40] Parliamentary scrutiny in EC/EU affairs in Spain has never been strong in practice, owing to the reduced institutional role of the parliament *vis-à-vis* the management of certain policy areas by the government. Post-Maastricht developments have confirmed this situation, except for specific issues of great relevance for the general public, which had its origin in EC decisions (for example, the reform of certain CMOs within CAP, fisheries, and the re-conversion of the coal and shipbuilding industries). The main parliamentary activity in relation to EC/EU matters has been government control, while legislative activity has been secondary. Parliamentary control mechanisms operate on the legislative process to incorporate EC rules into Spanish statutes,[41] through the control of Spanish government representatives in EC institutions and by the implementation of EC decisions by the public authorities for which the Spanish government is responsible. The broad positive consensus among the major political parties towards the process of European integration also underlies the limited participation and activity of the parliament in this field.[42] The parliament's role, apart from its symbolic connotations, is basically reactive and limited to the reception of information given by the government or other administrative bodies. Such information is generally granted after the definition of the Spanish official positions by the government.

The constitutional provisions concerning the involvement of the Spanish national parliament in European affairs are rather scarce because of the preponderance of the executive in the management of international and EC/EU affairs. The main role of the parliament concerns the ratification of international treaties.[43] The negotiations leading to the adoption and signature of an international treaty are exclusively led by the central government without any prior mandate from the national parliament. From a legislative perspective, the Spanish parliament limits itself to debating and approving, always at the initiative of the government, the regulatory measures needed to adapt internal law to European provisions. It is remarkable that an annual parliamentary debate on EC/EU affairs has never been established,[44] though the general aspects of European integration, in the early years after accession, and more specific policy oriented issues at present, have always been among the issues dealt with in wider political debates. There is, however, an important number of oral and written questions, as well as interpellations and motions subsequent to interpellation, presented to the government, in both the plenary sessions and in some of the sectoral committees of both chambers.[45] Informative sessions are thus the most important parliamentary control activity in EC/EU affairs, on the basis of the information given by the executive, whether on its own initiative or on that of the chambers. The plenary session of the Congress of Deputies holds a meeting after every summit of the European Council in order to be informed by the president of the government about the result of the negotiations.[46] The president also reports to the Congress and responds to the questions posed by the parliamentary leaders on such issues. Such interaction generally helps to create the necessary consensus with a view to the production of agreements on resolutions and recommendations aiming at guiding the Spanish negotiating positions in Brussels.

The Secretary of State for Foreign Policy and the European Union also appears bi-monthly before certain bodies of both chambers – the Joint Committee for the European Union and the Senate's Budget Committee – in order to answer questions by deputies and senators on EC/EU-related issues. Most of the sectoral Committees of the Congress[47] actually control the application and enforcement of EC legislation in their respective fields. The main parliamentary organ dealing with EC/EU affairs is the Joint Committee Congress/Senate for the European Union (Comisión Mixta para la Unión Europea),[48] the successor to the Joint Committee for the European Communities.[49] It is composed of an equal number of Congress deputies and senators[50] and reflects the relative strength of the political groups within the two chambers. The number of representatives is variable, agreed upon by the Cortes, in order to guarantee the presence of all parliamentary groups. The function of presidency over the committee is normally delegated by the President of the Congress or the First Vice-President of the Chamber.[51]

This non-legislative committee is the only parliamentary body which has direct and regular links with the EP and hence it plays a vital role in ensuring that the Cortes are kept informed of activities and developments in the European institutions. It has not generally been considered as an important parliamentary committee, in perpetual competition with other committees, especially that of foreign affairs. While the government has always used it as its main means of communication with the parliament, the opposition does not tend to consider it as its main device for government supervision.[52] The committee holds regular meetings,[53] some for general information and others on specific issues. Oral questions posed by the committee tend to be of a sectoral nature. With the exception of some appearances of administrative officers at their own request, and of the regular, institutionalised appearance of the Secretary of State for Foreign Policy and the European Union, every appearance takes place on request from the opposition groups. The committee has located its field of action between ex post and ex ante control of the executive action within the Council of the European Union.[54]

The senate has not been especially involved in EC/EU affairs except for questions and interpellations addressed to the government on EC issues affecting the Autonomous Communities, such as those related to the Structural Funds or the CoR. After the ratification of the TEU, the senate took the decision to set up a special committee to report on regional participation in Europe. However, it is before the senate's Budget Committee where the Secretary of State for Foreign Policy and the European Union regularly reports on a bi-monthly basis.

The Spanish Autonomous Communities and other sub-national actors

The Spanish Autonomous Communities implement Community policies within their own areas of competence according to the constitutional distribution of powers. The adaptation of regional legislation already in force prior to Spain's accession affected only Catalonia and the Basque Country. In a similar way to the situation on a national scale, regional governments remain the main actors for decision-making and management of EC/EU-related affairs. Nevertheless, regional parliaments, traditionally excluded from the management and control of these areas, have started recently to expand their activities in this field. Apart from debating the general or sectoral impact of the process of European integration for the respective Autonomous Community, regional parliaments regularly adopt resolutions or recommendations addressed to the regional government with a view to influencing both its internal policy and the relationship with the central government and administration.

Most regional parliaments have set up permanent parliamentary committees of a non-legislative nature in order to monitor developments in EU affairs.[55] These parliamentary committees are based on the model of the Joint Committee for the European Union. The regional minister co-ordinating the EC/EU affairs[56] reports on a regular basis to the committee and responds to the questions and interpellations posed by its members. These committees have in certain cases established formal relations with the CoR or with similar committees in regional parliaments of other Member States.[57] In 1994, three regional parliaments[58] for the first time adopted regional laws establishing procedures to participate in and control the management of the Structural Funds by the regional governments in its different stages – project selection, programming, financial execution. This is a further step with regard to the control mechanisms set up by the national Cortes.[59]

Each of the seventeen Autonomous Communities has created a department which deals exclusively with EC/EU affairs. These departments, which vary considerably in size and administrative relevance – as does their title and management status – are situated within one of the regional ministries (Consejerías) and tend to be located in the regional capital. The regional ministry concerned varies from one community to another, though it is usually a Directorate-General or service reporting to the regional Minister of the Presidency.[60] The organisation of the regional administrations for EC/EU affairs is directly related to the management of the Structural Funds.[61] The exception is the more complex cases of the Basque Country[62] and Catalonia. Most of the regional governments[63] have opened a Representation Office in Brussels with the main aim of keeping up to date with the latest EU developments, particularly those affecting the regions. However, there is a strong difference in the legal form, status and level of autonomy from the regional government. These regional offices – as well as the external activities, but not foreign relations, of the Autonomous Communities[64] – have been granted firm legal support by Decision 165/1994 of the Constitutional Court. The Representation Offices have started to create loose co-operation and co-ordination structures among themselves in terms of their relationship with the CoR, the EP or the Commission, always under the supervision of the Permanent Representation of Spain to the European Union.

Hierarchies, levels and channels of co-ordination with regard to EU policy-making

Co-ordination of policy between the central government ministries is organised by the Secretariat of State for Foreign Policy and the European Union. Apart from the Ministry of Foreign Affairs, other ministries with horizontal competences[65] have also started to play a co-ordinating role in terms of the Spanish participation in the EC/EU decision-making process, owing to the relative loss of comparative political weight experienced by the MAE. The Interministerial Conference for the European Union (Conferencia Interministerial para la Unión Europea)[66] is presided over by the Secretary of State for Foreign Policy and the European Union and includes representatives (Under-Secretaries, or Subsecretarios) of every ministry, as well as the Deputy Director of the Cabinet of the President of the Government. Its vice-presidents are the Secretary of the Delegated Committee for Economic Affairs and the General Secretary for Foreign Policy and the European Union. It meets on a fortnightly basis and is used to resolve disagreements between ministries, though it essentially co-ordinates economic affairs and provides information.[67] The political relevance of the Interministerial Conference arises from the monopoly of unified external action exerted by the Ministry of Foreign Affairs.

In the event that no final agreement can be reached with regard to economic issues, the matter can be submitted to the Governmental Delegated Committee for Economic Affairs (Comisión Delegada para Asuntos Económicos), which groups the economic oriented ministries under the co-ordination of highest-rank officials of the Ministry of Economy and Finance. The Minister of Foreign Affairs and the Secretary of State for the European Union attend this committee when it deals with EC/EU affairs, and so in most cases. In case of further conflict between ministries, negotiating positions in Brussels are settled through informal contacts among the Permanent Representatives, officials of SEPEUE and of the ministries involved. The Ministry for the Public Administrations co-ordinates the Governmental Delegated Committee for Autonomic (regional) Policy (Comisión Delegada para Política Autonómica), which from 1996 has increasingly intervened in the definition and co-ordination of the Spanish EC/EU policy with the Autonomous Communities. Finally, there is a Monitoring and Co-ordinating Committee for affairs related to the ECJ (Comisión de Seguimiento y Coordinación de Asuntos relacionados con el TJCE), composed of representatives of the Cabinet of the President, SEPEUE, and the Ministries of Justice, Economy and others specifically involved. This committee studies all proceedings brought against or by Spain before the ECJ.

The implementation of Community policies by the lower levels of the Spanish public administration has received growing awareness and specialisation with the general aims of improving the implementation structures, intra-governmental co-ordination and co-operation with regional administrations. Community pressures and suggestions have thus had a consistent impact on Spanish administration and its internal procedures.[68] This general trend should not hide the growing difficulty of implementing Community decisions in Spain owing to the transfer of competences to the Autonomous Communities, the disruption of formal traditional co-operation schemes between public administrations and the compelling need to meet higher standards.[69]

As regards regional participation in the EC/EU decision-making process,[70] several steps have been taken in recent years, mainly owing to the parliamentary support received by the socialist and conservative governments from the Catalonian (currently also Basque and Canarian) nationalist parties. The initial structure of information transfer never satisfied Catalonia and the Basque Country, which always wanted their own representatives to have more autonomy with respect to the Permanent Representation. Regions and central government institutionalised regional participation in Community affairs by means of the Conference on Community Affairs (Conferencia para Asuntos relacionados con las Comunidades Europeas), set up at ministry level, which will be assisted by a permanent working group, the Committee of Co-ordinators on Community Affairs (Comisión de Coordinadores para Asuntos Comunitarios). At the same time, the conference initiates and monitors regional participation in each Community policy through the specific Sectorial Conferences Government–Regions already existing.[71] The Council of Fiscal and Financial Policy of the Autonomous Communities (Consejo de Política Fiscal y Financiera de las Comunidades Autónomas) co-ordinates, among the general economic interests of the regions, those relating to the EC (relations with the ECOFIN, Structural Funds).

Despite the establishment of the conference, the regions continue to develop bilateral contacts with SEPEUE, which acts as their real partner for the defence of regional interests. Agreements and relations between the regions and SEPEUE have grown considerably. The Autonomous Communities have insisted on the need to include regional representatives in the Commission's advisory committees and the possibility that a regional minister could represent Spain in the Council meetings when regional competences are concerned.[72] Co-ordination between the major EU institutions and the regional departments dealing with EC affairs is arranged by SEPEUE. In 1997 a new delegate for the autonomous communities Affairs was appointed within the Spanish Permanent Representation to the European Union, whose aim is to co-ordinate the relationships between the regional offices in Brussels, the transmission of information to them and the definition and defence of the regional interests by the Spanish delegations in the EC/EU decision-making process. Spanish regional representatives within the CoR have so far played an important and active role. Some Spanish regions are part of transnational co-operation agreements with their partners from other Member States.[73]

Interaction between the national and Brussels levels

Spain has traditionally adopted an integrationist approach in relation to its negotiating positions within the EC/EU decision-making process. The Spanish government has traditionally kept good contacts with the European Commission and the EP. Such an integrationist approach has not stopped Spain from securing its national interests, especially in the institutional field, however; much of this is related to Spain's position between the 'large' and 'small' Member States. Spain has supported the Commission's points of view on most procedural issues. Nevertheless, it has also traditionally rejected (for example, at the 1996–97 IGC) the extension of majority voting to certain sensitive areas, such as the Structural Funds and the Environment. The co-ordinating role of the Spanish Permanent Representation, closely connected with the Ministry of Foreign Affairs, is crucial, both for the different national government departments and for the regional Representation Offices. Apart from informal contacts within political parties and parliamentary bodies, there has been no special effort by the Spanish institutions to establish closer links with the EP. However, the EP has had a growing public relevance and its profile in the media has been considerably enhanced in recent years following the debates on certain 'hot' issues, such as olive oil, CMO reform, budgetary reform, and the Commission's vote of no-confidence.

The parliamentary Joint Committee for the European Union also participates in the meetings of COSAC and bilateral meetings with delegations or bodies from the EP or other national parliaments of the Union. The President of the Congress/delegation of the Joint Committee for the European Union regularly attend meetings between the President of the EP and the representatives of the national parliaments. This occurs at the invitation of the current Presidency. The purpose of the meeting is to review the network of relations among parliaments and to suggest ways in which links can be improved. Spanish deputies and senators do not generally have other permanent channels of communication with the EU institutions apart from the Secretariat of State for the European Union, their respective political parties and personal contacts with MEPs.

The Spanish Constitutional Court vis-à-vis the implementation and control of EC legislation

The Spanish Constitutional Court has not dealt in a large number of cases directly concerning EC law. Most of the legal doctrine speaks of its 'lack of interest' or even 'reluctance to interpret' the Community legal order.[74] The Spanish Constitutional Court, a major organ of the Spanish institutional structure, has paradoxically developed its jurisprudence on the interpretation and application of EC law. This is carried out within the framework of its frequent interventions in constitutional disputes relating to the impact of Community acts on the internal division of powers between the central government and the Autonomous Communities.[75] The Spanish Constitutional Court has always defended its incompetence to decide on the compatibility between national law and EC law on the grounds of the non-constitutional rank of such legal conflict.[76] This implies that the Constitutional Court refuses to control the application of Community law, except for the protection of fundamental rights. Decision 28/1991 attributed the controversial term 'conflict of infra-constitutional norms' to such legal controversies, which was abandoned in Decision 180/1993 and reinstored in Decision 45/1996, much to the regret of the Spanish legal profession.[77] The jurisprudence of the Spanish Constitutional Court in the period 1993–98 (apart from the famous Decision 165/1994 concerning the Office of the Basque Government in Brussels[78]) has not varied with regard to its control of the application of EC law.[79]

On the other hand, in the field of fundamental rights, the Spanish Constitutional Court has accepted that the EC legal order might complement the scope of certain constitutional provisions in this field, by means of the extension of its application to non-nationals[80] or the interpretation to be given to sex discrimination.[81] However, the Constitutional Court has refused to accept, unlike its German and Austrian counterparts, that the arbitrary denial by a judge to initiate a preliminary ruling procedure before the ECJ might constitute a violation of the constitutional fundamental right to a fair trial.[82] The Constitutional Court itself has refused, though not categorically, to initiate preliminary ruling procedures before the ECJ. Finally, regarding disputes between the central government and the Autonomous Communities, the constitutional court has frequently been obliged to solve problems arising when both levels of government claim exclusive competence to enforce Community directives on shared matters according to the constitution and the respective Statutes of Autonomy (Estatutos de Autonomía). The Constitutional Court has insisted throughout this period in its traditional doctrine that the accession of Spain to the Union has not meant any reassignment of internal powers to the benefit of the central government. The Autonomous Communities remain responsible for the effective enforcement of such legislation, while the central government does so only for the negotiation of such agreements at supranational level and for the global guarantee of their fulfilment.

The Spanish courts vis-à-vis the implementation and control of EC legislation

The impact of EC law on Spanish society has been of great significance in the vast majority of economic sectors. Most of the Spanish legislation originally enacted to regulate for the first time several aspects of economic activity (e.g. competition law, insurance law, company law, environmental law, and consumer protection) directly derives from EC legislation. The adaptation of Spanish courts to Community law has been slow – as well as its use and allegiance by lawyers and prosecutors – but progressive with regard to both its interpretation and application. It could be stated that the situation in 1999 regarding the application of EC law by the Spanish courts was of full familiarisation and general acceptance of their role within the Community legal order.[83]

The number of preliminary ruling procedures initiated by Spanish courts has steadily increased to a current total number of ca. 50 procedures. Between 1986 and 1993 an extremely low number of preliminary rulings were initiated. This was especially the case until 1989,[84] mostly owing to the unawareness or misuse of the procedure by national judges. Since 1993, the trend has risen.[85] Some of these procedures are accumulated or withdrawn at a later stage of the process before the ECJ. The General Council of the Judiciary (Consejo General del Poder Judicial) and the main Lawyers' Associations systematically offered until 1996 specific courses and seminars addressed to magistrates, judges and lawyers on the application of EC law. In fact, some of the preliminary rulings initiated by Spanish judges have given course to crucial decisions of the jurisprudence of the ECJ (i.e. *Marleasing*, *Michelletti*, *FOGASA*, *Bordessa*). Not only the ordinary judges, but also the Supreme Court[86] and, especially, the High Courts of the Autonomous Communities (Tribunales Superiores de Justicia) have initiated such procedures. That has also been the case of two non-jurisdictional organs such as the Competition Defence Body (Tribunal de Defensa de la Competencia) and the Central Economic–Administrative Court (Tribunal Económico–Administrativo Central). The fact that most of such procedures arise from regional courts is a good sign of their dynamism and compliance with EC law, despite their recent creation.[87] Most Spanish courts having initiated a preliminary ruling procedure before the ECJ have later fully complied with the Court's decision within the further internal legal procedure.[88]

The Autonomous Communities have not been granted the right by the central government to directly defend their interests before the ECJ. Finally, certain organs recently created within the Spanish public administration of semi-jurisdictional nature[89] have started to co-operate fruitfully with the European Commission concerning the application of EC law.

Overall trends: the impact of the TEU on the political and administrative system

It could be stated that the level of 'Europeanisation' of the Spanish politico-administrative system has followed a progressive linear trend to its present position. The number of permanent civil servants in Brussels increased on a regular basis until the period of the last socialist government (1993–96), mostly due to administrative needs and restructuring caused by scope differentiation; their number has scarcely varied in recent years. On the other hand, the number of civil servants sent to Brussels from the national government departments has continued to increase, though not on a permanent basis. The effect of the implementation of the national plans for the restructuring of public administration and the ongoing transfer of competences to the Autonomous Communities has to be taken into account when comparing global figures. The level of 'Europeanisation' of the Spanish administrative varies significantly from the national to the regional and local levels. Nevertheless, the situation has in general terms stabilised, with the exception of certain Autonomous Communities with a lower attribution of competences. The EC/EU dimension is currently present into all departments of the different political levels. Continuity and deepening of the ongoing trends are the key issues concerning the assignment of the administration and coordination of EC/EU affairs to the various public bodies and institutions.

Both the Spanish Permanent Representation to the EU and SEPEUE have expanded their functioning structures to the maximum levels. Internal redistribution of competences merely reflects the increasing specialisation and professionalisation of their services and departments. The intermediate levels of the national administration within ministries or autonomous bodies are by far the least 'Europeanised'; their modernisation and reform is closely linked to the permanent process of internal redistribution of powers with the regional levels and the creation of new co-ordinating bodies. In any case, the global reform of the Spanish public administration is the last chapter, continuously postponed,[90] to be accomplished to create the full modernisation of the Spanish political system.

The management and administration of EC/EU affairs has increasingly become a major battlefield in the internal power disputes between administrative departments. This occurs between ministries especially with regard to the management of the Structural Funds and EC programmes and initiatives. However, it also occurs within the ministries themselves. At the same time, the need for co-ordination structures frequently transforms the EC/EU dimension in a common and neutral basis for interaction between different departments. This is particularly relevant in ministries with competences of a purely vertical nature, for example JHA and Public Health, which traditionally delegated all internationally related affairs to a single internal department.

On the other hand, both the definition and financing procedures of certain EC policies have caused internal rearrangements within the Spanish politico-administrative system, resulting that former strictly technical departments have now acquired a new political dimension. The EU institutions have also contributed to this polarisation of competences by requiring a single partner on the national level in terms of the negotiation and implementation processes. The European Commission has constantly encouraged the national level of the Spanish public administration to incorporate the regional administrative levels in the EC/EU decision-making process, since the Autonomous Communities will increasingly become responsible for the implementation of EC legislation.

Finally, it can be stated that no major changes at the administrative level can be observed when comparing the situation under the socialist governments and the current conservative one. The exception is the global trend towards the re-nationalisation of certain EC/EU policies and their management, derived both from the less integrationist approach shown by the Partido Popular and President Aznar towards the process of European integration and the general situation in other EU Member States. The relative decline of the co-ordinating and policy-defining role of the Ministry of Foreign Affairs could also explain the recent subtle trend towards more independent approaches to EC/EU affairs on the part of certain ministries, such as Agriculture, Economy and Finance, and Public Works.

Conclusions: from adaptive newcomer to controversial mainstreamer

General assessment on the 'post-Maastricht' changes in the Spanish political system

The Spanish politico-administrative system has been widely affected by the Treaty of Maastricht, but not in a disruptive way. On the contrary, the adoption and implementation of the TEU have simply contributed to the reinforcement, deepening and acceleration of reform processes already under way.[91] Furthermore, the most relevant changes in the management of EC/EU affairs by the Spanish administration do not directly derive from the implementation of the Treaty itself, but either from external complementary aspects or as a direct result of long-time prior developments. The implementation of the Treaty of Maastricht in Spain has run parallel to two simultaneous political processes. The first is the acceleration of the redistribution of powers between the national and the regional level (1993–99).[92] The second concerns the setting up of new departments and administrative bodies to deal with sectoral policies not previously managed at the corresponding level.[93] In general terms, it could be stated that the Treaty of Maastricht has clearly reinforced the role of the executive, at both national and regional level, in the EC/EU decision-making process. Only relative changes have occurred to enhance the role of the parliamentary bodies or that of the Autonomous Communities in their relationships with the central authorities concerning the protection of their interests. Thus, it can be agreed that the European integration process has had a negative impact on both the horizontal and vertical division of powers. Most units or bodies related to EC/EU affairs have changed their respective denominations. In some cases, new legislative acts or decrees adopted in

1994 or 1996[94] have reinforced or redefined their rights and competences (e.g. SEPEUE, Joint Committee for the European Union, and the Interministerial Conference for the European Union).

The Ministry of Foreign Affairs has retained its major co-ordinating role for all matters related to the Union, while the Ministry of Economy and Finance has considerably increased its policy scope, principally owing to management of the Structural Funds and the importance of the budgetary and financial provisions of EC/EU policies. The new policies introduced at European level by the TEU have generalised the EC dimension – hence the creation of specialised units – in all Ministries and their participation in the various co-ordinating bodies. A general trend towards further specialisation in certain units and incorporation of EC-related issues to the activities of the vast majority of administrative departments can readily be acknowledged. The implementation of the subsidiarity principle has not had any major direct impact on Spanish participation in the EC/EU decision-making process.

The definition of Spain's access to the third stage of EMU as a major all-embracing political objective by Aznar's government brought an overwhelming presence of EC/EU-related considerations into the national political debate and the administrative activity of most departments after 1997. The enactment of intergovernmental co-operation in the JHA field within the TEU also enhanced Spain's international police and judicial co-operation and opened a new policy area of great relevance and dynamism for Spain's national interests, such as immigration, and the fight against terrorism and drug trafficking. Not so much can be said of CFSP; the expectations raised by the new EU Mediterranean policy after the Barcelona Conference have not led to major results. The reinforcement of Spanish–Latin American relationships since 1990 were influenced not so much by Spain's membership of the Union, but by other factors, both political and economic.[95]

While the Spanish administrative level has not changed excessively in institutional terms[96] – despite the general acceptance that the impact of European integration has implied growing public management competitiveness – clear changes can be acknowledged at the political level. The public role, political relevance and selection of ministers and their teams of collaborators already takes into account the EC/EU dimension of their competences.[97] A clear distinction has been drawn within the Spanish representatives in Brussels between the technical level, where total continuity has presided over the change from the socialist to the conservative government, and the political level. President Aznar followed in the steps of his predecessors in most aspects of European policy. The management style has been different, focusing on team approaches and specific advances rather than overall strategies, and Spain's bilateral relationships with other members states of the Union – especially Portugal, France, and to a lesser extent, Italy and the United Kingdom – have considerably improved. Bilateral annual meetings have become increasingly institutionalised with Germany, France, Italy, Portugal and Morocco.

European integration has clearly produced more benefits than losses for Spain in terms of financial resources and political influence.[98] EC membership has also had a consistent impact on most Spanish public administrations whose procedures and structures have undergone a far-reaching process of adaptation to conform to Community standards. During the period after the adoption of the TEU (1993–99), previous politico-administrative trends and processes were reinforced or deepened, though not always as a direct result of the process of European integration itself. It could be said that the level of Spain's national participation has become more significant, especially on the political level and less so on the administrative one, yet without becoming too dominant. The number of meetings with national participation as well as the number of national civil servants posted to Brussels has begun to stagnate at the high level already achieved. The legislative output clearly differs from one policy field to another, though this might still be the result of the relatively recent enforcement of the Treaty of Maastricht and the features of the decision-making processes assigned to each of these policy fields. However, the changes and evolution experienced by the Spanish politico-administrative system concerning the process of European integration, and its participation in the EC/EU decision-making process imply long-term structural growth and policy differentiation. This is particularly the case at the administrative level. This long-term trend has sometimes been overshadowed by cyclical ups and downs,[99] which mostly happen at the political level, owing to external or indirect variables. In any case, the interaction of public instruments from several state levels linked with the respective 'Europeanisation' of national actors and institutions can easily be seen at its full extent in the Spanish case, particularly since 1995. The struggle for participation of national representatives and institutions takes place both horizontally (government, parliament and ministries) and vertically (government and the Autonomous Communities) on the Spanish national level and on the European one.

Both Spanish national and regional actors are increasingly taking part in the EC/EU legislative process and have experienced an extensive process of adaptation of their internal procedures. The increased rights for participation and co-decision have been used intensively by such actors. However, the internal Spanish political situation also clearly interferes with these processes, accelerating or slowing them down: the preference for certain instruments or decision procedures does not exclusively depend on the rhythm of the process of European integration itself. Finally, the increasing role of public opinion – though still not very relevant in the Spanish case – should also be taken into account.

The major pending issues and weaknesses of Spanish participation in the EC/EU decision-making process are the definition of a new effective model for the participation of the Autonomous Communities in all stages of the process. This still depends on the relative political strength of the nationalist/regionalist parties and their political alliances with the nationwide political forces. The improvement of the functioning of the co-ordinating bodies is also vital. The policy process still appears highly fragmented and insufficiently co-ordinated, both horizontally and vertically.

Perspectives for the future: the 1996–97 IGC and other EU negotiation processes

Spain played a relevant and high-profile role in most phases of the 1996–97 IGC.[100] Its priorities with regard to the revision of the Maastricht Treaty were made public in Autumn 1996, some months after the accession of the Partido Popular (PP) to power, and were mostly the result of general consensus among the major political parties.[101] Continuity presided both over the content of the proposals and the nomination of the non-political members of the negotiating team.[102] The main Spanish proposals,[103] apart from the maintenance of the clear separation between the IGC negotiations and the EMU process, were: support for the incorporation of a new Title on Employment; the creation of an area of freedom, security and justice, together with the reinforcement of the role of Europol and judicial co-operation on a European scale. However, there are still many controversial issues for the Spanish general public and the media. The prohibition of the analysis of political asylum requests by EU nationals[104] and the reinforcement of the CoR serve as examples. Yet there remain more: the simplification of the co-decision procedure; the establishment of an effective common security and defence policy by means of the prospective integration of the WEU within the EU; the European Convention on Human Rights (ECHR) before the ECJ; equality between men and women; the encouragement and co-ordination of voluntary organisations; and the creation of a permanent statute for the ultra-peripheral and island regions (i.e. the Canary Islands). Although Spain did not provide any written proposal on the weighting of votes in the Council or the number of members of the Commission, it did block these institutional issues owing to national interests.[105]

Finally, Spain firmly rejected certain proposals by other Member States which would have affected its national interests, especially those of a wider notion of the principle of flexibility and the re-drafting of the conditions of application of the principle of subsidiarity. On the other hand, Spain defended the extension of majority voting exclusively to certain individual areas, with a total rejection of such extension in the cases of management of the Structural Funds, social protection and management of water resources. Spain has also played or started to play a high-profile role in the negotiation processes concerning EC budgetary reform and the accession of new Member States, owing to the fact that it is currently the only large Member State with a conservative political party in power.[106] Spain has felt obliged to lead the position and interests of the so-called 'cohesion countries' in relation to the proposals of the northern countries for budgetary reform.

Prime Minister Aznar achieved a major internal political success with the entry of Spain into the third phase of EMU.[107] The successful performance of Aznar's economic policies and the relative lack of internal social tensions (apart from the new scenario created by the complex Basque peace process), has strengthened his position. The new role to be played within the European conservative political parties and among their leaders, and the experience accumulated in the European and international arenas since 1997 are also the foundations of Aznar's solid internal negotiating position. The co-ordinating role of the 'cohesion countries' has been strongly reinforced by means of close contact with the Portuguese and Greek governments.

At first glance, Spain is one of the Member States to have its national interests most negatively affected by the results of the EC budgetary reform. The management and effectiveness of the Structural Funds in the Spanish economy started to have its full effect only in recent years. Co-ordination, both vertical and horizontal, among the different administrative levels with regard to EU affairs still needs reinforcing and global improvement. Spain therefore seeks to extend as long as possible its present status as a net recipient state in financial terms, in order to further reduce the economic gap among its regions and in comparison with other Member States. The re-nationalisation of the traditionally integrationist Spanish policy towards the process of European integration seems inevitable, at least in the short term, given the current European political scenario. Spain's concerns regarding the enlargement of the Union towards Central and Eastern Europe are mostly motivated by the potential financial and institutional repercussions.[108] Contacts at the highest political level between the Spanish government and governments of some of the candidate countries, such as Poland and the Czech Republic, confirm this impression. The access of Spanish economic actors to such new markets will be reduced and unlikely to develop further. Historical and cultural links with such countries are also not very close. Spain could be in the position to condition the enlargement on the maintenance of a certain status quo within the present institutional and financial set-up of the Union.

Notes

1 The Accession Treaty was officially signed in Madrid on 12 June 1985, while the Organic Law of Authorisation LO 10/85, 2 August 1985, was published in the Spanish *Official Journal* (BOE), 8 August 1985.

2 See documents and political speeches in: Antonio Moreno Juste, *España y el proceso de construcción europea* (Barcelona: Ariel Practicum, 1998); and Raimundo Bassols, *España en Europa. Historia de la adhesión a la CE (1957–85)* (Madrid: Ed. Política Exterior, 1995).

3 Both chambers of the Spanish Parliament, the Congress and Senate, unanimously granted their authorisation for the ratification of the Accession Treaty on 26 June 1985.

4 See *El País*, Special Issue 228, 'Europeos', 2 July 1995; and 'Encuesta de opinión sobre los españoles en la Unión Europea', 21 June 1996, pp. 26 ff.

5 Particularly, the left-wing coalition Izquierda Unida (IU) and some of the nationalist/regionalist political parties, and, to a lesser extent, individual members of the right-wing Partido Popular (PP). See VV.AA., *La izquierda y Europa. Una aproximación crítica al Tratado de Maastricht* (Madrid: Izquierda Unida/Los Libros de la Catarata, 1992).

6 Spain has adopted very definite national negotiating positions, especially with regard to the maintenance of the Structural and Cohesion Funds.

7 See Carmen Garcia, 'Les groupes d'intérêt espagnols et la Communauté Européenne', in: Dusan Sidjanski and Ulrich Ayberk (eds), L'Europe du Sud dans la Communauté Européenne (Paris: PUF, 1990), pp. 115, 150; Mariano Baena del Alcázar, 'Groupes de pression et Administration en Espagne', in: *Annuaire Européen d'Administration Publique*, 1992, p. 137; and Emiliano Alonso Pelegrín, *El Lobby en la Unión Europea. Manual sobre el buen uso de Bruselas* (Madrid: Ediciones ESIC, 1994).

8 See Richard Gillespie, Fernando Rodrigo and John Story. *Las relaciones exteriores de la España democrática* (Madrid: Alianza, 1996).

9 Among others, the inclusion of the European citizenship provisions within the TEU or some of the key concepts of the co-operation in the JHA fields. See VV.AA., *España y el Tratado de la Unión Europea* (Madrid: COLEX, 1994), pp. 7–55; *Comité Organizador de la Presidencia Española del Consejo de la Unión Europea, Prioridades de la Presidencia española del Consejo de la Unión Europea* (Madrid: BOE, 1995); and VV.AA., *España y la negociación del Tratado de Amsterdam, Biblioteca Nueva* (Madrid: Ed. Política Exterior, 1998), pp. 35–58.

10 See M. Ramírez Jiménez, *Europa en la conciencia española y otros estudios* (Madrid: Trotta, 1996).

11 The length of such transitional periods, depending on the different policy areas and even product markets, ranged from five to seventeen years, being in some cases later reduced or renegotiated.

12 Especially the fisheries issues after the conflicts with Canada (1993) and Morocco (1995, 1999), and the enlargement negotiations with Norway.

13 The pursuit of a special status for the Canary Islands and its tax regime is to be explained in terms of the political support granted to Aznar's government by the Canarian nationalist parties.

14 Namely, the Catalonian centre-right coalition Convergencia i Uniò (CiU), the Basque Conservative party Partido Nacionalista Vasco (PNV) and the Canarian centre coalition Coalición Canaria (CC).

15 See VV.AA., *El tercer pilar de la Unión Europea. La cooperación en asuntos de justicia e interior* (Madrid: Publicaciones del Ministerio del Interior, 1997), pp. 9–22; and VV.AA., 1998, *op. cit.*, pp. 61–108.

16 See Rafael Arias Salgado, 'La política europea de España y la Conferencia Intergubernamental de 1996', in: *Política Exterior*, No. 47/1995, pp. 38–46.

17 See Angel Boixareu Carrera, 'Aspectos generales y principios básicos de la Unión. Subsidiariedad y suficiencia de medios', in: VV.AA., 1994, *op. cit.*, pp. 55–86.

18 See Araceli Mangas Martín, 'Le droit constitutionnel national et l'intégration européenne: Espagne', in: Jürgen Schwarze (ed.), *XVII FIDE Kongress (Berlin, October 1996) – Ergebnisse und Perspektiven* (Baden-Baden: Nomos, 1997), pp. 206–230.

19 Spain's entry into the Union coincided with the negotiation and enforcement of the SEA, hence the immediate implementation of its institutional and procedural changes.

20 It was accomplished by means of Organic Law 10/1992 of 28 December 1992, published in the *Spanish Official Journal* (BOE), No. 312, 29 December 1992.

21 See Pablo Pérez Tremps, *Constitución española y Comunidad Europea, Cuadernos de Estudios Europeos 11* (Madrid: Civitas, 1994).

22 Declaración del Tribunal Constitucional, 21 July 1992, on the possible incompatibility between Article 8B TEU and Article 13.2 of the Spanish Constitution, *Boletín de Legislación Extranjera*, 147–148, pp. 89–97.

23 Dictamen de la Comisión Permanente del Consejo de Estado, 9 April 1992, on the constitutional implications of the possible ratification of the TEU, in: *Boletín de Legislación Extranjera*, 149–150, pp. 81–88.

24 See among others Araceli Mangas Martín, 'La Declaración del Tribunal Constitucional sobre el artículo 13.2 de la Constitución (derecho de sufragio pasivo de los extranjeros). Una reforma constitucional innecesaria o insuficiente', in: *Revista Española de Derecho Internacional*, No. 2/1992, p. 38; and Francisco Rubio Llorente, 'La Constitution espagnole et le Traité de Maastricht', in: *Revue Française de Droit Constitutionnel*, No. 12/1992, pp. 351–361.

25 By means of Organic Law LO 9/1998, 16 December 1998, published in the *Spanish Official Journal* (BOE), 17 December 1998. Several amendments to the text of the Organic Law were proposed and later rejected by the Basque Nationalist Party with regard to further involvement of the Autonomous Communities in the decision-making process related to EC affairs. The ratification law includes an additional provision accepting the automatic jurisdictional competence of the ECJ concerning preliminary rulings in the field of judicial and police co-operation in criminal matters.

26 What initially was merely reduced to the implementation of specific Community policies (agriculture and fisheries) and the management of the Structural Funds can nowadays be already ascertained as the definition of full 'European policies' at the regional level. The participation and representation

of regional interests within the national EC/EU decision-making process was considerably enhanced – though still far from the demands and expectations of the Autonomous Communities – after Maastricht by means of the setting up of various State–Regions co-ordinating bodies and the appointment of a Counsellor for Autonomic ('Regional') Affairs within the Spanish Permanent Representation to the European Union.

27 All socialist and conservative governments from the 1993 general elections onwards relied upon the parliamentary support of the Catalonian nationalist coalition CiU.

28 For an updated overview of the Spanish politico-administrative system, see Michael T. Newton and Peter J. Donaghy, *Institutions of Modern Spain: A Political and Economic Guide* (Cambridge: Cambridge University Press, 1997).

29 SEPEUE was in fact established in February 1981, long before negotiations for accession had been concluded, under the denomination of the Secretariat of State for the Relationships with the European Communities (Secretaría de Estado para las Relaciones con las Comunidades Europeas, SERCE). This key institution for the Spanish EC/EU decision-making process was after 1986 called the Secretariat of State for the European Communities (Secretaría de Estado para las Comunidades Europeas, SECE) and after 1993 the Secretariat of State for the European Union (Secretaría de Estado para la Unión Europea, SEUE).

30 That was also the case with the State Legal Service for the Court of Justice of the European Communities (Servicio Jurídico del Estado ante el Tribunal de Justicia de las Comunidades Europeas).

31 It used to include two Directorates-General – the Directorate-General for Technical Co-ordination in European Affairs (Dirección general de Coordinación Técnica Comunitaria), dealing with internal policy, including more technical and economic matters, and the Directorate-General for EU Legal and Institutional Affairs (Dirección general de Coordinación Jurídca e Institucional Comunitaria), concerned with external, more political affairs, including the interpretation of EU legislation.

32 This latter also comprises a new Under-Directorate for Legal Affairs (Subdirección de Asuntos Jurídicos), which globally supervises the legal aspects of the whole Spanish EC/EU decision-making process, as well as acting before the ECJ on behalf of the Spanish government.

33 By far the most important of the latter for Spain is the ERDF, dealt with by the Sub-Directorate General for Management and Administration (Subdirección general de Gestión y Administración), a division of the Directorate-General for Planning (Dirección general de Planificación). In turn this Directorate-General is responsible to the General Secretariat for Planning and Budgets (Secretaría general de Planificación y Presupuestos). Some EC initiatives such as RECHAR, STRIDE, ENVIREG and PRISMA are directly handled by the MEH.

34 This Ministry also collaborates with the National Institute for Employment (Instituto Nacional de Empleo, INEM) and the Ministry of Education, Science and Culture through the Fund for the Promotion of Employment (Fondo para la Promoción del Empleo) for the management and promotion

of certain EU schemes and initiatives in this field (e.g. EUROTECNET). It also collaborates with three Institutes from the former Ministry – currently Secretariat of State – of Social Affairs (Secretaría de Estado de Asuntos Sociales): the Institute for Young People's Affairs (Instituto de la Juventud, INJUVE), the Institute for Women's Affairs (Instituto de la Mujer) and the Institute for Social Services (Instituto de Servicios Sociales, INSERSO).

35 The Guidance Section of the Fund is managed by the National Institute for Agrarian Reform and Development (Instituto Nacional de Reforma y Desarrollo Agrario, IRYDA), which is also responsible for administering bids and payments of the LEADER initiative. The Guarantee Section of the EAGGF is administered by the Fund for the Organisation and Regulation of Agricultural Products and Prices (Fondo de Ordenación y Regulación de Productos y Precios Agrarios, FORPPA), though actual payments under this scheme come from the National Service for Agricultural Products (Servicio Nacional de Productos Agrarios, SENPA). Both FORPPA and SENPA are autonomous commercial bodies. The IFOP is independently administered by the Fund for the Regulation and Market Organisation of Fish and Marine Products (Fondo de Regulación y Organización del Mercado de Productos de la Pesca y Cultivos Marinos, FROM).

36 The Department for the Organisation and Establishment of Professional Training (Area de Ordenación e Implantación de la Formación Profesional), formerly in charge of EUROTECNET, and the Secretariat of State for Universities and Research (Secretaría de Estado de Universidades e Investigación), formerly in charge of COMETT and other initiatives, are at present jointly responsible for the LEONARDO programme; the Sub-Directorate General for International Co-operation (Subdirección general de Cooperación Internacional), formerly in charge of LINGUA and TEMPUS, together with the Secretariat-General of the Universities Council (Secretaría general del Consejo de Universidades) are responsible for the SOCRATES programme.

37 Mainly through the Centre for Industrial Technological Development (Centro para el Desarrollo Tecnológico Industrial), though all activities in this field are co-ordinated by the Interministerial Committee for Science and Technology (Comisión Interministerial de Ciencia y Tecnología, CICYT), which also acts as a monitoring agent for Spanish involvement in the programmes.

38 These activities were previously managed by the Directorate-General for Environmental Policy within the former Ministry of Public Works, Transport and Environment.

39 Spain has tabled numerous proposals in this field and led the debate for the communitarisation of certain areas within the former third pillar. Some political parties and civil associations working in the fields of immigration and asylum have expressed their reluctance about some of the measures and decision-making procedures of the EU third pillar.

40 See Manuel Cienfuegos Mateo, 'El control de las Cortes Generales sobre el Gobierno en asuntos relativos a las Comunidades Europeas durante la década 1986–1995', in: *Revista de las Cortes Generales*, No. 38/1996, pp. 47–99.

41 Until the Reform Law of 1994 it was not the case with administrative decrees.
42 Only certain Congress deputies of the left-wing coalition Izquierda Unida and of some of the Basque, Catalonian and Canarian nationalist parties have actually developed dissenting strategies on EC affairs within the parliamentary bodies. See Beatriz Alvarez-Miranda Navarro, 'Integración europea y sistemas de partidos en el Sur de Europa: despolarización y convergencia', in: *Revista de Estudios Políticos*, No. 3/1994, pp. 143–167.
43 According to Articles 93, 94 and 96.2 of the Spanish Constitution, and, among them, those relating to the transfer of competences to supranational organisations. Different voting majorities are required depending on the specific types of international treaties. See Pérez Tremps, 1994, *op. cit.*, pp. 121 ff.
44 As is the case of the so-called 'State of the Nation' or 'State of the Autonomous Communities' annual parliamentary debates.
45 It should be underlined that at least one-third of these questions still pose general or institutional problems.
46 This practice was institutionalised after the meeting of the European Council held at the end of the first Spanish Presidency of the Council (1989).
47 Such as the Committee on Agriculture and Fisheries, the Committee on Foreign Affairs, the Committee on Industry or the Committee on Public Works.
48 See Manuel Cienfuegos Mateo, 'La Comisión Mixta para la Unión Europea. Análisis y balance de una década de actividad en el seguimiento de los asuntos comunitarios', in: *Gaceta Jurídica de la CE*, D-27, 1997, pp. 7–69.
49 This latter was created by the law of 27 December 1985. Its name, and, to some extent its functions, were changed by the law of 19 May 1994 following Spain's parliamentary ratification of the TEU.
50 That was not the case before, with a larger number of congress members.
51 Relevant politicians have assumed in practice the co-ordinating role of the committee in recent legislatures: Isabel Tocino, currently Minister for Environment; Pedro Solbes, former Minister of Economy and Finance and current member of the European Commission.
52 However, it has been, in recent years, an atypical and rather relevant committee of growing importance, because its action encompasses the totality of government policies. Among the rights granted to the committee by the law of 1994 are the following: to receive, via the government, legislation proposals emanating from the EP in sufficient time to be properly informed or to examine such proposals; to request a full debate on such proposals if it should consider them necessary; to request the appearance of a government member before the committee to inform it on the outcome of bills approved by the Council of the European Union; to be informed by the government about the general lines of its European policy; to draft reports on matters relating to the European Union; and to establish co-operative links with their counterparts in the parliaments of other Member States of the Union.
53 There is an average number of 40–50 sessions per legislature, thus more than one meeting per month.
54 The opposition has repeatedly demanded that the committee become a body

of advice prior to government adoption of decisions within the Union. The government in turn has always maintained that the speed required by the EC/EU decision-making process makes it impossible to seek parliamentary support or authorisation for each decision. According to a proposal of resolution presented in November 1993 by the opposition PP, the Joint Committee for the European Union was closely involved in the preparation of the 1996–97 IGC; a major consequence of such involvement was the Committee Resolution of 21 December 1995 which contained guidelines agreed by all parliamentary groups on the Spanish position for the IGC negotiations.

55 Such as the Comisión para el seguimiento de la Unión Europea y de Actuaciones Exteriores in Catalonia, the Comisión Permanente para Asuntos Europeos in Madrid or Asturias.

56 Normally the regional Minister for the Presidency or of Economy and Finance.

57 The first meeting of regional Parliaments of Member States of the European Union was held in 1998 in Oviedo (Asturias) – a final result of which was the so-called 'Declaration of Oviedo' – and created a permanent follow-up Committee initially presided by Ovidio Sánchez Díaz, former President of the regional Parliament of Asturias (Junta General del Principado).

58 Those of Cantabria, Madrid and Aragón. See VV.AA., *Incidencia del Tratado de la Unión Europea sobre la Comunidad de Madrid* (Madrid: Publicaciones de la CAM, 1993).

59 See David Ordoñez Solís, *Fondos estructurales europeos. Régimen jurídico y gestión administrativa* (Madrid: Marcial Pons, 1997).

60 In some of the larger regions, like Andalusia or Catalonia, these departments have even established some offices at provincial level.

61 While the ERDF regional office is normally located within the Directorate-General for Planning of the regional Ministry of Economy and Finance or is even administered by the specific Directorate-General for Community Affairs, the EAGGF regional office is usually to be found in the appropriate Directorate-General of the regional Ministry of Agriculture; the European Social Fund (ESF) office is most commonly located in either the regional Employment Agency or in the regional Ministry of Labour.

62 See VV.AA., *Euskadi en la Unión Europea* (Bilbao: Publicaciones de la Fundación Sabino Arana, 1994).

63 With the current – but not for too long – exceptions of La Rioja and Castile-La Mancha.

64 Jorge Pueyo Losa and Maria Teresa Ponte Iglesias, *La actividad exterior y comunitaria de Galicia: La experiencia de otras Comunidades Autónomas* (Santiago: Fundación Alfredo Brañas, 1997).

65 Such has been the case in recent years in the Ministry of Economy and Finance and the Ministry for the Public Administrations.

66 Formerly Interministerial Conference for Community Affairs (Conferencia Interministerial para Asuntos Comunitarios).

67 The fact that the officials of SEPEUE are recruited within the different ministries facilitates the co-ordinating role of the Interministerial Conference.

68 See David Ordoñez Solís, 'La ejecución del Derecho Comunitario Europeo en España', in: *Cuadernos de Estudios Europeos*, 10 (Madrid: Civitas, 1994).

69 See Susana Galera Rodrigo, *La aplicación administrativa del derecho comunitario en España* (Madrid: Civitas, 1998).

70 See among others VV.AA., *Comunidades Autónomas y Comunidad Europea. Relaciones jurídico-institucionales* (Valladolid: Publicaciones Cortes de Castilla y León, 1991); VV.AA., *La participación de las Comunidades Autónomas en los asuntos comunitarios europeos* (Madrid: Publicaciones del Ministerio para las Administraciones Públicas, 1995); Alan Arias Martín, *Comunidades Autónomas y elaboración del Derecho Comunitario Europeo* (Oñati: IVAP, 1998).

71 The functions of the conference were revised by means of the 1990, 1994 and 1996 agreements between the central government and the regions.

72 While the first request is already in force *vis-à-vis* the functioning of around fifty-five Commission's advisory committees, the second is still far from being agreed and is subject to lengthy negotiations between the government and the regions.

73 Such as the Four Motors for Europe or the European Conference of Capital Regions.

74 See, among others, José Julián Izquierdo Peris, 'El Tribuunal Constitucional como órgano de garantía del Derecho comunitario en España', in: *Gaceta Jurídica de la CE*, Bol-87, 1993, pp. 15–29; Javier Roldán Barbero and Luis Miguel Hinojosa Martínez, 'La aplicación del derecho Comunitario en España (1996)', in: *Revista de Derecho Comunitario Europeo*, 1, 1998, pp. 5–49; and Santiago Martínez Lage, 'El Tribunal Constitucional y las cuestiones prejudiciales comunitarias', in: *Gaceta Jurídica de la CE*, Bol-117, 1996, pp. 1–3.

75 In fact, the first cases indirectly related to EC legislation date only from 1988 and 1989 and solve some of the disputes initiated by the autonomous communities of Catalonia, the Basque Country and Galicia. The major decisions of the Spanish Constitutional Court with regard to the interpretation and application of EC law were nevertheless taken in 1991 and 1993.

76 In a somewhat similar way to the French Conseil Constitutionnel. The possible contradiction between national and EC norms cannot be interpreted as a case of non-compliance with a constitutional provision and therefore should be analysed as a mere conflict of non-constitutional laws to be solved by the ordinary judge.

77 See Mangas Martín, 1992, *op. cit.*, p. 209.

78 One of the most high-profile decisions (Decision 165/1994) of recent years was taken in 1994 by the Spanish Constitutional Court, which enabled the Basque government to open a delegation in Brussels with an official character, thus depending directly from the Regional Ministry of Presidency (Consejería de Presidencia), for the management of the external aspects related to the EC decision-making process within its statutory competences.

79 The Constitutional Court insisted in 1996 on its previous idea that the EC legal order was not part of the 'constitutional corpus' and therefore not fully subject to its jurisdictional competence. One of its Magistrates, Professor

González Campos, reacted to such an interpretation given in Decisions 46/1996 and 147/1996 by means of two respective dissenting opinions.

80 Decision 130/1995.

81 RA 1301/1994.

82 RA 2304/1994.

83 See Muriel Le Barbier- Le Bris, *Le juge espagnol face au droit communautaire* (Rennes: Apogée, 1998).

84 Diego Javier Liñán Nogueras and Javier Roldán Barbero, 'La aplicación judicial del derecho comunitario en España (1986–1989)', in: *Revista de Instituciones Europeas*, No. 3/1989, p. 885.

85 Diego Javier Liñán Nogueras and Alejandro Valle Gálvez, 'Crónica sobre la aplicación judicial del derecho comunitario en España (1 de julio de 1989–31 de diciembre de 1990)', in: *Revista de Instituciones Europeas*, 3, 1991, pp. 989 ff; Diego Javier Liñán Nogueras and Manuel López Escudero, 'Crónica sobre la aplicación judicial del Derecho Comunitario en España (años 1991 y 1992)', in: *Revista de Instituciones Europeas*, No. 1/1994, pp. 221; Diego Javier Liñán Nogueras and Javier Roldán Barbero, 'The Judicial Application of Community Law in Spain', in: *Common Market Law Review*, No. 6/1993, pp. 1135 ff and Diego Javier Liñán Nogueras and Margarita A. Robles Carrillo, 'La aplicación judicial del derecho Comunitario en España (años 1993, 1994 y 1995)', in: *Revista de Derecho Comunitario Europeo*, No. 1/1997, p. 127.

86 Though in very rare cases by its Third Senate and even expressing serious doubts about its effective competence to do so.

87 Major controversies with regard to the incorrect application of EC law by Spanish courts have been paradoxically caused, apart from the reasonable cases of individual lower judges, by the Supreme Court, owing to its reluctance to fully accept the conditions of application of the principles of supremacy and direct effect of EC law.

88 The public relevance of the ECJ for the Spanish general public – which has never been too high despite the Spanish nationality of its President – has increased considerably in recent years owing to certain major decisions affecting Spanish interests, such as the fisheries conflict with the United Kingdom and, particularly, the so called 'Strawberries' decision which condemned France for attacks against Spanish lorries carrying agricultural products.

89 Such as the Competition Defence Body, the Commission for the Regulation of the Electric Market (Comisión Reguladora del Mercado Eléctrico) and the National Commission for the Stock Exchange Markets (Comisión Nacional del Mercado de Valores).

90 And that seems to be also the fate of the legislative proposals for a new 'Estatuto de la Función Pública', because of the lack of political consensus and the preservation of corporatist interests.

91 See Francesco Morata, 'Spain: Modernization through Integration', in: Kenneth Hanf and Ben Soetendorp (eds), *Adapting to European Integration. Small States and the European Union* (London: Longman, 1998), pp. 100–115.

92 Mostly owing to the loss of the absolute majority in the national parliament

by the PSOE and the PP and their political dependence on the parliamentary support of the centre-right nationalist parties (PNV, CiU, CC).

93 For example, Ministry of Social Affairs, Ministry of Environment, Secretariat of State for Sport, Secretariat of State for Development Co-operation, Secretariat of State for Migrations and Secretariat of State for Tourism.

94 At the time of the formation of the respective new governments and the signature of political agreements among several political parties.

95 A considerable expansion and penetration of Spanish firms within Latin American markets took place after 1996. See the article 'The New Conquistadores' in: *Financial Times*, 2 July 1999, p. 21.

96 Apart from the redefinition of functions within the departments of SEPEUE or the Permanent Representation of Spain to the European Union.

97 It is to be noted that Spain's leading politicians in the field of international affairs have all been professionally directly related to the process of European integration.

98 See Amparo Almarcha Barbado (ed.), *Spain and EC Membership Evaluated* (London: Pinter, 1993).

99 This was particularly relevant in the first months of Aznar's term in office and within the IGC negotiations leading to the adoption of the Amsterdam Treaty.

100 The document 'Bases para una reflexión' prepared by the Spanish government and made public during its 1995 Presidency of the Council, together with the initiatives undertaken by Carlos Westendorp as Chair of the Reflection Group, helped to define the agenda and general framework for the development of the negotiations.

101 As contained in the Resolution of the Joint Committee for the European Union, 21 December 1995 (BOCG, Serie A, No. 82, 29 December 1995).

102 Internal debate arose only with regard to the so called 'asylum protocol'.

103 Spain presented twenty-nine official written proposals, three of them jointly with other Member States. Ten of them were finally incorporated into the new text of the Treaty, adopted with minor changes. The other nine proposals were tabled during the last stage of the negotiations without having been officially codified.

104 These three proposals were to be understood within the framework of the fight against the Basque terrorist group ETA in its international dimension.

105 The enforcement period for the Ioannina compromise was therefore extended and Spain accepted the insertion of a political Declaration stating that its particular case would be taken into account at the moment of further institutional reform owing to future enlargements of the Union.

106 Aznar's leadership within the European People's Party has been strongly reinforced in recent months.

107 This was one of the major points of the electoral programme of the PP on which Aznar placed most of his political energies at one time. Such a result has been accompanied by good economic results regarding inflation rates, employment growth, public deficit and interest rates.

108 See Carmela Martín, *España en la nueva Europa* (Madrid: Alianza, 1997).

Select bibliography

The text (English translation) of the Constitution of Spain can be found at the University of Richmond's constitution finder at http://confinder.richmond.edu/. Further sources on government and parliament of Spain can be found at Government www.la-moncloa.es or at Parliament www.congreso.es.

VV.AA. (1994) *España y el Tratado de la Unión Europea* (Madrid: COLEX).

VV.AA. (1995) *La participación de las Comunidades Autónomas en los asuntos comunitarios europeos* (Madrid: Publicaciones del Ministerio para las Administraciones Públicas).

VV.AA. (1998) *España y la negociación del Tratado de Amsterdam, Biblioteca Nueva* (Madrid: Ed. Política Exterior).

Almarcha Barbado, Amparo (ed.) (1993) *Spain and EC Membership Evaluated* (London: Pinter).

Bassols, Raimundo (1995) *España en Europa. Historia de la adhesión a la CE (1957–85)* (Madrid: Ed. Política Exterior).

CEOE (1996) Diez años de España en la Unión Europea (I y II), Informes y Estudios de CEOE 75 (Madrid: Publicaciones CEOE).

Gillespie, Richard, Rodrigo, Fernando and Story, John (1996) *Las relaciones exteriores de la España democrática* (Madrid: Alianza).

Molina del Pozo, Carlos F. (eds) (1996) *España en la Europa comunitaria. Balance de diez años* (Madrid: CEURA).

Morata, Francesc (1998) 'Spain: 'Modernization through Integration', in: Kenneth Hanf and Ben Soetendorp (eds), *Adapting to European Integration. Small States and the European Union* (London: Longman).

Moreno Juste, Antonio (1998) *España y el proceso de construcción europea* (Barcelona: Ariel Practicum).

Newton, Michael T. and Donaghy, Peter J. (1997) *Institutions of Modern Spain. A Political and Economic Guide* (Cambridge: Cambridge University Press).

Ordoñez Solís, David (1994) *La ejecución del Derecho Comunitario Europeo en España, Cuadernos de Estudios Europeos 10* (Madrid: Civitas).

Pérez Tremps, Pablo (1994) *Constitución española y Comunidad Europea, Cuadernos de Estudios Europeos 11* (Madrid: Civitas).

9 *Andrea Szukala*

France: the European transformation of the French model

Introduction: 'Maastricht' as a major challenge

Since Maastricht the politicisation of European 'high politics' promises to be a very hazardous political venture in France. A newspaper headline such as this from 1991: 'Government and MPs concerned about French indifference to European integration',[1] would be inconceivable today. It is not exaggerated to presume that Maastricht stands for a fundamental shift in how the French political system copes with the internal challenges of 'Europeanisation'.

Many political scientists still like to switch to French studies today, because the case of France serves as an excellent ideal type.[2] Indeed, France is often cited as an example when it comes to clashes of 'state-centric' national political systems with the pluralistic multi-level system that is the European Union. The characteristics of the 'French model' are: the centrality of the state in mediation procedures; specific forms of interest representation and a privileged place for the central state level to enforce and implement policies.[3] The conclusions of such analyses of systemic 'clashes' are persistently the same: owing to internal centralisation and the government-dominated procedures in 'external' relations, socio-economic actors in state-centric systems are said to be less qualified to do business in multi-level networks. Therefore policy-making performance at the implementation stage tends to suffer while policy deficits are subsequently higher. Even if the classification of France as a state-centric or state-corporatist model is still valuable, these categories should blind us to the major political and institutional changes the system has already achieved since 1985. It is undoubtedly true that the French polity suffered and still suffers from enormous system stress, but our perception is that today these systemic tensions have ceased to play a more important role in France than they do in other European countries. Actually – and perhaps in contrast to other systems – the state level always plays a major role in ensuring a degree of smoothness and intensity in adaptation processes. Since the central state is still constantly seeking to interpose itself in mediation processes, it acts as a kind of gatekeeper for multi-level integration in numerous domains. Its readiness to accept the permeability of political processes is a core variable for the explanation of the breaking up of the 'sovereignty shells' that so many French politicians furiously defended after the famous attacks from Schäuble and Lamers in autumn 1994.[4]

The events of recent years have been characterised by a great variety of responses to very different phenomena such as the integration boost of the SEM, the Maastricht Treaty and a changing European and international environment.[5] One should not pretend to be able to establish causal links from those interlocked processes to specific systemic answers. But a tentative strategy may be, while enumerating and describing the structural changes the French polity underwent between 1992 and 1999, to take into consideration the positions on which no change took place at all, and to search for missing factors. The core hypothesis of this chapter is that many of the revisions and adaptations the 'model' endured during the 1990s were a function of *governmental preferences*. These preferences include: restructuring the domestic debate after Maastricht, the preservation of the core assets of French 'statism' (strong public services, preservation of a certain state role in economic politics) and the implementation of domestic reforms that are partly aimed at strengthening France's position towards its European partners. The relative weakening of France's 'natural' European leadership after 1989 made it increasingly necessary – even for Europe's 'strongest' state – to be able to mobilise domestic political and socio-economic interests to defend its role as a significant player. The analysis parts from the observation that after a period of disorientation and piecemeal reform during the 1980s, when a new European regulatory culture led to dysfunctions and a weakening of the French administrative state and its relations with business,[6] state actors re-entered the game in the mid-1990s to try to fashion the 'Europeanised' French state in their own style.

Fundamentals and institutional specifics of policy-making after Maastricht

Five main developments mark the further progress of 'Europeanisation' and the new institutional arrangements since 1992. After the painful experience of referendums, French public opinion, when compared with other European countries, now has a better accommodation with Europe. However, political parties – notably on the right wing – are still haunted by the split between 'yes' and 'no' votes in September 1992. At the governmental level, the two heads of the executive are trying out a new internal balance in European policy-making; 'semi-presidentialism' is less and less a valuable model for classifying the French system of government.

At the same time the special relationship between the executive and the parliament, which is typical of the Fifth Republic's 'rationalised parliamentarism', seems to have undergone a fundamental change. However the attempts to preserve a kind of bureaucratic centralisation in Paris–Brussels interactions (from the 'state' to the 'Union') have become more explicit. Since administrative actors are still desperately seeking to cover and to supervise the whole range of European activities, actors such as the prime minister are progressively implicated, and a 'normalisation' of government and politicisation has emerged. This is not without consequences for the strategies of those involved in interest intermediation, which have traditionally been characterised by a strong tendency towards pressure politics through elite interaction with the European level. The continuous and important impact of the central level as a gatekeeper for Franco-European interactions is above all true for the regional level, which is still strongly supervised and confined by state actors, especially when distributional issues are at stake.

Risking the debate: public opinion and parties under stress

The impact of the 'Maastricht' conflict on public opinion and on party political cleavages was still perceivable during the 1995 presidential election and the third cohabitation (since May 1997). The entire process from the Maastricht referendum in 1992 and its 48 per cent 'no' votes, up to the conclusion of the Amsterdam Treaty and its ratification in March 1999, represents more or less a development from refusal and a strong downward trend at the beginning of the 1990s, to accommodation with the inevitable. Nevertheless this process is not at all linear. More so than other Member States French public opinion suffers from a kind of 'overload' with regard to the European dimension so that from time to time, conflictual issues tend to provoke eruptive system shocks which may alienate a generally positive tendency.

The parties' first reaction after the Maastricht referendum consisted of a desperate attempt to pacify the political game and to focus on internal issues. Whereas the left wing was fully absorbed by the end of Mitterrandism and the reconstitution of the Socialist Party after the loss of power in 1993, the governing right-wing coalition had to find a consensus on a candidate for presidential elections and to implement EMU. This turned out to be a difficult political project. The deficit-spending Balladur politics prior to the 1995 presidential elections had led to a stagnation of the French economy in the run-up to the third stage of EMU and therefore France risked not meeting the criteria at all. From this perspective, spring 1994 marked an outstanding low in French 'European' opinion with only 39 per cent of the population thinking that integration was beneficial to France.[7] This late 'post-Maastricht blues' coincided with a dramatic increase in France's public deficit (6 per cent), a downswing in

Gross Domestic Product (GDP) and a dramatic unemployment rate (12.5 per cent). These circumstances were not least due to the hard-line interest rate policy of the German Bundesbank. Indeed, since the crash of the EMS in 1993, France saw itself as being forced into the kind of machinations that culminated in the conclusion of the unpopular 'Stability Pact' in 1997. The important controversial debate on the social costs of monetary integration began at that time.[8] This forcefully split parties, separating the 'integrationnistes' from so-called 'souverainistes', namely national republicans and social Gaullists, who built a coalition against a so-called neo-liberal 'pensée unique'. In the 1995 presidential election, concerns about the preservation of a high level of social protection ranked second among the voters' preferences.[9]

After the election of Jacques Chirac in 1995, the newly installed Juppé government (1995–97) finally had to take a painful U-turn by launching rigorous budgetary cuts.[10] This abrupt policy change in the middle of 1995 made the costs of the introduction of the Euro particularly manifest in the eyes of French citizens.[11] Since then the French inclination towards the Union has again dropped to only 46 per cent of persons stating that it was 'a good thing for France' in autumn 1996.[12] Anticipating further implementation conflicts and uncertainties for the conservative governmental coalition, Chirac switched towards an even more critical distance with EMU and decided at the beginning of 1997 to bring about a premature dissolution of the National Assembly to preserve 'his' majority from a defeat in 1998. Even if the electoral campaign converged on the 'Europe Sociale' issue shared by all important parties involved,[13] the governmental coalition was ultimately broken up by its traditional internal rivalries, a successful Front National (14.9 per cent in 1997 national election's first round) and a quite forceful European cleavage. The 1994 European elections had already made it quite obvious that owing to the Maastricht conflict the fragmentation of the French right would persist.[14] The bitter quarrels after the loss of power in 1997 as well as after the regional elections in 1998, viewed in the context of the European elections in 1999, show that today the French right is severely disoriented and unable to deal coherently with European challenges. A solely voter oriented perspective permits the preservation of some kind of common bottom line, namely with regard to the important rural interests who are concerned about changes to the status quo in the Union's CAP. But when it came to a parliamentary vote on another core issue, the passage to the third stage of EMU,[15] Gaullists appeared once again unable to maintain a sufficient level of partisan cohesion adequate to the problem at stake. Obeying their party leader Séguin, parliamentarians of the neo-Gaullist Rassemblement pour la République (RPR) risked categorically refusing French passage to the third stage, had not President Chirac's intervention prevented the worst.

Yet the actual Socialist Party (PS) – having come through a period of painful reconciliation with the so-called 'Mitterrandie' – can still be seen as largely pro-integrationist. But even if key members of the Jospin government have solid European convictions (e.g. Elisabeth Gigou, Dominique Strauss-Kahn, Martine Aubry) and while the rest of the left-wing 'souverainistes' have had to retire to political clubs,[16] Socialist governmental policy differs from the 'old' approach. Whereas Mitterrand's European policy was characterised by functionalism combined with a great deal of voluntarism and symbolism,[17] the new approach appears to be more pragmatic in terms of interest formulation, in contrast with other European governments. The core preferences of the government have been made explicit since June 1997. France's main concern is still a rapid achievement of EMU conditional on four factors: an 'economic government' as a counterweight to the ECB; the inclusion of southern EU members in EMU; the establishment of obstacles to a Euro-overrating (i.e. preventing 'monetary dumping' with regard to the dollar and the yen); and employment and economic growth criteria to counter-balance the Stability Pact's severe monetary and budgetary standards.[18] With regard to European constitutive policies, France's adhesion to the Amsterdam acquis is not at all unconditional either: the ratification law consists of two articles, which describe the treaty's institutional provisions as inept and which make further EU Treaty reform an obligatory premise for enlargement.[19] A new European rhetoric is gaining ground which does not underline France's European challenges (as in the Mitterrand years), but which emphasises the growing importance of a genuine French contribution to the European project.

This current pragmatism is combined with a proactive governmental policy on French public opinion. As the 'age of symbols is over',[20] there is a continuous attempt to explain France's European interests and advantages to the – since 1997 – less and less Eurosceptic public. The 1998 campaign on the introduction of the Euro was largely supported by the national media and above all, was furthered by Finance Minister Strauss-Kahn, who continuously underlined the fact that it was the Euro-Zone that protected France from the most severe effects of the Asian crisis (the Euro as a 'bouclier monétaire'). As a result, French public opinion was among the most Euro-enthusiastic in the second half of 1998: 69 per cent of persons stated that the introduction of the Euro was a 'very good' or a 'good' thing, compared to 56 per cent in Germany, 66 per cent in Spain, 67 per cent in Italy and 49 per cent in the United Kingdom.[21]

The organisational cohesion of French parties is feeble compared to that of parties in other systems. If there are sub-units for European affairs, they do not have a relevant impact on day-to-day policy-making. Still, the capacity of high-ranking political personalities to bring about shifts in French public opinion cannot be underestimated. As shown above, the developments from 1992 to 1999 are not marked only by economic conjuncture, but also by the different degrees of governmental accommodation with the European venture. The stabilisation and normalisation which has been discernible since the re-accession to power of a party that is more accustomed and therefore 'fitter' to deal with those challenges, is similarly observable in the context of institutional adaptations and the evolution of the system of government. In this perspective the ups and downs of public opinion after 'Maastricht' also characterise a period of governmental policy-learning. In France it appears to be increasingly difficult to search for gains in national support for government – e.g. in the parliamentary arena – at the expense of the European level.[22] Notably in a centralised system, where governmental actors at European and national levels are most obviously the same, this strategy risks producing additional negative outcomes at the national level. Therefore in France, where – in the eyes of the citizen – European issues today are a major part of the national political game,[23] shifting blame to the European level is an increasingly difficult strategy.

The two heads: a new relationship between president and prime minister
The core element of French European policy-making was seen as the strong proclivity to an executive-dominated style when it came to political intercourse with the 'exterior'. The anxiety to preserve a homogenous image of one national interest and one sovereignty towards the outside stood at the centre of a quite Rousseaunian concept of interest representation. That is why the paradoxical French sharing of powers between the prime minister and the president always attracted many foreign policy analysts. But today more and more students of French foreign policy tend to recognise that the political and academic perception of the president's role in European politics is not free from simplification.[24] Indeed the reality of genuine European policy-making in the 1990s was not as strongly affected by 'cohabitation' as some may have stipulated. In 'high politics' a very firm sense of solidarity regarding the preservation of France's rank and influence among its European partners helped to surmount the potential cleavages between the prime minister and president in almost any situation.[25] Owing to the changing character of day-to-day European politics, the president's policy-making functions are constantly diminishing; in power-political terms the Chirac presidency is a failure.[26]

The relative weakness of the president is accentuated by his minor role in economic policy. The importance of EMU as the major European venture of the 1990s generated a more and more significant role for the prime minister and the cabinet, and a pre-eminent role for the ministers of Finance and the Economy. Therefore the changing patterns of executive European policy-making are not solely a result of the actual president's weaknesses, rather they elucidate the long-term consequences of the Maastricht integration boost, and a decline of presidential power in general. This development is implied in the institutional logic of the Vth Republic, that – under certain political circumstances – imposes a partial limitation of presidentialism.[27]

The Elysée's information tools have turned out to be too antiquated to cope with the complexities of modern governance: the presidential 'absolutisme inefficace'[28] is built on a system of counsellors centralised at the general secretariat of the presidency. Since 1985 the President has had at his disposal a small European unit that prepares bilateral meetings, European summits and Franco-German meetings. But in the end, the Elysée's General Secretary, who depends almost entirely on the secondment of civil servants from ministerial departments, cannot provide the organisational resources to fulfil the autonomous management and co-ordination tasks that would allow a president to govern this area of policy. From the first to the third periods of cohabitation, the president's isolation from the General Secretary of Government (Secrétariat Général du Gouvernement, SGG), the interface for ministerial co-ordination, made him more and more unsuited to intervene in day-to-day politics, even if traditionally his close connection with the head of the General Secretary for Inter-ministerial Co-ordination (Secrétariat Général du Comité Interministériel, SGCI) gave him a certain oversight of ministerial activities at the European level. Today – apart from the grand bargains such as treaty reforms, in foreign/defence policy and in his power to 'go public' (as does President Chirac when farmers' interests are at stake) – the French president is more or less a 'lame duck' in European politics. The 1995 reform, one of the major constitutional modifications following Maastricht,[29] may be understood as a reaction to this curtailment. The extension of the presidential referendum according to Article 11 of the French Constitution to any bill 'which deals with reforms relating to the economic and social policy of the nation and to the public services contributing thereto' is also an attempt to recover power in EMU-related domains.[30] Consequently, as a reciprocal gesture, the actual government – still assuming cohabitation until 2002 – seems to rely on a silent parliamentarisation of the Vth Republic to legitimate its increasing claim for executive power.[31]

Changes in executive–legislative relations: a revaluation of parliament

The European integration process has always had a reputation for creating a 'democratic deficit' in terms of a de-parliamentarisation of policy-making. Still, in 1996 a French analyst published an article entitled: 'The European Union: An Opportunity for the French Parliament to Recover Powers?'[32] Was France to be the only country where integration leads to power gains at the legislative level? It is evident that the basic pattern of the Vth Republic's 'parliamentarisme rationnalisé' is not very conducive to the effective exercise of the functions of control, legislation and interest aggregation. Legislative functions are delegated competencies, the parliament has no organisational autonomy and the government disposes of a set of strong instruments to overrule a disobedient assembly (e.g. 'Vote bloqué', 'Question de confiancc').

Yet the first functional organ to monitor French European policy-making at the parliamentary level – the Delegation for European Affairs – was created by the Senate in 1973. A similar body was created by the National Assembly in 1979, just after the first direct elections to the EP. As the number of permanent committees is constitutionally fixed (Article 43(2) of the French Constitution) and as the existing committees had made little use of the expertise provided by the new 'Délégations pour les Affaires des Communautés Européennes' (18 members per chamber), their performance had been more or less a failure. They had no relevant competencies and were permanently overlooked by governments, which felt absolutely unshackled in their diplomatic practice of 'foreign' policy-making in Brussels.

Finally, at the beginning of the 1990s parliamentarians began to feel a certain pressure from below: the SEM and later EMU caused socio-economic upheavals that the constituency oriented French parliamentarians could no longer ignore. Likewise the importance of the transfer of political competencies became so great that a growing part of parliamentary work was explicitly induced from above, i.e. from the European level. This awakened parliamentary elites. The first step consisted of a rudimentary reform of the delegations' general role to inform parliament on European matters. In 1990 membership doubled, governmental information policy became more systematic and the Ministers for European Affairs gained an informed parliamentary forum to present governmental policy via the organisation of periodic hearings (Loi 90–385, 10 May 1990).

But the real breakthrough occurred in the context of constitutional reform, on which the final ratification/referendum of the Maastricht Treaty was conditional. The preceding decision of the Constitutional Council (Conseil Constitutionnel, DC 92–308, 9 April 1992)[33] had stated non-conformity with the Constitution because certain Treaty provisions such as the formulation of a common visa policy, affected 'the essential conditions for the exercise of national sovereignty'. This ruling brought the two chambers of parliament into a veto position which they – above all the senate – used in a quite proficient way and against the government's initial dispositions. As a result, parliament extended its power to call into question the constitutional conformity of ratification laws (Article 54 of the French Constitution) and a revised system of parliamentary screening and controlling European secondary law-making emerged, which is based on a new Article 88(4) of the French Constitution:

> The Government shall lay before the Assembly and the Senate any proposals for Community instruments which contain provisions which are matters for statute as soon as they have been transmitted to the Council of the Communities.
>
> Whether Parliament is in session or not, resolutions may be passed under this article in the manner laid down by the standing orders of each assembly.

Article 88(4) gives the parliament for the first time the constitutional right to be informed, to scrutinise and to intervene – via the tabling of resolutions – in the conduct of French EC policy.[34] These are comparatively strong instruments when viewed in the light of the feeble powers of which the assemblies dispose in most of the 'internal' policy-making domains. Nevertheless, motions of 'no confidence' remain the only parliamentary instrument that allows a relatively spontaneous intervention of parliament into current executive decision-making.[35] The subsequent significant constitutional reforms (Loi organique 95–880) aim to provide the parliament with opportunities to fulfil its role as a 'European' actor by extending the session period and by loosening the governmental monopoly on the parliamentary agenda. Surprisingly the government has paid much attention to the implementation and effectiveness of the new mechanisms. The prime minister pointed out in several 'circulaires' to his ministers that negotiations in Brussels are inconceivable without taking into consideration the positions of the assemblies.[36] These changes mark a quite fundamental shift in executive–legislative relations in the Vth Republic.

Parliamentarians have made regular but not excessive use of this new instrument. Between 1993 and 1997, on 970 European proposals transmitted to the assemblies, 139 parliamentary resolutions were tabled. Most of them were in the domains of budgetary questions (24 resolutions), foreign trade (22), energy (13), telecommunications (12) and agriculture (10). Parliament involves itself very much in domains which are under exclusive Community competence, above all in foreign trade, where the European Commission – an international actor in its own right – is severely scrutinised and supervised by the national parliament. The National Assembly has made more active use of the new instrument of government control than the Senate (Table 9.1).

Problems arise when it comes to disagreements as to which issues constitute 'matters for statute' following Article 88(4) of the French Constitution. Which legislative proposals must the government transmit to the assemblies and what are the domains where parliamentary intervention is not allowed? Particularly conflictual issues include the domains

Table 9.1 Tabling of parliamentary resolutions, 1993–April 1997

Year	*National Assembly*	*Senate*
1993	13	8
1994	29	13
1995	23	9
1996	22	13
1997 (April)	6	3

Source: Statistiques Parlementaires, *Bulletin de l'Assemblée Nationale/ Bulletin du Sénat* (1993–97).

of the second and third pillars (CFSP and JHA), the interinstitutional agreements and Commission communications.[37] Finally, parliament has shown a great readiness to step into fields outside the EC framework and therefore to violate the boundaries of Article 88(4), e.g. when potential additional EU/EC competencies appear in the Commission's green or white papers or when Agenda 2000 was published. It is quite evident that a limitation of parliamentary control over genuine legislative proposals in pillar one is not in accordance with the definition of the statutory domain given by Article 34 of the French Constitution. On the other hand, important EC decisions may not touch the legislative domain at all while being incendiary in political terms, e.g. the decisions on prices and market organisation in the CAP. An irregular governmental practice of transmitting proposals gave rise to further suspicions surrounding the government's strategy. French parliamentarians legitimately call into question the general exclusion of CAP decisions, when at the same time the proposals on the reorganisation of wine and fruit markets – where the French government may have found it difficult to defend a hard-line status quo policy at the EU level – have exceptionally been submitted to parliamentary scrutiny.[38]

The new instrument is quite complicated to handle because the organisational challenge of establishing a European 'superstructure' within the constitutionally bounded Vth Republic's assemblies was a difficult puzzle. The National Assembly opted for a system which is based on the European Affairs Delegation as the major pillar. Given the quite consensual working style of delegations, one can easily conclude that the tabling of resolutions is not a technique exploited by the opposition to undermine governmental business in Brussels. However, some analysts observe an ideological–instrumental division of labour between parliament and the executive, 'that offered new political levers to both, whether on the domestic or on the international stage',[39] and provided an opportunity to contain the forceful right-wing anti-European faction by granting it a position within the parliamentary arena. The strong increase of governmental general declarations on European policy-making in the First

Chamber from five (1984–90) to fifteen (1991–97)[40] demonstrates the changing political mentalities and the strengthening of the link between parliament and the executive. Today, the National Assembly and the Senate have become full players in their own right in French European policy-making.

Administrative co-ordination and interest intermediation in European policy-making

In a context of increasing domestication, the French Constitution's Article 20 gives the government a more and more manifest role to play in European policy-making. Almost all ministries have had to further their institutional adaptation since the beginning of the 1990s, but in contrast to other Member States, none of them exercises a core function in horizontal co-ordination. Even if the Minister for Foreign Affairs (as well as the Minister for Finance) has many horizontal insights, it would be quite exceptional for such a minister to deal with an EC issue from start to finish. In addition neither minister is responsible for the co-ordination of Paris-Brussels policy-making.

The Foreign Affairs ministers are normally elected by the president. Even during cohabitation periods, the choices of Raimond (1986), Juppé (1993) and Védrine (1997) had the support of the head of state.[41] The ministry's organisational set-up is threefold: the General Directorate for Political and Security Affairs covers mainly CFSP issues, the General Directorate for European Economic Affairs treats issues such as EU trade policy and representation in international economic organisations, and the Directorate for Judicial Affairs represents France in trials at the ECJ.[42] The corresponding tasks of the minister himself lie in his presence within the General Affairs Council and subsequent executive EU organs, of course the ministry has privileged access to the French Permanent Representation in Brussels. However since the introduction of a European Affairs Ministry at the end of the 1970s, the European Affairs Minister has often acted as a substitute for the Minister for Foreign Affairs.[43] As the former minister is integrated into the Foreign Affairs Ministry, s/he does not have a specific portfolio, but prepares and co-ordinates the French presidencies, monitors public opinion and deals with European campaigning (as did Guigou at 'Maastricht') as well as the information of political and economic actors at the domestic level and in Brussels (e.g. Cresson, Barnier). Since Maastricht, the Ministers for European Affairs are explicitly charged with establishing 'a close dialogue with MEPs and delegates at the Committee of Regions in order that the government's concerns may be incorporated into the work of these two institutions'.[44] The responsibilities assigned to the Jospin government's European Affairs Minister Pierre Moscovici comprised the full range of questions concerning European integration, including institutional questions and the process of defining the CFSP.

Today almost all departments have established units that deal exclusively with European matters.[45] The management of European programmes such as the ESF and the ERDF is provided by the Ministry of Labour/Social Affairs and the Home Affairs Ministry, respectively. Problems mainly arise when these units are set up in a mode that interferes with the hierarchical patterns of intra-ministerial co-ordination in France. Indeed, the fact that functional units (in highly Europeanised ministries such as agriculture there may be several sub-units) dealing with European issues operate horizontally clearly does interfere with this hierarchical pattern and can lead to overlapping responsibilities and potential conflicts. This artificial 'Europeanisation' – creating new administrative strata dealing especially with European Affairs – is expanding and deeply penetrating the ministerial hierarchies: more than half of the ministries have created 'cellules européennes' even at the 'bureau' level.[46] Moreover it is a standard operating procedure that in the case of intersectoral conflicts, the ministerial 'cabinet' serves as a clearing-house. The cabinets are at the heart of French ministries and are composed of young, brilliant bureaucrats and personal assistants trusted by their minister. At this top level of bureaucracy, the organisational differentiation for European matters is more functional. Today most French ministers appoint within their cabinets a special counsellor for European Affairs who may shape and streamline the department's position in case of internal frictions and who represents the department's interests at interministerial meetings within the SGCI.[47] In a top-down perspective the creation of European sub-units at very low levels of the administrative hierarchy seems to be advantageous. As ministerial problem-solving 'à la française' always comprises the cabinet's opportunity to overrule hierarchical steps and to bypass the department's directors, special access points for European matters would seem to make sense. However some observers consider the expansion of cabinets' tasks to be one of the great flaws of the French system. This is not only because such expansion constitutes the driving force behind the politicisation of the French central administration, but also because it promotes the diffusion of decision-making points for civil servants who have to interact not only with their regular superiors but also with many ministerial collaborators to bring about a decision.[48]

Given the complexity of interministerial co-ordination tasks, France opted early on for a strong and centralised system at the domestic level to guarantee coherent interest representation at the European level. The linchpin of this politico-administrative co-ordination is the famous governmental secretariat, SGCI. Its responsibilities comprise the whole range of EC activities, enlargements and – since 1994 – pillar three policies, Schengen, the Dublin Convention and any other convention following Article 31 (ex Article K.3).[49] The SGCI's general secretary regularly fulfils a double function as he or she has often additionally been a counsellor within the prime minister's or president's cabinets (e.g. de Silguy for Prime Minister Balladur and Guigou for President Mitterrand). The structure serves as a link between the ministerial departments and parliament in Paris and the French Permanent Representation at Brussels. It works under the sole and therefore uncontested authority of the prime minister. The failure of its brief inclusion into the Ministry for European Affairs at the beginning of the 1980s was not only for functional reasons but may also have been a result of the rivalry and mistrust between the different ministerial 'elite corps' (e.g. Inspection des Finances, Corps des Mines) in France.[50]

One cannot underestimate the weight and the power of the SGCI which seems to dominate all stages of the French European policy-making process. Since the ratification of the Maastricht Treaty it has not only fully integrated pillar three politics, but has also increasingly centralised control over the implementation stage and over co-ordination in the context of adjudication. Likewise one should not overlook the attention paid by the SGCI to the French presence within European institutions. This is not only a power-political concern but reflects equally the recurrent French tendency to control national civil servants and their opaque activities in Brussels.[51] SGCI is a lean administrative unit and from the conclusion of the SEA to the ratification of the Treaty of Amsterdam, its staff has grown by about one-third. Given the many tasks it must undertake, this is not at all excessive. The co-ordination duties of SGCI have steadily increased with the multiplication of actors and policies at the EU level: furthermore, instead of recognising the difficulties of dealing with the entire scope of EU policies – except for CFSP – by opting for a diversification after Maastricht, the SGCI has extended and strengthened the coercive functions which it has always exercised over ministerial departments. The growing impact of transnational administrative interaction[52] is perceived as a threat to the 'coherence of French positions'. Thus the SGCI controls and supervises the activities of national actors, e.g. in the following areas:

- The information which ministries send to French MEPs.
- Any ministerial 'chargés de mission' who contacts an MEP is obliged to send an exact report stating what has been presented as 'the French position' to the SGCI.
- Any document transferred by the Home Office – which is responsible for regional policy and structural funds – to the Committee of Regions must be dispatched by the SGCI.[53]

Given this extremely elevated degree of centralised co-ordination, it is not surprising that the prime minister has tended to play an increasingly active role in the context of internal European bargains and as an arbiter between the different ministerial departments. Since the establishment of the Vth Republic, the prime minister has intervened only as chairman of interministerial arbitrage sessions in exceptional circumstances, mainly because of the technicality of most European matters and the opportunity to make issues 'remonter à l'Elysée'.[54] But today's limitation of presidentialism and the revaluation of the prime minister's role are both part of a 'normalisation' process that makes the SGCI a perfect forum for political action as is any other domain at the domestic level (Table 9.2).

Table 9.2 Personnel and activities of the SGCI, 1958–97

Interministerial Committee's arbitrage sessions, chair: prime minister	*Number of civil servants at SGCI*	*Interministerial working sessions*
1958–75: 4	1971: 88	
1976–81: 4	1988: 133	1991: 1090
1982–93: 0	1992: 147	1992: 1136
1994–97: 21	1997: 175	1997: 1700

Source: Sauron (1998), pp. 14 f.

'Traditional' interest intermediation in France is characterised by elite networks and pressure politics among high-ranking economic actors at the senior levels of the administrative hierarchy.[55] Anglo-American 'lobbying' techniques that consist of the provision of detailed practical information to the civil servant dealing with the specific technical matter are used rather rarely. However, this is the prevailing policy style at the European level. As Vivien Schmidt puts it: 'Although French civil servants might have felt at home with the centralised hierarchical style with which the Commission President, Jacques Delors, ran the Commission and dealt with Directorates General, they were not attuned to the overall decision-making process.'[56] Large agencies, which are still quite at least partially in state ownership, have their own Brussels representations (e.g. Enérgie de France, Renault) and benefit at the same time – for the reasons of 'copinage' described above – from privileged access to French EU actors. By contrast, small and medium-sized enterprises (SMEs) and other actors are doubly disadvantaged; one of their few access points being the French employers' representation in Brussels. State actors increasingly perceive the deficient comprehension of mediation styles as indirectly weakening France's position in negotiations.[57] Apart from their representation in corporatist structures such as UNICE, non-governmental actors perform poorly in day-to-day lobbying at the 'lower' levels of the EC administration. French socio-economic interests may therefore be absent from important informal networks, where the early stages of decision preparation take place. As regards the representation of labour interests, the picture is even worse. Prior to 1999, France's second trade union, the communist Confédération Générale du Travail (CGT), with about 650,000 members, was completely absent from the European Trade Union Confederation (ETUC). Given the extension of social partners' competencies through the 'Social Dialogue' (Social Protocol of Maastricht Treaty) and the impact of subsequent EC legislation in France, this is quite an extraordinary situation. The position of French trade unions looks even worse when compared to the powerful representation of German trade unions at the Brussels level.[58]

This lacuna is now fully recognised and therefore since the beginning of the 1990s there has been a growing tendency of the French government to supervise and to 'coach' national economic and social actors in Brussels. French state actors increasingly interpose in business interactions at the EU level and try to smooth the integration of national economic actors into Brussels decision-making and to make them more familiar with a pluralistic mode of interest representation.[59] The institution that plays a key role in this context is the Permanent Representation in Brussels. Apart from the normal working routines of any Member State's Permanent Representation, the French Permanent Representation fulfils further functions. Since Cresson's invention through a 'Groupe d'études et de mobilisation' (GEM), which was designed to encourage interactions between the politico-administrative world and economic actors, the Permanent Representation has played an important role in training and in the provision of information, e.g. on Structural Funds and programmes on behalf of SMEs. Today the 'Cellule Entreprises et Coopération' absorbs about 11 per cent of the Permanent Representation's personnel.[60] Since 1996, economic actors who experience difficulties when doing business within the SEM, have had the opportunity to call for support at the Bercy ministry's 'Mission Marché Unique'. This new organ is an administrative structure situated at the 'Direction des Relations économiques extérieures' (DREE), that co-operates with the Permanent Representation, the SGCI, the European Commission and Bercy's regional and Europe-wide centres for economic expansion. An important task of this unit is to take other Member States before the ECJ, when French SMEs are confronted with problems owing to non-compliance with EC law (above all in public procurement matters).[61]

At the same time, the government tends to set up better access structures for the French economy and civil society at the national level, mainly through the intensive governmental promotion of Euro-Info-Centres (affiliated with the regional chambers of commerce). Following an initiative of Elisabeth Guigou, another structure, 'Sources d'Europe', has been set up in Paris which serves almost the same purpose. It is important to note that 'Sources d'Europe' is a unique construction as it results from a common initiative of the European Commission and the French government and is financed by the Commission, the EP and the French government.

The sub-national level: European re-centralisation of regional politics?

Despite the 'Deferre laws' on decentralisation introduced at the beginning of the Mitterrand era,[62] France still counts among the most centralised systems in the Union. That is why – apart from representation in the CoR – a role for French regions is still almost non-existent in European decision-making, their functions being confined to the implementation of EC programmes addressed specially to them.

One of the great achievements of the 1982 reforms was the valuation of autonomous 'departemental' executives and administrations, represented by the Conseils Généraux. This could have been an incentive for French state actors in regional politics, above all the interministerial unit attached to the Ministry for Regional Planning and the Prime Minister (Délégation à l'Aménagement du Terretoire et de l'Action Régionale, DATAR), to choose the newly empowered 'departements' as their major counterparts for the implementation of EU policy. But the French state opted, on the contrary, for its own representatives at the sub-national level by charging regional civil servants with supervising the execution of EU programmes and managing the distribution of funds. The political linchpin of this system are the regional 'préfets', who co-ordinate the interaction between regional and departmental actors and the 'services déconcentrés', the central state's field services (e.g. the regional directions of the Labour Ministry), controls the assignment of funds and supervises the implementation of EC programmes. The choice of 'genuine' regional actors to participate in the regional set-up of EC programmes is often conditional on the existing structures within the framework of the state–regions contract and the subsequent five-year plans. Those contractual policies fit very well with the regulative modus operandi of EU regional schemes.[63] Eligibility for funding is assessed through a database, the 'Document unique de programmation' (DOCUP), administrated by the territorial services of the central administration. Officially there is no opportunity for sub-national units to interact directly with the EU level without being supervised by central state actors. Demands for funding must always be sent to regional 'préfets' and when it comes to the allocation of European funds, the recipient must sign a convention with the French state services that explains 'the conditions of implementation of the project'.[64] Thus the central administration acts as a ubiquitous interface between the Commission and the regional level and uses this position as a source of power. The structural funds have been the central factor for the reorganisation of the 'services déconcentrés'. DATAR, as the only access point to the EU level, has enhanced its status after a loss of influence at the beginning of the 1980s.[65] Today, links to the state field services are a much more promising strategy for obtaining subventions than the regular intercourse with autonomous regional administrations. As Balme and Jouve (1996) put it: 'Paradoxically, the main effect of the Europeanisation of local government seems [to be] the regionalization of the state, not an emerging regionalism.'[66] Even if the French regions have gained some weight as political units, because they are a target for European policy-making,[67] Europeanisation has also led to a re-centralisation of power and not to a systematic mobilisation of sub-national actors as the European Commission may have intended. This may help to explain why more and more regions have established their own representations in Brussels: by 1997 about twenty regions or associations of regions had done so (e.g. 'Bureau Alsace', 'Bureau de coopération des régions Centre-Atlantique').

The national policy-cycle: the central state as a gatekeeper

It is no longer adequate today to speak of separate Brussels and Paris stages of Community negotiation; rather it is now the case that any aspect of the policy-cycle can simultaneously involve any of the different levels of government (Figure 9.1).[68]

The preparation and making of decisions

Normally a proposal for a directive is communicated by the Commission to the Permanent Representation, which transmits it by fax to the SGCI. The Secretariat fulfils the functions of dispatching when it determines and contacts the relevant ministries demanding written observations. Already at this stage of the process, the sectoral specialists are invited to compose a detailed report on the impact on national legislation. The relevant ministry ('ministère chef de file') will usually be equally concerned when it comes to the presentation of bills at the transposition stage of the policy-making process.

Before the proposals are officially forwarded to the assemblies, a kind of pre-selection has to be accomplished (is the proposal 'legislative' in terms of Article 34 of the French Constitution?). This expertise, which had to be reorganised in 1993, is provided mainly by the Council of State (Conseil d'Etat), now an important national actor as it plays a core role in improving the parliament's chances of becoming a full player in the EC legislative process.[69] That is why today the reports of the Conseil d'Etat on the legislative or regulative quality of a proposal have to be published.[70] In addition, following the initiative of Juppé, all 'legislative' proposals – even those from pillars two and three – are transmitted to the assemblies, which, in the case of non-EC proposals, are allowed only to adopt 'conclusions' and not to table 'resolutions' (that give rise to the parliamentary reserve described

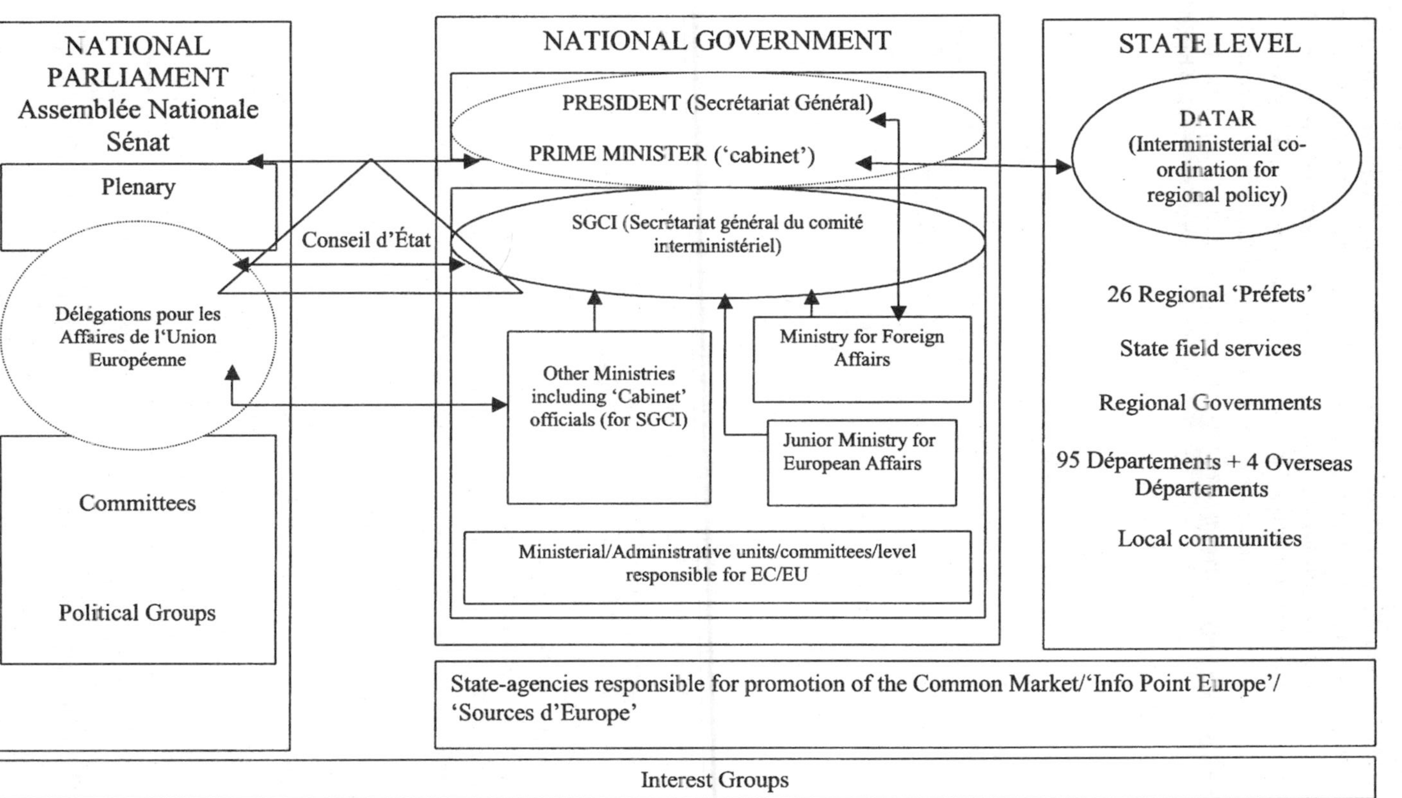

Figure 9.1 The national level of European decision-making – France

below). The Conseil d'Etat has fifteen days to provide its analysis, while the relevant ministries draw up lists of legislative texts that may have to be modified following Community legislation in the affected domain. A broader 'étude d'impact juridique' may be carried out by the ministry 'chef de file' within a period of one month if the legislative consequences of a European text seem to be particularly important.[71] The ministerial analysis should focus, among other things, on the legitimacy of the proposal regarding the principle of subsidiarity (Table 9.3).

Table 9.3 Statistics concerning the legislative impact of European proposals following the rulings of the Conseil d'Etat (Article 88(4)), 1993–98

Year	*1st (EC) pillar*	*2nd (CFSP) pillar*	*3rd (JHA) pillar*	*Total number*	*Legislative (according to Article 34 or the constitution)*
1993	994	0	0	994	179
1994	1038	0	141	1179	172
1995	1060	2	985	2045	213
1996	1221	77	1445	2743	192
1997	1136	78	1019	2233	214
1998	1144	145	926	2215	277

Source: Sauron (1998, p. 107; 1999, p. 200).

In cases of a probable legislative transposition the SGCI transfers the ministerial positions to the General Secretary of Government (SGG) and the Conseil d'Etat submits its report. The SGG co-ordinates general governmental work in any domain of state activity. If the SGG states a necessity of legislative involvement, it sends the Community proposal to the presidents of the two assemblies. The proposals are notified, published as parliamentary documents and mentioned in the French Official Journal.

At the administrative level, the negotiating ministerial experts periodically transfer information on the progress of deliberations to the SGCI, the Conseil d'Etat and the Ministry for European Affairs. A unique position can be maintained at all levels of negotiation (expert groups, COREPER and the Council of Ministers). Consultations are systematically controlled by the SGCI and by the prime minister's cabinet as a last recourse. This is due above all to the practice of involving the same few persons during all three stages of negotiation.[72] Since 1994 the assemblies have explicitly had to be informed of the current agenda of the Council of Ministers. But one major lacuna resented by the assemblies is the fact that they are not informed by the French government of COREPER's agenda. Therefore two-thirds of decision-making, the 'A-points' decided upon at the COREPER level and only rubber-stamped by the Council, pass rather unnoticed despite – or possibly because of – the conflictual nature of many of these issues.[73] Nevertheless, regular working contacts between ten sectoral specialists at the National Assembly's 'Division des Communauté et de l'Union européenne' (sub-unit of the European Affairs Department) and their counterparts at the Permanent Representation in Brussels, seem to be the dominant method of parliamentary information gathering.[74]

Given the large number of legislative proposals, the assemblies have had to find a way of reducing the risk of a European 'overload'. A second modification in the National Assembly's Standing Orders (RAN) Article 151 in 1994 underlined the eminent function of the parliamentary delegation in this context (of minor importance in the Senate).[75] The National Assembly's delegation examines all texts that have been transmitted by the SGG (Table 9.4).

Table 9.4 The National Assembly's checklist for European legislation

1	Treaty basis of proposal, voting procedures at the Council, involvement of EP
2	Date of transmission at the Council/date of reception at the parliament's presidency
3	Reasons for EU activity/subject matter/content
4	National legislation engendered
5	French and other Member States' positions
6	Agenda[a]

Note: [a] See Assemblée Nationale, *Le Nouveau Règlement de l'Assemblée Nationale* (Paris, 1994), pp. 124f.

One of the most important criteria for parliamentary evaluation of a proposition in the Senate is the attention paid to the subsidiarity principle.[76] The delegations formulate 'conclusions' of which their chambers/permanent commissions are informed and which may or may not suggest further implications for the decision-making process. Since 1994 in the National Assembly, the delegation may instantly nominate its own 'rapporteur d'information', who is able to submit an immediate proposal for a 'resolution' (two-thirds of the resolutions tabled at the National Assembly have this origin). Following this, any proposals must pass through a permanent commission in order to come into force (time limit: four weeks, Standing Orders Article 151–2).[77] Anyway in most cases – even if the formal denomination of a rapporteur occurs only at the permanent commission level – the competent MP is also a member of the European Affairs delegation. Before autumn 1998 only six resolutions had emanated autonomously from a permanent commission as the initiatory body in the National Assembly.[78] Thus in contrast to the Senate, the National Assembly's delegation has seemingly acquired perhaps not the statute but at least the functions of a European affairs committee. Finally, the relevant commission adopts the resolution directly provided that, within eight days, the government and the presidents of the standing commissions, delegations and political groups have not called for a floor session (40 per cent of resolutions debated, 1993–97).[79] When it comes to the tabling of a resolution, the SGCI has to be informed at an earlier stage.

The follow-up at the Brussels-level is twofold:

- If the Council intends to put the subject matter on its agenda in less than fourteen days, the SGCI instructs the Permanent Representative to intervene and to assert a 'parliamentary reserve'
- If the Council intends to put the subject matter on its agenda in more than fourteen days, the SGCI instructs the Permanent Representative to try to demand a postponement until a 'prise de position du Parlement français'.[80]

One European proposal may give rise to several parliamentary initiatives, which are pooled at the level of the relevant commission. However, there is no special instrument available to parliament with which it may closely observe further decision-making under the EP's co-decision procedure. Nevertheless, the SGCI provides a full service for the French MEPs. It sends a 'note de cadrage' detailing the interministerial positions as early as possible, before the EP becomes fully involved in the legislative process. Since 'Maastricht', every ministry has appointed a ministerial 'chargé de mission' for EP matters (a full-time civil servant at the Ministries for Agriculture, Transport and Industry) who is charged with transmitting a memorandum and a 'tableau indicatif de vote' on the legislative proposition in question, to the SGCI's 'Parlement' (PARL) department. These memoranda are sent to the leaders of the parliamentary groups at the EP and all eighty-seven French MEPs receive a 'lettre circulaire', that indicates the French position. It is curious to note that because of the new role played by MEPs in EC law-making since 'Maastricht', they are 'better' informed than national parliamentarians on French governmental preferences and positions defended at COREPER and the Council of Ministers. Neither the National Assembly nor the Senate regularly receive 'explanatory memoranda' that could help them to seize early on the relevant issues at stake. This may be one of the reasons behind the strong parliamentary attempt to integrate French MEPs into the work of the 'Délégations'.[81] It might also explain why the French Senate – following an initiative of its president Poncelet – has recently inaugurated a Brussels office in order 'to be better associated and better informed about law-making in the European institutions.'[82]

Decision implementation and monitoring

Until 1986 there was no central co-ordination of the implementation of EC policies in France. But the shortcomings, especially in the context of the SEM programme and the growing number of cases at the ECJ, have made the need for a reorganisation of the application of EC law rather urgent.

In 1989 a report from the Council of State (Conseil d'Etat) underlined certain deficiencies which Prime Minister Rocard attempted to reduce. In a 'circulaire' from January 1990, he underlines the sectoral responsibilities for the correct application of EC directives and regulations in ministerial departments but equally evokes a strengthening of the SGCI's functions in monitoring EC law in France. Here again, as in its co-ordination functions in the preparation and making of decisions, the SGCI sees its responsibilities reinforced rather than decentralised.

After the adoption of a directive, the SGCI sends the text to the SGG and the affected ministries. Three months later the administration must present an agenda for transposition and application. The agenda is set provided that the SGCI, the SGG and the ministries give their assent (if not, the prime minister intervenes). As shown for the stages of decision preparation and decision-making, the (1994) 'études d'impact juridique' and the analysis of the Conseil d'Etat may contribute to a consideration of implementation difficulties even prior to the final deliberations at the Community level. Any legislative text is followed up by the SGCI from the Commission initiative through to a trial at the ECJ.[83]

After notification of the application measures, the SGCI controls implementation, manages the interministerial agenda and observes the parliamentary legislative process.[84] Parliament is again involved following the constitutional distinction between legislative and regulative spheres. Even if since 1995 there has been a formal obligation for government to enlighten the European legislative source in the French 'projet de loi' explicative note, parliament is not systematically informed of the European impact of proposals. Nevertheless, the greater transparency of the decision-making process at the EU level leads to greater political pressure on the government to be more accountable. This is particularly the case on issues for which ministers cannot prove to have negotiated successfully at the European level after the tabling of a parliamentary resolution in Paris (See the example of the voting rights directive). However, genuine parliamentary legislative initiatives ('proposition de loi') transposing EC directives into French law, still remain exceptional.[85] Finally, an increasing number of 'last-resort' actions by interest groups can be observed at the decisive stage of the Franco-European policy-making process. For example, small producers and other social groupings which are unable and/or unwilling to act at the European level attempt to obstruct the correct application of EC law not only in interactions with enforcing administrations (see the 'Strawberry War')[86] but also by influencing the national representation. Indeed, the 'outcry' of French huntsmen against the provisions of the EC directive on the protection of wild birds and subsequent national initiatives provides a famous example of such voter orientation.[87] In this perspective the strengthening of parliament's role perhaps marks an alteration of French regulative culture, which was traditionally based on the flexibility of the implementing administrations[88] rather than on the integration of concerned groups at an earlier stage of the decision-making process, such as at the parliamentary level.

Decision adjudication: the politics of preliminary rulings

The French Constitution, in general, is orientated towards treaties which, together with subsequent legislation, are more or less exempt from constitutional challenge. Whereas the Constitutional Council (Conseil Constitutionnel) is not competent to examine the conformity of statutes to the stipulations of a treaty,[89] the Council of State (Conseil d'Etat) has achieved a slow but significant accommodation with the inevitable. This has occurred first, through the establishment in 1989 of the superiority of the EC Treaty over national lex posterior in the Council of State's '*Nicolo*'-ruling.[90] Later the superiority of regulations in the '*Boisdet*' ruling and even that of directives in '*Rothmans International*' was established. However, the '*Costa/Enel*' doctrine of direct effect is still not fully accepted and, theoretically, European law has to be explicitly incorporated into the body of national rules to be effective. This approach (the refusal to give up the 'gatekeeping' role) still influences French politics surrounding the implementation of treaty reforms.[91]

In the early 1990s France was among the less compliant countries in the EU: from 1993–95 it occupied first place in respect of presumed treaty infringements.[92] But despite some exceptional cases of non-compliance, e.g. in the women's night-work case,[93] the situation improved at the end of the decade. In the case of ECJ actions against France, interministerial co-ordination is again provided by the SGCI. The Foreign Affairs Ministry's lawyers represent French interests at the ECJ. But most of the ECJ rulings originate not from treaty infringement but from the domain of preliminary rulings, in co-operation with the national courts.

Since the mid-1990s the French government had a quite proactive policy on preliminary rulings that culminated in 1997 in a monitoring arrangement which more or less bound the French courts to governmental processes. The Minister for Justice's European department (SAEI) in co-operation with the SGCI, organises control of the 'appropriateness' when courts bring Article 234 ECT matters before the ECJ. The SGCI also intervenes, organising interministerial meetings to define a common strategy concerning the question raised,[94] and – if necessary – to 'reformulate the preliminary ruling suggested by the party from which the demand for a ruling emanates'.[95] The independence of French courts to request the ECJ to give a ruling thereon seems to be of minor importance, e.g. when French budgetary interests are at stake.

The underlying principle of such measures, i.e. the notion of a unique 'French interest' that is to the common advantage of all citizens, provides an interesting perspective on the functions of EC law within the Member States. The abrupt downward trend in French courts' referrals to the ECJ from 1995 onwards is surely part of a general trend at that time, but it undoubtedly marks a policy that has been repeatedly described as being characterised by a 'culte de cohérence'.[96]

Conclusion: changes after Amsterdam? The transformation of government in France

The ratification of the Treaty of Amsterdam – as with the Treaty of Maastricht – was conditional on constitutional reform resulting from a decision of the Constitutional Council.[97] The ruling referred to the non-conformity of the Amsterdam Treaty with the Constitution because certain treaty provisions, such as the use of QMV on asylum policy, affected 'the essential conditions for the exercise of national sovereignty'. The governmental 'projet de loi' for the constitutional reforms, adopted a very low profile compared to the important changes brought up by the last 'European' constitutional revision. Eventually, the assemblies voted for a quite consensual and un-political revision that produced only small effects on the making of European policy in France. Article 88(2) of the Constitution was amended to integrate the transfer of competencies in asylum policy. Article 88(4) was revised in such a manner that all documents (EC and EU) containing provisions which were matters for statute were to be placed before the assemblies as soon as they had been transmitted to the Council of Ministers. This new regulation modified the day-to-day practice of parliamentary scrutiny as it broadened the opportunities for tabling resolutions to second and third pillar issues.[98] The ratification law itself took the quite exceptional form of a political statement as it posed in Article 2 'des progrès substantiels dans la voie de la réforme ... afin de rendre le fonctionnement de l'Union plus efficace et plus démocratique' as a precondition for further enlargement.[99] It is important to bear in mind that once again, France did not opt for a constitutional 'general clause' that would have made future treaty revisions easier to implement. In contrast to the German Constitution's Article 23, for example, Article 88(2) of the French Constitution still strictly confines constitutional adaptation to the competencies enumerated in the present Treaty.

This attitude represents a phenomenon that is typical for governmental policy on procedures in French European policy-making. In this context, the ratification of the Maastricht Treaty marks a turning point. From a quantitative perspective, institutional adaptation processes after 1992 seem to be inflationary compared to those of the 1980s. What were the major challenges encountered by the French model during this period? Two general efforts mark the behaviour of governments and political elites: first, a pro-active policy through an opening up of the decision-making structures when French bargaining positions may be at stake, and secondly, a greater centralised control over French actors when the differentiation and multiplication of opportunity structures risks the dissolution of 'the coherence of French positions' into multiple multi-level interactions. The impelling underlying force seems to be to regain control over the 'Europeanisation' process in France and not to lose oversight of regulation processes at the European level.

The opening up of the political game is manifest with regard to a number of factors including: public opinion; the 'normalisation' of Franco-European policy-making owing to the limitations of presidential power; the empowerment of parliament; the politicisation by prime ministerial intervention in interministerial bargaining on European affairs; the acceptance of the EP as a full player in EU politics; the establishment of channels of influence at the administrative level and the desperate attempts of state actors to teach lobbying techniques that can make French actors more suited to multi-level networking. On the other hand there has been a manifest strengthening of governmental coercion of the two players that have gained new influence through direct access points provided by the Union: the national courts and the regions. It is not at all accidental that the central state explicitly interposes itself as a gatekeeper in the two domains where EU players tend to bypass the national state as a relevant actor. As a result of this, reform processes that have been undertaken in a strictly national modernisation perspective – such as in the case of decentralisation – have been partly undermined. Compared to these transformations, systemic stability is prevailing above all at the level of administrations and interministerial co-ordination. The SGCI, as the central organ in Paris–Brussels interactions, still seeks to absorb and to centralise most EU policy-making tasks at the stages of policy formulation and decision-making. Instead of opting for sectorisation to combat implementation deficits at the lower levels of administration, it has chosen to centralise policy-making at the implementation stage.

Indeed this interpretation of systemic adaptation parts company from a top-down analysis that assumes rational governmental behaviour. However, institutional and political choices have not always produced the anticipated outcomes and syncretistic changes of institutional and behavioural patterns are emerging at all levels of French politics and society. If our approach was useful for the comprehension of more or less rational strategies of government, it similarly uncovers the first 'unintended consequences' of the pro-active opening up of the state- and executive-centred system. In this perspective, the effects of the 'Maastricht' conflict that marked the end of executive-dominated 'foreign policy' style in French

European policy-making and which prevented the government from being able to shift blame to the European level may serve as one of the best examples. Another illustration is the changing character of French parliamentarism that today alters executive–legislative relations in an unforeseen and unintended way and which is alienating the institutional scheme of the Vth Republic. Regarding the process of 'Europeanisation' at the politico-institutional level, today's France is an example of a quite successful transformation of governance. But if subsequent societal and cultural processes operate at the same speed, this may still be open to debate.

Notes

1 See *Le Monde*, 21 June 1991, p. 7.

2 See Frans van Waarden, 'Über die Beständigkeit nationaler Politikstile und Politikinhalte', in: Roland Czada and Manfred G. Schmidt (eds), *Verhandlungsdemokratie, Interessenvermittlung, Regierbarkeit* (Opladen: Westdeutscher Verlag, 1993), pp. 191–212.

3 See Pierre Muller, 'Entre le local et l'Europe: la crise du modèle français des politiques publiques', in: *Revue Française de Sciences Politiques*, No. 42, April 1992, pp. 275–297.

4 See CDU/CSU-Fraktion des Deutschen Bundestages, *Reflections on European Policy*, Bonn, 1 September 1994.

5 The difficult redefinition of France's role is resumed by Stanley Hoffman, 'French Dilemmas and Strategies in the New Europe', in: Robert Keohane and Joseph Nye (eds), *After the Cold War. International Institutions and State Strategies in Europe* (Cambridge Mass.: Harvard University Press, 1993), pp. 127–147.

6 See Vivien A. Schmidt, 'Loosening the Ties that Bind: The Impact of European Integration on French Government and its Relationship to Business', in: *Journal of Common Market Studies*, No. 2/1996, pp. 223–254.

7 See *Eurobarometer*, No. 42, Luxembourg 1994.

8 See, for example, Viviane Forrester, *L'horreur économique* (Paris: Fayard, 1996).

9 In 1994 53 per cent of French felt that there was not enough state intervention in France, compared to 48 per cent in 1990 and 29 per cent in 1985. See Elisabeth Duproirier and Gérard Grunberg, 'La déchirure sociale', in: *Pouvoirs*, No. 73, April, 1995, pp. 143–157 (here pp. 153 ff.).

10 See John Keeler and Martin Schain (eds), *Chirac's Challenge. Liberalization, Europeanization, and Malaise in France* (London: Macmillan, 1996).

11 Not least in autumn 1995 when during the 'évènements' in the context of the social security system's reform public transport broke down for weeks. See the special issue on 'The Movements of Autumn', in: *French Politics & Society*, No. 14/1996.

12 *Eurobarometer*, No. 46, Luxembourg 1997.

13 See Andrea Szukala, 'Frankreich', in: Rudolf Hrbek (ed.), *Die Reform der*

Europäischen Union. Perspektiven und Positionen anläßlich der Regierungskonferenz (Baden-Baden: Nomos, 1996), pp. 80 ff.

14 There are four French right-wing groups in the EP, of which some or all members are explicitly anti-Europeans: two RPR-Gaullists in the I-EDN-group, Mouvement pour la France (MPF), Majorité pour l'Autre Europe, Front National.

15 National Assembly, 24 April 1998.

16 Such as the allies of Jean Pierre Chévènement's Mouvement des Citoyens, Max Gallo and Didier Motchane in the Fondation Marc-Bloch founded in March 1998. This club is equally open to right-wing 'souverainistes' coming from an RPR faction established around the journal 'Une Certaine Idée' and to personalities attached to Pierre de Villier's Mouvement pour la France.

17 See Francoise de la Serre, 'La politique européenne de François Mitterrand: innovante ou réactive?', in: Samy Cohen (ed.), *Mitterrand et la sortie de a guerre froide* (Paris: PUF, 1998), pp. 109–125, esp. pp. 112 ff.

18 See *Le Monde*, 7 June 1997, p. 2.

19 See Conclusion.

20 See Interview with Foreign Affairs Minister Védrine on Franco-German relations and European integration, in: *Libération*, 24 November 1998, pp. 8 f.

21 See *IPSOS 1998*, survey realised on behalf of the European Affairs Ministry.

22 See interview with a civil servant at the National Assembly, 30 September 1998.

23 See *IPSOS 1998*, *op. cit.*

24 See Marie-Christine Kessler, *La politique étrangère de la France. Acteurs et processus* (Paris: Presses de Sciences Po, 1999), p. 193.

25 Any of the three difficult European negotiations during the three cohabitation periods (1986–88 SEA, 1993–95 GATT, 1997 Stability Pact) were achieved in a consensual mode. See also Jean Massot, *Alternance et Cohabitation sous la Vième République* (Paris: La Documentation Française, 1997).

26 See Jean-Marie Colombani, *Le Résident de la République* (Paris: Stock, 1998).

27 See Olivier Duhamel, *Le Pouvoir Politique en France* (Paris: Presses Universitaires de France, 1991), p. 35.

28 Samy Cohen, 'Diplomatie. Le syndrome de la présidence omnisciente', in: *Esprit*, No. 9/1990, pp. 55–67. See also Jean-François Revel, *L'Absolutisme Inefficace ou: Contre le Présidentialisme à la Française* (Paris: Plon, 1992).

29 See Jean-Louis Quermonne, 'Chronique d'une Révision Constitutionnelle Improvisée: A propos de la Loi Constitutionnelle du 4. Aout 1995', in: *French Politics & Society*, No. 4/1995, pp. 1–11.

30 The French Constitution of 4 October 1958, authorised translation of the Ministry of Foreign Affairs, updated edition, 1996. During cohabitation periods the presidential referendum is a blunt sword, because it is conditional on a governmental initiative.

31 See Circulaire du 6 Juin 1997, *Journal Officiel* du 7/6/1997.

32 Louis Dubouis, 'The European Union: An Opportunity for the French Parliament to Recover Powers?', in: *European Monographs*, No. 11/1996, pp. 49–63.

33 Decision No. 45, in: Louis Favoureu and Loïc Philip, *Les Grandes Décisions du Conseil Constitutionnel* (Paris: Dalloz, 1997).
34 See Franco Rizzuto, 'The French Parliament and the EU: Loosening the Constitutional Straitjacket', in: Philip Norton (ed.), *National Parliament and the European Union* (London: Cass, 1996), pp. 46–59.
35 There has been only one vote of 'no confidence' on governmental European policy after Maastricht concerning the reform of the CAP. See *Journal Officiel* – Assemblée Nationale/Débats, séance du 1 Juin 1992, pp. 1741–1763.
36 See Circulaire du 21 Avril 1993 relative à l'application de l'Article 88(4) de la Constitution, *Journal Officiel* du 22/4/1993; Circulaire du 19 Juillet 1994 relative à la prise en compte du Parlement français dans l'élaboration des actes communautaires, *Journal Officiel* du 21/7/1994.
37 Delegations are more or less able to 'control' the governmental transmission practice, because apart from the implications in Article 88(4) (of the French Constitution) procedure they are still fulfilling their 'traditional' general information functions: following Loi No. 94–476 du 10 Juin 1994, government has to provide them with all documents concerning pillar two and three issues, but of course the chambers are not allowed to table resolutions on matters, that have been 'filtered out' by the Council of State: normally they present simple 'conclusions'.
38 See Senate's report No. 281, session 1997–98: Sur une révision de l'article 88–4 de la Constitution, rapporteur: Lucien Lanier.
39 Notably used by government during the IGC preparing the Treaty of Amsterdam, see Bertrand Benoît, *Social-nationalism: An anatomy of French Europscepticism* (Ashgate: Aldershot, 1997), p. 56.
40 See *Bulletin de l'Assemblée Nationale*, Statistiques 1984–97.
41 See Alain Guyomarch, Howard Machin *et al.*, *France in the European Union* (London: Macmillan, 1998), p. 47.
42 See Circulaire du 21 Mars 1994, *Journal Officiel* du 31/3/1994.
43 See Christian Lequesne, *Paris–Bruxelles* (Paris: Presses de Sciences Po, 1993), pp. 59–77.
44 See Circulaire du 21 Mars 1994, *op. cit.*
45 See Christian Lequesne and Philippe Rivaud, *The Politico-Administrative Institutions of France and the European Union. Towards Fusion?* (Manchester: Manchester Papers in Politics, 1998), Annexes.
46 See Jean-Luc Sauron, *L'application du droit de l'Union européenne en France* (Paris: La Documentation Française, 1999), p. 59.
47 See Lequesne, 1993, *op. cit.*, pp. 31 ff.
48 See Rapport au Premier Ministre, L'Etat en France. Servir une Nation Ouverte sur le Monde (Paris : La Documentation Française, 1995), pp. 118 ff.
49 See Circulaire du 21 Mars 1994, *op. cit.*
50 See Marie-Christine Kessler, *Les Grands Corps de l'Etat* (Paris: PUF, 1994), pp. 94 ff.
51 See earlier warnings from Rocard: Circulaire du 22 Septembre 1988, *Journal Officiel* du 15 Octobre 1988.
52 See Wolfgang Wessels, 'Administrative Interaction', in: William Wallace (ed.), *The Dynamics of European Integration* (London: Pinter, 1952), pp. 241–292.

53 See Circulaire du 21 Mars 1994, *op. cit.*
54 Christian Lequesne, 'Coordonner la Politique Européenne de la France', in: *Projet*, No. 4/1987, pp. 41–56.
55 See the classical study from Ezra N. Suleiman, *Politics, Power, and Bureaucracy in France: The Administrative Elite* (Princeton: Princeton University Press, 1974).
56 Schmidt, 1996, *op. cit.*, p. 234.
57 This is also due to the still quite unchallenged view that French economic actors are bounded by principles of 'national interest', See Elie Cohen, 'Dirigisme, politique industrielle et rhétorique industrialiste', in: *Revue Française de Sciences Politiques* No. 2/1992, pp. 210–243.
58 See 'La ruée vers l'Europe des syndicats français', in: *Libération*, 29 June 1999, p. 22.
59 See Michel Clamen, *Bruxelles au jour le jour. Petit guide des négociations communautaires* (Paris : La Documentation Française, 1996).
60 See the Organigram of the French Permanent Representation at 1 April 1998.
61 See 'La Mission Marché Unique de la Direction des Relations économiques extérieures', in: *Les Notes Bleues de Bercy*, 134, 1–15 May 1998, pp. 1–7 (here p. 6).
62 See Jean-Claude Douence, 'The Evolution of the 1982 Regional Reforms', in: John Loughlin and Sonia Mazey (eds), *The End of the French Unitary State?* (London: Cass, 1995), pp. 10–24.
63 See Arthur Benz, 'Politikverflechtung ohne Politikverflechtungsfalle – Koordination und Strukturdynamik im europäischen Mehrebenensystem', in: *Politische Vierteljahresschrift*, No. 3/1998, pp. 558–589 (here pp. 556 ff.).
64 Richard Skrzypczak, *Collectivités locales. L'Europe partenaire* (Paris: La Documentation Française, 1997), p. 76.
65 See Hugues Portelli (ed.), *La décentralisation française et l'Europe* (Boulogne: Pouvoirs Locaux, 1993).
66 Richard Balme and Bernard Jouve, 'Building the Regional State: Europe and Territorial Organization in France', in: Lisbeth Hooghe (ed.), *Cohesion Policy and European Integration: Building Multi-Level Governance* (Oxford: Oxford University Press, 1996), pp. 219–255 (here p. 223).
67 See Patrick Le Galès and Christian Lequesne (eds), *Les paradoxes des régions en Europe* (Paris: La Découverte, 1997).
68 See Wolfgang Wessels, 'Institutions of the EU System: Models of Explanation', in: Wolfgang Wessels and Dietrich Rometsch (eds), *The European Union and the Member States: Towards Institutional Fusion?* (Manchester: Manchester University Press, 1996), pp. 20–36.
69 See Yann Aguila, 'Le rôle du Conseil d'Etat', in: Henri Roussillon (ed.), *L'article 88–4 de la constitution française. Le rôle du parlement dans l'élaboration de la norme européenne* (Toulouse: Presse de l'Université des Sciences Sociales de Toulouse, 1995), pp. 161–171.
70 See Letter from the Prime Minister to President of Assembly's Delegation, 10 July 1995, in: Assemblée Nationale, *L'Assemblée Nationale et l'Union Européenne*, Paris, pp. 121 f.
71 See Circulaire du 21 Mars 1994, *op. cit.*

72 See Jean Luc Sauron, *Droit communautaire et décision nationale* (Paris: LGDJ, 1998), p. 67.
73 Interview with a National Assembly civil servant, 30 September 1998. See on the politics of 'false A-points': Jeffrey Lewis, 'Is the 'Hard Bargaining' Image of the Council Misleading? The Committee of Permanent Representatives and the Local Elections Directive', in: *Journal of Common Market Studies*, No. 36/1998, pp. 479–504 (here pp. 493 ff.).
74 Interview with a National Assembly civil servant, 30 September 1998.
75 See Assemblée Nationale, *Le Nouveau Règlement de l'Assemblée Nationale* (Paris, 1994).
76 Interview with a Senate civil servant, 2 October 1998.
77 The Amsterdam Treaty stipulates in its protocol No. 9, that a six-week period has to be respected between the Commission's transmission of a legislative proposal to Council and the EP and the inscription at the Council's agenda.
78 Interview with a National Assembly civil servant, 30 September 1998.
79 This disposition constitutes an significant weakening of the governmental prerogatives concerning the parliamentary agenda-setting (Article 48 of the French Constitution).
80 Circulaire du 19 Juillet 1994, *op. cit.*
81 Notably during the IXth legislature, when French MEPs participated actively in the National Assembly's work on the reorganisation of fruit and wine markets, see Assemblée Nationale, 1994, *op. cit.*, p. 79.
82 Sénat, *Bulletin d'informations rapides*, No. 727, 25 Mai 1999, p. 31.
83 See Sauron, 1999, *op. cit.*, pp. 57 ff.
84 For more details on implementation of EC decisions in France, see Andrea Szukala, 'Europäische Mehrebenengesetzgebung und nationale Non-Compliance', in: Stephanie Pfahl *et al.* (eds), *Institutionelle Herausforderungen im Neuen Europa* (Opladen: Westdeutscher Verlag, 1998), pp. 243–274.
85 See *Proposition de loi* No. 469 du 3 mars 1997 sur la responsabilité du fait des produits défectuex.
86 French farmers destroyed Spanish lorryloads while the French police present took no action (see Judgement of the ECJ: C-265/95, Commission/France).
87 Judgement of the ECJ: C-166/97, Commission/France. See Yves Mény, 'France', in: Heinrich Siedentopf and Jacques Ziller (eds), *Making European Policies Work*, National Reports, Vol. 2 (London: Sage, 1988), pp. 279–373.
88 See Vivien A. Schmidt, *From State to Market? The Transformation of French Business and Government* (Cambridge: Cambridge University Press, 1996), Chapter 7.
89 See DC No. 74/54 du 15 Janvier 1975, Réceuil, 1975, pp. 19 ff.
90 See Edward Tomlinson, 'Reception of Community Law in France', in: *Columbia Journal of European Law*, No. 1/1995, pp. 183–231.
91 See conclusions: the ratification of the Amsterdam Treaty.
92 See Europäische Kommission, 13. Jahresbericht an das Europäische Parlament über die Kontrolle der Anwendung des Gemeinschaftsrechts 1995, KOM (96), p. 126.
93 For the second time in social policy, the ECJ is called on to impose a penalty payment: see European Commission, Press Release, 23 April 1999.

94 See Circulaire du Garde des Sceaux du 25 Mars 1997.
95 Sauron, 1998, *op. cit.*, p. 188.
96 See Clamen, 1996, *op. cit.*, pp. 80 ff.
97 See DC 97–394 du 30 Décembre 1997.
98 See Annexe 'Projet de loi constitutionnelle': Décrét du 30 Décembre 1998, tendant à soumettre un projet de loi constitutionnelle au parlement réuni en Congrès, *Journal Officiel* du 31/12/1998.
99 See the common declaration of Belgium, Italy and France annexed to the Amsterdam Treaty, see Loi 99–239 du 23 Mars 1999, *Journal Officiel* du 25/3/1999.

Select bibliography

The text (English translation) of the constitution of France can be found at the University of Richmond's constitution finder at http://confinder.richmond.edu/. Further sources on government and parliament of France can be found at Government www.france.diplomatie.fr or at Parliament www.assemblee-nat.fr.

Balme, Richard and Jouve, Bernard (1996) 'Building the Regional State: Europe and Territorial Organization in France', in: Lisbeth Hooghe (ed.), *Cohesion Policy and European Integration: Building Multi-Level-Governance* (Oxford: Oxford University Press), pp. 219–255.

Guyomarch, Alain and Machin, Howard *et al.* (1998) *France in the European Union* (London: Macmillan).

Hoffman, Stanley (1993) 'French Dilemmas and Strategies in the New Europe', in: Robert Keohane and Joseph Nye (eds), *After the Cold War. International Institutions and State Strategies in Europe* (Cambridge Mass.: Harvard University Press), pp. 127–147.

Ladrech, Robert (1994) 'Europeanization of Domestic Politics and Institutions: The Case of France', in: *Journal of Common Market Studies*, No. 32/1994, pp. 69–88.

Lequesne, Christian (1993) *Paris–Bruxelles. 'Comment se fait la politique europénne de la France'* (Paris, FNSP).

Lequesne, Christian and Rivaud, Philippe (1998) *The Politico-Administrative Institutions of France and the European Union. Towards Fusion?* (Manchester: Manchester Papers in Politics, EPRU 3/98).

Mény, Yves and Muller, Patrice *et al.* (eds) (1996) *Adjusting to Europe. The Impact of the EU on National Institutions and Policies* (London: Routledge).

Rizzuto, France (1996) 'The French Parliament and the EU: Loosening the Constitutional Straitjacket', in: Philip Norton (ed.), *National Parliament and the European Union* (London: Cass.), pp. 46–59.

Sauron, Jean-Louis (1998) *Droit communautaire et décision nationale* (Paris: LGDJ).

Sauron, Jean-Louis (1999) 'Le contrôle parlementaire de l'acitivité gouvernementale en matière communautaire en France', in: *Revue Trimestrielle de Droit Européen*, No. 2/1999, pp. 171–200.

Schmidt, Vivien A. (1996) 'Loosening Ties that Bind: The Impact of European

Integration on French Government and its Relationship to Business', in: *Journal of Common Market Studies*, No. 34/1996, pp. 223–254.

Tomlinson, Edward (1995) 'Reception of Community Law in France', in: *Columbia Journal of European Law*, No. 1/1995, pp. 183–231.

10 *Brigid Laffan*

Ireland: modernisation via Europeanisation

Introduction: EU membership as part of the National Project

Membership of the European Union since 1973 represented for Ireland the achievement of a roof or a shelter for its national project of modernisation. Following a re-assessment of Ireland's economic policy in 1958, when a decision was taken to pursue external-led economic growth financed by multinational investment, membership of the large European market with its CAP became highly desirable. Economic growth was necessary to alleviate the political and social consequences of low incomes, emigration, high unemployment and low productivity. The highly conscious change marked a reversal of protectionist economic policies. EU membership was about providing Ireland with the opportunities to 'catch-up' economically with mainstream Europe, to make Ireland more like urbanised, industrialised Europe and thus less like the kind of Ireland the original state-builders wanted to construct. EU membership was also likely to help in relation to the traditional concerns of Irish nationalism, notably by providing a multilateral context within which to tame or modify its asymmetrical political and economic relationship with the United Kingdom. Hence European integration was regarded from the beginning as a positive-sum game by the Irish state elite and Irish society. In Europe, Ireland was attempting to consolidate its economic and political independence and re-discover its society's internationalist traditions.

The period since joining the Union largely confirmed the early expectations of membership. In the Union, Irish politicians and policy-makers adapted with relative ease to the demands of multi-level governance. They had a keen sense that for a small state the 'pooling of sovereignty' actually enhanced autonomy and freedom of action. There were few reservations in Ireland about traditional doctrines of sovereignty. Apart from the question of military alliances, there was an easy fit between domestic concerns and the Union's policy regimes, which enabled successive Irish governments to appear 'communautaire', at least when seen from the perspective of the preferences of the Danes or the British. This was confirmed in 1985 at Milan, when Ireland was the only new Member State to vote with the 'inner six' on the question of treaty change. From the outset, Ireland's two main political parties – Fianna Fail (FF) and Fine Gael (FG) – favoured membership of the EU. The Labour party (LAB), which opposed membership in the 1972 referendum, quickly accepted the democratic choice of the Irish electorate but remained vigilant on such issues as neutrality and neo-liberal market integration. It did not take a formal position on the SEA in the 1987 referendum but supported the TEU in 1992. The Democratic Left (DL, which dates from 1992 and formally integrated with the Labour Party in 1999), a party further to the left of the Labour Party, opposed the TEU but supported the Treaty of Amsterdam. Of the remaining parties in Parliament, the Green party (G) and a republican party, Sinn Fein, are the only two parties to continue to oppose treaty change in the Union. There has thus been a gradual but reluctant acceptance of EU membership across the political spectrum. EU membership did not lead to any divisive splits in Ireland's political parties. An expert survey carried out in 1992 on party attitudes shows where the parties lie on closer relationships with the Union; it remains largely accurate apart from the shift in the position of DL (see Table 10.1).

Table 10.1 Expert survey on Irish party positions

Oppose close relations with the Union											*Support close relations with the Union*								
1	2	3	4	5	6	7	8	9	10	11	12	13	14	15	16	17	18	19	20
			SF		WP		G		DL				LAB		FF		PD	FG	

Source: Laver (1994), p. 164.

At a popular level, the Irish electorate has ratified each EU Treaty by a comfortable majority since 1972 and has thus given its consent to the deepening of integration since the mid-1980s. Acceptance of Ireland's involvement in European integration appears well rooted in the Irish body politic and in surveys over many years, well over 80 per cent of respondents believe that membership has been good to Ireland. In *Eurobarometer* 48 (autumn 1997), 88 per cent of Irish respondents felt that Ireland had benefited from membership; this was a far higher proportion than for any other Member State. Support for Ireland's membership of the Union is not accompanied by a high level of knowledge about EU affairs. Ireland ranks just above the Union average in such knowledge, with 59 per cent of Irish respondents to *Eurobarometer* surveys displaying low or very low knowledge of the EU.[1]

There is remarkable consistency in the policy domains that were accorded a high priority by Ireland in the Union. From the outset, emphasis was placed on the CAP and the need to develop cohesion policies at EU level to assist Europe's peripheral areas to catch-up. In addition to these, priority was given to sectoral policies and EU regulation that were likely to have an impact on Ireland's competitive position and on regulatory frameworks at national level. The Internal Market programme was thus accorded a high priority because of the weight of EC legislation and the need to prepare the Irish industry and the service sector for the competitive shock of the 1992 programme. The TEU marked a further deepening of integration with the inclusion of provisions on a single currency, the CFSP and pillar three. Rather than dislodging the high-ranking policies of the past, the TEU simply added additional priorities and concerns. The Programme for Government (FG, LAB and DL) in 1994 and the 1997 FF and Progressive Programme for Government highlighted the following themes:

- *EMU:* Commitment to the public debt philosophy and targets set out in the Maastricht Treaty (Government Programme, 1994)[2] and support for the full observance of the Maastricht criteria across Europe (Government Programme, 1997).[3] Full consultation with the exposed sectors of the economy about the potential problems faced by them in the single currency zone.
- *Structural Funds:* Emphasis on the need to maximise sustainable and long-term employment as a result of the projects undertaken (Government Programme, 1994). The need to negotiate the continuation of EU structural funds so as to avoid or mitigate any sudden shock to the Irish economy (Government Programme, 1997).
- *Social policy:* Support for the Social Charter and the improvement of working and living and working conditions (Government Programme, 1994).
- *Small states:* Need to protect the interests of smaller Member States in any institutional reform. (Government Programme, 1997).
- *The Presidency in 1996:* Ireland took over the Presidency in the latter half of 1996 after a succession of large-state presidencies. It was determined to show that small-state presidencies could manage the business of the Union in an effective manner.

Of the above, adaptation to the single currency and the reform of the Structural Funds had the highest political and official priority. Domestic adaptation to the challenge of competition and Ireland's vulnerability as a small open economy, was not however, unproblematic. Ireland had, perhaps, the worst economic performance in Europe during most of the 1980s, as a result of international recession, which was reinforced by a dramatic domestic adjustment to reduce public finance and balance of payments deficits and reduce inflation. By the mid-1980s, Ireland's economic and social strategy was in ruins and its hope of prospering in the Union was in considerable doubt. Ireland had to find the institutional and cultural capacity to overcome the failure of the 1980s. Without this the opportunities offered by the internal market and a deepening of integration would have been lost. Gradually there was a recognition by government and the key representatives of the two sides of industry that 'membership of the Community does not reduce the need for clear Irish policy aims and methods. In particular, membership of the Community does not diminish the need for a national ability to identify solutions to national problems – even where these required Community policies or action.'[4] Thus a key concern of this period was to ensure that Ireland's domestic policies were congruent with membership of a highly competitive market regime.

Irish efforts to manage 'Europeanisation' and internationalisation evolved through a form of neo-corporatism known as 'social partnership'. This began in 1987 with the Programme for National Recovery (1987–90) and was followed by three subsequent programmes – the Programme for Economic and Social Progress (PESP 1990–93), the Programme for Competitiveness and Work (PCW 1994–96) and Partnership 2000 (1997–2000). The programmes involved agreement between employers, trade unions, farming interests and the government on wage levels in the public and private sectors and on a wide range of economic and social policies. The content of all programmes were negotiated in the context of EU developments and the need to ensure that Ireland adjusted to the demands of economic integration. The partnership approach, together with an expansion of EU spending programmes in Ireland, produced the much-needed recovery from the disastrous early and mid-1980s. From 1992 onwards, Ireland consistently out-performed its EU partners in terms of economic growth, employment creation and the growth of exports. As a result, per capita incomes in Ireland converged rapidly with the Union. EU finance was critical in helping Ireland create the human and physical infrastructure which fuelled economic growth and recovery. This meant that at the end of the 1990s, Ireland had to re-position itself, as it was no longer the poor peripheral state that joined in 1973. It is now a successful competitor for growth and employment creation.

Constitutional changes following the TEU

Article 29.4.3, which was inserted into the Irish Constitution in 1972 after a referendum on the question of EU membership, enabled the state join the European Community and conferred constitutional immunity on measures 'necessitated' by such membership. It did not, however, enable the Irish state to take on new constitutional and legal obligations without recourse to the people in a referendum, if the Union was taking on significant additional powers. The TEU was judged by the government to require a referendum in Ireland to amend the Irish Constitution, given the significance of the single currency project. The TEU referendum was the thirteenth referendum to amend the Irish Constitution, and the third on the Union. The referendum campaign was led by the incumbent government, a FF–PD coalition which had been formed in February 1992 under the leadership of Albert Reynolds, the leader of Fianna Fail. The Government White Paper on the TEU was launched in April 1992 with an accompanying guide to the main features of the Treaty. The tone of the government White Paper was very supportive of the TEU and recommended ratification by the Irish electorate. The main message was that membership of the Union conferred substantial economic, political and social benefits on Ireland and that 'staying out could only be devastating'.[5] The stage was set for another routine EU referendum in Ireland. This occasion was, however, disturbed by a High Court and Supreme Court case on abortion and by the Danish 'no' vote in June 1992. During the negotiations on the TEU, the Irish government had insisted on the inclusion of a protocol to the Treaty which stated that no provision in the Treaty could override the eighth amendment to the Irish Constitution which protected the life of the unborn and gave constitutional protection to a legal prohibition on abortion facilities in Ireland. The protocol became embroiled in controversy because of a case in the Irish High Court and Supreme Court (February–March 1992) about the right of a fourteen-year-old alleged rape victim to travel to the United Kingdom to have an abortion. The constitutional uncertainty arising from the case meant that the TEU protocol was the subject of considerable suspicion by both the pro- and anti-abortion lobbies. The public campaign was dominated by contention about the impact of the protocol on women's rights and not on the substance of the Treaty itself. Following the Danish 'no' vote in June, the government moved quickly to reiterate its commitment to a 'yes' vote in Ireland. In Parliament, the Taoiseach argued that:

> The reasons for a 'yes' vote in our case are clearly in evidence, with the overwhelming endorsement given by this House and the Seanad recently, as well as by the full spectrum of economic and commercial interests including employers, trade unions and farming bodies.[6]
>
> Do those who advocate a 'No' vote here tell us how we would cope with the sort of pressures which have hit Denmark today? Could we as an even smaller and less wealthy economy withstand the outflow of investment funds which would follow?[7]
>
> I cannot emphasise sufficiently that a resounding 'Yes' will be important here to enhance our standing in Europe and strengthen our position in EC negotiating fora.[8]

In the event, the TEU was passed by a sizeable majority (69.1 per cent 'yes', 30.9 per cent 'no'). Ireland was thus in a position to assume the legal and constitutional obligations of the Treaty and once more the commitment of the Irish people and not just the state elite to Ireland's membership of the Union was confirmed. Apart from constitutional change, the TEU did not in itself lead to any major institutional or procedural changes in Irish Government (Figure 10.1).

The national policy-cycle: the EU as a reference guide for internal reform

Overall, EU business was grafted onto the pre-existing pattern of public policy-making in Ireland through a process of what might be called 'internalisation'. Because of the political consensus in Ireland on Europe and the high level of support for membership in the first referendum, Irish civil servants did not face the challenge of participating in EU policy-making in a hostile political or parliamentary environment. They did not have to control, disguise or attempt to contain the impact of EU policy at national level. Rather successive governments and the senior civil service were largely free to chart Ireland's course in the Union. This allowed them to be open to the multiple streams of 'Europeanisation' coming from Brussels.

The central actors in the management of Ireland's EU policies are the incumbent government and senior civil servants in central administration. Irish administrative adaptation was based on the primacy of the 'lead department' for each area of EU policy that fell within its responsibility. The primacy of the 'lead department' reflected Irish administrative culture, which accorded considerable latitude to the sectoral ministries, notwithstanding the doctrine of collective responsibility and the role of the cabinet in co-ordinating public policy. Individual departments are responsible for those areas of EU policy that fall within their functional competence. Responsibility implies the preparation of Ireland's negotiating position, attendance at Commission committees and advisory groups, negotiations in Council working parties and subsequent implementation of law or spending programmes. The impact of the Union is thus uneven across the system with some ministries entrenched in the Union's policy processes and others with a periodic and more intermittent interest. As new areas develop at EU level, national ministries are brought into the Union's policy process. A distinction needs to be made between the overarching, multi-sectoral and sectoral departments. The Departments of Foreign Affairs, Finance and the Taoiseach (Prime Minister's Office) are the main overarching departments. The Department of Finance had the longest tradition of involvement in EU business from the early 1960s, whereas the Department of Foreign Affairs was transformed by membership. The importance of the Finance Ministry has been enhanced by its management of structural funds and its responsibility for EMU preparations. The role of the Taoiseach's Department was accentuated by the development and growing importance of the European Council. From the beginning, the Department of Agriculture was the main sectoral

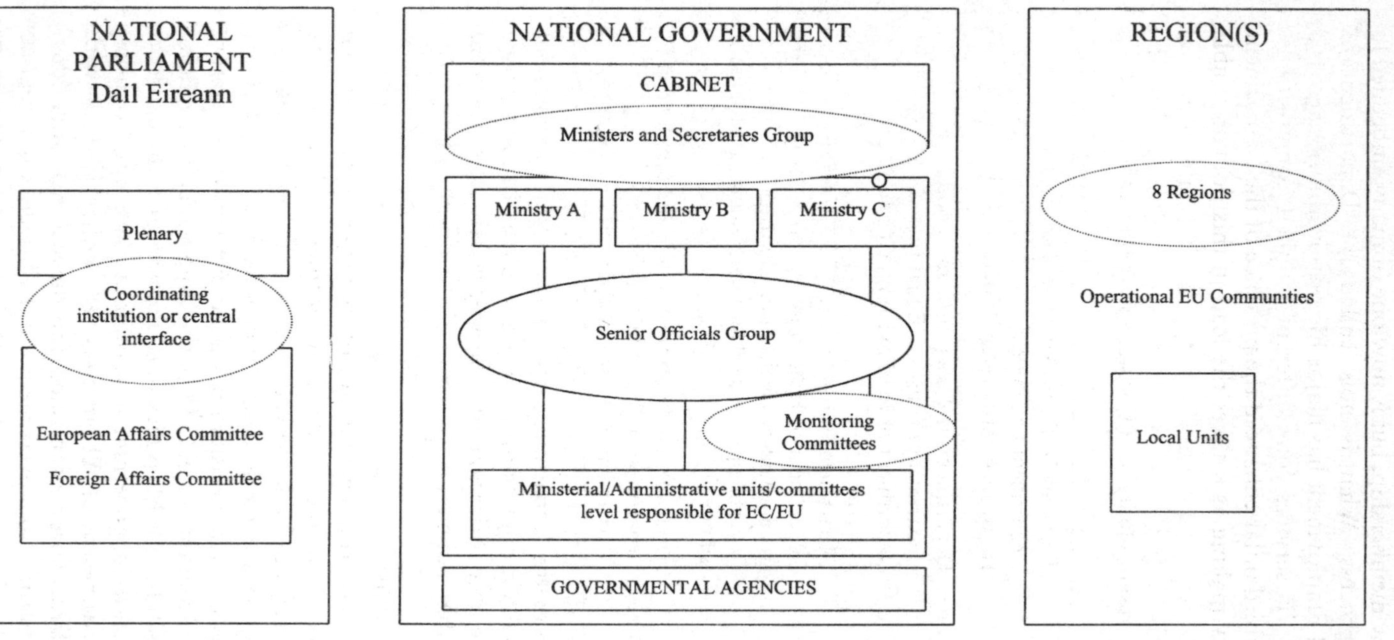

Figure 10.1 The national level of European decision-making – Ireland

department affected by membership, but is now one of many embedded in the Union's policy process. What is now called the Department of Enterprise, Trade and Employment has major EU responsibilities across a range of EU policies; it services four different Council compositions. Developments in the third pillar enhanced the presence of the Department of Justice in EU policy-making as it takes the lead in this domain (Table 10.2).

Table 10.2 Ministerial responsibility for EU matters in the central administration

Overarching ministries	Taoiseach's (Prime Minister) Department Department of Finance Department of Foreign Affairs
Sectoral ministries with one distinctive policy area	Department of Agriculture and Food Department of Justice, Equality and Law Reform Department of the Environment and Local Government Department of the Marine and Natural Resources Department of Education Department of Health and Children Department of Arts, Heritage, Gaeltacht and the Islands
Sectoral ministries with multiple EU responsibilities	Department of Enterprise, Trade and Employment Department of Public Enterprise Department of Tourism, Sport and Recreation

With the exception of the Department of Defence, all departments of state have been gradually brought within the ambit of the Union's governance structures. The intensification of 'Europeanisation' is apparent across the range of public policies.

The government and cabinet

The cabinet has the primary responsibility for the management of national and EU policy. The core principle of cabinet government in Ireland is the doctrine of collective responsibility which ensures that the cabinet as a whole takes responsibility for its decisions and individual ministers are expected to support government decisions in public. A pronounced feature of Irish government formation since 1982 is the dominance of coalition governments. Responsibility for EU policy does not appear to have been a major source of tension in government formation, nor are coalition governments any less cohesive on EU matters. EU policy is dealt with through the normal procedures established for the cabinet. Individual ministers bring memoranda to government on EU issues that require monitoring or agreement by the government. Departmental ministers are responsible for those areas of EU policy that fall within the ambit of their departments. They represent their departments in the EU's ministerial Councils and oversee the implementation of EC laws and programmes. The key ministers are the Ministers for Foreign Affairs, Finance, Agriculture, Justice and Enterprise, Trade and Employment. In most governments since the mid-1980s, there has been a practice of having a Minister of State (junior minister) with a European responsibility attached to the Foreign Ministry or the Taoiseach's Department or both. The government elected in June 1997 is the first government, in over a decade, not to have a minister with this responsibility.

The pillar structure introduced by the TEU did not have any discernible impact on Ireland's policy style or the management of EU business, other than to further increase the salience and reach of EU affairs. The most significant extension in the first pillar was the single currency project which became the responsibility of the Department of Finance. Its tasks in relation to EMU included budgetary policy so that Ireland could meet the convergence criteria, participation in EU committees dealing with the evolution of single currency rules and policies and domestic preparation for the advent of the Euro. In 1995, the Single Currency Officers' Team (SCOT) was established to prepare for the introduction of the Euro in the Irish public sector. This was followed by the Euro Changeover Board, which is responsible for the technical aspects of the changeover and information programmes for companies and the wider society. The extension of pillar one activities to new policy areas such as public health, culture, education, civil protection, tourism and consumer protection was absorbed into the workload of existing government departments and state agencies.

Responsibility for the second pillar remained with the Political Division of the Department of Foreign Affairs which had been responsible since 1973 for European Political Co-Operation (EPC). As CFSP dealt essentially with traditional areas of foreign policy, the Political Division had less involvement, than the Economics Division, with government departments on the domestic side. CFSP remained largely within a relatively small and closely-knit policy community in the diplomatic service. The sensitivity of security policy in an Irish context, however, ensured that there was considerable public and parliamentary scrutiny of Ireland's activities under the CFSP umbrella. As a direct consequence of the TEU, Ireland assumed observer status at the WEU in 1993 together with Denmark but remained outside the Partnership for Peace of NATO (PFP). In January 1999, the government took a decision to join PFP. The Department of Justice took the lead role on pillar three issues with the Department of Foreign Affairs playing a subsidiary role. Again this was a domain that remained largely outside cut and thrust of domestic policy-making.

The national parliament

Following membership of the Union, the Oireachtas lost the 'sole and exclusive power of making laws' bestowed on it by Article 15.2.1 of the Constitution. Like other parliaments in the Member States, the Oireachtas sought to qualify its loss of law-making powers by establishing mechanisms to oversee the government's behaviour. Besides being to some extent accountable through the traditional mechanisms of parliamentary questions and debates, the government is also committed to placing a report on EU developments before the Houses of the Oireachtas twice yearly. These reports generally arrive too late for parliament to give serious consideration to the issues they raise. They are however, a useful overview of developments in the Union for those deputies committed to tracking EU business.

In 1973 the Oireachtas established the Joint Committee on the Secondary Legislation of the European Communities, as a watchdog committee on EC matters. Since Ireland did not have a strong tradition of parliamentary committees, this committee was something of a novelty at the outset. It had twenty-five members (eighteen deputies and seven senators), with the political parties represented in proportion to their strength in the Oireachtas. Its terms of reference allowed it to examine and report to the Oireachtas on Commission policy proposals, legislative proposals, EC laws, regulations made in Ireland under the European Communities Act 1972, and all other legal instruments that flow from EC membership. Between 1988 and 1992, the Committee published twenty-six reports, the largest number of any parliamentary committee.

The Joint Committee suffered from a number of constraints that impede the work of all parliamentary committees. Its terms of reference were very restricted, so it concentrated most of its energies on secondary legislation and did not maintain a systematic overview of the flow of EU policies through the legislative process. Nor could it examine major changes in the European landscape, notably the collapse of communism and German unification, that would shape the Community of the 1990s. In the work that it actually did, it was hampered by a weakness of both financial and human resources. Neither the members nor the secretariat of the committee had the legal or technical expertise to examine many of the complex issues involved in EC law and policies; the many time pressures on Irish politicians do not allow them to develop the kind of expertise required for a thorough examination of EU policies.

In response to these difficulties the FF–LAB government established a new Joint Oireachtas Committee on Foreign Affairs in the spring of 1993. This subsumed the work of the previous Committee on Secondary Legislation, and also covered a much broader agenda encompassing the state's foreign relations as a whole. The establishment of a Foreign Affairs Committee brought Irish parliamentary practice into line with other parliaments in Western Europe. The terms of reference of the Committee established in 1993 allowed the Committee to:

- Scrutinise the estimates of the Department of Foreign Affairs and International Co-Operation.
- Analyse and report on all aspects of Ireland's international relations including its co-operation with developing countries and Ireland's membership of the European Communities.
- Receive and debate the Government Annual report presented to both Houses of the Oireachtas.
- Send for persons, but information need not be provided to the Committee if a Member of the government certifies in writing that such information is confidential.
- Engage the services of consultants and specialists.

Irish members of the EP including Northern Ireland may attend the Committee but not vote.[9] The Foreign Affairs Committee meets once every two weeks and has four sub-committees; it published seven reports between December 1993 and October 1995.

A separate Joint Committee on European Affairs was re-established in March 1995 as part of the 1994 Programme for Government, because the work of the Foreign Affairs Committee left it with inadequate time for the scrutiny of European law and wider EU developments. This meant that the Foreign Affairs Committee no longer carried a European brief although ambiguity remains concerning the CFSP. Both Committees ceased to exist in June 1997 when the Parliament was dissolved and were re-established in autumn 1997 by the new Parliament. The terms of reference of the European Affairs Committee enable it to:

- Consider such matters arising from Ireland's membership of the European Communities.
- Consider programmes and guidelines prepared by the Commission, acts of the EC Institutions, regulations under the 1972/95 European Communities Acts and other instruments necessitated by membership of the Communities.
- Consider matters referred to it by the Houses of the Oireachtas.
- Represent the Irish Parliament at COSAC.[10]

The European Affairs Committee meets in plenary session once a fortnight and has one sub-committee which deals with EC secondary legislation. Ireland's fifteen MEPs have the right to attend the Committee and to participate in the discussions. It is difficult to judge the effectiveness of the Committees as they are of relatively recent origin and have been established at a time when there is an attempt to professionalise and enhance the committee structure of the Irish Parliament. Neither Committee has adequate research and administrative back-up to develop independent thinking on foreign and European issues. The Committees are heavily dependent on briefing papers from the Department of Foreign Affairs and on external consultants. Attendance at the Committees is patchy, given the constituency duties of Irish parliamentarians. There is some overlap and hence tension between the Committees on areas such as the CFSP. The terms of reference of the Committees allow the Foreign Affairs Committee to request a joint meeting with the European Affairs Committee on matters of common activity. The Committees have contributed to greater openness and accountability on foreign policy matters, meetings are usually held in public and successive ministers and officials have attended and given evidence. The Committees have also provided a focus for the attentive public in this domain. A small coterie of deputies and senators has become engaged in foreign policy matters. The Government White Paper concluded that these committees have 'significant powers and are important instruments for maintaining the democratic accountability of foreign policy in Ireland'.[11] The involvement of the European Affairs Committee in COSAC has also exposed Irish parliamentarians to practices in other Member States.

The regions

The Union has had an ambiguous impact on territorial politics in Ireland. The Commission's support for partnership as a principle of government began to loosen the highly centralised nature of Irish public policy-making and add a territorial and not just sectoral element to the operation of the Structural Funds. The management of the Structural Funds which was contained within the narrow confines of central government and the large state-sponsored bodies has evolved to include diffuse interests including local authorities, community groups, environmental groups and the social partners, all in search of a slice of the Brussels pie. EU monies created a new kind of politics which encouraged people to look both below and beyond the state. Access to EU monies gave community groups additional authority and leverage *vis-à-vis* central government; on the other hand, the availability of EU largesse reinforced clientelism, a central feature of the political culture.

In 1988 seven sub-regional review committees were established to oversee the operation of the Community Support Framework (CSF) in each of the eight regions. These were largely an administrative expedient which added a weak regional layer to the implementation of the CSF and thereby satisfied the Commission about the operation of the 'partnership principle' in Ireland. These were replaced in 1994 by eight Regional Authorities with the task of co-ordinating the provision of public services in each territorial unit. Provision for the authorities was made in the Local Government Act 1991. Each Regional Authority has an EU Operational Committee (OP) which operates alongside and partly within the

Authorities, sharing the same secretariat. The EU Operational Committees meet once each quarter. Whereas the committees established in 1989 were cosmetic in nature, they have gradually carved out a presence for themselves in the policy process. The OPs from the eight regions, operating together, have established the right to have two seats on the national Community Support Framework Monitoring Committee and two seats on each of the nine OP Monitoring Committees. The Regional Authorities have taken advantage of Community Initiatives to get funding for forty programmes in their regions. Institutionally, the Regional Authorities are positioned between the heavily resourced central and local governments and lack the formal attributes of public power, such as staff and significant budgets. There are only twenty-nine full-time members of staff working for the regional Authorities with a total budget of IEP 1.6 million per annum.

The future of the Regional Authorities depends on what is likely to happen *vis-à-vis* structural spending. Given Ireland's exceptional economic performance during the 1994–99 period, Ireland as a whole cannot continue to benefit from Objective One status of the Cohesion Funds and faces a drop in receipts from the Union's regional policies during the next financial period. As a consequence, the government formally took a decision to pursue an application to EUROSTAT, the Statistical Services of the Union, for a change in Ireland's status as a single region for the purposes of the structural funds.

The government decided to divide the country into two regions, one consisting of the current sub-regions of the West, Border, the Midlands and counties Clare and Kerry and the other consisting of the rest of the country. The intention was that the Western region would be eligible for Objective One status and the rest of the country would be in transition from Objective One. The reclassification of Ireland into two regions was dependent on a decision by EUROSTAT, which endorsed the division with some changes to the territorial reach of the regions proposed by the government. Two new regions have been established with responsibility for administering the regional dimension of Ireland's national plan from 2000 to 2006. It remains to be seen just how much autonomy the Department of Finance in Dublin will allow to the regions over the life of this plan.

The local dimension

The 1994–99 Community Support Framework placed particular emphasis on the regeneration of local communities, particularly urban and rural areas blighted by high levels of unemployment and social exclusion. The decision to emphasise the local dimension of development stemmed from an understanding that disadvantage and social exclusion had to be tackled at a local level within the urban and rural communities. It reflected and promoted the explosion of community initiatives and innovation in Ireland in the 1990s. Local development initiatives followed the 'partnership model' promoted by the EU Commission throughout Europe. The approach was to empower local communities to tackle their problems and improve the quality of life. New institutional structures – Area-Based Partnerships and County Enterprise Boards – have been established. EU money was channeled through three sub-programmes:

- local enterprise;
- integrated development of disadvantaged areas;
- urban and village renewal.

The first sub-programme was implemented through thirty-five County Enterprise Boards which had a brief to support small and micro-businesses by financing feasibility studies and start-up grants. The aim was to engender a spirit of enterprise and entrepreneurship at local level. The second sub-programme is the responsibility of Area Development Management (ADM) Ltd. ADM Ltd. channeled financial support to area-based partnerships and community groups which were attempting to deal with social exclusion and long-term unemployment. In response to the initiative, thirty-eight partnerships were established in both urban and rural Ireland. In addition, thirty-two community groups benefited from the local development initiative. The Structural Funds were used to assist those communities making a collective effort to provide training, education and work experience for the long-term unemployed. The third sub-programme was designed to assist urban and village renewal in Ireland's cities, towns and villages. The evolving nature of the Union had an important impact on the willingness of the Irish public service to engage in experimentation and micro-social interventions.

Other actors

Given the reach of the Union's policy remit, interest groups in Ireland have been drawn into the Brussels arena and are active in trying to influence government policy in different EU sectors. The employers', trade unions and agricultural interest groups have privileged access to government through the system of social partnership. The Irish Business and Employers' Confederation (IBEC) is very active in EU policy and maintains an effective presence in Brussels with its office the Irish Business Bureau. The farming groups are also very active in Brussels with an office and easy access to the Irish Agricultural Ministry. The trade unions do not maintain an office in Brussels because of the cost implications but are active at national level and in the ETUC. All other interests active in Irish politics at national level have learnt to play the Brussels game, notably, the women's groups, environmentalists and the wider voluntary sector. The Irish Organisation for the Unemployed has developed a discernible presence in Brussels. Irish interests have little difficulty in playing multi-level politics and are no longer focused only on the national government; it remains a key player for them, but only one of many.

Decision-making on the national level

Assessment of how decisions are made in Ireland on EU matters requires a distinction between routine day-to-day items of EU policy and the non-routine or 'high-politics' issues. With regard to the routine day-to-day decisions in the Brussels system, the Irish approach is characterised by considerable sectoral autonomy and delegation to the desk officer. Within each government department, EU business is delegated to the division dealing with the substantive area of policy at national level. Hence a distinction is not drawn between Irish company law and EC company law. The Company Law division of the Department of Enterprise, Trade and Employment deals with both. Each division is responsible for preparing and servicing each Council working party that falls within its domain and will be called on to provide briefing material for COREPER, other high-level groups or Ministerial Councils as the need arises. The linkages are largely internal to each department and their representatives in the Permanent Representation in Brussels. Cross-cutting issues that transcend departmental boundaries are led by the key department with ad hoc committees to manage the interdepartmental dimension of such issues. The underlying norm of the Irish system is that its officials must 'sing from the same hymn sheet' in Brussels and must consult across the system before going to Brussels: the Irish system is one of informal effectiveness.

The management of the 'big dossiers' differs from that pertaining to the routine decisions. In the case of the salient dossiers, the Irish system becomes highly formalised, centralised and hierarchical in that all actors up to and including the cabinet will be involved. Resources are directed towards tracking the negotiations at every phase and adapting strategy to suit the flow of the negotiations. The 1996 presidency, the IGC and the Agenda 2000 negotiations are all examples of issues that were treated as 'big dossiers' and handled in a 'hands-on' fashion. Agenda 2000 provides a useful illustration of how decision are taken in Ireland. In 1997 an interdepartmental committee, chaired by Foreign Affairs, was established to co-ordinate the responses of the various departments to the Commission's proposals. This group did the ground work for the Group of Senior Officials (GSO) and the Ministers and Secretaries Group (MSG) during the latter half of 1997 and 1998. The Department of Foreign Affairs issued all instructions to Irish negotiators in all working groups and high-level groups dealing with Agenda 2000 and carefully tracked the domestic debate in all of the Member States through its embassies. The issues went to cabinet on numerous occasions during this period; the MSG met six times in 1997 and a further seven times in 1998. The Taoiseach, as head of government, engaged in a series of bilateral visits to explain the Irish position at the end of 1998 and in the run-up to the Berlin Council. In December 1998, the Taoiseach established an Expert Technical Group (ETG) consisting of the key officials in the Departments of Foreign Affairs, Finance, Enterprise, Trade and Employment, and Agriculture. This group met seven times in the lead-up to Berlin. The role of the Department of Foreign Affairs was to ensure consistency and coherence in the Irish position and to track what was happening in the other Member States. The Department of Finance took the lead on the Structural Funds and Agriculture fought to defend the gains of the 1992 MacSharry reform of the CAP. The Irish managed the negotiations in a sequential manner and did not attempt to trade off Structural Funds against agriculture. Rather, it took whatever deal was on offer at any one time and went on to handle the next phase of the negotiations. Given Ireland's changing position in the Union, those involved in the negotiations felt that they had got a very good deal, especially on agriculture.

Co-ordination

The operating principle of the 'lead department' does not obviate the need for co-ordination in the Irish system. The autonomy of individual departments breaks down when an issue has implications for a number of government departments or has no obvious home in the domestic administration. For example, environmental taxes clearly involves Environment, Finance, and Enterprise and Employment, and views are likely to differ across these departments on the merits of such taxes. Hence processes are needed to deal with issues that cross-sectoral or interdepartmental boundaries. Co-ordination is also necessary to ensure coherence in national policy in relation to the 'history-making decisions' or the 'big dossiers', as discussed above. Co-ordination is achieved at the apex of the Irish system by the cabinet, which is responsible for the broad thrust of public policy. The Irish cabinet system is not buttressed by an extensive committee system. At an administrative level, day-to-day co-ordination is the responsibility of the Economics Division of the Department of Foreign Affairs which has a watching brief over all EU policies. The division is responsible for co-ordinating briefs for the General Affairs Council, the main co-ordinating council in the EU system and 'A points' for other Councils. It also had primary responsibility for the interdepartmental European Communities Committee which was chaired by the Assistant Secretary responsible for the Economics Division. This Committee was ultimately replaced in March 1987 by a successor committee chaired by the Minister of State for European Affairs, Maire Geoghegan-Quinn attached to the Taoiseach's Department. The committee was essentially a committee of senior civil servants with a political chair, which met monthly and was responsible for the co-ordination of Ireland's approach to the strategic aspects of Community business at this time. In 1989, this committee became a planning committee, responsible for organisational and logistical functions, for the 1990 Irish Presidency. Its policy co-ordination functions were superseded by a Ministerial Group for the Presidency established by the then Taoiseach, Mr Charles Haughey. Mr Haughey also established an MSG to co-ordinate the preparation of the National Plan for Delors I and to negotiate the CSF. This committee represented an institutional innovation by bringing together key cabinet ministers and senior officials. Once the Presidency was over, there was no standing mechanism for co-ordination at either ministerial or senior official level other than ad hoc co-ordination groups working on the IGCs and related dossiers. In 1992, the Taoiseach Albert Reynolds re-established the Committee, this time under the chairmanship of Minister of State, Tom Kitt, as the so-called Kitt Committee. This format has since been superseded by the MSG which took over responsibility for the preparations of the Irish Presidency in 1994–95. Notwithstanding changes in the committee structure in central government, the MSG appears to have become a permanent feature in the political/administrative landscape. The MSG is serviced by a GSO who prepare the papers which form the core of its deliberations. The Committee meets on average once a month but has no pre-ordained cycle of meetings. There are also a number of interdepartmental groups on such issues as Agenda 2000 and comitology, among others. The Irish system of interdepartmental co-ordination differs from the other Member States in being less institutionalised and less stable, although the Ministers and Secretaries format appears to have become institutionalised (Table 10.3).

Table 10.3 Evolution of co-ordination mechanisms in the Irish central administration, 1973–94

European Communities Committee (1973–87)
Chair and Secretariat: Assistant Secretary DFA/DFA Secretariat

European Communities Committee (1987–90)
Chair and Secretariat: Minister of State for European Affairs/Taoiseach's Department

Ministers and Secretaries Group (1988–90)
Chair: Taoiseach Department

European Communities Committee (1992–94)
Chair: Taoiseach's Department

Ministers and Secretaries Group (since 1994)
Group of Senior Officials (since 1994)

The Permanent Representation

A central feature of organising for Brussels is the role of the Permanent Representation Centre. The Representation is the control centre for Ireland's formal dealings with the Union's policy process. The Irish Centre consists of civil servants drawn from the Department of Foreign Affairs and all of the home departments dealing with Brussels. As the tentacles of EU policy spread, so too has the staffing of the Representation which draws its staff from a wide range of home departments. The Permanent Representative and his Deputy are career diplomats, who in addition to managing the internal running of the Representation, are Ireland's representatives on COREPER I and II. Since 1973, Ireland has had five Permanent Representatives in Brussels and a number of those have served also as deputies in the Representation. At present Foreign Affairs has twelve staff in Brussels: Finance (three), Enterprise and Employment (three), Transport, Energy and Communications (three), Tourism and Trade (two), Agriculture (two), Revenue Commissioners (two) Health (one), Social Welfare (one), Environment (one), Marine (one) and Justice (one). There are thirty-two administrators, in contrast to twenty-two in 1978. Apart from Luxembourg, with seven, Ireland has the smallest Representation (Table 10.4).

Although formally the pathway for information and instructions from Dublin to Brussels should pass through the Department of Foreign Affairs, the domestic civil servants in Brussels tend to deal directly with their home departments, while keeping Foreign Affairs informed. Civil servants at the Representation exercise a Janus-like role between the Union and the domestic 'faces'. They are primarily responsible for ensuring that Irish interests and preferences are put forward in the policy process but they are also a critical source of intelligence on the attitudes of the other Member States and on the flow of negotiations. They are well placed to advise Dublin when a deal looks like coming to fruition and when concessions must be made. The Representation is also the 'early-warning' nucleus of the system. Officials in the Representation Centre must establish good working relations with the Irish Cabinet, Commission services, other representations and the Council Secretariat because such relations are the lifeblood of successful negotiations. The Permanent Representative returns to Dublin for meetings of the MSG and their advice would carry considerable weight in the development of Ireland's negotiating strategies.

Relations with the Commission and the EP

As a small state, the Irish have traditionally regarded the Commission as an ally. It is seen as an institution that has an obligation to take the interests of all states into account and to balance the demands of the larger and more powerful states. As a result, the retention of an Irish Commissioner

Table 10.4 The Irish Permanent Representation, 1967–97

Year	*Head of mission*	*Deputy Permanent Representative*	*Counsellor*	*First Secretary*	*Third Secretary*
1967	1		3		1
1968	1		3		1
1969	1		3		1
1970	1		3		1
1971	1		3	3	
1973	1		7	7	
1974	1		7	12	1
1975	1	1	7	14	1
1976	1	1	7	14	
1977	1	1	7	12	
1978	1	1	7	12	
1979	1	1	7	14	1
1980	1	1	7	14	
1981	1	1	7	13	2
1982	1	1	8	12	2
1983	1	1	8	12	2
1984	1	1	8	12	2
1985	1	1	8	12	2
1986	1	1	8	10	2
1988	1	1	8	8	
1989	1	1			
1990	1	1			
1991	1	1	9	10	2
1992	1	1	10	11	2
1993/94	1	1	9	10	2
1995/96	1	1	8	15	1
1997	1	1	8	16	2

Source: State Directory, Annual, Government of Ireland.

is regarded as a core aspect of policy on the institutional development of the Union. With regard to the services of the Commission, the Irish Administration has developed very close links with the spending directorates because of their involvement in the national monitoring committees for the Structural Funds and with DG6 – Agriculture. All departments with responsibility for EU policy have bilateral dealings with the Commission and these tend to be relatively free of conflict, although tensions have arisen in the state aids sector with DG4. Relations with the EP are far less intensive. Successive Irish Presidencies have accorded considerable importance to maintaining close links with the EP during the period of the Presidency but this has not translated into the building of close links at an official level. There are systems in place to brief Irish MEPs, but little tracking of the activities of EP committees.

Judicial control of EC law

The transposition of EC law into Irish law is usually by means of Statutory Instrument or secondary legislation. Primary law is used only for major changes in legislation required by EU membership. Between membership in 1973 and 1996, 956 statutory instruments were enacted under the 1972 European Communities Act; 1994 was the year with the highest number of statutory instruments with a total of eighty-nine (Table 10.5). In 1994 the use of statutory instruments was challenged in the Supreme Court (*Meagher* v. *Minister for Agriculture*) when the plaintiff challenged the validity of a Statutory Instrument which had appealed an Irish statute. The Supreme Court found that the sheer number of EC directives necessitated the use of statutory instruments even when statutes of the Oireachtas would be repealed. This issue was examined by the Review Group on the Constitution in its 1996 Report. It considered that the extensive use of Statutory Instruments contributed to an 'information deficit' and possibly a 'democratic deficit'. It argued that 'the use of statutory instruments ensures speedy and effective implementation of EC law but often at the expense of the publicity and debate which attends the processing of legislation though the Oireachtas'.[12]

Table 10.5 The use of Statutory Instruments in Ireland, 1973–96

Years	*No. of Statutory Instruments*
1973–77	111
1978–82	180
1983–87	152
1988–92	229
1993–96	284
Total	956

Source: Developments in the European Communities, 1974–1996.

In the period 1993–97, the ECJ gave judgements in five cases that had been referred to it for a preliminary ruling. Of these, two cases were sent by the Supreme Court, two by the High Court and one by the Dublin District Court. Two cases dealing with the milk super-levy were taken by individual farmers and the Irish Farmers' Association. There were two commercial cases dealing with export refunds and the definition of a 'maintenance creditor' and the final case related to the impounding of a aircraft owned by the Federal Republic of Yugoslavia arising from the sanctions against that state. None of the cases involved major issues of constitutional law.

Conclusions

The TEU did not represent a dramatic 'Europeanisation' of the Irish political system. Rather it represented an additional layer to the Union's constitutional fabric which in turn further enmeshed the national in the European and the European in the national. It was another step in the deepening relationship between the young Irish state and the evolving Union. The expansion in the scope of the Union – EMU, pillar three – marked a further deepening and widening of the reach of the Union into national policy-making and politics. There is clear evidence of a linear progression in the expansion of the policy scope of the Union with the evolution from market to money in the TEU. The Danish 'no' may be evidence of the 'pendulum' in action but it had little impact on the attitude of the Irish Government and senior policy-makers. Their commitment to membership of EMU in the first wave never wavered despite the prospect of the United Kingdom remaining outside. The underlying commitment to membership as the best shelter for the Irish state and economy is deeply embedded in the attitudes of senior policy-makers. This is not to say that they wish to be subsumed in a European federal state. They want to maintain as much autonomy at national level within the constraints of an integrating market and continue to have a clear sense of 'Ireland Inc.'. There is an ongoing concern to ensure that policy regimes developed at EU level suit Irish needs and the Irish model of economic development. There is no desire to import the continent's high social costs and high levels of corporate taxation. Thus while in the past the Irish may have argued for 'more Europe', this may well change as Ireland's re-positions itself in the EU system as a more prosperous state and society.

Perspectives for the future

Ireland is at a cross-roads in its relationship with the Union as it moves from its status as a peripheral state to one with a successful model of economic development. Ireland benefited greatly from the single market in two ways. First, as an export-driven economy, a level playing field and open markets are in Ireland's interests. Second, Ireland seemed to attract a disproportionate amount of the flow of US capital into Europe as a consequence of the '1992' programme. Ireland was able to benefit from both these developments because it had in place a system of social partnership that kept the economy competitive in this phase of integration. Given the speed and newness of Irish convergence, there is still uncertainty among the state elite about the sustainability of economic growth and the future prospects of the Irish economy. On the one hand, all of the indicators point to continuing growth, albeit at a lower level, and unemployment levels at or below 3 per cent. On the other hand, decades of relative economic failure are difficult to overcome. Irish politicians and policy-makers are going through a period of reflection about Ireland's future place in the Union and the kind of Union that will suit Ireland. Although this is a challenging period of Ireland's relations with the Union, it is happening in a far more benign environment than the early 1980s when Ireland was facing failure on all fronts.

Notes

1 See Richard Sinnot, 'Knowledge of the European Union. Irish Public Opinion Sources and Implications', Occasional Paper, 5 (Dublin: Institute of European Affairs, 1995), p. 34.
2 See Ireland, *Government Programme* (Dublin 1994).
3 See Ireland, *Government Programme* (Dublin 1997).
4 See 'Ireland in the European Community. Performance, Prospects and Strategy', Report No. 88 (Dublin, National Economic and Social Council, 1989), p. 218.
5 See *Ireland. A Government of Renewal* (Dublin, December 1994).
6 See Irish Parliament: *Dail Debates*, 3 June 1992, p. 1356.
7 See Irish Parliament: *Dail Debates*, 3 June 1992, p. 1356.
8 See Irish Parliament: *Dail Debates*, 3 June 1992, p. 1357.
9 See Irish Parliament: *Dail Debates*, 28 April 1993, pp. 1641–1642.
10 See Ireland, *European Affairs Committee, Terms of Reference* (Dublin, 1997).
11 See Ireland, 'Challenges and Opportunities Abroad': *White Paper on Foreign Policy* (Dublin: Stationery Office, 1996), p. 333.
12 See Constitutional Review Group, *Report of the Constitution Review Group* (Dublin: Stationery Office 1996).

Select bibliography

The text of the Constitution of Ireland can be found at the University of Richmond's constitution finder at http://confinder.richmond.edu/. Further sources on government and parliament of Ireland can be found at Goverment www.irlgov.ie or at Parliament www.irlgov.ie/oireachtas/frame.htm.

Arkins, Audrey (1990) 'Legislative and Executive Relations in the Republic of Ireland', in: Philip Norton (ed.), *Parliaments in Western Europe* (London: Frank Cass), pp. 90–102.

Constitution Review Group (1996) *Report of the Constitution Review Group* (Dublin: Stationery Office).

Girvin, Brian (1993) 'Social Change and Political Culture in the Republic of Ireland', in: *Parliamentary Affairs 1993*, pp. 380 ff.

Ireland (1996) 'Challenges and Opportunities Abroad', *White Paper on Foreign Policy*, Pn 2133 (Dublin: Stationery Office).

Ireland (1997) *Ireland, An Action Programme for the Millennium* (June).

Keatinge, Patrick and Brigid Laffan (1996) 'Ireland in International Affairs', in:

J. Coakely and M. Gallaghre (eds), *Politics in the Republic of Ireland* (Dublin: PSAI Press).

Laver, Michael (1994) 'Party Policy and Cabinet Portfolios in Ireland 1992. Results from an Expert Survey', in: *Irish Political Studies,* No. 9/1994, pp. 157–164.

Sinnott, Richard (1995) 'Knowledge of the European Union: Irish Public Opinion Sources and Implications', Occasional Paper, 5 (Dublin: Institute of European Affairs).

11 *Flaminia Gallo and Birgit Hanny*

Italy: progress behind complexity

Introduction: integration as a stabilising factor

Since the beginning of the European integration process the Italian membership of the Community seems to have been perceived by masses and elites as a kind of higher political good – scholars even speak of the Union as a 'collective myth' for Italian society.[1] Besides the deficits in the country's day-to-day performance in EC policies – e.g. in the implementation of EC law – Italian society has broadly shared basically positive attitudes towards the European integration process and its outcomes in the pre- and post-Maastricht years.[2] Questioned by *Eurobarometer* over a long time period, large majorities (+ 70 per cent) believed membership of the Union to be generally beneficial for the country.[3] Since 1950, membership of the Community has been seen as an inalienable stabilising factor for Italian democracy with its characteristic governmental instability and the strong structural differences between north and south. Furthermore, EC membership has been seen as essential for the development of Italian economic welfare and its generous social system.[4] Throughout the history of European integration one can observe a tendency among Italian political actors to justify internal reforms or unpopular decisions – such as cuts in pension and health systems – with demands from the European level and as necessary for keeping Italy in the 'heart of Europe'.[5] Furthermore, Italian governments have traditionally preferred federalist designs for the future of the Community, they have supported the institutional strengthening of the EP, a far-reaching 'communitarisation' of several policy areas, and have been ready to accept continuous transfers of competencies and tasks from their own political and constitutional system up to the European level.[6]

The strange combination of a broad but diffuse support for the European integration process, shared by masses and elites, with the weak performance of the Italian political and administrative system in the day to day policy-cycles of the Community, is often referred to as paradoxical, abnormal or even schizophrenic. It has been seen as a major reason for the loss of credibility among Italian negotiators and the consequent narrowing of their room for manoeuvre on both the European and the national levels.[7]

In the immediate post-Maastricht period public debates in Italy were not dominated as much by the ratification of the TEU as they were by other issues, such as the crisis and change in the Italian party system because of the so called 'Tangentopoli' scandals and their judicial prosecution, the emergence of new political actors such as Silvio Berlusconi, the heated battle against organised criminality and the beginning of massive Albanian immigration. Major attention in the media, newspapers and public debates was dedicated almost entirely to the so-called 'Maastricht criteria' for the completion of EMU and the possibility of Italian participation at the beginning of stage three.[8] After 1992 all Italian governments adopted strict financial discipline in order to deal with the precarious situation of public finances and with the aim of reaching most of the macroeconomic criteria in time.[9] This new stability oriented style in Italian economic and financial policy was mainly shaped by so-called 'technocratic' actors – among them the monetary experts L. Dini and C.A. Ciampi – who had participated in the negotiations for EMU. Such technocrats were able to increase their influence by taking advantage of the elite changes in the party system and the disciplining pressure of the Maastricht criteria for the country's economic behaviour.[10] A more severe economic policy – including unpopular reductions in public expenditure and even a special Euro tax – was justified by the government in terms of Italy's need to 'keep up with Europe' and was also supported by the parliamentary opposition, trade unions and employers.[11] The first broad public debate concerning the possible economic and social risks for Italy in paying too high a price for its participation in EMU took place in 1996. It shed light upon some rather critical comments and anti-Maastricht sentiments among the Italian population.[12] The decrease in public support for the European integration process, and for Italian participation within it, demonstrated by 1997 *Eurobarometer* data, might have been a consequence of these debates. For the first time in over two decades, fewer than 50 per cent of citizens believed that Italy benefited from its membership of the Union.

The ratification of the Treaty of Maastricht and its consequences

On April 1992, the Italian government presented the draft ratification law on the Maastricht Treaty to the Senate of the Republic. On October 29 1992 a large majority in the Italian Chamber of Deputies – 403 positive votes of 467 parliamentarians present (compared with 630 members in total) – fulfilled its part in the ratification of the Maastricht Treaty without any debate involving the wider public. Nevertheless, the ratification law, which was finally approved by the Senate on 3 November 1992, was accompanied by several declarations of government intent. For example, the government was obliged to work towards the correct application of the subsidiarity principle, the elimination of the democratic deficit in EU decision-making, a coherent method of monitoring the national finances and the information of the Italian Parliament prior to European Council meetings. The parliament decided to proceed with the approval of the ratification law in the short term, because the TEU was seen both as an important achievement in the European integration process and as a step which might be endangered by the French and Danish referendum results.

The TEU extended the competencies of the European Communities by establishing EMU, for example, and by introducing the concept of European citizenship. Thus, during the first parliamentary reading of the draft ratification law, MPs engaged in discussions concerning the EU's democratic deficit, its social aims and the co-ordination of fiscal policies.[13] There were also questions raised as to the extent to which Article 11 of the Constitution provided a sufficient legal base for the TEU to produce its effects on Italian law, national sovereignty and on the organisation of the state. The Italian Parliament decided that the limitation of sovereignty through the new economic policy could be based on this Article 11 of the Constitution. Furthermore, it declared that the constitutional provisions for the active and passive electorate should be modified in order to allow EU citizens to vote legitimately in Italy, as foreseen by Article 19 (ex Article 8b) ECT. The possibilities of amending the Constitution, of modifying several of its articles or of introducing a general provision that would affirm the supremacy of Community law over national law, were also taken into consideration but have not been realised so far.[14]

With the ratification of the Maastricht Treaty, the Italian government declared that it would take the initiative for the constitutional amendments discussed. Since then, the Italian Parliament has promoted two major attempts at constitutional reform with regard to Italy's relationship with the Union. The first was presented during the XI legislature in 1993, when the Chamber of Deputies' Committee for Community Policies and the Senate's Constitutional Affairs Committee suggested, first, that parliament be given the power to influence government activities both at the preparatory stage and within the EU institutions and secondly, that the regions be allowed to participate in the elaboration of European regional policies. In addition, parliament proposed the insertion of an article in the Italian Constitution which would explicitly constitutionalise the EC treaties. This proposal lapsed because of the anticipated dissolution of the XI legislature.[15] The second proposal, put forward by the Parliamentary Committee for Constitutional Reforms, established in

1997, included three articles concerning Union–Italian relations. These provided some declarations of principle codifying constitutional jurisprudence and some innovations, such as a procedure to accept further limitations of sovereignty and definitions of the role of the two chambers of parliament in Community policies and the role of the regions in shaping and implementing Community law.[16] As the different political parties were not able to find a compromise on other aspects, such as the modalities to appoint the Head of the State and the autonomy of the judicial system, the whole reform project failed, including the part concerning relations with the Union.

Although the TEU was not the only reason behind attempts to adapt the Italian political system to its European environment, one can nevertheless observe its direct impact in a number of areas. First, the establishment of the CoR favoured ongoing changes in the relationship between the Italian regions and the central government in the preparation and implementation of Community policies, as will be described below. With regard to EMU, legislation was devised in Italy stating that the national central bank would carry out its tasks within the European System of Central Banks (ESCB). The norms that had to be revised were those concerning the competencies of the Governor of the Bank of Italy, the role of the state in the issuing of banknotes, the control of the annual budget of the Central Bank, the fixing of minimum income percentages to be set aside as reserves and powers for the Treasury to inspect and supervise the sessions of the various organs of the Central Bank.[17] Generally speaking, the approach followed was not simply to abrogate the norms incompatible with EC law, but to reproduce the dispositions of the TEU and of the ESCB Statute in the national legislation. Another aspect requiring an immediate adaptation of the Italian legal system was the right of EU citizens to vote in their country of residence, provided by Article 19 (ex Article 8b) ECT. A national decree was therefore approved, establishing that EU citizens living in Italy had to register their intention to vote eighty days before the elections to the EP.[18]

The national policy-cycle: the search for full Italian participation in EU policy-cycles

In 1989 the Italian Minister for European Affairs described the situation of his country in EC policy-cycles as follows: 'It is not unusual that prior to the negotiation ... the necessary support is not forthcoming from analysis which might put forward alternatives and predict results. Consequently, we are sometimes bound to take a particular stance which goes against our interest but which we first collaborated in defining.'[19] Such considerations led, from 1987 onwards, to the adaptation of structures and procedures for preparing and implementing EC decisions within

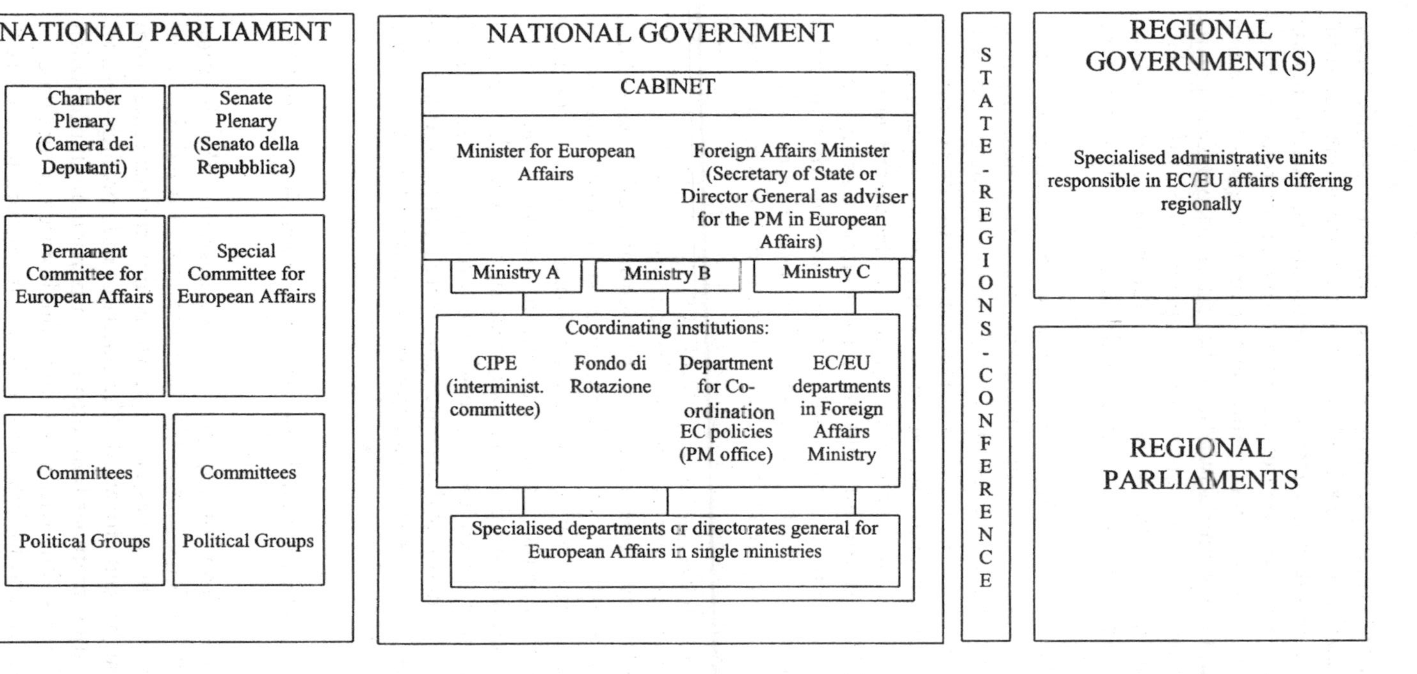

Figure 11.1 The national level of European decision-making – Italy

the Italian political system (Figure 11.1). The reforms began with two laws: the legge Fabbri No. 183/1987 and the legge La Pergola No. 86/1989, both concerning Italian participation in the normative processes of the European Communities and the co-ordination of the national actors involved.[20] The latter introduced an annual legge comunitaria (Community law) that is on the one hand a cyclical instrument for the incorporation of EC decisions and always contains a list of European regulations, directives or decisions with an indication of the respective method of incorporation/implementation to use. On the other hand, the legge comunitaria serves as a vehicle for further improvements to the structures and procedures of Italian administrative and political units dealing with European affairs.[21] The reforms were intended either to introduce or to strengthen mechanisms for co-ordination and co-operation among different actors in the national arena, including ministerial, regional and local administrations and parliamentary bodies. The aim was to reduce fragmentation and to establish closer links between those actors preparing European decisions and those asked to implement them.[22] The incorporation procedures for EC law and the relationship between government and parliament in this regard were further central aspects of the reforms.[23] During the 1990s the set of regulations and provisions for the internal preparation and implementation of EC/EU policies was enriched not only via the annual legge comunitaria, but also through several – sometimes even contradictory – provisions of other laws or decrees. Examples of these include the Law No. 400 of 1988 concerning the organisation of the prime minister's administrative infrastructure, and the Decree of the Prime Minister No. 150 of 1990, regulating the structure and tasks of the department for the co-ordination of European affairs in the prime minister's office.[24] The two so-called 'Bassanini Laws' of 1997 must also be mentioned. They represent another important reform project in the Italian political system, introducing a kind of administrative federalisation of the system which, if put fully into practice, would change profoundly the relationship between the central government and the regional and local levels in EC/EU affairs. All these reforming laws pointed at procedures among and competencies of institutional actors and administrative units at the national and sub-national Italian levels with regard to EC/EU policies in general; no distinction was drawn between the different kinds of EC/EU decisions, specific policy fields or EC/EU procedures.

These different legal texts reflected a gradual change in thinking from the traditional interpretation of EC/EU membership as a domain of foreign policy and therefore of the Foreign Affairs Ministry, towards a more issue-related attitude. The call for a more efficient and effective implementation of EC law in particular, led to a clearer definition of tasks and competencies of the parliament and the regions, at least in the national parts of the European policy-cycle. At the same time, the older rules for the Foreign Affairs Ministry and other governmental bodies remained unchanged.[25] Consequently, between 1987 and 1997 there was no coherent adjustment of structures and procedures within the different administrative units involved in the national preparation and implementation of EC/EU policies. Rather, a complex patchwork of functions and competencies, of co-ordinating mechanisms and formalised information channels was put into practice.

In the post-Maastricht period, the participation of Italian administrative and political actors in the preparation, writing, implementation and control of EC legislation and the national implementation of the treaty itself, has been shaped by the set of regulations described above. But – as will be shown below – the establishment of actors, structures and new units dealing with European affairs in the Italian political system in the early 1990s cannot be seen as direct consequence of the Maastricht Treaty. From the outside, there have been no observable, formal structural reactions or systematic adaptations within the Italian political–administrative system either to the different kinds of decision-making procedures introduced at the European level by the Maastricht Treaty or to the changed position of institutional actors such as the EP. Indeed, Italian administrative and political actors are characterised by a highly fragmented, pluralistic and sector oriented style of work at the domestic and European levels. Nevertheless, one could assume that many of these actors do take into consideration the procedural changes at the European level during their day-to-day work and are likely to adapt their strategies when struggling for access and opportunities to advance their particular interests and needs.

The central government and the ministerial bureaucracy as key players

In the immediate post-Maastricht period, almost all Italian ministries introduced special units dealing in some way with policies that were negotiated or regulated in EC policy-cycles.[26] The Associazione Nazionale per l'Informazione e la Documentazione Europea in 1994 counted about 140 directorates general or departments in the central ministerial apparatus that were involved in the national preparation and/or implementation of EC decisions.[27] Among those units, four in particular officially have major co-ordinating tasks: first, the Comitato Interministeriale per la Programmazione Economica (CIPE), the Interministerial Committee for Economic Prospects, which is considered to be a 'heavyweight' among the Italian interministerial committees; second, the Fondo di Rotazione, a special unit of the Finance Ministry, which organises and controls financial transactions related to EC policies such as the national use of structural funds; third, the Minister for European Affairs and fourth, the department for the co-ordination of the Community policies in the prime minister's administration. There are also specialised co-ordinating units of the Foreign Affairs Ministry dealing with EC/EU affairs.[28]

For the national preparation of EC policies, two scenarios seem to be typical. The less frequent of the two occurs when an issue negotiated at the European level is of interest to only one ministry. The latter prepares the Italian contribution, which afterwards should be channelled via the specialised units of the Foreign Affairs Ministry in Rome to the Italian Permanent Representation in Brussels.[29] In the second scenario, in which the issue concerned spans the competencies of more than one ministry, the co-ordinating bodies mentioned above should produce a coherent Italian contribution. Formally it is the responsibility of the CIPE, in which the Minister for European Affairs also takes part, and the co-ordination department of the prime minister's office to integrate the different positions in the ministerial administration.[30] In reality, the effectiveness of these mechanisms is considered to be low. This is because the CIPE deals mainly with the economic and financial implications of different EC policies, while two of the more recent additions to the administrative system, the Ministry of European Affairs (which is without portfolio) and the co-ordinating unit in the prime minister's office, occupy a rather weak position with regard to the co-ordination of national preparation of EC policies.[31] The prime minister is not obliged to appoint a separate Minister of European Affairs – for example this position in the Dini cabinet of 1995–96 was held by the Finance Minister in office, thereby weakening the position of the co-ordination department in the ministerial bureaucracy.[32] This department, in theory, has a variety of tasks related to the Italian performance in EC/EU policy-making. It should take the initiative for co-ordinating the activities of the Italian government, the ministerial administration and the regions and provinces in the national preparation and implementation of EC law. Furthermore it should take responsibility for all governmental activities related to the Common Market and be the national interlocutor for the European Commission for technical and legal aspects of the implementation of EC law.[33] Whoever holds the position of Minister of European Affairs is also responsible for the regular information of the regions and the parliament on EC/EU matters in line with the provisions of the laws indicated above.[34]

The overlapping of old and new co-ordination mechanisms and competencies in the Italian preparation of EC/EU policies seems to provoke the resistance of former central actors – such as the units of the Foreign Affairs Ministry. Such actors, at least during the national preparation phase, tend to a certain extent, to ignore the competencies of the Minister of European Affairs or the co-ordination department of the prime minister.[35] The Minister of European Affairs may take part in Italian delegations when policies related to the Common Market are negotiated, while the co-ordination department of the prime minister has no formal direct access to the European level: the units of the Foreign Affairs Ministry seem to defend their privileged position in this regard.[36] The members of Italian delegations participating in EC policy-making are proposed by the different ministries and are officially appointed by the Foreign Affairs Ministry.[37] In the optimal case, these delegation members meet at the national level or co-ordinate their positions with the help of communication technologies before participating in meetings at the European level. However, co-ordination efforts are often made much later within the Italian Permanent Representation.[38] Since 1990 the Foreign Affairs Ministry has had to open its representation in Brussels to other ministries, to the Italian central bank and also to regional administrations and is therefore composed nowadays of officials from several administrative units.[39]

The reality behind the formal attribution of competencies and co-ordinating tasks still shows a strongly fragmented access for different ministerial units to the European level. Many such units have direct contacts with their Brussels counterparts and quite often ignore the formal competencies of co-ordinating bodies at the national level, thus permitting sectoral interests to reach the Brussels arena.[40] Therefore, tendencies towards 'Europeanisation' and 'sectoralisation' of the ministerial administration during the process of European integration and the typical administrative pluralism of the Italian political system seem to have mutually reinforced each other.[41] One major problem for the definition of coherent national positions within the ministerial administration in the preparation phase of EC policies seems to be a kind of 'privatisation' of information. This means that important details concerning preparation for European-level decisions and the effects of and difficulties with the implementation of other similar decisions are always well known somewhere in the administrative apparatus at the national or the regional and local level in Italy. However, such details are seldom spread among all interested actors in the system.[42] The existing formalised channels of information do not seem to produce a sufficient flow of documents and knowledge.

While for the preparation of EC law within the ministerial bureaucracy, none of the formal co-ordinating actors is able to ensure the effective integration of different views, the situation is slightly different with regard to the incorporation of EC law. There is a kind of division of labour between on one hand, the Foreign Affairs Ministry and its permanent representation, as actors trying to dominate the preparation phase, and, on the other, the co-ordination department for Community policies in the prime minister's office, which has a more decisive role during the implementation phase.[43] The prime ministerial department for Community policies organises the drafting of the annual legge comunitaria, the main instrument for introducing EC decisions into the national legal system. This legge must be presented at the beginning of each year to the Italian parliament by the respective Minister of European Affairs or the prime minister him or herself.[44] The individual parts of this legge are initially drafted in the ministry mostly affected by an EC regulation, directive or decision. They are then brought together into one draft law under the co-ordination and legal supervision of the department for Community policies and with the help of phone, faxes and ad hoc interministerial meetings.[45] Officials of the co-ordination department argue that difficulties and delays in the preparation of this draft seem to depend on the degree of conformity of the EC provision with the specific features of the Italian legal system. Once the draft of the legge comunitaria has found its way through the parliamentary incorporation procedure, the implementation of EC law is no longer dealt with by the co-ordination department for Community policies or another central unit, but rather it follows the same logic as ordinary Italian laws do, depending on the performance of different ministerial, regional or local bodies.[46] Only in the case of requests and complaints from the European Commission does the department for the co-ordination of Community policies in the prime minister's office return to the scene. It then examines the case from a judicial point of view, locates the responsible administrative units and insists on the problems being solved.[47] The department in this case has no competence to give instructions but can react by introducing respective legal provisions in the draft of the legge comunitaria of the following year or presenting the problem to the government.[48] Furthermore the department under discussion has two specialised offices for the Common Market and Community programmes. These offices take part in several interministerial committees dealing with these topics under the supervision of the CIPE as the main committee for such matters.[49] With regard to the organisation of financial transactions related to EC policies, the Fondo di Rotazione – which is also supervised by the CIPE – seems to have become a successful instrument of control, fighting the improper use of funds and ensuring the continuous collection and publication of all information related to its field of activity.[50] Generally speaking, in the post-Maastricht period, one can observe a shift of activities and co-ordinating competencies in the national preparation and implementation of EC policies from the Foreign Affairs Ministry, which dominated the scene for decades, to the prime minister's offices. The effect of this – at least in the short and medium term – has been an intensification of administrative fragmentation and of the struggle for direct access to the EC policy-cycle at the European level.

The parliament struggling for influence

Since 1965, the Italian government has been obliged only to present an annual report on European affairs to the parliament. But the formal information rights of the two houses of parliament have been significantly extended with the reform laws since 1987. Now the parliament has the de jure possibility to be regularly informed about EC law which is in preparation or has just been decided upon at the European level. It also has the right to ask the government or individual ministers for an evaluation of the conformity of EC law with the national legal system, to hear the government or individual ministers on concrete policy issues and to be informed about the general development of the Union and the Italian system as part of it. Furthermore the parliament has the right to submit comments on these matters to the government.[51] With the annual community laws (legge comunitaria) of 1996 and 1998 the Italian parliament strengthened its information rights during the preparation phase of Community decisions of all kinds and must now be informed before a draft is negotiated at the European level. During the first half of the 1990s these formal rights and channels of information were used only occasionally and seem not to have led the Italian parliament to a more influential position in the national preparation of EC law. Government reports were presented sporadically and contained only general remarks that were far from enabling the members of the houses to discuss details of the different aspects of EC policies. Following the legge Fabbri and its improvement in the Community Law No. 128 of 1998, the parliamentary committees and the regions should receive regularly, and promptly, all the draft EC decisions that the Minister of European Affairs receives from the permanent representation via the Foreign Affairs Ministry in Rome. But this procedure seems to last too long and many of the documents do not even reach the respective committees of both chambers of the Italian parliament.[52] One reason seems to be the overloading of the office within the prime minister's administration which must support the Minister of European Affairs and the co-ordination department for Community policies in the transmission of information to the parliament and the regions.[53] Although members of the parliamentary committees on European affairs are specialists in EC policies and would have a wide-ranging knowledge in this regard, only a few official opinions have in fact been presented to the government on occasions when draft EC decisions have been discussed in the parliamentary committees.[54]

Both the Senate and the Chamber of Deputies in the course of the reforms of the preparation and implementation of EC policy at the national level, have modified their internal structures in order to improve parliamentary procedures especially with regard to the incorporation of EC law.[55] In 1988, as a consequence of the legge Fabbri, the Senate amended its rules of procedure, expanding the rights of the committee for European affairs (Giunta per gli affari delle Communitá Europee) and in 1990 the Chambers of Deputies established a special commission for European Community affairs (Commissione speciale per le politiche comunitarie). This latter got the status of a permanent commission in

1996 and the name was changed into commission for European affairs (Commissione per le politiche dell'Unione Europea), which did not mean any change in its competencies and tasks. Both units have internal co-ordinating tasks in dealing with the annual legge comunitaria which is usually examined by different parliamentary committees. Furthermore – together with the commissions for external affairs in both chambers – they exert parliamentary control over governmental activities and deal with all kinds of information received by the parliament concerning the policy-cycles of the Union in general.[56]

The adaptations of the parliamentary structure and the extension of its formal rights of access to and information on the national preparation of EC policies has not yet led to a more active role for parliamentarians in Italian–European policies. With regard to the incorporation and implementation of EC law, with the instrument of the legge comunitaria, the procedures in both houses were improved and the parliament regained some control over the activities of the ministerial bureaucracy in comparison to the former unsystematic delegation of legislative competencies to the government for the incorporation of EC decisions.[57] Although this delegation of competencies to the government is still used quite often, the parliament is now able to gain more control over the process.[58] It can do so by indicating the legal and/or administrative methods to be used as well as setting deadlines and obligations for the government to report on the ongoing implementation process for each individual directive, regulation or decision. The procedure for the legge comunitaria is thus comparable to that of the annual budget law[59] and has led to more structured parliamentary procedures with the effect that the Italian incorporation performance with regard to EC law has been decisively improved in the immediate post-Maastricht period.[60] So far, the Italian parliament has not found a similarly structured way to deal with policy field of the Union not covered by formal legal processes of the ECT – such as CFSP and the JHA field. Different interested commissions and committees of both chambers – together with the specialised bodies mentioned above – exert information and consultation rights (e.g. by inviting members of the national government and EP or expressing observations and recommendations as a reaction to the government addresses in parliament). Since 1993, a joint parliamentary committee with members of both chambers has the task of controlling the implementation and the functioning of the Schengen agreement as well as observing related activities within the Union. Though all these parliamentary bodies have developed a wide range of activities and produce a remarkable amount of observations and comments, their influence in the preparation of European decisions in the CFSP and JHA fields appears to be low. It depends on the importance of the information the government presents to the parliament in this regard.

The regions on the European scene

With regard to EC policies, the relationship between the central political institutions in Rome and the Italian regions and autonomous provinces has over a long period been rather conflictual and characterised by centralist tendencies. It has involved on the one hand the limitation of regional activities in EC/EU affairs to the national arena, both legally and in practice, and on the other, demands from the sub-national actors to become more involved in the preparation of EC law. One reason behind this conflict is the direct impact of European decisions on sub-national structures and the legal competencies of these actors.[61] With the first reform laws of 1987, the role of the Italian regions, in comparison to their former very marginal position in the national preparation and implementation of EC law, began to change.[62] Information rights for the regions and new mechanisms for the co-operation of national and sub-national administrative units were established. The aim here was to ameliorate problems associated with the incorporation and implementation of EC law and to institutionalise regional access to the national preparation of such decisions.[63] But the utilisation of these rights and structures seems to have caused some problems. As with the parliament, the Italian regions and autonomous provinces should receive all the drafts of EC legislation in preparation from the government, or to be more precise, from the Foreign Affairs Ministry via the Minister of European Affairs, on which they may comment afterwards. But this opportunity was seldom taken by the regions and autonomous provinces during the first half of the 1990s.[64] The regional opinions expressed are not binding for the central government and might therefore encounter difficulties in being taken seriously into consideration in a ministerial bureaucracy that already has problems with internal co-ordination when dealing with EC affairs.[65] Furthermore the regions seem to receive draft EC laws only at the point when these drafts have already been pre-negotiated at the European and national ministerial levels. Therefore any eventual regional input would most likely be too late to be effective. The legge comunitaria of 1998 introduced an obligation for the government to inform the parliament and the regions and autonomous provinces at an earlier stage, and to indicate the expected date of a decision on a draft law at the European level.[66] In reality, only part of the EC decisions in preparation ever reached the Italian sub-national level during the first half of the 1990s.[67] A major problem for the Italian regions and autonomous provinces is that quite often EC policies in certain areas – such as agriculture – overlap with some of their original legislative and regulative competencies,[68] which have been increasingly undermined as the number of EC regulations incorporated into the Italian legal system has risen.[69] The sub-national level usually is asked to implement these kind of decisions as an extension of the central administrative structures, because it is the latter that are responsible to the European Community.[70]

Since the reforms of 1987, the role of sub-national actors has been strengthened particularly with regard to the incorporation and implementation of EC law. The regions and autonomous provinces are now allowed to incorporate EC decisions of different kinds that affect their exclusive legislative competencies without waiting for a law or regulation of the central institutions, and since 1998 they may do the same for matters falling under their secondary or competitive legislative competence.[71] In practice, the central institutions quite often seem to ignore the possibility of leaving the incorporation and implementation of EC law and decisions to the sub-national level. Furthermore – as the central government always has prerogative rights – it is felt that there is a risk of higher cost when implementing European decisions autonomously at the sub-national level and when actors at this level are required to adapt their own provisions in line with national acts.[72]

In order to enforce co-operation between the regions and the central government in the case of communications and decisions of the Council of Ministers or the European Commission which affect Italian regional or provincial competencies, the possibility has been introduced, through the legge La Pergola, of the presidents of the regions or autonomous provinces taking part as advisors in the respective central government sessions.[73] A permanent conference of the regions and the State (Conferenza permanente tra lo Stato e le regioni) was also introduced in 1988 which should establish closer relations and a better flow of information between the centre and the sub-national level, as well as guaranteeing regional access to the preparation of EC policies within the national arena. This conference is the only formal structure in the Italian political system in which national and sub-national governmental actors take part together, but it seems not to have satisfied the expectations mentioned above.[74] It can be convoked by the prime minister at least twice a year, whenever he or she thinks it to be necessary, and it should deal with EC policies affecting regional competencies. In addition, since 1998 the regional presidents and those of the two autonomous provinces are entitled to call for a session on European affairs within the state–regions' conference. The latter's comments on EC law in preparation are not binding on the government and the special sessions on European affairs that should take place at least twice a year, were held only twice between 1989 and 1994, while during three general meetings the conference dealt only occasionally with EC-related matters.[75] At least in the short term the state–regions conference has not become an effective instrument for co-ordinating national and sub-national positions and needs. Commentators also point to a lack of political determination at the national level to allow regional and local actors to become more involved in the preparation of EC policies; a certain resistance by formerly dominant ministerial units has also been observed.[76]

Nevertheless owing to changes of the rules since 1987, Italian regions and autonomous provinces are now officially allowed to have their own regional offices in Brussels and to maintain direct contacts with administrative units and political actors at the European level, but only with regard to EC policies affecting regional competencies. Regional officials belong to the staff of the Italian permanent representation in Brussels and regions and autonomous provinces may co-operate with other European regions or local units. The relevant changes concerning regional relations with EU institutions are laid out in the Decree of the President of the Republic of 31 March 1994.[77] It established that regions may have relations with offices and directorates of EU institutions without either the previous agreement of, or prior communication with the Italian government. Thus, from a juridical point of view the regions were facilitated not only in implementing EC law but also in obtaining information directly from the European level. Nevertheless the realisation of these provisions for the participation of the regions in European decision-making seems to have encountered some difficulties.

The changes to the internal and external roles of sub-national political and administrative actors – especially the regional or provincial governments – show a certain trend towards regionalisation of the Italian participation in EC policy-cycles. This dynamic, in the immediate post-Maastricht period, might have been reinforced through the development of a stronger regionalist profile of the Union itself. This might have occurred as a result of pressures in Italy, from Northern Italian anti-establishment parties, to introduce a federal system by the so-called Leghe and through the increasing demands of some Italian regions and autonomous provinces to be given more chances to participate in the preparation of EC law at the national and European levels.[78]

EC law and the national legal system: the long road towards the acceptance of the supremacy of EC law

Though the European integration process had a deep impact on the constitutional system of the Member States and although constitutional modifications were seen as necessary in Italy following the signing of the Community treaties, such constitutional changes have not actually taken place. The evolution of the Italian constitutional system as a result of the progress of European integration is reflected more by the examinations and sentences of the Italian Constitutional Court than by modification of Italian law. Likewise, developments which originate in the European treaties have found their major interpreter in the jurisprudence of the ECJ, which has been called not only to apply these provisions but also to clear up discrepancies between European and national laws and to distinguish between the competencies and roles of the different levels of government.

Since the establishment of the EEC, three phases in the complex relationship between the Italian and the Community's legal system can be identified. In the first phase of the integration process, the Italian Constitutional Court used Article 11 of the constitution to affirm the legitimacy of the treaties for the national law system. In a second phase, marked by the customs union, the development of more policies such as the CAP and the growing powers of EC institutions to adopt regulations, the Italian Constitutional Court, through its judgement No. 183 of 1973, affirmed the two fundamental principles of the European legal construction: the direct applicability and the supremacy of EC regulations over national law. Before this decision, Italy infringed the provision of Article 249 (ex Article 189) ECT establishing the direct application of EEC regulations.[79] The third phase began with judgement No. 170 of 1984.[80] In particular, the jurisprudence of the Constitutional Court in this period affirmed:

1 The obligation of Italian judges not to apply national rules which contradicted directly applicable EC norms
2 The direct implementation not only of regulations and directives but also of interpretative judgements and declarations of non-fulfilment of the ECJ
3 The possibility for EC law (and regulations) to derogate from constitutional norms and to replace them in the delimitation of competencies between state and regions
4 The obligation of the public administration not to apply rules incompatible with directly applicable EC law.

The evolution of the Italian Constitutional Court's jurisprudence was completed with judgement No. 168 of 18 April 1991.[81] After the affirmation of the direct applicability of EC regulations and the constitutional supremacy of EC legal sources over national ones, it accepted the request of the ECJ to be able to send questions of compatibility with EC norms that are directly applicable to common Italian judges. Thus, the Constitutional Court accepted to a loss of control over these matters in favour of ordinary Italian judges, with the ECJ having established a direct interface among these actors. In the post-Maastricht period, this attitude was confirmed in the order No. 536 of the Constitutional Court in December 1995. The common judges now have to resolve problems of interpretation and validity of norms by appealing directly to the ECJ.

Conclusion: structural weakness persists

The Maastricht Treaty was one element among others reinforcing an ongoing adaptation process in the national Italian system to the necessities of being a member of the developing Union. Therefore, the beginning of a new reform activism in Italy was marked not by the Maastricht Treaty but by national laws introduced from 1987 onwards. These laws led to a substantial improvement in Italian participation in EC and later EU policy-cycles and in the internal preparation and implementation of European decisions.[82] In the immediate pre- and post-Maastricht period several attempts at procedural and administrative adaptations could be observed, which are linked to the European integration process in general and not explicitly to the TEU.

The reasons behind this Italian reform activism in EC/EU affairs since 1987 include, on one hand, the rather low incorporation rate of EC decisions into the national legal system that quite often led to infringement procedures and sentences against Italy under Article 226 (ex Article 169) ECT. On the other hand, the administrative incapacity – and sometimes possibly political unwillingness – to implement EC policies effectively was perceived by scholars and political actors to be closely linked to a weak Italian performance in the day-to-day preparation of common decisions at the European level. As a result, these decisions were quite often far from being national priorities and the peculiarities of the Italian administrative and legal system might have caused even more difficulties in their implementation.[83] The dynamics of the integration process at the end of the 1980s, with the realisation of the SEA, the completion of the Internal Market Programme, the consequent demands among Italian economic elites to improve the implementation of these developments and the approaching negotiations on EMU made these shortcomings too pressing for the Italian political and administrative actors even prior to the approval of the Maastricht Treaty.[84]

The structural characteristics of the political system were perceived as major causes of these difficulties and therefore reform, as referred to above, was clearly necessary. In the preparation of EC decisions at the national level, the high degree of administrative fragmentation was seen to lead to rather incoherent, even contradictory, positions among Italian actors from different ministries when negotiating at the European level, and to a lack of intra-ministerial co-ordination. It also prevented a fine-tuning between the preparation of decisions and their implementation at the national level.[85] With regard to the incorporation and effective implementation of EC decisions, the reforms aimed to ensure co-operation between governmental bodies and the Italian parliament, and between government and regions or provinces as well as introducing parliamentary incorporation procedures, the implementation of which partly coincided that of the Maastricht Treaty.

From a technical, efficiency oriented perspective on Italian participation in EC/EU policies, the reforms and the impact of the Maastricht Treaty have not (yet) led to greater efficiency in the co-ordination of administrative units at the national level or to more effectiveness in internal preparation and implementation of European decisions. Italian participation in the EU policy-cycle as well as in constitutional revision of the Union after Maastricht thus still shows two faces. There is political rhetoric of pro-Europeanism besides an administrative and legal reality showing a high degree of interadministrative struggle for access to the European level. In the years shortly before and after the TEU more and more former 'outsiders' such as the regions and the parliament became involved in the national EC-related decision processes – which does not automatically mean that these actors really got more influence on decisions taken. The high-regulating, 'baroque' legal system still allows overlapping competencies among interested administrative units and political institutions, tolerating the lack of transparency of the Italian political system in general and also in European policy making.

During the 1996–97 IGC leading to the Amsterdam Treaty, it could be observed that, in terms of both economic and foreign and security policy, 'Europe' had become the main point of reference for Italian foreign policy interests and actions. The Italian government's constant attention to the attitudes and position of its most influential European partners was a good case in point. Italy's prime ministers in all aspects of foreign affairs have come to look to Bonn rather than Washington. In the European environment, Italy still finds a point of reference for its domestic reforms ranging from cuts in public spending to the future of the Italian welfare system. Secondly Italy was confronted with a process of marginalisation and exclusion from some European initiatives such as the Bosnia Contact Group and in policy fields that were thought to be of interest for the country. One result was Italy's negative attitude towards the directoires that in the 1980s tended to exclude it from the circle of more influential Member States of the Union. Italian political actors in constitutional negotiations at the European level therefore prefer 'core groups' within the Union's institutional framework, with precise 'opting-in' clauses, rather than allowing the creation, outside the Union, of new clubs which lack clear mechanisms of delayed participation. Thirdly, Italian political, administrative and economic actors at the highest level of government, parties, ministries and the economy, have acknowledged the importance of the Union in its role as an external binding factor for domestic reforms.

If this is true of the reforms in public spending policies tied to the Maastricht macroeconomic criteria, it might also be useful for the overdue modernisation of Italy's institutional set-up. Finally, Italy's position at the crossroads of the two major crisis points in the Euro-Mediterranean region justifies its requirement of a new security and defence policy as a response to the changes taking place in this environment. The threats perceived to come from that region cannot be seriously countered through the creation of merely occasional alliances such as, most recently, the Southern European countries' alliance engaged in the Albanian mission: from the Italian perspective they would instead require a more active role for the Union. Hence, during the 1996–97 IGC, public statements issued by the Foreign Affairs Minister Lamberto Dini and prime minister Romano Prodi emphasised Italy's support for a stronger institutional framework in the political dimension of the Union. In other words, the focus was on institutional reform of the Community pillar of the Union (the EP's powers, majority voting and so on), the creation of more effective institutions dealing with CFSP and, finally, the adoption of common policies for immigration and asylum (the so-called third pillar). From the Italian perspective, the Treaty of Amsterdam introduced several relevant innovations, but important reforms remain on the negotiating table. As a consequence, at the end of September 1997, Italy, Belgium and France presented a joint declaration to be enclosed in the protocol on the institutions with the prospect of the enlargement of the Union, affirming that the reinforcement of the institutions is seen as an indispensable condition for the conclusion of the first accession negotiations and that they are 'determined to give the fullest effect appropriate to the protocol'. Since then, the Italian position has remained unchanged.[86]

In view of future intergovernmental conferences and of its day-to-day policy-cycles, Italian participation and performance will still be marked on the one hand, by complex internal structures and administrative and regional struggles for access to those fora where the decisions are taken, and on the other, by far reaching, pro-European visions for the future development of the Union and Italy's part in this process. Within these margins the Italian actors involved have taken advantage even of their often quite inefficient and ineffective participation in EC/EU policy-making for the stabilisation and modernisation of the country's political and economic system over recent decades. There is a high probability that this mechanism will work for the future as well.

Notes

1 See Sergio Romano, *Guida alla politica estera italiana* (Milano: Rizzolini 1993), p. 192.

2 See Sergio Pistone, 'Italien und die westeuropäische Integration nach dem Zweiten Weltkrieg', in: Wolf D. Gruner and Günther Trautmann (eds), *Italien in Geschichte und Gegenwart* (Hamburg: P. Krämer, 1991), pp. 225 ff; Maria Valeria Agostini, 'Italy and its Community Policy', in: *The International Spectator*, No. 4/1990, p. 351; Istituto Affari Internazionali, *L'Italia*, 1990, p. 254; Emile Noël, 'Italia – CEE. Vizi e virtù di un membro fondatore', in: *Relazioni Internazionali*, June 1990, p. 99.

3 See European Commission, *Eurobarometer*, 'Public opinion in the European Union, Trends 1974–1992, April 1993; European Commission, *Eurobarometer*, 39, June 1993; 41, July 1994; 43, October 1995; 45, December 1996; 47, October 1997.

4 See Maurizio Cotta, 'European Integration and the Italian Political System', in: Francesco Francioni (ed.), *Italy and EC Membership Evaluated* (London:

St Martin's Press 1992), p. 210; Franco Bruni and Mario Monti, 'Auf dem Weg zur Wirtschafts- und Währungsunion', in: Maurizio Ferrera and Elfriede Regelsberger (eds), *Italien und die Bundesrepublik Deutschland – Antriebskräfte der europäischen Integration* (Bonn: Europa Union Verlag, 1990), pp. 139–146; Paolo Guerrieri and Pier Carlo Padoan, 'Two Level Games and Structural Adjustment. The Italian Case', in: Conference on 'Global and Domestic Factors in International Cooperation', 3–4 April (Trento, 1989), p. 29; Maurizio Ferrera, 'The Politics of EC Membership. An Explanation of Some Italian Paradoxes', in College of Europe (ed.), *The Institutions of the European Community after the Single European Act* (Bruges, 1990), p. 3.

5 See David Hine, 'Italy and Europe. The 1990 Presidency and the Domestic Management of European Community Affairs', in: Centre for Mediterranean Studies Occasional Paper, No. 3 (Bristol, 1991), p. 37; Cotta, 1992, *op. cit.*, p. 210; Agostini, 1990, *op. cit.*, p. 345; Carlo Maria Santoro, 'Dove va la politica estera italiana? Cinque ipotesi su una media potenza', in: *Relazioni Internazionali*, No. 1/1989, p. 97.

6 See Giuseppe Vedovato, *Italienische Außenpolitik. Grundzüge, Entwicklungen, Analysen* (Bonn: Europa Union Verlag, 1984), p. 121; Marco Giuliani, 'Il processo decisionale italiano e le politiche comunitarie', in: *Polis*, No. 2/1992, p. 330; Benedetta Rizzo, 'Comunità Europea', in: Luigi Vittorio Ferraris (ed.), *Manuale della politica estera italiana 1947–1993* (Roma/Bari: da terza, 1996), pp. 103, 152 ff., 162 ff., 325, 333.

7 See Florence Zampini, 'L'Italie en amont du manquement . . . Un problème de compétence entre l'executiv, le parlement et les régions', in: *Revue trimestrielle de droit européen*, No. 2/1994, p. 196; Antonio Tizzano, 'La nouvelle loi italienne pour l'execution des obligations communautaries', in: *Revue du marché commun*, 339, August–September 1990, p. 532; Istituto Affari Internazionali (ed.): *L'Italia nel processo di integrazione europeo. Problemi e progressi* (Roma: Istituto Affari Internazionali/Franco Angeli, 1989), p. 1; Marco Giuliani, 'Italy', in: Dietrich Rometsch and Wolfgang Wessels (eds), *The European Union and Member States. Towards Institutional Fusion?* (Manchester; Manchester University Press, 1996), pp. 105–133; Hine, 1991, *op. cit.*, pp. 20 f.

8 See Martin Bull and Martin Rhodes, 'Between Crisis and Transition. Italian Politics in the 1990s', in: *West European Politics,* No. 1/1997, p. 8; Carlo Masala, 'Italienische Europapolitik 1994–1997. Interessen, Widersprüche, Perspektiven', *Stiftung Wissenschaft und Politik*, June 1997, p. 7; Giacomo Vaciago, 'Italy. EMS Discipline, Fiscal Imbalance', in: James Forder and Anan Menon (eds), *The European Union and National Macroeconomic Policy* (London: Routledge, 1998), p. 124; Bruno Coquet, 'Italie, l'Europe coute que coute', in: Observations et diagnostics économiques, *lettre de l'OFCE*, 165, 26 June 1997, p. 1.

9 See Günther Trautmann, 'Italiens Finanz- und Wirtschaftspolitik im Hinblick auf die Europäische Währungsunion', in: *Aus Politik und Zeitgeschichte*, No. 28/1998, p. 16; Vincent della Sala, 'Hollowing Out and Hardening the State. European Integration and the Italian Economy', in: *West European Politics*, No. 1/1997, p. 24; Maurizio Ferrera, 'Italiens Europapolitik im Jahr von

Maastricht', in: Susanne Wilking (ed.), *Deutsche und italienische Europapolitik. Historische Grundlagen und aktuelle Fragen* (Bonn: Europa Union Verlag, 1992), p. 111; Vaciago, 1998, *op. cit.*, p. 127.

10 Bull and Rhodes, 1997, *op. cit.*, p. 9; Vaciago, 1998, *op. cit.*, p. 127; Sala, 1997, *op. cit.*, pp. 24, 29.

11 See Trautmann, 1998, *op. cit.*, pp. 18 f.; Sala, 1997, *op. cit.*, pp. 16, 20; Istituto Affari Internazionali (ed.), 'Italy', Revision of Maastricht, Report I, April 1994, Report II, Summer–Autumn 1994, Report III, Winter–Spring 1995 and Report IV, Summer–Autumn 1995.

12 See Coquet, 1997, *op. cit.*; Aldo Rizzo, 'L'Italia e la moneta europea', in: *Affari Esteri*, Vol. 28, 112, 1996, pp. 727 ff.; Istituto Affari Internazionali (ed.), 'Italy', Revision of Maastricht, Report VI, July–December 1996.

13 See the draft ratification law and the related government report, A. S., XI, No. 153.

14 See Massimo Luciani, 'La Costituzione italiana e gli ostacoli all'integrazione europea', in: *Politica e diritto*, 1992, p. 557.

15 See Commission for Community policies of the Chamber of Deputies and Commission of constitutional affairs of the Senate: 'Relazione alla Proposta di legge costituzionale', 5 August 1993 and 'Indagine conoscitiva sui problemi connessi all'attuazione del Trattato di Maastricht, Documento Conclusivo', 23 October 1993 (internal report).

16 For a deeper analysis, see Bengt Beutler, Roland Bieber *et al.*, *L'Unione Europea, Istituzioni, Ordinamento e Politiche, Edizione italiana a cura di Valeria Biagiotti* (Bologna: Il Mulino, 1998).

17 See *Gazzetta Ufficiale della Repubblica Italiana (GURI)*, No. 295, 19 December 1997.

18 See 'Disposizioni urgenti in materia di elezioni al Parlamento Europeo', No. 408, 24. June 1994, *GURI*, No. 148, 27 June 1994.

19 See on the *La Pergola* case, Onorato Sepe, 'The Case of Italy', in: Spyros A. Pappas (ed.), *National Administrative Procedures for the Preparation and Implementation of Community Decisions* (Maastricht: EIPA, 1995), p. 334.

20 See Law No. 183 ('Fabbri') 16 April 1987, Supplemento Ordinario alla *GURI*, No. 109, 13. May 1987; Law No. 86 ('La Pergola'), 9 March 1989, *GURI*, No. 58, 10 March 1989; Camera dei Deputati, *La legge comunitaria*, 1995, p. 17; Mario P. Chiti, 'L'amministrazione per il coordinamento dell politiche comunitarie nelle recenti riforme', in: *Rivista Italiana di Diritto Pubblico Comunitario*, 1991, p. 13; Adriano Raffaelli, 'I rapporti CEE-Regioni in applicazione delle direttive comunitarie', in: Istituto Affari Internazionali (ed.), *Ricercha. La Regione nel processo di integrazione europeo* (Roma, 1989), p. 3; Massimo Morisi, *L'attuazione delle direttive CE in Italia. La legge comunitaria in parlamento* (1992), p. 17; Vincenzo Guizzi, 'L'attuazione delle direttive in Italia', in: Camera dei Deputati (ed.), *Comunicazione. Secondo Congresso della associazione europea per la legislazione. L'attuazione delle direttive comunitaria in Italia* (Roma, 24–25 March 1995), p. 1; Sepe, 1995, *op. cit.*, p. 334; Associazione Nazionale per l'Informazione e la Documentazione Europea (ed.), *Pubblica amministrazione e Comunità Europea. Un Modello per l'Italia, Roma* (1994), p. 53; Sergio Bartole, 'Novità e problemi applicativi del disegno di legge La Pergola

per l'attuazione delle direttive comunitarie', in: *Foro Italiano*, IV (Roma, 1988), p. 498; Mario P. Chiti, 'Regionalismo comunitario e regionalismo interno. Due modelli da ricomporre', in: *Rivista Italiana di Diritto Pubblico Comunitario*, No. 1/1992, p. 45.

21 Presidenza del Consiglio dei Ministri, *Schema di disegno di legge concernente: legge comunitaria 1998* (Roma, 19 February 1998); Camera dei Deputati, Servizio Rapporti Comunitari (ed.), *L'attuazione delle direttive comunitarie in Italia, Secondo Congresso della Associazione europea per la legislazione (EAL)*, (Roma, 24–25 March 1995); Vincenzo Guizzi, *Manuale di diritto e politica dell'Unione Europea* (Napoli, Milano: Editioriale Scientifica, 1994), pp. 502–506; Claudio de Rose, 'Guida alla lettura della legge comunitaria 1994', *Consiglio di Stato*, No. 1/1996, pp. 121–131; Gerardo Pelosi, 'La Camera verá la maxi-Comunitaria', in: *Il Sole 24 Ore*, 110, 23 April 1998, pp. 22–23.

22 See Associazione Nazionale, 1994, *op. cit.*, p. 56; Morisi, 1992, *op. cit.*, pp. 16 f.; Hine, 1991, *op. cit.*, p. 26; Zampini, 1994, *op. cit.*, p. 215; Sepe, 1995, *op. cit.*, p. 334.

23 See Giuliani, 1996, *op. cit.*, p. 119; Morisi, 1992, *op. cit.*, pp. 16 f.; Guizzi, 1995, *op. cit.* p. 6.

24 See Law No. 400, 23 August 1988, *GURI*, No. 214, 12 September 1988, Decree of the Prime Minister, No. 150, 30 April 1990, *GURI*, No. 139, 16 June 1990.

25 See Mario P. Chiti, 'Der Vertrag über die Europäische Union und sein Einfluß auf die italienische Verfassung', in: *Der Staat*, No. 1/1994, p. 19; Guizzi, 1995, *op. cit.*, p. 5; Raffaelli, 1989, *op. cit.*, p. 12; Claudio Franchini, *Amministrazione italiana e amministrazione comunitaria. La coamministrazione nei settori di interesse comunitario* (Padova: CEDAM, 1993), p. 117; Paolo Caretti, 'La nuova disciplina della partecipazione dell'Italia al processo normativo comunitario e delle procedure di esecuzione degli obblighi comunitari, dettata dalla l. n. 86 del 1989 alla prova. La prima 'legge comunitaria' (legge 29 dicembre 1990, n. 428)', in: *Rivista italiana di diritto pubblico comunitario*, No. 1/ 1991, p. 335.

26 See Claudio Franchini, 'L'integrazione europea e il governo delle politiche comunitarie in Italia. Organizzazione amministrativa e rapporti con le comunita europee', in: Centro nazionale di prevenzione e difesa sociale (ed.), Congresso su 'Il mercato unico europeo. Pubblico e privato nell'Europa degli anni '90' (Milano, 15–18 February 1990), p. 331.

27 See Associazione Nazionale, 1994, *op. cit.*, pp. 21–45.

28 See Agostini, 1990, *op. cit.*, p. 352; Ferrera, 1990, *op. cit.*, p. 6; Franchini, 1993, *op. cit.*, pp. 44, 47 f.; Morisi, 1992, *op. cit.*, pp. 50 ff.; Sepe, 1995, *op. cit.*, pp. 339 f.; Teofano Felicolo, 'Il fondo di rotazione per l'attuazione delle politiche comunitarie', in: *Mondo Agricolo* 23–24 June 1994, pp. 17 f.; Spyros A. Pappas, 'The European Partnership through National Administrative Procedures for the Preparation and Implementation of Community Decisions', in: Spyros A. Pappas (ed.), *National Administrative Procedures for the Preparation and Implementation of Community Decisions* (Maastricht, EIPA, 1995), p. 37.

29 See Senato della Repubblica, Giunta per gli Affari delle Comunità Europee

(ed.), *Indagine conoscitiva sulla partecipazione dell'Italia alle fasi formativa ed applicativa del diritto comunitario* (Roma: Tipografia del Senato 1991), pp. 22, 63.

30 See Senato della Repubblica, 1991, *op. cit.*, pp. 63, 239; Franchini, 1993, *op. cit.*, pp. 47 ff.; Maria Valeria Agostini, 'The Role of the Italian Regions in Formulating Community Policy', in: *The International Spectator*, No. 2/1990, p. 88.

31 See Ferrera, 1990, *op. cit.*, Hine, 1991, *op. cit.*, p. 34; Marinella Gualdesi Neri, 'La politica d'integrazione europea', in: Istituto Affari Internazionali (ed.), *L'Italia nella politica internazionale, anno 1990–1991* (Roma: Instituto Affari Internazionali/Franco Angeli, 1993), p. 157.

32 Information by officials of the Dipartimento per il coordinamento delle politiche comunitarie, office of the prime minister (Rome, 10 April 1996); see also Franchini, 1993, *op. cit.*, p. 62.

33 See Decree of the Prime Minister, No. 150, 30 April 1990, *GURI*, No. 139, Article 2, 16 June 1990; Zampini, 1994, *op. cit.*, p. 224.

34 See Pappas, 1995, *op. cit.*, p. 37.

35 See Hine, 1991, *op. cit.*, pp. 29, 32; Sepe, 1995, *op. cit.*, p. 325; Mario P. Chiti, 'Il coordinamento delle politiche comunitarie e la riforma degli apparti di governo', in: *Quaderno* No. 1, 1989–90, p. 245.

36 See Chiti, 1989–90, *op. cit.*, p. 254; Franchini, 1993, *op. cit.*, p. 44.

37 See Istituto Affari Internazionali, 1981, *op. cit.*, p. 77; Sepe, 1995, *op. cit.*, p. 335.

38 See Guizzi, 1994, *op. cit.*, p. 471.

39 See Hine, 1991, *op. cit.*, p. 32; Maria Valeria Agostini, 'L'attività internazionale e comunitaria dei Länder, delle Regioni, dei Cantoni e delle Comunità autonome. Il caso Italiano', in: Università di Madrid, Università dei Paesi Baschi (eds), *L'attività internazionale e comunitaria dei Länder, delle Regioni, dei Cantoni e delle Comunità autonome* (Madrid, 1994), p. 368.

40 See Chiti, 1989–90, *op. cit.*, p. 245.

41 See Claudio Franchini, 'L'amministrazione italiana e la CEE. La fatica di stare in Europa', in: Paul Ginsborg (ed.), *Stato dell'Italia* (Milano: B. Mondadori, 1994), pp. 503 ff.

42 See Associazione Nazionale, 1994, *op. cit.*, pp. 66–79.

43 See Sepe, 1995, *op. cit.*, pp. 324, 339; Pappas, 1995, *op. cit.*, p. 37.

44 See Law No. 86, 9 March 1989.

45 Information by officials of the Dipartimento per il coordinamento delle politiche comunitarie, Office of the Prime Minister (Rome, 10 April 1996).

46 See Jacques Ziller, 'The Implementation of European Community Policies in the Member States', in: Heinrich Siedentopf and Jacques Ziller (eds), *Making European Policies Work. The Implementation of Community Legislation in the Member States* (London: Sage, 1988), p. 141; Kieran St C. Bradley, 'The Increase of Effectiveness. Problems of Implementation', in: Christian Engel and Wolfgang Wessels (eds), *The European Union in the 1990s – Ever Closer and Larger?* (Bonn: Europa Union Verlag, 1993), p. 83.

47 Information by officials of the Dipartimento per il coordinamento delle politiche comunitarie, Office of the Prime Minister (Rome, 10 April 1996).

48 See Branca Marzio, 'Il Dipartimento per il coordinamento delle politiche

comunitarie', in: Presidenza del Consiglio dei Ministri; Dipartimento per la Funzione Pubblica (ed.), *La riforma della pubblica amministrazione. Atti delle commissioni e dei comitati di studio. La pubblica amministrazione e l'Europa*, No. VI (Rome, 1994), p. 58.

49 *Ibid.*, pp. 54–57.

50 See Ministero del Tesoro; Ministro per il Coordinamento delle Politiche Comunitarie (ed.), *Bollettino Bimestrale del Fondo di Rotazione per l'attuazione delle politiche comunitarie, Ragioneria Generale dello Stato*, 1–6, 1990–94.

51 See Giuliani, 1996, *op. cit.*, pp. 117 f.; Vincenzo Guizzi, 'Parlamento italiano e comunità europea nei meccanismi introdotti dalle nuove norme dei regolamenti parlamentari', in: *Rivista di diritto europeo*; No. 2/1991, p. 295; Norme generali sulla partecipazione dell'Italia al processo normativo comunitario e sulle procedure d'esecuzione degli obblighi comunitari', in: Senato della Repubblica (ed.), *Atti del 1. corso di aggiornamento per i funzionari della carriera direttiva del senato della repubblica* (Roma, 1992), pp. 330 f.

52 See Salari, 1992, *op. cit.*, p. 332.

53 See Law No. 400, 30 April 1990.

54 See Paul Furlong, 'The Italian Parliament and European Integration – Responsibilities, Failures and Successes', in: Philip Norton (ed.), *National Parliaments and the European Union* (London: Frank Cass, 1995), p. 43.

55 See Sepe, 1995, *op. cit.*, p. 328.

56 See Guizzi, 1995, *op. cit.*, pp. 7 f.

57 See Alberto Predieri, 'Prefazione. Una legge comunitaria nello Stato prefederativo', in: Massimo Morisi (ed.), *L'attuazione delle direttive Ce in Italia. La 'legge comunitaria' in Parlamento* (Milano: Giuffrè, 1992), p. xxxi; Sepe, 1995, *op. cit.*, pp. 326 f.

58 See Vincenzo Guizzi, 'La legge La Pergola No. 86/89. Una impostazione nuova del circuito decisionale e operativo Italia-Comunità', in: *Rivista di Diritto Europeo*, No. 1/1990, p. 9.

59 See Morisi, 1992, *op. cit.*, pp. 55, 61, 140.

60 See: European Commission: *Annual Reports on Monitoring the Application of Community Law*, 1990 COM (91) 321Final, 1991 COM (92) 136Final, 1992 COM (93) 320Final, 1993 COM (94) 500Final, 1994 COM (95) 500Final.

61 See Agostini, 1992, *op. cit.*

62 See Agostini, 1990, *op. cit.*, p. 88; Chiti, 1994, *op. cit.*, p. 21; Antonio Ruggeri, 'Prime osservazioni sul riparto delle competenze stato-regioni nella legge 'La Pergola' e sulla collocazione di quest'ultima e della legge comunitaria nel sistema delle fonti', in: *Rivista italiana di diritto pubblico comunitario*, 2, 1991, p. 727.

63 See Enzo Balboni, 'Un nuovo regionalismo fra lo Stato e l'Europa', in: *Il Mulino*, 338, anno XL, November–December 1991, p. 1070; Enzo Cannizzaro, 'La legge comunitaria per il 1990 e il D.D.L. per il 1991', in: Massimo Morisi (ed.), *L'attuazione delle direttive CE in Italia. La 'legge comunitaria' in Parlamento* (Milano: Giufrè Editore, 1992), p. 219.

64 Information by officials of the Italian Senate, Rome, 12 December 1995 and of the Autonomous Province of Trentino-Südtirol, Bozen, 3 June 1998.

65 See Agostini, 1990, *op. cit.*, p. 88.
66 See Senato della Repubblica, 1991, *op. cit.*, p. 61.
67 *Ibid.*, p. 75.
68 'Competitive' or 'secondary' legislative competencies means that the Italian regions or the autonomous provinces share certain legislative and regulative rights with the central institutions that in this case sets guidelines and principles for the sub-national legislators. For certain policy areas the Italian regions and autonomous provinces have also 'exclusive' or 'primary' legislative or regulative competencies under Article 117 of the Italian constitution.
69 See Walter Obwexer, 'Die Auswirkungen des Gemeinschaftsrechts auf die Hoheitsbefugnisse der lokalen Gebietskörperschaften', in: Diensteinheit für Studien der Autonomen Region Trentino-Südtirol (ed.), *Europäische Gemeinschaftliche Dimension und regionaler Kontext im Hinblick auf die Europäische Union* (Trient: Druckerei und Vervielfältigungsdienst der Autonomen Region Trentino-Südtirol, 1994), p. 185.
70 *Ibid.*, pp. 147 f.
71 See Law No. 126, 24 April 1998, Article 13, Disposizione per l'adempimento di obblighi derivanti dalla appartenenza dell'Italia alle Comunità Europee. Legge comunitaria 1995–1997, *GURI*, *Supplemento Ordinario*, No. 104, 7 May 1998.
72 See Obwexer, 1994, *op. cit.*, p. 163.
73 See Law No. 86, 9 March 1989, *GURI*, No. 58, 10 March 1989.
74 See Agostini, 1990, *op. cit.*, p. 89; Maria Chiara Sacchetti, 'L'organizzazione regionale per la gestione degli affari comunitari. Profili generali', in: Presidenza del Consiglio dei Ministri, Dipartimento per la Funzione Pubblica, *La riforma* (1994), p. 163.
75 See Sacchetti, 1994, *op. cit.*, p. 163.
76 *Ibid.*, pp. 163 f.
77 See Decree published in: *GURI*, No. 167, 19 July 1994.
78 See Riccardo Vuillermoz, 'Les régions italiennes face au processus d'integration juridique communautaire', in: *Europe en formation. Les cahiers du fédéralisme*, 304, 1997, pp. 39 ff.
79 See Puglisi, 'La pratica riproduttiva nella normativa italiana di attuazione dei regolamenti della Comunità economica europea', in: *Giustizia Civile*, No. 6/1981, p. 271.
80 As published in: *Rivista di diritto internazionale*, 1984, p. 360.
81 As published in the *Rivista di diritto internazionale*, 1991, p. 108.
82 See Hine, 1991, *op. cit.*, p. 35; Sepe, 1995, *op. cit.*, p. 334.
83 See Sepe, 1995, *op. cit.*, p. 334.
84 See Hine, 1991, *op. cit.*, p. 30; Istituto Affari Internazionali: I rapporti fra il quadro Istituzionale nazionale e quello internazionale, con particolare riguardo a quello comunitario. Ricerca condotta dall'IAI per conto del CNEL (Roma, 1981), p. 135; Gianni de Michelis: 'Le priorità italiane sulla scena internazionale', in: *Relazioni Internazionali*, December 1989, p. 84.
85 See Gaetano d'Auria, 'L'administration italienne et l'intégration européenne', in: *Annuaire Européen d' Administration Publique*, Vol. IX, 1986, p. 76; Fausto Capelli, 'Die Anwendung des Gemeinschaftsrechts in Italien', Zentrum für Europäisches Wirtschaftsrecht, Vorträge und Berichte, 29 November

1992, p. 6; Philip Daniels, 'Trends in Italian European Policy, 1985–1990', in: *Italy. The European Community and the 1990 Presidency*, Centre for Mediterranean Studies Bristol, Occasional Paper, No. 3, 1991, p. 13.

86 See Camera dei Deputati, Commissione III: 'Indagine Conoscitiva sulla revisione del trattato di Maasstricht anche in vista dell'allargamento dell'UE', 3 December 1997, Atti Parlamentari, XIII Legislatura.

Select bibliography

The text (English translation) of the Constitution of Italy can be found at the University of Richmond's constitution finder at http://confinder.richmond.edu/. Further sources on government and parliament of Italy can be found at Government www.aipa.it, or at Parliament http://www.camera.it.

Agostini, Maria Valeria (1990) 'Italy and its Community Policy', in: *The International Spectator*, No. 4/1990, pp. 347–355.

Associazione Nazionale per l'Informazione e la Documentazione Europea (ed.) (1994) *Pubblica amministrazione e Comunità Europea. Un Modello per l'Italia* (Roma: Editore SIPI).

Chiti, Mario P. (1991) 'L'amministrazione per il coordinamento dell politiche comunitarie nelle recenti riforme', in: *Rivista Italiana di Diritto Pubblico Comunitario*, pp. 11–31.

Franchini, Claudio (1993) *Amministrazione italiana e amministrazione comunitaria. La coamministrazione nei settori di interesse comunitario* (Padova: CEDAM).

Furlong, Paul (1995) 'The Italian Parliament and European Integration – Responsibilities, Failures and Successes', in: Philip Norton (ed.), *National Parliaments and the European Union* (London: Frank Cass), pp. 35–45.

Giuliani, Marco (1996) 'Italy', in: Dietrich Rometsch and Wolfgang Wessels (eds), *The European Union and Member States. Towards Institutional Fusion?* (Manchester: Manchester University Press), pp. 105–133.

Guerrieri, Paolo and Padoan, Pier Carlo (1989) 'Two Level Games and Structural Adjustment. The Italian Case', in: *Conference on 'Global and Domestic Factors in International Cooperation*', Trento, 3–4 April, pp. 1–41.

Guizzi, Vincenzo (1994) *Manuale di diritto e politica dell'Unione Europea* (Roma: Editoriale Scientifica).

Morisi, Massimo (1992) *L'attuazione delle direttive CE in Italia. La legge comunitaria in parlamento* (Milano: Giuffrè Editore).

Pappas, Spyros A. (ed.) (1995) *National Administrative Procedures for the Preparation and Implementation of Community Decisions* (Maastricht: EIPA) (esp. the chapters by Spyros A. Pappas and Onorato Sepe).

della Sala, Vincent (1997) 'Hollowing Out and Hardening the State. European Integration and the Italian Economy', in: *West European Politics*, 1/1997, pp. 14–33.

Senato della Repubblica, Giunta per gli Affari delle Comunità Europee (ed.) (1995) *Indagine conoscitiva sulla partecipazione dell'Italia alle fasi formativa ed applicativa del diritto comunitario* (Roma: Tipografia del Senato).

Vuillermoz, Riccardo (1997) 'Les régions italiennes face au processus d'integration juridique communautaire', *Europe en formation. Les cahiers du fédéralisme*, 304, pp. 21–41.

12 *Danielle Bossaert*

Luxembourg: flexible and pragmatic adaptation

Participating in European integration to strengthen national autonomy[1]

With 406,000 inhabitants and a surface area of 2.586 km^2, Luxembourg is by far the smallest Member State of the European Union. The highly positive attitude of the Luxembourg people towards the Union, expressed, for example, in the *Eurobarometer* surveys which are carried out on a regular basis, can be explained not merely by Luxembourg's history, but also by the specific characteristics related to its small size. In this sense, the European Union as a community of peace contributed substantially to both strengthening Luxembourg's oft-challenged national autonomy[2] and to compensating for the disadvantages of the small national market. As one of the founding states, Luxembourg has gained many advantages from membership of the Union which have quite significantly contributed to a strengthening of its own sovereignty. In particular, those elements of the Union's 'architecture' which are based on the principle of supranationality, which guarantee rights of participation and co-decision for the smaller states, have contributed considerably to ensuring that Luxembourg has an influence disproportionate to its size. Normally, an isolated state such as Luxembourg – which has no political weight to speak of, has few natural resources and is more than 95 per cent dependent on imports and exports – would hardly be noticed as a sovereign state in European and international circles. In this context, the other Member States now recognise and respect the Grand Duchy as a partner, not least because of the active presence and willingness to participate of Luxembourg politicians, diplomats and public servants in the European Council, the Council of Ministers and its related expert groups. This also helps Luxembourg to better protect and look after its own vital interests.

Since the beginning of the integration process, political parties and interest groups consider EU membership an unquestionable necessity for reasons related to security policy and economy. In this context it is also interesting to note that in recent years the employees' organisations have become aware of the advantages of better mutual consultation. Thus, in 1996 the two largest trade unions, the socialist OGBL (Onofhëngege Gewerkschaftsbond Lëtzëbuerg) and the Christian LCGB (Lëtzëbuerger Chrëschtleche Gewerkschaftsbond), established a joint office in order to better safeguard Luxembourg's interests within the ETUC. Both parties in the government (the Christian Social Party and the Democratic Party) as well as the main opposition parties (the Socialist Party and the green parties) openly follow a course in favour of integration. Accordingly, the deepening of the European integration process is carried by a broad consensus. For instance, Luxembourg was one of the first states to ratify the Maastricht Treaty by a large majority, and thus openly demonstrated its deep commitment to the introduction of a single European currency, a CFSP and progress in the JHA area.

However, even the smallest Member State is sometimes susceptible to reservations about the idea of integration. In particular, the concept of citizenship of the European Union, which was introduced by the Maastricht Treaty, according to which EU citizens have the right to vote and to stand as candidates in municipal and European elections throughout the Union, caused alarm about foreign domination among the Luxembourg population. It was feared that this might jeopardise the peaceful co-existence of the Luxembourg and foreign population and that this right could change the current political balance of power.[3] Later, however, this concern, which was connected with the fear of losing national identity, proved to be unfounded, especially since only a few EU citizens exercised this right.

As the smallest Member State, Luxembourg is quite sensitive on matters that directly affect its extremely vulnerable economic structure and its most important sectors such as finance, the iron and steel industry, etc. Luxembourg therefore does not support harmonisation efforts at any price in the field of taxes or the introduction of capital gains tax. Two other key national interests concern the question of the seats of the European institutions and the observance of the principle of equal rights as regards representation in these institutions. Nevertheless, despite these sensitivities, the strongly pro-European attitude of the Luxembourg population is primarily based on the view that its national interests are best looked after in a supranational community of solidarity and common values. Indicative of this is the fact that the ratification of the last two EU treaties (Maastricht in 1992, Amsterdam in 1997) did not encounter any insurmountable constitutional problems. Since 1956, the transfer of sovereign rights to a supranational community has been regulated by Article 49a of the Luxembourg Constitution, which stipulates that competences reserved for legislative, executive and judiciary powers can be temporarily transferred by treaty to institutions under international law. The right of EU citizens to vote and stand for election at municipal and

European levels, as introduced by the Maastricht Treaty, was the only change requiring Articles 52 and 107 of the Constitution to be amended.

Luxembourg's policy priorities in the Union: active deepening and discrete mediating

Luxembourg's policy regarding the Union shows an exceptionally high degree of continuity. Apart from some minor shifts of emphasis, which are mainly caused by the different personalities of the leading politicians, there has hardly been any difference between the principal European policies of the Christian Social governments under Pierre Werner (1959–74; 1979–84), Jacques Santer (1984–95) and Jean-Claude Juncker (since 1995), and those of Gaston Thorn's Democratic government (1974–79). With their clearly pro-European attitudes, these governments have contributed considerably to strengthening and promoting further integration. For example, in the early 1990s, it was the proposal developed under the Luxembourg Presidency, which was strongly oriented towards political compromise between the United Kingdom and the other Member States, which prevailed over the far more idealistic Dutch plan and served as a basis for the formulation of the Maastricht Treaty.

Prominent Luxembourg politicians such as Joseph Bech, in the early years, made great contributions to the further development of the European integration process as active co-developers or discrete mediators. In this respect it is worth mentioning the three-stage plan to build EMU, developed in the 1970s under the leadership of Pierre Werner, as this played an important role in the field of financial policy. In the late 1990s, the negotiating skills of the Prime Minister Jean-Claude Juncker brought about German–French agreement at a time when the stability pact on budget deficits was being developed, and thus helped to further EMU. Luxembourg's European policy focuses primarily on a deepening of the integration process while safeguarding vital national interests. During the 1996–97 IGC, the government supported first and foremost the consolidation of the Internal Market through the introduction of EMU and the reinforcement of the second and third pillars. However, it vigorously opposed both a Europe *à la carte* and any weakening of the European Commission. Jean-Claude Juncker has particularly favoured monetary union, to which he committed himself with great perseverance and which is considered in the Grand Duchy as an indispensable preliminary stage for a CFSP. Of course, with respect to this close co-operation on monetary policy, we should not overlook the fact that the establishment of the ECB has given Luxembourg a considerably greater say in matters than it has ever had before, especially when considering that since its accession to the Belgian–Luxembourg Economic Union[4] in 1921 it had given up part of its monetary sovereignty.[5] In the Luxembourg government's declaration on ratification of the Maastricht Treaty, former Prime

Minister Jacques Santer stated that monetary union was significant for Luxembourg since it would now become a partner with equal rights in a Union managing a common currency and defining a common monetary policy.[6] In contrast to larger countries such as Germany or France, which are characterised by extremely complex structures of domestic interests, the vital interests of a small state such as Luxembourg which, moreover, is spared from internal disputes as far as Luxembourg's European policy is concerned, are less extensive. This of course has the advantage that in certain areas it may be more ready to compromise and can often act as mediator between conflicting interests.

Looking to the future, a question that arises in particular for Luxembourg is that of its position within a European Union which will one day comprise twenty or more Member States, mostly from Central and Eastern Europe. In this context the Grand Duchy will of course be required to defend its position as an active founding member with the same rights and obligations as the large states. Consequently, during the 1996–97 IGC the government vehemently argued that – both now and in the future – all the Member States should be represented in all institutions (Council of Ministers, Commission, EP, ECJ, Court of Auditors, Presidency, etc.), so that they can actively participate in the decision-making process. Understandably, this topic is a high priority for the smallest Member State, all the more so since attempts were made in the run-up to the institutional reforms to reduce the disproportionately strong influence of small states. In this respect the Grand Duchy vigorously resists any attempts to marginalise its position, by unequivocally voicing its opinion on equal representation in the principal institutions. Hence, Luxembourg is not prepared to give up 'its seat' in the European Commission or its right to the rotating Presidency of the Council, while in essential areas such as treaty amendments, citizenship of the Union, taxes, accession, etc. it remains in favour of maintaining unanimity in the Council of Ministers. Another key element in Luxembourg's European policy since the Juncker government came to power is the aim of achieving better consultation with both Benelux partners, Belgium and the Netherlands, and to extend this to various policy areas in coming years.

The national policy-cycle: pragmatic and flexible adaptation to the EU treaties

Luxembourg is a unitary central state with only two administrative levels (national and municipal) (Figure 12.1). Unlike most EU Member States, it has no regional or intermediate authorities. Without exception, EU policy is prepared, decided on and implemented centrally. In the consensus oriented democracy of Luxembourg, great importance is attached not only to the mostly informal involvement of the parliament in the decision-

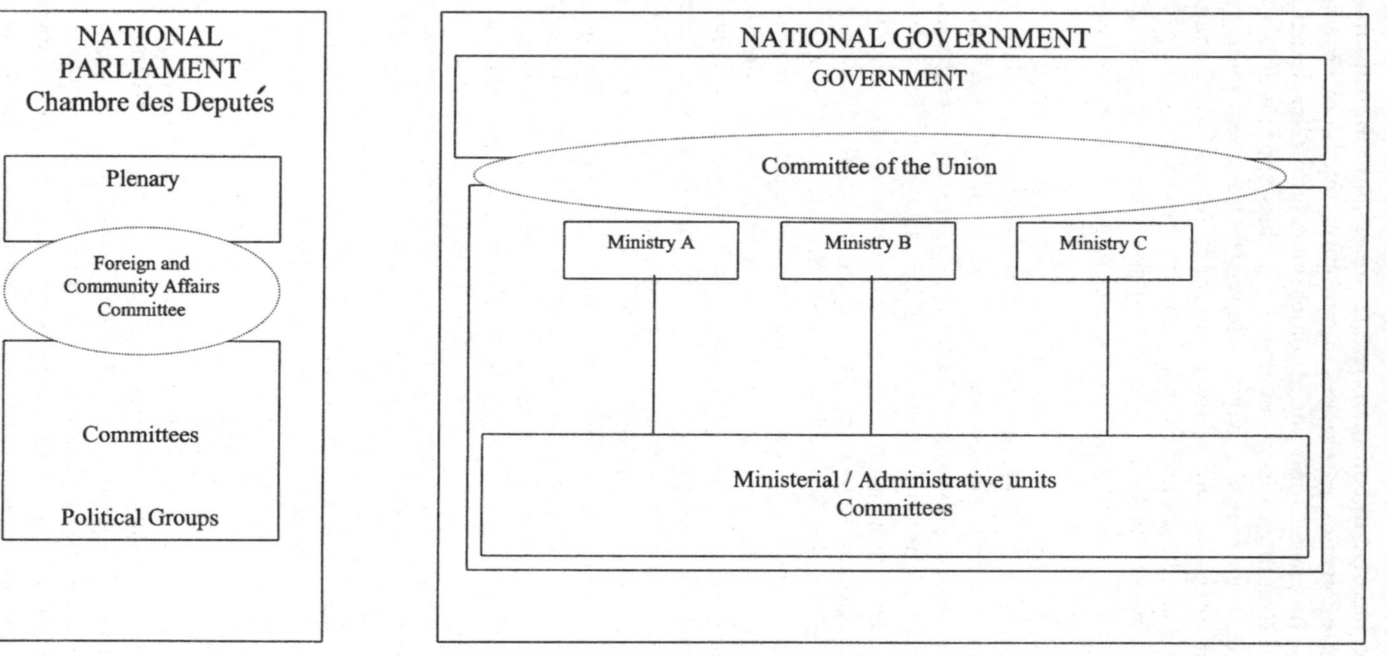

Figure 12.1 The national level of European decision-making – Luxembourg

making process, but also to consultation and provision of information to the relevant interest groups, employees' organisations, etc. in order where possible to find consensual solutions. Another important characteristic of political life in Luxembourg is its small size, which is apparent from the fact that the total staff of the public administration does not exceed 11,800 civil servants. This structural feature is naturally a determining factor, which affects the organisational capacities as well as the co-ordination mechanisms of the Grand Duchy. Some of the most distinctive characteristics will be discussed below.[7]

Decision-making processes at national level

Perhaps the most striking characteristic of political life in Luxembourg is the manageability of relations. In this sense, nearly all decision-makers who deal with EU policy know each other personally. This almost daily and direct contact, along with Luxembourg's democracy which is based on compromise, is advantageous insofar as the degree of bureaucratisation in the co-ordination of the various ministries is much lower than in the larger states and in that the flow of paperwork stays within reasonable limits. For instance, the result of these simplified channels of communication is that Luxembourg has relatively few permanent and regularly meeting co-ordination structures. And where such interministerial bodies do exist, they are characterised particularly by the fact that they are linked to a direct interest, as in the case of an IGC, and that they are usually only of a temporary nature. Another feature is that co-operation between the various administrations in Luxembourg is characterised by a low degree of competitive behaviour, which can also be put down not only to the frequent consultations, but also to the fact that there are so few internal 'cleavages'. Therefore, political decision-makers usually agree in principle that it is better for the country's interests for them to agree on a negotiating position rather than block a national decision unnecessarily by stirring up interministerial rivalries.

Dominance of decentralised decision-making processes

Owing to the closeness of the relationships, the hierarchical decision-making processes in Luxembourg are considerably shorter and more flexible than in larger states. Usually, the officials who are in charge of a certain EU dossier have a large degree of independence in their field and, when working within their ministry, they will generally co-operate with their minister, with whom they have direct contact in person or by telephone. Of course, this considerable 'room for manoeuvre' gives officials an enormous sense of responsibility and requires considerable expertise in their own field, all the more so since, owing to the limited staff resources, they often have to manage several fields at the same time. The result of the visibly growing number of working groups, expert committees and other bodies at EU level is therefore that civil servants participate in various groups on account of their many different functions. What characterises ideal Luxembourg officials is not so much their marked expert knowledge but mainly their broad education and ability to quickly familiarise themselves with new fields of work.

Personnel shortages as well as the consensual development of the democracy have a decisive influence on the working style of the different administrations. In view of the additional workload associated with the advancing process of European integration, one of the main challenges for Luxembourg is to ensure a smooth and satisfactory functioning as regards the preparation, decision-making and implementation of EU policy, without, however, having to make unnecessary additions to the staff.[8] So far the government has solved this dilemma mainly by taking a pragmatic and flexible approach, characterised by a distribution and organisation of tasks which is targeted primarily at respective requirements and not so much at strict observance of areas of competence and the exact application of rules.[9] A good example of this style of adaptation according to practical needs is the Presidency of the EU Council of Ministers, whose successful management in Luxembourg is not merely the result of a tightly structured and well-organised administrative machinery, but also, and chiefly, of the flexible working methods, the strong motivation and positive work attitude of officials as well as the availability of young college graduates or diplomats currently abroad. A consequence of this flexible approach is that the Luxembourg administration has so far proved to be extremely resistant to fundamental organisational and procedural restructuring, and that the institutionalisation of co-ordinating bodies is far less advanced than it is, for example, in federal states which often have extremely complicated co-ordination mechanisms.

The government and the administration

European policy in the consensual democracy of Luxembourg is formulated by coalition governments, which are characterised by extraordinary stability and continuity. The Prime Minister Jean-Claude Juncker (Chrëschtlech-Sozial Vollëkspartei, CSV), can already look back on more than fifteen years of experience in government, while Pierre Werner (CSV) was able to make his mark on the country as Prime Minister for a total of twenty years and Jacques Poos (Lëtzëbuerger Sozialistesch Arbëchter Partei, LSAP) led the Ministry of Foreign Affairs for a long period as well. Besides many years of extensive experience at EU level, another characteristic of Luxembourg's decision-makers is the fact that they usually manage several important ministries. A good example of this multifunctional approach of Luxembourg politicians is again Juncker, who in the previous legislative period was the Minister of Employment, Minister of Finance and Prime Minister at the same time, and represented

Luxembourg in these capacities in several important EU Councils of Ministers. This strong presence naturally gave him a deep insight into key decision-making processes. Despite the enormous workload, this combination of key functions in a single person can be advantageous in that energy-consuming and decision-blocking rivalries and disputes over competences between these key ministries can be avoided.

Nevertheless, Luxembourg has not been completely exempt from the question of competence in European policy in recent years. For instance, the coalition partner (LSAP) which held the post of Minister for Foreign Affairs, particularly criticised the Prime Minister's overly strong interference in EU policy, arguing that he was overstepping his limits as primus inter pares. However, since the formation of the coalition government between the Christian Social Party (CSV) and the Democratic Party (Demokratesch Partei, DP) in June 1999, this question has again been pushed into the background. As a result of Luxembourg's specific structural characteristics, the administration is characterised by a marked decentralisation and considerable autonomy on the part of the individual ministries. However, in 1993, with the appointment of a European Correspondent in all ministries, a first step seems to have been made towards better more formalised co-ordination in the implementation of EU law and a more efficient treatment of the European dossiers. Besides keeping track of major European issues, the responsibilities of European Correspondents also include monitoring the correct application of EU law.

Most of the responsibility for preparing, deciding on and implementing EU dossiers rests with the competent ministries, while co-ordination lies within the scope of responsibility of the Ministry of Foreign Affairs.[10] Although this ministry cannot exert control over other ministries, its role as a 'go-between' – scouting Luxembourg's policy interests between the Permanent Representation in Brussels and the national administration – should not be underestimated. Important communications between the 'technical' ministries and the EU bodies usually go through the Ministry of Foreign Affairs. Commission proposals for EU legislation are sent to the competent ministry (or ministries) to be worked on. After the latter have added their comments to the dossier, the content of which now represents the official negotiating position of Luxembourg, sometimes including a special report from the Ministry of Foreign Affairs, it is passed on to the Permanent Representation. Where there are varying points of view between the 'technical' ministries, the Ministry of Foreign Affairs can call on an interministerial advisory body of senior civil servants, which is formed on an ad hoc basis, and which will then try to define a strategy. If agreement still cannot be reached or if the dossier in question is of such vital importance that it affects the national interest, the government's Council of Ministers may become involved, which will then decide on Luxembourg's position. Besides the weekly Council of Ministers meeting, the Union Committee (Comité de l'Union), which meets every two weeks under the chairmanship of the Ministry of Foreign Affairs, is the most important co-ordinating body in Luxembourg. At the meetings of this body, attended by ministers and their colleagues concerned with an item on the agenda, all topical issues (institutional questions, Agenda 2000, etc.) are discussed. In Luxembourg's consensual democracy, interest groups affected by a directive on the Union's rolling agenda are also consulted in the preparatory and decision-making phases. A new trend in recent years has been the improved consultation and co-ordination regarding Luxembourg's national position as a result of increased informal consultation with the two Benelux partners. With regard to the 2000 IGC, the three partner states again wanted to lay out their common proposals in a memorandum concerning the further development of the Union. Their aim, of course, is not least to be able to better protect the interests of smaller countries within the institutional structure.

In the decision-making phase, the national officials dealing with a dossier usually participate in the relevant working groups at European level with each official covering about two–three groups. The Ministry of Foreign Affairs sends about thirty-five of its total staff members[11] to meetings in Brussels. The implementation of EU directives is a matter for the ministries in whose area of competence the contents of a directive or any other EU legal act fall. In accordance with the internal rules on the management of dossiers requiring implementing measures[12] laid down by the Ministry of Foreign Affairs, the respective ministries are urged to ensure both that the act in question is correctly implemented and that time limits laid out in a directive are observed. According to the statistics, the Grand Duchy, with its implementation rate of 94.4 per cent, is now twelfth within the Union.[13] This small distance behind its partners is partially due to a shortage of staff in the administrations, which has become particularly apparent during the Luxembourg Presidencies. Such a responsible and prestigious task demands so much of the administrative machinery of a small country that the entire routine legislative process relating to domestic policy slows down considerably during this time. In the case of actions for infringement of the EC Treaty,[14] Luxembourg was sixth[15] in 1998 with a total of eight cases, while in the period between 1953 and 1998 it was taken to court in eighty-six cases.[16]

So far, the new Treaties (Maastricht and Amsterdam) have given rise to some small organisational and institutional adjustments in Luxembourg. Judging from the coalition agreement of the new CSV–DP government,[17] it is to be assumed that some additional adjustments will be made in the coming years, for example as regards interministerial co-ordination, co-operation between parliament and government, information and communications policy, etc.

In the context of the establishment of EMU the conversion of the Luxembourg Monetary Institute (Institut monétaire luxembourgeois) into a Central Bank with the same competences and the same legal status as equivalent institutions in the other Member States, has been of paramount importance. The Monetary Institute in existence up to that point did not have all the competences of a central bank owing to Luxembourg's monetary union with Belgium. All decisions concerning EMU fall within the jurisdiction of the Ministry of Finance, which also deals with tax policy in general and EU tax harmonisation in particular.

In the Ministry of Foreign Affairs, the further development of a common foreign and security policy through the Treaty of Maastricht led to a limited expansion in order to cover the twenty-five working groups of the European Council. A very recent adjustment, which is not due to the increasing influence of European integration on the national level, but rather to the dissolution of the Ministry of Defence after the formation of the new government, concerns the transfer of the competence for defence policy from the Ministry of Defence to the Ministry of Foreign Affairs in order to do justice to the increasing importance of the defence policy dimension within the Union. Another adjustment brought about by the Maastricht Treaty was the transfer of the asylum and immigration policy from the Ministry of Foreign Affairs to the Ministry of Interior. However, as regards matters covered by pillar three and Schengen, for example, the Maastricht Treaty did not bring any major changes, and so these remained within the Ministry of Justice, according to the principle that the ministries covering a certain field of expertise at national level will be responsible for the same area at European level.

The Permanent Representation

The Permanent Representation in Brussels has a key role when it comes to the formulation of Luxembourg's European policy. Not only does it hold a high position within the Luxembourg administration, but the weight of its opinions also has considerable influence in the development of Luxembourg's negotiating positions. With an average length of service of ten–fifteen years, most of the accredited diplomats in the Belgian capital have a thorough knowledge and considerable experience in the field of European affairs. The great value attached to the Permanent Representation by the Luxembourg government is also clear from its constant expansion and the considerable investments made in it.[18] Since 1997 the Representation has a better infrastructure, as it has a seat in the House of Luxembourg[19] near the EU institutions. Parallel to this development in terms of space, its staff has increased from approximately five diplomats in 1995 to a current total of twelve. All officials come from the Ministry of Foreign Affairs with the exception of a representative from the Ministry of Finance, a representative from the Ministry of

Employment and Social Affairs, who deals exclusively with social affairs and labour market policy, a representative from the Ministry of Justice, who is responsible for the third pillar and a representative from the Ministry of Economic Affairs, whose work area covers all financial and fiscal affairs.

During the presidencies, which are extremely labour-intensive for a small state, the limited number of staff must be supplemented with young academics and temporarily seconded diplomats. Without these, the smooth organisation and coordination of around 1,600 meetings at ministerial, ambassador and expert level during the last presidency in 1997 could hardly have been achieved. The manageable size of the Representation also means that in its routine tasks Luxembourg concentrates primarily on those areas which are of direct importance to protecting its interests. For instance, it is more than reasonable to assume that the small Luxembourg administrative machinery would not have the same expertise on all technical issues as, for example, a bureaucracy which is the size of those in France or Germany. In this respect, the shortage of staff and material resources is linked to a certain selectiveness in working methods. In its relations with the most important EU institutions – the Council of Ministers, Commission and Parliament – Luxembourg is also characterised by this selective approach, in which respect it attaches special importance to its close contacts with the Council Secretariat and the Commission. This is, of course, all the more important as Luxembourg cannot be represented in all working groups and is therefore dependent on the availability of reliable information. On the other hand, its relations with the EP are not as close and its contact is less frequent.

The Chamber of Deputies

The Chamber of Deputies comprises sixty delegates, most of whom also have a job in addition to having a seat in parliament. For this position they receive a compensation as well as, at a later stage, an addition to their regular pension. Members of Parliament have only a very limited administrative and scientific staff, which means that whenever there is a great deal of work it is often difficult for them to familiarise themselves with each specific field in their subject area. This also applies to technical questions on EU matters; the result is that systematic consideration of all proposals from Brussels is not possible.[20] Furthermore, the fact that Luxembourg Members of Parliament are elected at national level has not always increased their willingness to take initiatives regarding EU affairs.

The main share of the work of the Luxembourg parliament takes place in twenty-three committees with eleven members each on average, while responsibility for European policy lies with the Committee for Foreign and European Affairs, which consists of thirteen members. So far, repeated attempts to create a specific advisory body dealing only with

European affairs have failed. One of these plans was aimed at creating a consultative committee comprising the six members of the national parliament and six MEPs. The reason why none of these plans could be realised is connected, on the one hand, with the fact that the establishment of another body would have further increased the workload of individual Members of Parliament and, on the other hand, that it would have been difficult to demarcate the area of competence between this committee and the Committee for Foreign and European Affairs.[21]

The involvement of the Chamber of Deputies in preparing, deciding on and implementing EU policy has developed only to a limited extent in Luxembourg and, according to the new coalition agreement between the CSV and the DP, is likely to expand in the future. The first concrete proposal for stronger parliamentary involvement in the European legislative process aims at involving the Committee for Foreign and European Affairs, which is responsible for European policy, at an earlier stage in the decision-making process by informing it of the government's initial official position regarding important proposals for a directive.

Until now, relations between the government and the legislature in the area of information and consultation have developed without the parliament having been actively involved in the law-making process. The progress made mainly concerns the improved provision of information by the government and the regular briefing of parliament before and after summit meetings, during the IGC or in the case of important decisions taken by the Minister for Foreign Affairs. These meetings always end with a parliamentary debate. Another form of this provision of information is the sending of all relevant EU documents such as white papers, green papers, etc., to the Chamber of Deputies. However, with a view to the increasing extension of EU competences to new fields and with the transfer of national competences to European level, the Chamber of Deputies has become somewhat more active in relation to Europe since the Amsterdam Treaty. In order to integrate EU policy more efficiently into the work of the committees, it was decided that, in European matters, the individual committees would be given the responsibility for those sectors for which they are also responsible at national level. As a result, many of the existing committees set up their own sub-committees which deal exclusively with EU topics.

The desire for a stronger and more efficient involvement of the Chamber of Deputies in EU policy, which has grown more acute particularly in recent years, was not limited only to the parliament. An important initiative came from the government in 1996 when it put the Luxembourg MEP Charles Goerens in charge of writing a report on the future role of national parliaments in the Union. In Goerens' opinion, a charter should be incorporated into the Treaty which, on the one hand, ensured that governments imposed minimum obligations on national parliaments and, on the other hand, strengthened the obligations of the EU institutions towards the EP. Some of his proposals, which also concerned Luxembourg, aimed to improve co-operation between MEPs and national Members of Parliament, for example through the participation of MEPs in thematically relevant meetings of national committees, through the right of MEPs to ask questions of the competent ministers, and through the closer involvement of MEPs in the national committee for Foreign and European Affairs. The fact that, in the future, changes will be made in the co-ordination between government and parliament in Luxembourg is also underlined by the new government programme which envisages stronger participation of the Chamber of Deputies in the EU decision-making process.

The regional level

For a small state like Luxembourg, which as regards its size is comparable to the smallest German Bundesland (Saarland), it would be a luxury and surely also too expensive to have an intermediate or regional level of government with its own competences and administration. Below the central state level, the Grand Duchy is composed of three districts and 118 local communities. In each district, a senior civil servant, appointed by the Grand Duke, supervises the implementation of laws, regulations, etc. as well as the administrative management of local finance. This centralist, unitary state structure without powerful regional players naturally facilitates the government's pro-integrationist course towards European integration which reflects more or less the interests of the whole population.

Conclusion: Luxembourg – condemned to a pro-active integration strategy

In the smallest EU Member State, active and committed co-operation with the European institutions is considered a necessity which increases Luxembourg's visibility and strengthens the protection of its interests in Europe and in the world. From this viewpoint, the Treaties of Maastricht and Amsterdam were considered by the public as quite far-reaching, although the expansion of matters dealt with by the EU has not led to fundamental feelings of resentment at the further loss of sovereign rights. The existing consensus among the political elite that national interests can best be safeguarded in a supranational community has not been shaken. As regards the Amsterdam Treaty, it was even suggested that the communitisation of some fields, such as common foreign and security policy and asylum and immigration policy, would not go far enough to solve current problems.

The uncomplicated attitude of the Luxembourg people towards the new treaties is also reflected in the pragmatic adaptations of the national institutions to the extended European agenda. Even after the latest treaty modifications, the internal co-ordination of EU policy is still characterised by a small degree of institutionalisation of co-ordination bodies, while the various ministries and the individual officials in particular have considerable decision-making power and autonomy, and interministerial conflicts are kept within limits. The restructuring of the administration has, up to now, been rather a flexible adjustment to acute requirements, as for example in the case of the introduction of the European correspondents. However, as set out in the new government's coalition agreement, some adjustments are expected in the future. Besides more efficient interministerial co-ordination and improved bilateral relations, the policy on information and communication between the institutions and between the state and the citizens should also be improved. These reforms aim in particular to strengthen the coherence of Luxembourg's EU policy and to defend its national interests more effectively in a Europe which is becoming increasingly complex. For instance, in the course of the enlargement of the Union to the east, the smallest Member State must pay particular attention to ways of increasing its visibility and its room to manoeuvre within an enlarged Union by developing contacts with its neighbours and its traditional allies.

In this context it is also interesting to note that the employees' organisations have become aware of the advantages of better mutual consultation. Thus, in 1996 the two largest trade unions established a joint office in order to better safeguard Luxembourg's interests within the ETUC.

With the growing importance of the European level an increased need for co-ordination and co-operation between the national institutions has also arisen in Luxembourg. However, while on the one hand, this need has not developed in the same way as in large states, on account of the small size of the country and the simpler communication channels, on the other hand the growing complexity and abundance of subjects to be dealt with also requires certain adjustments to be made, such as, for example, a better distribution of tasks and a clearer organisational structure.[22] This is, of course, not always so simple for an administration the size of that of a city, particularly since it will never have access to the same specialised and technical expertise as an administration the size of Germany or France. The individual official in Luxembourg often has to deal with a whole range of special issues which in other states are spread over several departments. With the further deepening of the Union, the responsibility and workload of the individual official is likely to increase rather than decrease, especially since it will not be possible to increase the number of staff accordingly owing to high costs.

However, this specific problem of small size is not expected to become acute in the near future because Luxembourg has fewer national key interests than large states and because it can specialise mainly in these key areas. However, owing to the limited capacity of its small administration as well as its very small size, it will in the future still have to rely on competent politicians with a strong personality who will look after both national interests and Community interests. A great challenge for the Grand Duchy will therefore continue to be that of compensating for its small size and the associated structural disadvantages through active and committed co-operation in the European integration process.

Furthermore, with regard to Luxembourg's ability domestically to deal with the deepening of the European integration process, it should be emphasised that the small size of the country's administration with its highly informal communication structures and the predominance of generalists rather than specialists, has until now had many advantages (little need for institutionalised co-ordination structures, a pragmatic and flexible approach towards European integration, etc.). On the other hand, however, it should be pointed out that owing to the increasing complexity and specialisation of the working areas, it is very difficult to make prognoses for the future. In this context and without questioning the strategy of flexible and pragmatic adaptation, we can only conclude in a very general way that Luxembourg is increasingly becoming aware of the need for better co-ordination and communication structures,[23] as can be seen, for instance, in the coalition agreement of June 1999. A development in that direction would therefore be considered as an indication of the stronger influence of the European level on the national level.

Notes

1 I would like to thank Marc Ungeheuer, Deputy Permanent Representative of Luxembourg to the European Union and Victor Weitzel, Press Attaché of Jacques Poos, the former Ministry of Foreign Affairs, for their valuable support with regard to this chapter.

2 In the more than 150 years of the state's existence, its national independence was challenged several times by Belgian, German and French 'Annexionsversuche'.

3 This should chiefly be considered against the backdrop of the fact that in some municipalities the majority of the population consists of foreigners.

4 The economic union with Belgium, established in 1921, also meant a currency union with a common currency (the Belgian franc), the predominance of the Belgian National Bank (Banque Nationale de Belgique) and a common commercial policy.

5 A striking example is the 8.5 per cent devaluation of the Belgian franc in February 1982 by the Belgian government without prior consultation of the Luxembourg government.

6 See the declaration by Prime Minister Jacques Santer on the ratification of

the Maastricht Treaty of 22 April 1992 in the Chamber of Deputies.

7 See Martine Nies-Berchem, 'L'administration luxembourgeoise et les débuts de l'administration européenne', in: Gilbert Trausch and Edmée Croisé-Schirtz (eds), *Le Luxembourg face à la construction européenne* (Luxembourg: Saint-Paul, 1996), pp. 147–160; Jean-Marc Hoscheit and Malou Weyrich, Luxembourg, La mise en oeuvre des directives communautaires', in: Heinrich Siedentopf and Jacques Ziller (eds), *Making European Policies Work*, Vol. II (Maastricht: EIPA, 1988), pp. 521–569.

8 At present, about one in three employees in Luxembourg works for the state, while the industrial sector and the services sector increasingly have to rely on foreigners to meet their staff needs.

9 See Simone Merten-Beissel, 'Administration luxembourgeoise et l'intégration européenne', in: Charles Debbasch (ed.), *Administrations nationales et l'intégration européenne. Proceedings of the colloquium in Aix in October 1986* (Paris: Presses du CNRS, 1987); Editions du Centre national de la Recherche Scientifique, p. 49 *et seq.*

10 See Marc Bichler, 'The case of Luxembourg', in: Spyros A. Pappas (ed.), *National Administrative Procedures for the Preparation and Implementation of Community Decisions* (Maastricht: EIPA, 1994), pp. 371–386.

11 More than one-third of total staff (120) of the Ministry of Foreign Affairs.

12 See Bichler, 1994, *op. cit.*, p. 382.

13 See Implementation Report, May 1998. In this context, it should be pointed out that the differences between the first position and the twelfth position are small.

14 The following statistics concern Articles 169, 170, 171, 225 of the ECT, Articles 141, 142, 143 of the EAEC Treaty and Article 88 of the ECSC Treaty.

15 Belgium and France were last with twenty-two cases, while Denmark, Finland, Sweden and the United Kingdom were the 'model pupils' with only one case.

16 Belgium, on the other hand, had the most cases: a total of 225.

17 See *Déclaration gouvernementale*, declaration by Prime Minister Jean-Claude Juncker, of 12 August 1999 in the Chamber of Deputies, pp. 4–5, 8–9.

18 These investments are the most significant the state of Luxembourg has ever made abroad.

19 The 'House of Luxembourg' also accommodates the Luxembourg Embassy in Belgium, the Consulate and the Representation to the WEU.

20 See Gaston Stronck, 'Luxembourg', in: Roger Morgan and Clare Tame (eds), *Parliaments and Parties* (London: Macmillan, 1996), p. 171.

21 See *ibid*, p. 169.

22 In the context of administrative reform, improvements in the organisational structure are planned, as well as a more specific distribution of tasks in general.

23 See *Déclaration gouvernementale*, declaration by Prime Minister Jean-Claude Juncker, of 12 August 1999 in the Chamber of Deputies, p. 9.

Select bibliography

The text (English translation) of the constitution of Luxembourg can be found at the University of Richmond's constitution finder at http://confinder.richmond.edu/. Further sources on government and parliament of Luxembourg can be found at Government www.gov.lu/ or at Parliament www.chd.lu/.

Calmes, Christian and Bossaert, Danielle (1996) *Geschichte des Grossherzogtums Luxemburg von 1815 bis heute* (Luxembourg: Saint-Paul).

Clesse, Armand (1998) 'Les petits pays et l'intégration européenne', in: *Les petits pays et le processus d'intégration européenne*, Colloquium 18 février 1998, Institut Royal supérieur de défense (Bruxelles 1998).

Kirt, Romain and Meisch, Adrien (1993) *Innovation – Intégration, Mélanges pour Pierre Werner* (Luxembourg: Saint-Paul).

Lepszy, Norbert and Woyke, Wichard (1985) *Belgien, Niederlande, Luxemburg. Politik – Gesellschaft – Wirtschaft* (Opladen: Leske & Budrich).

Merten-Beissel, Simone (1997) 'L'administration luxembourgeoise et l'intégration européenne', in: Charles Debbasch (ed.), *Administrations nationales et intégration européenne* (Paris: Presses du CNRS).

Stronck, Gaston (1996) 'Luxembourg', in: Roger Morgan and Clare Tame (eds), *Parliaments and Parties* (London: Macmillan).

Trausch, Gilbert, Croisé-Schirtz, Edmée and Nies-Berchem, Martine (1996) *Le Luxembourg face à la construction européenne*, Centre d'études et de recherches européennes Robert Schuman (Luxembourg, 1996).

13 *Ben J.S. Hoetjes*

The Netherlands: a former founding father in search of control

Introduction: a mature member's second thoughts

The involvement of the Dutch in European integration dates back to the 1950s, and so do the Dutch attitudes towards it. Over the years, they have changed, but there is also a long-standing support for the overall process of European integration. A clear distinction, however, should be drawn between the elite and the general public. For the general public, European integration in the 1950s was a good cause, to be left to the experts and to the elite. Until the mid-1960s, when the system of pillarisation[1] was still in force, the general public was quite willing to leave politics to its pillarised elites (Catholic, Protestant, Socialist or Liberal-Conservative). Within the political elite, there was hardly any disagreement about European integration, and the general public played its role as a 'captive audience'.

In the mid-1960s, relations between the voters and the elite, and within the elite, became less predictable. New parties emerged, and 'floating voters' became more important in the elections.[2] In the 1970s, public opinion and political discussion were radicalised. Remarkably, however, this change did not affect the Union. European integration remained a highly technical, specialised and politically uninteresting field. Notions about integration were rather vague. There was, at least, an implicit assumption that Dutch identity and Dutch political institutions would remain in place, and that the integration process would deliver considerable benefits, especially in economic terms.[3] With the decline of ideology and political participation in the 1980s, European integration became a matter of 'positive indifference'. After the end of the Cold War, ideological controversies subsided, or virtually disappeared. The public at large lost interest in politics altogether. Only very down-to-earth and close-to-home issues such as safety in the streets, the stock exchange, career openings, private business, etc. could draw the public's attention.

Against this 'post-modern' background, the mid-1990s showed more and more signs of Euroscepticism and Eurocynicism. Gradually, European integration came to be criticised as 'too costly', 'wasteful', 'un-democratic', etc. Business people remained quite positive about the Union, but in other circles, positive indifference was replaced by controversy, or by negative indifference.

The Dutch state and the integration process: the constitution and national politics

The ratification of the EU treaties (Maastricht and Amsterdam) created no constitutional problems. Although international treaties require the assent of parliament, the Dutch Constitution permits the granting of legislative and/or executive powers to international bodies created to carry out international treaties (Article 92). Therefore, neither Maastricht nor Amsterdam required a constitutional amendment. Both treaty ratifications as such, did not generate a serious discussion in parliament. Because of this smooth and silent approval, it took some time before Dutch politics and administration became aware of the consequences of the Maastricht Treaty. Specifics will be presented later, but in general there was a rather hurried and haphazard reaction to the Union as the new supranational level of government. Meanwhile, some important political changes took place in the 1990s. One was the decline in ideological identity, especially among the left. Another, related to the first, was the emergence of new coalitions. The 1994 parliamentary elections brought losses for the social democrats and the Christian Democrats, and gains for the liberal conservatives and the leftist liberals. The new 'purple' coalition government led by the social democrat Kok left the Christian Democrats in opposition – an event unprecedented since the First World War. After the 1998 elections, a second 'purple' government was formed.

The policy programme of the new government did not represent a radical break with the previous government (Christian Democrat/social democrat coalition), but there were some interesting changes from an EU perspective. For one thing, the Christian Democrats no longer represented the Netherlands in Brussels. Personalities such as Lubbers disappeared, and the long-standing Christian Democratic commitment to Europe was replaced by social democratic and liberal commitments. Personalised animosities, e.g. Lubbers' failure to become President of the Commission, could be put aside. Something else was also obvious: new, and more critical attitudes towards the Union would soon present themselves.

In terms of personnel, the trio of Lubbers–van den Broek–Dankert (Prime Minister, Minister of Foreign Affairs, State Secretary for European Affairs) was replaced by Kok–van Mierlo–Patijn. Patijn (liberal conservative) took a low profile, and concentrated on the organisational and diplomatic side of EU work. Van Mierlo (left liberal) took a higher public profile, preferring broad 'philosophical' views on world affairs, and –

interestingly – stressing closer relations between the Netherlands and France. Kok, however, took the actual lead in Dutch EU affairs. Being on close personal terms with Helmut Kohl – in spite of party differences – he managed to improve Dutch–German relations, both bilaterally and within the Union. In the background, the Queen and especially her husband Prince Claus von Amsberg, contributed further to the Dutch commitment to the Union and to close relations with Germany.

The second 'purple' coalition in 1998 involved the same parties, but some new personalities. The Kok–van Mierlo–Patijn group was succeeded by the trio of Kok–van Aartsen–Benschop. Kok and Benschop belonged to the social democratic party while van Aartsen was a liberal conservative. Although this implied a stronger social democratic weight in EU affairs, it should be taken into account that Benschop did not have any EU experience – he was the election campaign manager for the social democrats. Van Aartsen, on the other hand, was Agriculture Minister in the former 'purple' coalition. As such, he acquired considerable EU experience. He has a reputation for down-to-earth political skill and as a 'general manager' more than a 'career diplomat'. Furthermore, he has close links with the (liberal conservative) Minister of Finance, Zalm, who strongly asserted himself in EU affairs after 1994 – he was also the Finance Minister in the previous government. Next to the Prime Minister and the Minister of Foreign Affairs (assisted by the State Secretary for European Affairs), the Ministry of Finance plays a strategic role, both in domestic politics (co-ordinating all public finance) and in EU affairs.

Dutch policy priorities in the Union: a rethinking of governments and political parties

For the Dutch government, the Maastricht Treaty and the new European Commission in 1994 were two 'dramatic moments ' of rude awakening to the political realities of Europe in the 1990s. In the negotiations for Maastricht, the Dutch presidency took a strongly pro-federal position which proved untenable and had to be discarded in a rather embarrassing way. The TEU's three-pillar structure was a Luxembourg–French design,[4] forced upon an unwilling and disgraced Dutch presidency. For the Dutch, Maastricht is remembered vividly as 'Black Monday'[5] – a major diplomatic failure, and a trauma, especially for the Foreign Ministry. The Dutch, therefore, have tended to overlook the enormous progress of European integration brought about by the TEU.

In the negotiations for the new Commission in 1993–94, Prime Minister Lubbers campaigned rather openly for the Commission Presidency. When this failed – the post went, rather humiliatingly, to the Luxembourg Santer – he campaigned for the position of NATO Secretary-General, and also failed. These two experiences, on the one hand, created ill-feelings especially among the Christian Democrats – the bitterness of 'a founding-father of the EU, who is no longer listened to'. This may well have contributed to the electoral discredit of the Christian Democrats in 1994 and 1998. On the other hand, they also forced the Netherlands to re-think its approach and priorities in the Union. This re-thinking process has not yet come to an end, but since 1994 some overall changes have emerged. First, there is now an explicit commitment to the national interest. Before 1994, the Netherlands always declared their full and explicit commitment to the cause of European integration – implicitly assuming that this was the best way to serve the national interest. After 1994, the government publicly stated its desire to promote its national interest in Europe, including Dutch business interests.

Secondly, a higher priority is given to financial issues in the Union. The presidency of the ECB was won by the Dutch social democratic banker Duisenberg, after a sustained and extensive campaign. In the discussions about EU finance, the Netherlands sided with Germany in favour of reducing national contributions. Owing to the CAP reforms, the Netherlands had become a net-payer rather than a net-receiver, and Finance Minister Zalm decided to take a hard 'I want my money back' line. Compared to the 1980s, this was a remarkable reversal of both the position and the tone of the Dutch in the Union.

Thirdly, there is a stronger emphasis on coalition-building inside the Union – something to which the Dutch government was not accustomed. Instead of simply just balancing-off the major Member States, or assuming the moral authority of the Netherlands, the government has to look for groupings within the Union. Depending on policy areas, these groupings may vary – e.g. in environmental affairs the Scandinavian countries are potential partners whereas in monetary matters, Germany is a possible ally. Currently, the Foreign Ministry is developing a more systematic approach to coalition-building in Europe.

Aside from these general changes, one can also see a pattern in the specific Dutch policy priorities.[6] The traditional commitment to pillar one integration continues: full support is given to economic and monetary integration (Single Market, EMU, convergence criteria and the stability pact), to a more efficient and reformed CAP, and also to a stronger EU environmental policy. However, in social affairs the Dutch take a more low-key approach. Whenever the harmonisation of social security legislation in the Union might threaten the Dutch competitive position in terms of productivity or production costs, the Dutch government is reluctant. The Dutch also supported the Barber Protocol, aimed at the restriction of EU-wide equal rights provisions, mainly for financial reasons. Furthermore, Dutch support for EU employment programmes and policies is rather ambivalent. For ideological reasons, the social democrats proclaim their commitment, but since unemployment in the Netherlands is much lower than elsewhere in the Union, there is little interest in strong financial support for EU employment programmes. The reduction of public expenditure, and the creation of jobs are among the major Dutch domestic policy goals. Only if EU policies are supportive of these will they be embraced.

In the second pillar (CFSP) the Dutch have shown a strong support for peace-keeping activities under the Petersberg missions and for various forms of aid to conflict-ridden countries, e.g. the former Yugoslavia. The fight against poverty by means of international aid should prevent, or reduce the influx of refugees and immigrants into the Union. The Dutch government also supports the expansion of the Commission's powers in the second pillar.

Only since 1997 has the third pillar received explicit attention, e.g. in government declarations in parliament, budget debates etc. with the Ministry of Justice taking the lead. Pillar three has been a late developer but has recently grown in importance. This is clearly related to the increased political salience of crime and safety in the Netherlands. Immigration has also become a major political issue – again, bringing in the Ministry of Justice and the third pillar.

On the political party scene, one can observe a major change in policies towards the Union especially in the liberal-conservative Volkspartej voor Vrijheld en Democratie (VVD).[7] Its former unquestioning commitment to European integration, especially from a business perspective, was challenged, within the party, by a new nationalism promoted by party leader Bolkestein. In the socialist Partei van de Arbeid (PvdA) there is some leftist intellectual flirting with 'post-modern nationalism', but there is a clear commitment to European integration with increasing attention paid to social security and unemployment. Leftist liberals, as well as Christian Democrats, remain clearly committed to the integration process, including a federal Union. Only among the small parties on the far left – not the Green Party, but especially the Socialist Party (former Marxist) – and on the far right – orthodox Calvinist parties – can one find a clear rejection of the Union.

The subsidiarity principle, as it appeared in official EU policies, did not create a great stir in Dutch political thinking. Although in origin it is a Christian Democratic concept – with its roots in Catholic political philosophy – it was unknown in Dutch ideological discussion. In fact, however, it fits quite well with current administrative thinking in the Netherlands. The Dutch state is a 'decentralised unitary system' with historical roots in a confederal republic. Local and provincial autonomy have historically been very strong, and the continuous budget cuts over recent decades have only encouraged central government to shift powers – and burdens – to lower levels. In Dutch policy discussions, therefore, the preference for the downward-shifting of powers sounded quite familiar. By itself, this preference is part of the older tradition of consociational democracy in the

Netherlands. The tradition of 'pillarisation' has, since the 1960s, been secularised and is now called the Dutch 'polder model', but the basic idea of leaving as much power as possible in the hands of smaller, constituent units, has remained.[8] Thus, subsidiarity may have sounded unfamiliar, but substantially it belonged to the 'automatic reflexes' of Dutch administrative and political culture.

In the Dutch policy-cycle, the interministerial Review Committee on Commissions Proposals – the Beoordelingscommissie Nieuwe Commissievoorstellen (BNC) – was established to review proposals from the European Commission from the viewpoint of subsidiarity.

The national policy-cycle: adapting to trauma, and catching up

Since the Netherlands has a decentralised unitary system[9] with a relatively weak intermediary, provincial level of government, we can distinguish between the national level on the one hand, and the 'lower levels' on the other (Figure 13.1). We then deal with political parties and interest groups and, finally, we look for patterns of change since Maastricht. When analysing national involvement in EU policies, one can distinguish between government and parliament. For both, there is the question of involvement in the preparation of EU policies, the actual making of decisions, their implementation and, finally, the control of implementation. In this last phase, an important role is also played by the judiciary.

Government: politicians and civil servants

In practice, it is very difficult to pinpoint the exact beginnings of EU policy preparation.[10] The Commission's advisory committees, Council of Ministers working groups, EP committees (since Amsterdam), or informal discussions, seminars or conferences provide the breeding ground for policy ideas or initiatives. For a national government it is very important to have well-organised links with these 'breeding grounds'. Moreover, these links are needed for the formal policy preparation process, i.e. 'feeding' the national representatives with the necessary expertise and instructions for Council decision-making.

Within each ministry in the Netherlands, there is a unit in charge of international and/or EU affairs.[11] In some cases, it has a strong position as a directorate, e.g. Agriculture, Economic Affairs, Environmental Affairs, Finance; sometimes it has the status of a bureau or a division (afdeling) (e.g. Justice, Transport and Water), and sometimes it is placed in a co-ordinating position close to the secretary-general (e.g. Interior).

The position of these units has changed over the years. In general, this has been consolidated (e.g. Economic Affairs, Agriculture, Finance), or strengthened considerably (e.g. Justice, Interior). In the ministries with a long-standing EU involvement, EU affairs have become an established

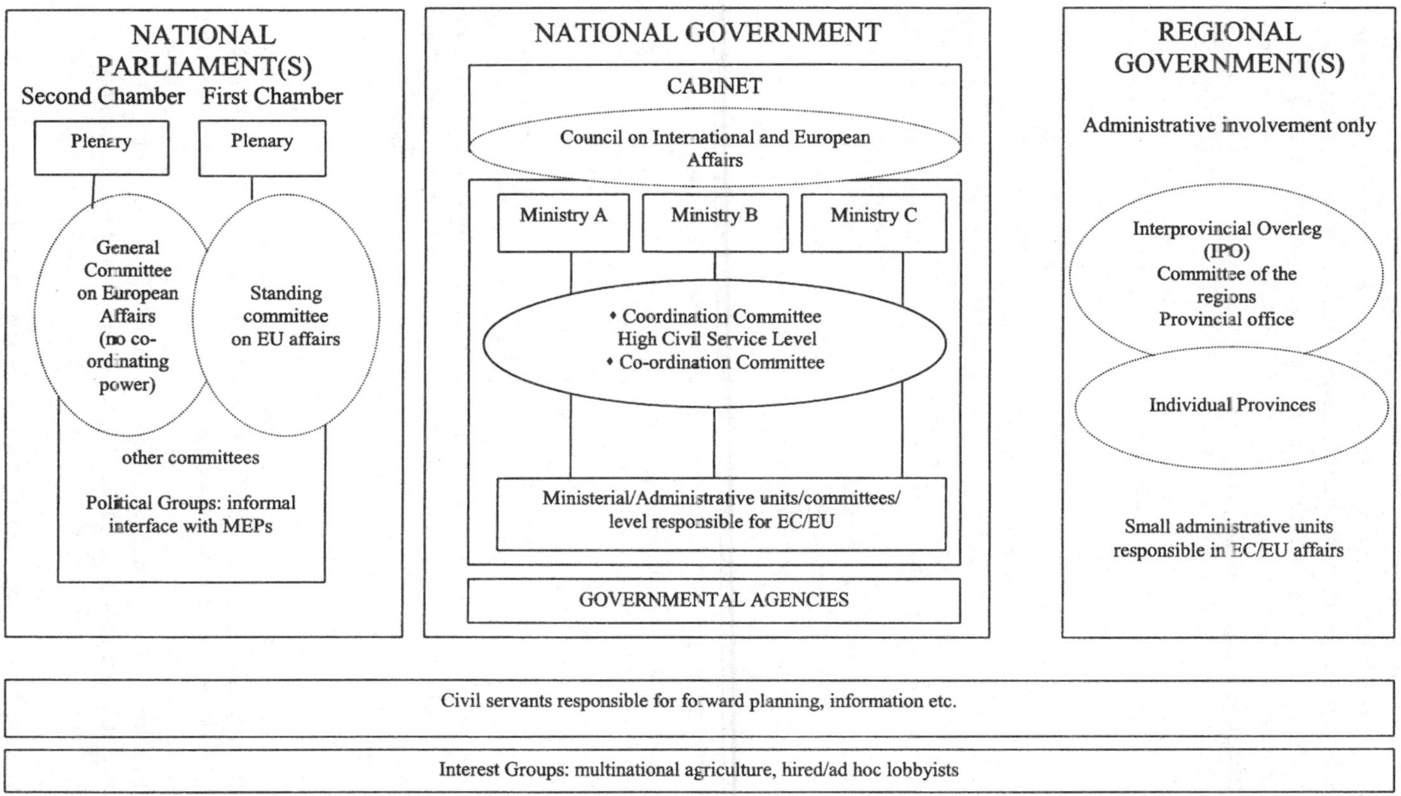

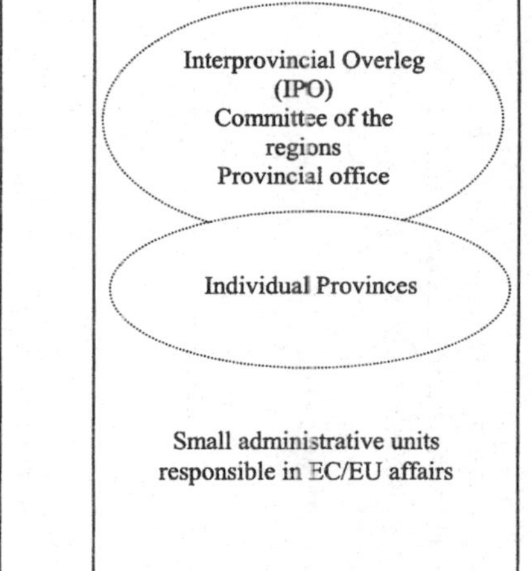

Figure 13.1 The national level of European decision-making – The Netherlands

specialisation for a specific unit. In the more recently 'Europeanised' ministries the EU units are small and are charged with increasing awareness of the Union throughout their organisation.

The views of the ministries on EU policies are presented in the (frequent) meetings of interministerial bodies: the Co-Ordination Committee (CoCo), the Review Committee on new Commission Proposals, and the Co-Ordination Committee at High Civil-Service Level (CoCoHAN).[12] All ministries are represented in these committees and they are chaired by the Ministry of Foreign Affairs' Directorate for Integration in Europe (in charge of EU as well as other multilateral European organisations).

The CoCo was established in the early 1960s, after an interministerial struggle over the leadership in EEC affairs. Economic Affairs, which had been involved in European integration since the late 1940s (Marshall Program, OECD, ECSC), lost out to Foreign Affairs, which won the leading position in Dutch EEC policy. For specific aspects of the EEC, especially trade and agriculture, a privileged/autonomous status was, however, given to the ministries of Economic Affairs and Agriculture.[13] In Dutch coalition politics, it is impossible for a single ministry to impose its will on a policy area where other ministries are involved.

The BNC was created more recently, in order to carry out 'subsidiarity testing' on Commission proposals, i.e. to give a preliminary judgement as to whether a proposal deserved to be developed by the Commission at all, or whether it should be handed over to the national government.[14] CoCoHAN was created after the trauma of Maastricht in 1992. It was felt that the involvement of the very top-level civil servants would prevent future policy failures. Whereas CoCo consists of the heads of ministerial EU units, the EU Director from the Foreign Affairs Ministry and a representative of the Dutch Permanent Representation, CoCoHAN involves the secretary-generals of all the ministries, plus the Permanent Representation director himself and the Secretary of State for Foreign Affairs. CoCo and CoCoHAN provide the Dutch Permanent Representation with instructions for meetings of the EU Council of Ministers. However, since there is also a strong political dimension to the Union, the Dutch position is also prepared at the political level, i.e. in a committee of the Council of Ministers: the Council on International and European Affairs – Subdivision on Europe (REIA-E). REIA-E is chaired by the Prime Minister, and consists of all cabinet ministers. Some sub-groups, e.g. Foreign Affairs–Union, Agriculture, Economic Affairs and the Prime Minister, have their own preparatory meetings for REIA-E at the political level. Policy preparation in the bureaucracy is thus paralleled by political preparation – with the Secretary of State-Foreign Affairs–Union as the linch-pin.

Moving from policy preparation to decision-making, one has to acknowledge the strategic role of the Dutch Permanent Representation in Brussels. Between 1986 (SEA) and 1992, the Permanent Representation expanded rapidly, so that all ministries now have at least one representative. Before the TEU's three-pillar structure was in place, all ministries had joined in the 'race for Brussels'. The Ministry of Foreign Affairs is formally in charge of the Permanent Representation; its head is a career diplomat, and all views/instructions from individual ministries have to be channelled through it.[15] However, Agriculture and ECOFIN are exempted from this rule and can make their own policies in the Council – under the pillar one procedures. In the third pillar, the K4 committee has carved out its own competence in preparing Council meetings.

These exceptions indicate the serious problems of co-ordination and control in the Permanent Representation.[16] They are not unique to the Netherlands, but they are aggravated by Dutch coalition politics, which offers much autonomy to individual ministries. The Dutch prime minister is always a 'primus inter pares', unable to impose his views on others, and the Minister of Foreign Affairs is usually more interested in international politics and diplomacy than in the technical specifics of EU policy proposals.

The Dutch Permanent Representative, therefore, has a very difficult task. Not only does a great deal of policy preparation escape his view – there are many contacts between ministries of Member States which bypass the head of the Permanent Representation – but also his control – as some important ministries have succeeded in creating a reserved 'policy space'. For them, the Permanent Representation serves mainly as a technical facility in Brussels.

Only a strong Minister of Foreign Affairs, or – even better – a coalition between a strong Foreign Affairs Minister and the Prime Minister, can reduce the Dutch problems of co-ordination and control in EU policymaking. The present government, where the Prime Minister has strong European ambitions, the Secretary of State has close links with the Prime Minister and the Minister of Foreign Affairs has an interest in weakening the autonomy of Agriculture, for example, demonstrates some interesting illustrations of this struggle for control. Policy failures in the past, and the increasing need for some success in the Union, should stimulate the Dutch not only to find coalition partners among the other Member States, but also to settle their internal differences and to speak with one voice in the national interest.

Concerning the implementation of EU policies and the control of implementation, the record of the Netherlands is rather mixed – quite unlike what one might expect from this founding father of European integration. Table 13.1 shows the number of EU directives implemented, the number of delays, infringement procedures and verdicts of the ECJ against the Netherlands concerning non-implementation, for the years 1990–97.[17]

Table 13.1 (Non-)implementation of EU directives by the Netherlands, 1990–97

Year	Implemented (started by Commission)	Delayed	Infringement	Court case + verdict
1990	66	70	31	4
1991	90	71	41	10
1992	149	73	45	6
1993	141	79	41	5
1994	123	35	18	2
1995	82	31	18	0
1996	73	32	6	0
1997	89	33	19	0

Compared to earlier data,[18] Table 13.1 shows that the 'race for 1992' to implement the White Paper was ultimately successful in the Netherlands. The Dutch government has considerably increased the number of directives implemented since 1990, and kept up a high implementation record after the 1992 obligations had been fulfilled, i.e. until 1994. In the process, the balance between directives implemented and directives delayed (deadline passed) also shifted in favour of implementation: the number of deadlines passed remained below the number of implemented directives, and this 'positive gap' increased.

Nevertheless, the number of Commission notifications of delay remained quite high until 1993, as did the number of infringement procedures started by the Commission. Only after 1994 did implementation problems decrease, at least in statistical terms. Overall, however, in 1997 the Dutch record of implementation, including infringements and ECJ cases, was much better than in 1990. Even so, there were several serious cases of implementation failure, or even blunders. One of them was the EU nitrate directive of 1991, where the Dutch government tried, in vain, to obtain an exemption for its cattle farmers (cows and pigs). As a result, Dutch farmers found themselves in flagrant violation of EU nitrate norms, sometimes 400 per cent above the permitted levels, and the government was unable to enforce the rules. After a rather dramatic episode of farmers' protests (1996) followed by widespread swine fever (1997), the Commission officially and publicly notified the Dutch government of violation (1998).

Another case was the so-called '*Securitel*-list', i.e. the non-implementation of the ECJ verdict in 1996, which stated the obligation of national governments to notify the European Commission of national rules concerning technical product specifications. In 1997, it turned out that more than 350 rules of this type had not been duly notified, and could therefore be declared invalid. The Ministries of Economic Affairs and

Justice, after some panic, and a parliamentary debate, took emergency measures to correct this lapse. Thus, problems of implementation have remained, and they are caused by several factors. One is the technical complexity of many matters, which are accessible only to very few specialised civil servants – if one of them falls ill, implementation can be delayed considerably. Another factor is the translation into Dutch which is sometimes rather weak, owing to staffing problems in the Commission. Sometimes, also, there is disagreement and stalemate as to which ministry has jurisdiction over a particular EU directive. Also, there is the Dutch desire for consensus, consultation and legal perfectionism – related to consociational democracy and Calvinism – which makes for cumbersome time-consuming procedures. Finally, the implementation of EU rules does not have a high priority in Dutch government. Since the administration is increasingly under stress (budget cuts, staff reductions), the implementation of EU rules, which is politically unattractive, soon lags behind. The impact of the '1992 campaign' was clear, but the TEU with its new policy fields did not affect implementation directly. Implementation and control belong to the pillar one policy-cycle – all, then, depends on the legislative productivity of the EU in the first pillar.

The second and third pillars do not produce EU legislation, but, at most, they lead to international treaties. The implementation and control of such treaties is, on the one hand, a phenomenon with a long tradition – much longer than the implementation of EU legislation. On the other hand, it uses different mechanisms of control. There may be good reason to take a new look at this, because the third pillar in particular, produces many conventions, but this falls beyond the scope of this chapter. For the Netherlands, it seems at first sight that the second and third pillars do not present serious problems of implementation.

Another form of control over EU policy implementation is the requests by national Courts of Justice for advice from the ECJ concerning applicability of EC law: the 'preliminary rulings'. The Dutch courts have always been quite active in this field, compared to other Member States. From 1988 to 1997, the number of Dutch preliminary rulings increased from 19 to 54 (annual figures: 19, 28, 16, 21, 21, 43, 38, 30, 18, 54). There is a considerable time-lag between an EC law's entry into force, the starting of a national court case, and a preliminary ruling.[19] Furthermore, when analysing the topics of the Dutch preliminary rulings, one finds no clear link with the Maastricht Treaty. Indirectly, as argued above, the increasing productivity of EU pillar one legislation is bound to bring an increase in preliminary rulings in the medium and long term. A final remark concerning control: the Dutch Court of Accounts in 1998 complained about the difficulties of controlling the spending of EC Structural Funds in the Netherlands, and called for a closer collaboration with the European Court of Auditors (ECA). The problem behind this is that the competence of the Dutch Court of Auditors is restricted to the implementation of Dutch legislation, and therefore it does not have full control over EC spending (based directly on EC law) in the Netherlands. In the management supervision of spending there is an adequate involvement of all actors (local, regional, national, EC), but in the field of accounting, control and reporting, some 'border problems' have not yet been solved, and delays or gaps can occur, in spite of the good working relations between the Dutch Court of Auditors and the ECA.

Parliament: parties, committees and MEPs[20]

The involvement of the Dutch parliament in the EU policy-cycle is very weak: it takes place, if at all, in the very last phase of implementation and control. The Ministry of Foreign Affairs reports every three months to parliament (second chamber) about the implementation of EU legislation, and parliamentary debate about the Union is mostly triggered by implementation problems – protests against Dutch legislation based on EC law, or against Dutch legislation which violates EC law. These debates follow the familiar lines of opposition versus government without, however, going into the substantive reasons for EC policies, or into the Dutch position in the Union. Aside from some grumblings or disbelief, parliament concludes by agreeing that EC rules have to be complied with. The vast majority of EC rules are overlooked by parliament altogether, in spite of the fact that more than half of Dutch legislation (and, in agriculture or environment, for example, almost all legislation) is of EC origin. EC policies, therefore, are given 'much too little attention, and much too late'.

Parliamentary interest in and frustration with the Union is nevertheless weak and recent. Only in the mid-1980s were steps taken to increase parliamentary interest by creating a Standing Committee for European Affairs (1986). Quarterly reporting on EU implementation started in 1989, at parliamentary request, and since 1991 the 'fiches' dealing with EU decisions and issues have been made available to the Dutch parliament.

The interest of the Dutch parliament in the role and the work of the EP, was and is mostly of an informal nature – i.e. following party lines. Every political party wants to maintain a certain control over its representatives in the EP and to be informed about 'what goes on in Brussels'. After all, recruitment of EP candidates is in the hands of the national parties, who want to keep an eye on their performance, if only to decide about their future value for the party. Numerous informal contacts therefore exist between MEPs and their colleagues in the Dutch parliament – not only before 1979 when the dual mandate and the indirect election of the EP existed, but also since then. Within some parties, contacts were somewhat institutionalised (e.g. the agenda of the Labour MEPs was/is sent to the Labour representatives in the Dutch parliament), but on the whole, contacts remain intensive but informal. The performance of MEPs, however, is judged not only along party lines, but also along national lines: an MEP's ability to serve the national interest is highly appreciated in the Dutch parliament.

During the 1980s the Dutch parliament drifted further away from the EP, mainly because the dual mandate disappeared. EP membership became a separate, full-time job – on paper. In practice, it became a nomadic existence, well-paid but formally distant from national politics. The Standing Committee on EU Affairs, for example, consisted of members of the Dutch parliament only; the meetings of COSAC therefore involved a different 'circuit' than that of the Dutch MEPs. More and more, contacts between the Dutch parliament and the EP came to depend on the personal, informal initiative of the MEPs.

The increasing powers of the EP since the SEA provoked some efforts to increase Dutch parliamentary interest in EU policy-making and the Maastricht Treaty strengthened these efforts. In 1994 the Standing Committee on EU Affairs became a General Committee on EU Affairs with a mission to increase awareness of EU matters among all MPs. Furthermore, the First Chamber of the Dutch parliament also established a Standing Committee on EU Affairs. Dutch MEPs are asked for advice more frequently, and in 1996 the Dutch parliament (Second Chamber) created a special 'question time' for EU matters. In 1996–97, a weekly Euro-consultation was started, involving Standing Committees of parliament (not only the EU committees), ministers and Dutch MEPs. All major parties have institutionalised their contacts with their MEPs through co-ordination meetings, steering groups, committees for foreign affairs (Labour, Christian Democrats), the systematic presence of MEPs at Dutch parliamentary meetings (conservative liberal) or 'fraction' meetings (leftist liberals). Plans to formalise these contacts at the parliament level, by creating 'mixed committees' of the EP and Dutch Parliament, are supported by the major parties, but have not yet materialised. On the whole, then, the Maastricht Treaty and the Dutch Presidency during the conclusion of the Amsterdam Treaty had a stimulating impact on parliamentary interest in the Union.

The provinces and municipalities

The Dutch 'decentralised unitary state' is sub-divided into twelve provinces and 548 municipalities.[21] Their governmental structure consists of an executive (Queen's Commissioner or a Mayor) and an elected assembly (council). This is also the case for the sixty-six water boards, another important lower level of government in the Netherlands. The involvement of these lower levels in EU affairs is, in practice, restricted to their administrations. The elected assemblies are not involved in the Union, apart from 'recreational activities' such as excursions to the EP, etc. At the municipal level, there are numerous 'twinning' arrangements – in the past mostly with Third World counterparts, but increasingly within Europe, especially Eastern Europe – but this is outside the direct scope of the Union.

The Maastricht Treaty had a substantial impact on provincial and local involvement in EU policies. Before the TEU, provinces or municipalities made an occasional effort to benefit from EU programmes and/or from the Structural–Regional Funds. Rotterdam, for example, obtained support from the Renaval programme in the 1980s, and the province of Friesland benefited from agriculture-related Structural Funds. Official as well as informal contacts with the Commission (e.g. Friesland with DG VI) and/or with MEPs, were the main channel to promote their interests in Brussels. This competitive struggle for financial benefit increased, if only because of the continuing domestic budget cuts. As the Union expanded its activities, it became more and more interesting for individual Dutch provinces, municipalities and water boards. On top of this, the creation of CoR, and of the JHA pillar, offered municipalities and provinces official entry to the EU policy-making scene – as a group, at an earlier stage, and in a modest way.

The SEA, the Schengen Agreement and the ensuing creation of the third pillar were the reasons behind the expansion of the Dutch Permanent Representation. A representation of the Ministry of the Interior was added in 1990 (at first one, later two officers, plus a third pillar specialist from the Foreign Ministry). Its task was to participate in the negotiations on behalf of the Interior Ministry, mainly in police and internal security co-operation, but also to represent the interests of local and provincial administrations, and especially to inform them about the requirements of the 'Europe 1992' programme. Because of 'Europe 1992', some of the larger cities established organisational units for EU affairs, and a Common Information Point for municipalities and provinces was established by the Ministry of Interior, the Dutch Association of Municipalities (VNG), and the Inter Provincial Consultative Agency (IPO).

The CoR[22] was created mainly at German and Belgian insistence. When it became operational in 1993 there was a slight panic among Dutch provinces and municipalities who were hardly prepared, and had very little EU expertise. The Ministry of the Interior wanted the Dutch CoR delegation (twelve members) to represent only the administrative units/levels with a democratically accountable executive. In practice, this boiled down to the provinces and municipalities – the water boards, for unknown reasons, were left out. Also, it was decided that the seats were to be divided between municipalities and provinces. Thus, one finds six representatives of the Dutch municipalities (most of whom are mayors, the others are elected aldermen) and six representatives of the provinces (most of whom are elected deputies, the others are Commissioners of the

Queen – one of them is the chairman of the delegation). In geographical terms, the CoR offers a strong representation of the periphery of the country, i.e. the southern, eastern and northern provinces. The IPO acts as the secretariat for the Dutch CoR delegation while, the VNG acts as the most influential interest group.

In terms of policy input, however, the Dutch CoR delegation was confronted with very difficult circumstances. The CoR had great difficulty putting itself on the EU map – competing with both ECOSOC and the EP. Also, the prospect of a diminishing Dutch share of the Structural Funds proved a severe handicap for an organised and effective input in EU structural policy-making. Successes were very hard to achieve, and therefore the CoR delegation also turned to lobbying at the implementation stage. As mentioned above, there were some benefits for Dutch municipalities and provinces in the 1980s. In the early 1990s, the province of Flevoland obtained Objective One status, qualifying for substantial support until 1999, albeit at a very high political cost in the public's eyes. Support for this wealthy region seriously undermined the credibility of EU Structural Funds.

For the immediate future, Dutch municipalities and provinces are looking for EU support in the fields of urban problems, crime and safety, immigrant minorities and social integration. Commission initiatives and programmes – URBAN, INTERREG, RESTRUCT, LEADER – are increasingly addressing Dutch concerns. Transport and infrastructure also figure highly on the municipal and provincial list, and there is also an increased awareness of the EU's importance for environmental regulation, which belongs to the local/provincial competence.

Lobbying by Dutch municipalities and provinces to a large extent takes place in a competitive and rather haphazard fashion. Rotterdam, Amsterdam and the Hague have sizeable units for international affairs, and a common office in Brussels, which is also used by the three western provinces. Recently, this office has become available for all the provinces, which used to have their own separate, individual offices.

The most active provinces, surprisingly, are not the three western ones, but the two larger 'peripheral' ones: Gelderland in the east and Noord-Brabant in the south. The municipalities, aside from the 'big three', are mostly represented by the VNG, which has a sizeable international division. However, there is also a great deal of individual activity: the enthusiasm and commitment of a mayor or alderman is often crucial for success in Brussels. MEPs rooted in specific regions are also mobilised for provincial or municipal lobbying. As the importance of the EP in EU policy-making increases, their role becomes more important. In this respect, the Maastricht and Amsterdam treaties have substantially changed the life of a Dutch MEP.

Parties and interest groups

After the 'Europe 1992' campaign and the Maastricht Treaty, there was a considerable, but mostly temporary, increase in activity from different interest groups towards the EU institutions, especially the EP.[23] The increase in powers of the EP in the policy-making process, however, was overestimated – access to the Commission, and to the Council, which basically means, to the national capitals, has remained the most important way to influence policy-making and/or implementation.

Patterns of behaviour among Dutch political parties and interest groups have apparently not changed much.[24] The major parties have maintained their policy on the Union except for the 'nationalist' challenge among the conservative liberals. A newcomer among the anti-EU parties was the Socialist Party. The emergence of a strong European platform, e.g. for the EP elections, remains a temporary affair. Among the interest groups, the trade unions since Maastricht are giving more attention to the Union, for example, the Barber Protocol, the Social Protocol, and majority voting/co-decision in the first pillar have made them aware of the importance of involvement at the earliest stages of decision-making. Larger companies, especially multinationals, are highly aware of the strategic importance of EU rules concerning competition, health, safety, or the environment, and of EU programmes and initiatives concerning R&D. Dutch agriculture has changed its organisational structure – becoming less corporatist – but has maintained its presence in the CAP, and in COPA.

In terms of interest representation, some of the Dutch MEPs have close links with Third World groups (socialists), trade unions (socialists), transport and trade (orthodox Calvinists) or agriculture (Christian Democrats, liberal conservatives). However, more and more lobbying activity is contracted out to consultancy offices, lawyers, accounting firms, etc. in Brussels, for reasons of cost effectiveness and flexibility. These professional brokers have one interest in common, to restrict direct access to the EU policy-making cycle. Their 'vested interest in complexity' is hardly compatible with the desire for more transparency and democratic accountability in EU policy, and controversy about their role is likely to emerge.

Changing patterns after Maastricht and Amsterdam?

By way of overview, it can be stated that a major change in Dutch involvement in the Union since Maastricht has been the increased attention given to the Union in the administration, especially at the national level. The Dutch Presidencies of Maastricht and Amsterdam were triggers creating a dramatic, but temporary, increase in political attention and administrative input. For most ministries, the Dutch Presidencies brought a 50 per cent increase in EU personnel input – followed, of course, by a clear dip.

However, for the Dutch administration, the Maastricht episode provided a lesson which had been learned by the time of the Amsterdam Presidency. After the 'failure' of Maastricht, preparations for 'Amsterdam 1997' were made in a very thorough way. Elaborate and careful views on the Union were developed, after taking into account the views of the other Member States. Ambitions for 'Amsterdam' were presented as low key so that 'success was guaranteed'. This approach required more, and sustained, attention from the administration, especially the Ministry of Foreign Affairs. However, in other ministries, too, the post-Maastricht era brought a further organisational adaptation, enabling stronger involvement in EU policies. Afterwards, the policy problems related to the Union – especially *Securitel*, concerning the non-implementation of the ECJ verdict in 1996 – sent a strong message to the Dutch administration – that the neglect of EU policies can create serious problems of non-compliance for a (national) government. EU policies are not only an important resource for solving problems – e.g. EU assistance was essential in the 1997 swine fever crisis – but they also provide a regulatory framework which has to be taken into account at all times.[25] In reality, the Union has become 'the new roof on the Dutch house of government'. The introduction of the Euro will further stimulate this awareness.

Next to the administrative adaptation, there was also a change in public opinion and party politics. A more explicit promotion of the national interest, and a focusing on financial issues was added to the traditional Dutch commitment to European integration. This change is clearly related, with some time lag, to the change of the Netherlands' status from a net receiver to a net payer in the Union. Public opinion and party views have come to recognise the new realities of the 1990s. The change is also related to a general shift in the public mood towards domestic 'close-to-home' issues such as crime, safety, and – even in the open society of the Netherlands – the control of immigration. The outside world is no longer regarded only in positive, idealistic terms. This new line of thinking has demonstrated itself both in the debate about institutional reform of the Union, and in the reform of EU finances. The Dutch have declared an unwillingness to reduce their representation in the institutions (EP, Commission, Council of Ministers). Without aiming for the next Commission Presidency explicitly, they are not willing to do without 'their' one commissioner – in the portfolio distribution there is some flexibility for negotiation.

In EU finances, the reduction of the Dutch contribution has a high priority. In the national budget, accepted by parliament, the Dutch financial input into the Union has already been reduced dramatically. It constitutes an unprecedentedly tough starting position in the negotiations. In the discussions concerning CAP reform, the re-structuring of the EU Structural Funds and other Agenda 2000 items, a considerable compensation will be demanded in exchange for Dutch agreement. The close relationship with Germany, however, imposes certain limits on Dutch obstinacy.

Conclusion: the Netherlands – less willing but more able within the EU?

How 'Europeanised' is the Dutch administration?

After Maastricht, all Dutch ministries adapted their internal organisation and created, at least on paper, close links with the Union. The actual 'Europeanisation' of organisational culture, often lagged behind, but since 1990 there has been an organisational upgrading of EU units, as well as an increase in the attention paid by management to international and EU affairs. In the Dutch administrative culture of the 1990s, the Union was central. An interesting case was the Ministry of the Interior, the latecomer in EU affairs. In organisational terms, it made the necessary adaptations even before Maastricht, but within the ministry, EU awareness is spread rather thinly and unevenly – it is strong in the Police and Internal Security directorates but weak in the Provincial/Municipal Supervising and Funding directorates. After several 'policy accidents' related to the Union, measures were taken to prevent such events from occurring again. A reorganisation within the ministry upgraded the EU division in the hierarchy, but considerable effort is still needed to integrate awareness of the EU into the ministry's 'domestic' culture. Another interesting indication of the 'Europeanisation' of the Dutch administration is the number of secondments from the ministries to the Commission.[26] This number is modest, i.e. between thirty-three and fifty-nine per year between 1993 and 1998 from the thirteen ministries. Most secondments (five–fifteen per year) are from the Ministries of Agriculture, Economic Affairs and Foreign Affairs. Traffic and Water, Housing and Environment, and Finance send around five persons per year, while the other ministries send fewer than this. These figures reached a high point in 1993, fell between 1993 and 1995, but rose again after 1996. The 1993 level (fifty-nine), however, had not yet been reached by 1998 (fifty-one). There is no clear relationship between the number of secondments to the Commission and the signing of the Maastricht and Amsterdam Treaties.

How 'fit' are the Netherlands for the post-Maastricht Union?

Are the Netherlands 'willing and able' to play a role in the new phase of EU development, and to face its challenges? This question can be answered quite positively – with some specifications and provisos. The specific role of the Netherlands will depend on the rethinking of its foreign policy, which is currently in process. The Netherlands will look for new partnerships and coalitions within the Union. While it takes the national interest as an explicit starting-point, in order to create new coalitions it will nevertheless have to make some sacrifices and compromises. The Netherlands' close relationship with Germany is likely to become a cornerstone of Dutch foreign policy – and this will offer both possibilities and restrictions for the Dutch position. In terms of EU enthusiasm, the Dutch no longer want to play the moral leading role among the Member States. In the discussion about institutional reform and the accession of new members, therefore, they are likely to take a cautious approach, preferring consolidation and 'cleaning up' rather than expansion and new dynamism. The vulnerable spot in the Dutch position is popular legitimacy of the Union. Turnout at EP elections decreased in the 1990s, and the Union is increasingly seen as a financial institution which is not able to handle its finances in a proper manner. It has the 'political sex appeal' of a bank-cum-lawyers' office, i.e. virtually zero. For the Dutch role in EU affairs, this implies that for most of the time, the public will not pay much attention and will give implicit room for manoeuvring. But when the public does pay attention, this will be negative, unless a great effort is taken to explain the value of the Union for the solution of the country's social, political, economic, environmental and other problems.

Future perspectives: debates surrounding the Union

Political discussion about the Union in the Netherlands follows the general shift in public opinion: politics is considered relatively uninteresting, e.g. compared to sports, or 'high society', and is therefore a matter for the opinion of a small elite of students, public servants, politicians, etc. Within politics, attention focuses on personalities and money, and less on social problems or ideals. In EU matters, much public attention was given to the 'race for the European Central Bank presidency' (the Duisenberg lobby), the introduction of the Euro, the Dutch contribution to EC finances, the 'fraud, corruption and mismanagement' of EC funds and the financial 'extravagance' of the EP. In the run-up to the 1999 EP elections, the political parties developed their platforms, with especially the leftist liberals, the social democrats and the Christian Democrats stressing the need to transcend national thinking. The conservative liberals took a more national approach: 'don't throw away good Dutch money'. Aside from this, the EU has been called upon, more often than in the past, to assist in solving the major problems of Dutch politics: crime and safety, immigration, maintaining the health care system, and traffic congestion and the transportation system, including airports, highways and railways. There is an opportunity, therefore, for the Union to prove its 'added value'. Furthermore, the Union is, and in future will be, called upon more frequently in matters of market policy and competition policy, such as mergers and market access for such things as public transportation, telecommunications, banking and insurance.

For the Dutch economy, the Dutch state is far too small: transnational thinking and action have been strong in Dutch business for centuries, and will be only strengthened by the development of the Union. The introduction of the Euro in particular, will stimulate further, international transactions, in both the private and the public sector. Monetary issues, therefore, will loom large in Dutch discussions about the Union. The ECB presidency has been won, the introduction of the Euro is in full swing, but there is concern about the solidity of the Euro in the future, i.e. the ECB's policies. A stronger Dutch input into the ECB's actions – present and future – might well be worth a concession in some other EU field for the Dutch government.

In short, the Dutch foreign policy mix of peace, profits and principles[27] is likely to shift in favour of profits, with a rather puritanical approach towards thriftiness, cleanliness and solid finance – or even a certain 'miserliness' (the Dutch expression is krenterigheid). The moral chord has certainly not disappeared, but for the time being, it produces a different music.

Notes

1 For the model of 'consociational democracy' see Arendt Lijphart, *Democracy in Plural Societies – A Comparative Exploration* (New Haven: Yale University Press, 1977).

2 See Rudy B. Andeweg, *Dutch Voters Adrift – On Explanations of Electoral Change 1963–1977* (Leiden: Proefschrift, 1982).

3 See Ben Hoetjes, 'The Netherlands', in: Dietrich Rometsch and Wolfgang Wessels (eds), *The European Union and the Member States. Towards Institutional Fusion?* (Manchester: Manchester University Press, 1996), pp. 155–184.

4 See Johan Willem Lodewijk Brouwer and Alfred Pijpers, 'Nederland en Luxemburg. Eeen grote en een kleine mogendheid?', in: *Internationale Spectator*, No. 1/1999, p. 33.

5 For a detailed account of 'Black Monday' see Michel van Hulten, 'Zwarte Maandag – kroniek van een gemiste kans', in: Hans Labohm (ed.), *De waterdragers van het Nederlandse Europa-beleid – terugblik op 40 jaar DGES* (Den Haag: SDU, 1997), pp. 193–210.

6 See Anjo G. Harryvan and Jan van der Harst, 'Verschuivingen in het Nederlandse Europa-beleid', in: *Transaktie*, 26, 1997; Staatscourant, Troonredes, The Hague, September 1989–1997; Dutch priorities on the eve of the 1996 IGC, The Hague, February 1996.

7 See Gerardus Arnoldus van der List, *De macht van het idee – de VVD en het Nederlandse buitenlands beleid 1948–1994* (Leiden: DSWO Press, 1995); Isaac Lipschits, *Verkiezingsprogramma's 1989/1994/1998* (Groningen: Documentatiecentrum Nederlandse Politieke Partijen, 1989/1994/1998).

8 See Lijphart, 1977, *op. cit.*

9 See Jan Kooiman and J. Breunese, 'The Netherlands', in: Donald Cameron

Rowat (ed.), *Public Administration in Developed Democracies – A Comparative Study* (New York, Basel: Dekker, 1988), pp. 237–254; Jan Willem van Deth and Jan C.P.M. Vis, *Regeren in Nederland – het politiek-bestuurlijke bestel in vergelijkend perspectief* (Assen: Van Gorcum, 1995).

10 Compare the metaphors of 'primeval soup' (Ursuppe) and 'nested games'. See Jeremy J. Richardson (ed.), *European Union – Power and Policy-Making* (London: Routledge, 1996), pp. 3–21.

11 See *Staatsalmanak* (The Hague: SDU, 1990–98) and the internal papers by Ben Hoetjes *et al.* (The Hague: Clingendael Institute, 1998).

12 See Jan Marinus Meeuwis van den Bos, *Dutch EC-Policy-Making. A Model-Guided Approach to Coordination and Negotiation* (Amsterdam: Thesis Publishers, 1991), especially on CoCo.

13 See Hans Labohm (ed.) *De Waterdragers van het Nederlandse Europa-beleid – terugblix op 40 jar DGES* (Den Haag: SDO, 1997).

14 In the Dutch case, reference to the provincial or municipal level has not (yet) occurred.

15 And onward to COREPER, before entering the Council meetings.

16 See Vincent Wright, 'The National Co-Ordination of European Policy-Making. Negotiating the Quagmire', in: Jeremy Richardson (ed.), *European Union. Power and Policy-Making* (London: Routledge, 1996), pp. 148–169.

17 See Vergaderstukken Tweede Kamer, vergaderjaren 1990–91, 1991–92, 1992–93, 1993–94, 1994–95, 1995–96, 1996–97, 1997–98; *Publicatieblad Europese Gemeenschappen*, 1988–1998.

18 See Hoetjes, 1996, *op. cit.*, see also Kenneth Hanf and Ben Soetendorp (eds), *Adapting to European Integration. Small States and the EU* (Harlow: Longman, 1998).

19 See *Publicatieblad Europese Gemeenschappen*, 1988–1998.

20 See Algemene Commissie voor Europese Zaken, *Tweede Kamer en Europese besluitvorming*, The Hague, 1995; Algemene Commissie voor Europese Zaken, *Europese informatievoorziening*, The Hague, March 1998. See also Leendert Jan Bal, 'Parlementaire verantwoordelijkheid voor Europese besluitvorming', in: *Internationale Spectator*, No. 5/1996; Peter Bursens, 'Belangenbehartiging bij het Europese Parlement', in: *Internationale Spectator*, No. 3/1997; Marinus C.P.M van Schendelen, 'Cue Processes and the Relationship between the European Parliament and the Dutch Parliament', in: Valentine Herman and Marinus C.P.M. van Schendelen (eds), *The European Parliament and National Parliaments* (Westmead: Gower, 1979).

21 See Theodorus Adrianus Jacobus Toonen, 'Gevolgen van de Europese eenwording voor openbaar bestuur: Europa vraagt om binnenlands bestuur', in: *Namens*, No. 4/1992, pp. 52–55; Ben Hoetjes, 'Éen Europees-bestuurlijke verdieping. De Nederlandse provincies en de EU', in: *Internationale Spectator*, No.7–8/1999; Jens Joachim Hesse and Rolf R. Kleinfeld, *Die Provinzen im politischen System der Niederlande* (Opladen: Westdeutscher Verlag, 1990).

22 See also Theodorus Adrianus Jacobus Toonen, C. Mariette and S. Glim, 'A Country without Regions in the Committee of the Regions', in: Jens Joachim Hesse (ed.), *Regionen in Europa* (Baden-Baden: Nomos, 1994), pp. 75–99.

23 See Bursens, 1997, *op. cit.*
24 See W. J. Veenstra, 'De Partij van de Arbeid en Europa', in: *Internationale Spectator*, April 1997.
25 During the swine fever crisis, for example, the Commission severely criticised the Dutch veterinary measures – and had to be listened to.
26 *Source:* Bureau Internationale Ambtenaren, The Hague.
27 See Joris J. C. Voorhoeve, *Peace, Profits and Principles. A Study of Dutch Foreign Policy* (The Hague: Nijhoff, 1979).

Select bibliography

The text (English translation) of the Constitution of the Netherlands can be found at the University of Richmond's constitution finder at http://confinder.richmond.edu/. Further sources on government and parliament of the Netherlands can be found at Government www.postbus51.nl or at Parliament www.parlement.nl.

Andeweg, Rudy B. (1982) 'Dutch Voters Adrift – On Explanations of Electoral Change 1963–1977' (Leiden: Proefschrift).

Bos, Jan Marinus M. van den (1991) Dutch EC-Policy-Making. A Model-Guided Approach to Coordination and Negotiation (Amsterdam: Thesis Publishers).

Brouwer, Jan Willem Lodewijk and Pijpers, Alfred E. (1999) 'Nederland en Luxemburg: een grote en een kleine mogendheid?', in: *Internationale Spectator*, No.1/1999, pp. 31–36.

Deth, Jan Willem van and Vis, Jan C.P.M. (1995) *Regeren in Nederland – het politiek-bestuurlijke bestel in vergelijkend perspectief* (Assen: Van Gorcum).

Hanf, Kenneth and Soetendorp, Ben (eds) (1998) *Adapting to European Integration. Small States and the EU* (Harlow: Longman).

Hoetjes, Ben J.S. (1996) 'The Netherlands', in: Dietrich Rometsch and Wolfgang Wessels (eds), *The European Union and Member States. Towards Institutional Fusion?* (Manchester: Manchester University Press, 1996), pp. 155–184.

Labohm, Hans (ed.) (1997) *De waterdragers van het Nederlandse Europa-beleid – terugblik op 40 jaar DGES* (Den Haag: SDU).

Toonen, Theodorus A.J. and Glim, Mariette S. (1994) 'A "Country without Regions" and the Committee of the Regions', in: Jens Joachim Hesse (ed.), *Regionen in Europa* (Baden-Baden: Nomos), pp. 75–99.

Voorhoeve, Joris J.C. (1979) *Peace, Profits and Principles. A Study of Dutch Foreign Policy* (The Hague: Nijhoff).

Wijk, Rob de (1998) 'Randvoorwaarde of beleidsterrein? Europa in de verkiezingsprogramma's', in: *Internationale Spectator* No. 3/1998.

14 *Otmar Höll, Johannes Pollack and Sonja Puntscher-Riekmann*

Austria: domestic change through European integration

Introduction: ambivalence as 'Leitmotiv'

Austria's attitude towards the (West) European integration process after 1945 has been ambivalent at best.[1] The Second Republic was designed as a democratic system, based on political pluralism and party competition. However, its political culture and its real character (Realverfassung), because of its strong corporatist elements, developed into the typical features of the specific 'Austrian model'. The first steps towards post-war recovery and re-integration into the international community were largely shaped by participation in the European Recovery Programme. The amazing economic success of the first decades after the occupation by the four Allies (until 1955) helped to create a stable socio-political environment. In contrast to the harsh conflicts of the interwar period the emergence of a consensus oriented society was a major task resulting in a pact between parties, chambers, employers and trade unions called the 'social partnership'.[2]

In its international orientation membership in the UN (1955) and in the Council of Europe (1956) was achieved shortly after the State Treaty in May 1955 was signed and the Constitutional Law on permanent neutrality as the condition for regaining independence was adopted. Together with the socio-economic success story these factors formed the basis of a so far unknown strong popular identification with the 'Austrian Nation'.[3] While it maintained a rigid attitude on military aspects of permanent neutrality, Austrian politicians showed a more flexible stance in interpreting neutrality with regard to economic and ideological dimensions. Austria not only signed a customs and price agreement with the ECSC in 1956 in the framework of GATT, but also entered into negotiations with the EEC in order to establish independent agreements on tariff reductions, dispute resolution committees and economic policy harmonisation in 1960.[4] As for the rest of the European neutrals (Switzerland, Sweden and Finland) at that time membership in the EEC was viewed as incompatible with permanent neutrality. These countries co-operated in setting up the European Free Trade Association (EFTA) of the so-called 'Outer Seven'.[5] Since NATO membership of Great Britain and Norway did not bother the neutrals in the EFTA framework, EEC membership may have been seen as economically too far-reaching for them.

Against a completely changing political and economic background full EC membership was first demanded by the Federation of Austrian Industrialists in May 1987.[6] The Austrian People's Party, Österreichische Volkspartei (ÖVP), the smaller of the two coalition parties, followed suit. After all provincial governors, as well as the four institutions of the system of social partnership, had come out in favour of EC membership in March 1989, the Social Democratic Party – Sozialdemokratische Partei Österreichs (SPÖ) – finally decided to vote for the application which was subsequently lodged in July 1989.[7] This development was only logical for the ÖVP under Foreign Minister Alois Mock, who was an early and enthusiastic advocate of European integration, whereas the SPÖ underwent a certain change in its stand on Europe. It was Chancellor Franz Vranitzky who convinced the party of the gains of EC membership.

The Austrian government's re-orientation was motivated primarily by economic considerations. It accepted the consequences of membership for the national decision-making processes, and for various policy fields, especially in the realm of the economy, social security, environment and democratic policy. Foreign and military security arguments, by comparison, began to feature more prominently only with the collapse of the Soviet Union and the beginning of the war in former Yugoslavia.[8] Austria forged ahead on the question of membership at a time when the governments of Switzerland, Sweden and Finland still perceived neutrality and EC membership as incompatible.[9] For many analysts, especially those who were acquainted with the traditional Austrian foreign policy profile of 'active neutrality policy', this came as a surprise. In retrospect, it is worth mentioning that Austria applied for membership at a time when the European Community was pushing heavily towards integration in many fields, including defence cooperation, especially since the TEU. In June 1992, the Austrian government declared its 'preparedness to participate in the CFSP and in its dynamic development actively and in a spirit of solidarity'.[10]

Membership of the Union required far-reaching constitutional changes for Austria, a two-thirds majority in the 'Nationalrat' (the Austrian Parliament), but also approval by the 'Bundesrat' (second chamber of the Austrian Parliament), and finally a popular referendum.[11] Considering that there was quite strong popular opposition (between 38 per cent in spring 1989 and more than 40 per cent in 1991 and 1992 against membership), and two opposition parties strongly arguing against accession, the task for the government to convince the population was not small.[12] Moreover, membership in the EEA, which was achieved on 1 January 1994, was not regarded as a suitable substitute for full membership of the Union – it was merely taken as a tiresome but necessary prerequisite, also providing the government with arguments in favour of accession. Taking over two-thirds of the acquis communautaire without participation in the decision-making institutions of the Union was seen as foolish.

Austria's membership negotiations began on 1 February 1993 and were concluded on 1 March 1994. The areas of greatest domestic political concern to the government were agriculture, transit traffic and regulations restricting the sale of property in Alpine regions.[13] Reflecting the internal politics of the grand coalition, the Austrian negotiating team was officially led by the Foreign Minister Alois Mock (ÖVP) and the State Secretary in the Chancellor's Office, Brigitte Ederer (SPÖ). The Austrian negotiation positions had mainly been a matter of co-ordination between the government, the social partners and the provinces, while the parliament, despite participation and having information rights, remained outside.

A referendum on membership was obligatory under the Constitution and was called by the government for 12 June 1994, well in advance of the Scandinavian countries. The referendum debate was characterised by a marked and stable elite consensus on the desirability of EU membership. Main opponents were the right-wing and populist Austrian Freedom Party, the Freiheitliche Partei Österreichs (FPÖ),[14] the Green Party as well as the weak Austrian Communist Party. The FPÖ under Jörg Haider tried to stir up and exploit popular sentiments. Sections of the trade unions and farmers, extra-parliamentary initiatives (Anti-Transit Movement) and some other grass roots organisations formed by more or less prominent individuals, also opposed EU membership. Yet, because of the large heterogeneity of interests a common position among these groups was not achieved. Compared with the Scandinavian countries, opinion polls in Austria since application indicated a relatively clear, albeit volatile, majority in favour of membership that dwindled temporarily during the critical phases of the entry negotiations in the winter of 1994. Yet the extent of the need for domestic adjustments was deliberately played down by the elites, in fear of risking a minority result in the referendum. The Austrian objectives remained the same: guaranteeing sustainable economic growth and securing political manoeuvrability and influence of the country. On voting day turnout was 82.4 per cent, 66.6 per cent voting in favour of EU membership and only 33.4 per cent against.[15] After the parliamentary ratification process was concluded, Austria joined the Union on 1 January 1995.[16] The most important legal consequences of accession were the adaption of parts of the EU acquis which had not already been integrated with EEA membership. What was clear from the beginning was that the balance between government, parliament and the social partners would shift in the direction of the former. The parliament was expected to lose its legislative monopoly,[17] and the public service would come under mounting pressure. The 'social partnership', the system which had served Austria so well in the 1960s and 1970s but which has become a burden to modernisation, would change substantially as well.

The national policy-cycle: from consociational to competitive democracy?

With EU membership the perception of the Austrian society as being composed of quite stable relationships of relatively equal interest groups was suddenly superimposed by the reality of antagonisms between the 'winners' and 'losers' in the integration process (Figure 14.1). The idea of being an 'island of the blessed' began to be replaced by a more intense power struggle, with the coalition parties SPÖ and the ÖVP trying to maintain their political influence on society.[18] The addition of a new (European) tier in policy-making saw the opposition parties FPÖ, LIF (Liberal Party) and the Green Party demand a voice as well. The opposition was able to underpin its demands with the results of the 1994 federal elections; the two government parties combined lost more than 12 per cent and, consequently, their previous two-thirds majority in Parliament. This enabled the opposition to press for strong controlling rights for the Austrian parliament in EU issues. Post-war consociational patterns of governance came under strain, driving the system towards greater competition and confrontation.[19] Some parts of the governing Austrian political elites expected EU membership to be a catalyst for structural reform. In order to increase their influence within the complex EU system, a more anticipatory policy-making style and swifter decision-making procedures had to be developed. The traditional, sometimes sluggish consultations among the 'social partnership' institutions – the Federal Chamber of Labour, the Austrian Federation of Trade Unions, the Presidential Conference of Chambers of Agriculture, the Austrian Chamber of Business, and interest groups – were seen not to enable the Austrian political system to deal efficiently with the complex multi-level system of the Union.

In order to adapt the domestic decision-making structures to EU membership, three major problems had to be tackled: how to co-ordinate the governmental policy-making process; how to involve the regions in it; and how to secure parliamentary scrutiny of government policy within the Union. However great the aims to modernise the Austrian corporatist system, the results have still to be seen as its continuity. The two coalition parties (SPÖ/ÖVP) decided on a system of formal equality. Today EU

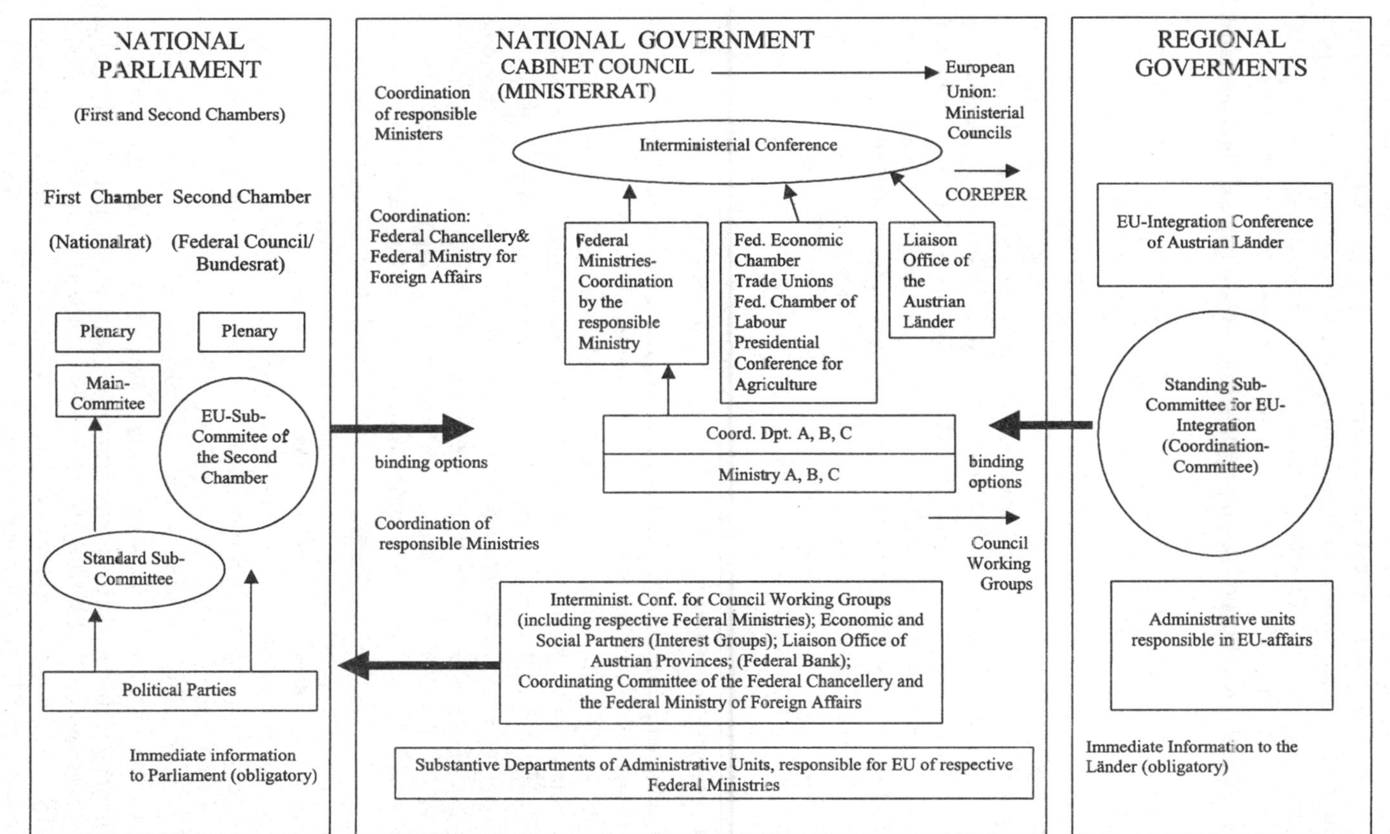

Figure 14.1 The national level of European decision-making – Austria

policy is co-ordinated by the Federal Chancellery and the Foreign Ministry, the former being dominated by the SPÖ, the latter by the ÖVP. From a legal point of view, co-ordination within the Austrian government is necessary only to the extent that a European issue compels several ministerial areas to take action in a particular question. This is mainly due to the differences in the distribution of competencies on the European level and in the Austrian bureaucracy. The political agreement to share the responsibilities and merits to a far greater extent than in the past was politically formalised in the coalition agreement of 1994 and a separate statute from 1996.[20]

The federal government

Once a week the government discusses the Austrian position for the next meetings of the Council of the European Union. Under a special item on the agenda the respective member of the government reports 'about the subjects which for implementation need a governmental decision by law in the form of an oral or written cabinet address before the meeting of the Council of the European Union where the decision is taken at the latest'.[21] The purpose of the cabinet address is the description of the subject as well as a justification of the Austrian position. The coalition agreement also demands a permanent information exchange between the ministries; owing to the potential role of the so-called Main Committee of the Parliament granted by constitutional law, the heads and directors of the parliamentary groups of the government parties were granted the right of participation and speech in the Austrian cabinet meetings.

The position of the permanent representative in COREPER I and II is co-ordinated in a weekly jour fixe where all ministries, the Austrian National Bank, the Austrian Statistical Office, the League of cities and municipalities, the Standing Committee of the Austrian Länder and the 'social partners' take part. As a general rule for common working groups a system of periodic change in the chair was fixed between the parties.

The federal government in agreement with the Main Committee of the Parliament nominates the candidates for the European Commission, the ECJ, the Court of First Instance, the EIB and the ECA. This procedure constitutes a constitutional novelty because for the first time the parliament (in form of the Main Committee) takes part in personnel decisions of the government. On the other hand the Austrian President was granted an information right only.

The presidential element of the Austrian constitution has – contrary to some expectations before accession – not been strengthened. After a short disagreement between the Austrian Chancellor Franz Vranitzky and the Austrian President Thomas Klestil on the occasion of the Corfu Summit in June 1994, regarding who should be appointed as the main representative at European Council meetings, the latter was limited to his constitutional role – i.e. without specific competences in European politics.[22]

The parliament

In comparison with other national parliaments the Austrian parliament is provided with strong constitutionally embodied participation rights in the field of EU policy.[23] Articles 23e and 23f were introduced in a constitutional amendment in December 1994 regulating the rights of information and opinion. Thus, Morass (1996) talks about a 'special constitutional democratic legitimation' by the parliament.[24] Today this assessment appears to require some revision. The government is obliged to inform the parliament (i.e. its Main Committee) about 'any initiatives' within the Union.[25] Parliamentary scrutiny not only includes legislative initiatives but also political ones and encompasses all three pillars. Positions by the Main Committee bind the government. An escape clause can be invoked by the government if there are 'compelling reasons of integration policy' (Article 23e §2B-VG). EU decisions which require constitutional changes necessarily require an advance agreement with the parliament. Whereas the Main Committee is supposed to deal with questions of a supranational nature (i.e. first pillar subjects), the Foreign Policy Committee of the Austrian Parliament is responsible for intergovernmental questions, such as the CFSP and possible changes in the Community Treaties. There is no direct co-ordination between the two committees but coherence can be reached through personal union or in the so-called Preparatory Committee, which tries to stem the information avalanches coming from the bureaucracy. These parties and the Klubreferenten (secretaries of the parliamentary groups) meet usually the day before the Main Committee comes together and pre-select the incoming information and draw up an agenda for the Main Committee which consists of representatives of all parties.

What in theory looks like a remedy for the lamented democratic deficit in EU-related domestic policy-making turns out to be of limited use in practice. Setting a tight scope for negotiations would impede the manoeuvrability of the acting minister and contradict the widespread practice of package deals in the European Union. On the other hand the parliament simply cannot cope with the enormous amount of information – which may serve a certain strategy of the bureaucracy to neutralise it.[26] In addition, the parliament depends on the reports of the participating agents and has no possibility of getting first-hand information owing to the complex, multi-level system of the Union. In 1995, the parliament was informed of 17,317 European projects. Though this number looks quite large, one must not forget that it comprises proposals of legislative acts, reports, opinions, invitations for meetings, agendas, requests for preliminary rulings, to name only a few. Around 70 per cent of the documents derive from the Council of the EU, 20 per cent from the European Commission, 7 per cent from the Permanent Representation of Austria in Brussels, 1 per cent from the ECJ, 1 per cent from the EP and 1 per cent from the ECA. Around one hundred became the subject of deliberation in the Main Committee, which finally issued eighteen opinions. Between 1996 and 1997, 37,624 projects were conveyed to the Main Committee. Of these, 106 were dealt with and eleven statements were made. Considering that the Main Committee comprises twenty-nine members, even a very selective approach can handle only a fraction of the important issues.

The Länder

From the outset the nine Austrian Länder realised their changing political role with regard to prospective EU membership. To secure their influence on the federal level they pressed for a structural reform of the federal system. The Landeshauptleute (state governors) made their approval for accession dependent on a successful reform of the federal system.[27] On 8 October 1992 a 'Political Agreement on the Reform of the Federal State' was signed between the Länder and the federal government which included a general commitment to a redistribution of competences in accordance with the principle of subsidiarity, a reform of the financial transfer system and the establishment of the Bundesrat as the representation of the Länder, similar to the German model. A joint commission was to develop concrete proposals, but no agreement has been reached thus far. The Landeshauptleute removed the linkage after the overwhelming result of the referendum on EU membership, in order to deflect responsibility had the referendum failed.

Concerning the Länder, the federal government has been constitutionally bound to inform them about all EU questions 'which affect their independent sphere of action or may otherwise be of interest to them'.[28] The Länder can issue a simple or qualified opinion from which the government can still deviate for important integration reasons, but it has to justify its decision within eight weeks. Additionally the federal government can transfer its participation in the EU Council of Ministers to a representative nominated by the Länder (Article 23d §3). Foreseeing their shrinking influence without close co-operation, the Länder founded the 'Integration Conference of the Länder,' comprising the Landeshauptleute and the Standing Committee of the Länder. In practice, the Standing Committee plays only a marginal role since it is not provided with sufficient resources to cope with the enormous information overflow. Reflecting the strategy of the EU Commission to bypass the federal governments, some of the Austrian Länder have opened Representation Offices in Brussels in order to improve their opportunities for lobbying.

The social partners and administrative agencies

To compensate the 'social partners' for their loss of influence in Austrian EU policy-making, the government parties in 1994 agreed on the so-called 'Europaabkommen' (Agreement on Europe) which guaranteed them participation in 'important' and 'relevant technical questions'. At first the federal government tried to secure their official involvement in the various working groups of the Council of Ministers. However, the equal participation in these groups failed because it would have been an infringement of EC law (Article 203 TEC) which states that only representatives of the government have the right of vote and speak.

The challenge for the Austrian administration has been twofold. The first concerns the implementation of the acquis communautaire in the Austrian legal system after accession to the EEA in 1994, and intensifying with full-scale membership in the Union. Siedentopf and Ziller (1988) pointed to the importance of early preparation for the successful implementation of EC law in the national legal systems. Since 1987 the Austrian federal government has taken care of adapting the domestic legal system to conform to EC law: a guideline was issued which demands a check of all government bills regarding this conformity. With the Austrian accession to the EEA, around 1,600 EU regulations were taken over. However, the 1996 report of the Commission on the implementation of EC law shows a total of 819 complaints against Austria which is an improvement of about 14 per cent compared with 1995 (1,145 cases).[29] Unfortunately, in the same period the Austrian share of non-implemented or poorly implemented directives rose by 15 per cent. Concerning the implementation of Internal Market directives, Austria occupied last position in 1996 and 1997. The reasons for this delay are manifold: the federal distribution of competences; the strict constitutional principle of legality, which demands a legal determination for any state actions; and the still strong tradition of 'social partnership'. Furthermore, the implementation of the acquis demanded far-reaching changes in Austrian economic administrative law. This occurred at the same time as a staff reduction in public administration was under way for budgetary reasons. In November 1997, 10 per cent of the directives were notified as not implemented. However, in May 1998, a big leap took Austria to the seventh position, and only 5 per cent remained unsettled.[30]

Concerning Austria's applications for preliminary rulings of the ECJ, a significant growth can be observed. In the first year of membership Austria requested two preliminary rulings. In 1996, this increased to six. In comparison to Sweden and Finland this is quite a standard development (Sweden: 1995, 6, 1996, 4; Finland: 1995, 0, 1996, 3).[31] However, in 1997, the Austrian cases rose to thirty-five whereas Sweden asked for four and Finland for six.[32] One possible explanation might be that the awareness of the Austrian judges concerning Community law is to some degree higher than that of the other new Member State judges.

The second challenge for the administration involves participation in the policy-making process at the European level. The highlight in terms of workload and publicity was the Austrian Presidency of the Council of the European Union in the second half of 1998, following the United Kingdom and preceding Germany. Since presidencies have significantly grown in importance in terms of co-ordinating European politics as well enhancing the visibility of the Union, the Austrian presidency was well prepared by the government administration. In order to cope with the everyday business of the presidency, the administration created co-operation structures between all ministries, installing a regular meeting of all high officials (Sektionsleiterkonferenz). The management of the presidency was, in short, a success story. The same appears to be true of the public spectacle during the various formal and informal summits. The 'Europeanisation' of the public administration during the Austrian Presidency of the Council was an invaluable asset.[33] However, as to the political achievements of the Presidency, a more sceptical judgement is appropriate. The two main goals could be summarised by the slogans proposed by the government: Austria aims at the role of an 'honest broker' in the policy process and it wants to achieve greater 'fitness' of the Union, particularly in view of the coming enlargement.

The list of projects ranging from the creation of jobs to the protection of the environment contained such a variety of important themes that one could hardly qualify them all as priorities for a six-month Presidency. Furthermore these topics represented quite an unequal choice, the introduction of the Euro being at that stage largely a technical issue, while the negotiations on the Agenda 2000 and the enlargement were objects of political controversy. During the opening ceremony, though, the Austrian Chancellor Viktor Klima and the Vice-Chancellor Wolfgang Schüssel placed the accent mainly on enlargement, while the Minister of finance Rudolf Edlinger pointed to tax harmonisation as being his priority.[34]

On a first assessment of the Austrian EU Presidency we may draw some initial conclusions. To begin with, many of the points listed in the above programme did not result in concrete policies or action owing to the underlying problems involved. The political and economic preconditions of some goals also made the success of some projects impossible – for instance, Agenda 2000, or the compromise of the Berlin Summit, which did not permit serious reform of the financial system to adapt to EU enlargement.

Disappointingly, the Austrian initiatives in the process of EU enlargement towards Central and Eastern Europe, as well towards Cyprus, did not lead to agreements about concrete time schedules. Beyond the Commission's screening the applicants' strategies for implementing the acquis communautaire and what has been achieved, enlargement policy appears to lack a strong political will by key players among the Member States. This is partly due to the self-imposed budget constraints as a result of the Treaty of Maastricht and the Stability Pact, and partly to the urgent, yet unanswered, need for institutional reforms. At the same time, the postponement of negotiations on Agenda 2000 to the German Presidency was closely linked to the question of enlargement. Interestingly, the Austrian 'Programme of the EU Presidency' vaguely touched upon this highly delicate issue when it referred to the Conclusions of the Summit in Cardiff (June 1998). It made a point that part of the problem was addressing equal distribution of financial contributions by Member States. However, the Austrian programme did not provide any solutions to this problem. Although any expectations of finding such indications in an official paper might be too high, one could speculate about the links between this omission and the lack of results at the Vienna Summit in December 1998. Whether this lack of concrete results corresponds with the traditional Austrian corporatist system of avoiding conflict remains an open question.

Conclusions: the persistence of ambivalence?

To assess the changes in the Austrian policy-making process induced by European integration is somewhat difficult owing to the relatively short period of EU membership. Like all institutional change, the adaptation of national institutions, rules, norms and forms of behaviour to the European reality occurs at a rather slow pace, and such changes are far from easy to measure. Assessments which might hold true for some institutions cannot be simply applied to others; in order to corroborate any judgements on the changes occurring in the Austrian institutional arrangements, more in-depth studies on different dimensions of the transformation process are needed.

The easiest part of the task of describing the changes Austria has undergone since the beginning of EU membership in 1995 concerns constitutional amendments. Owing to the specific power constellation after the national election of 1994, in which the governing parties lost their two-thirds majority, the opposition parties won the game in the negotiations on the role of the parliament in the EU policy-making process. However, what appeared to be a victory of the legislature over the executive quite quickly turned sour for two reasons. First, the Main Committee of the Parliament was overwhelmed by the sheer quantity of EU proposals it had to deal with. Secondly, the 'power of tradition' saw members of the ruling parties in parliament uphold government positions. Thus, for the time being the Austrian situation reflects the developments that have occurred in most of the Member States: European policy-making is the privilege of the executive.

Regarding more general changes in the decision-making process, including the whole set of intermediary powers, assessment necessarily remains more speculative. As has been stated above, the system of 'social partnership' that has been the main pillar of Austrian consociational democracy has been put under considerable pressure. It is, however, important to note that owing to international competition, at least part of this strain had already surfaced in the mid-1980s. Changes in the Austrian political and economic elites *vis-à-vis* EU membership may also be interpreted as a strategy to cope with more general developments on global markets. Moreover, the shifts in economic ideology within the SPÖ towards greater liberalism as well as the change in leadership from Bruno Kreisky to Franz Vranitzky in 1986,[35] who downplayed the international role of neutral Austria, have to be considered. However, changes in the 'social partnership' require some distinctions. While it is safe to assess that the system of consensus-building between capital and labour has lost much of its attraction, EU membership has provoked interesting shifts of power within the institutional arrangement of the 'social partners'. Those representing large industries, which had emerged through privatisation, grew in importance at the expense of those lobbying for SMEs. With regard to those representing labour interests, it can be said that the traditionally powerful Austrian union (Österreichischer Gewerkschaftsbund) has been stripped of power, in particular when negotiating the 1996 and 1997–98 budgets, in order to satisfy the convergence criteria of the Maastricht Treaty. For the first time in the history of the Second Republic, labour representation was not involved from the outset, but only after they had expressed considerable protest against the new procedures. Yet extrapolating from this experience, a more general assumption about the end of Austrian corporatism might turn out to be an exaggeration.

The most impressive change in Austrian institutions appears to relate to the party system. Yet, here again a cautionary tale has to be told in that the erosion of the two-party system owing to the growth of a strong third force (the FPÖ) and to the emergence of two smaller ones (the Greens and LIF), is only partly linked to the 'Europeanisation' of the Austrian policy-making process. The persistent growth of the 'New' Radical Right, the FPÖ, in the 1990s, must be assessed in terms of its anti-European stance. During this period, it increased its percentage of votes, from 5–6 per cent to approximately 25 per cent at the federal level, and to a sensational 42 per cent in a provincial election in 1999. The success story of the FPÖ is also owing to the fact that the enthusiasm professed by Austrian citizens in the referendum on EU membership in 1994 rather quickly declined in the wake of the restrictive budget policy compelled by the construction of EMU. The main parties ruling the state in a 'grand coalition' failed to control their electorate by neglecting the need for a truly public European discourse. As a matter of fact, after they had won the referendum,

'Europe' disappeared from their communications with the public and returned only during their EU Presidency in the second half of 1998. In terms of public debate, the Presidency was dominated by superficial elements rather than communicating the actual nature of the supranational polity to the public.

However, the Presidency produced important results with regard to the 'Europeanisation' of the Austrian administration. The Presidency was professionally organised and involved significantly larger parts of the bureaucracy than had previously been the case. As one high official of the Ministry of Foreign Affairs explained in a conference in March 1999 on the outcomes, in that six-month period, the Austrian actors did not 'make the Union fitter for the future' – as was stated by a poster slogan of the government – but the intensive involvement in European affairs made the Austrian bureaucracy 'fit for the Union'.[36] The proficiency of the administration was nonetheless achieved at the expense of clear political strategies with regard to the important questions challenging the Union at the time, such as Agenda 2000 or institutional reform.

Moreover, the Austrian EU Presidency was marked by an ambivalent attitude towards EU enlargement in that a special commitment was pronounced in public and seemingly countervailed in action. The ambivalence is also the result of the growing Radical Right in Austria which fiercely opposes EU enlargement. Less visible, though not less important, are the changes in the Austrian judiciary in implementing a European legal order superseding the national order. The studies available in this field show that some of the greatest implementation difficulties may pertain to any legal reform. However, other difficulties appear to be specific to the 'Europeanisation' of judicial activity. In particular, resistance to or neglect of European laws is repeatedly argued on the basis that these laws contradict the principle of legality dominating the Austrian system. Thus, experts in EC law warn against the increasing lack of legal certainty. Here again, further in-depth studies are needed in order to assess the quantity and quality of non-compliance.

With regard to the changes Austria has undergone since the beginning of its EU membership, one final remark must be made about the EP elections in June 1999. The results underlined Austrian ambivalence toward the Union. Turnout was perilously low (49 per cent) when compared to national elections, despite corresponding to the EU average. Interestingly, the very visible and controversial election campaign did not lead to a greater interest of the public in EU institutions: in a survey, 20 per cent of non-voters mentioned the insignificance of the EP. However, most of the competing parties considered the election as a rehearsal for the national election in October 1999, and failed to define their themes in 'European' terms. In view of the war in Yugoslavia, neutrality largely dominated the campaign, both positively as well as negatively. While the SPÖ and the

Greens argued in favour of neutrality, the People's Party, the FPÖ and the Liberals denied the importance of the subject in a European election. However, one significant change occurred in this debate, at least in terms of rhetoric. The discourse on NATO membership, pursued by the three latter parties, shifted to a call for an independent European security system without NATO. Interestingly, EU enlargement did not play a great role, not even in the positions of the Radical Right, which in fact lost 4 per cent compared to the previous European election of 1996.

By way of conclusion, a clear-cut judgement on the form and degree of the transformation of the Austrian political and economic system as a result of European integration is far from possible. As to the question of whether the political system has been transformed from a consociational to competitive democracy, two answers may be proposed: the first pointing to the fact that at least part of this transformation occurred before EU membership; the rise of the FPÖ can also be interpreted as a reverberation of a more general European development of the Radical Right. The second answer is driven by a more sceptical view of the sustainability of this change. The same holds true for the attitude towards European integration: while on a macro-level the commitment to the European Union is still impressive, the micro-level adaptation to the new order is difficult to measure. The 'power of tradition' continues to influence the mentality and behaviour not only of ordinary people but also of the elites in politics, economy, the judiciary and the scientific community. It may well take another five years in order to tell whether the elites have been able to become the gravitational centre of a sustainable process of transformation.

Notes

1 See Michael Gehler and Wolfram Kaiser, 'A Study in Ambivalence. Austria and the European Integration 1945–95', in: *Contemporary European History*, No. 1/1997, pp. 75–99; Michael Gehler and Rolf Steininger (eds), *Österreich und die europäische Integration 1945–1993. Aspekte einer wechselvollen Entwicklung* (Vienna, Cologne, Weimar: Böhlau, 1993); Heinrich Schneider, *Alleingang nach Brüssel. Österreichs EG-Politik* (Bonn: Europa Union Verlag, 1990).

2 The literature about social partnership is numerous, see, for example, Peter Gerlich, 'A Farewell to Corporatism', in: Kurt R. Luther and Wolfgang Müller (eds), *Politics in Austria: Still a Case of Consociationalism?* (London: Cass, 1992), pp. 132–146; Emmerich Tálos, 'Corporatism – The Austrian Model', in: Volkmar Lauber (ed.), *Contemporary Austrian Politics* (Boulder, Co.: Westview Press, 1996), pp. 103–123; Günter Bischof and Anton Pelinka, Austro-Corporatism. Past, Present, Future, *Contemporary Austrian Studies*, Vol. 4 (New Brunswick, London: Transaction Books, 1996).

3 See the contributions of Felix Kreissler, *Der Österreicher und seine Nation.*

Ein Lernprozeß mit Hindernissen (Vienna: Böhlau, 1984); and Ernst Bruckmüller, *Österreichbewußtsein im Wandel. Identität und Selbstverständnis im Wandel* (Vienna: Signum, 1994).

4 See Hans Mayrzedt and Waldemar Hummer (eds), *20 Jahre österreichische Neutralitäts- und Europapolitik (1955–1975)* (Vienna: Braumüller, 1976).

5 Apart from Austria these countries comprised Great Britain, Sweden, Norway, Denmark, Switzerland and Portugal.

6 This demand was supported by an expert judgement on the compatibility of Austrian neutrality with EC membership. See Waldemar Hummer and Michael Schweitzer, *Österreich und die EWG. Neutralitätsrechtliche Beurteilung der Möglichkeit der Dynamisierung des Verhältnisses zur EWG* (Vienna: Signum, 1987).

7 See Rolf Kaiser, *Basic Institutional Options for National EU Coordination* (SIGMA-Arbeitspapier) (Vienna, 1995); Christian Schaller, 'Zur Diskussion um den österreichischen EU-Beitritt', in: Emmerich Tálos and Gerda Falkner (eds), *EU-Mitglied Österreich. Gegenwart und Perpektiven: Eine Zwischenbilanz* (Vienna: Manz, 1996), pp. 17–32.

8 Note that Austria's preparations for accession had already started before democratic resolutions in Eastern Europe and before the USSR changed its foreign policy behaviour – see Jeffrey Lantis and Matthew F. Queen, 'Negotiating Neutrality: The Double-Edged Diplomacy of Austrian Accession to the European Union', in: *Cooperation and Conflict*, No. 2/1998, pp. 152–182.

9 See Helmut Kramer, 'Austrian Foreign Policy from the State Treaty to European Union Membership', in: Kurt R. Luther and Peter Pulzer (eds), *Austria 1945–1995* (Dartmouth: Aldershot, 1996) pp. 161–180 (here p. 173).

10 See Peter Jankowitsch, 'The Process of European Integration and Neutral Austria', in: Sheila Harden (ed.), *Neutral States and the European Community* (London: Brassey's, 1994), pp. 35–62 (here p. 57).

11 EU membership was generally considered to fundamentally affect various central constitutional principles, such as the democratic and federal principles, amounting to a so-called Gesamtänderung (total revision) of the Constitution, that according to Article 44 requires a referendum in addition to a two-thirds majority in Parliament.

12 The FPÖ since 1991–92 changed from a strong pro-accession party to an opposing stance. The Greens were also against membership.

13 On negotiations see Francisco Granell, 'The European Union's Enlargement Negotiations with Austria, Finland, Norway and Sweden', in: *Journal of Common Market Studies*, No. 1/1995, pp. 117–141.

14 The FPÖ changed its position towards the European integration only in 1991–92. It has previously been an ardent supporter of the integration process. Among other reasons the sudden change of Jörg Haider led to the formation of the splinter group of the Liberal Forum (LIF) in February 1993.

15 See Wolfram Kaiser, 'Die EU-Volksabstimmungen in Österreich, Finnland, Schweden und Norwegen: Folgen für die Europäische Union', in: *Integration*, No. 2/1995, pp. 76–87.

16 For an exact picture of voting behaviour see the disaggregated figures in:

Anton Pelinka, *Austria. Out of the Shadow of the Past* (Boulder, Co.: Westview Press, 1998), p. 67.

17 See Heinrich Neisser, 'Parlamentsreform und Europäische Union', in: Peter Gerlich and Heinrich Neisser (eds), *Europa als Herausforderung. Wandlungsimpulse für das politische System Österreichs* (Vienna: Signum, 1994), pp. 43–69.

18 Between 1945 and 1995, the two parties combined always managed to attract between 94.4 and 66.4 per cent of the votes. The dominance of these two parties is strongly linked to the high level of organisation in the party system (in the 1970s around 30 per cent of the population were party members). However, in the 1980s, new political mobility and the subsequent erosion of the party state system significantly altered this arrangement.

19 See Pelinka, (1998) *op. cit.*, p. 71.

20 See the Circular of the Federal Chancellery and the Ministry of Foreign Affairs, 19 January 1996, Part I.

21 See Statute of the Austrian Government (Vienna, 1996).

22 However, it is only because the constitution is quite imprecise in that respect that this quarrel emerged.

23 See Michael Morass, 'Österreich im Entscheidungsprozess der Europäischen Union', in: Emmerich Tálos and Gerda Falkner (eds), *EU-Mitglied Österreich. Gegenwart und Perspektiven: Eine Zwischenbilanz* (Wien: Manz, 1996), pp. 32–49, esp. p. 39. The Austrian model to involve the parliament in EU politics is discussed in Torbjörn Bergmann, 'National Parliaments and EU Affairs Committees. Notes on Empirical Variation and Competing Explanations', in: *Journal of European Public Policy*, No. 4/1997, pp. 373–387; Stefan Griller, 'Zur demokratischen Legitimation der Rechtsetzung in der EU', in: *Journal für Rechtspolitik*, No. 3/1995, pp. 164–179.

24 See Morass, 1996, *op. cit.* p. 39.

25 With the reform of the standing order of the National Council 1996 a special European Committee (being itself a sub-committee of the Main Committee) was founded.

26 See Gerda Falkner and Wolfgang C. Müller (eds), *Österreich im europäischen Mehrebenensystem. Konsequenzen der EU-Mitgliedschaft für Politiknetzwerke und Entscheidungsprozesse* (Wien: Signum, 1998).

27 The Länder asked for more participation in the EU policy process, and a general strengthening of the executive. The federal government made far-reaching suggestions ranging from fiscal sovereignty in certain areas for the Länder, the strengthening of the regional parliaments (Landtage) and even the setting up of Constitutional Courts in the Länder. The Länder rejected all suggestions. See Peter Pernthaler and Gert Schernthanner, 'Bundesstaatsreform 1994', in: *Österreichisches Jahrbuch für Politik* 1994 (Wien, Oldenburg: Verlag für Geschichte und Politik, 1995), pp. 559–595.

28 See Article 23d B-VG.

29 See Communication of the European Commission, COM [97] 299Final, II.A.

30 See Press communiqué of the European Commission, 18 May 1998.

31 See *General Report of the European Commission on the Activities of the European Union* (Luxembourg, 1996, 1997, 1998).

32 See *General Report of the European Commission on the Activities of the*

European Union 1996, p. 513; 1997, p. 481; 1998, p. 431.

33 This fact was constantly stressed by senior officials of the Austrian administration during a conference hosted jointly by the Research Unit for Institutional Change and European Integration of the Austrian Academy of Sciences and the Austrian Institute for International Affairs on 'The Austrian Presidency of the European Union: Assessment and Perspectives', Vienna 19–20 March 1999. Conference report forthcoming, available at www.iwe.oeaw.ac.at.

34 See 'Austria Plans Push for Tax Harmonisation', in: *Financial Times*, 2 July 1998, p. 1.

35 Although the period of the so-called 'small coalition' of SPÖ and FPÖ under Chancellor Fred Sinowatz has been relevant for certain domestic reasons, it may be dropped from our considerations in this text.

36 See Stefan Lehne in his speech at the Conference 'Austria's EU-Presidency. Assessments and Perspectives', Austrian Academy of Sciences, 19–20 March 1999.

Select bibliography

The text (English translation) of the Constitution of Austria can be found at the University of Richmond's constitution finder at http://confinder.richmond.edu/. Further sources on government and parliament of Austria can be found at Government www.austria.gv.at or at Parliament www.parlinkom.gv.at.

Bischof, Günter and Pelinka, Anton (eds) (1996) 'Austro-Corporatism. Past, Present, Future', in: *Contemporary Austrian Studies*, Vol. 4 (New Brunswick, London: Transaction Books).

Falkner, Gerda and Müller, Wolfgang C. (eds) (1998) *Österreich im europäischen Mehrebenensystem. Konsequenzen der EU-Mitgliedschaft für Politiknetzwerke und Entscheidungsprozesse* (Wien: Signum).

Holzinger, Gerhart (1997) 'Umsetzung und Anwendung des Gemeinschaftsrechts in Österreich', in: Siegfried Magiera and Heinrich Siedentopf (eds), *Die Zukunft der Europäischen Union* (Berlin: Duncker & Humblot), pp. 87–104.

Kaiser, Wolfram (1995) 'Austria in the European Union', in: *Journal of Common Market Studies*, No. 3/1995, pp. 411–425.

Lantis, Jeffrey S. and Queen, Matthew F. (1998) 'Negotiating Neutrality: The Double-Edged Diplomacy of Austrian Accession to the European Union', in: *Cooperation and Conflict*, No. 2/1998, pp. 152–182.

Neisser, Heinrich (1998) 'Die Mitwirkungsbefugnisse des Nationalrates im Entscheidungsprozeß der Europäischen Union', in: Heinz Schäffer *et al.* (eds), *Staat – Verfassung – Verwaltung*. Festschrift für Friedrich Koja (Vienna, New York: Springer), pp. 335–355.

Pelinka, Anton (1998) *Austria. Out of the Shadow of the Past* (Boulder, Co.: Westview Press).

Potacs, Michael and Pollak, Christian (1996) 'Österreichischer Landesbericht', in: Jürgen Schwarze (ed.), *Das Verwaltungsrecht unter europäischem Einfluss* (Baden-Baden: Nomos), pp. 733–785.

Puntscher-Riekmann, Sonja (1999) 'The Politics of Ausgrenzung, The Nazi-Past and the European Dimension of the New Radical Right in Austria', in: Günter Bischof, Anton Pelinka and Ferdinand Karlhofer (eds), *The Vranitzky Era in Austria* (New Brunswick, London: Transaction Books), pp. 78–105.

Tálos, Emmerich and Falkner, Gerda (eds), *EU-Mitglied Österreich. Gegenwart und Perspektiven: Eine Zwischenbilanz* (Wien: Manz).

Siedentopf, Heinrich and Ziller, Jacques (1988) *L'Europe des Administrations? La mise en oeuvre de la législation communautaire dans les Etats Membres* (Brussels: Bruylant).

Wieser, Thomas and Kitzmantel Edith (1990) 'Austria and the European Community', in: *Journal of Common Market Studies*, No. 4/1990, pp. 431–449.

15 *Maria João Seabra*

Portugal: one way to Europeanisation

Introduction: from enthusiasm via Euro-pessimism towards active support

Portugal joined the European Communities in 1986, following a process of negotiations that had lasted eight years. The request for membership was made in March 1977, at a time when the country was still deeply engaged in the process of democratic transition. Internally, the European option was considered to be decisive to the consolidation of democracy. Shortly after the 25 April 1977 coup d'état, the democratic parties, and especially the socialist party (Partido Socialista, PS), began to use the slogan 'Europe is with us', which played a major role in the consolidation of Portuguese democracy.

This political option was clearly supported by the Portuguese people. Although pro-European parties had always won, there was also strong support in opinion polls at both the national and the European level. Until 1992, it can be said that the Portuguese were much more 'European' than the government. From 1986 to 1992, the Portuguese government chose a low-profile European policy. Deeply concerned with the economic impact of integration and with the negotiations of the Structural Funds (Delors Packages I and II), the government had a very cautious position towards the development of political union. This is clearly demonstrated by the positions adopted at the 1991 IGC. While favouring the single currency and economic and social cohesion, the Portuguese government opposed the inclusion of any kind of federal commitment and was not very supportive to the establishment of a CFSP, especially its security and defence dimensions. At that time, however, opinion polls showed that the Portuguese were ready to support these developments.

Until 1992, all three major political parties were strongly pro-European, and the Communist Party was the only one to support anti-European positions. This situation changed with a new leadership in the small Christian-Democratic party (Centro Democrático Social and the

Partido Popular, CDS–PP) In the general elections of 1991, it was the fourth party with 4.4 per cent of the vote.[1] From a traditionally federalist approach, the party moved to an anti-European position. During the debate on the ratification of the TEU, the CDS–PP advocated a referendum[2] and developed a nationalistic rhetoric on the loss of Portuguese sovereignty. This new position created the conditions for a wider debate on European affairs in Portugal but has also contributed, together with the 1992–93 economic crisis, to a certain decrease of public support for the European integration process. This bout of 'Euro-pessimism' is now in the past, largely owing to the economic and social development the country has experienced since, and participation in the single currency. The majority of the Portuguese interest groups support the European integration process. Although concerned with the impact of the single market and of common trade policy on Portuguese economy, which has led to demands of increased transitional periods and derogations, the major agriculture and industry organisations did not develop an anti-European attitude. Trade union associations have adopted different positions. The Workers General Union (União Geral de Trabalhadores, UGT) has traditionally been more supportive of the European Union than the Portuguese Workers' Confederation (Confederação Geral dos Trabalhadores, CGTP).

Constitutional changes

The participation in European integration has forced several changes in the Portuguese Constitution.[3] Drafted in the aftermath of the revolution, the 1976 text was the result of the political and economic upheavals that characterised the Portuguese transition and that were incompatible with full membership of the European Communities. The first revision took place in 1982 and settled the role of the armed forces in the political system: the Council of Revolution, a military-run institution that monitored the constitutionality of laws, was abolished and replaced by the Constitutional Court. Although this is not directly connected with the perspective of EC accession, full membership would obviously not have been possible without the constitutional regulation of political–military relations. At the same time, the first revision paved the way for the future accession to the Union. Although a general clause providing for the possibility of transferring sovereign rights was not included, the amended constitutional text did provide a framework in which Community regulations could be adopted with no further change.

The second revision was concluded in 1989 and concentrated mainly in the economic aspects of the constitution. The 1976 text stated that the process of nationalisation was irreversible which was incompatible with the participation in the European process.[4] The 1992 reform was a direct consequence of the TEU. In spite of the general framework agreed in

1982, the major pro-European parties came to the conclusion that the constitutional text should be revised prior to ratification of the TEU, and the Portuguese Parliament therefore decided to amend the constitution. Four major amendments were made: the inclusion of a new norm allowing the joint exercise of powers within the Union;[5] the right of citizens of EU member countries to vote and to be elected to the EP; the re-definition of the role of the Portuguese Central Bank; and the reinforcement of the role of the parliament in reviewing Portugal's participation in European integration. The third revision was clearly an up-date of the Portuguese Constitution according to the developments at the European level. The amendments, however, did not create any kind of automatic mechanism to transfer powers to the Union.

The latest revision of the Constitution, which took place in 1997, was related to strictly internal questions. As far as the Union is concerned, an amendment was made on the role of the Central Bank, in order to allow for participation in the single currency.[6] Another amendment concerns the referendum. Following the signature of the TEU, the question was raised of whether a referendum, upon ratification, should be called. Prominent in the public debate in Portugal,[7] this issue re-emerged as a part of the political agenda of the 1995 general elections. Both the Partido Socialista and the social democratic party (Partido Social-Democrata, PSD) promised to hold a referendum on the ratification of the new treaty that would emerge from the 1996 IGC. With the agreement between these two parties, the Constitution was changed again in 1997. The articles on the referendum state that issues of relevant national interest, which must be the subject of international agreement, can be subject to a referendum. Although strictly speaking this is not a change wrought by participation in the Union, it is a consequence of the uneasiness that followed the debate on Maastricht and of the subsequent adaptation of the Portuguese political system. It reflects the need to overcome the 'permissive consensus' and to establish mechanisms to increase the perceived legitimacy of Portugal's participation in the Union. The process to hold a referendum on the Amsterdam Treaty took place in 1998 but the Constitutional Court ruled that the question was unconstitutional, and so the referendum actually did not take place. The Amsterdam Treaty was ratified by parliament in January 1999.

The evolution of Portuguese political priorities

Since 1986, the Portuguese political priorities with regard to EU policy-making has somewhat evolved owing to both domestic and European reasons. Since accession, the Portuguese government concentrated its efforts on regional development policies and the management of Structural Funds. Fisheries policy also received a high level of attention, since this sector was one of the most affected by integration. Externally, the Portuguese priorities were directed towards Africa and Latin America.[8] The new policies introduced by the TEU forced the government to adjust its own priorities: EMU and the participation in the single currency turned into one of the top Portuguese priorities.

The domestic political changes also affected the ranking of priorities. The socialist party won the 1995 general elections.[9] Despite the fact that both the socialists and the social democrats have always shared the same views on the Portuguese participation in the European process, the new socialist government introduced some changes to Portugal's European policy. The commitment to participating in the single currency from the outset was maintained by the new government, as well as the emphasis on social and economic cohesion. The main change occurred in the political dimension of the Union. The programme of the PS government emphasised the need to reinforce this. The socialist government's positions during the 1996–97 IGC,[10] on the CFSP and on integrating the WEU into the Union, differs from the previous government. Another difference is the importance attached to the EP, namely through support to the extension of the co-decision procedure. Co-operation on JHA is another priority of the present government, especially on such issues as drug trafficking, organised crime, terrorism and illegal migrants.

In 1999, the negotiations on the financial framework were at the top of the government's priorities and economic and social cohesion continued to be a key element of its European policy. Another delicate issue is the institutional reform of the Union. Although open to reform, the Portuguese government is unwilling to accept drastic changes in the present pattern of power-sharing. The current debate on voting weight, double majority, the composition of the Commission, the number of the MEPs and the rotation of the presidencies is seen as posing a direct threat to one of the basic principles of the European process: equality among states. The socialist government abandoned the traditional Portuguese attitude in the Union. From a very reactive and passive presence, the new government adopted a more active and constructive participation, trying to be present in the discussions of all the dossiers, which enlarged the scope of the Portuguese political action in the Union.

The national policy-cycle: centralisation and Europeanisation

The Ministry for Foreign Affairs has a major role in dealing with EU issues (Figure 15.1). Within the ministry, the Secretariat of State for European Affairs (SSEA), which until 1994 was named Secretariat of State for Community Affairs, deals with all EC/EU matters with the exception of the CFSP. Bilateral relations with European countries, including fellow EU Member States, also fall outside the scope of the SSEA. The change in name reflects the changing nature of the issues being dealt with at the

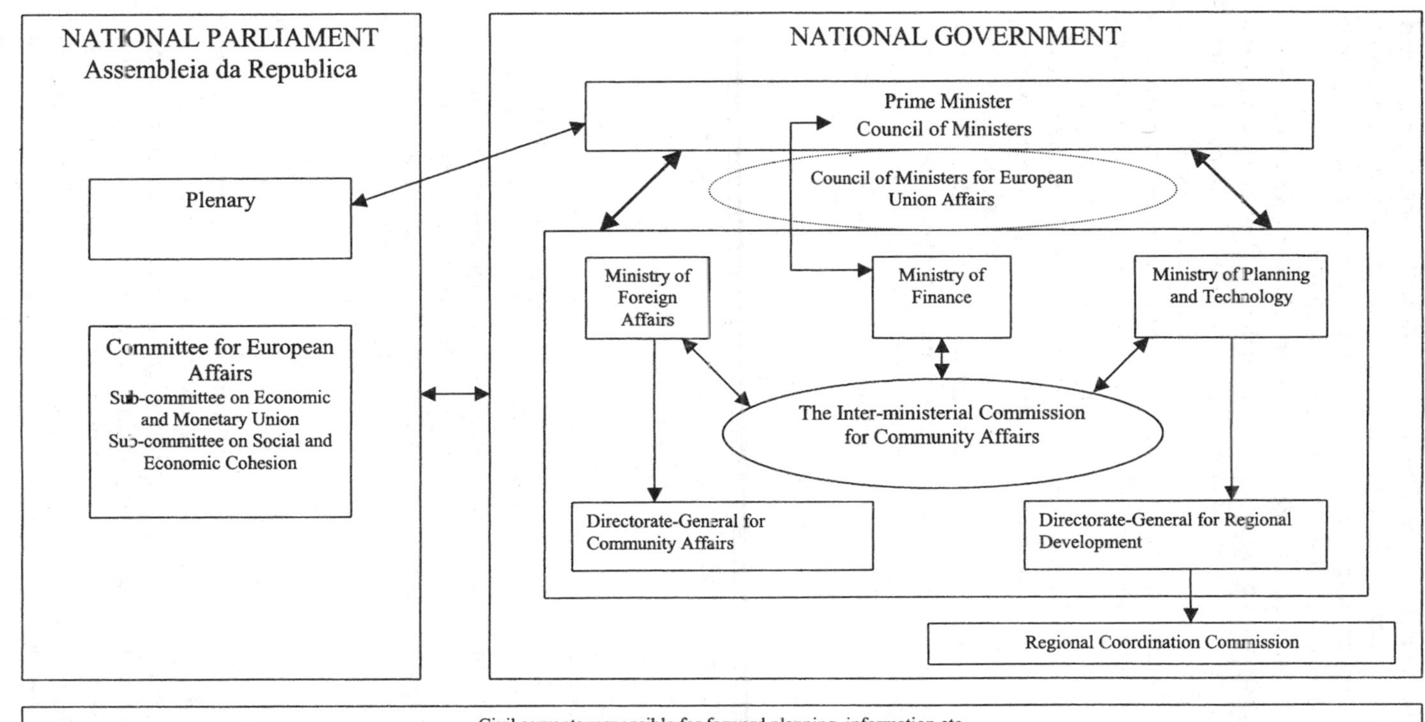

Figure 15.1 The national level of European decision-making – Portugal

European level. The Secretary of State is responsible for the Directorate-General for Community Affairs, the Interministerial Commission for Community Affairs and for the National Co-Ordinator for Free Movement of People in the European Space.

The Directorate-General for Community Affairs co-ordinates the actions on Community matters.[11] It includes ten units (direcção de serviços). The unit on Community institutions supports the participation of the members of the government in the European Council, General Affairs Council and other ministerial-level meetings, overviews the activity of the EP and of the ECOC and follows the issues related to the Union's decision-making process. The juridical unit monitors the legislative adaptation and co-ordinates the cases in the ECJ. The economic and financial unit is responsible for the follow-up of the application of all policies related to social and economic cohesion. The unit of agriculture and fisheries deals with the CAP and the fisheries policy. The unit on the Internal Market, deals with the issues of the free movement of people, goods, services and capital. The unit on foreign relations deals with the relations between the Union and third countries and organisations. The unit on intra-European relations is responsible for the relations of the Community with European non-Member States, including the EEA. The unit on bilateral relations is responsible for co-ordinating relations with Member States on Community issues. The other two units deal with scientific, technological and industrial issues and with documentation, information and training, including the adaptation of the Portuguese administration to the requirements of the European Communities.

The co-ordination between all the ministries is made by the Interministerial Commission for Community Affairs, which also includes representatives from the two autonomous regions, Azores and Madeira, and from the Prime Minister's office. The post of National Co-ordinator for Free Movement of People in the European Space was created in 1996 and is a direct consequence of the TEU and the Schengen Agreement. Until 1996, K4 committee affairs and co-ordination on Schengen were handled by two separate entities. To guarantee coherence and efficiency, the government decided to set up this institutional body, which functions in the Ministry for Foreign Affairs, in co-ordination with the corresponding departments of the Justice and Home Affairs Ministries. The creation of the CFSP also produced some changes in the structure of the Ministry of Foreign Affairs.[12] The 1994 administrative reform of the ministry created the unit of Common Foreign and Security Policy which 'inherited' the European Correspondent Service. According to their own competencies, all the other ministries are involved in EC/EU matters. Apart from the Ministry of Finance, that deals with all the ECOFIN issues and is one of the most directly involved in European affairs, another important ministry is the Ministry of Planning and Territorial Administration. This ministry is responsible for planning and carrying out actions related to EU Structural Funds and initiatives. The Directorate-General for Regional Development shares the Commission of Management of the Structural Funds and is the interlocutor of the Cohesion Fund and the ERDF. The Ministry of Labour and Solidarity handles the ESF and all Community initiatives related to job creation and training in co-operation with the Ministry for Education.

With the TEU, the Ministries of Justice and the Ministry of Home Affairs were forced to adjust to the third pillar. Even if third pillar and Schengen affairs are mostly dealt with by the national co-ordinator for free movement, the services functioning under these ministries, including the police, the courts and the migration and border control services (Serviço de estrangeiros e fronteiras) are now much more involved in the preparation and implementation of EU legislation. The development of JHA co-operation also generated a need to have counsellors at the Portuguese Permanent Representation in Brussels.

To co-ordinate the action of all the ministries and establish the priorities of Portuguese European policy, the government created special cabinet meetings known as the Council of Ministers for European Union Affairs. The council meets once a month, and is attended by all cabinet ministers, the Secretary of State for European Affairs and the representatives of the central government (Ministro da República) in Madeira and the Azores. This is the highest co-ordinating body of the Portuguese system, and it concentrates mainly on the definition of the strategic goals of the Portuguese government.

The relations between Portugal and the European institutions

Since accession, the Portuguese authorities have chosen the Commission as the most important ally in the Union. A small, peripheral country, much less developed than most of the other Member States, Portugal has always tried to gain Commission support. As far as the EP is concerned, there are no special relations. Furthermore, at the time of the 1991 IGC, Portugal still opposed increasing the EP's powers. Only in 1996 did that position change, with the support of the extension of the co-decision procedure. The attention paid to the EP, however, is likely to grow. This is owing to its increasing powers after the coming into force of the Amsterdam Treaty, but also because of the election of Mário Soares, the former Portuguese President, the leading candidate of the socialist party in the June 1999 European elections. The choice of Soares to lead the socialist team reflected the will to upgrade the political importance of the EP.

At this point, the Portuguese political parties attach much more importance to the European parties than the government does to the EP. One interesting example is the change in the Portuguese social democratic party's political group. Originally, it had joined the Liberal Group but it moved to the European People's Party in 1996.[13] This choice was justified by the affinity in European policy and also by the fact that the European People's Party (EPP) is much stronger than the ELDR (European Liberal, Democrat and Reform Party).

Parliamentary control

The TEU includes a declaration on the improvement of the participation of national parliaments in EU activities. In order to keep with that declaration, the 1992 constitutional revision included a new paragraph stating that parliament has the competence to monitor and to evaluate the participation of Portugal in the process of European integration.[14] Concomitantly, the government is required to submit to the Assembly of the Republic, at appropriate times, information concerning the integration process. Finally, in 1997 a new article was added according to which parliament is required to give its opinion, as provided by law, on matters that are pending decision within the organs of the Union that have a bearing on their exclusive legislative powers.[15]

Law No. 20/94 states that parliament will review and evaluate Portugal's participation in the process of construction of the Union, through a regular process of exchange of information and consultation between parliament and government. Each year, the government will present a report to parliament, which will enable it to review Portuguese participation in the process of the construction of the Union. That report must provide information concerning the resolutions adopted in the previous year by European institutions having an impact on Portugal and the measures put into practice by the government as a result of those resolutions. A parliamentary debate with the government occurs during each six-month presidency of the European Council.

The Parliamentary Committee for European Affairs is mandated to review and globally evaluate EU matters. The committee evaluates all the subjects of interest to Portugal within the framework of the European institutions. It encourages greater participation by parliament in the activities undertaken by the European institutions, and stimulates exchanges between the national Parliament and the EP. The committee proposes reciprocity, as appropriate, and regular meetings with interested members of the EP, in particular those elected in Portugal. The committee also appoints the Portuguese representatives to COSAC from the national Parliament, and assesses COSAC's activities and findings.

Within this new legal framework, the Parliamentary Committee for European Affairs has increased its activities. Two sub-committees, one on EMU and another on Economic and Social Cohesion, have been created, and the dialogue with the government has been improved. The Foreign Minister meets with the committee after each European Council, and the

Secretary of State for European Affairs holds a similar meeting with the committee after each General Affairs Council. The finance minister and the minister for planning also hold frequent discussions with the committee, especially to discuss budgetary issues and the management of structural funds. These meetings are not a legal requirement, and the reason behind them is twofold. First, there is an awareness of the need to involve the parliament more deeply, and secondly, the government requires the support of the other parliamentary caucuses; it must therefore, increase work with the Parliament. This situation was particularly important for the approval of the budget, in order to comply with the convergence programme and fulfil the criteria for participating in the single currency.

Despite these improvements, the Portuguese Parliament still lags behind in terms of having an effective control over EU issues. The effectiveness of its role is still too dependent on the willingness of the government to co-operate. It has the power to sanction government action within the Union, but not to keep the government from taking political decisions or, conversely, to recommend particular action to be taken. Furthermore, even if it is duly informed on the Union's legislative proposals it does not have the power to oblige the government to follow parliamentary positions.

The role of other actors

The Portuguese political system does not leave much room for effective participation in EC/EU affairs of institutions other than the central government. The government and the central administration are clearly the main actors. The action of political parties is felt mainly through Parliament. It has become the practice that the prime minister receives the leaders of the parliamentary political parties before each European Council. The two autonomous regions of Madeira and the Azores have their own political and administrative statutes and their own institutions of self-government. These regions have the ability to programme and manage the Structural Funds, which in the mainland is an exclusive competence of the central government. This is the reason why their representatives attend the meetings of the Interministerial Commission for Community Affairs. Contrary to what happens with regions of other EU Member States, neither the Azores nor Madeira has set up offices in Brussels.

The administrative structure of mainland Portugal is highly centralised. The government tried to pass legislation to create administrative regions in the country, which could have some political powers and certainly influence in the policy-cycle. A referendum was held in October 1998 and the majority voted against this regionalisation process.[16] The Union was an argument used during the campaign of the referendum; the political parties and citizens' movements opposing the creation of regions argued frequently that the division of the country would diminish Portuguese bargaining power in the Union. Behind this position was a conception of competitive lobbying by the regions in Brussels. The opponents of regionalisation were apprehensive about a possible fragmentation of the Portuguese bargaining power, given that Portugal is such a small country.[17]

Although lacking effective autonomous powers, there are regional branches of central government that play a role in the policy-cycle, especially in the administration of the structural funds. Mainland Portugal is divided in five regional co-ordination commissions – North, Centre, Lisbon and Tagus Valley, Alentejo and Algarve. They are responsible for the preparation and co-ordination of the regional development programmes and for monitoring the programmes of social and economic development within each of the regions. These entities, however, are branches of central government and if they have a role in the preparation of policies, the final word belongs to Lisbon.

As far as the civil society is concerned, Portugal's accession to the Union is a parallel process to the development of civil society. The number of NGOs and professional associations is growing, as well as the importance these organisations attach to the European process. Especially important is the participation in European-wide networks. These organisations – some of them, such as business associations, which have established offices in Brussels – try to influence the EC/EU legislative process, both in Portugal and in Brussels. At the same time, the government also tries to get the support of these organisations for its policies. The prime minister receives the major interest groups and trade unions associations before each European Council.

Conclusions: progressive 'Europeanisation' of the civil societies

The adaptation of the Portuguese administration to the new political and economic internal circumstances was parallel to the process of integration in the Union. It is difficult to say, in same cases, whether the changes were internally or externally induced. Right after the request for membership, the changes introduced in the Portuguese administration tried to cope with the demands of integration. The correlation between internal changes and European integration has increased with the TEU. In fact, the TEU led to a substantial reform in the Portuguese constitution and it has changed the role of the Parliament in the control of the EC legislation. At the same time, almost all the ministries had to create or adapt their services and institutions even those traditionally less 'Europeanised', such as the police forces and the judicial authorities. Even if the Foreign Ministry continues to be the major player on European issues, the other ministries are progressively becoming more involved. The co-ordination structure, however, did not change drastically. It is the same since the accession and it has been evolving without major upheavals. The same applies for the preparation of decisions and policies, still mainly concentrated in the ministers and secretaries of states and not so much in the administration.

The coming into force of the Amsterdam Treaty is likely to produce some changes, but not to the same extent as the Maastricht Treaty. The same is true for the single currency, which will probably cause the Ministries of Finance and of Economy to reform their structure to some extent. So far, the Portuguese membership of the Union has been a success story. Politically, administratively and socially, Portugal is evolving and adapting to the evolution of the Union itself. But the Union is also enlarging its scope and it will probably become increasingly demanding. On the one hand, the greater involvement of more ministries can produce rivalries, requiring a greater co-ordination effort. On the other hand, the concentration of the preparation of decisions almost exclusively at the political level could not be enough to cope with Union requirements.

The Portuguese case also shows that domestic political change is still influential in the definition of European policies. The new government has changed the attitude *vis-à-vis* EC/EU dossiers and has contributed to a broader range of internal actors involved in the process, although in a very informal way. It is also interesting to note the different profiles of Portuguese prime ministers. While Aníbal Cavaco Silva – Prime Minister from 1985 to 1995 – had a low profile in the European scene, António Guterres has a much higher profile, and this obviously has a bearing in enhancing the role of Portugal. Portuguese civil society is also learning how to deal with European integration. Following democratic transition, Portuguese civil society became more active and organised; civil society organisations now tend to act not only in Portugal but also in the European institutions. In the near future, civil society, through its organised representatives, is likely to play an increasing role in Portugal's European policies.

Perspective for the future

The Portuguese position on the 1996–97 IGC concentrated mainly on three basic issues: institutional reform, social Europe and JHA. At the institutional level, the main concern was the preservation of the country's relative power: the voting weight at the Council, the composition of the Commission, the rotation of the Presidency. Another concern was the interpretation of subsidiarity and the introduction of the flexibility clause. Portugal also stood for the simplification of decision-making mechanisms and the extension of the co-decision procedure with the EP. Another priority was social Europe and co-ordination of employment policies. Portugal supported the partial communitarisation of the third pillar, and concentrated on issues such as drug-trafficking, organised crime, terrorism and illegal flows of immigrants. The Portuguese government also paid special attention to the promotion of human rights and the fight against discrimination. The protection of the peripheral regions and the recognition of their specificity, which has a direct impact on the Azores and Madeira, were also of particular concern.

The Amsterdam Treaty did not generate any special divergences amongst the political parties. Following the rather peculiar incident of the referendum, the Treaty was ratified in January 1999. Afterwards, Portugal was deeply involved in what was probably the most difficult negotiation since the accession: the Agenda 2000 and the financial framework for 2000–06. Portugal tried to maintain the present level of financial flows and opposed attempts to link the cohesion fund to the participation in the single currency. Prime Minister António Guterres has constantly stressed that the Union was facing dangerous times with the emergence of strong selfish, national attitudes. The Portuguese position is especially difficult because the country is overwhelmingly dependent on the structural funds. While other cohesion countries can obtain significant resources from the CAP, Portugal on the contrary is a net contributor in terms of agricultural policy. Another important topic is the phasing out of the Lisbon region. Until recently, the whole of the country qualified for Objective One, but the Lisbon region is now over the 75 per cent threshold.

The internal political debate on Agenda 2000 was very strong, with opposition parties urging the government to veto proposals that could be detrimental to Portugal. The government, nevertheless, chose to be very cautious with the threat of vetoing. The outcome of the negotiations was rather positive to Portugal, which managed to keep the same amount of funds as in the second CSF.

It was the government's position to de-link budgetary negotiations with the enlargement process. The Portuguese government fully supports accession of the CEE countries; since the Community supported the Portuguese democratic consolidation process and economic development it should therefore play the same role in Central and Eastern Europe. It is quite clear that the negotiations on the financial framework are not, in Portugal's view, about a competition for funds between present and future members but rather about a concern for perceived gaps between north and south, and richer and poorer Member States in the EU.

Notes

1 The change in the European policy of CDS–PP granted the party much better electoral results: in the 1994 European elections it reached 12.5 per cent of the vote and 9.1 per cent in the 1995 general elections.

2 At that time, the Portuguese Constitution barred any referendum on international treaties.

3 For a complete overview of the constitutional reforms, see José Magalhães, *Dicionário da Revisão Constitucional* (Lisbon: Europa-America, 1989) and José Magalhães, *Dicionário da Revisão Constitucional* (Lisbon: Europa-America, 1999).

4 Following the attempted coup of 11 March 1975, the banking and insurance sectors were nationalised as well as the major industrial companies.

5 Article 7 §6. Provided that there is reciprocity, Portugal may enter into agreements for the joint exercise of the powers necessary to establish the Union, in ways that have due regard for the principle of subsidiarity and the objective of economic and social cohesion.

6 Article 102: 'The Bank of Portugal, in its capacity as a central bank, shall carry out its functions in accordance with the law and with the international rules to which the Portuguese State is bound.' The reference to the omission of currency was eliminated.

7 The demand to hold a referendum on the ratification of the TEU was largely made by its opponents, but not exclusively. The then President of the Republic, Mário Soares, also argued that the Maastricht ratification would be a good occasion to consult the Portuguese on the participation of Portugal in the Union. The two major parties, the socialists and the social democrats, however, refused to change the constitution in order to allow the referendum.

8 The importance that Portugal and Spain gave to Latin America, and their willingness to bolster the importance attached by the Union to that region was clearly expressed in the Treaty of Accession, which included a 'common statement of intent in relation to the furthering of relations with the countries of Latin America'.

9 It was the first time since the Portuguese accession that the government had changed (the PSD had won the 1985, 1987 and 1991 general elections).

10 Portuguese document to the Inter-governmental Conference www.minnestrangeiros.pt/politica/europeia/engindex.html

11 The Directorate General for Community Affairs was created in 1985, under the designation Directorate-General of the European Communities. The change of name took place in the framework of global restructuring of the Foreign Ministry, in 1994.

12 See Pedro Sanchez da Costa Pereira, 'Portugal. Public Administration and EPC/CFSP – A Fruitful Adaptation Process' in: Franco Algieri and Elfriede Regelsberger (eds), *Synergy at Work, Spain and Portugal in European Foreign Policy* (Bonn: Europa Union Verlag, 1996), pp. 207–229.

13 CDS–PP was a member of the EP but it was expelled after becoming an anti-European party.

14 Added to Article 166; now in Article 163, following the 1997 revision.

15 See Article 161.

16 The referendum was held 8 October 1998. The 'no' vote won, with 63.5 per cent of the votes.

17 Another argument used was the fear that some of the Portuguese regions could fall into a sphere of influence of the border Spanish regions.

Select bibliography

The text (English translation) of the Constitution of Portugal can be found at the University of Richmond's constitution finder at http://confinder.richmond.edu/. Further sources on government and parliament of Portugal can be found at Government www.pcm.gov.pt or at Parliament www.parlamento.pt.

Lopes, José da Silva (ed.) (1993) *Portugal and EC Membership Evaluated* (London: Pinter).

Matos, Luís Salgado de Matos (1992) 'O sistema político português e a Comunidade Europeia', in: *Análise Social*, No. 118–119 (Lisbon: ICS).

Pereira, Pedro Sanchez da Costa (1996) 'Portugal: Public Administration and EPC/CFSP – A Fruitful Adaptation Process', in: Franco Algieri and Elfriede Regelsberger (eds), *Synergy at Work, Spain and Portugal in European Foreign Policy* (Bonn: Europa Union Verlag).

Vasconcelos, Álvaro (ed.) (1995) *Portugal no Centro da Europa – Propostas para uma reforma democrática do Tratado da União Europeia* (Lisbon: Quetzal).

Vasconcelos, Álvaro and Antunes, Luís Pais (1996) 'Portugal', in: Dietrich Rometsch and Wolfgang Wessels (eds), *The European Union and Member States. Towards Institutional Fusion?* (Manchester: Manchester University Press).

16 *Karl Magnus Johansson*

Sweden: another awkward partner?

Introduction: reluctant yet faithful

Scholars of the European Union must lift the lid off the 'black box' of domestic politics to understand the behaviour of Member States in the integration processes. In this chapter, we will move inside the Swedish polity by analysing domestic constraints and institutional characteristics. The overarching aim is to capture the fundamentals of Sweden as an EU member, thereby identifying the primary actors involved in the policy-cycle. Joining late, Sweden has faced strong pressures of adaptation both at the state and societal levels. As the Union has advanced and become an increasingly complex organisation, countries seeking membership and new Member States are faced with a more difficult and steeper learning curve than the founding members. At the same time, latecomers are in a position to learn from the experiences of others.

Sweden joined the Union in January 1995. The decision to seek membership can be seen as a logical consequence of the interdependence between the strongly export-reliant Swedish economy and the West European economies.[1] Although officially neutral, Sweden has since long been strongly associated with West Europe, both economically and politically.[2] Swedish economic forces actually joined the Common Market before membership was formally and politically approved. Just like in Britain and Denmark, membership has been justified primarily by the political elites on economic grounds, which provided the rationale for requesting membership in the first place and provoked unrealistic expectations of economic benefits and thereby continued to haunt the elites, broadly in favour of membership. It is also important to emphasise that Sweden entered the Union at a time of economic recession.

At the same time, however, there clearly were political determinants behind the decision to apply for membership. The argument of increasing political influence was often employed by political leaders when arguing the case of joining the Union.[3] Leading social democrats pointed out that the nation state is no longer enough and that meant cross-national borders had to be found.[4] In other words, those leaders were willing to 'trad[e] off some of their de jure sovereignties for a guaranteed say in effective policy-making'.[5]

The matter of full EC membership rose to the top of the Swedish political agenda in a short period of time. The governing social democrats took a decisive step in this direction in October 1990, in the context of the management of an acute economic crisis. Later that year, the parliament (Riksdagen) voted in favour of applying for EC membership by 289 votes to 28, with the reservation that it must be in a form compatible 'with the retention of neutrality'.[6] The membership application was handed to the Dutch EC presidency in the Hague on 1 July 1991.

The negotiations for Sweden's accession to the Union were formally opened on 1 February 1993 and outstanding issues were resolved in March 1994. Overall, the deal reached in 1994 was not a bad one for Sweden. As Miles (1998) has argued, 'the Swedish negotiators, for the most part, gained a generous agreement from the Community and this was primarily due to the concerns of both sides at the size of domestic opposition to the country becoming a full member'.[7] It seems, therefore, that the Eurosceptical public may be more of an asset than a liability for Swedish negotiators and decision-makers, playing two-level or even multi-level games in multiple arenas.[8] That public opinion provides a safety valve was also shown in connection to the social democratic government's justification for not joining EMU in the first wave. During the accession negotiations and since, Sweden has highlighted particularly Swedish issues and has been allowed to leave a distinct Swedish imprint on the common EU agenda. The importance to strike a good deal with the Union has been considered especially urgent to compensate for the weak support for European unity in Swedish public opinion.

In fact, *Eurobarometer* data has confirmed that the Swedes are the most Eurosceptic of all citizens in the Union. This situation results in restricted room for manoeuvre for Swedish decision-makers and will continue to do so given the persistence of anti-EU sentiments among the Swedes. It appears that European integration has become a new cleavage in Swedish politics.[9] The pattern of party support and opposition to EU membership still reflects the position of the referendum in November 1994. Accordingly, the Left Party and the Green Party are against, at least nominally, whereas the Social Democratic Party, the Liberal Party, the Moderate Party, the Christian Democratic Party and the Centre Party remain principally in favour. At the same time, however, there is opposition to supranational integration within all the Swedish political parties. Although there has been a consensual style to Swedish EU policy, especially when supposedly 'national interests' are at stake, the political priorities are very much those of the social democrats. From the outset, a priority was to turn away the debate from institutional issues in particular. As a non-member at the time, Sweden was not in a formal position to influence the contents of the Maastricht Treaty. Nevertheless, leading social democrats were critical of the focus on institutional reform and monetary union. They wanted to put other issues on the EU agenda, notably employment. At the same time, politicians across the political spectrum seemed happy about the insertion in the treaty of the subsidiarity principle, conveniently defining it in terms of 'nearness'.[10]

The social democrats have invested enormously in committing the Union to a Swedish-style active labour market policy. Accordingly, employment had top priority in the 1996–97 IGC, resulting in a separate title on employment in the Amsterdam Treaty.[11] Predictably, this was considered a victory by the Swedish social democrats.

In the IGC, Sweden emphasised issues presumed to be of concern, such as equal opportunities between men and women, consumer protection, the environment, and openness, or transparency, in addition to employment.[12] Sweden reluctantly accepted the flexibility clause, which implies that those Member States that want to could go on with co-operation and integration without having all partners on board.[13] For Sweden, as one of the smaller EU members, the notion of flexibility was seen as favourable for the larger Member States, eventually forming a hard core, but it was stressed that flexibility would be of limited use given the right of veto and also for reasons of solidarity among Member States. The Swedish government was also opposed to changes in the rules for QMV in the Council and to changes in the composition of the Commission.

One can detect a growing awareness on the part of the Swedish government that supranationalism in the sense of strong EU institutions and decision-making procedures could be advantageous for the relatively smaller Member States, fearing the emergence of a directoire among larger states. However, this is difficult to communicate in a country where the influence of Sweden in the Union is widely measured in terms of the number of votes, presently four, in the Council. Accordingly, the Swedish government has been reluctant to discuss deepening – that is, institutional reforms necessary or desirable in order to extend the number of EU members. Sweden has been an enthusiastic and unequivocal supporter of EU enlargement, performing the role of an advocate for the Baltic states.

For the foreseeable future, the Swedish policy of non-participation in military alliances, with the aim of making it possible for the country to remain neutral in the event of a war in its vicinity, is likely to remain unchanged. However, the social democratic government has adopted a more pragmatic attitude towards existing alliances and joint operations, while rejecting proposals for a common defence in the Union along the lines of collective security.

Unlike Britain and Denmark, Sweden has no formal 'opt-out' from the third stage of EMU. Whether or not Sweden will join will also depend on the positions of the other Member States which decided not to join in the first wave, notably the decision by the British government. The reticent government position on EMU reflects the divisions in the social democratic party and also an overall anti-federalist attitude.

There is a basic anti-federalist sentiment in Sweden, a unitary state, and in the political parties. In this regard, there is a deep-rooted 'nation state logic' behind Swedish membership of the Union.[14] The broad support in favour of the welfare state and feelings of uniqueness, some say 'welfare chauvinism', imply that the instincts of most Swedes are that they would lose from closer integration in a federalist direction. Accordingly, the Union has been seen by the public largely as a threat rather than as an opportunity:

> To many voters, the immediate and very visible costs associated with the Europeanisation of Sweden far outweigh the potential but diffused benefits of membership, as professed by various establishment figures. The people of Sweden were inspired by their political authorities to turn their backs on the Continent of Europe some fifty years ago. In spite of the best efforts by the new generation of leaders to draw public attention back to this traditional focus of interest, most Swedes (across party lines, but more so the young and women than the middle-aged and men) tend to remain sceptical.[15]

Sweden stayed out of the two world wars and many of the ideas underpinning the EU project, such as the subsidiarity connected with Catholic social teachings, are unknown to most Swedes, few of whom identify with this project. In short, neither crucial parts of general European history nor basic ideas are shared between Sweden and the continental countries which originally launched the project of European integration.

Against this background, it might be argued that Sweden is and will remain another 'awkward partner' in the Union, or a 'reluctant European'.[16] Paradoxically, however, Swedish compliance with EC legislation is among the highest of all the Member States and Swedish representatives seemingly do their best to behave well in the Union, both administratively and politically.[17] As a Member State, Sweden must, however, be considered aloof from the 'heart of Europe' not only geographically but also ideologically.

The national policy-cycle: identifying the primary actors

The primary concern of this section is to discuss the institutional characteristics and changes following from the Swedish EU membership and the adjustments to the EU policy-cycle. The most important actors involved in the policy-making process will be identified. Formally, the obvious actors are the government and the public administration as well as the

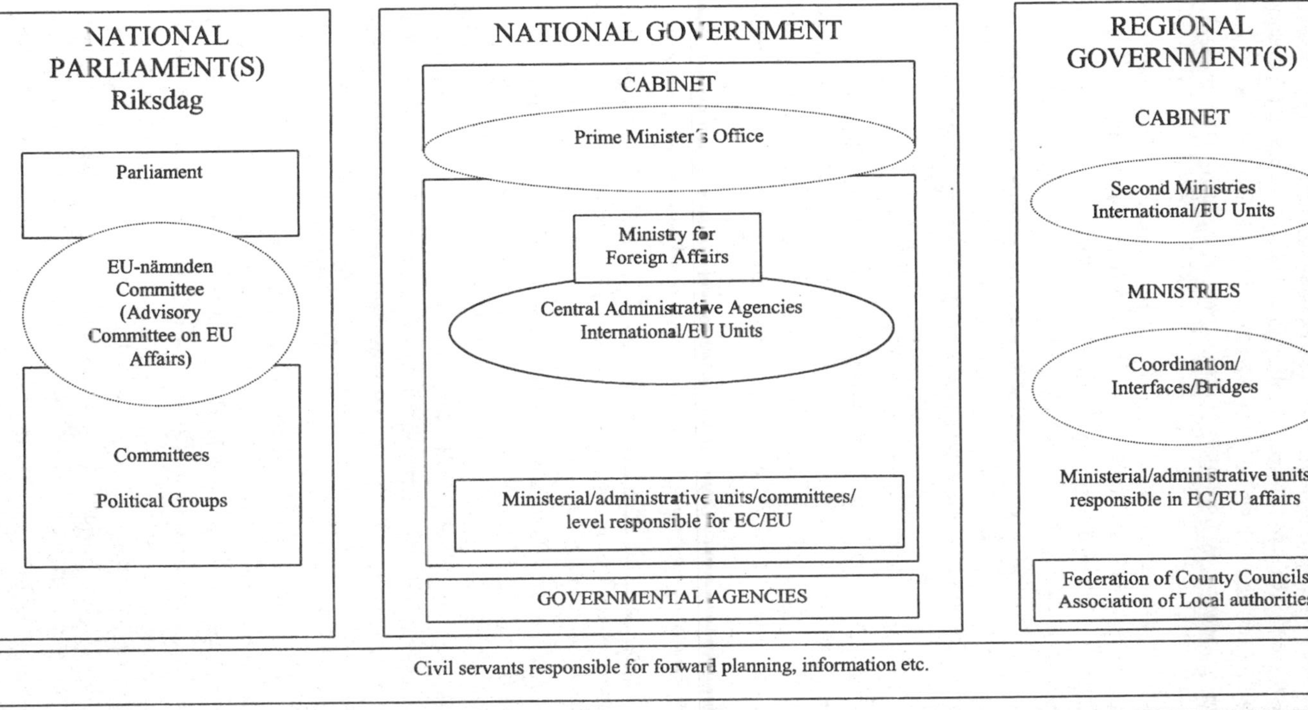

Figure 16.1 The national level of European decision-making – Sweden

parliament. In addition, there are non-governmental actors such as interest groups, political parties and the media.

Although there is an old tradition of local government, and renewed regionalisation, the Swedish unitary polity must be considered as relatively centralised compared to several of the other EU Member States, especially the federal or semi-federal states. In the making of Swedish policies towards the Union, the degree of centralisation is striking. However, there is a certain fragmentation at the central level insofar as there is an interministerial rivalry and, perhaps inevitably, problems of co-ordination. The institutions dealing with the Union in one way or the other are continuously adjusting to the EU policy-making process, and this appears to be the situation for the institutional set-up in general.

The central government and administrative agencies

In an age of globalisation, few if any issues are completely domestic. And in the light of Europeanisation an increasing number of policy areas must similarly be handled by government sections other than foreign ministries which thereby lose some of their control of exchanges across borders. This situation may reflect a general waning of influence and prestige for foreign ministries. In Sweden, the Ministry for Foreign Affairs has traditionally had a somewhat superior position compared to other ministries. The Ministry had the privilege of defining neutrality and non-alignment. However, this privilege has no longer the same meaning and importance as it used to have. And the involvement in the EU policy-making process has added to the rivalry in the direction of Sweden's external relations in general.

The search for smooth horizontal interministerial co-ordination must be seen in the light of the relationship between the Ministry for Foreign Affairs and other ministries. Given the rivalry noted above, in reality as well as potentially, the Ministry for Foreign Affairs was naturally keen on having the co-ordinating function. Accordingly, the main co-ordinative unit, the EU secretariat, was placed there. Officially, however, this was considered a cross-ministerial body, with the staff seconded from other ministries as well. On a cross-ministerial basis, there is also a group for EU affairs among state secretaries, the most high-ranking civil servants in the ministries. When a new social democratic government was formed in March 1996, the widespread impression was that the new Prime Minister and his office (Statsrådsberedningen) would take a firmer grip on the co-ordination of EU affairs.[18] An indication of this was that the position of Minister for European Affairs, placed in the Ministry for Foreign Affairs, was abolished. At the same time, however, one of the state secretaries in the Ministry for Foreign Affairs was to specialise on the Union, thereby reducing the burdens on the Ministry for Foreign Affairs. On balance and in terms of influence, the winner from these changes seems to have been the Ministry for Foreign Affairs.

However, one of the reorganisations of the government office in connection with the formation of the social democratic cabinet after the September 1998 general election concerned co-ordination of EU affairs. Although the EU secretariat would be retained in the Ministry for Foreign Affairs, a co-ordinative unit would at last be established in the Prime Minister's Office and a state secretary appointed. The then Minister for Foreign Affairs, Lena Hjelm-Wallén, the longest-serving of the present ministers, was appointed Deputy Prime Minister, with overall co-ordination responsibilities. These changes, also made in view of the Swedish Presidency of the Union during the first half of 2001, must be interpreted as a recognition of the organisational deficiencies concerning the co-ordination of EU affairs so far. It remains to be seen to what extent the new arrangements will run smoothly, ensuring effective co-ordination. There is still a potential for co-ordination problems: following the October 1998 cabinet formation, there are three ministers in the Ministry for Foreign Affairs, all of whom deal with the Union in one way or the other. The head of the ministry, the Ministry for Foreign Affairs, represents Sweden in the General Affairs Council. There is still a Minister for Foreign Aid, and the Minister for Trade, previously in a separate ministry, co-ordinates Sweden's Baltic Sea policies, which are of high priority for the cabinet but through this division of work seemingly, and perhaps unfortunately, separated from EU affairs.

The relative influence between different bodies cannot be explained only with reference to structural conditions, however. Another factor is the degree of personal commitment to the Union. That some key persons in the Ministry for Foreign Affairs have turned out to be very committed and capable with regard to EU affairs and bargaining, contributes to their influential position. And it is obvious to any observer that the Prime Minister since March 1996, Göran Persson, has not shown a great interest in EU affairs, at least not during the years of his first cabinet and before that as Minister for Finance.[19]

Thus, the Swedish involvement in the EU policy-cycle has revealed a democratic and constitutional problem in regard to the relationship between politicians and civil servants to the extent that Swedish policy-making *vis-à-vis* the Union has been driven by unelected bureaucrats rather than politicians. That several politicians at the ministerial level apparently are not interested in EU affairs results, in turn, in a lack of political backing. This could be frustrating for officials speaking on behalf of the Swedish government in various working groups, committees and pre-Council meetings. The ambiguity that has characterised the Swedish position-taking in the Union, notably in the Council, is to the detriment of Sweden's overall influence and has, therefore, a political cost. Such ambiguity makes a Member State an unpredictable ally. For successful negotiation outcomes, civil servants negotiating on behalf of the Swedish government have called for clarity and political backing.

It goes without saying that the Swedish Permanent Representation to the Union underwent an expansion of staff owing to membership. According to a report in the Ministry for Foreign Affairs, only the Greek representation was larger than the Swedish in June 1998. Then, ninety-one people worked at the Swedish Representation in Brussels. Out of fifty-two civil servants altogether, twenty-four were from the Ministry for Foreign Affairs and twenty-eight from other ministries. Again, there is a divide between the Ministry for Foreign Affairs and other ministries in that the Brussels-based civil servants either are career diplomats or more or less specialised officials from ministries such as the ministries for finance, agriculture or environment. Specialised experts, on a temporary basis, are also seconded from central administrative agencies. In addition to the horizontal co-ordination at the ministerial level, there is the vertical co-ordination between ministries and central administrative agencies. The linkages between them have become more dense because of EU membership. Since Swedish ministries are relatively small, as measured by the number of staff, they have to rely on assistance and expertise from the specialised administrative agencies and, generally speaking, increasingly so the more technical the issues are. The closer contacts and interlinkage between Swedish ministries and central administrative agencies have constitutional implications given the latter's formally independent status.[20] This status has a long tradition in Sweden and is likely to be maintained for the foreseeable future, just like the principle of collegial decision-making in the cabinet and the system of common deliberations (Gemensam beredning) between two or more ministries in general and in budgetary matters in particular.

Swedish government structures – in regard to communication, steering and co-ordination both horizontally and vertically – have thus been deeply affected by the necessary adjustments to the EU policy-cycle. Furthermore, EU membership has given rise to a new kind of relationship between the government and the parliament.

The parliament

Law-making and scrutiny are two of the functions of any parliament, and these functions are both directed towards the government. EU membership has diminished the overall legislative influence of parliaments, including the Swedish Riksdag. However, an awareness of this diminished role has acted as an incentive for new ideas in regard to governmental relations. Looking at other models, mainly the Danish, of how to scrutinise the government's handling of EU affairs, the Swedish parliament set up the Advisory Committee on EU Affairs (or the EU Advisory Committee).[21] It follows from its name that the committee is a forum for consultation with the government, which has to inform the Riksdag about all matters which are to be dealt with by the Council and has to confer about Sweden's positions on important matters more generally.[22] Formally, the powers of the committee are limited since it is advisory unlike the Danish model, cannot bind a minister in regard to the Council negotiations. Nor can the committee submit issues under deliberation to the chamber for plenary debates.

Nevertheless, the committee exercises a real influence, which is impossible to measure, insofar as the committee's recommendations are taken into consideration. If a minister does not follow the advice given by the committee, the matter could actually be scrutinised by the Committee on the Constitution and a 'no confidence' vote could be taken in the chamber.[23] It is also interesting to note, given that IGCs are formally between governments, that the government regularly consulted with the committee during the 1996–97 IGC.[24]

The committee, which regularly convenes on Fridays and behind closed doors, is attended by the relevant minister, and his or her advisers, or exceptionally by state secretaries and under-secretaries of state if ministers are unable to attend. Who the relevant minister is depends, of course, on the nature of the issue to be dealt with in the Council the following week.

That government representatives come before the committee so late in the policy-cycle is one of the major deficiencies in the ways in which government–parliament relations over EU matters have been organised so far. A related problem is that the issue-specific information primarily is provided by the government, mainly through the EU secretariat and before then from the Swedish Representation in Brussels. However, the committee has direct communication with different units in the entire government office. That the background information to the committee is provided by the government implies that it could be filtered when it arrives in parliament. The question arises to what extent the information is reliable and sufficient. Even though relations are said to be good, the committee does not completely rely on the government which seems to be a healthy scepticism from a body with scrutiny of government as one of its key functions.[25] For this reason, the committee, through its secretariat, has established alternative sources of information.

One source is the cabinet of the Swedish Commissioner. Other sources are various data bases and documentation from other parliamentary units dealing with EU affairs, notably those of the other Nordic Member States with which the Swedish committee exchanges information and occasionally holds joint meetings both among staff and committee members. Information is also provided by the twenty-two Swedish MEPs.[26] The fact that the government tends to focus on the Council and to ignore what goes on in the EP implies that the information from the government rarely includes briefs about proceedings in the EP and its agenda.

However, the relationship between Swedish MEPs and the Riksdag, notably the EU Advisory Committee, has been somewhat tense in that some of the MEPs wanted access to the committee, on a more formal basis, but were denied it. Also the proposal, serious or not, that Swedish MEPs could be invited to attend debates on EU matters in the chamber was turned down. Instead, the channels of communication between the Swedish parliament and the Swedes in the EP are primarily upheld by the political parties and the party groups in the Riksdag.

The direct channels of communication between the party groups in the Swedish Riksdag and the Swedish MEPs enable committee members to get first-hand information from party colleagues at the European level of politics. Thereby, one can identify a strategy seeking to bypass the central government. Such a bypassing strategy is also employed by sub-national governments and by a host of non-governmental actors.

Sub-national governments

The sub-national levels of the Swedish body politic, mainly the regional level, are undergoing a transformation. Although some changes were initiated before Swedish membership of the Union, some of the most apparent signs of Europeanisation of the Swedish polity are related to regionalisation and the new dynamics of regional self-government. Such processes refer to networks of transaction, communication and organisation across state borders. Maps have been redrawn and there are experiments with new regional authorities in some parts of the country, including Scania, West Sweden, the County of Kalmar and the island of Gotland. It is beyond doubt that these changes have been reinforced by processes of 'Europeanisation' in general and EU membership in particular. Not least, the principle of subsidiarity provided an opportunity for further decentralisation and regionalisation, and the Structural Funds and the establishment of the CoR have also contributed to this development.

To an increasing extent, units at the sub-national level of government and public administration become transborder, or transnational, actors. Specifically, there are the trans-regional exchanges across the Öresund between Denmark and Sweden.[27] There are also the wider exchanges across the Baltic Sea. Both the Öresund area and the Baltic Sea area have gained EU financial assistance, specifically through the INTERREG programmes. A small secretariat of Interreg II C is located in the town of Karlskrona, and a larger secretariat of that programme is located in Rostock, Germany. Another illustration is provided by the regional lobbying *vis-à-vis* EU institutions.[28] One example of representation centres in Brussels of different Swedish regions and associations of local authorities, or communes, is the South Sweden European Office. Swedish sub-national governments are also represented, with altogether twelve members, in the CoR. These members are formally appointed by the Swedish central government, but they are nominated by the Federation of County Councils (Landstingsförbundet) and the Association of Local Authorities (Kommunförbundet).

The outward-looking regional and local authorities have brought a new kind of relationship between public authorities and societal actors, for example through chambers of commerce. In other words, processes of regionalisation and Europeanisation at large may give rise to strengthened partnerships between the private and the public.

Where the Swedish central government has been reactive in its dealings with the Union, sub-national governments have in many cases appeared to be pro-active. Thereby, one can identify patterns of 'paradiplomacy', 'microdiplomacy' and 'multi-level governance'. Just like parliamentarians and political parties, as mentioned above, sub-national governments employ influence strategies, often through networking, bypassing the central level of government and its hierarchical structures. The same situation applies to the multiplicity of non-governmental actors which appear in EU policy-making in one way or another.

Non-governmental actors and interest groups

Non-governmental actors are involved in patterns of informal European integration. They thus exercise transnational strategies of influence and play an agenda-setting role. Such actors could go through central government and public administration or bypass these by targeting EU institutions and policy-makers directly. These strategies could also be combined and their effectiveness varies between the phases of the EU policy-making process. Given the corporatist tradition of Sweden, strong and centralised interest organisations have been part of the policy-making process. The central organisation for blue-collar workers is the Swedish Trade Union Confederation (Landsorganisationen) and for white-collar workers the Swedish Confederation of Professional Employees (Tjänstemännens Centralorganisation) and the Swedish Confederation of Professional Associations (Sveriges Akademikers Centralorganisation). These organisations have a joint office in Brussels. The central organisation for employers is the Swedish Employers' Confederation (Svenska Arbetsgivareföreningen), which has a joint representation centre in Brussels together with the Swedish Trade Council (Industriförbundet). It is important to emphasise that both of these Brussels offices were in place several years before Sweden became an EU member. However, since Sweden joined the Union the organisations mentioned above could become full members of the ETUC and UNICE, respectively. And the Federation of Swedish Farmers (Lantbrukarnas Riksförbund), which also has an office in Brussels, became a full, and active, member of COPA.

Swedish interest organisations, primarily those mentioned above, are indirectly represented in the EU's Social Dialogue and directly in

ECOSOC, with altogether twelve seats. And even though Swedish interest groups were active in the European arena before Sweden became an EU member, their overall lobbying in Brussels and Strasbourg has increased considerably since 1995. The same situation applies for 'new' social movements such as the environmental groups, some of which have linked-up with umbrella organisations, or Euro-lobbies, notably the European Environmental Bureau (EEB).

Political parties

Correspondingly, Swedish political parties have linked-up with Euro-parties and co-operate actively with like-minded parties on a transnational basis.[29] By 'Euro-parties', I mean the European parties called for in the Maastricht Treaty (Article 138a). At another organisational level, there are the EP party groups. Again, it is stressed that these informal integration processes on the part of Swedish non-governmental actors were set in motion before Sweden formally became an EU member.

In fact, the Swedish Social Democratic Party became a founding member of the Party of European Socialists (PES) in 1992. For their part, the Moderates and the Christian Democrats became full members of the European People's Party (EPP) in 1995, they had previously been affiliated with this Euro-party. A similar situation applies for the Liberal Party, which is a member of the European Liberal, Democrat and Reform Party (ELDR). While there is no Euro-party for the leftists, formerly Communists, they sit in the leftist group in the EP. The Greens, however, are members both of the Green Group in the EP and the European Federation of Green Parties (EFGP), which like the ELDR was founded in 1993. The Centre Party is represented with one seat in the ELDR group in the EP, but is not a member of the ELDR party. For a governing party like the Swedish Social Democratic Party, the involvement in a Euro-party like the PES provides channels for access to other governing parties. Specifically, there are the PES pre-meetings to European Council summits and the group of Sherpas – that is, of personal representatives of party leaders sitting in government. These representatives seek to co-ordinate policies more broadly. Such concerted efforts have, for example, been made in the issue area of employment.[30] The Swedish Deputy Prime Minister, Lena Hjelm-Wallén, is a vice-president of the PES, and her predecessor as Swedish Foreign Minister, Margaretha af Ugglas, is a vice-president of the EPP.

Issues related to the Union have, more or less, disrupted the cohesion within the political parties represented in the Riksdag. Intra-party factionalism and conflicts are sometimes difficult to control for party managers. One strategy, most notably employed by the social democrats but also by other parties, is to contain intra-party divisions by avoiding clear-cut positions on different issues, such as EMU, and avoiding debate altogether.

This strategy of party management, which can be interpreted as a lack of leadership, slows down, if not actually hinders, Europeanisation.[31] Party attitudes are also formed in relation to the stance of the interest groups with which the parties are related, such as trade unions in the case of the social democrats, employers for the Moderates and agriculture for the Centrists. Arguably, the vacillating position of the latter party reflects a cost-benefit analysis for the agricultural sector as a whole, with many small-scale farmers suffering from the increased competition. However, the Federation of Swedish Farmers came out in favour of EU membership. Their connection to industry may explain the strongly pro-EMU position of the Moderate Party, historically a conservative party. However, there is a growing dissent within the party over the single currency. The Christian Democrats and the Centrists are divided over the issue, whereas the Liberal Party is almost at one in its favourable position. Both the leftists and the greens insist that Sweden should stay out of the third stage of EMU and that the matter should be decided by a referendum, the sooner the better.

The media

The impact of the media on Swedish policies towards the Union is also impossible to measure. However, the media shapes public opinion, and very much so in a Eurosceptic direction given the focus on detailed EU standardisation and legislation reportedly affecting Sweden negatively. The media, thereby, impacts indirectly on the government's policies and provides a further domestic constraint.

The quality of media reporting with regard to the Union varies enormously. The two leading daily newspapers, *Dagens Nyheter* and especially *Svenska Dagbladet*, generally contain highly qualitative reports and commentaries. They are widely read by the political elites. Both of these newspapers are non-socialist, as are most of the Swedish newspapers. Accordingly, the leading articles tend to be critical towards the approaches to the Union on the part of the Swedish government. This may have contributed to the government's more active approach, at least rhetorically, since the formation of a new cabinet in October 1998. Reports in the foreign media may also have had the same effect, especially when they have compared Swedish behaviour in the Union to the allegedly more effective and active Finland.[32] In effect, also the media, through opinion formation across borders, appears as a non-governmental and transnational actor. Such actors exert informal power.

Conclusions: an adaptive but largely reactive and defensive member

Looking into the future, we should recall the Statement of Government Policy presented by the Prime Minister in October 1998, which put an heavy emphasis on the role of Sweden in the Union and Europe at large.

'Sweden will actively contribute to the shaping of Europe's future. Membership of the European Union makes it possible for Sweden to work for a continent characterized by democracy, solidarity and openness. The presidency of the EU in 2001 will be a new milestone in our work in the EU.'[33] This might be interpreted as a recognition that Sweden, during the early years in the Union, has been insufficiently active and therefore may have missed opportunities that could have been seized. The new message might also be interpreted as an effort to try to convince the public of some of the advantages of being an EU member.

The cabinet still suffers fundamental constraints from a lukewarm public opinion, however. And having done badly in the September 1998 general election, the social democrats entered into negotiations and built a kind of informal coalition with the the two most Eurosceptic parties in parliament. At least in their rhetoric, those two parties want Sweden to leave the Union. The partnership with them became increasingly strained in connection with the campaign for the June 1999 European elections.

Although there have been, and still are, apparent problems of adjustments and co-ordination, both administrative and political agencies have proved capable of learning and on the whole are fit for the task of representing Sweden in the Union. At the same time, it is fair to say that the Swedish learning process has been slower than the Finnish. At least to some extent, this can be explained by organisational factors. Organisationally, there have namely been weaknesses in the Swedish government office in terms of a machinery for co-ordination and an anticipatory capacity for strategic thinking. There clearly is a myopia and preoccupation with day-to-day politics.

How 'fit' is Sweden? A learning curve

Sweden's approaches to EU affairs during the first years of membership can be characterised as largely reactive rather than pro-active and anticipatory; a defensive attitude to European integration has prevailed. This situation has had negative effects for co-ordination, both horizontally among ministries and vertically between ministries and central administrative agencies. In addition, and perhaps most importantly, Sweden has been an unpredictable partner in the Union. There have probably been many missed opportunities for effective coalition-building, which is very much the name of the game. This situation has also diminished Sweden's overall EU influence.

The 'nation state logic' underpinning Swedish membership has resulted in a method of organisation that is basically intergovernmental rather than supranational. In the light of the metaphor of the 'inside' and the 'outside', the EU is primarily seen as something 'outside', that is, beyond national borders and spatially separated from the national territory. In a deeper sense, therefore, 'the Swedish nation has not adapted to the requirements of EU membership or even to the wider movement toward a transnationally defined human existence'.[34]

That the intergovernmental rather than the supranational image has prevailed in Swedish thinking towards the Union is indicated by the prominent, although diminishing, role of the Ministry for Foreign Affairs and traditional diplomacy with regard to EU affairs. The Swedish government has similarly tended to focus on the basically intergovernmental Council rather than the supranational institutions of the Commission and the EP. In many ways, Sweden has been affected by processes of 'Europeanisation'. This is illustrated by the membership of political parties in Euro-parties and of interest groups in Euro-lobbies, as well as by the European activities of regional and local authorities and by the increasing number of personnel dealing with EU affairs at different levels of government. One can identify an 'institutional fusion' in that there is a close 'intermesh' between institutions at the European level and at the national and sub-national levels of politics.[35] However, the Swedish central government fundamentally maintains the control of deliberations on EU affairs. It is the central government that provides background information to parliament and sets the rules, overall, for local and regional self-government. And despite the inherent spillover dynamics of being an EU member, no transfer of national sovereignty can occur without the accord of Member States' governments.

Nevertheless, the Swedish central government is a victim of conflictual pressures emanating from the supranational and the sub-national levels of government. There are, in fact, parallel processes of 'Europeanisation' and nationalisation, in the case of Sweden, in so far as membership of the Union provides policy-makers with the task of formulating national positions and vital interests. This double-edged challenge constitutes a paradox of being a Member State in the Union and is often overlooked by scholars in the field of 'Europeanisation'. In short, European integration brings about counter-reactions and countervailing forces.

Given the 'nation state logic' underpinning EU membership, Sweden is and will remain, regardless of the colour of the government, an obstacle to those forces that want the Union to develop in a federalist direction. This implies that Sweden's membership even makes it more likely that the Union will develop further into a 'multi-speed' or 'hard-core', and perhaps fragmented, entity. EU Member States should not be dealt with as unitary entities, or monoliths. In addition to the external constraints, a government like that of Sweden suffers internal, domestic constraints and these have to be identified if we are to understand the behaviour of Sweden as a Member State. Given the nature of the domestic constraints, Sweden will add to the cyclical ups and downs of European governance and is likely to remain, by and large, an 'awkward partner', at least in the eyes of committed European federalists.

Notes

1 For accounts of the factors explaining the decision to seek membership, see Jakob Gustavsson, *The Politics of Foreign Policy Change. Explaining the Swedish Reorientation on EC Membership* (Lund: Lund University Press, 1998); Magnus Jerneck, 'Sweden – The Reluctant European?', in: Teija Tiilikainen and Damgaard Petersen (eds), *The Nordic Countries and the EC* (Copenhagen: Political Studies Press, 1993); Cynthia Kite, 'Scandinavia Faces EU. Debates and Decisions on Membership 1961–1994', University of Umeå, *Research Report*, No. 2/1996; Paul Luif, 'On the Road to Brussels. The Political Dimension of Austria's, Finland's and Sweden's Accession to the European Union', *Laxenburg Papers*, No. 11/1995; Lee Miles, *Sweden and European Integration* (Aldershot: Ashgate, 1997); Bengt Sundelius, 'Changing Course. When Neutral Sweden Chose to Join the European Community', in: Walter Carlsnaes and Steve Smith (eds), *European Foreign Policy: The EC and Changing Perspectives in Europe* (London: Sage, 1994).

2 See Mikael af Malmborg, *Den ståndaktiga nationalstaten. Sverige och den västeuropeiska integrationen 1945–1959* (Lund: Lund University Press, 1994).

3 See Kerstin Jacobsson, *Så gott som demokrati: Om demokratifrågan i EU-debatten* (Umeå: Boréa, 1997).

4 See Gustavsson, (1998) *op. cit.*, Chapter 8; Karl Magnus Johansson, 'Tracing the Employment Title in the Amsterdam Treaty. Uncovering Transnational Coalitions', in: *Journal of European Public Policy*, 1/1999, p. 90.

5 See Wolfgang Wessels, 'An Ever Closer Fusion? A Dynamic Macropolitical View on Integration Processes', in: *Journal of Common Market Studies*, No. 2/1997, p. 289.

6 See Lee Miles, 'Sweden and the Intergovernmental Conference. Testing the Membership Diamond', in: *Cooperation and Conflict*, 4/1998, p. 184.

7 *Ibid.*, p. 221.

8 See Miles, 1998, *op. cit.*, p. 184.

9 See Henrik Oscarsson, 'Den svenska partirymden. Väljarnas uppfattningar av konfliktstrukturen i partisystemet 1956–1996', University of Gothenburg, Department of Political Science, 1998.

10 See Magnus Jerneck, *Subsidiaritetsprincipen i EU* (Stockholm: Fritzes, 1995).

11 See Johansson, 1999, *op. cit.*

12 See Ulf Bernitz, 'Amsterdamfördraget-utformning, betydelse och flexibel integration', in:: Ulf Bernitz *et al.* (eds), *Europaperspektiv 1998. Årsbok för Europaforskning inom ekonomi, juridik och statskunskap* (Stockholm: Nerenius och Santérus, 1998); Rutger Lindahl, 'The Swedish Debate', in: Josef Janning *et al.*, 'The 1996 IGC-National Debates (2): Germany, Spain, Sweden and the UK', The Royal Institute of International Affairs, Discussion Paper, No. 67/1996.

13 See Gunilla Herolf (ed.), 'EU Enlargement and Flexibility, The Swedish Institute of International Affairs', *Conference Papers*, No. 23/1998.

14 See Johansson, 1999, *op. cit.*

15 See Magnus Ekengren and Bengt Sundelius: 'Sweden. The State Joins the European Union', in: Kenneth Hanf and Ben Soetendorp (eds), *Adapting to*

European Integration: Small States and the European Union (London, New York: Longman, 1998), p. 146.

16 The question if Sweden is a 'reluctant European' has been posed by Jerneck, 1995, *op. cit.* See also Toivo Miljan, *The Reluctant Europeans. The Attitudes of the Nordic Countries Towards European Integration* (Montreal: McGill–Queen's University Press, 1977). It is mainly Britain that has been considered an 'awkward partner', specifically in a book title by Stephen George, *An Awkward Partner. Britain in the European Community*, Second Edition (Oxford: Oxford University Press, 1994).

17 It is important to emphasise that much of the acquis communautaire was integrated into Swedish law through the EEA. This made the accession negotiations easier and has contributed to Sweden's high degree of compliance with EC law and Single Market directives. In addition, one could point to cultural factors and to the relatively centralised Swedish political system.

18 It is interesting to note that a working group set up by the non-socialist government of 1991–94 actually suggested, similar to the British example, that the primary co-ordinative function should be placed in the Prime Minister's Office were Sweden to become an EU member. In 1997 the entire government office, consisting of the ministries, the Prime Minister's Office and the Office for Administrative Affairs, became a common authority.

19 Unlike the former Prime Minister and the leader of the Moderate Party, Carl Bildt, who is a devoted European. Bildt would have to define policies in the light of a Eurosceptic public were he again to become prime minister, however. In fact, there is opposition to EMU within his own party as well.

20 See Bengt Jacobsson, *Europa och staten: Europeiseringens betydelse för svensk statsförvaltning* (Stockholm: Fritzes, 1997); *Statskontoret* No. 6/1996, EU-medlemskapets effekter på svensk statsförvaltning: Samordning, organisation och arbetsformer i statsförvaltningens EU-arbete.

21 See Hans Hegeland and Ingvar Mattson, 'To Have a Voice in the Matter. A Comparative Study of the Swedish and Danish European Committees', in: *The Journal of Legislative Studies*, No. 3/1996; Hans Hegeland and Ingvar Mattson, 'Delegation and Accountability in Multi-level Parliamentary Democracy. The Swedish Parliament and the European Union', *Journal of Legislative Studies* No. 00/1900, 1 (2000). See also Torbjörn Bergman, 'National Parliaments and EU Affairs Committees. Notes on Empirical Variation and Competing Explanations', in: *Journal of European Public Policy*, No. 3/1997.

22 As regulated in the Swedish Riksdag Act (Chapter 10, Article 5): 'The Government shall keep the EU Advisory Committee informed of matters before the Council of the European Union. The Government shall also confer with the Advisory Committee concerning the conduct of negotiations in the Council prior to decisions which the Government deems significant and on other matters as determined by the Advisory Committee.'

23 In 1998 the Minister for Trade was criticised by the Committee on the Constitution, whose chairman also was a member of the EU Advisory Committee, because an official at the Swedish representation to the EU, voting on an issue dealing with tourism, apparently did not take the advice of the EU Advisory Committee into account.

24 The committee met several times at the final stage of the concluding IGC negotiations in Amsterdam in June 1997, having telephone conferences with the Minister for Foreign Affairs and chief negotiators.

25 In 1998 the Committee on the Constitution criticised the government for providing unsatisfactory background information with regard to a specific environmental issue.

26 See Martin Brothén, 'Parlamentariker emellan. Om kontakter mellan svenska riksdagsledamöter och EU-parlamentariker', manuscript, University of Gothenburg, Department of Political Science, 1998.

27 See Magnus Jerneck, 'East Meets West: The Öresund Area – A Case of Transnational Region-Building', in: Janerik Gidlund and Magnus Jerneck (eds), *Differing Eurogames for Nordic Territories* (Stockholm: Norstedts Juridik, 1999).

28 See Janerik Gidlund and Magnus Jerneck, *Komplex demokrati: Regional lobbying i Bryssel* (Stockholm: Norstedts Juridik, 1999).

29 See Gullan Gidlund, *Partiernas Europa* (Stockholm: Natur & Kultur, 1992); Magnus Jerneck, 'De svenska partiernas utlandsförbindelser-från internationalisering till europeisering?', in: Knut Heidar and Lars Svåsand (eds), *Partier uten grenser?* (Oslo: Aschehoug, 1997); Karl Magnus Johansson, *Transnational Party Alliances. Analysing the Hard-Won Alliance Between Conservatives and Christian Democrats in the European Parliament* (Lund: Lund University Press, 1997).

30 See Johansson, 1997, *op. cit.*

31 See Karl Magnus Johansson and Tapio Raunio, 'Partisan Sources of European Union. Comparing Finnish and Swedish Political Parties', in: *European Journal of Political Research*, No. 2/2001, pp. 225–249.

32 In a strongly critical front-page article in the *Frankfurter Allgemeine Zeitung* (7 September 1998), Sweden was depicted as a 'foreign policy dwarf' with a wait-and-see policy towards the Union, notably over EMU, common employment and common defence. Contrasting the Swedish approach to the Finnish, it was stated that the Swedes, more than three years into the membership, still look upon the Union as an alien body (Fremdkörper).

33 www.regeringen.se/info_rosenbading/regeringsforklaring/981006eng.html.

34 Ekengren and Sundelius, 1998, *op. cit.*, p. 146.

35 See Wessels, 1997, *op. cit.*; Dietrich Rometsch and Wolfgang Wessels (eds), *The European Union and Member States. Towards Institutional Fusion?* (Manchester: Manchester University Press, 1996).

Select bibliography

The text (English translation) of the Constitution of Sweden can be found at the University of Richmond's constitution finder at http://confinder.richmond.edu/. Further sources on government and parliament of Sweden can be found at Government www.regeringen.se or at Parliament www.riksdagen.se.

Ekengren, Magnus and Sundelius, Bengt (1998) 'Sweden. The State Joins the European Union', in: Kenneth Hanf and Ben Soetendorp (eds), *Adapting to*

European Integration. Small States and the European Union (London, New York: Longman).

Gustavsson, Jakob (1998) *The Politics of Foreign Policy Change. Explaining the Swedish Reorientation on EC Membership* (Lund: Lund University Press).

Jacobsson, Kerstin (1997) *Så gott som demokrati. Om demokratifrågan i EU-debatten* (Umeå: Boréa).

Jerneck, Magnus (1993) 'Sweden – The Reluctant European?', in: Teija Tiilikainen and Damgaard Petersen (eds), *The Nordic Countries and the EC* (Copenhagen: Copenhagen Political Studies Press).

Kite, Cynthia (1996) 'Scandinavia Faces EU. Debates and Decisions on Membership 1961–1994', University of Umeå, *Research Report*, No. 2/1996.

Luif, Paul (1995) 'On the Road to Brussels. The Political Dimension of Austria's, Finland's and Sweden's Accession to the European Union', *Laxenburg Papers*, No. 11/1995.

Malmborg, Mikael af (1994) *Den ståndaktiga nationalstaten: Sverige och den västeuropeiska integrationen 1945–1959* (Lund: Lund University Press).

Miles, Lee (1997) *Sweden and European Integration* (Aldershot: Ashgate).

Sundelius, Bengt (1994) 'Changing Course: When Neutral Sweden Chose to Join the European Community', in: Walter Carlsnaes and Steve Smith (eds), *European Foreign Policy: The EC and Changing Perspectives in Europe* (London: Sage).

17 *Kenneth A. Armstrong and Simon Bulmer*

The United Kingdom: between political controversy and administrative efficiency

Introduction: once a latecomer always a latecomer?

European integration has represented one of the most fundamental challenges for politics in the United Kingdom since 1945. Integration has highlighted the problems of, and possibilities for, the re-orientation of foreign policy as part of the United Kingdom's post-war descent from world power status. The 'Monnet method' of supranational integration raised constitutional concerns for a state which had elevated territorial integrity and parliamentary sovereignty to key normative principles of its institutional order.[1] Integration has at different times divided the main political parties internally as well as being a source of division between them, from the ratification of accession right through to the present. Levels of public support for integration have been among the lowest of all Member States. And yet the business of preparing, making and implementing European policy has been characterised by considerable efficiency at the official level.

For the United Kingdom as for the other Member States the result has been a pattern of 'fusion': 'trends of merging public resources at several state levels, leading to increasing complexity, a lack of transparency and difficulties in reversing the development'.[2] However, this fusion has not led to a homogenisation of patterns of European policy-making within the Member States. The British approach remains distinctive. Its political and legal institutions are outside the continental mainstream, and its European policy discourse remains distinctive. But that is not to say that there has been no impact of EU membership. The UK constitution is in the process of undergoing major reform as part of the Blair government's political agenda of modernisation. European integration is among the stimuli for this change.

Political context

The United Kingdom was not a founder member of the European Communities. Neither of the two main political parties was prepared to engage with European organisations that went beyond intergovernmental forms of co-operation. Under the Conservative Macmillan government a policy change took place, resulting in the decision to apply in 1961 for membership of the Communities. This decision was contested within the government and opposed by many in the Labour Party. Following the 1963 rejection of the British application by President de Gaulle, the Wilson Labour government made a renewed application in 1967 which met the same fate. Following de Gaulle's retirement in 1969 the international climate for UK accession improved and it was the incoming Heath Conservative government which was able to agree terms of entry. Once terms had been finalised, the Heath government faced the task of securing the passage of the accession agreement (the European Communities Bill) in Parliament. The government had to contend with a significant group of dissenting MPs within its own party; out of a highly contested situation the internal party factionalism on integration developed that has persisted in various forms to the present.

Based on a lack of political consensus, EU membership has been dogged by two other factors. First, no real vision has been presented by successive British governments of what form European integration should take, there has been much greater clarity on what was not wanted from integration.[3] In consequence, a persistent feature of the United Kingdom's relationship has been one of 'backing into integration' out of fear of isolation, with other states taking the initiative. UK (prime) ministers have been seriously lacking in 'the vision thing' where European policy has been concerned – Mrs Thatcher's support in the early 1980s for the Single Market Programme was a notable exception.[4] Beyond that – and prior to the 1997 Blair government – proposals for strengthening integration have been of a pragmatic nature. Second, successive UK governments have had to contend with an acquis communautaire that did not reflect British interests most notably the principles of the CAP and the EC budgetary arrangements. These substantive policy issues could rally parliamentary opposition to the Union in the same way as miscellaneous threats to sovereignty. European integration has been a 'poisoned chalice' for all governments, from Heath to Major. Whether the Blair government is able to avoid the same fate will depend on how it handles the policy of British participation in the single currency.

If we examine governmental priorities and attitudes towards the last three exercises in treaty reform we are able to capture the first of the two problems. In 1985 the SEM White Paper was adopted at Milan and the IGC was set up that led to the SEA. The position of Mrs Thatcher's Conservative government was one of support for the SEM: a policy which she could regard as market liberalisation of the kind she advanced domestically. Her government was much more reserved about the SEA, especially the institutional reforms.

The strategy in the negotiations leading to the Maastricht Treaty was not radically different, although much more complex owing to greater intrusion of domestic political divisions. Mrs Thatcher was deeply concerned by German unification but did not draw the conclusion that it should act as a spur to deeper integration. She made clear her opposition to monetary union in 1990, a position which was fully in line with her more sceptical policy on the Union in the late 1980s, as outlined in Bruges in 1988. Her negative position on EMU was one of the factors which led to a leadership challenge against her in the Conservative Party and culminated in her replacement in December 1990 by John Major. The new prime minister's effort to put 'Britain at the heart of Europe' was compromised by the presence of key figures in his Cabinet who were opposed to deeper integration. Two key integrationist advances in the Maastricht Treaty – EMU and the Social Chapter – were subject to British opt-outs. Concerned about the loss of national sovereignty, the Major government was one of the key advocates of subsidiarity being introduced as a guiding principle in the Maastricht Treaty. A notable exception to this position was the British initiative to strengthen the powers of the ECJ so that it could fine states which flouted EC law. Increased powers for the EP and greater use of QMV were not among the government's wishes but were regarded as a necessary part of the Maastricht 'deal'. The subsequent ratification of the Treaty brought the government, re-elected in April 1992 with a much reduced majority, to the brink of defeat.

With Major still in power, and a vocal group of rebellious Eurosceptic backbenchers, the British government played a rather obstructionist role in the IGC preparing what became the Amsterdam Treaty. The breakdown of relations with EU partners over the handling of the outbreak of 'mad cow' disease (CJD) entrenched positions further. The government's policy was largely defensive, for instance in blocking increased use of QMV and further powers for the EP. In those areas where it made initiatives, they were largely to limit, or roll back, supranational powers, for example in its proposals to limit the powers of the ECJ. The IGC effectively ground to a halt as partner states hoped for a change of government at the May 1997 British general election. The incoming Labour government of Tony Blair proved more flexible: accepting, inter alia, more QMV, increased powers for the EP and signing up to the Social Chapter.[5]

As can be seen from the above episodes the United Kingdom has been a somewhat reluctant participant in these three exercises in EU constitutional revision. The Blair government's wish to play a much more positive role in integration has been borne out to some degree, as in proposals for a European defence identity. However, non-participation in the single currency places the United Kingdom on the sidelines of the EU's key integrationist programme.

What are the key European policy priorities of the Blair government? The two specific manifesto commitments were:

- To hold a referendum on participation in the single currency
- To lead reform of the Union.[6]

The latter of these refers to a range of proposals, including: rapid completion of the single market; a high priority for enlargement of the Union to CEE countries and Cyprus, with accompanying institutional reforms; reform of the CAP and of the Common Fisheries Policy; greater openness and democracy in EU institutions and support for a proportional voting system in national elections to the EP; retention of the veto on matters of national interest but extension of QMV in a limited number of areas; and signing up to the Social Chapter.[7]

Having proved more flexible in the IGC than its predecessor, Chancellor Gordon Brown in late 1997 set out the conditions under which the government would recommend joining the single currency. It then made progress towards putting its other commitments into action during the Presidency. The overall position of the Labour government remains one of commitment to a Union composed of sovereign states but it is more prepared to see the Union as an 'opportunity structure' than Major's government.

Constitutional context

The principal characteristics of the British political system are as follows:

- Until summer 1999 it was a unitary state; it is now an *asymmetrically devolved* one (i.e. there is limited devolved power in England, and the powers devolved to Scotland and Wales differ from one another).
- It is a *constitutional monarchy*, with the formal seat of power residing in the Queen in parliament (parliamentary sovereignty).
- Parliamentary sovereignty embodies the principle that the *government-in-parliament* has the ultimate power to make or unmake any law (i.e. no law can bind a successor parliament).
- There is *no formal, written constitution* and *no British Constitutional Court* vetting parliamentary legislation or acting as a check on government.
- The English *legal tradition* (common law) differs from that of continental Europe.
- The rules of the Westminster electoral system tend to ensure *single-party majoritarian government*.
- The institutional structure of the state encourages the conduct of *adversarial politics* in Westminster between government and opposition parties.
- The Prime Minister has considerable potential power resources, and

can call upon the *centralised machinery of Whitehall*, co-ordinated through the Cabinet Office, to reinforce leadership.

- The direct involvement of the state in *economic governance* is relatively limited by comparative European standards.
- The *civil service* is well qualified, under pressure to be efficient, and theoretically neutral (i.e. subservient to the objectives of whatever party is in power).
- State power has traditionally been concentrated on *central government*, with local government having a weak position.
- The United Kingdom nevertheless comprises different *national identities* (Scots, Welsh, etc.) as well as the complex situation in Northern Ireland.
- Finally, the *constitutional order* – of England in particular – has evolved peacefully over many centuries, with no breach of territorial or constitutional integrity.

This constitutional order has been stable for much of the post-war period. However, the Labour government embarked on several major reform exercises, which we discuss at the end of the chapter.

The national policy-cycle: a Rolls Royce machinery with erratic politicians at the wheel?

The conduct of the United Kingdom's European policy is dependent on the politicians at the head of government being able to put the machinery of government to effective use (Figure 17.1). The latter has sometimes been regarded as a very smooth, 'Rolls Royce' operation. At times, however, this Rolls Royce has been described as having a lunatic at the wheel, as dogmatic political positions have been adopted on the substance of European policy. The latter situation has been most likely to occur when 'parliamentary arithmetic' makes the House of Commons a key veto point in the formulation of European policy. Thus, we have argued that two broad patterns of European policy conduct can be identified in the United Kingdom.[8] Under circumstances of a small parliamentary majority, we argued that continued British sensitivity to issues of sovereignty could result in issues of European policy being handled in a highly symbolic, rhetoricised manner and following the logic of adversarial parliamentary politics. However, we also argued that much European policy did not trigger these sovereignty concerns and was consequently conducted at a more technical level.

We do not wish to depart from that analysis, which we feel offers a valid explanation for the bulk of the period of UK membership since 1973. But we do need to point out the very special circumstances enjoyed by the Blair government. It was elected in 1997 with a majority of 179 seats.

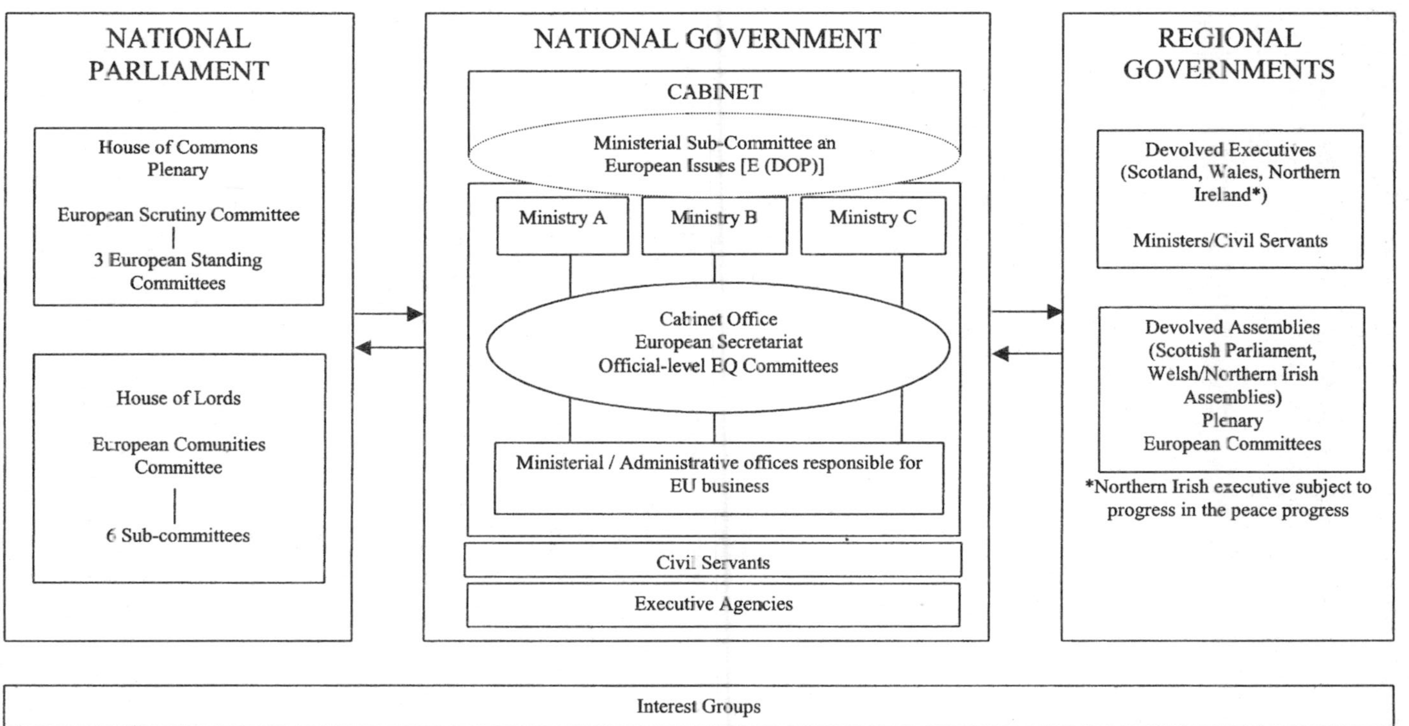

Figure 17.1 The national level of European decision-making – United Kingdom

Furthermore, generational turnover among Labour MPs reduced the number of Eurosceptics in the party. Hence the government had a commanding majority and it is unlikely that parliamentary veto points will play a major part in the formulation of European policy. This situation is a big departure from the circumstances prevailing for the Major government, revealed most dramatically in his difficulties in securing the ratification of the Maastricht Treaty but evident also in a range of other issues, including the domestic handling of relations with the Union over CJD.[9]

What is the contemporary machinery for the making and controlling of European policy?[10] The principal institutional link between national politics and the Union is through the national governments, which are often seen as occupying the role of 'gatekeepers'. This designation derives from their central institutional role at the intersection of national and European decision-making. British central government comprises different levels, of course, and it is important to be alert to these in what follows. Thus, the growth of the European Council since 1975 has brought with it a major involvement on the part of heads of government. The ministerial level is extremely active in the various formations of the Council of Ministers. The civil service is active in the preparation and implementation of policy. It is also involved at the European decision-making stage by supporting the appropriate national minister or through participation in COREPER and related committees and working groups. The involvement of civil servants in EU negotiations may occur in the form of the Whitehall-based officials. Equally, the role of the UK Permanent Representation in Brussels (UKREP) must be considered. Finally, civil servants and ministers have an involvement in transposing Community law into national law where this is necessary. Implementation and application of EC law is a separate task which falls to central government; central government agencies;[11] local authorities (and, post-devolution, to devolved authorities in Scotland, Wales); and – depending on the peace process – in Northern Ireland.

There are two apparently contradictory patterns evident in the management of British European policy. One is a pattern of *centralisation*. Its centripetal features find expression in:

- the co-ordination of European policy by the Cabinet Office European Secretariat (COES, whose origins date back to the 1960s);[12]
- co-ordination at political level by a ministerial sub-committee on Europe, whose origins date back to the original application for membership;
- the growth of prime ministerial involvement, especially following the creation of the European Council in 1975;
- a strong information-sharing value within the British civil service.

The other trend is more *centrifugal*, and can be seen in other features, such as:

- the problems of co-ordinating the sheer volume of business that emanates from the Union;
- the emergence of 'mini-hubs' for co-ordination: in the Foreign and Commonwealth Office (FCO) for the CFSP, in the Home Office for JHA, and in the Treasury for EMU;
- the tensions which may develop between devolved executives and central government in London.

Hitherto – and certainly when compared with other Member States – the centripetal dynamics have prevailed. However, much business does not necessitate government-wide co-ordination, and this work is carried out in a more decentralised way.

The role of the Prime Minister

The Prime Minister has many policy areas beyond the Union to attend to. However, important tasks include dealing with the Union in the run-up to regular European Council sessions, regular EU items on the agenda of Cabinet meetings, and frequent bilateral summits with EU counterparts. In comparative terms the Prime Minister has considerable power resources. They may be used in connection with European policy under two particular sets of circumstance: where European policy is contested within Parliament and perhaps also in the Cabinet; and where a European policy initiative is pursued. The former situation led John Major (1990–97) to expend much effort on European policy, e.g. in finding a negotiating line on Maastricht or in trying subsequently to agree a policy (of keeping options open) on UK participation in EMU. Given the parliamentary salience of European policy for most of the period since 1973, the Prime Minister must have good antennae for picking up signals from the political environment. The latter situation was more typical of Heath (1970–73), who made accession a government priority. It is also worth noting that prime ministers have considerable scope for limiting the discussion of policy in areas that they wish to keep as a domaine réservé. Participants in her cabinets have noted that this practice was used by Mrs Thatcher to restrict discussion of European policy.[13] The Prime Minister's staff in 10 Downing Street will provide support for this European policy business but the principal adviser on European policy is the head of the COES.

The role of departmental ministers

By comparison with the Prime Minister, the involvement of several departmental ministers is more continuous, since it is neither dependent on the relatively infrequent meetings of the European Council nor on the fluctuating political salience of European policy issues. The Foreign Secretary, the Minister of Agriculture and the Chancellor of the

Exchequer are particularly affected in this way, with annual meetings of 'their' Council of Ministers formation into double figures. The key ministers are those in the ministerial sub-committee, known as (E(DOP)) under the Blair government and as (OPD(E)) under Major. The formal reporting structure of this sub-committee is via the Foreign Secretary, as Chair, to the full Ministerial Committee on Defence and Overseas Policy (DOP) but, more usually, direct to the Cabinet itself, where there is a regular EU agenda item.

The European dimension of ministerial work has not been an 'easy ride' for several of the incumbents. Among the casualties of senior office on European policy-related grounds have been: Michael Heseltine/Leon Brittan (1986), Nigel Lawson (1989), Nicholas Ridley (1990) and Sir Geoffrey Howe (1990) under Mrs Thatcher and Norman Lamont under Major. These upheavals normally arose from contested views on European policy on the part of individual politicians.

Civil service departments

The lions' share of European policy is conducted at the specialist level within the individual ministries. Moreover, all departments now have EU business, from the Ministry of Agriculture Fisheries and Food (MAFF, since 2001 DEFRA) – arguably the most 'Europeanised' ministry – to the more peripheral Ministry of Defence and the Department of Culture, Media and Sport. The key players, however, are the FCO, the Department of Trade and Industry (DTI), MAFF and the Treasury. Our attention is focused initially on the policy- and decision-making stages, that is to say, on the period up to formal decision-making in the EU institutions.

The decision to integrate EC affairs into the existing organisational structure of the ministries was taken in summer 1971 when, following a review of other countries' systems, Prime Minister Heath decided that there would be no Ministry for Europe but, rather, all ministries should 'think and act European'.[14] Co-ordination was entrusted to the Cabinet Office's European Secretariat, which was considered to be a more neutral agency than the FCO for bringing together the wide spectrum of ministerial views, since the latter's expertise lay in diplomatic matters. The COES is staffed by some nine senior staff who are seconded from those ministries which are most affected by EC matters but the head is always from a home department – counter-balancing the FCO appointment of the Permanent Representative in Brussels. It acts 'as a clearing house for the dossiers that go to ministers as well as providing guidance for departments on others'.[15] Its co-ordinating role comes to the fore when Whitehall-wide negotiations are under way, such as for IGC negotiations or enlargement. In co-ordination there is a strong norm that policy should be agreed early and thereafter the whole of Whitehall should 'sing from the same hymn-sheet'. The secretariat's tasks also include the preparation of negotiating tactics: a task facilitated by a Friday meeting of relevant ministries, attended by the Permanent Representative. The head of the European Secretariat is particularly influential in co-ordinating governmental policy and, in addition, briefs the prime minister prior to sessions of the European Council. Staff from the COES chair official level committees: EQO, comprising senior officials (formerly known as EQS), and EQO at middle-ranking level. The former meets infrequently but the latter often, although the meetings are often ad hoc. The members of these committees are part of an EQ network, among whom key papers on European policy are distributed. Special sub-committees may be set up separately from these two, for example to co-ordinate on IGCs or enlargement. It is also worth noting that there is a separate lawyers' network within central government, chaired by the Cabinet Office Legal Adviser, who is located in the Treasury Solicitor's Department. It has its own committee, known as EQO(L) and meets frequently, chiefly to co-ordinate on legal advice or on EU litigation.

For the purposes of cross-national comparison, it should be pointed out that the Cabinet Office is the part of the government responsible for putting into practice the principle of collective cabinet responsibility. It functions in an anticipatory mode; it does not have to contend with intra-coalition negotiations; nor does it expect to devote large parts of its time to solving crises which have already reached the Cabinet, since its role is to pre-empt them. These characteristics set it apart from most of its counterparts elsewhere in the Union.

The FCO plays a more technical kind of co-ordinating role. It shadows most policy areas and leads on institutional developments and CFSP in its EU Departments. It is formally responsible for UKREP in Brussels. It also assumes a greater role in policy co-ordination when the United Kingdom holds the Presidency, and will set up a special Department for about eighteen months. In 1999 it absorbed bilateral relations with European partners into its EU command structure.

Other ministries have had to accommodate the European dimension in a significant manner. MAFF/DEFRA is a prime example because of the extent to which national agricultural policy is integrated into the CAP. Already in 1982 it was estimated that some 200 MAFF officials travelled to Brussels each month.[16] The DTI's responsibilities within the Union are extensive and include the majority of the Single Market Programme, trade, regional policy and research and technology policy. Under the Blair government a Minister for Trade and Competitiveness in Europe was appointed – Lord Simon, formerly Chief Executive of BP. His responsibilities include the DTI's European Directorate as well as responsibility for the Euro Preparations Unit, which is located in the Treasury. The Treasury itself is a key ministry, including responsibility for budgetary policy and monetary union. Its strict budgetary rules have an impact on all Whitehall departments which have responsibility for programmes spending resources for the EC budget.[17] The Home Office has become a more significant player in European policy with the growth of JHA co-operation.

The Scottish, Welsh and Northern Ireland Offices also warrant comment, for they have often been neglected in studies of European policy-making in the government. Prior to devolution in summer 1999, at which point their roles changed, they had a twofold responsibility. On the one hand, they represented their particular territorial interests at the policy-making stage, whether at ministerial or administrative level. On the other hand, they supervised policy implementation in their own territories. For instance, the existence of the separate Scottish legal system often necessitates different implementing legislation from the rest of the country. In Scotland and Wales devolved executives took on these functions from July 1999. At the time of writing the peace process in Northern Ireland had not made sufficient progress for a similar planned development to take effect there.

Other agencies

All these departments and ministers are engaged in the preparation of policy. There will be consultation of other agencies outside the departmental structure of government as the need arises. The Bank of England is an obvious case in point in respect of EMU. It was granted autonomy by Chancellor Gordon Brown in 1997; however, this decision was presented much more as a decision designed to facilitate a sound monetary policy. The move does, of course, have implications for joining the single currency. UK competition agencies are consulted on European competition policy, for instance; the Health and Safety Executive (HSE) on EU legislation in that domain; the Civil Aviation Authority (CAA) on air transport liberalisation policy; and so on. Customs and Excise and the Inland Revenue, two agencies responsible to Treasury ministries, have a significant involvement in European policy.

The role of UKREP

UKREP is a key component of European policy-making. It acts as an intelligence-gathering body, keeping ministries briefed on developments in the supranational institutions. But its involvement becomes more critical in the decision-making stage, where the Ambassador, the Deputy Permanent Representative and other officials undertake key preparatory work with their counterparts in the Council hierarchy, pending formal ministerial approval. UKREP has generally had a staffing level of some fifty senior officials: one of the larger Permanent Representations in Brussels and drawn from ministries across Whitehall. As already noted, the Permanent Representative returns to Whitehall on Fridays to discuss the tactics and strategy of British policy at a Cabinet Office meeting with interested ministries. This regular participation in Whitehall's European policy-making is indicative of the latter's centralised nature. The involvement of the UK government in negotiations has been summarised well by Peter Pooley, formerly the senior MAFF official in UKREP: '[T]he British are more predictable. They are very well briefed, they are very articulate, it's very easy to get hold of and understand their point of view. It's relatively more difficult to change it.'[18] This last comment highlights the fact that a highly co-ordinated European policy such as the United Kingdom's may bring inflexibility in negotiations within the Union. This situation – a product of the institutional characteristics of EU policy-making within the United Kingdom – may be compounded by the adversarial norms which British politicians bring with them to the Council and the European Council that do not emphasise the more consensus-building dynamics in the EU intergovernmental institutions.

Developments post-Maastricht

Maastricht-related developments in EU policy-making have been of much less significance than for certain other states, such as Germany. There has been no fundamental re-arrangement of the government machinery. The principal change has been the reinforcement of three subsidiary co-ordination hubs under the umbrella of the COES machinery.

On EMU, both in the IGC negotiations leading to Maastricht and thereafter, the Treasury has served as a co-ordinating 'mini-hub'. Under the Conservatives contacts were with the Bank of England at a technical level and between the Chancellor and the Prime Minister at the political level (owing to the sensitivity of the issue within the government). Under Labour the DTI was brought in rather more, with the need for British industry and commerce to prepare for the Euro even without UK participation. The creation of an EMU Preparations Unit within the Treasury has been the main institutional change. On JHA co-operation the Home Office has taken on the role of 'mini-hub', reflecting the fact that the UK representative on the K4 Committee is from that Department. Other ministries and agencies involved include the Lord Chancellor's Department (i.e. the law officers) and Customs and Excise. The staffing compliment of the Home Office has grown considerably in order to deal with JHA business. On CFSP the existing 'mini-hub' around the FCO has been reinforced somewhat, with the Ministry of Defence becoming more involved with the advent of negotiations on security and defence policy. Beyond these developments there has been no fundamental change, although there has been some adjustment to parliamentary procedures.

Regions and other sub-national actors

The involvement of central government administration in Scotland, Wales and Northern Ireland pre-devolution has been outlined above. In England central government has the so-called 'government offices' in the regions, such as the English North-West, and their creation was partly stimulated by the Union, notably the growth of the Structural Funds. Prior to summer 1999 there have been no directly elected assemblies above the level of local authorities, but regional governance is becoming an increasingly significant development across the United Kingdom.

Parliament and policy-making

The role of parliament in shaping British European policy has three aspects. First, the House of Commons is recognised as a 'talk' parliament rather than as a 'work' parliament. It is not especially attuned to the influential scrutiny of proposals emanating from the Commission. Secondly, the government's institutional origins lie in its majority in the House. Ministers thus need to be conscious of those EU developments which might encounter serious criticism within the House. As already indicated, this anticipatory function becomes even more critical when the government-in-office holds only a small majority. The third aspect is the work of the House of Lords, where business tends to be oriented towards detailed scrutiny. The focal point of the work of the House of Commons lies in oral reports, debates and questions relating to the Union. In the first category fall, for example, the reports made by the Prime Minister following a meeting of the European Council. Parliamentary questions may be asked of ministers or the prime minister on European matters, although it would be difficult to attribute any significance to these upon the ultimate pattern of negotiations in the Council of Ministers. The European Scrutiny Committee monitors proposals from Brussels and decides whether fuller debate is necessary, normally in one of three European Standing Committees established for the debate of different domains of EC legislation. However, such standing committees rarely capture public attention and party discipline generally ensures a fairly smooth passage. Commission documents have to be deposited with the committees within forty-eight hours of their formal receipt by the government and the lead department is expected to submit an Explanatory Memorandum as the government's evidence to Parliament within ten days. Amongst the weaknesses of the scrutiny system are pressure on timing, and problems discussing proposals before they are formalised. JHA and CFSP business was excluded until reform in November 1998.

A further means of control is an agreement with the government that no minister should agree to legislation in the Council if the scrutiny committee has not been consulted: the so-called 'scrutiny reserve' power, from which JHA and CFSP business were also excluded until November 1998. The 1998 reforms were part of the Labour government's parliamentary modernisation programme, pursued by the House's Modernisation Committee.

The work of the House of Lords is conducted in the Select Committee on the European Communities. This (1998–99 session) comprised six sub-committees according to policy area. The Committee's reports are thorough and highly regarded in the United Kingdom and elsewhere in the Union. Parliamentary control over EC legislation was for many years far from perfect; indeed, it was not until 1989 that the House of Commons Scrutiny Committee was permitted (i.e. by government) to look at anything other than formal EC proposals. Thus the SEA could not be considered prior to ratification, nor could the work of the IGC in which it had been negotiated. The Maastricht Treaty has certainly contributed to the pressure for reform of parliamentary procedures on EU business but it was as part of Labour's manifesto commitment to reform that momentum gathered pace in 1998.

Policy implementation

It has become the convention to describe the United Kingdom as a combative negotiator in the Council of Ministers but a good performer in terms of the subsequent implementation of EC law. One explanation for the latter has been civil service centralisation and efficiency. Moreover, there are in the United Kingdom no institutional features discriminating against EC legislation; as it has been pointed out, administrators may not even be aware of the origins of the legislation.[19] Indeed, the importance of the administrative context may be developed further; the centralised nature of the UK administration may contribute to the positive performance. By contrast, a federal state may create longer chains of command. But arguably as important is the culture embedded in the British public administration. Although the British administrative machinery is not populated by staff with a legal training, there is nevertheless a strong assumption that laws are made to be put into practice.

Transposition and compliance

In the previous section we suggested that the United Kingdom's administrative structures tend to ensure the positive implementation of EC obligations. Of course, the transposition of Community legislation is but one form of compliance. Breaches of Community law may occur through transgressions of directly effective Treaty provisions, such as the rules on free movement. Or Community rules can be implemented, but incorrectly applied by the relevant national agencies. In this way, there are no straightforward indicators of how well the United Kingdom complies with its obligations. That said, we can point to some indicators:

- In terms of direct actions brought before the ECJ for failure to fulfil obligations, forty-one cases were brought against the United Kingdom between 1973 and 1998. This compares with 225 cases against

Belgium, 122 against Germany, 185 against France and a massive 355 against Italy.

- Few cases make it all the way to the ECJ. The majority of cases are resolved after the Commission has sent a Member State a letter of formal notice (the first stage in bringing infringement proceedings under Article 226 (ex Article 169) ECT. Between March 1998 and March 1999, twenty-one letters of formal notice were sent to the United Kingdom (compared with thirty to Belgium, thirty-one to Germany, fifty-two to France and forty-three to Italy) for alleged breaches of SEM rules.
- As regards implementation of SEM directives (in terms of the Commission's Single Market Scoreboard), the United Kingdom has a higher implementation rate than Belgium, France and Italy, but a poorer performance compared with Germany.

Approached with appropriate caution, it is evident from the above that the United Kingdom appears to have a good compliance record. However, it is important to stress that much of the life of EC law can be found in the use made of EC law arguments by litigants before their national courts. The statistics above give no indication of the qualitative significance of EC law within the national legal orders.

EC law in the UK courts

It is evident from previous sections that UK membership has resulted in institutional adaptation and evolution within the domestic administrative order. Adaptation and evolution within the national legal order is a more complex question. In its early jurisprudence, the ECJ itself made clear that national legal orders were to provide the structures, processes and remedies for the enforcement of Community law rights. It has, however, moved from such a position of complete procedural autonomy to recognise that features of the national legal orders may create barriers to the effective protection of Community law rights. In this way, while there has been no harmonisation of legal orders in institutional and procedural terms, national impediments to the effective protection of EC rights have been removed. Two UK cases are significant in this respect. In *Marshall II*, a national limitation on the amount of compensation to be paid for a breach of the Equal Treatment Directive was found by the ECJ to prevent the effective protection of EC rights.[20] In *Factortame I*, the House of Lords, following a preliminary ruling from the ECJ,[21] set aside a national constitutional rule preventing the granting of interim relief against the Crown. Perhaps the most important intrusion into the national legal orders has been the ECJ's creation of the doctrine of state liability for breaches of Community obligations. In the United Kingdom, the possibility for obtaining damages against the Crown for public wrongs has historically been very limited. But as a result of the ECJ's *Brasserie du Pêcheur/Factortame* ruling,[22] the English courts have awarded compensation to Spanish fishermen who suffered loss as a consequence of the United Kingdom's discriminatory system for the registration of fishing vessels.

Developments in the availability of remedies are a visible manifestation of the impact of EC law in the United Kingdom. Less visible is the more routine use of EC law arguments in the UK courts. It is clear that litigants may seek to use arguments derived from EC law to supplant or even replace domestic legal discourse. The use of EC law in the national courts has been enhanced in the public law sphere by a distinct legal evolution in the form of the 'application for judicial review'. The accompanying liberalisation of the rules of locus standi together with an enhanced ability to seek the remedy of a 'declaration' have been harnessed by individual litigants and pressure groups to seek declarations that public bodies have acted contrary to Community law. The impact of EC law upon the United Kingdom cannot, therefore, be traced back to simple moments of Treaty revision like the Maastricht or Amsterdam treaties. Rather, the dynamics of change are driven by a mixture of developments within the broader Community legal order; changes within the domestic legal arena; and the unpredictable flow of litigation in national courts.

Closing the door to the ECJ?

One means by which we might test the willingness of UK courts to engage with and accept EC law is to consider the use of the preliminary ruling procedure under Article 234 (ex Article 177) ECT. Although eagerness in seeking rulings from the ECJ may be considered to be indicative of a willingness to accept EC law, the converse is not necessarily true. Indeed as integration proceeds, national courts should feel themselves able to correctly apply EC law without the need for a ruling. Comparison between different Member States is difficult not least because of the differences in date of accession. By 1998, courts or tribunals in the United Kingdom had sought 269 preliminary rulings. Of these, twenty-three were sought by the highest civil court (the House of Lords) and ten by the English Court of Appeal.[23] The remaining 236 rulings were sought by lower courts or tribunals. By comparison, French courts have sought 594 rulings, Italian courts 581 rulings, while the German courts have sought 1,113 rulings. Even taking accession dates into account it is evident that the UK courts do not make as much use of the Article 234 ECT procedure as their EU partners. It has been suggested that lower courts use references to the ECJ as part of a strategy of judicial empowerment, while the higher courts may seek to restrict the use of references. It is true that the English Court of Appeal attempted to establish a restrictive approach to the use of references in the 1970s, but there is evidence that these guidelines have not been followed subsequently. Indeed, the English courts seem well aware of the advantages in seeking a ruling at an early stage if this is appropriate.

EC law and the UK constitution

At first sight it may seem paradoxical that a state like the United Kingdom, whose constitutional order is premised upon a dualist approach to international law coupled with a strong principle of parliamentary sovereignty, does not evidence strong conflicts between national and EC law. This paradox may seem more acute when one thinks of the difficulties encountered in France and Germany. That is not to say that reception of Community law is unproblematic – rather that the courts have generally sought to avoid conflicts.[24] As Craig has noted, UK courts have accepted their obligations under Community law using a number of techniques:

- By reasoning from national constitutional law itself, fulfilment of EC obligations can be viewed as an expression of the will of Parliament as expressed in the European Communities Act which gives effect to UK membership.
- Interpretative techniques can be used to avoid conflicts – although some judges have cautioned against distorting the language of UK statutes.
- In *Factortame I*, the House of Lords accepted the functional logic of the ECJ in the sense that the UK court set aside a national rule which prevented the effective protection of Community law rights.

That the English courts have accepted the functional rationale of the ECJ – i.e. the effectiveness justification for giving effect to Community law – does not necessarily imply that the courts accept the more normative rationale of the ECJ. Another way in which the constitution shapes UK membership concerns the whole process of negotiating and giving effect to international treaties in the first place. The United Kingdom, unlike its EU partners, does not possess a codified Constitution but rather a set of constitutional practices and constitutional norms deriving from a variety of sources. The power to negotiate and ratify treaties is an exercise of the royal prerogative; a power which is vested in the Executive and carried out in practice by government ministers. Parliament has no formal role in the ratification of treaties leading to the paradox that while Parliament has sought to increase its supervision of the Executive in the day-to-day decision making process of the Union, it has little power to supervise the Executive as regards the ratification of treaties. As a matter of constitutional practice under the so-called 'Ponsonby Rule', the texts of treaties are laid before Parliament for at least twenty-one days prior to ratification, and this will normally prompt a debate on the treaty.

Nonetheless, Parliament has only the possibility of expressing disapproval of the treaty (with no direct consequences) or more significantly of using a debate to force a motion of no confidence in the government (with the hope of precipitating a change in government). While the Executive may be responsible for the negotiation and ratification of treaties, any changes in the national legal position as a consequence of such treaties can be brought about only through an Act of Parliament. There is, therefore, potential for the Executive to ratify a treaty but for parliament to fail to enact laws to provide for the obligations contained in a treaty. This would itself amount to a violation of the Vienna Convention on the Law of Treaties. Therefore, it is normal practice for the required legislation to pass through parliament in advance of treaty ratification by the Executive.

The United Kingdom's relationship with the Union is regulated through the European Communities Act 1972, and with each treaty revision, amendment has been made to the Act. However, the Bill to give effect to the Maastricht Treaty created an opportunity for political battles both within and between the main UK political parties.[25] In short, the Bill to amend the 1972 Act became the subject of wrecking amendments proposed by Eurosceptic Conservative MPs and by the then Labour Opposition seeking to inflict damage on an increasingly beleaguered Conservative Administration. After the then Conservative government made approval of its Maastricht negotiations a matter of confidence in the government, the necessary resolution was passed, and the Bill was ultimately enacted as law.

Once the Act came into force, attempts to block the Maastricht Treaty continued through resort to the courts. It follows from the principle of the sovereignty of Parliament that the UK courts cannot call into question the validity of an Act of Parliament. Thus, challenge was brought by Lord Rees-Mogg to the executive act of ratification of the Maastricht Treaty,[26] rather than to the validity of the European Communities (Amendment) Act itself. This challenge, however, failed. The legal action met the same fate as the 1971 challenge to the United Kingdom's decision to accede to the European Communities in the first place,[27] namely a reassertion of the distinct constitutional roles played by the Executive and the Judiciary. In short, the English courts do not have the ability to seek to enforce national democratic approval of the foreign policy acts of the Executive. In the absence of strong parliamentary controls over the Executive in this field, the result is a relatively poor set of constitutional controls when compared to the United Kingdom's European partners.

Legal fusion?

To talk of 'legal fusion' in the EU context is to court controversy. It is undoubtedly true that UK membership of the Union has had consequences for national legal orders in terms both of the acceptance of the doctrinal jurisprudence of the ECJ and the incorporation of the material law of the Treaties and secondary legislation. But this is not the same as legal convergence or legal fusion. National laws and institutions may remain tightly coupled to social processes within the nation state.[28] While national institutions can adapt to accept rather than repel Community law, this is not the same as assuming the convergence of legal orders. In any event, we live in a world of greater complexity than the simple interaction of Community and national law. Globalisation forces can create new divergences. Thus, while the legal order of the United Kingdom may be fused to that of the Union, this relationship is one of mutual influence, adaptation and evolution.

Conclusion: moving towards the continental mainstream?

The argument thus far has been that the United Kingdom has an efficient machinery at official level, but one which has been at times subject to doctrinaire political positions, especially when parliamentary veto points have been in play. The Labour government elected in 1997 and re-elected in 2001, however, has called into question this interpretation. It has done so in two respects. It has adopted a more pro-European policy, exemplified by Blair's constructive European policy and engagement with fellow Centre-Left governments in the Union, a situation already clear at the EU level with agreement on the Amsterdam Treaty. Domestically, the absence of parliamentary veto points was clear with the smooth ratification of the treaty. It is chiefly the government's equivocation on joining the single currency that harks back to the United Kingdom's ambiguous stance of earlier periods. However, at the same time domestic constitutional reforms may call into question the existing efficient machinery. To examine this aspect we need to focus on the constitutional agenda of the government and its interaction with EU policy-making.

Perspectives for the future

The Labour government came to power in 1997 with an extensive commitment to constitutional reform.[29] Many of the proposed reforms have a European policy dimension, although the stimuli for them were principally domestic. Once fully operationalised, the making and implementation of European policy will have undergone fundamental change as part of reform UK politics. The proposals (status in brackets) include:

- *Scottish and Welsh devolution* (legislation enacted, elections to the new bodies in May 1999; powers transferred to assemblies/executives on 1 July 1999).
- The creation of a *power-sharing executive in Northern Ireland* as part of the peace process (legislation enacted and assembly elected but

executive's creation is contingent on the political situation including decommissioning of paramilitaries' weapons).

- A *directly elected London mayor* to head a new Greater London Authority (GLA) and the creation of regional development agencies and (indirectly elected) regional assemblies in England (in progress).
- Introduction of *proportional representation election systems* for the devolved assemblies and the EP (all used in 1999) and a referendum on whether to reform the electoral system for Westminster (not yet scheduled).
- Incorporation of the *Convention of Human Rights* (enacted).
- *Independence for the Bank of England* (enacted).
- Modernisation of the *House of Commons* (in progress – proposals and White Paper, with reforms on European business mentioned above).[30]
- Reform of the *House of Lords* (legislation on first stage in session 1998–99).
- The promise of a *freedom of information bill* (draft bill introduced for consultation in spring 1999).

These are major changes. They will have a transformative impact on the UK political system generally and the making of European policy specifically. Their full ramifications cannot be judged at the time of writing. What is clear on a general level, however, is that the United Kingdom's constitutional order is moving much closer to the continental mainstream. Coalition government, such as in Scotland, will become less unusual in the United Kingdom. Multi-level governance is now a political feature, and the Union may come to be seen as one level of government among several. EU and foreign policy are retained powers of the UK government but policies such as agriculture, the environment and regional development are devolved, so relations between the devolved executives and London may become politicised over European policy. The presence of a minority Labour administration in Wales and a Labour–Liberal Democrat coalition in Scotland reduces the scope for political clashes with London of the kind more likely had the Scottish National Party (SNP) taken power in Edinburgh. Nevertheless, there will be domestic tensions over European policy where policy issues have a territorial dimension, and the smooth administrative machinery may even be weakened, as devolved executives serve different political masters. The United Kingdom's good record on implementation may be challenged now that some legislation is to be implemented by devolved authorities rather than purely in Westminster.

It is difficult to judge exactly where all these developments will lead: the politics and public administration of European policy in the United Kingdom are both 'in play' as the country enters the new millennium.

Notes

1 See Simon Bulmer, 'Britain and European Integration: of Sovereignty, Slow Adaptation, and Semi-Detachment', in: Stephen George (ed.), *Britain and the European Community. The Politics of Semi-Detachment* (Oxford: Clarendon Press, 1992), pp. 1–29.

2 Wolfgang Wessels, 'An Ever Closer Fusion? A Dynamic Macropolitical View on Integration Processes', in: *Journal of Common Market Studies*, No. 2/1997, p. 267.

3 See most notably the Major government's White Paper in 1997: Foreign and Commonwealth Office, 'A Partnership of Nations: The British Approach to the European Union Intergovernmental Conference 1996', Cm 3181 (London: HMSO, 1996).

4 See the statement of HM Government's policy in 'Europe – the Future', in: *Journal of Common Market Studies*, No. 1/1984, pp. 74–81.

5 For more detail, see Simon Bulmer, 'European Policy. Fresh Start or False Dawn?', in: David Coates and Peter Lawler (eds), *Labour into Power* (Manchester: Manchester University Press, 2000).

6 *New Labour because Britain Deserves Better* (London: Labour Party, 1997).

7 For fuller examination, see Bulmer, 2000, *op. cit.*

8 See Kenneth Armstrong and Simon Bulmer, 'United Kingdom', in: Dietrich Rometsch and Wolfgang Wessels (eds), *The European Union and Member States. Towards Institutional Fusion?* (Manchester: Manchester University Press, 1996), pp. 253–290, esp. p. 262.

9 On the former, see David Baker, Andrew Gamble and Steven Ludlam, 'The Parliamentary Siege of Maastricht 1993. Conservative Divisions and British Ratification', in: *Parliamentary Affairs*, No. 1/1994, pp. 37–60.

10 In the outline that follows our account rests on the machinery prior to devolution.

11 Under the 'Next Steps' reforms, introduced by the Conservatives, one aim was to achieve a much clearer distinction between policy-making functions, retained in the ministries, and policy implementation, hived off to agencies.

12 On the historical origins of the machinery, see Simon Bulmer and Martin Burch, 'Organising for Europe: Whitehall, the British State and European Union', in: *Public Administration*, No. 4/1998, pp. 601–628.

13 Interview with former Cabinet minister.

14 Bulmer and Burch, 1998, *op. cit.*, p. 612.

15 Geoffrey Edwards, 'Central Government', in: Stephen George (ed.), *Britain and the European Community. The Politics of Semi-Detachment* (Oxford: Clarendon Press, 1992), p. 84.

16 Quoted in Edwards, 1992, *op. cit.*, p. 73.

17 See Bulmer and Burch, 1998, *op. cit.*, p. 618–619.

18 Quoted in Edwards, 1992, *op. cit.*, p. 76.

19 Philip Butt, Alan and Christina Baron, 'The United Kingdom', in: Heinrich Siedentopf and Jacques Ziller (eds), *Making European Policies Work, Vol. II, National Reports* (London: Sage, 1988), p. 639.

20 Case C-271/91, *Marshall* v. *Southampton and South-West Hampshire AHA* (No. 2) [1993] ECR I-4347.

21 Case C-213/89, *R* v. *Secretary of State for Transport ex p. Factortame* [1990] ECR I-2433.
22 Cases C-46/93 and C-48/93, *Brasserie du Pêcheur/Factortame* [1996] ECR I-1029.
23 No specific indication is given by the ECJ of references from Scottish or Northern Irish courts. The number of rulings sought by the English Court of Appeal is inconsistent with previous ECJ statistical information used by us in Dietrich Rometsch and Wolfgang Wessels (eds), *The European Union and Member States. Towards Institutional Fusion?* (Manchester: Manchester University Press, 1996).
24 For an overview of the reception of EC law within the United Kingdom, see Paul Craig, 'Report on the United Kingdom' in: Anne-Marie Slaughter, Alec Stone Sweet and Joe H.H. Weiler (eds), *The European Courts and National Courts: Doctrine and Jurisprudence* (Oxford: Hart Publishing, 1998).
25 See Baker, Gamble and Ludlam, 1994, *op. cit.*, pp. 37–60.
26 *R* v. *Secretary of State for Foreign and Commonwealth Affairs ex p. Rees-Mogg* [1994] 1 All ER 457.
27 *Blackburn* v. *Attorney-General* [1971] 2 All ER 1380.
28 Günther Teubner, 'Legal Irritants: Good Faith in British Contract Law or How Unifying Law ends up in New Divergences', in: *Modern Law Review* No. 1/1998, pp. 11–32; Imelda Maher, 'Community Law in the National Legal Orders: A Systems Analysis', in: *Journal of Common Market Studies* No. 2/1998, pp. 237–254.
29 For an overview of current developments, see the Constitution Unit's web site http://www.ucl.ac/constitution-unit/.
30 The House of Commons Modernisation Committee published its White Paper (Cm 4095) on 11 November 1998. See www.coi.gov.uk/coi/depts/GCO/coi8036e.ok for a summary of the key reform proposals.

Select bibliography

The text of the Constitution of the United Kingdom can be found at the University of Richmond's constitution finder at http://confinder.richmond.edu/. Further sources on government and parliament of the United Kingdom can be found at Government www.fco.gov.uk or at Parliament www.parliament.uk.

Armstrong, Kenneth and Bulmer, Simon (1996) 'United Kingdom', in: Dietrich Rometsch and Wolfgang Wessels (eds), *The European Union and Member States. Towards Institutional Fusion?* (Manchester: Manchester University Press), pp. 253–290.

Buller, J. and Smith, Michael (1998) 'Civil Service Attitudes Towards the European Union', in: David Baker and David Seawright (eds), *Britain For and Against Europe. British Politics and the Question of European Integration* (Oxford: Clarendon Press), pp. 165–184.

Bulmer, Simon and Burch, Martin (1998) 'Organising for Europe – Whitehall, the British State and the European Union', in: *Public Administration*, No. 4/1998, pp. 601–628.

Bulmer, Simon and Burch, Martin (2000) 'The Europeanisation of British Central Government', in: A. W. Rhodes (ed.), *Transforming British Government, Vol. 1 – Changing Institutions* (London: Macmillan).

Drewry, Gavin (ed.) (1996) *Westminster and Europe. The Impact of the European Union on the Westminster Parliament* (London: Macmillan).

Edwards, Geoffrey (1992) 'Central Government', in: Stephen George (ed.), *Britain and the European Community: The Politics of Semi-Detachment* (Oxford: Clarendon Press), pp. 64–90.

Gregory, Francis (1983) *Dilemmas of Government: Britain and the European Community* (Oxford: Martin Robertson).

Slaughter, Anne-Marie, Stone Sweet, Alec and Weiler, Joe H.H. (eds) (1998) *The European Courts and National Courts – Doctrine and Jurisprudence* (Oxford: Hart Publishing).

Wallace, Helen (1996) 'Relations between the European Union and the British Administration', in: Yves Mény, Pierre Muller and Jean-Louis Quermonne (eds), *Adjusting to Europe. The Impact of the European Union on National Institutions and Policies* (London: Routledge), pp. 61–72.

III

Conclusion

18 *Jürgen Mittag and Wolfgang Wessels*

The 'One' and the 'Fifteen'? The Member States between procedural adaptation and structural revolution

Does the EU matter? Fundamentals before and after Maastricht

The growth and differentiation of the institutional and procedural system of the European Union has created considerable challenges for all Member States.[1] The very nature of the process of European integration is a continuing pooling of sovereignty, and a transfer of responsibilities and authorities, which has enlarged the range of policy areas dealt with by the Union through para-constitutional communitarisation. This process has led to institutional and procedural differentiation and a subsequent widening of the functional scope of integration in the form of sectoral differentiation. Moreover, this enlargement of the EU's policy-making scope has brought into play a growing number of governmental and non-governmental bodies dealing with public policy. We can also observe an increasing actor differentiation.

Within the individual Member States there is an ongoing reaction to these challenges of the developing EU system. A general survey of the fifteen national systems does not however, paint a clear and unequivocal picture. With regard to the results of earlier analysis[2] the impression which can be sketched from the empirical material is vague and sometimes even confusing, including both divergent and convergent patterns of national adaptation.

For a systematic overview we use a typology (see Figure 18.1) differentiating between 'strong' and 'weak adapters' at both the national and at the 'Brussels' level. Do we witness on the one hand strong national performers (horizontal axis, type 3) shaping clearly defined interests and preferences in their own capital with regard to European policies and the making of political decisions without much access to Brussels? Who are these strong protagonists in the interplay between various intra-state actors in one Member State? On the other hand, are there 'strong' players at the supranational level (vertical axis, type 2) making efficient use of the opportunities for access and influence in the Brussels arena without an

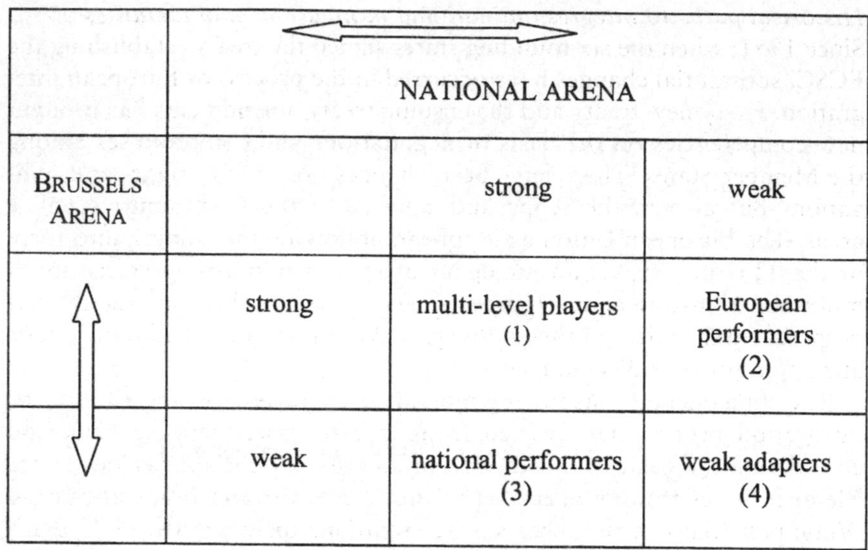

Figure 18.1 Models of Member States' adaptation

equivalent say in the national capitals?[3] Finally, do we observe 'strong multi-level' players (type 1) which are able to strengthen their access and influence on both levels and to make use of their position on each of these levels for strengthening their say on the other?

One finding is valid for all Member States: national institutions have made substantial efforts in order to cope with the requirements of the Union. As to the fundamental view on the European polity, all relevant actors in EU Member States are aware of the increasing importance of the Union and of the need to take strategic decisions on vital issues. Focusing on this observation, the central question is to what extent the trend towards 'Europeanisation' has had an effect on the Member States. How relevant are the EC/EU oriented procedures as well as the institutional and administrative set-ups for the Member States and for their constituencies? Have these procedures and set-ups led Member States to move towards becoming 'strong multi-level' players (type 1)? To what extent are national institutions involved in the policy-cycle of the European Union? Has there been a 'Europeanisation' of national institutions or a fusion of national and European institutions creating a persistent trend towards field 1? Do we observe a convergence between the various national models leading to stability in the EU system[4] or will our findings indicate a plurality of adaptation patterns such that a comparative view of Figure 18.1 would show many variations?

Historical paths to integration: national motivations and identities

Since 1951, when the six founding states signed the treaty establishing the ECSC, substantial changes have occurred in the process of European integration. Every new treaty and the ensuing treaty amendments has brought new competencies on the basis of negotiations and compromises among the Member States. There have been changes not only in rights and obligations but also in the scope and salience of the Community's policy areas. The European Union as it appears following the coming into force of the TEU in 1993 is an amalgam of several national interests and a multitude of historical developments. The success of this construction has perpetuated the effect of the EC/EU process, leading to a kind of magnetic attraction for outside countries.

The fundamental reasons for individual countries wishing to join the integration process have varied from case to case. Stepping back and considering the basic premises we can identify several approaches in the Member States from the very beginning of their respective memberships. While politicians in the three smaller founding members (B, LUX, NL)[5] have drawn their conclusions from the failure of their neutrality policies, the engagement of Germany was accompanied by the struggle for more acceptance and the need to regain sovereignty after the disastrous effects of the Second World War. A traditionally strong tendency towards multilateralism and the desire to overcome its social fragmentation have been the main reasons for the engagement of Italy in the integration process. French motives for participation were based to a certain degree on the belief that national interests – such as the political and economic control of Germany – could be realised most efficiently within a European set-up. Moreover, actors in France and the United Kingdom still subscribe to the belief that they should hold a position of political leadership that can be achieved to a certain degree through a European 'alliance'. The Danes were attracted to apply for Community membership primarily for economic reasons but were also motivated by a fear of isolation. Additionally, in Ireland the intention to achieve more independence from the United Kingdom should be stressed. On the other hand, Greece as well as Spain and Portugal, have linked their accession to the European project with the expectation of promoting the process of democratic consolidation after the demise of their authoritarian systems. The three latest newcomers were particularly motivated by economic reasons. However, in the case of Finland, geopolitical security interests have also played an important role 'because the decision to join the Western unity . . . had been beyond Finland's reach during the five long decades of the Cold War'.[6] The European Union has also been seen as an instrument for domestic modernisation. In several cases the challenges of the European level are highly welcome by the single Member States. Some of them consider the integration process as a gateway for their national projects of modernisation (A, GR, IR, NL), economic liberalisation (SF, S) or as providing the necessary guidance for overcoming particular regional problems such as the bi-national system of Belgium or the strong north–south cleavages in Italy. For a remarkable number of nations, 'opening the state' to the Union seems to provide the groundwork for necessary internal reforms.

Although the *finalité politique* of the integration process remains vague and ambiguous, the discourse on Europe in most Member States still embodies the expectation that the EU polity in general offers a better and safer future. The construction of these images and views continued in the 1990s and has even been somewhat reinforced by the new applicants. The Eurosceptic or minimalist states have continued to view their European engagement in terms of their own historical role and perception of a national future. The difficulties of adapting to a moving target are clearly visible and they remain high on the national agenda of an increasing number of states.

Despite this diversity of national motives a common groundwork for all Member States can be found. The idea of European integration has been promoted by a set of similar and common goals and aspirations such as the striving 'for the principles of liberty, democracy, respect for human rights and fundamental freedoms'[7] – but especially the search for economic benefits and the pursuit of national goals linked to a nation's identities and role in the world.

Priorities of the Member States: promoting 'national interests'

The vast majority of Member States have declared their agreement with the fundamentals of the European construction, implicitly assuming that this was the best way to serve their own national interests. However, with another upswing of Eurosceptic attitudes, governments in the 1990s reinforced arguments in favour of defending and pursuing vital national interests. The Maastricht process increased this trend in a considerable number of states, especially in such founding members as Germany, France and particularly the Netherlands, where the Maastricht Treaty was regarded as a 'dramatic moment' causing a 'rude awakening to the political realities of Europe in the 1990s'.[8] But 'even the smallest Member State', as is stated with regard to Luxembourg, 'is sometimes susceptible to reservations about the idea of integration'.[9] This emergence of more robust national attitudes can be seen as a direct or indirect consequence of the implementation of Maastricht, even in Member States considered as traditional supporters of the integration process.

Analysis of the fifteen Member States suggests that there are very heterogeneous interests in the policy domains of the European Union. These interests are linked closely to the peculiar structure and the geographical or organisational context of each Member State. Therefore, policy fields such as agriculture and fishery continue to be the highest-ranking domains in Ireland or Spain while other states are particularly interested in strong manufacturing bases or high export rates. Finland and Sweden, for instance, are engaged in an initiative on a 'Northern Dimension' of the Union while southern states such as Greece, Spain or Portugal are primarily interested in a continuation of the Structural and Cohesion Funds. These interests are difficult to categorise. National priorities are the product of particular intra-state structures and developments. Domestic issues are the prevailing issues. Thus, if we are looking at the 'real' actions of national governments, '(re)-nationalisation' of policies appears quite often to be more of a public relations affair than an actual change in policies pursued. Therefore, the same or similar policies are adopted and are promoted as 'good' European policy – or, as in more recent times, are described in terms of their national benefits. In the 1990s, most Member States gave a high priority to budgetary and monetary issues. Besides the demand for a reduction in national contributions to EU finances (D, NL, S, UK), the creation of EMU attracted particular attention in all countries. As far as security and defence are concerned, there are considerable differences between the positions of the founding Member States (B, D, F, I, LUX, NL) and the north-European countries (DK, S, SF, UK), which are either reluctant to participate in any military co-operation owing to the high priority given to national sovereignty and national defence, or because of a traditional policy of neutrality. The security initiatives of the Blair government since 1997 and the Helsinki decision on closer military co-operation therefore represent a fundamental change and might induce more adaptations of non-aligned countries.

Public opinion: from permissive consensus to reluctant acceptance

At first sight, we find in all Member States – with the exception of the United Kingdom and to a certain degree, Denmark and Sweden – a long-standing affective and, to a lesser extent, utilitarian support for the European enterprise. The integration process has been regarded for much of its history as a positive-sum game for many Member States. However, since the end of the 1980s and especially towards the mid-1990s this overall trend changed. Attitudes within Member States to the European integration process became more multi-faceted.[10] In several countries, more and more signs of Euroscepticism surfaced, causing heated debates concerning the benefits and costs of membership (A, D, DK, S, UK). The new and more sensitive issues of the Maastricht Treaty evoked more sceptical views and serious concerns among the general public about the democratic deficits of the European Union.[11] A commonly held view of the European enterprise was that its political aspects had their shortcomings while the economic side had been undoubtedly a success. The highest rates of support could be detected at the end of the 1990s in some of the original Member States (I, LUX, NL), on the Iberian peninsula (E, P) and particularly in Ireland. On the other hand, the lowest rates of support for EU membership are expressed in public opinion polls in some northern states (S, UK) and in Austria.[12] In nearly all Member States but especially in Germany and the northern states of the Union – and particularly with regard to EMU – there was a considerable gap between the attitude of elites and the rest of population. While political and economic elites are principally in favour of membership – as they see the benefits to be gained from the Community – the general public is less positive. Hence, in these Member States 'two worlds' can be observed: the general public discourse evolves according to its own mainly national logic on the one side as do the dynamics of the multi-level EU system on the other.

Whatever public opinion polls tell us specifically in each Member State, one major finding across the 'EU-fifteen' is that the increasing controversy concerning the development of European integration has not put the EU system itself into question. In view of the considerable changes in the international and European system since 1989 it is even more revealing that fluctuations in public opinion have basically not changed: pre-existing trends have thus not been reversed but have even been reinforced. Looking at the national end of the EU policy-cycle, the Brussels level of the EU polity seems to have become an essential day-to-day part of national political systems.

Such an observation offers a contribution to the issue of legitimacy.[13] That is, the surprising overall stability of the EU system might be due to the broad and intensive participation of national elites. Nevertheless, towards the end of the 1990s this tendency lost its dramatic impact. Though support for EU membership had not grown significantly, neither were there serious concerns about the European integration process as such. Instead, a 'positive indifference'[14] or a tendency towards 'accommodation of the inevitable'[15] has become the essential background for policy-making. The low voter turnout at the EP elections in June 1999 seemed to confirm this trend. Thus we might conclude that the public mood has changed from permissive consensus to 'reluctant acceptance'[16] or 'issue-related voice'[17] – with considerable variations within this broad trend.

Political parties: growing relevance of a 'European cleavage'?

As major national actors, parties are also slow and reluctant adapters. A vast majority of national parties support unconditionally, or to a large degree, the European integration process in general. The European policies of political parties in government are usually based on a broadly pro-integration attitude. Changes in government tend to have only limited impacts on the basic perceptions of European policies of the Member

States and on the methods of running the EU machinery. Strangely enough, this statement is also valid for eurosceptic, 'awkward'[18] or minimalist states. A higher degree of public distrust has only limited impact on governmental and administrative machinery. In no case has the forming of a new government led to a complete re-formulation of the national strategy on European integration.[19] Frequently, a consensus pervades in which both governmental and opposition parties approve of the integration process. Nevertheless, there is a small number of parties opposing further integration and, more importantly, in some cases an increasing internal party factionalism concerning the strategy towards European integration.

Since Maastricht, the debates on European policy in some Member States have brought about another cleavage in national party systems. The salience of both pro- and anti-European arguments have led to an additional dividing line between or within parties. Though attitudes towards European integration have become more differentiated, European matters play an increasing role in certain national party systems. A strict distinction between left or right oriented parties may be of limited use.[20] There are parties of the far right and left, ecological, regional or religious parties as well as conservative parties favouring re-nationalisation of particular policy fields. Recent election campaigns and the formation of anti-Europe-election platforms in some Member States (DK, F, UK) show this trend clearly. Negative feelings have been used by some parties, such as the Austrian FPÖ or the Swedish and orthodox Greek communists, to reinforce their anti-establishment strategies.[21] Moreover, pro-integration parties fear losses at the polls if their campaigns are too pro-European, especially if smaller parties stir up the national EU debate (DK, P, UK). As was seen in Finland in 1995, ruling parties have indeed paid heavily for their pro-European attitudes with considerable losses in the elections.

More important than the impact on party systems are the effects on individual parties. Differing attitudes towards Europe have led to increased tension within parties such as the French Gaullists, the British Conservatives and especially the parties in Sweden. Here, we observe 'opposition to supranational integration within all the Swedish political parties'.[22] Even (some) party splits can be attributed to the impact of European policy issues. The debate on Europe is thus often characterised more by intra-party rather than inter-party division. However, despite these cases the main trend is different: European integration, including major steps such as renouncing one's own currency, has not yet led to a new permanent cleavage in the party system or in political life in general. No persistent patterns can be identified EU-wide. Opposition parties with a critical view of the Union often discover, when coming into power, the utility of the EU system. An anti-European stance might be of importance for parties in some countries, but there is no united anti-EU front in the making. No 'anti-system party'[23] against the European Union has gained major relevance.

Except for some crises attracting media attention, most European policies and politics belong to the normalcy of everyday political life. The major dispute concerns the direction and the speed of this construction. Disputes about concrete issues often arise without leading to any kind of fundamental opposition.

Interest group politics: attraction by the European magnet

As has been revealed by the debate about pluralistic and corporatist interests, institutions and administrations in western political systems are closely linked to intermediary groups of different kinds.[24]

The participation of interest groups such as labour unions, employers' or farmers' associations or other NGOs represents an expression of specific societal interests. In some Member States these voluntary unions and corporate actors have developed considerable influence by using the informal channels of representative democracies in order to urge governments to act on matters of concern. For many, but not all interest groups, the expectation of access and more influence in Brussels has become a powerful magnet.[25] Taking the increased competencies of the European Union and its institutions into account, for several Member States 'Brussels' has gained more importance for the representation of organised interests while the significance of national political institutions and the domestic level has not decreased to the same degree.

Though there are many interest groups in each Member State, the most developed systems of such groups can be found in those Member States with (neo-) corporatist traditions, such as Austria, the Netherlands, Ireland, Germany and the northern states of the Community.[26] A growth in the formation and activities of interest groups – owing to the new challenges posed by the Union – is especially notable in Spain, France and apparently in Greece, where 'both industry and the unions have been increasingly using Europe not only as a lobbying field but also as a source for ideology formation'.[27]

The position of interest groups towards the European integration process is – very generally – positive. Nevertheless, there are some deviations depending very much on ideological and policy preferences – and also particularly on the sector. Thus, in the Finnish case, membership of the Union was opposed by farmers and the rural population owing to serious concerns about European competitors while industrial lobbyists were hoping for better access to the European market.[28]

Since the SEA and the Maastricht Treaty, interest groups have paid more attention to the European sphere because the EU institutions have made them aware of the importance of early-stage information and contacts. Larger companies, especially multinationals, are aware of the strategic importance of EU rules concerning competition, health, safety and environment, and of EU programmes and initiatives concerning R&D. Thus, the number of offices run in Brussels by the various interest groups continues to rise. Large corporations have their own delegations which in some cases include more staff than the offices of Europe-wide federations.[29]

Interest groups are still directing their attention primarily towards the European Commission. However, with the coming into force of the Maastricht treaty and the co-decision procedure, the EP has increasingly become a second point of contact in Brussels while the Council – which is less accessible – plays only a minor role for interest groups as they may turn instead to their governments in the national capitals. All in all, we can see that many have become active multi-level players in the semi-official, and even more in the informal and non-hierarchical networks.[30]

Constitutional provisions: smooth and limited adaptations

Looking at one major indicator for institutional change – the legal constitutions of Member States – the findings show again a modest rate of EC/EU-related revisions. The constitutions of the Member States are expressions of long traditions and historical identities of the respective nation. Participation in European integration and the adaptation of the relevant and valid community law, the 'acquis communautaire', has forced the Member States again and again to make incremental amendments to their constitutions. However, an overview of the constitutional changes in the fifteen national systems reveals that the rate and the salience of changes at the European level has not been matched by analogous structural revolutions in the Member States. One major conclusion is thus: political and administrative strategies have in all states been geared to use existing constitutional and institutional opportunity structures and to improve forms of intra-state co-ordination.

Constitutional changes have occurred only in some countries and are limited in scope and even more limited in their impact on the national policy-cycle. Changes are not linked specifically to the implementation of the Maastricht Treaty; rather, as in the Spanish case, they are related 'to the natural evolution and adaptation of the ... public administration to the requirements of the EC/EU decision-making process'.[31] Though European integration is among the incentives for constitutional change (A, D, F), there have also been adaptations or substantial changes as in the Netherlands (1983), Belgium (1993) or the United Kingdom (1998–99), which are not rooted in the challenges of the European treaties but in the deficiencies or shortcomings of national systems. In case of the United Kingdom they are explained as 'part of the Blair government's political agenda of modernisation'.[32]

The impact of Maastricht: a turning point for national fundamentals?

If we come back to the initial question concerning the impact of Maastricht, the latter has to be seen in the light of European history. Five steps and four subsequent periods which are defined by historical decisions to create, amend or revise the treaty can be identified: the ECSC, the Rome Treaty, the SEA, the Maastricht Treaty and – currently – the effects of the Amsterdam Treaty. The overall trend is clear and persistent: over fifty years, national actors have increasingly dedicated their attention to playing the EC/EU multi-level game both at home as well as in the European arena. The Maastricht Treaty has reinforced this trend. The TEU was the result of one year of negotiations between the different governments of the Member States. It had an immediate impact on the various actors and societies in the national systems. Though there are some Member States in which the impact of Maastricht was less substantial, in most states the TEU process attracted much attention. While the quasi-constitutional changes and reforms of the Maastricht Treaty have not been a turning point for the national systems, the changes brought about by Maastricht have reinforced pre-existing patterns. Furthermore new Member States have rapidly mobilised the necessary resources to compete successfully in all policy fields and in all stages of the policy-cycle.

Has Maastricht led to more convergence in the fundamentals? Our overview suggests several areas of convergence, especially concerning the basic reasons behind application for membership but also with regard to public opinion. Nevertheless a vast number of specific national characteristics remain. All in all, this survey adds to the conventional picture and reaffirms that some traditional insights are still relevant in the 1990s. In spite of substantial changes within the Community and the Union, and even after the major upheaval of the international and European political system in 1989, the historic legacy remains strong. In other words, the Member States or at least the political elites, define the *raison d'être* of the Union and its process of deepening and widening in terms of their own historical, geopolitical constellations and identities. Many Member States refer to their own history, such as in Ireland where it has been noted that 'in Europe, Ireland was attempting to consolidate its economic and political independence and re-discover its society's internationalist traditions'.[33]

In terms of reasoning about the fundamentals and the input dimension of a political system, there is a divided view concerning the extent to which the fifteen have become one: the debate about the *finalité politique* is still mainly influenced by national heritages. However, discussions concerning the future of Europe, which are often vague in nature, are nevertheless part of the debate on the general objectives of the Member States. The Member States' histories may differ but the future is broadly seen as a common endeavour. More specific visions of the Union are however, strongly influenced by national experiences. Thus, the European Union is supposed to become a Member State's own positive dream for the best of all worlds.

Do national institutions matter? The Member States in the EU policy-cycle

In comparison to the vast variety of political systems in the world, the European Union's Member States constitute a rather homogeneous group made up of what might broadly be described as 'liberal democratic systems'. Concerning their governmental structures, the fifteen Member States of the European Union generally fit into the category of parliamentary systems but with a wide range of variations. After the constitutional changes in Finland and Portugal only the French system could still be characterised as semi-presidential. Although there is a general trend towards convergence, there are still many divergences in the governmental structures of European states. They differ both between more consensual and more majoritarian patterns of policy-making as well as in terms of varying patterns of relations between central and regional levels.[34] Consensual traditions as in Austria, the Scandinavian states or the Netherlands, or federal structures as in Germany or Belgium, considerably influence the methods of policy-making adopted in the Member States. Such a typology allows for a comprehensive analysis of the fifteen national political systems and of the role, function and weight of their institutions.[35] However, rather than employing an extensive approach, our examination of the Member States' political systems focuses on the institutional framework and the relevant institutions with regard to the EU policy-making process without considering the particulars of each national system.[36]

Governments: national gatekeepers in European affairs?

Among governmental actors we observe a uniform instinct to seek out access and influence in EU policy-cycles and, at the same time, several processes of adaptation such as a shift in the intra-governmental balance.

In all Member States of the European Union, prime ministers or chancellors, as the heads of government, have become key actors in EU affairs. Particularly through their role as members of the European Council they are able to steer internal procedures and thus to lead the national decision-making process. The European Council and bilateral summits have even reinforced the role of those heads of government that were less powerful in the national arena. Given the need to act assertively and coherently in making key decisions, which are increasingly taken through the European Council, prime ministers have gained power *vis-à-vis* their colleagues. A shift in power towards heads of government can be observed in several Member States (DK, F, GR, SF), and even in such countries as the Netherlands where the formal status was traditionally that of a *primus inter pares*. As is the case in Italy, one can observe in many cases in the post-Maastricht period 'a shift of activities and co-ordinating competencies in the national implementation of EC policies from the Foreign Affairs Ministry, which dominated the scene for decades, to the prime minister's offices'.[37] Thus, the EC/EU process has changed the balance inside governments. In France this process has had a particular impact: 'The changing patterns of executive European policy-making are not solely a result of the actual president's weaknesses, rather they elucidate the long-term consequences of the Maastricht integration boost, and a decline of presidential power in general.'[38] Overall, the members of the European Council have become strong multi-level players.

Beyond a uniform basic instinct of governmental actors to attempt to gain access to the European 'policy-making process' we can identify certain directions. The European level is matched by the national governmental level particularly in the centralised countries of the Community (DK, F, GR, IR, LUX, P, S, SF, UK) where politicians of national governments have a powerful grip on EU affairs and where the EU-related bureaucracy is directly linked to the government in developing effective means for participating in the EU decision-making process (DK, F, UK). The more decentralised (E, I, NL) or federal countries (A, B, D) are characterised by a stronger involvement of the regional level, with the effect that in Belgium and Germany, regional ministers can participate in the Council of Minister's decision-making. Depending on the policy field and the issue at stake in the Council of Ministers, each national ministry and many departments therein are more or less intensively involved in the EC/EU decision-making process following traditional intra-state logics. In the Finnish case, for example, the 'key position of ministries and their officials mirrors the concrete exertion of powers and influence in the domestic EU process'.[39] Very roughly, we can differentiate between on the one hand, pioneer ministries such as those dealing with foreign affairs, finance, economics or agriculture, and on the other, newcomers such as ministries of environment, education, etc. Within those ministries which have a long-standing involvement in EU affairs, special units have been set up and consolidated, and have acquired a substantial role. Those ministries which have developed such units more recently, still have problems in establishing their position inside the national co-ordination machinery. Interestingly however, in all Member States we find within nearly every national ministry, a unit responsible for EU affairs. From the early days of European integration, departments of agriculture were the main ministries affected by membership, but nowadays they are only one of many embedded in the EU's policy process.

With the exception of defence, government ministries and, in many cases, administrative units within departments, have established their own EU resources and networks. Yet with the new plans for 'military crisis management'[40] even defence departments are becoming involved. The General Affairs Council of 15 November 1999 brought together for the first time in the history of the Union, the ministers of foreign affairs and defence. Sectoral differentiation – that is, the increasing number of policy fields dealt with by the EU – has therefore had remarkable effects. This fragmentation is also evinced by the increase in the number of committees operating on the same level as COREPER.[41]

With this decentralisation process within national governments, the need for hierarchical or co-operative co-ordination across policy sectors has grown.[42] Without exception all Member States substantially increased their internal co-ordination efforts in the 1990s. Foreign ministries remain formally the lead department in most (B, DK, E, F, GR, I, IR, LUX, P, S, UK) but not all Member States. Since the coming into force of the TEU, foreign ministers in several countries have lost some of their influence. Rivalries, particularly those between foreign ministries and economic/financial ministries concerning responsibility for the different EU pillars, have led to a more branched structure. Owing to the growing importance of EMU this shift has been accompanied by a greater role for finance ministers.

The number of policy fields at the EU level has thus promoted more sophisticated co-ordination between ministries. As ministries have been increasingly affected by European policies and as their desire to participate has grown, it has become necessary for governments to establish an effective system of interministerial and intra-ministerial co-ordination and co-operation in order to reach common viewpoints and to develop a coherent negotiation strategy. The way the Member States have dealt with this challenge reveals quite different patterns. A number of Member States adopt the practice of establishing special informal or ad hoc cabinet committees (E, F, I, NE, UK) while in others the cabinet as a whole takes on the task of formal co-ordination and decision-making (A, B, DK, IR, S, SF). A separate European ministry with far-reaching co-ordination competencies has not been established in any Member State. Though in some states (F, GR, I, SF, UK) sub-ministries with a moderate capacity for co-ordination have been created, in most Member States European policy is organised in a decentralised manner by the relevant specialised ministry.

While in Ireland we can detect a 'relatively light co-ordination',[43] such Member States as Denmark – which have developed 'elaborate co-ordination mechanisms'[44] – are known for their streamlined co-ordination machine (DK, F, P, SF). Developments after the coming into force of the TEU show that the mostly hierarchical methods of co-ordination are decreasingly able to cope with all issues, actors and information in the

European sphere. They have not prevented the 'subtle trend towards more independent approaches to the EC/EU affairs on the part of certain ministries',[45] that is, a tendency towards sectorisation and decentralisation. In Spain the existence of a central co-ordination body, the Secretariat of State for Foreign Policy and the European Union linked to the Ministry of Foreign Affairs, has not prevented interministerial conflicts and difficulties in defining positions in COREPER and the Council of Ministers. This tendency is still relevant after the internal reform of the 'Secretariat' in 1998.

Other countries such as Germany or Belgium are characterised by fragmented policy-making and have developed more complicated internal co-ordination mechanisms, with the result that their positions in Brussels are not always free of contradictions. In the Belgian case the federal authority, the regions and the communities concluded in March 1994 an agreement 'to organise a general co-ordination mechanism ensuring unity in the views expressed by Belgium'. According to this agreement, co-ordination 'must take place before each session of the Council of Ministers, whatever the field may be'.[46]

For a systematic approach to the differing models of co-ordination we propose the following set of categories. We take Figure 18.2 as point of departure. Can we observe with regard to European policies and the making of political decisions, a high or a low level of horizontal co-ordination, or do we find a small or large amount of horizontal functional decentralisation?

Without proper co-ordination, decentralised pluralist national positions are fragmented (Figure 18.2, type (3)). Often the German case is cited as an example of this type. In Germany, there exists 'no single

	⟺ Functional decentralisation		
Horizontal Co-ordination		low	high
⇕	low	unified (1)	pluralist-fragmented (3)
	High	(2) centralised	(4) horizontal consensus

Figure 18.2 Models of 'policy co-ordination'

decision-making centre but different levels interact in the decision-making process and compete for access and participation'.[47] Small governments might stay with unified positions. Given the functional scope and the political salience of the Union it is understandable that a 'one-hand' approach becomes less representative. In the case of a unified Member State (type 1), this exercise – so often tried in France – is not successful. The most interesting case is another one: the strategy of co-ordinating units, each of which have their own channels to Brussels. Two sub-types can be identified: a strong vertical hierarchy based on a central agency which is permanently supported by the political leadership (type 2), and horizontal co-ordination among equals based on consensus (type 4). The French and the United Kingdom's set-ups are normally cited as examples of the first case while the Dutch and Danish systems serve as examples of the second.

In the light of developments during the 1990s the differences among the Member States, though clearly still existent, might be less prominent than often stated: horizontal co-ordination seems to be overshadowed by an increasingly involved political hierarchy as in all Member States prime ministers have discovered the political importance of becoming involved. They have attempted to reduce fragmentation by introducing strong centralisation. Of course, this indirect effect works only when there is a sufficiently clear and stable political leadership. But nevertheless, a strong vertical hierarchy needs broad inputs from the specialised ministries and units.

Administrations: opening up to new challenges?

In general, bureaucratic structures are difficult to break up.[48] They form the basic patterns of a political system, which cannot be changed easily by governmental acts. However, with regard to the Union's institutional system, we cannot neglect the fact that national administrations are no longer restricted to their national spheres.[49] In all phases of the EU policy-cycle, i.e. decision preparation, decision-making, implementation and control, national administrations participate intensively.[50] Depending on the policy field and the issue at stake in the European Commission and Council of Ministers, ministries and departments are more or less intensively involved in the EC/EU decision-making process. They are, to an increasing extent, oriented towards Brussels and have considerable incentives to participate.

Interaction between European and national administrations has intensified and broadened since the early days of the Community. In several national systems, however, the process of negotiating the Maastricht Treaty was given special attention within national bureaucracies. In the Netherlands or Austria, the presidencies were 'the highlight in terms of workload and publicity'[51] and the starting point for a greater awareness among national administrations of the EU level. The realisation that carelessness with EU policies could cause serious problems became widespread and caused a change in national administrative cultures.

With regard to the policy-cycle it is difficult to identify precisely the starting point of EU policy preparation. For national administrations it is therefore important to have well-organised and permanent connections to institutions in Brussels, such as the advisory groups of the Commission, the working groups of the Council, the comitology committees and, more recently, the EP committees.

The connections of national administrations to Brussels are particularly necessary for the informal policy preparation process in the Commission and the formal process in the Council of Ministers and EP. In all Member States civil servants are therefore engaged in this very first stage of the policy-cycle. Administrative experts and sectoral specialists are involved in various types of preparatory committees (*groupe d'experts*). The contacts between the Commission and the national administrations are deliberate, either in permanent or in temporary groups. These contacts are activated by the Commission if and when the need arises. The delegation of national experts is part of the daily business of the national ministries and the responsible specified units. In some countries, such as Germany, the responsible units of the ministries co-ordinating the respective pre-reconciliation of the expert groups are not co-ordinated by any central institution. A characteristic feature of these administrations is the direct involvement of the responsible administrative unit in Brussels. This trend of decentralisation is favoured by the customary praxis of Community institutions to pay travel expenses for a limited number of national participants.

With regard to the decision-making phase of the policy-cycle, national administrators serve on various bodies of the Council of Ministers. Most important is the Committee of Permanent Representatives (COREPER). The main preparatory work of the Council is, however, carried out by specific working groups, which are established according to political sectors. In the immediate preparation of decision-making and preparatory drafting of EC legislation, national civil servants are involved in about 350 committees and working groups of the Council of Ministers.[52] Usually the participants are administrators from specialised ministries and, in some cases – according to the internal structure of the Member State – are accompanied by a civil servant from a regional administration.

With regard to the channels of access and influence in the Brussels arena, Permanent Representations play an important role in all Member States. They are key actors in the interplay between both administrations and governments on the one hand, and between the national and the Brussels level on the other. Civil servants within Representations often exercise – as in the Irish case – 'a Janus-like role between the EU and the domestic'.[53] Yet, Permanent Representations operate not only through a single government delegation but also liaise between different branches and levels of government, thus between the Council of Ministers and the Member State governments. In this context they influence the formulation of national points of view and negotiating positions. Between 1986 (SEA) and 1992, the Permanent Representations of the EU Member States expanded rapidly. The largest are those of Greece and Sweden, the latter being made up of ninety-one people.[54] At present, nearly all ministries of each Member State – with the exception of defence – have at least one civil servant attached to their national permanent representation in Brussels.[55] Foreign affairs ministries are formally in charge of the Permanent Representations which are headed generally by a professional diplomat. In some Member States this position is regarded as the most important status in a diplomatic career. All opinions and instructions from individual national ministries are supposed to be channelled through their Permanent Representations. However, there are manifold linkages between the ministries of Member States which evade the head of the Permanent Representation and also his control, as the example of the Netherlands shows. Here, 'some important ministries have succeeded in creating a reserved "policy space". For them, the permanent representation serves mainly as a technical facility in Brussels'.[56]

The third phase of the policy-cycle, the implementation of Community legislation at the European level, is carried out by the administrative units of the European Commission and by roughly 420 committees[57] which are in most cases established by the relevant legislative act for which they are responsible. There are various forms of these so-called 'comitology committees' in which the degree of formalised power of the national civil servants differs. Owing to the nature of the implementation committees, participating civil servants from the national administrations are in almost all cases working in the various ministries and specialised departments of ministries responsible for the policy field in question.

Altogether the administrative infrastructure in Brussels includes at least around 1,500 bodies of different characteristics. Assuming that each Member State sends an average of at least two civil servants or experts – in some cases even more as the example of Germany shows – there are about 40,000 national officials involved in many meetings per year.

The last phase of the policy-cycle – the monitoring of transposition and the control of binding decisions, also has a direct impact on national administrations. Legal considerations are becoming more and more relevant. Therefore, in Germany approximately twenty higher civil servants were exclusively specialised in European legal affairs in the mid-1990s. The Member States' Administrations are mostly concerned with EC directives which need to be incorporated at the national level within a certain time period. If time limits have not been adhered to, the European

Commission may take legal action against this non-compliance in order to enforce Community law. The Commission can deliver a reasoned opinion on the matter after giving the relevant Member State the opportunity to submit its observations. The various supervision and control mechanisms of the Commission laid down in the treaties thus lead to extensive consultation and co-operation procedures between the Commission administration and national – but also regional and local – administrations. Until the mid-1990s, the number of suits for non-compliance against Member States grew rapidly. Since then, the total sum has decreased, which can be explained by a learning process among national governments and administrations. Yet, in 1998 the Commission asked Member States to report on possible non-implementation in 1,101 cases on the basis of Article 226 (ex Article 177) ECT. In the same year, it delivered a reasoned opinion in 675 cases. If the Member States do not comply with the opinion of the Commission, the matter may be brought before the ECJ. In 1998, this occurred in 123 cases. The desire for a good compliance record and the implications of a negative judgement of the ECJ have forced specialised national administrators to push their national colleagues into conforming with the obligations of legal acts from the Community.

Summing up the governmental and administrative level, two parallel developments can be identified in nearly all Member States: more and more ministries and administrative units are becoming directly involved in the Brussels arena. They have often established their own links rather than being channelled through a national gatekeeping organisation. This decentralised move is matched – to different degrees among the Member States – by a co-ordination and centralisation strategy with other departments and ministries. These trends in Member States are evolutionary. We have found neither a radical revolutionary change in the governmental and administrative set-up of any country nor the construction of a new superstructure. But internal equilibria have been affected. We are witnessing increasing changes in the internal power balance. The influx of new actors and the stronger participation of old ones has led to new balances and coalitions both in the relations between states and within individual states, thereby reducing the relevance of foreign ministries but strengthening economic and financial departments and the role of prime ministers.[58]

It can be concluded that national actors, heads of government, ministers and administrations have overall proved to be active multi-level players and thus may be categorised as 'strong adapters'. All these actors have established their own channels of access and exercise their influence in all phases of the policy-cycle. Maastricht did not reverse but rather reinforced this trend. But what about national parliaments? Of specific interest is the question of how national parliaments have developed their position in the EU's multi-level game.

Parliaments: reactions to the warning lights of the TEU

In a large number of EU Member States (B, D, E, IR, LUX, NE, P) prior to the Maastricht Treaty, national parliaments were regarded as the victims of the integration process.[59] Owing to the growing supremacy of national governments in the European decision making process on the one hand, and because of governments' ability to use the knowledge and powers of their administrations on the other, national parliaments were either left outside the EU policy-cycle or were only marginally involved. Neither their financial nor their human resources could cope in any way with the increasing amount of EU legal acts – though in all national systems, formal legislative competencies are traditionally in the hands of parliaments. The role of national parliaments is particularly limited with regard to EC directives. Though such directives allow the Member States some room for manoeuvre in national transposition – in contrast to the directly applicable regulations – governments are very often not capable or willing to adapt the content of the respective act. In addition, some national parliaments have shown little interest in EU affairs, which can be explained to a certain extent by the complex internal structure of the some legislatures (D, F, NL). As the German case study illustrates, between 1980 and 1986 about 65 per cent of the EC documents considered by the Bundestag were already in force when they were debated for the first time.[60]

Since the coming into force of the Maastricht Treaty, perceptions have changed significantly.[61] National parliaments have recognised not only that the Union has acquired new policy fields and competencies, but also that they themselves are losing their traditional access and influence, especially in view of their scrutiny functions *vis-à-vis* governments. Aiming to move beyond the conventional instruments of parliamentary questions and debates, parliaments in all Member States have called for more influence over their governments. With regard to the EC/EU decision-making process, parliaments have asked to be informed earlier and more comprehensively about legislative proposals debated in the Council of Ministers. As became evident in the overview of national systems, a major step in improving the performance of national parliaments concerns their access to information.

The forms and implications of parliaments' attempts to increase their role differ across Member States. Nevertheless, some common features can be emphasised concerning constitutional changes, specific laws, declarations and reports. In some countries the new rights of national parliaments were based on constitutional revisions and amendments. Basic constitutional reforms due to the Maastricht Treaty have taken place in France and Germany. The amended Article 88(4) of the French constitution or Article 23 of the German Basic Law, which calls 'the Federal Government [to] inform the Bundestag and the Bundesrat comprehensively and as quickly as possible', are expressions of the parliaments' demands for more efficient participation. In Germany the new Committee on European Union Affairs can even be authorised by the Bundestag to take decisions for the Bundestag as a whole.

In the Belgian Chambre des Représentants, the Spanish Congreso de los Diputatados, the Irish Dáil Éireann, the Dutch Tweede Kamer and the Portuguese Assembleia da República, special laws and agreements between governments and parliaments were adopted in order to strengthen parliamentary scrutiny rights in European affairs. In the Netherlands the former Standing Committee for European Affairs became a General Committee on European Union Affairs with a mission to increase EU awareness among all MPs. In some countries the improvements to parliaments' role in European policy-making resulted frequently from their own declarations or reports which bound governments and improved the participation rights of the national parliaments (DK, E, I, NL, UK).

Moreover, parliaments have attempted to play a more effective part by strengthening the role of specialised committees. Though the establishment of committees on European affairs in all Member States had increased at the end of the 1990s, the impact of the newly established committees is still not as yet clear. One cannot overlook the possibility that rival parliamentary committees will be reluctant to allow the European dimension of their work to slip away into the hands of the new specifically EU-related committees. National parliaments, such as the Finnish for example, are following in the footsteps of Denmark where the Folketing is regarded as a policy-making assembly which has retained its position after entering the Community. The Danish parliament has exercised vast control over European policy. The Danish European Affairs Committee (the former Market Relations Committee) mandates its ministers in the Council. In Austria, the Constitution guarantees participation in cabinet meetings for the influential Main Committee of the Parliament and the heads of the parliamentary groups of the government parties.

It can be concluded that in nearly all Member States, national parliaments have strengthened their formal role in the EU decision-making process. Though decision-making continues to be primarily in the hands of governments, their room for manoeuvre in Brussels negotiations will be restricted to an increasing extent by national parliaments and particularly by their specialised committees. Some legislatures (DK, F, I, S, SF, UK) have even created their own points of contact in the EP's Léopold Building in Brussels. It seems that parliaments no longer simply follow their governments in European policy but try instead to prescribe their government's actions in EU policy-making. Some expect that the further development of the Union might not take place without a more active role for national parliaments, especially in the phases of preparation and control of EU decisions.

In this context increasing levels of interparliamentary co-operation can be seen. Since the end of the 1980s there have been regular meetings of the presidents and speakers of the national parliaments. Since 1989 national parliaments' specialised EU committees have met every six months in the framework of the so-called COSAC. The Amsterdam Treaty protocol on the role of national parliaments may alter COSAC's informal profile; it is remarkable that both the EP and the Council of Ministers have amended their rules of procedure in order to recognise national parliaments and COSAC as consultative bodies within the EU policy-making framework.[62]

National parliaments have learned and tried to cope with European challenges by adapting some of their procedures. Nevertheless, the relative weakness of national parliamentary institutions at the EU level cannot be overlooked. The patterns of national governments and administrations in preparing EU matters have been affected to only a limited degree. Continuous deficits in parliaments' ability to play the multi-level game reduce the influence of national deputies. The involvement of parliaments in the EU policy-cycle remains weak and largely reactive.

The overall trend of reinforcing the role of national parliaments in the ratification of the Maastricht Treaty might also be explained as a consequence of popular discontent. However, parliaments have not become an opposition force putting forward the critical views of the public. The logic of parliamentary government with the basic cleavage between the executive and the parliamentary majority on one side, and the parliamentary minority on the other, has not been replaced by a return to the classical division of power between executive and legislature. Indeed the incentives of the European arena have strengthened governmental actors and further reduced the influence of parliaments. The increased activities of some of the latter have not fundamentally shifted the institutional (dis-)equilibrium. Thus, at the end it is not an issue of resources but national parliaments have not been able to gain a decisive voice. Despite some constitutional changes most national parliaments have remained 'weak adapters' with regard to the European policy-cycle. Some have kept or gained a performance as national performers. Their influence is mostly notable – if at all – in the final phase of implementation and control.

Regions: new players in the multi-level game

As the range of policies dealt with by the Union has become wider, so the rights and competencies of regional as well as local bodies have been affected to an increasing extent.[63] While regions have specific – sometimes even autonomous – rights and tasks and are responsible for implementing legal acts, the growing number of acts and legislative activities of the Community in such fields as education, culture, research, health, environment, agriculture and fisheries has led to demands from regions in many countries (B, D, DK, E, F, I, NL, UK) for the right to participate more actively and efficiently in the EU policy-cycle. However, there are clear differences and even increasing divergences with regard to the extension of involvement of regional bodies in the respective national and EC contexts.

There has been much concern among the regions of Belgium, Germany, Austria and to some extent, Spain, owing to the federal structures of these countries. Amendments and revisions within the Union have induced the development of formalised rules and structures to assure participation rights for regions. Moreover, new instruments have been established with regard to the way EU policy is dealt with. In Germany nearly every regional ministry has its own desk officer for European affairs. After Maastricht, the German Länder and Belgian regions even succeeded in participating in the Council of Ministers and its working groups and committees of the Commission. Using the regulations of the new Article 203 of the TEU and the new Article 23 of the German Basic Law, German regions are able to appoint a delegate who represents the Federal Republic in the Council in such cases where sovereign, exclusive competencies of the Länder are concerned. In this process, the role of the German Bundesrat has also been reinforced, obtaining in certain constellations a veto position.

In Belgium the *Comité de concentration* with six national ministers and six representatives from the regional entities has become an important co-ordination body. In Spain the ongoing transfer of competencies to the Autonomous Communities has to be taken into account. Each of the seventeen Autonomous Communities has inaugurated a department exclusively dealing with EU affairs. In some autonomous regions of Spain the regional parliaments are even more active than the national parliament in seeking direct influence in Madrid and Brussels.

Elsewhere in countries which have a highly centralised structure, there are no regional bodies between the often well-equipped national and local governments. Replacing the seven former sub-regional committees in Ireland, eight regional authorities were established in 1994 to co-ordinate the provisions of public services in each territorial unit. After a very controversial debate on regionalisation – initiated by the struggle for further participation in the EU's structural funds in the period 2000–06 – Ireland has established a model dividing the country into two larger regions.

In some Member States where there are regional units with their own rights and competencies, such regions have had difficulties in articulating their views against national governments and have therefore only slightly improved their position with regard to EU affairs (F, I, NL). In Portugal – where there has been only a minor trend towards regionalisation as a result of EU membership – management of the Structural Funds lies in the hands of central government. Consequently, other channels of influence have been employed by the regions.[64] In Sweden and Finland several experiments with new regional authorities have been undertaken. It is interesting, however, that in Finland the regions earmarked for EU purposes are not identical with the formal state districts. Here, the 'regional councils function as promoters of regional interests with respect to the EU and are responsible for the implementation of its regional programmes'.[65]

Since the Maastricht Treaty – following the initiative of the German Länder and the Belgian government – CoR has given the regions a new forum to articulate their interests. Though there are considerable variations in the extent to which this body is used by the regions and municipalities, one cannot overlook the fact that owing to the limited institutional power of the CoR, some regions, particularly the German Länder, have employed other channels of access and influence.

In addition, more than eighty regions from within the Union maintain offices in Brussels, and many major cities have their own representatives there. Local bodies have been increasingly active in the European decision-making process and have partly established their own representatives in Brussels.[66] Since Maastricht, together with the regions, they have put pressure on governments, with some success, in order to extend their own competencies, especially concerning the Structural Funds.

The Union has thus become an important point of reference for regions and municipalities and has, to a certain extent, brought about a process of regionalisation in the Member States. Regional and local authorities have adapted their structures to the EU policy-making process. In particular, they have requested from central governments more competencies and greater participation in EU affairs. The changes in the more federally organised countries have mainly involved the participation of regional bodies via their national capital's channels of influence and co-operation rather than directly with the EU institutions.

Although in many Member States there have been no constitutional changes reinforcing the influence of regional governments, the effects of European integration have led to a partial institutional adaptation and some kind of an institutional learning. Thus traditional patterns or at least conventional views of national policy-making are being eroded, but to a limited degree as far as regions are concerned. Where regions do however have resources at their disposal – the German Länder or the Belgian regions might serve as examples – they have become effective players on both levels. Others have, however, remained confined to the national level – in many cases we observe 'weak adaptations'.

National courts: relevant actors in the policy-cycle

National courts can be qualified as political institutions since they are involved in institutional interaction within the EU system at the end of the policy-cycle, during the phase of implementing and controlling Community law. Courts become active when a case is brought before them and they pronounce their judgement on the basis of the national law, the EC treaties, previous judgements or established legal rules and principles. Thus also in an anticipatory view, they have an important indirect influence on the shaping of Community law and the institutional system as such, provided they do not 'stay away from politics' owing to the supremacy of national parliaments, as in the Danish case.[67]

In some Member States the courts were 'rather straightforward in accepting the mainstream principles of Community law' – 'even before accession', as has been the situation in Greece.[68] The most radical impact on the sovereignty of the Member States results from the gradual establishment of the supremacy of Community law. The ECJ has extended step by step its interpretation of the treaties, declaring that by creating a Community of unlimited duration and having its own institutions, the Member States have limited their sovereign rights.

Though many courts have expressed doubts – most famously in connection with the Irish ratification of the SEA and the judgement of the German Constitutional Court on the TEU – or stressed their right of review (A, B, D, E, I, S), the supremacy of Community law has generally been accepted.[69] It can be concluded – as in the case of the French *Conseil d'Etat* which examines the conformity of statutes to the provisions of a treaty – that the courts have 'achieved a slow but significant accommodation with the inevitable'.[70] In some states (DK, GR, P) either the relationship between Community and national law has not proved to be a major issue of legal dispute among national high courts or there have at least been no attempts to interpret the character of the Union in order to analyse the compatibility of national and European law. National courts have apparently accepted without any serious resistance the primacy of EC law and when needing to interpret the latter, they have referred to the ECJ. One highly important set of procedures which particularly concerns national institutions are the preliminary rulings made according to Article 234 (ex Article 177) ECT. These refer to decisions on the interpretation and application of the Community law in cases of uncertainty before the courts in Member States and which are referred to the ECJ by those courts: 'Where such a question is raised before any court or tribunal of a Member State, that court or tribunal may, if it considers that a decision on the question is necessary to enable it to give judgment, request the Court of Justice to give a ruling thereon.'[71] Such preliminary rulings are binding on national courts and form an important link between the ECJ and the Member States' courts. The use of such preliminary rulings varies considerably. By comparison, in 1998, British courts sought 269 rulings; Italian courts 581 rulings; French courts 594 rulings; and German courts sought as many as 1,113 rulings.

An indicator of the continuing differences between the Member States is the record of incorporation of EC legislation into national law. With regard to the frequency of legal proceedings against Member States, the trends of the 1980s continued. Those Member States with the then highest rates of infringement proceedings (B, DK, GR, F, I) had at the end of the 1990s – with the exception of Denmark – still the highest number of infringement cases. What is remarkable however, is that Denmark and the United Kingdom, with their broadly sceptical views of European integration, nevertheless have better records than such pro-integration Member States as Italy or Luxembourg. It would seem that this trend can be attributed only to a limited extent to political obstacles and a lack of efficiency – especially in the case of Luxembourg.

Regarding the total amount of infringements, the situation improved between 1991 and 1995 in nearly all Member States with, most importantly, a minimum of forty-four cases referred to the Court in 1994. Yet, until the end of the 1990s the total number again constantly grew, to 123 cases in 1998.

Though EC law 'remains a domain of specialists and a certain "elite"'[72] the growing amount of EC legislation and the number of cases involving Community law has increased the requirement in all Member States for national judges and lawyers, as well as national administrators, to be familiar with EC law (Table 18.1). In countries such as Ireland or Portugal special efforts have been undertaken to train the responsible staff. In the United Kingdom the impact on the national legal system has been stressed. The unspectacular but persistent involvement of national courts in the EC system is one of these basic trends which, to an increasing degree, links the national and the EU systems.[73] Thus – with all reservations in view of the specific character of national variations' – the court system might be characterised as belonging to the group of active multi-level players.

Do the European Union's Member States matter? Major findings on the 'Europeanisation' of Member States and the 'domestication' of the Union

The chapters on the 'One' and the 'Fifteen' tell a story full of complexities but also of some common and recurrent patterns. The evolution of the EU system as a whole has been considerable. There are ongoing changes and adaptations within both the European and the national systems. From analysing the institutional and procedural evolution of the European Union we have learned that the demands and challenges faced by national actors have grown considerably through several forms of differentiation. National governments, administrations, parliaments, regions and courts have had to face the processes and potential effects of para-constitutional

Table 18.1 Proceedings against Member States, by category, in comparative perspective, 1991–98

	Letters of Formal Notice								*Reasoned Opinions*								*Cases referred to the Court*							
State	1991	1992	1993	1994	1995	1996	1997	1998	1991	1992	1993	1994	1995	1996	1997	1998	1991	1992	1993	1994	1995	1996	1997	1998
B	71	110	98	77	80	72	93	88	46	22	26	41	19	62	33	78	8	6	7	10	6	20	18	20
DK	52	45	66	57	42	22	64	40	3	4	3	14	1	0	1	10	1	0	–	0	0	0	0	1
D	60	97	119	90	92	62	116	88	13	18	35	66	25	37	35	46	1	5	4	5	10	8	19	5
GR	88	112	125	96	113	58	109	95	48	30	41	85	26	51	23	51	9	4	4	17	12	17	10	16
E	79	127	107	86	81	59	104	78	30	39	28	53	15	30	23	36	2	5	5	9	6	9	7	6
F	54	111	106	90	97	88	157	121	15	10	39	49	17	46	49	94	4	1	2	8	6	11	15	23
IR	59	88	91	70	67	43	86	63	27	13	25	47	3	36	14	46	3	9	–	12	6	4	6	10
I	115	137	108	102	114	75	123	110	76	40	49	60	36	71	36	91	24	11	6	12	17	9	20	16
LUX	64	97	91	64	71	39	74	62	35	21	29	36	9	28	14	39	4	14	11	6	3	4	8	11
NL	62	73	75	73	59	32	65	28	23	16	22	20	4	9	11	23	7	5	5	4	0	2	3	3
P	86	116	125	96	115	54	116	80	84	22	40	54	22	49	35	57	2	1	–	5	4	6	14	5
UK	63	97	98	73	77	47	92	66	11	13	15	21	15	14	8	35	0	3	–	1	2	1	1	1
SF	–	–	–	–	2	290	78	52	–	–	–	–	–	0	8	16	–	–	–	–	–	0	0	1
A	–	–	–	–	4	132	109	76	–	–	–	–	–	2	38	38	–	–	–	–	–	1	0	4
S	–	–	–	–	2	69	75	54	–	–	–	–	–	0	6	15	–	–	–	–	–	0	0	1
Total	853	1210	1209	974	1016	1142	1461	1101	411	248	352	546	192	435	334	675	65	64	44	89	72	92	121	123

Note: In reading the columns it must be recalled that Greece joined the Community in 1981, Spain and Portugal in 1986 and Finland, Austria and Sweden in 1995.

Source: Table compiled by the authors on the basis of the *Annual Reports of the Commission to the European Parliament on Monitoring the Applications of Community Law.*

communitarisation as well as sectoral, procedural, institutional and actor differentiation.[74]

As a common reaction we can observe some persistent trends among the fifteen Member States. National systems in their overall set-up have moved into the European arena. Thus the institutional system of the Union – the 'One' – can be characterised neither as an isolated nor as a closed system. The European Union at the beginning of the new century is open to or has been opened by national institutions and actors, who are not restricted to their national sphere but rather, to an increasing extent, are oriented towards Brussels. Conversely actors from EU bodies have extended their reach of activities deeply in ever-wider fields previously the domain of sovereign nation states. This phenomenon of interaction and mutual influence between European and national institutions has become wider and more intense since the beginning of the integration process, and is continuing. The gains might be larger for some actors than for others, but winners and losers are broadly spread and the struggle for influence still continues in all member countries.

Vertical asymmetries: unbalanced co-evolution among levels

The 'Europeanisation' of national polities and the process of Member States becoming part of the EU polity is clearly documented by the regular patterns of interaction. But looking at the evolution of both levels we observe a vertical asymmetry. The rate of change in the Brussels arena has been faster than that at the national level. The overall impact of constitutional amendments and revisions leading to institutional and procedural adaptations has been limited and the strategies adopted by all national players in national political systems have not led to a major structural reorientation.

Experience so far shows that except for some actors – the German Länder or perhaps the French parliament – new constitutional frameworks and opportunities in the Member States have been used to only a limited extent. No elaborate adaptation strategy, which would be unknown or detrimental to the cornerstones of national systems, has yet been developed. We witness considerable intra-systematic adaptations owing to the differentiation challenges of the EU system, but no 'revolutions' in the set-up of national polities. Thus, we note that national reactions to the EU system have reached a certain prominence but they do not constitute a dramatic turn-around from traditional patterns of policy-making. Typically, we observe a mobilisation of established actors within the existing constitutional and institutional framework. This finding does, however, not exclude the apparently considerable changes in major policies of all Member States, which were directly influenced or at least reinforced by the evolution of the European Union. Active involvement in the Union has led to a considerable evolution of political cultures and policies, which were however outside the remit of this research.

There are two possible explanations of this asymmetry between levels. Either there is a considerable time lag, which would indicate a retarded adaptation by the fifteen Member States, or it might be that Member States are able to deal with these challenges by adapting their existing machinery and structures incrementally. This finding might therefore also explain a certain degree of satisfaction within Member States with their respective degree of adaptation to the complex EU system.

Winners and losers: towards mega-administrations?

In addition to the vertical asymmetries discussed above we also find differences in terms of adaptation to EU policy-making on the horizontal spectrum. Some groups of actors, particularly administrations and several regions, have been more successful adapters than others. Thus, they have been more successful in gaining access and influence – particularly than parliaments and most regions. The intensity of use varies considerably within and between Member States. Gains and losses depend not least on the way national actors have established their own channels to the EU level.

In the older Member States, parliaments and regions have reacted to the Maastricht Treaty and adapted their way of working through two parallel and mixed strategies: they seek formalised access and de jure influence over national governments both at the beginning and end of the EU policy-cycle. But to varying degrees these actors also step outside their national arena and establish their own access to the EU bodies and become part of network governance. Besides administrations, only interest groups have turned into active and efficient multi-level players.

Examples of strong national performers might include the governments of Greece and Portugal or some parliaments such as the Danish and, increasingly, the French. In these cases, constitutional and political resources could be better employed at the national level, but not in the Brussels arena. Strong EU performers without adequate national access are more rare. The Spanish comunidades might be examples of this model. The 'weak adapters'are unable or unwilling to play a stronger game at the national or the European level. The Italian regions and most parliaments might exemplify this type. Strong multi-level players are able to increase their access and influence at both levels and to use their position on one level for strengthening their say on the other. German and Belgian regions might develop into these kinds of actors. We can trace a persistent trend during the 1990s, particularly in terms of adaptations and reactions to Maastricht, towards stronger national performers.

Given this rise in salience it is surprising that some fundamental patterns of adaptation have not changed. Administrations have used existing set-ups to mobilise their resources for access and influence over an increasing scope of vital policy areas and over all phases of the policy-cycle. The masters of the treaty have installed and even reinforced an institutional set-up which has maintained and strengthened the strategic position of governments – especially prime ministers – and of administrations. Even in those states where European parliamentarians are participating on a permanent basis in EU committees of national parliaments, one cannot observe any kind of permanent, formalised interaction with the EU level. Parliamentarians of whatever level are not able to use their access and influence at one level for enhancing their role at the other. National bureaucracies have become the multi-level experts *vis-à-vis* their amateurish parliamentary masters. Parliaments are underprofessionalised – often they engage themselves too late and too little. Also, the CoR is no match for the influence that central governments can have over the game.

But even chancelleries and foreign offices are not gross winners, they are still the masters of amendment and revision of treaties – and with that the constitutional and institutional set-up. However, they are no longer masters of the normal use of these institutional incentives and constraints, they are no longer the exclusive 'chief negotiators'[75] or gatekeepers for the links between national and EU policy-cycles. The competition from administrators and lobbyists has reduced the margin of the executive's prerogative in extra-national policy-making.

We have seen a persistent extension in the participation of administrations and in the development of their role as active and strong multi-level players. Empirical trends towards a 'mega-administration'[76] are clearly visible, in and by which Community and national administrations link their channels of influence and merge their respective sources to create networks. In this process several variations can be discerned. A 'mega-technocracy'[77] or an 'expertocracy'[78] would serve as a benevolent 'epistemic community'[79] for a common good. This view would fit into functionalist thinking: the experts socialise and pre-decide what is 'good' for Europe. In more negative terms, national and European functionaries would form a 'mega-bureaucracy' in which they would follow their bureaucratic goals of maximising own resources. No more servants or agents of their governments, they monopolise the central channels of access and influence. As both levels are intrinsically interwoven, no control mechanism exists and the institutional equilibrium is shifted to these actors.

However, several features of the EU policy-cycle could put the validity of this argument in question. One is the rivalry among national administrations. Sectoral networks, with civil servants managing units, are competitors for access and power in areas of scarce resources. The staffing of Permanent Representations and the role of COREPER *vis-à-vis* other high-level bodies such as ECOFIN – formerly the monetary committee –

or the Political Committee of the CFSP structure are telling examples of administrative competition.

From asymmetries to differing degrees of adaptation: no imitation from divergent responses

Comparing adaptation processes, the rate of importing apparently successful components of other national systems is surprisingly limited. A screening of best practices is not pursued on a systematic level – and perhaps rightly so. The pictures sketched of particular Member States make clear that any simple imitation would be subject to the law of unintended consequences.

Several lines of thought have been presented in the 'goodness of fit' debate. Conventional wisdom stresses that administratively centralised and politically hierarchical machineries – such as those of the United Kingdom and France, for example – are clearly more successful than systems such as that of the FRG which is characterised as pluralist, fragmented, decentralised and non-hierarchical.[80] A later line of reasoning however, stresses structural congruencies between the EU system and the national systems. Puzzled by the apparently obvious successes of the FRG – that of 'failing successfully'[81] – the competitiveness of national positions was explained less by streamlined machinery but by broad and intensive participation. Given that major features of the FRG seem to be more congruent with some of the central characteristics of EU politics, the former is considered to be more competitive, at least in the long term. Pluralist and decentralised systems fit better into the pluralist system of the Union (Figure 18.3).

	Characteristics of the EU-System		
Characteristics of the national systems		Pluralist	Hierarchical
	Pluralist	Networking	Strong co-ordination
	Hierarchical	Decentralisation	Mobilisation

Figure 18.3 Models of adaptation strategies

After surveying the real variations on both levels, only cautious conclusions can be drawn. Both at the national and at the European level a simple answer is problematic. In view of national characteristics it is extremely difficult to make any serious and valid statements on who is more or less successful. Any blueprint for an optimal model is academically and politically risky. Best practices should be compared but carefully evaluated in terms of the relevant constitutional, institutional and political features, and the characteristics of the policy field concerned.

One issue is already linked to indicators of success. If we take the rate of implementation as a sign of the successful adaptation of national systems to the Union's legal output, we get a different rating than if we were to look at similarities of constitutional features or – another area of competition among actors – at the contents passed on specific policies. In certain areas the European Council and in others the Commission plays the role of a strong collective hierarchy. These policy areas therefore require different strategies among national actors when compared with those policy fields characterised by non-hierarchical networks. At the national level, systems which might look rather fragmented could turn out to be quite strong on certain issues where leadership can be mobilised on the basis of a large national or sectoral consensus. Certainly, the availability of different power resources might be of importance for a more successful policy, but this does not imply that smaller states are not competitive.

One more argument in the debate about dominating systems should be mentioned: perceived by some as being successful in constitutional decisions on the Union, German strategies might have created exactly the kind of EU set-up which fits best the German system. German models – autonomy of central banks, involvement of regions, ministerial autonomy in the sectoral councils, the judicial powers of the ECJ and the *Richtlinienkompetenz* of the European Council – can be seen as closer to those of consensus systems of a federal kind than those which exist in centralised systems of a majoritarian type. These latter systems are then forced by competition within the Union to evolve against long-established traditions towards pluralist or federalist lines. Thus, in the long term these dynamics would reinforce converging trends towards a multi-level consensus democracy. We could expect at least a more narrow band of variations.

Similarities among constitutional systems are open to debate. Perhaps the Union's institutional checks and balances might appear more similar to those of the French Fifth Republic in times of cohabitation than the German models presented above. A simple dichotomy between centralised/fragmented or consensus/majoritarian models thus lacks sufficient explanatory power, but might just serve as a starting point for further research.

It is therefore against all probabilities that an institutional and procedural device which has worked efficiently in one Member State will have the same effects in a different institutional and political environment.

The fact that imports will not work in the manner anticipated leads to the conclusion that operative lessons for applicant countries need to be drawn very carefully. The range of experiences gained by national actors in the present Union of fifteen is broad and offers many types of adaptation. However, as a precondition for any advice we need an in-depth analysis of the traditional structures and patterns of the country in question.

No convergence towards one hegemonic and dominating model

The finding of rather uniform reaction patterns with regard to the shift of awareness, attention and mobilisation of similar groups of actors should not hide another surprising pattern. The constitutional, institutional and administrative systems and their relative use have not converged into one model for all the Member States. Given that they have faced the same kind of challenges, the degree of convergence among the Union's constitutive units is rather small. Traditional national patterns are apparently flexible enough to cope with the European challenges and to be sufficiently complacent about the own performance inside the Union. Imports of apparently more competitive set-ups or procedures are rare. Competitive pressures have apparently only led to de facto harmonised mobilisation by the political market.

Each Member State pursues its own way into the Brussels 'space'. The Union remains as 'One' plus 'Fifteen' quite different component units – indeed in some cases the observations point to the reconfirmation and restoration of well-known national patterns in the adaptation process. Traditional key actors have used the challenges of Brussels to strengthen some of their familiar intra-state positions. This picture of strengthened conventional patterns is not however, without ambiguities. Some actors such as the German Länder and the French Assemblée have acquired roles which differ from those they played prior to the 1990s. The real effects are difficult to identify as yet. Sceptically it could be argued that the efforts of these actors have simply increased the complexity of national procedures without seriously affecting the national space and even without any relevance for the Brussels arena. Alternatively, it could be argued that there has been a long-term trend towards new institutional equilibria both at the national and at the European level.

This debate points to the basic problem of the 'no-convergence' thesis: the time span of our research might be too short. The autonomy of national central banks as a consequence of EMU, the upgrading of yet to establish regions due to Commission demands for structural funds and the Committee of Regions, the changing role of national parliaments in their relationships with governments owing to the need to reduce democratic deficits – all these elements might appear to be formal steps of minor importance to the established patterns of national polities which have simply been adapted but not overhauled as a consequence of the Union. However, we might also identify some initial dynamics towards an adaptation process in the long term which would converge into one specific type of Member State for the Union. The spilldown process from EU developments might be more persistent and relevant than we realise at the moment. The range of variations in the Member States' structures might become narrower in the future. This process would not lead to the development of a uniform type of Member State, but nevertheless the historical differences would lose their enduring strength and the major characteristics of the EU polity would then increasingly affect national structures and habits.

Another feature, which could be studied in depth, might be of long-term relevance for Member States. The broad involvement of many actors and a constitutionally driven – and needed – search for consensus could pave the way to a political and institutional culture quite different from an 'adversarial' culture.[82] Patterns of a consensual democracy would thus be dominant not only at the EU level, but might also spill down into national systems. The Community as a system of concordance might create or at least reinforce a dominant culture. If such a convergence was to make the 'life of the EU system easier' it would require additional research.

With these considerations in mind, our findings might also contribute to a dynamic theory on the evolution of (West-)European states.[83] In a long-term perspective, nation states have neither been 'rescued'[84] – though we observe strategies for restoring conventional role models – nor substituted by supranational institutions, as some federalists have suggested.[85] Even if we identify certain trends towards convergence there are difficulties in discerning in which direction this multi-level system is moving. No existing model – e.g. of conventional federations – offers a useful point of reference. The evolution of the national and the European levels does not follow any clear path towards a discernible *finalité politique*. We are thus observing the creation of a new kind of polity – not as a substitute for Member States but as some kind of a new stage in the evolution of West European states. If the fifteen evolve into one, this new system will have to be defined in a new way.

Theories revisited: a step towards fusion?

Our observations on the national systems as dependent variables raise the issue of explanations, i.e. of the validity of the four theoretical expectations following the (neo)realist, the (neo)federal/functional, the governance and the fusion assumptions. Although all four models are to some extent heuristic and ideal archetypes which describe reality in a schematic way, they are nevertheless helpful for classifying the evolution of the European integration process. Each model offers assistance, some insights, gains subsistence with regard to special matters and presents a positive theory explaining why and how this construction has evolved as it has, from the late 1940s up to the Amsterdam or Nice Treaty.

Yet, we come to the conclusion that, overall, the fusion theory is the most suitable for describing observations such as those we defined as 'Europeanisation', the ever-increasing institutional interaction and the limited systemic convergence. The development towards a federal system seems unlikely because national institutions aim to retain their influence. They will participate as long as it seems useful for the fulfilment of their tasks and their own survival. The constitutional dynamics of the Maastricht and Amsterdam treaties, of which (neo)functionalists and (neo)federalists would approve, have not worked. We could not identify enough indications of a clear shift towards strengthening a supranational regime. With regard to the Amsterdam Treaty and in view of the increase of parliamentary powers we have seen neither a development back to a (neo)realist model, limiting the institutions to the domestic level, nor a trend towards the governance model in which we would expect an erosion of the traditional politico-administrative systems of nation states. Governance analyses would need to bring the role of national parliaments and the EP into the research focus.

The intensive 'Europeanisation' can be seen as crucial ingredient in the fusion model in which national actors – voluntarily or involuntarily – create an irreversible process of pooling and merging policy instruments. The fusion process stresses the checks and balances between national and EU institutions in preparing, making, implementing and controlling binding decisions. It focuses on the mixing of national and EU competencies and the shared responsibility of institutions for the combined use of state instruments. According to this approach, a precise division of competencies and responsibilities is improbable and might even be seen as unnecessary. Instead, the fusion model emphasises the multitude of institutional interactions and co-operation.

The role of national governments and administrations in this process might help to explain the evolution of the system. The Union is the rational product of fundamental choices by member governments. Constituent steps in this process are the package deals through which Member States agree to invest competencies and resources into the political system. The Maastricht and Amsterdam treaties have been two among many fundamental agreements made by the Member States to use the Union for their own purposes. However, an emphasis on the role of national governments and administrations does not imply a submissive role for EU institutions. Indeed the latter are not only significant as agents for efficient and effective policy-making but have also developed their own institutional ambitions. According to neo-institutionalist approaches, EU institutions do matter in shaping the perceptions of national actors and in changing the context of the rational pursuit of national interests. States can remain the 'masters of the treaties' but they are transforming themselves in the very process. Indeed, they have become actors in their own right and with their own weight. The political space in Brussels is not only created by but also filled with national politicians and civil servants.

Yet, this fusion process has been asymmetrical. Change has been restricted to the governmental machinery, interest groups and to some degree courts among the fifteen. The fusion process has extended to some regions. But national parliaments have not become as deeply involved in the Brussels arena. The trend towards deparliamentarisation and bureaucratisation continues – though the dramatic impact of this development has decreased.

As to the future: an ever-continuing evolution without an optimum

The 1990s showed that the development of EU polity had not reached a final stage or even a 'local optimum'. The revisions and amendments of the Amsterdam Treaty as well as the working of EMU would lead us to expect a reinforced continuation of the basic trends. The Union in the first decade of the 3rd millennium will provide further challenges for national actors. With new Member States the number of important co-actors as veto players will increase. Given the Union's broader policy-making scope, national demands for influence will grow with key words such as 'transparency', 'democratic deficit' and 'legitimacy' being employed as a pretext for a higher degree of participation.

Following both national and European strategies for gaining access and influence, national actors will create additional structures and procedures. Actors on both levels have already demonstrated a large degree of ingenuity in developing incremental devices without creating new procedures or set-ups at the national level. We have not discovered any significant change in this conservative attitude among the major actors. If we extrapolate the major trends of the first decades – also in view of the new challenges – the EU polity will become even more complex. Thus the demands made of national actors will grow even further. A vicious circle between the claim for participation and the increase of complexity has set in and there are few signs that the present plans for improving efficiency and legitimacy will be more successful in moving the stronger multi-level players out of their positions. Neither a one-way-street towards re-nationalisation nor a continuous process of replacing national actors seems to be plausible.

The way in which the challenges of the political agenda up to the year

2000 are being dealt with both in the Union and the Member States would lead us to expect that the trends leading to and from Maastricht, Amsterdam and Nice will continue. Thus, there will be a continuation of the dilemma of creating an optimal balance between the perceived need for bold constitutional reforms to maintain efficiency and effectiveness, and the desire among Member States to participate and maintain control.

In the near future there might even be inexperienced incentives and more 'noise' in the system. With more partners, especially those applicant countries with a completely different historical tradition and with institutional patterns which have not been tested in multi-level arenas, the evolution of the Union and its Member States might take a different track in the future. The enlargement from fifteen to twenty-seven might oblige us to review the usefulness of the approach and to re-characterise the nature and the evolution of the 'beast'.

Notes

1 See Andreas Maurer and Wolfgang Wessels, 'The EU Matters: Structuring Self-Made Offers and Demands', Chapter 2 in this volume, pp. 33–36.

2 See especially Christoph Sasse, Edouard Poullet, David Coombes and Gérard Deprez, *Decision Making in the European Community* (New York, London: Praeger, 1977); Dietrich Rometsch and Wolfgang Wessels (eds), *The European Union and Member States. Towards Institutional Fusion?* (Manchester: Manchester University Press, 1996), esp. pp. 328–365; Yves Mény, Pierre Muller and Jean-Louis Quermonne (eds), *Adjusting to Europe – The Impact of the European Union on National Institutions and Policies* (London: Routledge, 1996); Maria Green Cowles, James A. Caporaso and Thomas Risse (eds), *Transforming Europe, Europeanization and Domestic Change* (Ithaca: Cornell University Press, 2000).

3 See Glenn Snyder and Paul Diesing, *Conflict among Nations, Bargaining, Decision Making and System Structure in International Crisis* (Princeton: Princeton University Press, 1977). Snyder and Diesing list as the maxim of civil servants 'to maintain or improve "access" and "influence" with the central decision maker'.

4 See for such a theoretical assumption Adolf Kimmel, 'Verfassungsrechtliche Rahmenbedingungen: Grundrechte, Staatszielbestimmungen und Verfassungsstrukturen', in: Oscar W. Gabriel and Frank Brettschneider (eds), *Die EU-Staaten im Vergleich. Strukturen, Prozesse, Politikinhalte* (Opladen: Westdeutscher Verlag, 1994), pp. 23–51 (here p. 23).

5 In this chapter, the following abbreviations are used for the respective Member States: A = Austria; B = Belgium; D = Germany (Deutschland); DK = Denmark, E = Spain (España); F = France; SF = Finland; GR = Greece; I = Italy; IR = Ireland; LUX= Luxembourg, NL = Netherlands; P = Portugal; S = Sweden, UK = United Kingdom.

6 Teija Tiilikainen, 'Finland: Smooth Adaptation to European Values and Institutions', Chapter 6 in this volume, p. 151.

7 Article 6 (ex Article 12) TEU.

8 Ben J.S. Hoetjes, 'The Netherlands: A Former Founding Father in Search of Control', Chapter 13 in this volume, p. 317.

9 Danielle Bossaert, 'Luxembourg: Flexible and Pragmatic Adaptation', Chapter 12 in this volume, p. 299.

10 See generally Bettina Westle and Oskar Niedermayer, 'Die Europäische Gemeinschaft im Urteil der Bürger – ein sozialwissenschaftlicher Untersuchungsansatz', in: *integration*, No. 4/1994, pp. 177–186 and Oskar Niedermayer and Bettina Westle, 'A Typology of Orientations', in: Oskar Niedermayer and Richard Sinnott (eds), *Public Opinion and Internationalized Governance* (*Beliefs in Government, Vol. II*) (Oxford: Oxford University Press, 1995), pp. 33–50. See also the annual contributions of Elisabeth Noelle-Neumann, 'Die öffentliche Meinung', in: Werner Weidenfeld and Wolfgang Wessels (eds), *Jahrbuch der Europäischen Integration 1998/99 ff.* (Bonn: Europa Union Verlag, 1999ff.), pp. 311–316.

11 See especially Cees van der Eijk *et al.* (eds), *Choosing Europe? The European Electorate and National Politics in the Face of the Union* (Ann Arbor: University of Michigan Press, 1996) and Karl Heinz Reif, 'Ein Ende des "Permissive Consensus"? Zum Wandel europapolitischer Einstellungen in der öffentlichen Meinung in den EG-Mitgliedstaaten', in: Rudolf Hrbek (ed.), *Der Vertrag von Maastricht in der wissenschaftlichen Kontroverse* (Baden-Baden: Nomos, 1993), pp. 23–33.

12 See for detailed empirical data the *Eurobarometer*, 53 (Spring 2000).

13 See for recent discussions Beate Kohler-Koch, 'Die Europäisierung nationaler Demokratien: Verschleiß eines europäischen Kulturerbes?', in: Michael Greven (ed.), *Demokratie – eine Kultur des Westens* (Opladen: Leske & Budrich 1998), pp. 263–288; Christopher Lord, *Democracy in the European Union* (Sheffield: Sheffield Academic Press, 1998); Wolfgang Wessels and Udo Diedrichs, 'Legitimacy for a New Kind of Parliament. The European Parliament in a Contested Polity', in: Thomas Banchoff and Mitchell Smith (eds), *The Contested Policy. Legitimacy and the European Union* (London, New York: Routledge, 1999), pp. 134–152; Fritz W. Scharpf, *Governing in Europe: Effective and Democratic?* (Oxford, New York: Oxford University Press (1999)); Philippe C. Schmitter, *How to Democratize the European Union ... And Why Bother?* (Lanham, Md., Boulder, Co., New York, Oxford: Rowman & Littlefield, 2000).

14 Hoetjes, Chapter 13, *op. cit.*, p. 315.

15 Andrea Szukala, 'France: The European Transformation of the French Model', Chapter 9 in this volume, p. 218.

16 Brigid Laffan, 'Ireland: modernisation via Europeanisation', Chapter 10 in this volume, p. 249.

17 Christian Franck, Hervé Leclercq and Claire Vandevievere, 'Belgium: Europeanisation and Belgium Federalism', Chapter 3 in this volume, p. 71.

18 Karl Magnus Johansson, 'Sweden: Another Awkward Partner?', Chapter 16 in this volume, p. 369.

19 See also Cees van der Eijk and Mark Franklin, 'European Community Politics and Electoral Representation: Evidence from the 1989 European Election Study', in: *European Journal of Political Research*, No. 19/1991,

pp. 111–123; Rudy Andeweg, 'The Reshaping of National Party Systems', in: *West European Politics*, Special Issue on: The Crisis of Representation in Europe, No. 3/1995, pp. 58–78.

20 See Simon Hix, 'The Emerging EC Party System? The European Party Federations in the Intergovernmental Conferences', in: *Politics*, No. 2/1993, pp. 38–49; Simon Hix, 'The Transnational Party Federations', in: John Gaffney (ed.), *Political Parties in the European Union* (London: Routledge, 1996), pp. 308–331; Oskar Niedermayer, *Europäische Parteien? Zur grenzüberschreitenden Interaktion politischer Parteien im Rahmen der Europäischen Gemeinschaft* (Frankfurt a.m., New York: Campus, 1983); Thomas Jansen, *Die Entstehung einer Europäischen Partei – Vorgeschichte, Gründung und Entwicklung der EVP* (Bonn: Europa Union Verlag, 1996).

21 See Andreas Maurer, 'Der Wandel europapolitischer Grundorientierungen nationaler Parteien in der Europäischen Union', in: Mathias Jopp, Andreas Maurer and Heinrich Schneider (eds), *Europapolitische Grundverständnisse im Wandel, Analysen und Konsequenzen für die politische Bildung* (Bonn: Europa Union Verlag, 1998), pp. 301–364.

22 Johansson, Chapter 16, *op. cit.*, p. 370.

23 See for the term Giovanni Sartori, *Parties and Party Systems, A Framework for Analysis, Volume I* (Cambridge: Cambridge University Press, 1976), pp. 132–133.

24 See Gerhard Lehmbruch and Philippe C. Schmitter, *Patterns of Corporatistic Policy Making* (London: Sage, 1982); Wolfgang Streeck (ed.), *Staat und Verbände* (Opladen: Leske & Budrich, 1994).

25 See in general Sonia Mazey and Jeremy Richardson (eds), *Lobbying in the European Community* (Oxford: Oxford University Press, 1993); Volker Eichener and Helmut Voelzkoew (eds), *Europäische Integration und verbandliche Interessenvermittlung* (Marburg: Metropolis, 1994); Beate Kohler-Koch and Rainer Eising (eds), *The Transformation of Governance in the European Union* (London: Routledge, 1999); Fritz W. Scharpf, *Games Real Actors Play, Actor Centered Institutionalism in Policy Research* (Boulder, Co.: Westview Press, 1997), esp. pp. 202–204; Hans-Wolfgang Platzer, 'Die europäischen Interessenverbände', in: Werner Weidenfeld and Wolfgang Wessels (eds), *Jahrbuch der Europäischen Integration 1996/97* (Bonn: Europa Union Verlag, 1997), pp. 273–276.

26 See Arend Lijphart, *Patterns of Democracy, Government Forms and Performance in Thirty-Six* Countries (New Haven: Yale University Press, 1999).

27 Nikos Frangakis and Antonios Papayannides, 'Greece: A Never-Ending Story of Mutual Influence Attraction and Estrangement', Chapter 7 in this volume, p. 173.

28 See Tiilikainen, Chapter 6, *op. cit.*, p. 150.

29 See for detailed statistics Wolfgang Wessels, 'The Growth and Differentiation of Multi-Level-Networks: A Corporatist Mega-Bureaucracy or an Open City?', in: Helen Wallace and Alasdair R. Young (eds), *Participation and Policy-Making in the European Union* (Oxford: Clarendon Press, 1997), pp. 17–41; Wolfgang Wessels, *Die Öffnung des Staates, Modelle und Wirklichkeit grenzüberschreitender Verwaltungspraxis 1960–1995* (Opladen: Leske & Budrich, 2000), pp. 353–357.

30 See for the term Adrienne Héritier (ed.), 'Policy-Analyse, Kritik und Neuorientierung', *PVS Sonderheft*, No. 24 (Opladen: Westdeutscher Verlag, 1993).
31 Felipe Basabe Lloréns, 'Spain: The Emergence of a New Major Actor in the European Arena', Chapter 8 in this volume, p. 186.
32 Kenneth Armstrong and Simon Bulmer, 'The United Kingdom: Between Political Controversy and Administrative Efficiency', Chapter 17 in this volume, p. 388.
33 Brigid Laffan, 'Ireland: Modernisation via Europeanisation', Chapter 10 in this volume, p. 248.
34 See for such an approach Arend Lijphart, *Democracies, Patterns of Majoritarian and Consensus Government in Twenty-One Countries* (New Haven: Yale University Press, 1984) and Lijphart, 1999, *op. cit.*).
35 See for a detailed analysis Gabriel and Brettschneider (eds), 1994, *op. cit.*; Wolfgang Ismayr, 'Die politischen Systeme Westeuropas im Vergleich', in: Wolfgang Ismayr (ed.), *Die politischen Systeme Westeuropas im Vergleich*, Second Edition (Opladen: Leske & Budrich, 1997), pp. 9–53; Yves Mény, *Government and Politics in Western Europe: Britain, France, Italy, Germany*, Second Edition (Oxford: Oxford University Press, 1993); Lijphart, 1999, *op. cit.*
36 See in this respect Simon Bulmer, 'The Governance of the European Union: A New Institutionalist Approach', in: *Journal of European Public Policy*, No. 4/1994, pp. 351–380; Hans Keman, 'Approaches to the Analysis of Institutions', in: Bernard Steuenenber and Frans van Vught (eds), *Political Institutions and Public Policy, Perspectives on European Decision Making* (Dordrecht: Kluwer, 1997), pp. 1–27; Simon Bulmer: 'New Institutionalism and the Governance of the Single European Market', in: *Journal of European Public Policy*, No. 3/1998, pp. 365–386.
37 Flamminia Gallo and Birgit Hanny, 'Italy: Progress Behind Complexity', Chapter 11 in this volume, p. 280.
38 Szukala, Chapter 9, *op. cit.*, p. 221.
39 Tiilikainen, Chapter 6, *op. cit.*, p. 153.
40 Presidency Conclusions of the Helsinki European Council, 10 and 11 December 1999.
41 See Martin Westlake, *The Council of the European Union* (London: Gale Group, 1996); Fiona Hayes-Renshaw and Helen Wallace, *The Council of Ministers* (New York: St Martin's Press, 1997).
42 See in general Scharpf, 1997, *op. cit.*, and Wessels, 2000, *op. cit.*, p. 252.
43 Brigid Laffan: 'Rapid Adaptation and Light Co-Ordination', in: Rory O'Donnell (ed.), *Europe, The Irish Experience* (Dublin: Institute of European Affairs, 2000), pp. 125–147) (here p. 136).
44 Finn Laursen, 'Denmark: In Pursuit of Influence and Legitimacy', Chapter 4 in this volume, p. 96.
45 Basabe Lloréns, Chapter 8, *op. cit.*, p. 201.
46 Franck, Leclercq and Vandevievere, Chapter 3, *op. cit.*, p. 78.
47 Andreas Maurer, 'Germany: Fragmented Structures Fitting into a Complex System', Chapter 5, in this volume, p. 117.
48 See classically Max Weber, 'Bureaucracy', in: Max Weber, *Economics and Society* (Tübingen: Mohr, 1947), p. 668.

49 See Christoph Knill, 'European Policies: The Impact of National Administrative Traditions', in: *Journal of European Public Policy* No. 18/1998, pp. 1–28.

50 See Maurer and Wessels, Chapter 2, *op. cit.*

51 See Otmar Höll, Johannes Pollak and Sonja Puntscher-Riekmann, 'Austria: Domestic Change Through European Integration', Chapter 14, in this volume, p. 346.

52 See Westlake, 1996, *op. cit.*; Hayes-Renschaw and Wallace, 1997, *op. cit.* and Maurer and Wessels, Chapter 2, *op. cit.*

53 Laffan, Chapter 10, *op. cit.*, p. 265.

54 See for the data Johansson, Chapter 16, *op. cit.*, p. 376.

55 See Michael Mentler, *Der Ausschuß der Ständigen Vertreter bei den Europäischen Gemeinschaften* (Baden-Baden: Nomos, 1996) and Wessels, 2000, *op. cit.*, p. 216.

56 Hoetjes, Chapter 13, *op. cit.*, p. 323.

57 See Christoph Demmke, Elisabeth Eberhöfer and Guenther F. Schäfer, 'The History of Comitology', in: Robin H. Pedler and Günther F. Schäfer (eds), *Shaping European Law and Policy. The Role of Committees and Comitology in the Political Process* (Maastricht: EIPA, 1996), pp. 61–83; Christian Joerges and Jürgen Neyer, 'From Intergovernmental Bargaining to Deliberative Political Processes: The Constitutionalisation of Comitology', in: *European Law Journal*, No. 3/1997, pp. 273–299.

58 See more detailed the conclusions in Wessels, 2000, *op. cit.*, pp. 413–434.

59 See Klaus Pöhle, 'Die Parlamente in der EG, Formen der praktischen Beteiligung', in: *Integration* No. 2/1992, p. 72–82; Tanja A. Börzel, 'Europäisierung und innerstaatlicher Wandel, Zentralisierung und Entparlamentarisierung', in: *Politische Vierteljahresschrift*, No. 2/2000, pp. 225–550.

60 See Wolfgang Ismayr, *Der Deutsche Bundestag. Funktionen – Willensbildung – Reformansätze* (Opladen: Leske & Budrich, 1992), p. 205.

61 The role of national parliaments in the legislative process of the Union has received special attention in the post-Maastricht period. For comparative research, see Andreas Maurer and Wolfgang Wessels (eds), *National Parliaments on Their Ways to Europe: Losers or Latecomers?* (Baden-Baden: Nomos, 2001); Torbjörn Bergman, 'National parliaments and EU Affairs Committees. Notes on Empirical Variation and Competing Explanations', in: *Journal of European Public Policy*, 3/1997, pp. 373–387; Philipe A. Weber-Panariello, *Nationale Parlamente in der Europäischen Union (*Baden-Baden: Nomos, 1995).

62 See Andreas Maurer, 'The European Parliament and National Parliaments after Amsterdam', in: Finn Laursen (ed.), *The Amsterdam Treaty: National Preference Formation, Interstate Bargaining, Outcome and Ratification* (2002).

63 See for a general overview Christian Engel, *Regionen in der EG, Rechtliche Vielfalt und integrationspolitische Rollensuche* (Bonn: Europa Union Verlag, 2000); Michael Keating and B. Jones, *The European Union and the Regions* (Oxford: Clarendon, 1995); Charlie Jeffery (ed.), Regional and Federal Studies, Special Issue, *The Regional Dimension of the European Union, Towards a Third Level in Europe?* (London: Routledge, 1996); Michael

Keating and Liesbet Hooghe, 'By-Passing the Nation State? Regions in the European Union', in: Jeremy Richardson (ed.), *European Union: Power and Policy Making* (London: Routledge, 1996), pp. 216–229; Rudolf Hrbek, 'Die Auswirkungen der EU-Integration auf den Föderalismus in Deutschland', in: *Aus Politik und Zeitgeschichte*, No. 24/1997, pp. 12–21; Beate Kohler-Koch, 'Leitbilder und Realität in der Europäisierung der Regionen', in: Beate Kohler-Koch, Bernhard Blanke *et al.* (eds), *Interaktive Politik in Europa, Regionen im Netzwerk der Integration* (Opladen: Leske & Budrich, 1998), pp. 231–253.

64 Maria João Seabra, 'Portugal: One Way to Europeanisation', Chapter 15, in this volume, p. 363.

65 Tiilikainen, Chapter 6, *op. cit.*, p. 159.

66 See Charlie Jeffery, 'Regional Information Offices in Brussels and Multi-Level Governance in the EU: A UK–German Comparison', in: *Regional and Federal Studies*, No. 2/1996, pp. 183–203; Detlef Fechtner, 'Die Länderbüros in Brüssel', in: *Verwaltungsrundschau*, No. 38/1992, pp. 157–159; Fabrice Larat, 'Prägende Erfahrung. Regionale Reaktionen auf europäische Politik', in: Kohler-Koch, Blanke *et al.* (eds), 1998, *op. cit.*, pp. 153–181 (here p. 180); Rudolf Hrbek and Sabine Weyand, *Betrifft: Das Europa der Regionen* (München: C.H. Beck, 1994).

67 Laursen, Chapter 4, *op. cit.*, p. 107.

68 Frangakis and Papayannides, Chapter 7, *op. cit.*, p. 174.

69 See especially the German Constitutional Court, Judgement of 12 October 1993, in: Andrew Oppenheimer (ed.), *The Relationship between European Community Law and National Law. The Cases* (Cambridge: Cambridge University Press, 1995). See for further discussion Günther Hirsch, 'Europäischer Gerichtshof und Bundesverfassungsgericht – Kooperation oder Konfrontation?', in: *Neue Juristische Wochenschrift* (1996), pp. 2457–2466.

70 Szukala, Chapter 9, *op. cit.*, p. 238.

71 Article 234 of the Treaty establishing the European Community (ex Article 177).

72 Franck, Leclercq and Vandevievere, Chapter 3, *op. cit.*, p. 86.

73 See Joseph H.H. Weiler, 'A Quiet Revolution, The European Court of Justice and its Interlocutors', in: *Comparative Political Studies*, No. 26/1994, pp. 510–534. Anita Wolf-Niedermaier, *Der Europäische Gerichtshof zwischen Recht und Politik* (Baden-Baden: Nomos, 1997).

74 See Maurer and Wessels, Chapter 2, *op. cit.*

75 See for this term Robert D. Putnam, 'Diplomacy and Domestic Politics: The Logic of Two Levels Games', in: *International Organization*, No. 3/1988, pp. 427–459 (here p. 457).

76 See for the term Harold K. Jacobson, *Networks of Interdependence, International Organizations and the Global Political System*, Second Edition (New York: McGraw Hill, 1984), p. 128; Wessels, 2000, *op. cit.*, pp. 107 f.; Andreas Maurer, Jürgen Mittag and Wolfgang Wessels, 'Theoretical Perspectives on Administrative Interaction in the European Union', in: Thomas Christiansen and Emil Kirchner (eds), *Administering the New Europe: Inter-Institutional Relations and Comitology in the European Union* (Manchester: Manchester University Press 2000).

77 Jacobson, 1984, *op. cit.*, p. 129.

78 Fritz W. Scharpf, *Demokratische Politik in der internationalisierten Ökonomie*, in: Michael Greven (ed.) *Demokratie – eine Kultur des Westens* (Opladen: Leske & Budrich, 1998), pp. 81–103 (here p. 91).

79 Peter Haas, 'Introduction: Epistemic Communities and International Policy Co-Ordination', in: *International Organization*, No. 1/1992, pp. 1–35 (here p. 3).

80 See for example Bulmer and Paterson, 1996, *op. cit.* pp. 9–32.

81 Hans Ulrich Derlien, 'Co-Ordinating German EU-Policy, Failing Successfully?', in Hussein Kassim, Guy B. Peters and Vincent Wright (eds), *National Co-ordination of EU Policy Making* (Oxford: Oxford University Press, 1999).

82 See Lijphart, 1999, *op. cit.*

83 Thus following the works of Charles Tilly (ed.), *The Formation of National States in Western Europe* (Princeton: Princeton University Press, 1975) and Stein Rokkan, 'Dimensions of State Formation and Nation-Building: A Possible Paradigm for Research on Variations within Europe', in: Charles Tilly (ed.), *The Formation of National States in Western Europe* (Princeton: Princeton University Press, 1975), pp. 562–600; Adrienne Héritier, Christoph Knill, Susanne Mingers and Martin Becka, *Die Veränderung von Staatlichkeit in Europa, Ein regulativer Wettbewerb, Deutschland, Großbritannien, Frankreich* (Opladen: Leske & Budrich, 1994). See for recent discussions especially Armin von Bogdandy, *Supranationaler Föderalismus als Wirklichkeit und Idee einer neuen Herrschaftsform, Zur Gestaltung der Europäischen Union nach Amsterdam* (Baden-Baden: Nomos, 1999).

84 See Alan S. Milward, *The European Rescue of the Nation State* (Berkeley: University of California Press, 1992).

85 Altiero Spinelli, Manifest der Europäischen Föderalisten (Frankfurt a.M.: Europäische Verlagsanstalt, 1958).

Select bibliography

Armstrong, Kenneth A. and Bulmer, Simon (1998) *The Governance of the Single European Market* (Manchester: Manchester University Press).

Battis, Ulrich, Tsatsos, Dimitris and Stefanou, Dimitris (eds) (1995) *Europäische Integration und nationales Verfassungsrecht* (Baden-Baden: Nomos).

Berranger, Thibaut de (1995) *Constitutions nationales et construction communautaire* (Paris: Librairie Générale de Droit et de Jurisprudence).

Bulmer, Simon (1994) 'The Governance of the European Union, A New Institutionalist Approach', in: *Journal of European Public Policy*, No. 4/1994, pp. 351–380.

Christiansen, Thomas (1998) 'Bringing Process Back in: The Longue Durée of European Integration', in: *Journal of European Integration*, No. 1/1998, pp. 99–121.

Craig, Paul and de Búrca, Craínne (eds) (1999) *The Evolution of EU Law* (Oxford: Oxford University Press), pp. 83–136.

Dinan, Desmond (ed.) (1998) *Encyclopaedia of the European Union* (Boulder, Co.: Lynne Rienner).

Duina, Francesco G. and Hall, John A. (1999) *Harmonizing Europe. Nation-States within the Common Market* (New York: State University of New York Press).

Hanf, Kenneth and Soetendorp, Ben (eds) (1998) *Adapting to European Integration. Small States and the European Union* (London: Longman).

Hix, Simon (1999) *The Political System of the European Union* (London: Macmillan), pp. 2–14.

Hoffmann, Stanley (1982) 'Reflections on the Nation State in Western Europe Today', in: *Journal of Common Market Studies*, Nos 1–2/1982, pp. 21–37.

Ismayr, Wolfgang (ed.) (1999) *Die Politischen Systeme Westeuropas*, Second Edition (Opladen, Leske & Budrich).

Jachtenfuchs, Markus and Kohler-Koch, Beate (eds) (1996) *Europäische Integration* (Opladen: Leske & Budrich).

Kassim, Hussein, Peters, Guy and Wright, Vincent (eds) (2000) *The National Co-Ordination of EU Policy* (Oxford: Oxford University Press).

Kohler-Koch, Beate (1996) 'Catching Up with Change. The Transformation of Governance in the European Union', in: *Journal of European Public Policy*, No. 9/1996.

Kohler-Koch, Beate and Eising, Rainer (eds) (1999) *The Transformation of Governance in the European Union* (London: Routledge).

Laursen, Finn and Pappas, Spyros A. (eds) (1995) *The Changing Role of Parliaments in the European Union* (Maastricht: EIPA).

Lijphart, Arend (1994) *Democracies, Patterns of Majoritarian and Consensus Government in Twenty-One Countries* (New Haven: Yale University Press).

Marks, Gary (1996) 'European Integration from the 1980s, State-Centric vs. Multi-level Governance', in: *Journal of Common Market Studies* No. 34/1996.

Marks, Gary, Hooghe, Liesbet and Blank, Kermit (1996) 'European Integration from the 1980's. State-Centric versus Multi-Level Governance', in: *Journal of Common Market Studies*, No. 9/1996, pp. 341–378.

Mény, Yves, Muller, Pierre and Quermonne, Jean-Louis (eds) (1996) *Adjusting to Europe. The Impact of the European Union on National Institutions and Policies* (London: Routledge 1996).

Moravcsik, Andrew (1999) *The Choice for Europe. Social Purpose and State Power from Messina to Maastricht* (London: UCL Press).

Norton, Philip (ed.) (1995) National Parliaments and the European Union, Special Issue of the *Journal of Legislative Studies*, Vol. 1, No. 3/1995.

Nugent, Neill (1999) *The Government and Politics of the European Union*, Fourth Edition (Durham, Md.: Duke University Press).

Pappas, Spyros A. (ed.) (1995) *National Administrative Procedures for the Preparation and Implementation of Community Decisions* (Maastricht: EIPA).

Peterson, John and Bomberg, Elizabeth (1999) *Decision-Making in the European Union* (Basingstoke, London: Macmillan, 1999).

Richardson, Jeremy (ed.) (1996) *European Union. Power and Policy-Making* (London: Routledge).

Risse-Kappen, Thomas (1996) 'Exploring the Nature of the Beast. International Relations Theory and Comparative Policy Analysis meet in the European Union', in: *Journal of Common Market Studies*, No. 1/1996.

Rometsch, Dietrich and Wessels, Wolfgang (eds) (1996) *The European Union and Member States. Towards Institutional Fusion?* (Manchester: Manchester University Press).

Sandholtz, Wayne and Stone Sweet, Alec (eds) (1998) *European Integration and Supranational Governance* (Oxford: Oxford University Press).

Trondal, Jarle (1999) 'Integration Through Participation – Introductionary Notes to the Study of Administrative Integration', in: *European Integration online Papers*, No. 4/1999 http://eiop.or.at/eiop/texte/1999–004.htm.

Wallace, Helen and Wallace, William (eds) (1996) *Policy-Making in the European Union* (Oxford: Oxford University Press).

Wallace, Helen and Young, Alisdair (eds) (1997) *Participation and Policy Making in the European Union* (Oxford: Oxford University Press).

Weber-Panariello, Philipe A. (1995) *Nationale Parlamente in der Europäischen Union – Eine rechtsvergleichende Studie zur Beteiligung nationaler Parlamente an der innerstaatlichen Willensbildung in Angelegenheiten der EU im Vereinigten Königreich, Frankreich und der Bundesrepublik Deutschland* (Baden-Baden: Nomos).

Weiler, Joseph H.H. (1999a) *The Constitution of Europe* (Cambridge: Cambridge University Press).

Weiler, Joseph H.H. (1999b) *The Constitution of Europe. 'Do the New Clothes have an Emperor?' and other Essays on European Integration* (Cambridge: Cambridge University Press).

Wessels, Wolfgang (1997) 'An Ever Closer Fusion? A Dynamic Macropolitical View on Integration Processes', in: *Journal of Common Market Studies*, No. 2/1997, pp. 267–299.

Wessels, Wolfgang (2000) *Die Öffnung des Staates, Modelle und Wirklichkeit grenzüberschreitender Verwaltungspraxis 1960–1995* (Opladen: Leske & Budrich), pp. 413–434.

Index

The key institutions of the European Union and the Member States are not listed in the index.